AGE DISCRIMINATION IN EMPLOYMENT ACT

A Compliance and Litigation Manual for Lawyers and Personnel Practitioners

Edited by Monte B. Lake

Equal Employment Advisory Council

Contributing Authors

Professor Alfred W. Blumrosen
Kay, Scholer, Fierman, Hays & Handler

Robert Coulson, Esq.
President, American Arbitration Association

Hon. Gilbert Drucker
Administrative Law Judge, Dept. of Health and Human Services, formerly Regional Solicitor of Labor, Chicago

Charles H. Edwards, III, Esq.
Chief of Staff, House Select Committee on Aging, U.S. House of Representatives

Ronald M. Gaswirth, Esq.
Gardere & Wynne

Ronald M. Green, Esq.
Epstein, Becker, Borsody & Green

Joseph Guerrieri, Jr., Esq.
Highsaw & Mahoney

Arthur E. Joyce, Esq.
Labor Arbitration and Litigation Counsel, General Electric Co.

Bernard T. King, Esq.
Blitman & King

Karl R. Kunze
President, Kunze Associates

Monte B. Lake, Esq.
McGuiness & Williams

Matthew M. Lind
Vice President of Corporate ATE Planning & Resources, The Travelers Insurance Company

Stephen R. McConnell, Ph.D.
Industrial Gerontologist, House Select Committee on Aging, U.S. House of Representatives

Malcolm H. Morrison, Ph.D.
Acting Chief, Research Support Staff, Employment Standards Administration, U.S. Dept. of Labor

George J. Pantos, Esq.
Vedder, Price, Kaufman, Kammholz & Day

Thompson Powers, Esq.
Steptoe & Johnson

Daniel M. Williams, Esq.
Supervising Attorney, Office of Field Services, Equal Employment Opportunity Commission

---

Copies of this manual may be ordered on a prepaid basis ($14.95 for EEAC members, $19.95 for non-members) from The Equal Employment Advisory Council, Suite 1220, 1015 15th Street, N.W., Washington, D.C. 20005. Telephone (202) 789-8650.

Foreword

Litigation under the federal Age Discrimination in Employment Act (ADEA) is perhaps the fastest growing area of employment discrimination activity. This is reflected in the Equal Employment Opportunity Commission's announcement that during fiscal year 1981 the Commission filed the largest number of suits under the ADEA since the Act's passage. Surveys of company labor counsel and personnel practitioners also indicate that age discrimination issues are demanding increased attention. As age-related employment issues and litigation have grown, the demand by lawyers and those with personnel responsibilities for information concerning the ADEA has been rapidly expanding.

In response to this demand, the Equal Employment Advisory Council, the American Bar Association's Commission on Legal Problems of the Elderly and Section on Labor and Employment Law, and The National Council on the Aging jointly sponsored a symposium on the ADEA on January 11–12, 1982, in Washington, D.C. The symposium represented an effort to educate both plaintiff and defense attorneys, as well as company personnel specialists, on the wide variety of legal, practical and policy considerations raised by the Age Discrimination in Employment Act. To achieve the co-sponsors' purpose of presenting diverse viewpoints on compliance and litigation issues, experts from the government, academia, the legal profession and private industry were brought together in a single public forum for a thorough discussion of the ADEA. The participants were asked to prepare papers providing a comprehensive treatment of current and significant questions related to their assigned topics.

This volume represents the collective work of the symposium faculty with an emphasis on issues arising in the private sector. Topics were assigned and papers edited in order to avoid unnecessary repetition while at the same time providing a thorough treatment of all relevant subjects. The manual is designed to serve as a resource tool for the lawyer and non-lawyer seeking guidance on the substantive and procedural requirements of the ADEA, pretrial and trial tactics from both the plaintiff's and defendant's perspectives, structuring company personnel policies to avoid age discrimination suits and developing and maintaining pension and benefit plans in compliance with the Act. In addition, it provides insight into current government and Congressional attitudes about the future of the ADEA.

We hope that *Age Discrimination in Employment Act—A Compliance and Litigation Manual for Lawyers and Personnel Practitioners* will be of assistance to those seeking to comply with the ADEA, as well as those facing the challenge of litigation.

Kenneth C. McGuiness, President
Equal Employment Advisory Council

March 1982

Table of Contents

	Page
Foreword	i

Part I: Litigation Under the ADEA

Substantive Requirements Under the ADEA 1
    Monte B. Lake

Procedural Requirements Under the ADEA 43
    Gilbert Drucker

Burdens of Proof Under the ADEA 68
    Alfred W. Blumrosen

Pretrial Tactics Under the ADEA
    Ronald M. Gaswirth 116
    Thompson Powers 140

Trial Tactics Under the ADEA
    Ronald M. Green 212
    Joseph Guerrieri, Jr. 228

EEOC's Enforcement Policies and Procedures 256
    Daniel M. Williams

Arbitration of ADEA Claims 269
    Robert Coulson

Part II: Compliance with the ADEA

Structuring Company Policies and Procedures to Avoid Age Discrimination Suits
    Arthur E. Joyce 276
    Karl R. Kunze 290

Structuring Employee Benefit Plans Under the ADEA
    Bernard T. King 307
    George J. Pantos 328

Creating Employment Opportunities for the Older Worker 349
    Matthew M. Lind

Part III: The Future of the ADEA

The Future of the ADEA: An Analysis of the Impact of the 1978 Amendments to the Act 357
    Malcolm H. Morrison

The Future of the ADEA: Pressure Builds to Abolish Mandatory Retirement 381
    Charles H. Edwards • Stephen R. McConnell

Part IV: Text of the ADEA and Applicable Regulations

The Age Discrimination in Employment Act of 1967, as amended 409
Pertinent Provisions of the Fair Labor Standards Act 420
Pertinent Provisions of the Portal to Portal Act 423
EEOC's Proposed Procedural Regulations, 29 C.F.R. Part 1626 429
EEOC's Substantive Interpretations, 29 C.F.R. Part 1625 432
EEOC's Recordkeeping Requirements and Administrative and
    Statutory Exemptions, 29 C.F.R. Part 1627 435
EEOC's Guidelines on Employee Benefit Plans, 29 C.F.R. Part 860 436

ADEA: A REVIEW OF THE SUBSTANTIVE REQUIREMENTS

Monte B. Lake*

---

* Partner, McGuiness & Williams, Washington, D.C. specializing in labor and equal employment law. As part of his practice, he serves as a counsel to and an officer of the Equal Employment Advisory Council. Mr. Lake has lectured on a variety of equal employment topics and is a co-author of EEAC's book <u>Preferential Treatment in Employment-Affirmative Action or Reverse Discrimination?</u> He has served as a Deputy District Attorney and Deputy Attorney General of the State of California. A graduate of the University of Pacific and the McGeorge School of Law at the University of Pacific, Mr. Lake is a member of the bars of California and the District of Columbia as well as the Litigation and Labor and Employment Law Sections of the American Bar Association.

The considerable assistance of Barbara Neilson, Esq., of the firm of McGuiness & Williams, is gratefully acknowledged.

TABLE OF CONTENTS

		Page
I.	INTRODUCTION	1
II.	PURPOSE AND SCOPE OF THE ADEA	1
	A. Purpose	1
	B. Scope	2
	1. Covered Business Entities	2
	2. Prohibited Conduct	4
	3. Relationship to State Law	6
	4. Relationship to Title VII of the Civil Rights Act and Fair Labor Standards Act	6
III.	EXEMPTIONS AND DEFENSES	9
	A. Age as a BFOQ	9
	B. Differentiations Based on Reasonable Factors Other than Age	16
	1. Description of the Defense	16
	2. Applicability of the Defense to Reductions in Force, Lay-offs and Discharges	18
	3. Economic Factors as a Defense	19
	4. The Determining Factor Test	21
	C. Discipline or Discharge for Good Cause	22
	D. Observing the Terms of a Bona Fide Seniority System or Employee Benefit Plan	23
	1. Definition of a Bona Fide Retirement Plan	23
	2. 1978 Amendments to Section 4(f)(2)	25
	3. The Legality of Incentives to Early Retirement	26
	E. Bona Fide Executives and High Policymakers	27
	F. Tenured Professors	28
	G. Bona Fide Apprenticeship Programs	29
	H. Good Faith Reliance on Administrative Regulations, Etc.	29
IV.	BURDEN AND ALLOCATION OF PROOF IN ADEA CASES	31
	A. Disparate Treatment Cases	31
	B. Disparate Impact Cases	38

ADEA: A REVIEW OF THE SUBSTANTIVE REQUIREMENTS

I. INTRODUCTION

The Equal Employment Opportunity Commission (EEOC) recently announced that it filed eighty-nine lawsuits under the Age Discrimination in Employment Act (ADEA) during fiscal year 1981, the largest number of suits filed by the government to enforce the Act since its passage. 1/ J. Clay Smith, Acting Chairman of the EEOC, declared that, "The rise in the number of ADEA lawsuits is a bold indicator of the seriousness of this problem to applicants, employees and the business community." 2/ Knowledge of the substantive requirements of the ADEA is therefore essential both for employees seeking to become aware of their rights and employers seeking to comply with the statute.

This paper provides an overview of the substantive requirements of the ADEA which affect employers and employees in the private sector. 3/ The purpose and scope of the ADEA and practices which are prohibited by the Act are discussed at the outset. Exemptions and defenses which may be asserted by employers and the burden and allocation of proof in lawsuits are then considered. Finally, some of the current issues under the Act will be highlighted throughout the paper.

II. PURPOSE AND SCOPE OF THE ADEA

A. Purpose

The Age Discrimination in Employment Act of 1967 4/ prohibits employment discrimination based on age by certain employers, employment agencies, and labor organizations. 5/ President Johnson recommended the ADEA in his Older Americans Message of January 23, 1967, stating:

> Hundreds of thousands, not yet old, not yet voluntarily retired, find themselves jobless

___

1/ 193 Daily Lab. Rep. A-1 (Oct. 6, 1981).

2/ Id.

3/ This presentation will therefore not discuss the provisions of the ADEA which prohibit discrimination by covered employment agencies, labor organizations, and federal agencies. See 29 U.S.C. §§ 623 and 633a.

4/ 29 U.S.C. §§ 621-634.

5/ 29 U.S.C. § 623.

3

- 2 -

> because of arbitrary age discrimination. Despite our present low rate of unemployment, there has been a persistent average of 850,000 people age 45 and over who are unemployed . . . . In economic terms, this is a serious--and senseless--loss to a nation on the move. But the greater loss is the cruel sacrifice in happiness and well-being, which joblessness imposes on these citizens and their families. Opportunity must be opened to the many Americans over 45 who are qualified and willing to work. We must end arbitrary age limits on hiring. 6/

According to section 2 of the ADEA, the statute was enacted "to promote employment of older persons based on their ability rather than age; to prohibit arbitrary age discrimination in employment; [and] to help employers and workers find ways of meeting problems arising from the impact of age on employment." 7/ Passage of the statute was motivated by congressional concerns about the difficulties encountered by older workers in retaining their jobs and regaining employment when they are displaced, the prevalent practice of setting arbitrary age limits which are unrelated to the employee's potential for job performance, and high unemployment among older workers. 8/

B. Scope

1. Covered Business Entities

The ADEA provides that it is unlawful for employers to discriminate on the basis of age against employees or applicants for employment who are at least 40 but less than 70 years old. 9/ The Act covers employers who are engaged in an industry affecting commerce 10/ as long as they have employed twenty or more employees "for each working day in each of twenty or more

---

6/ 113 Cong. Rec. 34743-44 (1967).

7/ 29 U.S.C. § 621(b).

8/ 29 U.S.C. § 621(a).

9/ 29 U.S.C. §§ 623(a) and 631(a). The provisions of the ADEA which prohibit age discrimination in federal employment do not specify an upper age limit. See 29 U.S.C. §§ 631(b) and 633a.

10/ The expression "affecting commerce" has been interpreted as coextensive with the commerce clause of the Constitution and has been broadly construed. See, e.g., Usery v. Manchester E. Catholic Regional School Bd., 430 F. Supp. 188 (D.N.H. 1977) (scope of term "affecting commerce" is broad enough to include activities of parochial school board).

calendar weeks in the current or preceding calendar year." 11/

If nominally separate corporations comprise an integrated enterprise, they will be considered to be a single employer, and the number of workers employed by each will be aggregated to determine whether the 20-employee threshold has been satisfied. 12/ Following the test developed by the NLRB and applied by some courts in Title VII cases, criteria used by several courts in ADEA cases to determine whether a parent and subsidiary or two other nominally distinct corporations should be deemed a single employer include whether there is an inter-relation of operations, common management, centralized control of operations, and common ownership or financial control. 13/

There are apparently no cases which consider the applicability of the ADEA to American corporations operating abroad. However, it has been held that, since the ADEA's definition of "employer" was patterned after Title VII, the courts may look for guidance to judicial construction of the term "employer" under Title VII. 14/ By analogy to Title VII cases,

---

11/ 29 U.S.C. § 630(b).

12/ See Linskey v. Heidelberg Eastern, Inc., 470 F. Supp. 1181, 1183 (E.D. N.Y. 1979); Marshall v. Arlene Knitwear, Inc., 454 F. Supp. 715, 719, (E.D. N.Y. 1978), modified, 608 F.2d 1369 (2d Cir. 1979). See also Woodford v. Kinney Shoe Corp., 369 F. Supp. 911, 916 (N.D. Ga. 1973) (parent may be held liable for discriminatory practices of its subsidiary if the parent so controls the subsidiary that the subsidiary is merely the agent or instrumentality of the parent); Brennan v. Ace Hardware Corp., 362 F. Supp. 1156 (D. Neb. 1973), aff'd, 495 F.2d 368 (8th Cir. 1974) (corporation with principal offices in Chicago and branch warehouses elsewhere considered single entity under ADEA). But see Hassell v. Harmon Foods, Inc., 336 F. Supp. 432 (W.D. Tenn. 1971), aff'd, 454 F.2d 199 (6th Cir. 1972) (per curiam) (parent and subsidiary not considered single employer).

13/ Linskey v. Heidelberg Eastern, Inc., 470 F. Supp. at 1184; Marshall v. Arlene Knitwear, Inc., 454 F. Supp. at 719. Accord: Radio & Tel. Broadcast Technicians Local 1264 v. Broadcast Service of Mobile, Inc., 380 U.S. 255-56 (1965) (under Labor Management Relations Act); Mas Marques v. Digital Equip. Corp., 637 F.2d 24, 27 (1st Cir. 1980) (under Title VII).

14/ Dartt v. Shell Oil Co., 539 F.2d 1256, 1259 (10th Cir. 1976), aff'd mem., 434 U.S. 99 (1977).

it appears that the ADEA may be found to be applicable to U.S. citizens serving American companies abroad. 15/

2. Prohibited Conduct

The ADEA prohibits covered employers from discriminating on the basis of age by failing to hire 16/, discharging 17/, denying employment opportunities 18/, or otherwise discriminating against

---

15/ Bryant v. International Schools Serv., Inc., 502 F. Supp. 472 (D.N.J. 1980); Love v. Pullman Co., 12 Empl. Prac. Dec. ¶11,225 (D. Colo. 1976). Under 29 C.F.R. § 860.20 of the Department of Labor's prior interpretations, however, the ADEA was considered to apply only to discriminatory acts in places over which the United States had sovereignty, territorial jurisdiction, or legislative control. This interpretation was not followed by the EEOC, whose guidelines are silent on this topic.

16/ See, e.g., cases challenging an employer's policy of not hiring employees who exceed a specified age, such as Murnane v. American Airlines, Inc., 26 FEP Cases 1537 (D.C. Cir. 1981), and Smallwood v. United Airlines, Inc., 26 FEP Cases 1376 (4th Cir. 1981), and cases challenging an employer's policy of not hiring employees with more than a specific number of years of experience, such as Geller v. Markham, 635 F.2d 1027 (2d Cir. 1980), cert. denied, 101 S. Ct. 2028 (1981) (Rehnquist, J., dissenting), all of which are discussed in detail infra.

17/ The ADEA abrogates the employer's traditional common law right to discharge an employee because of age. Sexton v. Beatrice Foods Co., 630 F.2d 478, 485 (7th Cir. 1980); LaChapelle v. Owens-Illinois, Inc., 14 FEP Cases 737, 739 (N.D. Ga. 1976). Under the common law "terminable at will" doctrine, an employment contract of indefinite duration could be terminated at the instigation of either the employer or the employee at any time, absent some statutory prohibition.

18/ See, e.g., Goodman v. Heublein, Inc., 645 F.2d 127 (2d Cir. 1981) (denial of promotion to different offices at the level of vice president because of age); Recinella v. Ford Motor Co., No. 8-71273 (E.D. Mich., Nov. 28, 1979) (employer successfully rebutted plaintiff's allegations of age discrimination in eligibility for promotion, management development, lateral transfer, and training programs); Polstorff v. Fletcher, 452 F. Supp. 17 (N.D. Ala. 1978) (violation of ADEA where federal employee was downgraded without being considered for other positions); Marshall v. Board of Educ., 15 FEP Cases 368 (D. Utah 1977) (violation of ADEA where employer refused to consider application of employee for

individuals in the protected age category with respect to compensation 19/, terms, conditions, or privileges of employment. 20/ The ADEA also forbids employer retaliation against an employee or applicant because he or she has opposed any practice prohibited by the ADEA or filed a charge, testified, assisted, or participated in an investigation, proceeding or litigation under the ADEA. 21/

Finally, the Act prohibits the publication of any employment notice or advertisement which indicates any "preference, limitation, specification, or discrimination, based on age." 22/ The EEOC has issued interpretations which indicate that the use of such phrases as "age 25 to 35," "young," "college student," "recent college graduate," "boy," "girl," or similar phrases in help wanted notices or advertisements deter the employment of older persons and will be deemed to violate the ADEA unless one of the exceptions discussed infra applies. 23/ Under the interpretations, the use of phrases such as "age 40 to 50," "age over 65, "retired person," or "supplement your pension" are also prohibited unless an exception applies, since they discriminate against other individuals within the protected group. 24/

---

administrative position because only one year was left before employee's mandatory retirement).

19/ See, e.g., EEOC v. Sandia Corp., 639 F.2d 600 (10th Cir. 1980), in which the court found a violation of the ADEA where employees were subjected to lengthening intervals between salary increases based on their increasing age.

20/ 29 U.S.C. §623(a). Employers are also prohibited from reducing the wage rate of any employee in order to comply with the Act.

21/ 29 U.S.C. § 623(d).

22/ 29 U.S.C. § 623(e).

23/ 29 C.F.R. § 1625.4, 46 Fed. Reg. 47726 (1981). In Hodgson v. Approved Personnel Serv., Inc., 529 F.2d 760 (4th Cir. 1975), the court found that the discriminatory effect of an advertisement is to be determined by the advertisement's context and not by "trigger words" such as "young." However, the court eventually held that ads which appealed to "recent college grads," "recent high school grads," and persons who were "one-two years out of college," or had "any recent degree" violated the ADEA.

24/ 29 C.F.R. §1625.4, 46 Fed. Reg. 47726 (1981). See also 29 C.F.R. § 1625.2 where the Commission states that it is unlawful to give preference based on age to employees within the ages of 40-70 covered by the ADEA.

Although a request that the applicant state his or her age is not viewed by the EEOC as a *per se* violation of the ADEA, it will closely scrutinize such a request to assure that it was made for a lawful purpose. 25/

    3.   Relationship to State Law

Section 14(a) of the ADEA provides that it does not affect "the jurisdiction of any agency of any State performing like functions with regard to discriminatory employment practices on account of age except that upon commencement of action under this Act such action shall supercede any State action." 26/ Floor debate and the commmittee reports at the time of the ADEA's amendment in 1978 made it clear that states were to retain the power to enact and enforce their own age discrimination laws. 27/ Since the ADEA merely establishes minimum federal standards, the states are not precluded from adopting more stringent standards. 28/ However, if state and federal law conflict, state law is preempted by virtue of the Supremacy Clause of the United States Constitution. 29/

    4.   Relationship to Title VII of the Civil Rights Act and Fair Labor Standards Act

As enacted, the ADEA is a hybrid, reflecting the influence of both Title VII of the Civil Rights Act of 1964, as amended,

---

25/ 29 C.F.R. § 1625.4, 46 Fed. Reg. 47726 (1981).

26/ 29 U.S.C. § 633(a).

27/ 124 Cong. Rec. S 4451 (daily ed., March 23, 1978) (remarks of Senators Javits and Williams); S. Rep. No. 493, 95th Cong., 1st Sess. 5-7 (1977); H.R. Rep. No. 950, 95th Cong., 2d Sess. 12 (1978). However, it should be noted that the provisions of the Employee Retirement Income Security Act (ERISA) have been held to preempt state laws which regulate employee benefit plans. See e.g., Hewlett-Packard Co. v. Barnes, 571 F.2d 502 (9th Cir. 1978), cert. denied, 439 U.S. 831 (1979). See also Malone v. White Motor Corp., 435 U.S. 497, 499 (1978) (dicta).

28/ 123 Cong. Rec. S 17293 (daily ed., Oct. 19, 1977) (remarks of Senators Allen, Chafee and Javits).

29/ See Gibbons v. Ogden, 22 U.S. (9 Wheat.) 1 (1824); EEOC v. County of Allegheny, 26 FEP Cases 1087, 1092 n. 19 (W.D. Pa. 1981).

and the Fair Labor Standards Act. 30/ As the Supreme Court has noted, the objective of the ADEA--elimination of discrimination from the workplace--and the employment practices which are prohibited by the ADEA parallel those of Title VII. 31/ However, the enforcement mechanisms established under the ADEA, unlike Title VII, are modelled after those found in the Fair Labor Standards Act (FLSA). 32/ There are therefore significant differences between the remedial and procedural provisions of the ADEA and Title VII. 33/ For example, amounts owing due to a violation of the ADEA are to be treated as "unpaid minimum wages or unpaid overtime compensation" under the FLSA, and the provisions of the ADEA are to be "enforced in accordance with the powers, remedies and procedures" of specified provisions of the FLSA. 34/ The ADEA and the incorporated provisions of the FLSA authorize actions by the Secretary of Labor (now the EEOC) 35/ on behalf of an aggrieved individual for monetary and injunctive relief, as well as private civil actions for "legal or equitable relief." 36/ In addition, the ADEA incorporates the defense of good faith reliance on administrative agency interpretations (discussed infra) and the statute of limitations set forth in the Portal-to-Portal Act, which also apply to actions under the FLSA. 37/

The hybrid nature of the ADEA has created considerable confusion among litigants, courts, and commentators concerning the extent to which the case law that has developed under Title VII is applicable to age discrimination actions. 38/ Some courts

---

30/ Lorillard v. Pons, 434 U.S. 573, 578 (1978).

31/ Oscar Mayer & Co. v. Evans, 441 U.S. 750 (1979) Lorillard v. Pons, 434 U.S. at 584.

32/ Lorillard v. Pons, 434 U.S. at 579; Marshall v. American Motors Corp., 475 F. Supp. 875, 883 (E.D. Mich. 1979).

33/ Lorillard v. Pons, 434 U.S. at 584.

34/ 29 U.S.C. § 626(b).

35/ As noted above, responsibility and authority for enforcement of the ADEA was transferred effective July 1, 1979, from the Department of Labor to the EEOC, pursuant to President Carter's Reorganization Plan No. 1 of 1978, 43 Fed. Reg. 19807 (1978).

36/ 29 U.S.C. § 626(b) and (c)(1).

37/ 29 U.S.C. § 626(e)(1), incorporating 29 U.S.C. §§ 255 and 259.

38/ This controversy is most evident in discussions of the proper burden and allocation of proof in ADEA cases, discussed in detail infra.

have concluded that the two statutes should be interpreted similarly, 39/ while other courts have found that the procedural and substantive differences between the two statutes warrant a different approach under the ADEA to such matters as the burden of proof and the use of statistics in establishing a prima facie case. 40/ Some courts have urged that different approaches be taken under the statutes by emphasizing the distinction between the invidious discrimination based on immutable characteristics (such as race and sex) of certain groups which Title VII seeks to prevent and the discrimination based on relative differences between all persons which the ADEA seeks to prevent. 41/ EEOC, the agency that is now charged with enforcement of both Title VII and the ADEA, has indicated that it will endeavor to interpret the ADEA in a manner consistent with Title VII, 42/ despite criticism that such a policy ignores the important procedural and substantive differences between the statutes. Perhaps the wisest approach has been taken by courts which have insisted upon examining the particular issues involved in an ADEA suit on a case-by-case basis in order to ascertain whether Title VII principles are relevant. 43/

39/ See, e.g., Loeb v. Textron, Inc., 600 F.2d 1003, 1015 (1st Cir. 1979); Murphy v. American Motor Sales Corp., 410 F. Supp. 1403, 1405 (N.D. Ga. 1976), modified on other grounds, 570 F.2d 1226 (5th Cir. 1978).

40/ See, e.g. Lindsey v. Southwestern Bell Co., 546 F.2d 1123 (5th Cir. 1977); Laugesen v. Anaconda Co., 510 F.2d 307 (6th Cir. 1975); Recinella v. Ford Motor Co., No. 8-71273 (E.D. Mich., Nov. 28, 1979); Mastie v. Great Lakes Steel Corp., 424 F. Supp. 1299 (E. D. Mich. 1976). See also Geller v. Markham, 635 F.2d 1017 (3d Cir. 1980), cert. denied, 101 S. Ct. 1028 (1981) (Rehnquist, J., dissenting).

41/ See, e.g., Laugesen v. Anaconda Co., 510 F.2d at 312 n. 4; Recinella v. Ford Motor Co., No. 8-71273 (E.D. Mich., Nov. 28, 1979); Williams v. City of San Francisco, 483 F. Supp. 335 (N.D. Cal. 1979).

42/ See the preamble to the EEOC's proposed procedural regulations under the ADEA, 46 Fed. Reg. 9970 (1981), and the preamble to the EEOC's proposed substantive interpretations under the ADEA, 44 Fed. Reg. 68858 (1979). The reference to consistent statutory interpretation of Title VII and the ADEA was deleted without explanation from the preamble to the final substantive interpretations appearing in 46 Fed. Reg. 47724 (1981).

43/ See, e.g., Gabriele v. Chrysler Corp., 573 F.2d 949, 953 (6th Cir. 1978), vacated on other grounds, 442 U.S. 908 (1979); Murphy v. American Motors Sales Corp., 410 F. Supp. at 1405.

III. EXEMPTIONS AND DEFENSES

The provisions of the ADEA identify four major exemptions from the Act's prohibitions. Practices which would otherwise be prohibited are legally permissible where (1) age is a bona fide occupational qualification reasonably necessary to the normal operation of the particular business; (2) the differentiation is based on reasonable factors other than age; (3) the employer is observing the terms of a bona fide seniority system or a bona fide benefit plan which is not a subterfuge to evade the ADEA; or (4) the employer is discharging or disciplining an employee for good cause. 44/ The ADEA, as amended in 1978, also allows the compulsory retirement of certain individuals who are between the ages of 65 and 70 and are tenured professors or are employed in bona fide executive or high policy-making positions. 45/ Finally, the Act incorporates the defense set forth in section 10 of the Portal-to-Portal Act which exempts employers from liability if they can plead and prove that the act or omission complained of was in good faith and in reliance upon an agency interpretation or policy.

Each of these exemptions and defenses will be examined in the subsections which follow, along with EEOC's exemption for bona fide apprenticeship programs. As a preface to this discussion, it should be noted that the ADEA has been held to be remedial legislation whose provisions should be liberally construed in order to effectuate the congressional purpose of eliminating age discrimination in employment. 46/ As a result, the exemptions and defenses under the Act have often been strictly limited in application. 47/

A. Age as a BFOQ

The ADEA provides that employers may discriminate on the basis of age if "age is a bona fide occupational qualification [BFOQ] reasonably necessary to the normal operation of the

---

44/ 29 U.S.C. § 623(f).

45/ 29 U.S.C. § 631(c) and (d).

46/ See, e.g., Holliday v. Ketchum, MacLeod & Grove, Inc., 584 F.2d 1221, 1229 (3d Cir. 1978); Vazquez v. Eastern Air Lines, Inc., 579 F.2d 107, 112 (1st Cir 1978); Dart v. Shell Oil Co., 539 F.2d 1256, 1260 (10th Cir. 1976), aff'd, 434 U.S. 99 (1977).

47/ See, e.g., Sexton v. Beatrice Foods Co., 630 F.2d at 486; Marshall v. Eastern Airlines, Inc., 474 F. Supp. 364, 368 (S.D. Fla. 1979). Accord Piedmont & Northern Ry. v. ICC, 286 U.S. 299, 311-12 (1932).

particular business." 48/ As one court has explained, "establishment of a BFOQ relating to age justifies an employer's violation of the heart of the ADEA, allowing him to apply a general exclusionary rule to otherwise statutorily protected individuals solely on the basis of class membership." 49/ The ADEA's BFOQ exception is similar to that of Title VII, which permits employers to avoid liability for otherwise prohibited employment practices where religion, sex, or national origin is a BFOQ reasonably necessary to the normal operation of the business or enterprise. 50/ The establishment of an age-related BFOQ has been treated by the courts as an affirmative defense, thereby requiring the employer to carry the burden of persuasion on that issue. 51/ Both the courts and the EEOC have indicated that the BFOQ exception is to be narrowly applied. 52/

The BFOQ defense has typically been raised in cases involving hiring policies and mandatory retirement practices for

---

48/ 29 U.S.C. § 623(f)(1).

49/ Marshall v. Westinghouse Elec. Corp., 576 F.2d 588, 591 (5th Cir. 1978).

50/ 42 U.S.C. § 2000e-2(e).

51/ See, e.g., Marshall v. Westinghouse Elec. Corp., 576 F.2d at 591; Arritt v. Grisell, 567 F.2d 1267, 1271 (4th Cir. 1977); Houghton v. McDonnell Douglas Corp., 553 F.2d 561, 564 (8th Cir.), cert. denied, 434 U.S. 966 (1977); Laugesen v. Anaconda Co., 510 F.2d at 313.

52/ See, e.g., Smallwood v. United Air Lines, Inc., 26 FEP Cases at 1378; Burwell v. Eastern Airlines, Inc., 633 F.2d 361, 370 n. 15 (4th Cir. 1980) (en banc), cert. denied, 101 S. Ct. 1480 (1981); EEOC v. City of St. Paul, 500 F. Supp. 1135, 1146 (D. Minn. 1980). In its interpretive guidelines, the EEOC states:

> Whether occupational qualifications will be deemed to be "bona fide" to a specific job and "reasonably necessary to the normal operation of the particular business," will be determined on the basis of all the pertinent facts surrounding each particular situation. It is anticipated that this concept of a bona fide occupational qualification will have limited scope and application. Further, as this is an exception to the Act it must be narrowly construed.

29 C.F.R. § 1625.6(a), 46 Fed. Reg. 47727 (1981).

bus drivers, firefighters, police officers, and airline pilots. The courts have not always applied the same standards in determining when the defense has been established, and in many cases have borrowed from decisions interpreting the BFOQ exception under Title VII. Two different tests have been formulated for determining what employers must show in ADEA suits in order to successfully defend a general exclusionary rule as a BFOQ, producing less than consistent results. One line of cases suggests that employers may establish a valid BFOQ simply by demonstrating that they have a rational basis in fact for believing that elimination of the age policy involved would increase the risk of harm to third parties or the public. 53/ Any increase in safety risk due to the employment of older persons, no matter how minimal, would be sufficient to establish an age BFOQ under this standard. For example, in Hodgson v. Greyhound Lines, Inc., 54/ the Department of Labor challenged the bus company's policy of refusing to consider the applications of persons who were 35 years of age or older for bus driver positions. Based upon evidence of the impact of degenerative changes associated with aging, the strenuous nature of the driving assignment given to new drivers, and statistics showing that older but less experienced drivers posed a safety risk, the court concluded that the company's maximum age hiring policy was permissible under the BFOQ exception. 55/

Similarly, in Murnane v. American Airlines, Inc., 56/ a court applying the Greyhound test held that a maximum hiring age policy requiring that new flight officers be less than forty years old was related to the maximization of passenger safety and was therefore reasonably necessary to the normal operation of the airline. In Murnane, American Airlines' "up or out" policy required that flight officers be terminated if they were not qualified to advance to co-pilot and captain positions after

---

53/ This test was first formulated in Hodgson v. Greyhound Lines, Inc., 499 F.2d 859 (7th Cir. 1974), cert. denied, 419 U.S. 1122 (1975).

54/ Id.

55/ See also Usery v. Tamiami Trail Tours, Inc., 531 F.2d 224 (5th Cir. 1976), in which a court (applying the second BFOQ test, discussed infra) faced with similar evidence supporting a BFOQ defense approved a bus company policy which precluded the employment of drivers who were between the ages of 40 and 65. The Tamiami court emphasized that employers engaged in businesses in which safety factors were important must be afforded substantial discretion in selecting factors which err, if at all, on the side of preserving lives.

56/ 26 FEP Cases 1537 (D.C. Cir. 1981).

receiving appropriate training; i.e., there was no possibility of becoming a career flight officer. The court concluded that the maximum hiring age policy was a BFOQ, emphasizing that "American's hiring policies, including the age forty guideline, might result in the death of one less person than were American required to abandon or modify these policies." 57/

A second line of cases sets forth a more stringent two-part BFOQ test based upon two prior Title VII cases involving sex discrimination charges, Weeks v. Southern Bell Telephone & Telegraph Co. 58/ and Diaz v. Pan American World Airways, Inc. 59/ The first part of the test requires that the employer prove either (a) that it has a factual basis for believing that all or substantially all persons within the affected age group would be unable to perform safely and efficiently the duties of the job involved; or (b) that it is impossible or highly impractical to deal with the persons affected by the rule on an individualized basis (i.e., individual examinations would not enable the employer to distinguish the qualified from the unqualified).

57/ Id. at 1540. A different result was reached in Aaron v. Davis, 414 F. Supp. 453 (E.D. Ark. 1976). In Aaron, the court found that the city had failed to establish that the BFOQ exception applied to justify the mandatory retirement of firefighters at age 62. The court emphasized that the public safety considerations involved differed from those at issue in the Greyhound case, where the risk was far greater that a slight error in the driver's judgment would produce tragic results. The court found no empirical justification for mandating retirement at age 62 and cautioned that "at no point will the law permit, within the age bracket designated by the statute, the fixing of a mandatory retirement age based entirely on hunch, intuition, or stereotyping, i.e., without any empirical justification." Id. at 461. Cases involving the forced retirement of firefighters have generally rejected the employer's assertion of a BFOQ defense. For example, in Johnson v. Mayor of Baltimore, 515 F. Supp. 1287 (D. Md. 1981), the court (applying the Tamiami BFOQ test, discussed infra), held that age was not a BFOQ for firefighters in Baltimore and therefore found that city code provisions requiring retirement at the age of 55 and 60 violated the ADEA. The court noted that exercise tolerance tests, supplemented by other tests and procedures, could be used to determine whether individual firefighters are capable of performing their duties. See also EEOC v. City of St. Paul, 500 F. Supp. 1135 (D. Minn. 1980) (age is not a BFOQ for fire chiefs).

58/ 408 F.2d 228 (5th Cir. 1969).

59/ 442 F.2d 385 (5th Cir. 1971), cert. denied, 404 U.S. 950 (1972).

The second part of the test 60/ requires that the job qualifications which are invoked by the employer to justify its discrimination be reasonably necessary to the essence of the employer's business. If a court determines that safety is the essence of the particular business involved in the case, it may evaluate the risk of harm to third parties or the public which may result if the age-related employment policy is discontinued.

This more stringent, two-tiered test was recently applied by the Court of Appeals for the Fourth Circuit in a factual context similar to that involved in the Murnane case. In Smallwood v. United Air Lines, Inc., 61/ the court considered a challenge to the air lines' policy of denying employment to flight officer applicants who were over 35 years of age. Significantly, United did not have an "up or out" policy for flight officers as was the case with American Airlines in the Murnane case, supra; it was thus conceivable that an employee could remain a flight officer indefinitely. 62/ The district court held that United had established a valid BFOQ defense. On appeal, the Fourth Circuit found that there was no significant evidence tending to show that all or substantially all new hires over 35 would be unable to perform safely or efficiently. Moreover, the court held that United had failed to establish the impossibility or impracticability of examining each individual for potentially disabling conditions. The air lines already had an effective physical examination program in place. The court further held that United failed to show a relationship between its rule and airline safety, and dismissed as irrelevant the argument that hiring older pilots would saddle it with economic burdens because the "period of peak productivity" of these pilots would be shortened. The court warned that "[e]conomic considerations . . . cannot be the basis for a BFOQ--precisely those considerations were among the targets of the Act." 63/

A modified version of the two-tiered test was employed by the district court in Tuohy v. Ford Motor Co. 64/ In Tuohy, a private company pilot was discharged when he reached 60 years of age. Ford claimed that the F.A.A. rule prohibiting commercial airlines from using pilots who were over the age of 60 established age as a BFOQ, thereby allowing it to terminate pilots in

---

60/ This test was first applied in an ADEA context in Usery v. Tamiami Trail Tours, Inc., 531 F.2d 224 (5th Cir. 1976). See also EEOC v. County of Santa Barbara, 27 FEP Cases 1480 (9th Cir. 1982).

61/ 26 FEP Cases 1376 (4th Cir. 1981).

62/ Id. at 1379 n. 7.

63/ Id. at 1379. See also 29 C.F.R. § 1625.7(f) where EEOC's guidelines limit the use of economic factors under the defense of reasonable factors other than age.

64/ 490 F. Supp. 258 (E.D. Mich. 1980).

its private air transportation system at age 60. Stressing the importance of safety in air transportation, the court held that the F.A.A.'s determination that it is not possible to use factors other than age to predict the likelihood of incapacitation constituted a complete defense to the age discrimination claim. The court urged that parts (a) and (b) of the first tier of the BFOQ test be made more flexible when safety factors are involved in order to take the public interest into account. The court concluded that, where safety factors are involved, employers need only be "reasonable" in their decisions to employ general age-exclusionary rules. 65/

The EEOC has further confused this area by developing yet a third, and perhaps a fourth, BFOQ test. Section 1625.6(b) of the Comission's interpretive guidelines 66/ states that employers asserting a BFOQ defense have the burden of proving that (1) the age limit is reasonably necessary to the essence of the business, and either (2) that all or substantially all individuals excluded from the job involved are in fact disqualified, or (3) that some of the individuals so excluded possess a disqualifying trait that cannot be ascertained except by reference to age. This test resembles the two-tiered analysis of the BFOQ test employed in the cases discussed above. Although the guidelines are ambiguous, it appears that the EEOC intends that this test apply to cases where public safety is not in issue. It is unclear why the EEOC selected this test for cases which do not involve public safety, since almost all of the cases in which this test has been applied have involved questions of public safety.

The last sentence of secion 1625.6(b) is particularly confusing. It provides that, "[i]f the employer's objective in asserting a BFOQ is the goal of public safety, the employer must prove that the challenged practice does indeed effectuate that goal and that there is no acceptable alternative which would better advance it or equally advance it with less discriminatory

---

65/ The court indicated that, where safety factors are not involved, employers should not be permitted to justify such rules merely by showing that they are reasonable; the rules should be "right" in the eyes of the finder of fact. Id. at 262-63. A somewhat contrary result was reached in Houghton v. McDonnell Douglas Corp., 553 F.2d 561 (8th Cir. 1977), cert. denied, 434 U.S. 966 (1978), in which the court held that the evidence presented by the company was insufficient to support an inference of diminished ability among 52-year old test pilots. The court emphasized that the plaintiff's evidence had shown that he was in excellent physical condition, the aging process occurs more slowly and to a lesser degree among professional pilots, and the accident rate of professional pilots decreases with age.

66/ See 46 Fed. Reg. 47727 (1981).

impact." It is unclear whether the latter test must be satisfied <u>in addition</u> <u>to</u> the three-element test, or whether it is an <u>independent</u> and <u>alternative</u> test. If it is an additional standard that must be satisifed, employers would find it substantially more difficult to establish a BFOQ in cases involving public safety issues despite the willingness of several courts to hold employers to a lesser standard of proof in such cases. 67/

If, on the other hand, EEOC has established the latter test as a separate and independent standard to be employed in cases involving public safety, it will be imposing a new standard in such cases. This standard appears to have been borrowed from Title VII cases in which policies having a disparate impact must be justified by a showing of business necessity. 68/ In borrowing the business necessity test from Title VII, EEOC's guideline misallocates the burden of proof by placing it on employers. The burden of proving the last part of the business necessity test, the availability of less discriminatory practices, properly rests with the plaintiff. 69/

To date, very few employers have raised BFOQ defenses in the context of businesses which do not involve considerations of public safety. In <u>Marshall v. Goodyear Tire & Rubber Co.</u>,70/ Goodyear admitted that it preferred applicants under the age of 40 for positions in its production department. The company contended that applicants over the age of 40 lacked the strength and stamina to perform the job in an economical, efficient and safe manner, and that age was therefore a BFOQ. However, the court found that the studies and data relied upon by Goodyear were not convincing and that many workers, once employed, continued to work into their 50's and 60's. The court concluded that the company had failed to carry its burden to show that it had a factual basis for believing that all or substantially all

---

67/ <u>See</u>, <u>e.g.</u>, <u>Hodgson v. Greyhound Lines, Inc.</u>, 499 F.2d 859 (7th Cir. 1974), <u>cert. denied</u>, 419 U.S. 1122 (1975); <u>Beck v. Borough of Manheim</u>, 505 F. Supp. 923 (E.D. Pa. 1981); <u>Tuohy v. Ford Motor Co.</u>, 490 F. Supp. 258 (E.D. Mich. 1980).

68/ Although some courts tend to lump the BFOQ and business necessity tests together, it is imperative that they be treated distinctly. B. Schlei and P. Grossman, <u>Employment Discrimination Law</u> 292 (1976); <u>Wilson v. Southwest Airlines Co.</u>, 26 FEP Cases 989 (N.D. Tex. 1981); <u>EEOC v. Marathon County</u>, 26 FEP Cases 1736 (W.D. Wisc. 1981). The business necessity defense only comes into play where an employment practice is facially neutral but has a discriminatory impact.

69/ <u>Dothard v. Rawlinson</u>, 433 U.S. 321, 329 (1977), <u>Albemarle Paper Co. v. Moody</u>, 422 U.S. 405, 425 (1975).

70/ 22 FEP Cases 775 (W.D. Tenn. 1979).

- 16 -

persons over 40 would be unable to perform the production duties safely and efficiently, employing the standard formulated in the Tamiami case. Based upon Goodyear and dicta in the cases discussed above, it is likely that courts will apply the BFOQ exception much more narrowly in situations which do not raise the possibility of safety risks to other persons, and will require strict compliance with the BFOQ test which is applied.

B. Differentiations Based on Reasonable Factors Other than Age

1. Description of the Defense

The ADEA provides that it is not unlawful for an employer to take any action otherwise prohibited under the Act if the differentiation is based on reasonable factors other than age (RFOA). 71/ It appears that Congress's intent in enacting the RFOA defense was to protect employers from liability for excluding older applicants or employees from employment opportunities where they are unable to perform or satisfy certain physical or other job requirements. 72/ Although the inability of individuals to satisfy employment requirements may in some cases be related to age, it is the inability to perform a test or satisfy a valid job requirement and not age that must be the determining factor in the employment decision. 73/

It is important to distinguish the RFOA from the BFOQ defense. As the Court of Appeals for the Fifth Circuit has explained, the RFOA defense is asserted as a denial of the plaintiff's claim of discrimination, unlike the BFOQ defense, in which the employer essentially admits that age was the determining factor in the employment decision and seeks to justify the use of the age-based criterion. 74/ Under the RFOA defense, "Plaintiff says that the employer fired him because of his age; employer replies, in effect, not so, plaintiff was fired for excessive absences, general inability, or some other non-discriminatory reason." 75/ Moreover, while the BFOQ defense is usually asserted with respect to a general exclusionary policy

---

71/ 29 U.S.C. § 623(f)(1).

72/ 113 Cong. Rec. S 15892 (daily ed. Nov. 6, 1967) (remarks of Sen. Yarborough).

73/ See, e.g., EEOC v. County of Allegheny, 26 FEP Cases 1087, 1091 (W.D. Pa. 1981).

74/ Marshall v. Westinghouse Elec. Corp., 576 F.2d at 591.

75/ Id.

based on age, the RFOA defense is available only on an individual, case-by-case basis. 76/

For example, in the recent case of Erwin v. Bank of Mississippi, 77/ the court held that an employee's inability to obtain cooperation from other bank officers, his failure to make requested changes in a training program, and his lack of technical banking knowledge constituted "reasonable factors other than age" upon which the bank could base a discharge decision. 78/ In other cases, courts have concluded that the elimination of the position held by an employee based on sound business reasons, 79/ an employee's lack of supervisory qualifications for a new position which subsumed his old job, 80/ intemperate and impolitic actions by an employee which breached corporate protocol, 81/ or an employee's lack of initiative, flexibility, and knowledge of sophisticated techniques, 82/ may serve as reasonable factors other than age to legitimize the discharge of employees within the protected class.

The case of Marshall v. Goodyear Tire & Rubber Co. 83/ is illustrative of the requirements imposed by courts when the RFOA defense is raised. Goodyear admitted that it preferred applicants

---

76/ EEOC v. Marathon County, 26 FEP Cases at 1738; Marshall v. Goodyear Tire & Rubber Co., 22 FEP Cases at 778. The EEOC's interpretations are in agreement with this view:

> No precise and unequivocal determination can be made as to the scope of the phrase "differentiation based on reasonable factors other than age." Whether such differentiations exist must be decided on the basis of all the particular facts and circumstances surrounding each individual situation.

29 C.F.R. § 1625.7(b), 46 Fed. Reg. 47727 (1981).

77/ 512 F. Supp. 545 (N.D. Miss. 1981).

78/ Id. at 805.

79/ Moses v. Falstaff Brewing Corp., 550 F.2d 1113 (8th Cir. 1977).

80/ Smith v. Farah Mfg. Co., 650 F.2d 64 (5th Cir. 1981).

81/ Sutton v. Atlantic Richfield Co., 646 F.2d 407 (9th Cir. 1981).

82/ Price v. Maryland Casualty Co., 561 F.2d 609 (5th Cir. 1977).

83/ 22 FEP Cases 775 (W.D. Tenn. 1979).

under the age of 40 for positions in its production department. The general basis of Goodyear's RFOA claim was that applicants for employment who were age 40 and above, as a class, lacked the strength, stamina and dexterity required to perform the jobs in an economical, productive and safe manner. The court held that the RFOA defense was not applicable to a class of applicants age 40 and over:

> [T]he defendant's claim of an RFOA defense under § 4(f)(1) [of the ADEA] based on the age of the applicants is invalid. A defense <u>based on age</u> will not entitle the defendant to claim an exception under <u>§ 4(f)(1) for differentiation based on reasonable factors other than age</u>. The defendant has intermixed its RFOA and BFOQ defenses. 84/

The court gave considerable weight to the Department of Labor's interpretations under the ADEA which indicated that, while physical fitness requirements based upon pre-employment examinations could support a differentiation based on reasonable factors other than age, a claim for a differentiation would not be permitted on the basis of an employer's assumption that every employee over a certain age usually become physically unable to perform the duties of a particular job. 85/

2. Applicability of the Defense to Reductions in Force, Lay-Offs and Discharges

The RFOA defense has often been asserted in cases in which a reduction in force has occurred due to a downturn in the employer's business, producing lay-offs, early retirements, or discharges. Courts in these cases pay particular attention to performance evaluations, since they usually play a crucial role in determining which employees will be affected by the reduction in force. 86/ Several courts have held that an employer may

---

84/ <u>Id.</u> at 778; <u>Accord</u>, <u>EEOC v. County of Allegheny</u>, 26 FEP Cases at 1091.

85/ 29 C.F.R. 860.105. These interpretations have no parallel in current EEOC interpretations, which superseded the Labor Department rules on September 29, 1981. <u>See</u> 29 C.F.R. § 1625.7, 46 Fed. Reg. 47724 (1981).

86/ For example, in <u>Mistretta v. Sandia Corp.</u>, 649 F.2d 1383 (10th Cir. 1981), the court held that the employer violated the ADEA when it terminated four older employees based on performance ratings that reflected age bias. However, the court found that the lay-offs of two other employees did not violate the ADEA even though one factor in their selection

establish the sufficiency of its process for terminating employees following a reduction in operations by showing that it conducted and relied upon a thorough evaluation process of the affected employees. 87/ The issue is not whether the evaluation of these employees was entirely accurate but instead "whether a thorough evaluation of all employees concerned was genuinely and honestly attempted." 88/ Many courts have upheld the validity under the ADEA of employee discharges in reduction in force cases, concluding that the affected employees were selected on the basis of legitimate, non-discriminatory reasons. 89/ To establish a violation of the ADEA, employees must show that the employer had either "consciously refused" to keep them on the job because of age or had "regarded age as a negative factor in such consideration." 90/

3. Economic Factors as a Defense

An issue specifically addressed by both DOL's original and EEOC's current guidelines is whether economic considerations related to the employment of older workers constitute reasonable factors other than age. 91/ Both interpretations disallow differentiations based on the fact that the average cost of employing older workers may be higher than that of younger workers. The only exceptions to this prohibition are provided under the guidelines interpreting section 4(f)(2) of the ADEA which govern employee benefit plans. 92/

---

for lay-off was their performance rating under the age-biased evaluation system, since their lay-off was in fact motivated by a severe decline in the particular work that they were qualified to perform.

87/ *Mastie v. Great Lakes Steel Corp.*, 424 F. Supp. 1299 (E.D. Mich. 1976); *Gill v. Union Carbide Corp.*, 368 F. Supp. 364 (E.D. Tenn. 1973); *Stringfellow v. Monsanto Co.*, 320 F. Supp. 1175 (W.D. Ark. 1970).

88/ *Mastie*, 424 F. Supp. at 1316.

89/ See, e.g., *Williams v. Gen. Motors Corp.*, 656 F.2d 120 (5th Cir. 1981); *Smith v. Farah Mfg. Co.*, 650 F.2d 64 (5th Cir. 1981); *Sahadi v. Reynolds Chemical Division of Hoover Ball & Bearing Co.*, 636 F.2d 1116 (6th Cir. 1980); *Mastie*; *Gill*; *Stringfellow*. But see *Mistretta v. Sandia Corp.*; *Schulz v. Hickok Mfg. Co.*, 358 F. Supp. 1208 (N.D. Ga. 1973).

90/ *Williams v. Gen. Motors Corp.*, 656 F.2d at 130.

91/ See DOL's superseded guideline at 29 C.F.R. § 860.103(h) and EEOC's current interpretation at 29 C.F.R. § 1625.7(f).

92/ The ADEA benefit guidelines were issued by DOL on May 25, 1979 and are found at 29 C.F.R. § 860.120. EEOC has seriously considered revising them but has not yet done so.

The courts considering this question have generally agreed with the agencies' approach, although some distinctions have been made. For example, the court in <u>Mastie v. Great Lakes Steel Corp.</u>, 93/ citing section 860.103(h), concluded that "an employer's arbitrary and across-the-board pronouncement that older workers are more expensive to employ than younger workers would be a flagrant violation of the Act." Such a <u>blanket exclusion</u> has been distinguished from cost evaluations done on an <u>individual</u> basis. The court interpreted section 860.103(h) as permitting differentiations on the basis of <u>individual</u> assessments of higher costs for older workers. To reach its conclusion, the court relied on the language of subsection (h) which only prohibits "general assertion[s]" about average costs.

The court in <u>Marshall v. Arlene Knitwear, Inc.</u>, 94/ takes an apparently contrary approach in holding that "where economic savings and expectation of longer future service are directly related to an employee's age, it is a violation of the ADEA to discharge the employee for those reasons." A similar approach was taken in the case of <u>Geller v. Markham</u>, 95/ a hiring case. In <u>Geller</u>, a school district adopted a facially-neutral hiring policy based on cost-cutting reasons that had a disparate impact on older employees as a class. The court cited prior section 860.103(h) in support of its rejection of the school district's budgetary-constraint argument.

In his dissenting opinion in the Supreme Court's denial of certiorari in the <u>Geller</u> case, Justice Rehnquist rejected the application of section 860.103(h) to facially-neutral employment policies predicated on budgetary considerations. His opinion was based on the conclusion that a hiring policy that favored those with less than five years teaching experience was not based on a "general assertion" that the average cost of employing older workers as a group is higher than younger workers. The policy in question made no reference to age and also significantly affected workers under 40 years of age. Because of the questions raised with respect to the application of disparate impact analysis under the ADEA in general, and in particular where facially-neutral economic factors are involved, section 1625.7(f) may be the subject of future litigation. 96/

93/ 424 F. Supp. 1299, 1319 (E.D. Mich. 1976).

94/ 454 F. Supp. 715, 728 (E.D. N.Y. 1978), <u>modified</u> 608 F.2d 1369 (2d Cir. 1979).

95/ 635 F.2d 1027, 1034 (2d Cir. 1980), <u>cert. denied</u>, 101 S. Ct. 2028 (1981).

96/ <u>See</u> "Burdens of Proof Under the ADEA" where this issue is more extensively discussed.

4. The Determining Factor Test

Although the above cases illustrate the distinctions between the RFOA and BFOQ defenses and types of considerations that are permissible in making personnel decisions, the question still remains as to what extent, if any, age may play a role in such decisions. Under the Department of Labor's interpretations, a plaintiff had to establish that age was a "determining factor" in an employment decision. 97/ This standard suggests that if age was one of several factors involved in an employment decision, it must have made a difference in reaching the decision. Thus, while a plaintiff need not show that age was the sole criterion used in an adverse personnel decision, he or she must show that, "but for" the employer's motive to discriminate on the basis of age, the adverse action would not have been taken. 98/ A substantial number of courts have adopted this approach. 99/

EEOC's recently revised substantive guidelines delete the determining factor language and state that, when age is used as a "limiting criterion," the defense that an employment practice is justified by a reasonable factor other than age is unavailable. 100/ It is unclear what is meant by the term "limiting criterion" and whether it implies that the determining factor test has been eliminated. EEOC's interpretation has been noted with approval in a recent decision. 101/ Because EEOC's new standard arguably represents an approach that conflicts with a contemporaneous one issued by the Department of Labor, it remains to be seen whether the courts will defer to it. 102/

97/ 29 C.F.R. § 860.103(c).

98/ See, e.g., Loeb v. Textron, Inc., 600 F.2d 1003, 1019 (1st Cir. 1979).

99/ See Spagnuolo v. Whirlpool Corp., 641 F.2d 1109, 1112 (4th Cir. 1981) cert. denied, 50 U.S.L.W. 3248 (1981); Kelly v. American Standard, Inc., 640 F.2d 974, 984 (9th Cir. 1981); Bentley v. Stromberg-Carlson Corp., 638 F.2d 9, 12 (2d Cir. 1981); Smithers v. Bailar, 629 F.2d 892, 897-8 (3d Cir. 1980); and Cleverly v. Western Elec. Co., 594 F.2d 638, 641 (8th Cir. 1979). The courts in both Loeb and Smithers in part relied on the Department of Labor's prior guidelines at 29 C.F.R. § 860.103(c).

100/ 29 C.F.R. § 1625.7(c), 46 Fed. Reg. 47727 (1981).

101/ EEOC v. Marathon County, 26 FEP Cases 1736, 1738 (W.D. Wis. 1981).

102/ See generally Mohasco v. Silver, 447 U.S. 807 (1980).

C. Discipline or Discharge for Good Cause

As a practical matter, the "good cause" defense is a more specific statement of the defense of reasonable factors other than age as it applies to discharge 103/ or discipline cases. The two defenses are often used interchangeably in ADEA cases in which a discharge claim is brought. 104/ Consequently, much of the foregoing analysis applicable to the RFOA defense is applicable to the defenses of discipline or discharge for good cause.

Section 4(f)(3) of the ADEA provides that it shall not be unlawful for an employer to "discharge or otherwise discipline an individual for good cause." 105/ The defense has been allowed, for example, where employers have shown that excessive tardiness by a discharged employee was the reason for termination rather than age, 106/ and where a sales manager failed to perform his duties satisfactorily. 107/ In such cases the defense of a reasonable factor other than age likewise could have been raised by the employers. As discussed more fully below in the section on the burden of proof, the employer would have the burden of producing evidence in support of these defenses in a disparate treatment case, but not the burden of persuasion, which remains with the plaintiff. 108/

103/ The defense also applies to instances in which the plaintiff quits but contends that he or she was constructively discharged from the position. Constructive discharge arises only when a "reasonable person would find conditions intolerable." Johnson v. Bunny Bread Co., 646 F.2d 1250, 1256 (8th Cir. 1981); Walter v. KFGO Radio, 26 FEP Cases 982, 985 (D. N.D. 1981).

104/ Marshall v. Westinghouse Elec. Corp., 576 F.2d at 591; (5th Kelly v. American Standard, Inc., 640 F.2d at 985.

105/ 29 U.S.C. § 623(f)(3).

106/ Brennan v. Reynolds & Company, 367 F. Supp. 440, 444 (N.D. Ill. 1973).

107/ Surrisi v. Conwed Corp., 510 F.2d 1088, 1090 (8th Cir. 1975). See also EEOC v. Marathon County, 26 FEP Cases 1736, 1738 (W.D. Wis. 1981).

108/ See Marshall v. Westinghouse Elec. Corp., 576 F.2d at 591.

D. **Observing the Terms of a Bona Fide Seniority System or Employee Benefit Plan**

  1. Definition of a Bona Fide Retirement Plan

Section 4(f)(2) of the ADEA provides that it is not unlawful for an employer to observe a bona fide seniority system or employee benefit or retirement plan which is not a subterfuge to evade the purposes of the Act, as long as the plan does not compel the involuntary retirement of employees prior to age 70. 109/ Most of the cases that have arisen under this section have involved employee challenges to company involuntary retirement policies that were adopted prior to the Act's amendment in 1978. 110/ The 1978 amendments to the Act raised the mandatory retirement age for non-federal workers from age 65 to 70 and clarified that employees cannot be involuntarily retired prior to that age.

Prior to the 1978 amendments many companies involuntarily retired employees before age 65 pursuant to some type of company retirement plan and defended challenges to their actions on the basis of section 4(f)(2). Litigation arising out of forced retirements generally raised the questions of whether the company "observed the terms" of the plan, whether the plan was "bona fide" and whether compulsory retirement was a "subterfuge" to evade the purposes of the ADEA.

The issue of whether the terms of a plan were "observed" has often arisen in the context of an employer retirement plan that allowed it the discretion to involuntarily retire employees without making early retirement mandatory for all employees.

109/ 29 U.S.C. § 623(f)(2). The exceptions to the age 70 rule for bona fide executives and high policy makers and tenured professors are discussed infra.

110/ Most of the cases arising under section 4(f)(2) involve questions concerning benefit plans as opposed to seniority systems. For a discussion of the application of section 4(f)(2) to a seniority system that was challenged as not being bona fide because its alleged purpose and effect was to create two classifications of employees based solely on age, see Morelock v. NCR Corp., 586 F.2d 1096 (6th Cir. 1978), cert. denied, 441 U.S. 906 (1979). See also EEOC guidelines on bona fide seniority systems at 29 C.F.R. § 1625.8. The Commission emphasizes that in any seniority system length of service is the key criterion for the allocation of employment opportunities between older and younger workers. Any seniority system that violates this principle by giving those employees with longer service who are covered by the ADEA lesser rights may be considered to be a subterfuge to evade the purposes of the Act.

Although the Supreme Court upheld the legality of bona fide mandatory early retirement plans adopted prior to the enactment of the ADEA in 1967, it did not address the question of whether discretionary plans were legal. 111/ Several courts of appeals have upheld the legality of discretionary plans. 112/

It has also been held that the language "observe the terms" of a bona fide benefit plan implies that there are express terms in the plan that provide for involuntary retirement. In Sexton v. Beatrice Foods Co., the court rejected the employer's argument that it observed the terms of a bona fide retirement plan when it involuntarily terminated employees prior to age 65 and provided them substantial retirement benefits, even though the plan itself made no provision for forced retirement by the company. 113/ The company had argued that the common law doctrine of termination at will provided it the right to retire employees prior to normal retirement age and that its actions were tantamount to bona fide retirement under the ADEA as long as retirement benefits were paid. The court disagreed and concluded the right to terminate at will is abrogated by the provisions of the ADEA that make age-based retirements that do not conform to the requirements of section 4(f)(2) of the Act illegal.

Retirement plans have generally been considered bona fide if they exist and pay substantial benefits. 114/ It has also been suggested that participants in a plan must be given notice of its provisions. 115/

111/ United Airlines, Inc. v. McMann, 434 U.S. 192, 197 n. 4 (1977).

112/ See, e.g., Carpenter v. Continental Trailways, 635 F.2d 578, 581 (6th Cir. 1980) cert. denied, 101 S. Ct. 2320 (1981); Gonsalves v. Caterpillar Tractor Co., 634 F.2d 1065 (7th Cir. 1980), cert. denied, 101 S. Ct. 1999 (1981); Marshall v. Hawaiian Tel. Co., 575 F.2d 763, 767 (9th Cir. 1978); Zinger v. Blanchette, 549 F.2d 901, 908 (3d Cir. 1977), cert. denied, 434 U.S. 1008 (1978).

113/ 630 F.2d 478, 486 (7th Cir. 1980). See also EEOC v. Baltimore & O. R. Co., 632 F.2d 1107, 1111 (4th Cir. 1980), cert. denied, 50 U.S.L.W. 3245 (1981); EEOC v. County of Santa Barbara, 27 FEP Cases 1480, 1415 (9th Cir. 1982); and Allen v. Colgate-Palmolive Co., 27 FEP Cases 1412 (S.D.N.Y. 1981).

114/ Carpenter v. Continental Trailways, 635 F.2d at 581; Marshall v. Hawaiian Tel. Co., 575 F.2d at 766; Brennan v. Taft Broadcasting, 500 F.2d 212, 217 (5th Cir. 1974).

115/ Sexton v. Beatrice Foods Co., 630 F.2d at 486. Cf. Marshall v. Atlantic Container Line, 470 F. Supp. 71 (S.D. N.Y. 1978).

To constitute a subterfuge to avoid the purposes of the Act, the Supreme Court has held that a company's conduct must involve a "scheme, plan, strategem, or artifice of evasion." 116/ The absence of an economic or business purpose does not, however, automatically convert an employer's retirement plan into a subterfuge. 117/ Plans adopted prior to the enactment of the ADEA, like that considered in McMann, cannot constitute a subterfuge, however; it becomes a factual question as to whether those that are adopted or amended thereafter are illegal. 118/

2. 1978 Amendments to Section 4(f)(2)

The 1978 amendments to the ADEA reflect Congress' intent to overcome the Supreme Court's decision in United Airlines, Inc. v. McMann and prohibit employers from forcing employees to retire prior to age 70. As a result, companies with retirement plans requiring retirement at any age prior to 70 had to amend them to conform to the new law. 119/ The amendments do not prohibit plans that allow employees to elect early retirement or that require retirement for reasons other than age. 120/

A major issue arising out of the amendment to section 4(f)(2) is whether it is to be applied retroactively to invalidate plans adopted prior to the amendment's passage. EEOC's guidelines take the position that the prohibition on involuntary retirement enacted on April 6, 1978 applies to lawsuits pending on that date or filed thereafter, that challenge involuntary retirements which occurred either before or after that date. 121/ A number of suits have challenged retroactive application of the amendment and almost all of the courts considering the issue have refused retroactive application and rejected the Government's position. 122/

116/ United Airlines v. McMann, 434 U.S. at 203.

117/ Id.

118/ Compare EEOC v. Baltimore & O. R. Co., 632 F.2d at 1113 (post-1967 amended plan a subterfuge) and Marshall v. Atlantic Container Line, 470 F. Supp. 71, 73 (S.D. N.Y. 1979) (post-1967 amended plan not a subterfuge).

119/ EEOC's interpretations of the effective dates of the 1978 amendments affecting retirement plans can be found at 29 C.F.R. § 1625.9.

120/ 29 C.F.R. § 1625.9(f).

121/ 29 C.F.R. § 1625.9(b)(2).

122/ See EEOC v. Shell Oil Co., 637 F.2d 683 (9th Cir. 1981); Carpenter v. Continental Trailways, 635 F.2d 578 (6th Cir. 1980); Jensen v. Gulf Oil Refining & Marketing Co., 623 F.2d

3. The Legality of Incentives to Early Retirement

An additional issue which arises under this exception concerns when, if ever, a "voluntary" early retirement may be deemed to be "involuntary" and thus a violation of the ADEA. As noted above, employees may voluntarily choose early retirement. 123/ A retirement is considered "voluntary" if it was "in no way compelled or coerced . . . because of [the plaintiff's] age or any other factor." 124/ For example, in Toussaint v. Ford Motor Co., 125/ the plaintiff claimed he was coerced into taking a special early retirement after his employer discriminatorily eliminated his position. The Tenth Circuit upheld the trial court's findings that the company's actions were not motivated by age but by "economic realities" and found that there was ample evidence that the retirement to which the plaintiff consented was a "studied choice by [plaintiff] as the preferred way out of a difficult situation." 126/ A contrary result was reached in Hays v. Republic Steel Corp., 127/ in which the court concluded that applications for pension benefits completed by the plaintiffs in lieu of or at the conclusion of a lay-off was not a defense to their ADEA action, since they did not make a voluntary choice. It appears that once a decision has been reached based on neutral principles to discharge an employee the employee may be offered early retirement as an alternative to discharge. 128/ It has even been held to be permissible for an employer to offer an employee who faces either discharge or early retirement enhanced

---

406 (5th Cir. 1980); Smart v. Porter Paint Co., 630 F.2d 490 (7th Cir. 1980); Sikora v. Am. Can Co., 622 F.2d 1116 (3d Cir. 1980); Gonsalves v. Caterpillar Tractor Co., 22 FEP Cases 967 (C.D. Ill. 1980), aff'd on other grounds, 634 F.2d 1065 (7th Cir. 1980), cert. denied, 101 S Ct. 1999 (1981). But see Davis v. Boy Scouts of Am., 457 F. Supp. 665 (D. N.J. 1978).

123/ 29 C.F.R. § 1625.9(f).

124/ Usery v. General Elec. Co., 13 FEP Cases 1641, 1645 (M.D. Tenn. 1976).

125/ 581 F.2d 812 (10th Cir. 1978).

126/ Id. at 816. See also, Ackerman v. Diamond Shamrock Corp., 27 FEP Cases 1563 (6th Cir. 1982).

127/ 12 FEP Cases 1640 (N.D. Ala. 1974), modified on other grounds, 531 F.2d 1307 (5th Cir. 1976).

128/ McCorstin v. United States Steel Corp., 621 F.2d 749 (5th Cir. 1980); Hannan v. Chrysler Motors Corp., 443 F. Supp. 802 (E.D. Mich. 1978).

retirement benefits conditioned on his retirement by a certain date, as long as the availability of the early retirement plan was not a basis for the discharge decision. 129/

E. **Bona Fide Executives and High Policymakers**

As broadly stated in the 1978 amendments to the ADEA, 130/ an employee is a bona fide executive or high policymaker and can be retired prior to age 70 if two requirements are satisfied: (1) The employee must be a bona fide executive or in a high policymaking position for the two years immediately preceding retirement, and (2) must have an annual retirement income of at least $27,000. EEOC's final interpretations of the amendment attempt to clarify the above requirements. 131/

Consistent with the legislative history of the 1978 amendments, 132/ EEOC interprets the definition of a bona fide executive in a restrictive manner and places the burden on the person invoking the exemption to establish that every element has been met. The Commission defines a bona fide executive by incorporating verbatim language from the Conference Report. 133/ The Report cites as examples of bona fide executives, the heads of a significant local or regional operation of a corporation heads of major departments or divisions of a corporation, at its corporate headquarters, and, in a large organization, the immediate subordinates of the heads of such divisions who exercise executive authority.

With respect to high policymakers, EEOC also adopts verbatim, the applicable provision of the Conference Report. 134/ There, high policymakers are defined as those who have no line authority but who play a significant role in the development of corporate policy. Employees with largely intellectual responsibilities that include evaluation of trends and issues, as well as

---

129/ Sutton v. Atlantic Richfield Co., 646 F.2d 407, 410 n. 4 (9th Cir. 1981) ("An employer's extension of extra-contractual benefits to an employee, who on neutral principles the employer has decided to seek his termination, is not violative of the ADEA").

130/ 29 U.S.C. § 631(c)(1).

131/ 29 C.F.R. § 1625.12, 44 Fed. Reg. 66791 (1979).

132/ 124 Cong. Rec. H2227 (daily ed. March 21, 1978) (remarks of Rep. Pepper).

133/ H. R. Rep. No. 95-950, 95th Cong., 2d Sess. 9 (1978).

134/ Id. at 10.

recommendation of policy direction to top executive officers, would fall within this definition. Examples cited by the Conference Report are the chief economist or research scientist of a corporation.

Assuming an employee satisfies the above definitions of executive or high policymaker, he or she also must have worked in such a position for the two-year period immediately before retirement. Under EEOC's interpretation, an employee who holds two or more different jobs during the preceding two-year period is subject to the exemption only if each job is an executive or high policymaking position. 135/

If the definition of either a bona fide executive or high policymaker is met, an employee still must satisfy the minimum retirement income test. Under section 12(c)(1) of the ADEA, an employee must be:

> entitled to an immediate nonforfeitable annual retirement benefit from a pension, profit-sharing, savings, or deferred compensation plan, or any combination of such plans, of the employer of such employee, which equals, in the aggregate, at least $27,000. 136/

The definitions of the key terms of immediate and nonforfeitable benefits, as well as the proper method of calculating the $27,000 annual retirement benefit, are somewhat complicated. A thorough explanation of EEOC's approach to determining the amount of an annual retirement benefit can be found in its current guidelines. 137/

F. Tenured Professors

The 1978 amendments to the ADEA raising the mandatory retirement age to 70 also carved out an exemption for college and university faculty members serving under a contract or similar arrangement which provides for unlimited tenure. 138/ This exemption was included because it was felt that younger professors, particularly women and minorities, would be denied teaching opportunities because the number of available faculty

---

135/ 29 C.F.R. § 1625.12(f).

136/ 29 U.S.C. § 631(c)(1).

137/ 29 C.F.R. § 1627.17.

138/ 29 U.S.C. § 631 (d). EEOC's interpretive guidelines covering this section can be found at 29 C.F.R. § 1625.11.

positions is closely related to the number of retirements. 139/ Unlike the exemption for executives and high policymakers, the college and university faculty exemption will terminate on July 1, 1982.

G. Bona Fide Apprenticeship Programs

Prior to EEOC's assumption of enforcement authority under ADEA, the Department of Labor exempted bona fide apprenticeship programs from the prohibitions of the ADEA. 140/ The exemption recognized that the placement of age limitations on the entry into such programs was necessary to provide young men and women training essential for skilled employment. After assuming enforcement responsibility under the ADEA, EEOC proposed to reverse DOL's longstanding exemption for bona fide apprenticeship programs. The Commission's proposed approach would have eliminated a blanket exemption and allowed exemptions on an ad hoc basis where legitimate reasons could be established. 141/

As finally issued, however, the EEOC's guidelines retain the broad exemption previously afforded by DOL. Consequently, employers may continue to limit entry into such programs to younger workers under specified ages. 142/

H. Good Faith Reliance on Administrative Regulations, Etc.

Section 10 of the Portal to Portal Act, which is incorporated into the ADEA, provides a defense to employers who prove that "the act or omission complained of was in good faith in conformity with and in reliance on any written administrative regulation, order, ruling, approval, or interpretation, [of the Commission] . . . or any administrative practice or enforcement policy of [the Commission] with respect to the class of employers to which he belonged." 143/ Before EEOC's assumption of enforcement of the ADEA, DOL issued a series of interpretations governing the scope and defining the elements of the "good faith reliance" defense. 144/

139/ S. Rep. No. 493, 95th Cong., 1st Sess. 8 (1977); 123 Cong. Rec. S17287 (daily ed. Oct. 19, 1977) (remarks of Sen. Chafee). For a discussion of some of the issues that have arisen under this exemption, see Levine v. Fairleigh Dickinson Univ., 646 F.2d 825 (3d Cir. 1981).

140/ 29 C.F.R. § 860.106.

141/ 45 Fed. Reg. 64212 (1980).

142/ 29 C.F.R. § 1625.13.

143/ 29 U.S.C. § 259.

144/ 29 C.F.R. § 790.13-.19.

Under DOL's guidelines, the opinion or regulation relied upon must be in writing and cannot be based on oral representations made by an agency representative. 145/ Moreover, an employer's reliance must be placed in good faith. Courts have generally used an objective rather than a subjective test to measure whether a company's reliance was made in good faith. 146/ The objective test has been defined as that which a reasonably prudent person would have done under the same or similar circumstances. For example, in Marshall v. Baptist Hospital, Inc., 147/ the court held that under the reasonable person test, a company could not have relied in good faith on public opinion letters and a Field Operations Handbook which were equivocal on the point in question when read in their entirety. Thus, an employer on notice that a ruling was not authoritative could not rely on it in good faith.

The question of what is an administrative regulation, order, ruling, approval, or interpretation is extensively covered in DOL's interpretation of the scope of the defense. 148/ No distinction is made between any of the terms, (i.e., between a regulation and an interpretation) for purposes of section 10 of the Act. It is important, however, that the regulation, interpretation, or opinion relied upon is specific enough to cover the particular employment practice in question 149/ and that the person providing the opinion is the designated representative of the agency, as opposed to an employee or other representative. 150/

The defense has arisen in ADEA cases in situations where employers have relied upon a DOL interpretive opinion concerning bona fide retirement plans under section 4(f)(2). For example, in Marshall v. Hawaiian Telephone Co., the court noted that if

---

145/ 29 C.F.R. § 790.13; Usery v. Godwin Hardware, Inc., 426 F. Supp. 1243, 1267-68 (W.D. Mich. 1976) (oral representations by compliance officer insufficient).

146/ 29 C.F.R. § 790.15; EEOC v. Baltimore & O. R. Co., 632 F.2d 1107, 1112 (4th Cir. 1980), cert. denied, 50 U.S.L.W. 3245 (1981); Mayhew, Inc. v. Wirtz, 413 F.2d 658, 661 (4th Cir. 1969).

147/ 473 F. Supp. 465, 478-79 (M.D. Tenn. 979).

148/ 29 C.F.R. § 790.17.

149/ EEOC v. Baltimore & O. R. Co., 632 F.2d at 1112; Pilkenton v. Applachian Regional Hospitals, Inc., 336 F. Supp. 334, 340 (W.D. Va. 1971).

150/ 29 C.F.R. § 790.19; Murphy v. Miller Brewing Co., 307 F. Supp. 829 (E.D. Wis. 1969), aff'd sub nom. Hodgson v. Miller Brewing Co., 457 F.2d 221 (7th Cir. 1972).

the company had involuntarily retired several of its employees pursuant to a bona fide pension plan in good faith reliance on a DOL interpretation (29 C.F.R. §860.110(a)), it would be immune from liability. 151/ Likewise, where an employer consulted with counsel and relied upon a published DOL interpretation concerning involuntary retirement prior to retiring several of its employees, a defense under section 10 was held to be available. 152/ If, however, the agency guideline in question is not specific enough to cover the particular facts involved in an employer's involuntary retirement of employees, thereby raising the question of whether the company could have objectively relied upon it in good faith in making its decision, the defense may be inapplicable. 153/

EEOC has proposed guidelines that would differ from those previously issued by DOL by imposing greater restrictions on the availability of the good faith reliance defense. 154/ In its proposed regulations, the Commission has attempted to articulate the circumstances under which the defense would apply. If adopted as proposed, the defense would be available only where an employer relies upon written documents designated as "opinion letters" which are signed by the Commission's General Counsel or upon Federal Register publications denominated as "opinion letters." 155/ Moreover, an opinion letter issued pursuant to EEOC's guidelines would be applicable only to the addressee and not other parties. 156/

IV. BURDEN AND ALLOCATION OF PROOF IN ADEA CASES

A. Disparate Treatment Cases

In a typical age discrimination suit brought under the "disparate treatment" theory of discrimination, an individual

---

151/ 575 F.2d 763, 767 n. 8 (9th Cir. 1978).

152/ Marshall v. Atlantic Container Line, 470 F. Supp. 71 (S.D. N.Y. 1979).

153/ E.E.O.C. v. Baltimore & O. R. Co., 632 F.2d at 1112.

154/ 46 Fed. Reg. 9970, 9972 (1981).

155/ Id.

156/ If such an interpretation is adopted, it may conflict with judicial precedent that has held that section 10 of the Portal to Portal Act allows a successor owner of a business to operate the business in the same manner as the predecessor who had obtained a ruling. See Martinez v. Phillips Petroleum Co., 283 F. Supp. 514, 527 (D. Idaho 1968), aff'd, 424 F.2d 547 (9th Cir. 1980).

plaintiff alleges that an employer treated him or her less favorably than other applicants or employees because of age. If a plaintiff who is relying on the disparate treatment theory is to prevail, proof of a discriminatory motive on the employer's part is essential. 157/ In this type of case, the overall burden of proving discrimination by a preponderance of the evidence rests at all times with the plaintiff. 158/ The plaintiff thus bears the ultimate burden of persuading the fact finder that age was a determining factor in the adverse employment decision. 159/ The burden may be satisfied by introducing evidence of discrimination, such as the employer's statements concerning the plaintiff's age; statistical evidence supporting the existence of a pattern of adverse employment decisions affecting older applicants or employees; or other circumstantial evidence indicating a preference for younger employees. 160/

Despite the differences between the ADEA and Title VII of the Civil Rights Act of 1964, 161/ courts have frequently followed Title VII precedent when faced with burden of proof

---

157/ See, e.g., Douglas v. Anderson, 27 FEP Cases 47, 49 (9th Cir. 1981).

158/ See, e.g., Goodman v. Heublein, Inc., 645 F.2d 127, 130 (2d Cir. 1981); Hughes v. Black Hills Power & Light Co., 585 F.2d 918, 919 n. 1 (8th Cir. 1978); Price v. Maryland Cas. Co., 561 F.2d 609, 612 (5th Cir. 1977); Mastie v. Great Lakes Steel Corp., 424 F. Supp. 1299, 1308 (E.D. Mich. 1976). Accord, Texas Dept. of Community Affairs v. Burdine, 450 U.S. 248, 254-56 (1981) (Title VII).

159/ See, e.g., Kelly v. American Standard, Inc., 640 F.2d 974, 984 (9th Cir. 1981); Smith v. Flax, 618 F.2d 1062, 1066 (4th Cir. 1980); Loeb v. Textron, 600 F.2d 1003, 1019 (1st Cir. 1979); Laugesen v. Anaconda Co., 510 F.2d 307, 317 (6th Cir. 1975). The strong weight of authority supports some version of the "age as determining factor" test. See Smithers v. Bailar, 629 F.2d 892, 896-97 (4th Cir. 1980); Goldman v. Sears, Roebuck & Co., 607 F.2d 1014, 1019 (1st Cir. 1979), cert. denied, 445 U.S. 929 (1980); Cleverly v. Western Elec. Co., 594 F.2d 638, 641 (8th Cir. 1979). But see Brennan v. Reynolds Co., 367 F. Supp. 440, 444 (N.D. Ill. 1973) (implies that a discharge will not be deemed to be for "good cause" under the ADEA if age is even one of a number of reasons for the discharge).

160/ See Walter v. KFGO Radio, 26 FEP Cases 982, 985 (D.N.D. 1981) and cases cited therein.

161/ See discussion above, pages 6-8.

issues under the ADEA. 162/ The Supreme Court recently clarified its earlier pronouncements concerning the allocation and order of proof in disparate treatment cases arising under Title VII:

> First, the plaintiff has the burden of proving by the preponderance of the evidence a prima facie case of discrimination. Second, if the plaintiff succeeds in proving the prima facie case, the burden shifts to the defendant "to articulate some legitimate nondiscriminatory reason for the employee's rejection." [Citation omitted.] Third, should the defendant carry this burden, the plaintiff must then have an opportunity to prove by a preponderance of the evidence that the legitimate reasons offered by the defendant were not its true reasons, but were a pretext for discrimination. 163/

The Court made it clear that the ultimate burden of persuading the trier of fact that the employer intentionally discriminated against the plaintiff remained at all times with the plaintiff. 164/

Many courts have applied this three-step proof process, first formulated in McDonnell Douglas Corp. v. Green, 165/ in cases arising under the ADEA. 166/ Certain modifications are

---

162/ It has, however, been noted that adoption of all Title VII law would be inappropriate because age is a progressive factor which all individuals must eventually face. See Laugeson v. Anaconda Co., 510 F.2d at 312, n. 4; Williams v. City of San Francisco, 483 F. Supp. 335, 344 (N.D. Cal. 1979); Mastie v. Great Lakes Steel Corp., 424 F. Supp. at 1306. See also Smith v. Farah Mfg. Co., 650 F.2d 64, 67 (5th Cir. 1981) (age discrimination is qualitatively different from race or gender discrimination).

163/ Texas Dept. of Community Affairs v. Burdine, 450 U.S. at 252-53, quoting McDonnell Douglas Corp. v. Green, 411 U.S. 792, 802, 804 (1973).

164/ Burdine at 253.

165/ 422 U.S. 792, 802-04 (1973).

166/ See Douglas v. Anderson, 27 FEP Cases 47, 49 (9th Cir. 1981); Smith v. Farah Mfg. Co., 650 F.2d at 67-68; Smith v. Flax, 618 F.2d at 1066; Loeb v. Textron, 600 F.2d at 1015; Kentroti v. Frontier Air Lines, 585 F.2d 967, 969 (10th Cir. 1978); Hughes v. Black Hills Power & Light Co., 585 F.2d at 919 n. 1; Marshall v. Westinghouse Elec. Corp., 576 F.2d 588, 590 (5th Cir. 1978); Rodriquez v. Taylor, 569 F.2d 1231, 1239 (3d Cir. 1977), cert. denied, 436 U.S. 913 (1978). Cf.

usually made in the McDonnell Douglas guidelines for the establishment of a prima facie case in order to tailor them to age discrimination suits which usually challenge the plaintiff's discharge. Courts have generally required plaintiffs in ADEA discharge cases to establish a prima facie case of discrimination by proving that they were (1) within the protected age group; (2) qualified to perform the job; (3) discharged, laid off, or forced to retire; and (4) replaced by an employee who was not included in the 40 to 70-year old protected class. 167/ Although these elements have been applied in proper cases, it has been recognized that they do not constitute "the alpha and omega of possible tests" under the ADEA. 168/ For example, the Court of Appeals for the Fifth Circuit, which originally issued the four-part test for prima facie cases under the ADEA, has repeatedly held that it is not necessary for a plaintiff who was laid off during a reduction in force to show actual replacement by a younger employee. 169/ Moreover, there is some case authority which would not foreclose the establishment of a prima facie case even where the plaintiff was replaced by an older employee or a younger employee within the protected class. 170/

Laugesen v. Anaconda Co., 510 F.2d at 312 (McDonnell Douglas guidelines may be applied to age discrimination cases but not automatically).

167/ See, e.g., Price v. Maryland Cas. Co., 561 F.2d at 612; Erwin v. Bank of Mississippi, 512 F. Supp. 545 (N.D. Miss. 1981); Sills v. Fort Pitt Steel Casting Co., 24 FEP Cases 927 (W.D. Pa. 1979). But see Douglas v. Anderson, 27 FEP Cases at 50 (modifying fourth element to generally require replacement by a substantially younger employee with equal or inferior qualifications).

168/ McCorstin v. United States Steel Corp., 621 F.2d 749, 753 (5th Cir. 1980).

169/ Williams v. General Motors Corp., 656 F.2d 120 (5th Cir. 1981); Smith v. Farah Mfg. Co., 650 F.2d at 67; McCuen v. Home Ins. Co., 633 F.2d 1150 (5th Cir. 1981); McCorstin v. United States Steel Corp., 621 F.2d at 753-54.

170/ See Douglas v. Anderson, 27 FEP Cases at 50 (replacement by even an older employee will not necessarily foreclose prima facie proof if other direct or circumstantial evidence supports an inference of discrimination); Sutton v. Atlantic Richfield, 646 F.2d 407 (9th Cir. 1981) (employee can establish a prima facie case even when that employee was replaced by someone within the protected age group); Loeb v. Textron, 600 F.2d at 1013 n. 9 (person might have been hired to ward off threatened lawsuit); Smith v. World Book-Childcraft International, Inc., 502 F. Supp. 96, 102 (N.D. Ill. 1980) (summary judgment for employer was precluded notwithstanding fact that plaintiff was replaced by person ten years older).

In determining whether the plaintiff has established a prima facie case, the main inquiry is whether the evidence is sufficient to support an inference of discrimination. 171/ In suits brought under the ADEA, this may be achieved by introducing evidence that identifies age as the "likely reason" for an adverse employment decision. 172/ Statistical evidence may be used to support a prima facie case in ADEA cases, as under Title VII, 173/ as long as the statistics upon which the plaintiff relies are compared to a relevant group. 174/ However, statistics concerning the age of workers may not be accorded as much weight as Title VII statistics concerning the sex or racial composition of the workforce. 175/ As the court noted in Mastie v. Great Lakes Steel Corp.:

> [T]he court further concludes and cautions that statistics in age discrimination litigation cannot be used exclusively to establish a prima facie case of age discrimination . . . . [T]here are persuasive reasons, in this court's opinion, for placing less weight on statistical evidence in age discrimination cases. Institutional, psychological, economic and physiological restraints to employing the aged suggest that statistics might not be a reliable indicator of an employer's compliance with the Act's proscriptions. 176/

Moreover, the Sixth Circuit has noted that "in the usual case, absent any discriminatory intent, discharged employees will more often than not be replaced by those younger than they, for

---

171/ See Texas Dept. of Community Affairs v. Burdine, 450 U.S. at 253-54 (Title VII); Douglas v. Anderson, 27 FEP Cases at 50 (ADEA).

172/ Douglas v. Anderson, 27 FEP Cases at 50.

173/ See, e.g., EEOC v. Sandia Corp., 638 F.2d 600 (10th Cir. 1980); Langesen v. Anaconda Co., 510 F.2d at 317; Hodgson v. First Fed. Savings & Loan Ass'n, 455 F.2d 818 (5th Cir. 1972); Schulz v. Hickok Mfg. Co., 358 F. Supp. 1208 (N.D. Ga. 1973).

174/ Lindsey v. Southwestern Bell Tel. Co., 546 F.2d 1123, 1124 (5th Cir. 1977).

175/ See Kephart v. Institute of Gas Technology, 630 F.2d 1217 (7th Cir. 1980); cert. denied, 101 S. Ct. 1418 (1981); Erwin v. Bank of Mississippi, 512 F. Supp. at 552; Morelock v. NCR Corp., 586 F.2d 1096 (6th Cir. 1978), cert. denied 441 U.S. 906 (1979).

176/ Mastie v. Great Lakes Steel Corp., 424 F. Supp. at 1320.

older employees are constantly moving out of the labor market, while younger ones move in." 177/ Therefore, although statistics may be helpful in establishing a prima facie case under the ADEA, their value may be more limited than in Title VII cases.

If the plaintiff establishes a prima facie case of discrimination, the burden shifts to the employer to "articulate some legitimate nondiscriminatory reason" for the adverse employment decision. 178/ It is well established that the burden that shifts to the employer is merely the burden of going forward with evidence; 179/ thus, the employer does not have to prove the absence of a discriminatory motive by a preponderance of the evidence. 180/ Several courts have accordingly held that an employer may adduce proof that the plaintiff was discharged for good cause, because of reasonable factors other than age, or under a bona fide seniority or benefit plan, in order to satisfy its burden of going forward with evidence of a legitimate, nondiscriminatory reason for the employment decision. The employer does not bear the burden of persuasion when these defenses are asserted, but must merely produce evidence. 181/

The EEOC's recently issued substantive interpretations of the ADEA create some uncertainty concerning the burden which is placed on employers who assert the RFOA defense. Section 1625.7(e) of the interpretations provides: "When the exception of

---

177/ Laugesen v. Anaconda Co., 510 F.2d at 313.

178/ Texas Dept. of Community Affairs v. Burdine, 450 U.S. at 253, quoting McDonnell Douglas Corp. v. Green, 411 U.S. at 802.

179/ See, e.g., Smith v. Farah Mfg. Co., 650 F.2d at 67; Goodman v. Heublein, Inc., 645 F.2d at 130; Marshall v. Westinghouse Elec. Corp., 576 F.2d at 592; Price v. Maryland Cas. Co., 561 F.2d at 612. Accord: Texas Dept. of Community Affairs v. Burdine, 450 U.S. at 254 (Title VII).

180/ Smith v. University of North Carolina, 632 F.2d 316, 337 (4th Cir. 1980); Marshall v. Arlene Knitwear, Inc., 454 F. Supp. 715, 728-29 (E.D.N.Y. 1978), modified, 608 F.2d 1369 (2d Cir. 1979). Accord: Board of Trustees of Keene State College v. Sweeney, 439 U.S. 24 (1978) (Title VII).

181/ Unlike the BFOQ defense, which is treated as an affirmative defense on which the employer bears the burden of persuasion, these defenses merely require the production of some evidence. See, e.g., Smith v. Farah Mfg. Co., 650 F.2d at 67 ("burden of rebutting an ADEA plaintiff's prima facie case requires no more than producing evidence that the employment decision was based upon reasonable factors other than age"). See also Marshall v. Westinghouse Elec. Corp., 576 F.2d at 591-92; Marshall v. Goodyear Tire & Rubber Co., 554 F.2d 730, 736 (5th Cir. 1977).

'a reasonable factor other than age' is raised against an individual claim of discriminatory treatment, the employer bears the burden of showing that the 'reasonable factor other than age' exists factually." 182/ There was no similar provision in the prior ADEA regulations issued by the Department of Labor.

Under EEOC's new test, it is unclear what is meant by the "burden of showing that the [RFOA] exists factually." In the preamble to the interpretations, the EEOC relied upon Loeb v. Textron 183/ as support for its approach under § 1625.7(e). In Loeb, the court recognized that the employer satisfies its burden of articulating a legitimate nondiscriminatory motive if he "simply 'explains what he has done' or 'produc[es] evidence of legitimate nondiscriminatory reasons,'" 184/ quoting Board of Trustees of Keene State College v. Sweeney. 185/ The Loeb court went on to conclude that the employer does not bear the burden to persuade the trier that it was in fact motivated by a legitimate reason and not by a discriminatory one, but rather bears the burden of production, "i.e., a burden to articulate or state a valid reason . . . ." 186/ In view of the language used by the court in Loeb and the judicially accepted standards of proof described above, it is unlikely that the EEOC intended that the burden of persuasion shift to the employer when it asserts an RFOA defense. It is logical to assume that the EEOC's ADEA interpreation simply requires that an employer produce some evidence that its action was based upon reasonable factors other than age.

Finally, if the employer in an ADEA disparate treatment case offers evidence that is sufficient to raise a genuine issue of fact that the adverse action was based upon legitimate reasons (such as good cause or reasonable factors other than age), it is up to the plaintiff to prove that the legitimate reasons proffered by the employer were not the employer's true reasons but are merely a "pretext or 'cover-up' for what was in truth a discriminatory purpose." 187/ Although "the reasonableness of the employer's reasons may of course be probative of whether they are pretexts," it must be understood that the "focus is to be on

---

182/ 46 Fed. Reg. 47724, 47727 (1981).

183/ 600 F.2d 1003 (1st Cir. 1979).

184/ Id. at 1011 (emphasis in original).

185/ 439 U.S. 24, 25 n. 2. (1978).

186/ 600 F.2d at 1011 (emphasis in original).

187/ Loeb v. Textron, Inc., 600 F.2d at 1012. See also Smith v. Farah Mfg. Co., 650 F.2d at 68.

the employer's motivation, . . . and not on its business judgment." 188/

B. Disparate Impact Cases

Under Title VII, employment practices which are neutral on their face but actually have the effect of denying employment opportunities to members of a protected group at a higher rate than those not belonging to a protected group are said to have a disparate impact. 189/ An inference of discrimination is often established through the use of statistical evidence which compares the composition of one group (for example, the racial make-up of the employer's workforce) with the composition of another group (the relevant labor market). 190/ It is not necessary under this theory to show an intent to discriminate on the employer's part; 191/ however, under the judicially-developed "business necessity" defense any employment practice which has a disparate impact is allowed to stand if it is shown to be related to job performance or to accurately measure job capability. 192/ If the employer shows that the employment practice is justified by business necessity and is related to successful job performance, the plaintiff is given an opportunity to show that other practices which have a lesser discriminatory impact would serve the employer's legitimate interests. 193/

The proper application of the disparate impact theory in age discrimination cases is unclear. The Second Circuit recently applied Title VII disparate precedent in an ADEA case challenging a school board's policy of hiring only teachers with less than a specified number of years of experience, finding that the plaintiff's statistical evidence established that the policy had a disparate impact. 194/ However, in his dissenting opinion from

---

188/ Loeb v. Textron, Inc., 600 F.2d at 1012 n. 6.

189/ Griggs v. Duke Power Co., 401 U.S. 424, 429-430 (1970).

190/ See Hazelwood School Dist. v. United States, 433 U.S. 299 (1977). International Brotherhood of Teamsters v. United States, 431 U.S. 324 (1977).

191/ See Griggs v. Duke Power Co., 401 U.S. at 432; Local 189, Papermakers v. United States, 416 F.2d 980, 989 (5th Cir. 1969), cert. denied, 397 U.S. 919 (1970).

192/ Griggs at 432.

193/ Dothard v. Rawlinson, 433 U.S. 321, 329 (1977); Albemarle Paper Co. v. Moody, 422 U.S. 405, 425 (1975).

194/ Geller v. Markham, 635 F.2d 1027 (2d Cir. 1980), cert. denied, 101 S. Ct. 2029 (1981) (Rehnquist, J., dissenting).

the denial of the school board's petition for a writ of certiorari, Justice Rehnquist pointed out:

> The policy under attack in this case . . . makes no reference to age. For budgetary reasons, a school board simply adopted a policy to hire teachers with fewer years of experience . . . . [T]he courts below found the Board's policy unlawful because it has a greater "impact" on teachers between the ages of 40 and 65 than it has on teachers under the age of 40. They reached this conclusion even though over 60% of all teachers under the age of 40 also have more than 5 years of experience and are detrimentally affected by the Board's policy. This Court has never held that proof of discriminatory impact can establish a violation of the ADEA, and it certainly has never sanctioned a finding of a violation where the statistical evidence revealed that a policy, neutral on its face, has such a significant impact on all candidates concerned, not simply the protected age group. 195/

Despite the uncertainty concerning the availability of the disparate impact theory in age cases, which is discussed in greater detail in "Burdens of Proof Under the ADEA," the EEOC has apparently taken the position that the theory is applicable. Section 1625.7(d) 196/ indicates that employers charged with using employee selection procedures or other employment practices which have a disparate impact on those in the protected age group will be required to defend them on the basis of business necessity and in light of the Uniform Guidelines on Employee Selection Procedures. 197/ The EEOC's adoption of the disparate impact

---

195/ 101 S. Ct. 2028, 2030 (1981) (Rehnquist, J., dissenting).

196/ 46 Fed. Reg. 47724, 47727 (1981). Section 1625.7(d) provides:

> When an employment practice, including a test, is claimed as a basis for different treatment of employees or applicants for employment on the grounds that it is a "factor other than" age, and such a practice has an adverse impact on individuals within the protected age group, it can only be justified as a business necessity. Tests which are asserted as "reasonable factors other than age" will be scrutinized in accordance with the standards set forth at Part 1607 of this Title [the Guidelines on Employee Selection Procedures].

197/ See 29 C.F.R. §§ 1607.1-.18.

approach in age cases is questionable in light of the above-described concerns raised by Justice Rehnquist. Moreover, the Commission's incorporation of the Guidelines on Employee Selection Procedures appears to be of doubtful validity, since the Guidelines and the related questions and answers exclude age from the types of discrimination covered. 198/

198/ 29 C.F.R. § 1607.2(D).

A REVIEW OF THE PROCEDURAL REQUIREMENTS OF
THE AGE DISCRIMINATION IN EMPLOYMENT ACT

Gilbert Drucker*
Michael W. Parker**

---

* Administrative Law Judge, United States Department of Health and Human Services, Office of Hearings and Appeals. Former Counsel for Employment Standards, U.S. Department of Labor. J.D., Chicago-Kent College of Law; Member of the Illinois and Federal Bars. In 1973, Mr. Drucker received the Ollie A. Randall Award of the National Council on Aging for the most significant American contribution to the field of aging. The views expressed here are those of the authors and do not necessarily represent the views of any agency or department of the United States.

** Student, the John Marshall Law School; B.A., Southern Illinois University 1978.

TABLE OF CONTENTS

                                                                                           Page

INTRODUCTION 1

I. PRIVATE LITIGANTS UNDER THE ADEA............................1

    A. The Charge...1
    B. The 180-Day Filing Requirement...........................4
    C. The Date The Alleged Unlawful Practice
       Occurred...6
    D. The Limitations Periods Applicable To
       Filing A Lawsuit..10
    E. The Relationship Between Suits By The
       Government And Suits By Private Litigants...............12
    F. The Federal-State Relationship In Sections
       7(d) And 14(b) Of The ADEA..............................13

        1. Generally...13
        2. The commencement of State proceedings in
           deferral States.....................................15

        3. The initiation of State proceedings and
           the 300-day filing period...........................16

    G. Class Actions...18
    H. Remedies and Attorney's Fees............................19

II. LITIGATION BY THE GOVERNMENT..............................21

       A. Conciliation..22

CONCLUSION...23

INTRODUCTION

As the graying of America has become more evident to the public, so too has the importance of the Age Discrimination in Employment Act (ADEA) 1/ become more vital in the battle against and in the understanding of age discrimination.

Before one can reach the substantive requirements of the ADEA one must first pass through the morass of its procedural requirements. Accordingly, this article will review the basic procedural requirements of the ADEA with special emphasis on the areas of greatest uncertainty and litigation. This review would not be complete without an analysis of the Equal Employment Opportunity Commission's (EEOC) proposed procedural guidelines. 2/ Because the basic procedural requirements under the Act differ for private litigants and the government, this article will generally discuss them separately. 3/

I. PRIVATE LITIGANTS UNDER THE ADEA

A. The Charge

With respect to private litigants under the ADEA, the initial procedural requirement is that a charge alleging unlawful discrimination be filed with the "Secretary." 4/ The purpose of

---

1/ The Age Discrimination in Employment Act of 1967, 29 U.S.C. § 621 (1976), as amended by the Age Discrimination in Employment Act of 1968, Pub. L. No. 95-256, 92 Stat. 189.

2/ Proposed EEOC Procedural Rules on Age Discrimination in Employment Act, 29 C.F.R. 1626 (1981).

3/ With respect to private litigants, the ADEA provides that no civil action may be commenced until 60 days after a charge alleging unlawful discrimination has been filed with the Secretary. 29 U.S.C. § 626(d) (1976).
   With respect to the government, the ADEA provides that the Secretary shall attempt to eliminate the discriminatory practice or practices alleged and effect voluntary compliance with the Act through conciliation, conference, and persuasion before any action is instituted. 29 U.S.C. § 626(b) (1976).

4/ 29 U.S.C. § 626(d) (1976), as amended by Age Discrimination in Employment Act Amendments of 1978, Pub. L. No. 95-256, § 4(d)(1), 92 Stat. 189.
   Prior to July 1, 1979, the Secretary of Labor was responsible for enforcement of the ADEA, but on July 1, 1979, the enforcement of the ADEA became the responsibility of the EEOC. Reorganization Plan No. 1 of 1978, 43 Fed. Reg. 19,807 (1978). Because the EEOC is now the agency charged with enforcement of the Act, all references to the "Secretary" now define the duty of the EEOC.

the charge is to provide the Secretary (hereinafter the EEOC) with sufficient information so that it may notify prospective defendants and eliminate the alleged unlawful practices through informal methods of conciliation. 5/

The form of the charge is to be a written statement which identifies the potential defendant and generally describes the action believed to be discriminatory. 6/ The applicable time limit for filing the charge with the EEOC is within 180 days of the alleged unlawful act of discrimination, 7/ or, in cases where there is an applicable state statute as described in the Act, within 300 days of the alleged unlawful practice or within 30 days after receipt by the individual of notice of termination of proceedings under State law, whichever is earlier. 8/

The EEOC has proposed regulations governing the submission of charges, the form and definition of a charge, the timeliness of a charge, the contents of and amendments to a charge, the notice of a charge, and the withdrawal of a charge. 9/ According to the proposed regulations, a charge means a written statement filed with the Commission (EEOC) by or on behalf of an aggrieved person which alleges that the named prospective defendant has engaged or will engage in actions in violation of the Act. 10/ Charges may be submitted in person or by mail to any of the District or Area Offices of the Commission, to the Headquarters of the Commission in Washington, D.C., or with any designated representative of the Commission. 11/ The proposed regulations state that a charge shall be in writing and shall name the prospective respondent and shall generally allege the discriminatory act(s). 12/ Oral charges delivered in person or by telephone

---

5/ H.R. Rep. No. 950, 95th Cong., 2d Sess. 12 (1978).

6/ 46 U.S.L.W. 56 (1978).

7/ 29 U.S.C. § 626(d) (1976), as amended by Age Discrimination in Employment Act Amendments of 1978, Pub. L. No. 95-256, § 4(d)(1), 92 Stat. 189.

8/ 29 U.S.C. § 626(d) (1976), as amended by Age Discrimination in Employment Act Amendments of 1978, Pub. L. No. 95-256, § 4(d)(2), 92 Stat. 189.

9/ Proposed EEOC Procedural Rules on Age Discrimination in Employment Act, 29 C.F.R. § 1626.3, 5-8, 11, 13 (1981).

10/ Id. § 1626.3.

11/ Id. § 1626.5.

12/ Id. § 1626.6. The form of the charge as indicated is entirely consistent with the legislative history. See text accompanying notes 5 and 6, supra.

reduced to writing by the EEOC satisfy the charge requirements. 13/
A charge may be amended to clarify, amplify, or allege additional acts unlawful of discrimination, and such amendments will relate back to the date the charge was first received; provided, however, that the amendments alleging additional acts unlawful of discrimination are related to or grow out of the subject matter of the original charge. 14/

A charge that has been amended shall not again be referred to the appropriate state agency. 15/ Upon receipt of a charge, the Commission has the duty to promptly notify the respondent that a charge has been filed. 16/ Finally, charging parties may request withdrawal of a charge; 17/ but because the Commission has independent investigative authority, 18/ it may continue any investigation and may secure relief for all affected persons notwithstanding a request by a charging party to withdraw a charge. 19/

13/ 29 C.F.R. § 1626.7(c)(3) provides that charges may be delivered to the EEOC in person or by telephone, and for purposes of determining the date of filing with the Commission, the date of such communication applies.
29 C.F.R. § 1626.8(b) states: "notwithstanding the provisions of paragraph (a) of this section, a charge is sufficient when the Commission receives from the person making the charge either a written statement or _information reduced to writing by the Commission_ that conforms to the requirements of Section 1626.6" (emphasis added).
The view that charges delivered orally but reduced to writing satisfy the notice requirement has been accepted by many courts under the former "notice of intent to sue" requirements. See, e.g., Pirone v. Home Ins. Co., 507 F. Supp. 1281 (D. N.Y. 1981) (an interview reduced to writing can be construed as an age discrimintion charge for limitations purposes; it is not explicitly required that an aggrieved individual personally file a charge. The charge may be initiated on his behalf); C.f. Hays v. Republic Steel Corp., 531 F.2d 1307 (5th Cir. 1976) (where oral complaint was not reduced to writing, the filing requirement was not satisfied).

14/ 29 C.F.R. § 1626.8(c).

15/ Id.

16/ 29 C.F.R. § 1626.11.

17/ 29 C.F.R. § 1626.13.

18/ 29 C.F.R. § 1626.4 provides that the Commission may, on its own initiative, conduct investigations of employers, employment agencies, and labor organizations.

19/ 29 C.F.R. § 1626.13.

B. The 180-Day Filing Requirement

As stated above, the charge is to be filed with the EEOC within 180 days of the alleged unlawful act of discrimination, or, if section 14(b) of the Act applies, within 300 days or 30 days after receipt by the individual of notice of termination of proceedings under State law, whichever is earlier. 20/ The failure to comply with these filing requirements has resulted in much litigation. The leading case in the area is Dartt v. Shell Oil Co., which addressed the question of whether the 180-day period might be tolled based on equitable considerations. 21/

In holding that equitable considerations will toll the 180-day requirement, the court noted the fact that a "notice of intent to sue" not filed within the specified period was not "jurisdictional," and hence not fatal to the plaintiff's suit. 22/ This view was adopted when the statutory requirement of a "notice of intent to sue" was amended in 1978 to require a "charge alleging unlawful discrimination." 23/ In light of the remedial nature of the ADEA and to best effect its purposes, a rule requiring outright dismissal of a plaintiff's suit was thought too harsh; rather, the failure to comply with the 180-day filing

---

20/ 29 U.S.C. § 626(d)(1) and (2) (1976). See note 33, infra. It should be noted, however, that under EEOC's proposed regulations (29 C.F.R. § 1626.7(a)) the Commission indicates that it will not reject charges as untimely provided that they are not barred by two and three years statute of limitations periods provided under the Portal to Portal Act of 1947.

21/ Dartt v. Shell Oil Co., 539 F.2d 1256 (10th Cir. 1976), aff'd. by an equally divided court, 434 U.S. 99 (1977).

22/ Before the 1978 amendments to the ADEA, § 7(d) required that a plaintiff file a notice of intent to sue. That language was amended and now the requirement is that a charge alleging unlawful discrimintion be filed with the Secretary. According to the House-Senate Conference Report that accompanied the Age Discrimination in Employment Act Amendments of 1978, H.R. Rep. No. 95-950, 95th Cong., 2d Sess. 12 (1978), the change in language was not intended to alter the basic purpose of the notice requirement. Therefore, the courts will interpret the requirement of ‑ "charge" no differently from the requirement of a "notice of intent to sue."

23/ H.R. Rep. No. 95-950, 95th Cong., 2d Sess. 12 (1978), states that the "charge" requirement is not a "jurisdictional prerequisite to maintaining an action under the ADEA..." and that "equitable modification for failing to file within the time period will be available to plaintiffs...."

requirement is subject to equitable tolling or estoppel. 24/
This has become the majority view. 25/

Even though the 180-day period for filing a charge alleging unlawful discrimination with the EEOC is subject to equitable modification, the safest course to follow is compliance. 26/ Equitable modification on the theory of failure to post notices as required under the ADEA or estoppel based on misrepresentation

---

24/ The court stated: "we do not contend that a filing of a notice of intent to sue is not a condition precedent to an action under the ADEA. However, the similarities between Title VII and the ADEA, the liberal reading of analogous time limitations in Title VII, the overly broad usage of the term 'jurisdictional' by courts interpreting section 626(d) of the ADEA, the remedial nature of the legislation, and the lack of legal training and guidance for many of the ADEA complainants lead us to conclude that while section 626(d)(1)'s notice of intent-to-sue requirement cannot be waived, the 180-day time limitation should be interpreted as being subject to possible tolling and estoppel." Dartt v. Shell Oil Co., 539 F.2d 1256, 1260 (10th Cir. 1976), aff'd. by an equally divided court, 434 U.S. 99 (1977).

25/ Bonham v. Dresser Industries, Inc., 569 F.2d 187 (3rd Cir. 1977), cert. denied, 439 U.S. 821 (1978); Wright v. State of Tennessee, 628 F.2d 949 (6th Cir. 1980) (enbanc); Kephart v. Institute of Gas Technology, 581 F.2d 1287 (7th Cir. 1978); Nielsen v. Western Electric Co., 603 F.2d 741 (8th Cir. 1979); Coke v. General Adjustment Bureau, Inc., 640 F.2d 584 (5th Cir. 1981) (enbanc); Naton v. Bank of California, 649 F.2d 691 (9th Cir. 1981); Dartt v. Shell Oil Co., supra.
  Other courts have held that analogous provisions for notice in Title VII, 42 U.S.C. § 2000e (1976), are subject to equitable modification. E.g., Laffey v. Northwest Airlines, Inc., 567 F.2d 429 (D.C. Cir. 1976), cert. denied, 434 U.S. 1086 (1978).

26/ The courts may be unwilling to find a factual basis for equitable modification. See Hays v. Republic Steel Corp., 531 F.2d 1307 (5th Cir. 1976) (employee's illness, even after oral complaints to the Department of Labor, was held not to excuse his failure to file timely); McCrickard v. ACME Visible Records, Inc., 409 F. Supp. 341 (W.D. Va. 1976) (allegations of misleading advice to employee's counsel did not excuse failure to timely file); Adams v. Federal Signal Corp., 559 F.2d 433 (5th Cir. 1977), and Skoglund v. Singer Co., 403 F. Supp. 797 (D. N.H. 1975). (In both cases, employees could not rely on employer's failure to post necessary ADEA notices where their job responsibilities involved the posting of notices or duty to determine necessary notices to be posted).

are largley undeveloped in the courts and similar fact patterns have led to different results. 27/ Therefore. a charge in writing which names the prospective defendant and generally describes the discrminatory act should be filed with the EEOC within 180 days of the alleged unlawful practice, in order to avoid any pitfalls.

C. <u>The Date The Alleged Unlawful Practice Occurred</u>

A vital issue concerning the filing of a charge with the EEOC is the date on which the alleged unlawful practice occurred. This date is key not only because it triggers the 180 or 300-day period for filing the charge, but also because it sets the starting date to compute the statute of limitations for filing a lawsuit. 28/ If the employee who is alleging wrongful

---

27/ Under the ADEA, an employer is required to post notices to be prepared by the EEOC which set forth information regarding the employees' rights under the ADEA. 29 U.S.C. § 627 (1976). It has been held that the failure to post such notices does not excuse the failure to comply with the 180-day notice or charge requirement. <u>Hiscott v. General Electric Co.</u>, 521 F.2d 632 (6th Cir. 1975); <u>Edwards v. Kaiser Aluminum & Chemical Sales, Inc.</u>, 515 F.2d 1195 (5th Cir. 1975); <u>Brohl v. Singer Co.</u>, 407 F. Supp. 936 (M.D. Fla. 1976). Other courts have held, however, that the failure to post notice as required under the ADEA is sufficient to warrant equitable tolling. <u>Bonham v. Dresser Industries, Inc.</u>, 569 F.2d 187 (3rd Cir. 1977), <u>cert. denied</u>, 439 U.S. 821 (1978); <u>Pirone v. Home Ins. Co.</u>, 507 F. Supp. 1281 (D. N.Y. 1981); <u>Skoglund v. Singer Co.</u>, 403 F. Supp. 797 (D. N.H. 1975) (the failure to post the notice required is sufficient to toll the period, but the facts presented did not warrant equitable tolling); <u>Bishop v. Jelleff Associates</u>, 398 F. Supp. 579 (D. D.C. 1974).

With regard to estoppel based on misrepresentation, one court has held that where an employer induced the employee to delay the filing of the notice until after the applicable period had expired, the employer may not assert the lack of timely filing as a defense. <u>Ott v. Midland-Ross Corp.</u>, 523 F.2d 1367 (6th Cir. 1975). <u>See also</u> <u>Naton v. Bank of California</u>, 649 F.2d 691 (9th Cir. 1981) (adopted rule that equitable modification in the form of estoppel is proper on showing of reasonable reliance on employer's representations).

28/ 29 U.S.C. § 626(d) (1976) sets out the requirements regarding the filing of the charge. 29 U.S.C. § 626(d), incorporates sections 6 and 10 of the Portal-to-Portal Act of 1947. 29 U.S.C. §§ 255, 295 (1976). The statute of limitations as specified therein is two years from the date of violation of nonwilful violations of the Act and three years from the date of violation for wilful violations. "Wilful" has been defined as a "knowing or voluntary act" as opposed to "a merely negligent act." <u>Olsen v. Southern Pac. Trans. Co.</u>, 480 F. Supp. 773 (N.D.

discrimination has been terminated or fired from his job, the circuit courts are split on whether the date the unlawful practice occurs is the date on which the employee receives unequivocal notice of termination, the employee's last day of work, or the employer's date of termination for administrative purposes. 29/ The liberal view guarantees the aggrieved employee the longest possible time period in which to file his charge, and fixes the date of the unlawful practice at the employer's date of termination for administrative purposes. This date has been held as the date on which the employer ceases to pay to the employee accrued vacation pay or periodic severance payments, or the date beyond which the employer refuses to extend insurance coverage. 30/

The restricted view, on the other hand, states that where there is a clear intention to discharge the employee of which the employee is aware and where the employer no longer accepts the services of the employee, the 180-day filing period begins to run, despite the fact that the employee is still receiving severance payments or extended insurance coverage. 31/ At the present time, a majority of the circuits follow this restricted

---

Cal. 1979); Bishop v. Jelleff Associates, 398 F. Supp. 579 (D. D.C. 1974).

29/ Moses v. Falstaff Brewing Corp., 525 F.2d 92 (8th Cir. 1975), and Flaherty v. Itek Corp., 500 F. Supp. 309 (D. Mass. 1980), hold that for purpose of filing the notice of intent to sue (charge alleging wrongful discrimination), the date at which the 180-day period begins to run is the date when the employee was terminated for administrative purposes and not the date when the employee was advised of his impending termination nor the date of the employee's last day of work. Contra, Wilkerson v. Siegfried Ins. Agency, Inc., 621 F.2d 1042 (10th Cir. 1980), and Bonham v. Dresser Industries, Inc., 569 F.2d 187 (3rd Cir. 1977), holding that where unequivocal of termination and the employee's last day of work coincide, notice of the alleged unlawful act will be deemed to have occurred on that date, notwithstanding the employee's continued receipt of certain employee benefits, such as periodic severance payments or extended insurance coverage.

30/ Moses, and Flaherty, supra. See also Davis v. Boy Scouts of America, 457 F. Supp. 665 (D. N.J. 1978) (where the court held that filing of the notice was timely because the employee was receiving retirement pay for some three weeks after his last day of work).

31/ Wilkerson, supra, at 1044; Bonham, supra, at 191. See also Payne v. Crane Co., 560 F.2d 198 (5th Cir. 1977) (where there was a clear intention to discharge the employee and such employee's services were no longer accepted, the unlawful practice occurred at such time for purposes of the notice requirement).

view. 32/ This restricted view applies to the 300-day filing period in so-called "deferral states" as well. 33/ Because of the disparate holdings among the various circuits, the diligent litigant should, if his case involves discharge, file his charge with the EEOC within 180 days or in deferral states, within 300 days of the date on which services to the employer end. 34/

The theory that where employment continues after an unlawful act of discrimination there is a continuing violation of the ADEA has received little support. 35/ The typical case is where an

---

32/ Wilkerson, (10th Cir.); Bonham, (3rd Cir.); Payne, (5th Cir.); Davis v. RJR Foods, Inc., 420 F. Supp. 930 (S.D.N.Y. 1976), aff'd without published opinion, 556 F.2d 555 (2nd Cir. 1977).

33/ Section 14(b) of the ADEA, 29 U.S.C. § 633(b) (1976) provides in relevant part: "In the case of an alleged unlawful practice occurring in a state which has a law prohibiting discrimination in employment because of age and establishing or authorizing a State authority to grant or seek relief from such discriminatory practice, no suit may be brought under section 626 of this title before the expiration of sixty days after proceedings have been commenced under the State law, unless such proceedings have been earlier terminated...."

34/ The view that the 180 or 300-day period begins upon the termination of services to the employer and not upon the termination of benefits to the employee was recently followed in Gray v. Mortgage Bankers Ass'n. of America, Inc., 492 F. Supp. 914 (D.D.C. 1980). In Gray, the employee submitted a letter of resignation at the insistence of the employer's new executive vice-president on January 9, 1978, to be effective April 30, 1978. However, no services were performed for the employer after January, 1978. The employee filed his charge on January 27, 1979, and argued that because he continued to receive paychecks through April 30, 1978, the 300-day period did not begin to run until that date. The court held the suit was barred, and found that the plaintiff knew he was being terminated and services to the employer ceased in January, 1978. It was on the date that services to the employer ended that the 300-day period began to run. Id. at 916.

35/ Where an employee who was laid-off and was not rehired sought to justify late notice to the Secretary with the argument that the failure to rehire was the wrongful act, the court held that the suit was barred for failure to give timely notice. There was no continuing violation of the ADEA in the absence of the repeated refusal of the employer to rehire the employee in accordance with a contractual obligation to do so. Woodburn v. LTV Aerospace Corp., 531 F.2d 750 (5th Cir. 1976). Accord, Cutright v. General Motors Corp., 486 F. Supp. 590 (W.D. Penn.

employee is laid-off and seeks to justify late notice to the EEOC with the argument that the failure to rehire was the wrongful act of discrimination. In these types of cases, the courts agree that claims arising from a lay-off accrue on the day the employee left work, and the day that the 180-day period begins to run is the day the employee left work. 36/ However, there is some contrary authority in the Title VII area. The failure to hire based on unlawful discrimination can constitute a continuing violation where an ongoing discrminatory policy is in effect. 37/

The extent to which Title VII cases can control the result in an ADEA case is somewhat unclear. Therefore, in termination

---

1980) (the mere failure to recall a laid-off employee is not a continuing violation of the ADEA, any claim arising from the lay-off accrued on the day the employee left work and not when he was subsequently placed on early retirement); Pierce v. Green Giant Co., 26 Emp. Prac. Dec. 32,074 (D.C. Tex. 1981) (even the fact that the employee continued to work on special assignment until retirement did not extend the time limit to file an age charge). But see Brennan v. Central Virginia Health Facilities, Inc., 7 Emp. Prac. Dec. 9173 (W. D. Va. 1973) (where each day that wages were withheld to employees such activity constituted a continuing violation sufficient to overcome a motion to strike the plaintiff's complaint).

36/ Id., Woodburn and Cutright, supra.

37/ Roberts v. North AM Rockwell Corp, 650 F.2d 823 (6th Cir. 1981); Rich v. Martin Marietta, 522 F.2d 333 (10th Cir. 1975), Macklin v. Spector Freight Systems, Inc., 478 F.2d 979 (D.C. Cir. 1973); Belt v. Johnson Motor Lines, Inc., 458 F.2d 443 (5th Cir. 1972); Bartmess v. Drewrys U.S.A., Inc., 444 F.2d 1186 (7th Cir. 1971), cert. denied, 404 U.S. 939 (1971).
These cases under Title VII of the Civil Rights Act of 1964, 42 U.S.C. §706(e), are relevant to ADEA cases because the notice requirements set out in both the ADEA and Title VII are similarly worded. Because of these similarities, courts refer to the Title VII interpretations for assistance in defining analogous provisions of the ADEA. See, e.g., Dartt v. Shell Oil Co., 539 F.2d 1256 (10th Cir. 1976), aff'd by an equally divided court, 434 U.S. 99 (1977) (establishing the equitable tolling of the 180-day notice requirement); Coke v. General Adjustment Bureau, Inc., 640 F.2d 584 (5th Cir. 1981) (en banc). See note 24 supra.
In Goldman v. Sears, Roebuck & Co., 607 F.2d 1014 (1st Cir. 1979), where an employee alleged violations of Title VII and the ADEA, the court held that in order to state a continuing violation, a complaint must indicate not only the injury, but also the fact that the discrimination is ongoing. The court was unwilling to find a continuing violation of the ADEA and Title VII where the employee was transferred from department to department in one of Sears' stores. Id. at 1018, 1019.

of employment situations the diligent litigant should seek to file the charge with the EEOC within 180 days or 300 days, in deferral states, of the date that services to the employer cease. Similarly, in situations where services to the employer continue or the employee is merely laid-off, the charge should be filed within 180 (or 300) days of any adverse action by the employer against the employee. 38/

D. *The Limitations Periods Applicable To Filing A Lawsuit*

Under the ADEA, a private litigant's right to file a lawsuit or civil action is subject to two time limitations--a 60-day period which begins after he files his charge alleging wrongful discrimination with the EEOC and a two-year statute of limitations for nonwilful violations of the Act or a three-year statute of limitations if the violation of the Act was wilful. 39/ The purpose of the 60-day period is to allow for conciliation efforts by the EEOC. 40/

If conciliation efforts by the EEOC fail and it brings an action on behalf of an aggrieved employee under the Act, the right of such aggrieved employee to bring a civil action

---

38/ See Coke v. General Adjustment Bureau, Inc., 640 F.2d 584 n.2 (5th Cir. 1981) (en banc) (date of demotion of employee is starting date for 180-day notice period, not date when employee could reasonably be expected to know demotion was for discriminatory reason).

39/ 29 U.S.C. § 626(c)(1) provides in relevant part: "any person aggrieved may bring a civil action in any court of competent jurisdiction for such legal and equitable relief as will effectuate the purposes of this Act..."
  29 U.S.C. § 626(d) provides that: "no civil action may be commenced under this section until 60 days after a charge alleging unlawful discrimination has been filed with the Secretary...." (now the EEOC, see note 4, supra.)
  29 U.S.C. § 626(e)(1) provides that: "Sections 6 and 10 of the Portal-to-Portal Act of 1947 shall apply to actions under this Act..." (see note 28, supra.)

40/ 29 U.S.C. § 626(d) provides in relevant part: "Upon receiving such a charge (from an "aggrieved person" or "individual") the Secretary (EEOC, see note 4, supra) shall promptly notify all persons named in such charge as prospective defendants in the action and shall promptly seek to eliminate any alleged unlawful practice by informal methods of conciliation, conference, and persuasion...." (emphasis added).
  The proposed EEOC Procedural Rules on Age Discrimination in Employment Act, 29 C.F.R. § 1626 (1981), at section 12 follow the language of 29 U.S.C. § 626(d), above, and require that conciliation by the EEOC be initiated.

terminates. 41/ If, on the other hand, an employee brings a civil action prior to the expiration of the 60-day period, either the suit will be dismissed, or an order will be entered directing that the suit be held in abeyance pending expiration of the 60-day period. 42/ In order for a litigant to avoid any problem with this 60-day waiting period, suit should not be filed any earlier. The courts have clearly stated that the 60-day requirement is jurisdictional either in the sense of subject matter jurisdiction or in the sense of a condition precedent to suit. Only in the latter case is equitable modification available and then only when special circumstances so warrant. 43/

With respect to the second time limitation on the private litigant's right to file a civil action, the courts have construed the term "wilful violation" as action taken by the employer involving knowledge or suspicion that the action taken might violate the ADEA. 44/

41/ 29 U.S.C. § 626(c)(1) (1976) provides: "the right of any person to bring such action [civil action] shall terminate upon the commencement of an action by the Secretary [EEOC] to enforce the right of such employee under this Act.

42/ Cannon v. University of Chicago, 559 F.2d 1063 (7th Cir. 1976), rev'd on other grounds, 441 U.S. 677 (1979), requires that any action commenced prior to the 60-day period shall be dismissed for want of jurisdiction. Id. at 1076, 1077.
    Rucker v. Great Scott Supermarkets, 528 F.2d 393 (6th Cir. 1976), on the other hand, states that the 60-day period is jurisdictional but only where the special facts of the case do not warrant equitable relief. Id. at 395, see also McCree, Circuit Judge (concurring).
    Gabriele v. Chrysler Corp., 573 F.2d 949 (6th Cir. 1978), vacated and remanded on other grounds, 442 U.S. 908 (1979), suggests that the proper course to follow where a suit is filed before the expiration of the 60-day period is that "the district court need not dismiss the complaint but should hold the case in abeyance for the requisite period of time." Id. at 956 n. 18. Gabriele also followed Rucker, supra in holding that § 626(d)'s requirements are a condition precedent to suit in federal court, but noncompliance does not deprive the court of power to hear the case. Id. at 955 n. 15.

43/ Rucker, supra, at 395, found no basis for equitable modification where the employee alleged a "good faith effort" to comply with the requirements of § 626(d).

44/ See Olsen v. Southern Pac. Trans. Co., 480 F. Supp. 773 (N.D. Cal. 1979). Olsen required only "substantial evidence that the employer knew or suspected that his actions might violate the ADEA." (emphasis added).

Other courts have used a similar formulation. 45/ The ordinary period is two years and three years where a wilful violation is found. The courts state that the purpose of the extra year in the case of wilful violations is to prevent an employer from delaying a lawsuit by misleading its employee as to his rights. 46/ It must also be mentioned that the statute of limitations is subject to tolling. 47/ The ADEA provides that while the EEOC is attempting conciliation, the period a private litigant retains the right to file a civil action is tolled, but not for a period in excess of one year. 48/ Thus, where the private litigant's right to bring a civil action has not been superceded by an EEOC court action on his behalf, in order to avoid the ambiguities surrounding "wilful violations," the private litigant should file his suit more than 60 days after the charge is filed and less than two years from the date of the alleged unlawful practice.

E. <u>The Relationship Between Suits By The Government And Suits By Private Litigants.</u>

Where the EEOC files a lawsuit to enforce the right of an employee under the ADEA, such employee's right to "bring" his own civil action is terminated. 49/ One reported district court decision has held that a prior ADEA suit filed by an aggrieved

---

45/ <u>Coleman v. Jiffy June Farms, Inc.</u>, 458 F.2d 1139 (5th Cir. 1972), provides that a "wilful violation" under the Fair Labor Standards Act of 1938, § 7 <u>as amended</u>, 29 U.S.C. § 207, and the Portal-to-Portal Act of 1947, § 6 <u>as amended</u> 29 U.S.C. § 255, is a "deliberate, voluntary and intentional act as distinguished from one committed through inadvertence, accidentally, or by ordinary negligence." <u>Id</u>. at 1142.

46/ <u>See</u> <u>Brennan v. Heard</u>, 491 F.2d 1, 3 (5th Cir. 1974). The employer would have reason to mislead or delay an employee when it knew that its actions were possibly violative of a statute prohibiting employment discrmination. <u>See</u> <u>Kelly v. American Standard, Inc.</u>, 640 F.2d 974 (9th Cir. 1981) (where the court distinguishes between a wilful violation for purposes of the statute of limitations and a "wilful violation" for purposes of the liquidated damages provision of section 7(b) of the ADEA. 29 U.S.C. § 626(b) (1976).

47/ 29 U.S.C. § 626(e)(2) (1976).

48/ <u>Id</u>. The section provides for tolling of the statute of limitations with respect to conciliations commenced after April 6, 1978. 29 U.S.C. § 626(e)(2) (1976), <u>as amended by</u> Age Discrimination in Employment Act Amendments of 1978, Pub. L. No. 95-256, 92 Stat. 189.

49/ 29 U.S.C. § 626(c)(1) (1976). <u>See</u> note 41, <u>supra</u>.

person is to be dismissed upon a subsequent filing by the EEOC on behalf of such person. 50/ The authors submit that this is unlikely to be the accepted view as it rests on a strained interpretation of the word "bring" contained in the ADEA and appears to be contrary to the purposes of the Act.

F. The Federal-State Relationship In Sections 7(d) And 14(b) Of The ADEA.

1. Generally

Perhaps the most vexing problem and the one which has generated the most litigation under the ADEA is the effect of the Federal-State relationship as set forth in Sections 7(d) and 14(b) of the ADEA. 51/ These sections in essence state that an

---

50/ Jones v. City of Janesville, Wis., 488 F. Supp. 795 (W.D. Wis. 1980). The employee filed a civil action on October 17, 1979. The EEOC commenced an action to enforce the right of the employee on October 19, 1979. The court noted that 29 U.S.C. § 626(e)(1) terminated the right of any person to "bring" an action. The court stated: "Bring is ambiguous. It may mean 'commence.' It may mean 'maintain.' It may mean 'bring or maintain.' I construe it to mean 'bring or maintain.'" The court went on to note that since Congress intended to bar an individual suit when the EEOC had previously commenced suit, it must have also intended that no private suit be maintained simultaneously with a suit filed by the EEOC. Id. at 797.

However, there are reasons why the court should allow for the maintenance of a private suit. As the court pointed out, the private attorney might receive reimbursement for his fees, thereby causing less of a burden to the private litigant. Also, the interests of the EEOC and the private litigant do not necessarily coincide; the EEOC would no doubt seek relief for other members of the protected group. For a result contrary to that reached in Jones, supra, see Shepperd v. National Broadcasting Co., 22 EPD ¶ 30876 (S.D.N.Y. 1980).

51/ Section 7(d) of the ADEA, 29 U.S.C. § 626(d) provides in pertinent part:

No civil action may be commenced by an individual under this section until 60 days after a charge alleging unlawful discrimination has been filed with the Secretary. Such a charge shall be filed:

(1) within 180 days after the alleged unlawful practice occurred; or
(2) in a case to which Section 14(b) applies, within 300 days after the alleged unlawful practice occurred, or within 30 days after receipt by the individual of notice of termination of proceedings under State law, whichever is earlier.

- 14 -

individual must file a charge within 180 days of the unlawful act or, in a case to which section 14(b) applies (i.e., a State which has a law prohibiting age discrimination with a State authority empowered to grant relief), within 300 days of the unlawful act or within 30 days of termination of the State proceedings, whichever is earlier. 52/

Section 14(b) states further that no civil action may be brought before the expiration of 60 days after proceedings have been commenced under the State law, unless such proceedings have been earlier terminated.53/ The question arises under section 14(b) as to which States meet the requirements. Section 1626.10 of the proposed regulations of the EEOC lists the States the EEOC considers "referral States." 54/

> Upon receiving such a charge, the Secretary shall promptly notify all persons named in such charge as prospective defendants in the action and shall promptly seek to eliminate any alleged unlawful practice by informal methods of conciliation, conference, and persuasion.

Section 14(b) of the ADEA, as set forth in 29 U.S.C. § 633(b), provides in relevant part:

> In the case of an alleged unlawful practice occurring in a State which has a law prohibiting discrimination in employment because of age and establishing or authorizing a State authority to grant or seek relief from such discriminatory practice, no suit may be brought under section 626 of this title before the expiration of sixty days after proceedings have been commenced under the State law, unless such proceedings have been earlier terminated: Provided,. . . (i)f any requirement for the commencement of such proceedings is imposed by a State authority other than a requirement of the filing of a written and signed statement of the facts upon which the proceedings is based, the proceeding shall be deemed to have been commenced for the purposes of this subsection at the time such statement is sent by registered mail to the appropriate State authority.

52/ Id.

53/ Id.

54/ Proposed EEOC Procedural Rules on Age Discrimination in Employment Act, 29 C.F.R. § 1626 (1981). § 1626.10 provides in relevant part:

§ 1626.10 Referral States.

(a) States to which all ADEA charges are referred: Alaska, California, Connecticut, Delaware, District of

2. The commencement of State proceedings in deferral States

Prior to the Supreme Court's decision in Oscar Mayer & Co. v. Evans, 441 U.S. 750 (1979), the circuits were split concerning the effect of the Federal-State relationship set forth in sections 7(d) and 14(b) of the ADEA. Specifically, the circuits were divided on the question of whether the commencement of State agency proceedings was mandatory in deferral States. 55/

One view held that it was unnecessary to file with the State agency in a deferral State, 56/ while the other view held that in order to maintain an action in federal court, prior resort to the State agency was mandatory. 57/

In Oscar Mayer, the Supreme Court resolved the conflict. It held that the commencement of state proceedings is mandatory in deferral states, but that this step may be taken after a federal court action is begun, and the federal action may be held in abeyance pending the outcome of the state proceedings. 58/

The effect of the holding is to require state proceedings in deferral states. A litigant, therefore, must file with the appropriate state agency if he wishes to pursue his federal

---

Columbia, Florida, Georgia, Hawaii, Idaho, Illinois, Iowa, Kentucky, Maryland, Massachusetts, Michigan, Minnesota, Montana, Nebraska, Nevada, New Hampshire, New Jersey, New Mexico, New York, Oregon, Pennsylvania, South Carolina, Utah, West Virginia and Wisconsin.

55/ Prior to Oscar Mayer & Co. v. Evans, 441 U.S. 750 (1979), there were two views concerning whether, in deferral States, the commencement of State proceedings by a private litigant was mandatory. See Holliday v. Ketchum, MacLeod & Grove, Inc., 584 F.2d 1221 (3rd Cir. 1978) (en banc) (no prior resort to state agency procedures is required as a precondition to commencing a federal action charging age discrimination under the ADEA); Evans v. Oscar Mayer & Co., 580 F.2d 298 (8th Cir. 1978), reversed and remanded, Oscar Mayer & Co. v. Evans, 441 U.S. 750. Contra, Reich v. Dow Badische Co., 575 F.2d 363 (2nd Cir. 1978), cert. denied, 439 U.S. 1006 (1979) (employee's failure to timely file complaint with state agency having authority over his age discrimination claim precluded maintenance of action is federal court).

56/ Holliday, supra, at 1230.

57/ Reich, supra, at 370.

58/ 441 U.S. 750, 764.

remedy. The litigant then will have to wait 61 days before initiating a civil action in federal court.

The dispositive factor in the Supreme Court's decision appeared to be the fact of the similarity between section 706(c) of Title VII and section 14(b) of the ADEA. 59/

Because 706(c) of Title VII had consistently been construed to require prior resort to state law, section 14(b), which is virtually identical in its terms to § 706(c), was construed to have the same effect. 60/

Another effect of Oscar Mayer is that an aggrieved individual may commence state proceedings at any time, with reference to only one requirement: that state proceedings be commenced within 60 days before federal litigation is instituted. 61/ Therefore, the failure to timely file with the state will have no effect upon a federal action, and the 60-day time period for bringing a civil action in federal court begins to run upon the "filing of a written and signed statement of the facts upon which the proceeding is based." 62/

    3. The initiation of State proceedings and the 300 day filing period.

The Supreme Court's decision in Oscar Mayer was clear in two respects: a deferral state litigant must file his claim with the appropriate state agency if he wishes to pursue or to continue to pursue his ADEA remedy, and such proceedings with the state agency need not be commenced within time limits specified by state law. 63/

59/ "Section 14(b) of the ADEA was patterned after and is virtually in haec verba with § 706(c) of Title VII (formerly § 706(b)), 78 Stat. 259, as redesignated, 86 Stat. 104, 42 U.S.C. § 2000e-5(c) . . . ." Oscar Mayer, supra, at 755.

60/ The court stated: Since the ADEA and Title VII share a common purpose, the elimination of discrimination in the workplace; since the language of § 14(b) indicates that its source was § 706(c), we may properly conclude that Congress intended that the construction of § 14(b) should follow that of § 706(c) . . . ." Oscar Mayer, supra, at 756.
    See also Love v. Pullman Co., 404 U.S. 522 (1972).

61/ Oscar Mayer, supra, at 759.

62/ See 29 U.S.C. § 633(b), note 51, supra.

63/ Oscar Mayer & Co. v. Evans, 441 U.S.750, 758, 759 (1979).

Thus, if a litigant's state complaint is dismissed as untimely, his federal remedy would not be impaired. 64/

However, the Supreme Court's decision in Oscar Mayer did not answer a key issue: whether a prospective plaintiff in a deferral state must file his charge with the appropriate state agency within 180 days of the alleged unlawful practice to be entitled to the extended filing period of 300 days to file his charge with the EEOC. 65/

64/ The rationale of Oscar Mayer appears to approve of the following procedural scenario as proper in a deferral state in order to preserve ADEA remedies:

1. A person aggrieved may file a charge with the EEOC, the appropriate state agency, or both concurrently.

   a. If the person aggrieved files his charge with the EEOC and the appropriate state agency concurrently, he must await the expiration of 60 days before he may bring a civil action. See §§ 7(d) and 14(b) of the ADEA.

   b. If the person aggrieved files his charge only with the EEOC, he must await the expiration of 60 days before he may bring a civil action. Id. According to Oscar Mayer such suit will not be dismissed but held in abeyance pending the necessary filing of a charge with the state agency.

   c. If the person aggrieved files his charge only with the appropriate state agency, he must wait 60 days unless the state proceeding terminates earlier and file a charge with the EEOC within the time limits of § 7(d)(2) of the ADEA, wait 60 days, and then file suit in federal district court.

2. As prescribed by Oscar Mayer, these minimum periods apply irrespective of the timeliness of the filing with the state agency under state law time limits. It should be stressed that even if the filing with the appropriate state agency is not timely under state law time limits it has no effect on the time limits for filing an action in the U.S. District Court as set out in sections 7(d) and 14(b) of the ADEA.

65/ See Ciccone v. Textron, Inc., 616 F.2d 1216 (1st Cir. 1980), vacated at 101 S. Ct. 311 (1980), which read Oscar Mayer as requiring a deferral state litigant to file a charge with the appropriate state agency within 180 days or forfeit the extended filing period of 300 days in which to file a charge with the EEOC. Accord, Ewald v. Great Atlantic & Pac. Tea Co., Inc., 620 F.2d

---

- 17 -

61

The circuits had split on this issue. 66/ One view held that if the deferral state litigant failed to commence proceedings with the appropriate state agency within 180 days, he should be treated the same as a nondeferral state litigant. 67/ The opposing viewpoint simply refused to read into the ADEA a requirement that a deferral state complainant file a charge with the appropriate state agency within 180 days in order to obtain the benefit of the extended period in which to file a charge with the EEOC. 68/

This split in the circuits appears to be resolved by the Supreme Court's decision in Mohasco Corp. v. Silver, 447 U.S. 807 (1980). Mohasco criticized the narrow view taken by the First and Sixth Circuits which denied a deferral state complainant 300 days in which to file a charge with the EEOC where state agency proceedings had not been commenced within 180 days. 69/ Accordingly, on remand from the Supreme Court, the First and Sixth Circuits held that "the longer period of 300 days is to be allowed for federal filing in deferral states." 70/

G. Actions

Class actions under Rule 23 of the Federal Rules of Civil Procedure are unavailable to private litigants under the ADEA. 71/ The ADEA incorporates section 216 of the Fair Labor Standards Act. That section allows private litigants to "opt

---

1183 (6th Cir. 1980); cf. Olson v. Rembrandt Printing Co., 511 F.2d 1228 (8th Cir. 1975) (Title VII).

66/ See Bean v. Crocker Nat. Bank, 600 F.2d 754 (9th Cir. 1980), which read Oscar Mayer as imposing no requirement that a deferral state litigant file his charge with the appropriate state agency within 180 days in order to obtain the benefit of the 300-day federal filing period. Accord, Davis v. Calgon Corp., 627 F.2d 674 (3rd Cir. 1980).

67/ Ewald, supra, at 1187.

68/ Bean, supra, at 758, 759.

69/ Mohasco Corp. v. Silver, 447 U.S. 807, 814, n.16, 19 (1980), expressly criticizing the view taken in Ciccone v. Textron, supra.

70/ Ciccone v. Textron, Inc., 651 F.2d 1 (1st Cir. 1981). Accord, Ewald v. Great Atlantic & Pac. Tea Co., Inc., n.1 (6th Cir. Jan. 6, 1981) (on remand). See also Avakian v. Trinity Memorial Hospital of Cudahy, Inc.,) 514 F. Supp. 1297 (E.D.Wis. 1981) (no 240-day limit).

71/ E.g., LaChapelle v. Owens-Illinois, Inc., 513 F.2d 286 (5th Cir. 1975).

- 19 -

into" an existing lawsuit. More specifically, section 216(b) provides that an employee may bring an action on behalf of himself and other employees who are "similarly situated" and who file written consents to join in the action. 72/ There is a conflict among the circuits with respect to whether each person who attempts to join in an action must satisfy the requirement of filing a charge with the EEOC. 73/ In light of the broad remedial purposes of the ADEA, the better view is that rigid technical compliance with the charge requirement is too harsh a construction, especially where the EEOC has already been put on notice of a class seeking relief. 74/ Where the EEOC is aware of a potential class of aggrieved individuals, requiring all members to file a charge alleging age discrmination would appear to be repetitive and burdensome to the courts, the aggrieved individuals, EEOC and the employer.

H. Remedies and Attorney's Fees

Section 7(c) of the ADEA provides that a person aggrieved may bring a civil action in any court of competent jurisdiction for such legal or equitable relief as will effectuate the purposes of the Act. 75/ Section 7(b) of the ADEA, 76/ incorporates the powers, remedies and procedures provided in sections 11(b), 16, and 17 of the Fair Labor Standards Act of 1938. 77/ Available remedies for a person aggrieved include back wages and benefits as well as an equal amount in liquidated damages. 78/ There is a split within the circuits as to whether damages for

---

72/ See Naton v. Bank of California, 649 F.2d 691 (9th Cir. 1981).

73/ McCorstin v. United States Steel Corp., 621 F.2d 749 (5th Cir. 1980) (class action could not be maintained where no "intent to sue letter," (now a "charge") was filed with the "Secretary of Labor" (now the EEOC) nor did members of purported class give notice of affirmative consent). Contra, Mistretta v. Sandia Corp., 639 F.2d 588 (10th Cir. 1980) (two timely charges filed with the "Secretary" were held sufficient to allow employees similarly situated to opt into the suit upon filing notice of affirmative consent despite no individual charges filed by the prospective class members).

74/ Mistretta, supra, at 594.

75/ 29 U.S.C. § 626(c).

76/ 29 U.S.C. § 626(b).

77/ 29 U.S.C. §§ 211(b), 216, 217.

78/ E.g., Kelly v. American Standard, Inc., 640 F.2d 974 (9th Cir. 1981).

pain and suffering are recoverable. Four circuits have held they are not; however, there is authority to the contrary. 79/ There are also two holdings which deny recovery for injury to reputation. 80/

The availablity of liquidated damages in addition to amounts recovered for back wages and benefits depends on a showing of a "wilful violation" of the ADEA. 81/ In order to establish a "wilful violation" under the ADEA the litigant must show a "knowing and voluntary violation of the Act" However, cases have held that although there is a wilful violation, a good faith defense is available to the employer in resisting a claim for liquidated damages. The better view appears to be to the contrary. 82/

The cases also address the question of an employee's duty to mitigate damages and the collateral source rule. An employee has the duty to seek other employment in order to mitigate damages. 83/ Amounts paid as unemployment compensation are also to be deducted from the back pay award in some circuits. 84/

79/ Rogers v. Exxon Research and Engineering Co., 550 F.2d 834 (3rd Cir. 1977), cert. denied, 434 U.S. 1022 (1978) (compensatory damages for pain and suffering including emotional distress are not recoverable); Walker v. Pettit Const. Co., 605 F.2d 128 (4th Cir 1979); Vazquez v. Eastern Air Lines, Inc., 579 F.2d 107 (1st Cir. 1978); Dean v. American Sec. Ins. Co., 559 F.2d 1036 (5th Cir. 1977), cert. denied, 434 U.S. 1066 (1978). Contra, Bertrand v. Orkin Exterminating Co., 419 F. Supp. 1123 (N.D. Ill. 1976); Cf. Kennedy v. Mountain States Tel. & Tel. Co., 449 F. Supp. 1008 (D. Colo. 1978) (punitive damages based upon intentional infliction of emotional distress held recoverable).

80/ Schlicke v. Allen-Bradley Co.., 448 F. Supp. 252 (E.D. Wisc. 1978); Dorsey v. Consolidated Broadcasting Corp., Radio Station WEMP, 432 F. Supp. 542 (E.D. Wisc. 1977).

81/ E.g., Wehr v. Burroughs Corp., 619 F.2d 276 (3rd Cir. 1980). Syvuck v. Milwaukee Boiler Mfgr. Co., Nos. 80-2851, 81-1022 (7th Cir. Nov. 24, 1981).

82/ See Kelly v. American Standard, Inc., 640 F.2d 974, 980 (9th Cir. 1981), and cases cited therein.

83/ Bucholz v. Symons Mfg. Co., 445 F. Supp. 701 (E.D. Wisc. 1978); Coates National Cash Register Co., 433 F. Supp. 655 (W.D. Va. 1977).

84/ Buchholz supra. Cf. Marshall v. Goodyear Tire & Rubber Co., 554 F.2d 730 (5th Cir. 1977) (discretionary with trial judge). Contra, Marshall v. Arlene Knitwear, Inc., 454 F. Supp. 715 (E.D. N.Y. 1978).

Severance pay and any amounts which can be shown to be earnable with reasonable diligence are also to be deducted from an award of back wages. 85/

With respect to attorney's fees, the ADEA incorporates section 216 of the Fair Labor Standards Act. 86/

That section provides for the award of attorney's fees to a prevailing plaintiff. 87/ Section 216 also authorizes a separate determination of fees in the event of appellate level legal services. 88/ One court, in the case of legal services performed at the administrative agency level, refused to award any fees, partly on the basis that the ADEA requires no administrative steps be taken, other than giving notice to the EEOC before filing a civil action. 89/

II. LITIGATION BY THE GOVERNMENT

Section 7(b) of the ADEA authorizes the EEOC, after first attempting conciliation, to file suit to enforce the right of an aggrieved person. 90/ Section 7(c)(1) of the Act provides that the right of any aggrieved person to bring a civil action shall terminate upon commencement of an action by the EEOC. 91/ Section 7(e)(2) provides that for the period during which the EEOC is attempting conciliation under section 7(b), the statute

---

85/ Marshall, supra, at 730.

86/ 29 U.S.C. § 216(b).

87/ See Cova v. Coca-Cola Bottling Co. of St. Louis, 574 F.2d 958 (8th Cir. 1978); Rodriquez v. Taylor, 569 F.2d 1231, 1250 n. 34 (3rd Cir. 1977), cert. denied, 436 U.S. 913 (1978).

88/ See Cleverly v. Western Elec. Co., 594 F.2d 638 (8th Cir. 1979, and case cited therein; Kelly v. American Standard Inc., 640 F.2d 974 (9th Cir. 1981); See also Houghton v. McDonnell Douglas Corp., 627 F.2d 828 n. 17 (8th Cir. 1980). In Houghton, the Eighth Circuit specifically held that the plaintiff and the EEOC were entitled to attorney's fees in litigation in all federal courts. The amount thereof was left to the discretion of the district court.

89/ Kennedy v. Whitehurst, 49 U.S.L.W. 1146 (3/24/81). But Cf. New York Gaslight Club, Inc. v. Carey, 447 U.S. 54 (1980) (Title VII litigants may recover fees incurred in state fair employment practice agency proceedings, if successful).

90/ 29 U.S.C. § 626(b). (Again, references to the "Secretary" in the Act define the duty of the EEOC).

91/ 29 U.S.C. § 626(c)(1).

of limitations shall be tolled but in no event for a period in excess of one year. 92/ Finally, section 14(a) provides that upon commencement of an action under the ADEA, such action shall supercede any state action. 93/

A. Conciliation

The major procedural requirement affecting the government under the ADEA is conciliation. The report of the conference committee on the 1978 amendments to the ADEA clearly stated that "conciliation" is not a jurisdictional prerequisite to suit. 94/ That report cited the case of Brennan v. Ace Hardware 95/ for the proposition that district courts have equitable jurisdiction to stay civil actions pending before them to permit conciliation. 96/ This principle has been followed by other courts. 97/ Equitable jurisdiction to stay proceedings pending the completion of procedural requirements was an approach taken by the Supreme Court when it decided the Oscar Mayer case. 98/

What constitutes conciliation is not free from doubt; however, the courts have stated that the essential elements are that the government should demonstrate the validity of its claim, despite the fact that the data is also available to the employer in its own files, and the government should respond in some way to the employer's contentions. 99/ The authors submit that this does not require a full trial of the alleged unlawful practices at the conciliation stage. Such a requirement would be contrary to the Act, which states that the purpose of conciliation is to "effect voluntary compliance...through informal methods of...conference, and persuasion." 29 U.S.C. § 626(b). Moreover,

---

92/ 29 U.S.C. § 626(e)(2).

93/ 29 U.S.C. § 633(a).

94/ See 46 U.S.L.W. 55 (5/9/78).

95/ 497 F.2d 368 (8th Cir. 1974).

96/ Id.

97/ See EEOC v. Fox Point School Dist., 24 Emp. Prac. Dec. 31, 408, 24 FEP Cases 668 (E.D. Wisc. 1980).

98/ 441 U.S. 750 (1979). The procedural requirement before the court in that case, however, was not conciliation, but prior resort to state administrative agencies in deferral states. See notes 55-64, supra.

99/ See Dunlop v. Sandia Corp., 13 FEP Cases 128 (D.C. N.M. 1975).

requiring a full trial at the conciliation stage would lead to innumerable delays and hamper enforcement of the Act.

The failure of the government to attempt to conciliate after receiving a timely charge would not bar a discharged employee from bringing his own action against an employer. 100/ This view is in accord with section 7(d) of the Act which states that an individual cannot commence a civil suit until 60 days after a charge has been timely filed. 101/

CONCLUSION

This procedural review of the ADEA has attempted to give all members of the public affected by the Act, as well as practicing members of the bar, a deeper insight into the major procedural requirements contained in the Act. If the authors have accomplished this goal, this article has served its purpose.

100/ Lundgren v. Continental Industries, Inc., 14 FEP Cases 58 (D.C. Okla. 1976); Woerner v. Bell Helicopter, 16 FEP Cases 480 (D.C. Tex. 1977).

101/ 29 U.S.C. § 626(d).

INTERPRETING THE ADEA: INTENT OR IMPACT

Alfred W. Blumrosen *

---

* B.A. 1950, J.D. 1953, University of Michigan. Professor
of Law, Rutgers--The State University of New Jersey; Of
counsel, Kaye, Scholer, Fierman, Hays & Handler, New
York. Chief of Conciliations, United States Equal
Employment Opportunity Commission, 1965-67; Consultant,
Equal Employment Opportunity Commission, 1977-79, on
reorganization, procedures, Uniform Guidelines on Employee
Selection Procedures, and Affirmative Action guidelines;
Consultant intermittently since 1967 to the United States
Departments of Labor, Justice, Housing & Urban
Development, Equal Employment Opportunity Commission,
state and local human rights agencies; advisor to private
parties in equal employment matters, 1973-77, 1979 to
present; author, Black Employment and the Law (1971) and
law review essays; labor arbitrator since 1957; Acting
Dean, Rutgers Law School, 1974-75. The views expressed
herein are those of the author, and not necessarily those
of any government agency.

TABLE OF CONTENTS

I. THE LEGISLATIVE HISTORY OF THE ADEA......................4

    A. The Secretary of Labor Reports........................5
    B. Congress Requests Action On The Report..............14
    C. The President's Message..............................14
    D. The "Findings And Purpose" In The Bill..............16
    E. The Congressional Hearings..........................17
    F. The Debate On The Floor.............................21
    G. "Solely" Because Of Age.............................22
    H. The Statutory Language..............................25
    I. The Initial Administrative Interpretation..........27

II. FROM 1967 TO THE 1978 AMENDMENTS........................28

III. THE NEW ADMINISTRATIVE INTERPRETATION....................31

IV. THE QUESTION OF POLICY..................................33

V. GELLER V. MARKHAM EXAMINED..............................37

VI. SOME PRACTICAL CONSEQUENCES OF CONFINING THE ADEA
TO THE "INTENT" STANDARDS...............................39

    1. Burden of Persuasion................................39
    2. Burden of going forward with Evidence:
       The Prima Facie Case................................40
    3. The "cost" justification............................42

VII. CONCLUSION..45

INTERPRETING THE ADEA: INTENT OR IMPACT

New statutes frequently define the conduct which is to be regulated in words of uncertain meaning. The interpretation of these words will determine the limits of the influence of the statute. 1/ In employment discrimination law, the crucial question is whether the statute prohibits conduct which is "intended" to restrict opportunities or whether it also prohibits conduct which has an "adverse impact" on opportunities of members of protected groups regardless of the employer's intent. 2/

This question of "intent" or "impact" may have major social ramifications. The "impact" definition of discrimination under Title VII of the Civil Rights Act of 1964 was a major factor in the increase in the employment opportunities for minorities and women during the 1970's. 3/ In

---

1   See Blumrosen, Toward Effective Administration of New Regulatory Statutes, 29 Ad. L. Rev. 87 (1977).

2   See generally Blumrosen, Strangers in Paradise: Griggs v. Duke Power Co. and the Concept of Employment Discrimination, 71 Mich. L. Rev. 59 (1973-2) [hereinafter cited as Strangers in Paradise].

3   See Blumrosen, Strangers in Paradise note 2, supra; Blumrosen, The Bottom Line Concept in Equal Employment

contrast, the "intent" standard defining race discrimination, which had been in effect from 1945 to 1970, made little difference. Without the "impact" test, it is unlikely that the equal employment opportunity issue would have commanded so much attention in the legal and industrial relations communities. This attention then produced profound revisions in employment practices.

This same potential for social change inheres in the the Age Discrimination in Employment Act.[4] Therefore, the question of "intent" or "impact" under the ADEA is of great practical and theoretical concern. If employers must eliminate employment practices which adversely affect employees between 40 and 70 and are not required by business necessity, there will be greater job protection for older workers than if the law prohibits only practices which are intended to restrict opportunities of older workers. Correspondingly, employer decision-making is restricted to a greater extent under the "impact" test than under the "intent" test. The lower court decisions[5] and the literature[6] have

---

[3] (Footnote Continued)

Opportunity Law 12 N. Car. C. L. Jour 1 (1980); Comptroller General, Further Improvement Needed in EEOC Enforcement Activity, p. 45, Apr. 9, 1981

[4] 29 U.S.C. 621 et seq.

[5] Geller v. Markham, 635 F.2d 1027 (2d Cir. 1980) (applies adverse impact standard); Loeb v. Textron, Inc., 600 F.2d 1003 (1st Cir. 1979) (applies method of proof in "intent" cases). But see Laugesen v. Anaconda Co., 510 F.2d 307 (6th Cir. 1975); Kephart v. Institute of Gas Technology, 23 FEP 1412 (1st Cir. 1980), Marshall v. Goodyear Tire & Rubber Co., 554 F.2d 730, 736 (5th Cir. 1977)(all expressing reservations about the significance of statistics because of the normal cycle of employment of persons of various ages.

[6] See e.g., O'Donnell, Lasser and Bailor, The Federal Age Discrimination Statute; Basic Law, Areas of Controversy and Suggestions for Complaince, 15 Wake Forest L. Rev. 1 (1979); (assumes adverse effect principle of Title VII applicable, no discussion of the issue); Player, Defenses under the ADEA, Misinterpretation, Misdirection and the 1978 Amendments, 12 Ga. L. Rev. 747 (1979) (assumes adverse effect principle of Title VII applicable, no discussion of the issue); Calille, Three Developing Issues of the

(Footnote Continued)

approached this question obliquely, and the Supreme Court has not addressed it at all in the 14 years since the ADEA was adopted.[7]

The Equal Employment Opportunity Commission, which recently acquired administrative enforcement authority under the ADEA,[8] has changed the "intent" standard of the original ADEA regulations into an "impact" standard.[9] The Second Circuit in Geller v. Markham[10] has recently adopted the "impact" standard overtly. Under these circumstances, it is appropriate to take a close look at the issues involved in de-

---

6   (Footnote Continued)

Federal Age Discrimination in Employment Act of 1967, 54 U. of Det. Jour. of Urban Law 431 (1977) (Discusses use of Title VII precedents, including use of statistics in making prima facie case (at p. 496), without discussing whether the case involves "effect" or "intent."); M. McKenry, Enforcement of Age Discrimination in Employment Legislation, 32 Hastings L. Jour. 1157 (1981) (Notes Problem of Differing Policies under the Two Acts.) Note, The Cost of Growing Old: Business Necessity and the Age Discrimination in Employment Act, 88 Yale L.J. 565 (1979), (The authors state, note 3, that, ". . . this note draws on judicial interpretations of comparable provisions and purposes of Title VII. There are important similarities between the two statutes, but also significant differences. . . .) Note, The Age Discrimination in Employment Act of 1967, 90 Harv. L. Rev. 380 (1976) (Discusses factual differences between age, and race/sex situations, but does not discuss whether the "effect test is applicable under ADEA.); Note, Proving Discrimination under the Age Discrimination in Employment Act, 17 Ariz. L. Rev. 494 (1975) (argues that the purposes of the two statutes are "analogous," that Congress did not make absence of intent a defense and that since "willful" violations are subject to increased damages, innocent violations were expected to produce liability.)

7   See Justice Rehniquist's dissent from the denial of certiorari in Geller v. Markham, 101 S. Ct. 2028 (1981).

8   Reorganization Plan No. 1 of 1978, 43 Fed. Reg. 19807, 92 Stat. 3781.

9   See text infra at notes ____.

10 635 F. 2d 1027 (2d Cir. 1980).

ciding whether the ADEA should be interpreted to proscribe employer actions which have "adverse impact" on persons in the protected age group as well as actions "intended" to restrict their opportunities.[11]

I. THE LEGISLATIVE HISTORY OF THE ADEA

The legislative history of the ADEA is a model of lucidity. In 1964, Congress requested the Secretary of Labor to report on problems of age discrimination. That report, submitted in 1965, explicitly distinguishes "arbitrary age discrimination" from "factors which bear more strongly on older workers as a group than younger workers." The report recommended that "arbitrary age discrimination" be prohibited and that the "other factors" be dealt with by manpower policy, not statutory prohibitions. Congress then demanded that these recommendations be presented in statutory form. The Secretary of Labor's report influenced a presidential statement, congressional committee reports, and most legislators who addressed the issue during the process of enacting the ADEA. This legislative history drives the reader to the conclusion that "intent" to discriminate on the basis of age was the gravamen of age discrimination, and that actions which have "adverse effect" on older workers were not to be considered illegal.

In contrast, the statutory language which expresses this congressional intention can easily be read as prohibiting employer conduct which has an "adverse effect" on employment opportunities of older workers. This language was copied verbatim from Title VII of the Civil Rights Act of 1964.[12] The Title VII language was interpreted to include the "impact" test in Griggs v. Duke Power Co.[13] This decision, although it was rendered in 1971, four years after the adoption of the ADEA, affords legitimate reason to contend that the same mean-

---

11 See United Steelworkers v. Weber, 443 U.S. 193 (1979); Bd. of Ed. of New York v. Harris, 101 S. Ct. 363 (1979); County of Washington v. Gunther, 101 S. Ct. 2244 (1981).

12 42 U.S.C. 2000e(2)(a). The fact that Title VII substantive provisions were incorporated "in haec verb" has been noted by the Supreme Court. Lorrilard v. Pons, 434 U.S. 575, 584 (1978). The Supreme Court notation has, in turn, been used to justify the application of Title VII principles under the ADEA. See Standjev v. Ebasco Services, Inc., 643 F.2d 914 (1981).

13 401 U.S. 424 (1971).

ing should be given the same words in the ADEA.[14] As a result, we are faced with a legislative history and statutory language which point in different directions on the issue of "intent" or "impact".

A. The Secretary Of Labor Reports

In the Civil Rights Act of 1964 Congress requested the Secretary of Labor to make a "full and complete study of the factors which might tend to result in discrimination in employment because of age. . ." and to report "such recommendations for legislation to prevent arbitrary discrimination in employment because of age as he determines advisable."[15] This provision was adopted to head off efforts -- largely but not exclusively -- by Southern Democrats to include Age Discrimination in Title VII in order to "overload" and thus "sink" the bill.[16]

Pursuant to the Congressional mandate, in June, 1965, Secretary of Labor Wirtz submitted a report entitled "The Older American Worker, Age Discrimination in Employment."[17] The report interpreted Section 715 as establishing two areas of study -- one relating to discrimination that was "arbitrary" and the other calling for a consideration of "factors which might tend to result in discrimination." This distinction permeates the legislative history of the ADEA. The Report begins by distinguishing racial discrimination from age discrimination:

---

[14] See Sands, Statutes and Statutory Construction, (4th Ed.) § 51.3, 73 Am. Jur. 2d. Statutes § 227.

[15] Pub. L. 88-352, Title VII, § 715, 78 stat. 265.

[16] In the House of Representatives, an effort to insert age as a prohibited category was made on the same day as sex was included in the statute. The effort was rejected, as it was in the Senate, in part by reference to the requirement that the Secretary of Labor study the subject. See 110 Cong. Rec. 2596-97, 99, (House). 13490-92 (Senate). The purpose of those who introduced "sex" into the statute is noted in County of Washington v. Gunther, 101 S. Ct. at 2258, n.4 (1981).

[17] U.S. Department of Labor, Report to the Congress on Age Discrimination in Employment under Section 715 of the Civil Rights Act of 1964 (1965), hereafter cited as Secretary's Report; reprinted, Hearings, note 28 infra, p. 201.

- 6 -

"The gist of the matter is that 'discrimination' means something very different, so far as employment practices involving age are concerned, from what it means in connection with discrimination involving -- for example -- race. It means in connection with the age question, furthermore, several different things.

"Employment discrimination because of race is identified, in the general understanding of it, with non-employment resulting from feelings about people entirely unrelated to their ability to do the job. There is no significant discrimination of this kind so far as older workers are concerned.

"The most closely related kind of discrimination in the non-employment of older workers involves their rejection because of assumptions about the effect of age on their ability to do a job <u>when there is in fact no basis for these assumptions</u>. It is this which Congress refers to, in Section 715 of the Civil Rights Act, as 'arbitrary discrimination.'

"A third type of discrimination -- which should perhaps be called something else entirely -- involves decisions not to employ a person for a particular job because of his age <u>when there is in fact a relationship between his age and his ability to perform the job</u>. The only reason for marking out this third area is that it clearly does exist so far as the age question is concerned, but does not exist so far as, for example, racial or religious discrimination are concerned.

"There is finally, so far as age is concerned, that kind of 'discrimination' which results when an employer turns an older man or woman away, not because of concern about the individual's ability to perform the work, but because of programs and practices actually designed to protect the employment of older workers while they remain in the work force, and to provide support when they leave

75

> it or are ill. Seniority and promotion -
> from - within systems, and pension and
> insurance programs, are a mark of civili-
> zation. They vastly enhance the dignity,
> the security, the quality of the later
> years of life in the United States.
> At the same time, ironically, they some-
> times have tended to push still further
> down the age at which employers begin
> asking whether or not a prospective employee
> is too old to be taken on.[18]

"Arbitrary discrimination" is equated in the report with employer policies of imposing "Specific Age Limits" on hiring:[19]

B. Arbitrary Discrimination: Specific Age Limits

> The most obvious kind of age discrimination
> in employment takes the form of employer policies
> of not hiring people over a certain age, without
> consideration of a particular applicant's indivi-
> dual qualifications. These restrictive practices
> appear in announced employer policies (e.g., in
> Help Wanted advertisements; or in job orders filed
> with employment agencies) or in dealings with appli-
> cants when they appear in the hiring office.[20]

Having canvassed the illogic and impropriety of such "arbitrary" age limits, the report states:

---

18 Secretary's Report, pp. 5-6.

19 The discussion of upper age limits for <u>hiring</u> is not accompanied by a similar discussion of age limits for termination although the discussion of state laws indicates that they covered discriminatory discharge employees because of age. Secretary's Report, p. 9 In United Airlines v. McMann, 434 U.S. 192 (1977) the Supreme Court majority noted that the "primary purpose of the bill was the hiring of older workers, 434 U.S. at 203, n.9."

20 Secretary's Report at 6. This emphasis on the word "arbitrary" was argued unsuccessfully to affect plaintiff's burden of persuasion in Marshall v. Goodyear Tire & Rubber Co., 22 FEP. 775 (W.D. Tenn. 1979). It was not argued with respect to the "intent" versus "impact" issue.

> "Consideration has been given in the preceding section to the arbitrariness of specific age limitations, indiscriminatorily applied. It is equally important to recognize the force of certain circumstances which unquestionably affect older workers more strongly as a group than they do younger workers."[21]

These circumstances included health factor differentials between younger and older workers, the lower educational attainment of older workers, changes in technology, possible lowerings of productivity and a "range of institutional arrangements that indirectly restrict the employment of older workers."[22] These institutional arrangements include the principle of promotion from within, seniority systems, costs under workmen's compensation law and costs in connection with pension and health insurance plans.

The report thus treats "arbitrary age limits" on hiring (and inferentially on termination) as one kind of problem and the other factors "which affect older workers more strongly as a group" as another kind of problem. Only the first is called "arbitrary age discrimination." The report concludes with the recommendation,[23] "Action to Eliminate Arbitrary Age Discrimination in Employment." Under that heading, it states:

> "There is persistent and widespread use of age limits in hiring that in a great many cases can be attributed only to arbitrary discrimination against older workers on the basis of age and regardless of ability. The use of these age limits continues despite years of effort to reduce this type of discrimination through studies, information and general education undertaken by the Federal Government and many States, as well as by nonprofit and employer and labor organizations.
>
> "The possibility of new nonstatutory means of dealing with such arbitrary dis-

---

21 Secretary's Report, p. 11.

22 Id. at 15.

23 Id. at 21, 22.

crimination has been explored. That area is barren.

"State experience with statutes prohibiting discrimination in employment on the basis of age indicates that such practice can be reduced by a well-administered and well-enforced statute, coupled with an educational program. It is clear from this experience that an educational program to promote hiring on the basis of individual merit is far more effective when provided for by statute.

"The elimination of arbitrary age limits on employment will proceed much more rapidly if the Federal Government declares, clearly and unequivocally, and implements so far as is practicable, a national policy with respect to hiring on the basis of ability rather than age.

"Such implementation should emphasize the role to be played by persuasion and education, both in general and in individual cases of alleged violations of policy, and should provide for action in the event that persuasion and education fail.

"Specific provision should be made for handling instances of alleged arbitrary discrimination where the facts of the case indicate that the older worker in question needs reeducation, training, counseling, or health and other services. In these cases, the individual should be referred to the appropriate programs for needed assistance. . .

"A clear-cut and implemented Federal policy against arbitrary discrimination in employment on the basis of age would provide a foundation for a much needed vigorous, nationwide campaign to promote hiring on the basis of ability rather than age."

Other recommendations in this report were intended to address institutional arrangements which worked a disadvantage to older workers,[24] to increase the availability of work for older workers[25] and to enlarge educational opportunities for older workers.[26] These separate and distinct recommendations reinforce the conclusion that the statutory prohibition on age discrimination was intended to prohibit only specific age limits for hiring or termination.

Although this report was written six years before Griggs was decided, the distinction that it contained between "arbitrary discrimination" and "factors which affect older workers more strongly as a group than they do younger workers," foreshadowed Griggs. The Report did not suggest that institutional practices which had an "adverse effect" on older workers should be declared illegal. On the contrary, it recommended that institutional pressures, such as those arising from pension systems, be eased by special programs which would not discourage hiring of older workers. The only practice which the report proposed to declare illegal was the setting of a specific age limit for hiring or termination in disregard of individual capacity. Such a practice would have to be "intentional" by its nature.

The Report distinguished the philosophy of the ADEA from that of Title VII of The Civil Rights Act of 1964 and associated legislation which dealt primarily with race discrimination. The Report noted:

> "Employment discrimination because of race is identified, in the general understanding of it, with non-employment resulting from feelings about people entirely unrelated to their ability to do the job. There is no significant discrimination of this kind so far as older workers are concerned."[27]

Thus from the beginning, age discrimination was viewed as a different phenomena from race discrimination --a phenomena that did not flow from a long history of prejudice and subordination but rather, flowed from contemporary assumptions that individuals at a certain age lost the capacity to engage in certain activities. The legal remedy

---

[24] Id. at 22.

[25] Id. at 23.

[26] Id. at 24.

[27] Id. at 2.

for such discrimination was the striking down of specific age barriers. The conventional definition of discrimination, the "intent" to act upon the basis of the proscribed characteristic, was sufficient to encompass the purpose set forth in the Secretary of Labor's report.

In the Fall of 1965 the Subcommittee on Labor of the House Committee on Education and Labor held hearings on "Employment Problems of Older Workers."[28] Secretary Wirtz had just published his report on the older American. His written statement included the following:[29]

> "First, we need to eliminate arbitrary age discrimination in employment where it exists. . . .
>
> * * *
>
> Second, we need action to adjust certain institutional arrangements where they work to the disadvantage of the older worker.
>
> Pension plan limitations were cited by some employers as a reason for not hiring older workers. . . .
>
> Similarly, promotion-from-within policies and staffing policies designed to maintain a work force age balance often restrict hiring to lower paid entry levels considered unsuitable for older workers.
>
> Seniority systems which protect workers with long service may -- where units were narrow and rules rigid -- result in layoffs of older workers with long service from one unit while new workers are being hired in another.
>
> Third area of action involves the

---

[28] Hearings on Employment Problems of Older Workers, on H. Rep. 10634 etc., Subcommittee on Labor of House Committee on Education and Labor, 89th Cong., 1st sess. (Aug. 25, 31, Sept. 1, 2, 1965).

[29] Id. at 21, 22.

- 12 -

increased availability of work by creating more jobs and improved matching of skills and jobs.

> The fourth and last area of action . . . calls for a new system of continued training and educational opportunity to prepare workers, while they are still employed, for job changes, to reduce their vulnerability to displacement, to protect them against discrimination, and to open the way to satisfying activity in retirement.

In his oral testimony he said:

> "It is a startling fact that about half of all job openings in this country are simply closed to people over 55 years of age. It is so startling a fact that it is the kind of thing that a person does not want to believe and, therefore, he is not going to believe, for the next year or two. It is a fact of the same kind that a quarter of the jobs in the country are closed to people over 45. . . The report is built really around two approaches to this problem. The specific assignment was to look at the matter of discrimination against workers on account of direct age discrimination."[30]

Then he said

> "I want to make a point in connection with this. There ought to be a different word in the English language to cover the situation we are talking about here.
>
> "The word 'discrimination' in employment has taken its color, its caste, now, from the problem as it arises in connection with racial discrimination. This is such a different problem from that, that it is unfortunate the same word is involved. There are elements of whatever you want to call it as far as racial

---

30   Id. at 24, 25.

- 13 -

>discrimination is concerned, elements of [,] well there is no point in characterizing them in this stage of the progress in that area, but it is quite different from what is involved here.
>
>"There is no antagonism on anybody's part toward an older person. Just none at all. Quite the contrary. And I say again it is too bad that we have to use the same word, because age discrimination is such a different kind of discrimination. It results, as far as our studies are concerned --this study of 500 firms and other studies -- from a basic misunderstanding of fact, and an assumption that people lose their power to contribute to an establishment of one sort or another, as age progresses."[31]

Later in hearing there occurred an exchange which confirms that legislation was aimed at specific age limits on hiring.

Congressman O'Hara asked Mr. Conway, the director of the New York Human Rights Agency whether he agreed that, "If the government were to tackle effectively the problem of discrimination on account of age in employment, that an essential element would be an out right prohibition on arbitrary discrimination on account of age?

>Mr. Conway: I believe this is absolutely essential. If there is a valid statute which gives powers of enforcement, then the prohibition becomes effective. . . .
>
>...I am very certain that in the State of New York we have accomplished much more by way of education; that is to say, conference with employers and this sort of thing because we had the big stick behind us. Absent that I think they would have listened to us very politely and gone on about their merry way, and because <u>traditionally they had fixed age limits</u>, they would remain at that point."[32] (Emphasis added)

---

[31] Id. at 26. Senator Javits' statement quotes the Secretary's report as does his oral testimony. Id. at 51, 52.

[32] Id. at 129.

B. Congress Requests Action On The Report

In 1966, Congress, in amending the Fair Labor Standards Act, included the following language:

> "The Secretary of Labor is hereby directed to submit to the Congress not later than January 1, 1967 <u>his specific legislative recommendations</u> for <u>implementing the conclusions contained in his report</u> on age discrimination in employment made pursuant to Section 715 of Public Law 88-352."[33] (Emphasis added)

This legislative direction emphasizes the importance of the Secretary's Report as the basic document shaping the thinking in Congress which led to the Age Discrimination Act. This is but the first of a chain of statements which link the Secretary's report directly to the statute as it was ultimately adopted.

C. The President's Message

The legislation that was proposed in 1967 which became the Age Discrimination in Employment Act was recommended to the Congress by President Johnson. President Johnson's statement on "Older Americans" concluded with a call for legislation to "prohibit arbitrary age limits in employment," a phrasing which echoed the distinction drawn in the Secretary of Labor's report.

On January 23, 1967 the President delivered a special message to Congress proposing programs for older people.[34]

He said:

> "One of the tests of a great civilization is the compassion and respect shown to its elders. Too many of our senior citizens have been left behind by the progress they work most of their lives to create. Too often the wisdom and experience of our senior citizens is lost or ignored. Many who are able and

---

[33] P. Law 89-601, Sec. 601, 606 (1966).

[34] Public Papers of the Presidents, Lyndon B. Johnson, Jan. 23, 1967, No. 12.

willing to work suffer the bitter rebuff of arbitrary and unjust job discrimination."[35]

After making proposals with respect to increase in social security benefits, increase in welfare benefits, tax reform, medicare, nursing and health care, the President discussed "job opportunities for the older American" and included the following statement:[36]

> "Opportunity must be opened to many Americans over 45 who are qualified and willing to work. We must end arbitrary age limits on hiring. Though 23 states have already enacted laws to prohibit discriminatory practices, the problem is one of national concern and magnitude.
>
> "I recommend that: -- the Congress enact a law prohibiting arbitrary and unjust discrimination in employment because of a person's age. -- The law cover workers 45 to 65 years old -- the law provide for conciliation and enforcement if necessary through cease and desist orders, with court review -- the law provide an exception for special situations where age is a reasonable occupational qualification, where the employee is discharged for good cause, or where the employee is separated under a regular retirement system. -- educational and research programs on age discrimination be strengthened."

The President went on to note

> "Employment opportunities for older workers cannot be increased solely by measures eliminating discrimination. Today's high standards of education, training and mobility often favor the younger worker. Many older men and women are unemployed because they are not fitted for the jobs of modern technology: be-

---

35   Id. at 32.

36   Id. at 37-38.

cause they live where there are no longer
any jobs, or because they are seeking
jobs of a bygone era. . . .

"I am directing the Secretary of
Labor to establish a more comprehensive
program of information, counselling and
placement service for older workers. . . ."

Again, the distinction first drawn in Secretary
Wirtz' report appears. The elimination of "discrimination"
would not, in the President's view, affect the "high standards of education, training and mobility [which] . . . favor
the younger worker." The "adverse effect" test of discrimination is implicitly rejected. Once again "arbitrary and
unjust" discrimination refers only to specific age limits.

D. The "Findings And Purpose" In The Bill

The statement of findings and purpose in the bill
which was originally introduced was adopted without change.[37]
One of these findings confirms the distinction discussed
above:

(2) the setting of arbitrary age limits
regardless of potential for job performance has become a common practice, and
certain otherwise desirable practices
may work to the disadvantage of older
persons;

The distinction between "arbitrary age limits" and practices
which "work to the disadvantage of older persons" expressed
in § 621(a)(2) reflects the basic distinction in the Secretary of Labor's report.

In addition, the last finding states:

(4) the existence in industries affecting commerce of arbitrary discrimination
in employment because of age burdens
commerce and the free flow of goods in
commerce.

It is only "arbitrary discrimination" and not "practices (which) may work to the disadvantage of older workers,"
which is stated in §4 to burden interstate commerce. This

---

[37] 29 U.S.C. 621(a)(2), (a)(4).

suggests that only "arbitrary discrimination" was the subject of the prohibitions in the law.

Section 621(b) states a threefold purpose of the law: "To promote employment of older persons based on their ability rather than age; to prohibit arbitrary age discrimination in employment; to help employers and workers find ways of meeting problems arising from the impact of age on employment."

This statement reflects that the distinction in the Secretary of Labor report was maintained by the Congress; prohibiting "arbitrary age discrimination" was separate from helping "employers and workers find ways of meeting problems arising from the impact of age on employment."[38]

E. The Congressional Hearings

Secretary Wirtz' written testimony in hearings before both House and Senate Committees[39] carries forward this concept that "arbitrary age discrimination" is the deliberate disregard of a worker's ability solely because of age. It focused on research and other programs to deal with

---

[38] This distinction is confirmed in the section by section analysis in the Senate report which was reprinted in the Congressional Record. S. Rep. 723, reprinted, 113 Cong. Rec. 31249 (Nov. 6, 1967), states "The section, in subsection (b), declares it to be the purpose of the Act to promote employment of older persons based on their ability rather than age, to prohibit arbitrary age discrimination in employment and to help employees and workers find ways of meeting problems arising from the impact of age on employment." (Id. at 31251) (Emphasis added) This statement makes clear that the policy statement in the ADEA did in fact refer to three distinct purposes -- the "ending of arbitrary age discrimination" was viewed as different from "helping employees and workers meet problems arising from the impact of age on employment." Assistance in meeting these problems was to come through the research and promotional activities and educational activities provided for in the act. Thus Congress envisioned that age might have an impact on employment even when "arbitrary age discrimination" was eliminated.

[39] See Hearings before the Subcommittee on Labor of the Senate Committee on Labor and Public Welfare on S.830 and s.788, March 15, 16 and 17, 1967, p. 8.

- 18 -

other aspects of the problems of older workers.

The hearings began with the introduction of bills, including S.830 which, with certain modifications, became the ADEA.[40]

Senator Javits' prepared statement quoted Secretary Wirtz "landmark report" on the older American worker:

> "an unmeasured but significant proportion of the age limitations presently in effect are arbitrary in the sense that they have been established without any determination of their actual relevance to job requirements and are defended on grounds apparently different than their actual explanation."

He recited the Secretary's recommendation for a clear and unequivocal announcement of national policy with respect to hiring on the basis of ability rather than age.[41]

Senator Jennings Randolph's statement[42] noted that Secretary Wirtz' report had,

> ". . . listed four steps which he deemed essential to insure an adequate beginning toward solving employment prob-

---

[40] Ibid. The record included a letter from the Undersecretary of the Department of HEW, Wilbur Cohen, dated March 20, 1967 which recommends favorable consideration of the bill. The letter cites both the President's message and the June 30, 1965 report of the Secretary of Labor on age discrimination. It quotes from the report that "the possibility of new non-statutory means of dealing with such arbitrary discrimination has been explored. That area is barren." It also quotes: "the elimination of arbitrary age limits on employment will proceed much more rapidly if the federal government declares, clearly and unequivocally, and implements so far as is practicable, a national policy with respect to hiring on the basis of ability rather than age." Assistant Director Rommel of the Bureau of the Budget also submitted a letter which referred to Secretary Wirtz' testimony of March 15, 1967 and recommended enactment of the bill.

[41] Id. at 23.

[42] Id. at 31.

- 19 -

>lems of older workers. One of these we are now considering in hearings, the Secretary has described as 'action to eliminate arbitrary age discrimination in employment.' The other three action steps recommended by the Secretary were (1) action to adjust institutional arrangements which work to the disadvantage of the older workers; (2) action to increase the availability of work for older workers and (3) action to enlarge educational concepts in institutions to meet needs and opportunities of older age."

This statement demonstrates an awareness of the distinction between "arbitrary" age limits and institutional arrangements which adversely affected older workers which was expressed in the Secretary's report.

In his oral testimony Secretary Wirtz stated

>"We faced a problem in connection with the development of this legislation in this testimony as to whether we should say unjust and arbitrary discrimination. Now, on the one hand, discrimination in itself connotes unjustness and arbitrariness.
>
>"To say 'unjust and arbitrary discrimination' leads to the question, what other kind of discrimination is there? We have left out of this bill the phrase, 'arbitrary', but discrimination throughout this bill means unjust and arbitrary discrimination if there is any doubt about that."[43]

The hearings resulted in House and Senate Committee Reports which cited the Secretary of Labor's Report and continued to focus on specific age limits.[44] The House Committee report stated:

>"The Committee further recognizes that

---

43 Id. at 43.

44 H.R. 805 90th Cong. 1st Sess., p.1 (October 23, 1967); S. Rep. 723, 90th Cong. 1st Sess., p.2 (Nov. 4, 1967).

in some industries, such as the railroad industry, a disproportionately high number of older workers are found in the work force (a Department of Labor report states that one sixth of railroad engineers are sixty-five and over.) In some cases, this has resulted from a decline in total employment in such an industry, coupled with the exercise of seniority rights. <u>The Committee does not intend that the legislation be administered in such a way as to worsen a situation as this, or to prevent an employer from achieving a reasonable age balance in his employment structure.</u> It is expected that the Secretary will recognize these particular situations and treat them according to their individual merits on a case by case basis."[45]

The opportunity to maintain a "balanced" labor force based on age which was recognized by both House and Senate Committees, is consistent with the Secretary of Labor's recognition that practices such as promotion from within which might have an adverse impact on the employment opportunities of older job applicants, would not be illegal. The employer who chose to "promote from within" could expect to maintain a "reasonable age balance" by hiring primarily younger employees. While a rigid refusal to hire older employees would violate the statute, the practices of promoting incumbent employees would not. Similarly, an employer whose employee age balance was similar to the railroad industry discussed in the Committee report could take action to redress such an imbalance which did not run afoul of the ban on specific age limitations. The achievement of a "reasonable age balance" necessarily means that termination rates will be higher among older workers to make room for younger

---

[45] H. Rep. 805, supra note 44, at p.7. The Senate Report, S. Rep. 723, note 44, supra. at p.7 took a similar view: "The committee further recognizes that in some industries a disproportionately high number of older workers are found in the work force. In some cases, this has resulted from a decline in total employment in such an industry, coupled with the exercise of seniority rights. The committee does not intend that the legislation be administered in such a way as to worsen a situation such as this."

ones.⁴⁶

F. <u>The Debate On The Floor</u>

The speeches on the floor in the House in support of the Bill echo the Secretary of Labor's report. One representative substantially quoted the part of the Secretary of Labor's Report where he distinguished the problem of age discrimination from race discrimination on the grounds that age did not involve bigotry.[47] Another quoted the part of the Report which distinguished between arbitrary age limits to be prohibited by law and misunderstandings by employers to be addressed by education and research.[48] Several of the speakers who supported the passage of the Age Discrimination Act referred at least once to the Secretary of Labor's report.[49]

Senator Javits, a moving figure in the adoption of the ADEA, said in the Senate:

> ". . . it is a sad day indeed when a man realizes that the world has begun to pass him by; that happens to all of us sooner or later. But it is surely a much greater tragedy for a man to be told, arbitrarily, that the world has passed him by, merely because he was born in a certain year or earlier, when he still has the mental and physical capacity to participate in it as energetically and vigorously as anyone else."[50]

This statement reinforces the concept that it was the specific and arbitrary age limit to which Congress directed its attention in the 1967 law.

---

[46] A point recognized in Laugesen v. Anaconda Co., 510 F.2d 307 (6 Cir. 1975) and Marshall v. Goodyear Tire & Rubber Co., 554 F.2d 730 (5th Cir. 1977).

[47] 113 Cong. Rec. 34742, (Rep. Burke).

[48] <u>Id</u>. at 34746 (Rep. Dent).

[49] <u>Id</u>. at 34741 (Rep. Perkins); 34742 (Rep. Matsonaga); 34742 (Rep. Dent).

[50] <u>Id</u>. at 31254.

- 22 -

Senators Javits and Yarborough agreed that the ADEA would not conflict with the employment discrimination provisions of Title VII. "I do not think this presents any particular problem. The Civil Rights Act of 1964 does not cover age discrimination and S. 830 does not cover racial or religious discrimination. The laws will operate completely independently of each other, as will the enforcement procedures."[51]

Senator Young then spoke about the evils of the specific ban on employment of persons of certain age[52] and the bill was passed.

G. "Solely" Because Of Age

There is other evidence in the legislative history supporting a more restricted reading for the ADEA then of Title VII. The Secretary's report and Senators' statements, including particularly Senator Javits', constantly spoke in terms of discrimination "solely" on the basis of age. In fact, there is what appears to be a carefully worked out colloquy of this matter on the floor.

Senator Javits:[53]

"Section 4 of the bill specifically prohibits discrimination against any 'individual' because of his age. It does not say the discrimination must be in favor of someone younger than age 40. In other words, if two individuals ages 52 and 42 apply for the same job and the employer selected the man aged 42 solely -- and I emphasis that word 'solely' -- because he is younger than the man 52 then he will have violated the act. The whole test is somewhat like the test in an accident case -- did the person use reasonable care. A jury will answer yes or no. The question here is: Was the individual discriminated against solely because of his age? The alleged discrimination must be proved and the

---

51   Id. at 31255.

52   Id. at 31256.

53   Id. at 31255.

burden of proof is upon the one who would assert that that was actually the case. Would the senator from Texas be kind enough to advise the Senate whether he agrees with that interpretation of the bill?

Sen. Yarborough. . .

"if two men applied for employment under the terms of this law, and one was 42 and one was 52, naturally, the personnel officer or employer would have a choice to make. But if they were of equal capability, or one was higher than the other, he could not turn either one down on the basis of the age factor, he would have to go into the capabilities, experience, of the two men, or he might have to give them a test, either manual or mental, or whatever test that particular personnel officer would require to see if they could do the work. The law prohibits age being a factor in the decision to hire as to one age over the other whichever way his decision went."

While Senator Yarborough's comment is slightly ambiguous, it reflects an affirmative answer to Senator Javits' inquiry. The use of the term "solely" in front of the term discrimination was common in the debate and Senator Javits' emphasis on the term did not produce any dissent from Senator Yarborough.

In 1964, Senator McClelland had sought to insert the word "solely" into the bill to prohibit race, sex, national origin and religious discrimination which ultimately became Title VII of the Civil Rights Act. This amendment was opposed vigorously by the supporters of the act. Senator Case said, "The difficulty with this amendment is that it would render Title VII totally nugatory. If anyone ever had an action that was motivated by a single cause, he is a different kind of animal from any I know of. But beyond that difficulty, this amendment would place upon persons attempting to prove a violation of this section, no matter how clear the violation was, obstacles so great as to make the Title completely worthless."[54]

---

[54] 110 Cong. Rec. 13837.

Senator Magnuson stated, "The difficulty is that a legal interpretation or a court interpretation of the word 'solely' would so limit this section as probably to negate the entire purpose of what we are trying to do."[55] The proposal was defeated. A similar proposal had been defeated in the House of Representatives.[56] Yet, three years later the same body accepted the concept that it was prohibiting discrimination that was based "solely" on age.

This reinforces the conclusion that the focus of the Congress in 1967 was on those specific and direct age limitations which the Secretary of Labor's report had outlined. Those age limitations are not subtle, they are brutal. "If you are over a certain age we will not employ you and when you reach a certain age we will fire you." To say that the firing had to have been "solely" because of those age limitations does not pose proof problems which arise if the discrimination involved was "subtle and illusive." The "sole cause" concept is the natural complement to a prohibition on fixed age limits for hiring and firing.

The consistent use of the word "solely" by major proponents of the legislation is further evidence that the Congress considered that it was eradicating the specific practice of rigid age limits rather seeking more generally to eliminate the adverse effect of employment practices on older workers. It is not conclusive in itself because it is common in civil rights debates to address evils which are said to be based "solely" on a characteristic which is sought to be protected. But, when coupled with legislative attention to specific age limits, it points to the concrete problem addressed by the law.

Thus, the legislative history leads to the conclusion that "arbitrary age discrimination" referred to specific age limits for hiring and, inferentially, for retirement. The bulk of the legislative history was directed at maximum age limits for hiring of new employees. The Report recognized that there were many other practices which had an adverse effect on older workers but which were not to be included within the concept of "arbitrary age discrimination." The focus on the specific age limits made it natural to condemn such limits as illegal when they were the "sole cause" of the alleged discrimination.

---

[55] Ibid.

[56] 110 Cong. Rec. 2728 (1964).

H. The Statutory Language

The congressional discussions did not focus on the particular form of words in the ADEA. Congress simply copied the words from Title VII replacing "race, color, religion, sex and national origin," with the word "age"[57] with respect to employers, labor organizations, employment agencies, publications and retaliation.

The words of § 623(a) of the ADEA do not clearly answer the question of whether the act is violated by proof of "impact" without proof of "intent":

> It shall be unlawful for an employer--
>
> (1) to fail or refuse to hire or to discharge any individual or otherwise discriminate against any individual with respect to his compensation, terms, conditions, or privileges of employment, because of such individual's age;
>
> (2) to limit, segregate, or classify his employees in any way which would deprive or tend to deprive any individual of employment opportunities or <u>otherwise adversely affect his status as an employee, because of such individual's age</u>.[58]
> (Emphasis added.)

Four years after the ADEA was enacted, the equivalent of § 623(a)(2) in Title VII (§ 703(a)(2)) was construed to incorporate the "adverse impact" definition of discrimination.[59]

The language of § 623(a)(2) after the "or otherwise" clause does support such a reading. But it is also possible to read it as relating to the <u>conditions</u> of employment, while the preceding language relates to the <u>existence</u> of employment. In this reading, both parts of § (a)(2) would relate to intentional conduct.

---

[57] 42 U.S.C. 2000e2(a).

[58] 29 U.S.C. 623(a)(1), (2).

[59] Griggs v. Duke Power Co., 401 U.S. 424 (1971); Dothard v. Rawlinson, 433 U.S. 321 (1977); Nashville Gas Co. v. Satty, 434 U.S. 136 (1977).

What was the interpretation of § 703(a) of Title VII in 1967 when Congress adopted its language in the ADEA? At that time, there were few District Court opinions on the merits in Title VII litigation.[60] One common understanding of the term "discrimination" was that it did require proof of "intent."[61] Thus, the legislators may be forgiven for using the substantive language of Title VII to express a narrower principle than that which the court later held was applicable under Title VII.[62] The language of the ADEA, without the gloss of Griggs, is consistent with the conclusion that Congress sought only to eliminate specific age barriers, be they directly articulated or be they implemented through a "subterfuge".[63]

---

[60] Two opinions on the merits of Title VII claims before December, 1967 were inconclusive on the possible scope of Title VII's definition of discrimination. See Bowe v. Colgate Palmolive Co., 272 F. Supp. 332 (S.D. Ind. 1967) rev. 416 F.2d 711 (7th Cir. 1969); Vogler v. McCarthy, Inc., 294 F. Supp. 368 (D.C. La. 1967), affirmed, sub nom Asbestos Workers Local 53 v. Vogler, 407 F.2d 1047 (5th Cir. 1969) In 1968, after the ADEA was adopted, the first major opinions were issued on this issue. They differed. In Quarrels v. Philip Morris, 279 F. Supp. 505 (E.D. Va. 1968) the continuing effects of prior discrimination were held by Judge Butsner to constitute discrimination. In Griggs v. Duke Power Co., Judge Gordon took the opposite view and held that a present intention to discriminate was necessary to show a Title VII violation, 292 F. Supp. 243 (1968) rev. in part, 420 F.2d 1225 (4th Cir. 1970) rev. in part 401 U.S. 424 (1971).

[61] See Bonfield, the Substance of American Fair Employment Practice Legislation I: Employers, 61 Nw. U. L. Rev. 901, 955-56 (1967) (Race); NOTE, Age Discrimination in Employment: The Problem of the Older Worker, 41 N.Y.U.L. Rev. 383 (1966) (Age).

[62] The "impact" test has been recognized since Griggs as a separate and distinct concept of Discrimination. See INt'l Bhd of Teamster v. United States, 431 U.S. 324, 335-36 n. 15 (1977); County of Washington v. Gunther, 101 S. Ct. 2242 at 2248 (1981).

[63] 29 U.S.C. 623(f)(2). See Justice White's explanation of "Subterfuge", United Air Lines v. McMann, 434 U.S. at 207 (1977).

I. The Initial Administrative Interpretation

The original administrative interpretation of the Act is consistent with this view.[64] While this interpretation does not sharply focus on the definition of discrimination, it does address both of the issues identified above: (1) Whether the statute is intended to deal only with purposeful discrimination and (2) whether that purposeful discrimination must be the sole cause of the harm done to the employee. The administrator's interpretations suggest that the employer's "purpose" is important. For example, in discussing the requirement in help wanted notices that an applicant state his or her age, the regulation says " . . . because the request that an applicant state his age may tend to deter older applicants or otherwise indicate a discrimination based on age, employment notices or advertisements which include the phrase "state age" or any similar term, will be closely scrutinized to assure that the request is <u>for a permissible purpose and not for purposes proscribed by the statute.</u>"[65] (Emphasis added). The phrase "for a permissible purpose and not for purposes proscribed by the statute," appears also in relation to questions concerning age in job applications.[66]

In discussing differentiations based on "reasonable factors other than age," the "sole cause" approach is modified by the interpretations; "the clear purpose (of the Act) is to insure that age, within the limits proscribed by the Act, is not a <u>determining factor</u> in making any decision regarding hiring, dismissal, promotion or any other term, condition or privilege of employment of any individual."[67] (emphasis added) This "determining factor" language has been adopted by many courts in their analysis of the required connection between age discrimination and the harm to the employee.[68]

---

[64] The interpretation issued by the acting wage hour administrator, Department of Labor, June 12, 1968, is at 29 C.F.R. 860.

[65] 29 CFR 860.92(d).

[66] Id. at 860.95.

[67] Id. at 860.103(c).

[68] See, e.g., Loeb v. Textron, Inc. 600 F.2d 1003 (1st Cir. 1979).

II. FROM 1967 TO THE 1978 AMENDMENTS

Thus, in 1967, at the time of the adoption of the ADEA, the language of § 623 was consistent with a conventional definition of discrimination which all concerned in the legislative process had understood. That definition required "intent" to act on the basis of age. Thereafter, events took place under Title VII which were to raise the questions about this definition.

The seminal event, of course, was the decision of the Supreme Court in <u>Griggs</u> v. <u>Duke Power Co.</u>, in 1971, which adopted the "adverse impact" or "disparate impact" test under Title VII. <u>Griggs</u> held that Title VII did not require proof of a discriminatory intent on the part of the employer whose practices adversely affected minority employees and were not justified by business necessity.[69] In 1973, the Court explained that this concept had been adopted to assure that "childhood deficiencies in education and background of minority citizens resulting from forces beyond their control, not be allowed to work a cumulative and invidious burden on such citizens for the remainder of their lives."[70] As previously noted, Secretary Wirtz' report had explicitly indicated that there was no "background of bigotry" in the age discrimination situation.

After <u>Griggs</u>, the next relevant event was the amendment of Title VII in 1972, to give the EEOC the power to institute suit in federal courts, and to expand its coverage. In the course of the legislative process leading to these changes, Committee reports in both houses noted that the law which had unfolded under Title VII had developed considerably beyond the understanding of discrimination that had existed in 1964:

> Employment discrimination, as we know today, is a far more complex and pervasive phenomenon. Experts familiar with the subject generally describe the problem in terms of "systems" and "effects" rather than simply intentional wrongs. The literature on the subject is replete with discussions of the mechanics of seniority and lines of progression, perpetuation of the present effects of earlier

---

69 <u>See</u> Strangers in Paradise, note 2, supra.

70 McDonnell Douglas Corp. v. Green, 411 U.S. 792, 806 (1973).

discriminatory practices through various institutional devices, and testing and validation requires. The forms and incidents of discrimination which the Commission is required to treat are increasingly complex. Particularly to the untrained observer, their discriminatory nature may not appear obvious at first glance. A recent striking example was provided by the U. S. Supreme Court in its decision in <u>Griggs</u> v. <u>Duke Power Co.</u>, 401 U.S. 424, 91 S. Ct. 849, 3 <u>FEP Cases</u> 175 (S. Ct. 1971), where the Court held that the use of employment tests as determinants of an applicant's job qualification, even when nondiscriminatory and applied in good faith by the employer, was in violation of Title VII if such tests work a discriminatory effect in hiring patterns and there is no showing of an overriding business necessity for the use of such criteria. It is increasingly obvious that the entire area of employment discrimination is one whose resolution requires not only expert assistance, but also the technical perception that a problem exists in the first place, and that the system complained of is unlawful.[71]

Thus the Congress when it amended Title VII in 1972 was aware of the broadening of the concept of employment discrimination under that statute. In 1978, when Congress amended the Age Discrimination Act, it did not refer to the broad interpretation that Title VII had by then received in such cases as <u>Griggs</u>. Rather, the sponsors addressed the problem of specific age limits on retirement and on the use of age as the "sole cause" of discrimination. For example, in the House of Representatives, Congressman Hawkins opened the debate with the following statement: "Congressmen Pepper, Findley, Weiss, and Waxman are to be commended for their tireless efforts to eliminate age as <u>the sole criteria</u> for hiring, firing, promotion or involuntary retirement."[72]

In the Senate, Senator Williams introduced the

---

[71] Rep. 92-238, 92d Cong. 1st. Sess. 8 (1971). To similar effect is S. Rep. No. 92-415, 92d Cong. 1. Sess. 5 (1971).

[72] 123 Cong. Rec. 29002 (1977).

debate as follows: "When Congress enacted the Age Discrimination in Employment Act in 1967, it determined that it would be our national policy to promote the employment of older workers between the ages of 40 and 65 by preventing discrimination in hiring, firing, and other conditions of employment based solely upon age".[73] Senator Javits said "It has always seemed unjustifiable to me to permit employees to be forced into retirement solely because they have reached an arbitrarily established age."[74]

The sharp focus on specific age barriers is reflected in the Senate report.[75] "The primary purpose of this legislation is to strengthen and broaden the provisions of the ADEA to insure that older individuals who desire to work will not be denied employment opportunities solely because of age. This would be done by raising the current upper age limit of 65 in the ADEA to age 70 and by clarifying an existing section of the Act to prohibit the mandatory retirement . . . of individuals within the protected age group. . . ." (Emphasis added)

These statements show the preoccupation of the Congress, not with practices neutral on their face which had an adverse effect because of age, but rather with specific practices which overtly restricted opportunities because of age. This is obvious in connection with moving the upper limit of the ADEA from 65 to 70. It is also true with respect to the amendment which reversed the result reached by the Supreme Court in McMann v. United Airlines.[76] McMann dealt with a pension plan which antedated the ADEA by many years and required retirement earlier than 65. The majority held that the plan was not "a subterfuge" to evade the purposes of the Act because it had been established many years before the enactment of the ADEA. The McMann decision thus created a loophole in the protection against compulsory retirement prior to the age of 65. Congress, concerned with the integrity of the minimum mandatory retirement age provisions of the original ADEA, amended the Act to close the "loophole".[77]

---

[73] Id. at 34294 (1977).

[74] Id. at 34297.

[75] S. Rep. No. 95-493, page 1, October 12, 1977.

[76] Supra note 63.

[77] The amendment reads "And no such seniority system
(Footnote Continued)

This further demonstrates the continued Congressional attention to one specific employer activity: the establishment or the maintenance of specific age limits for hiring or termination.

The Legislative History of the original ADEA and its amendments in 1978 are similar in that they both focus on specific age limits and on the concept that the Act was intended to prevent adverse personnel actions based "solely" on those age limits.

III. THE NEW ADMINISTRATIVE INTERPRETATION

Reorganization Plan #1 of 1978 transferred jurisdiction over the Age Discrimination Act to the Equal Employment Opportunity Commission,[78] and made it appropriate for the Commission to reexamine the ADEA interpretations of the Department of Labor. However, the Reorganization Act and the Plan do not provide the EEOC with the authority to treat the ADEA as if it had been amended to conform to Title VII Congress, which had treated the statutes so differently at the time of their adoption, permitted the transfer of ADEA to EEOC to facilitate the processing of "run of the mill" age cases, particularly when some Title VII complaint was joined to it. Nevertheless, in 1981, the Commission revised the administrator's interpretations, and sought to equate ADEA and Title VII.[79] The purpose of the EEOC effort was stated in the introduction to the proposed new interpretations: "It is the Commission's position that these proposed interpretations be interpreted in a manner which is consistent with Title VII of the Civil Rights Act of 1964."[80]

The proposed interpretation abandoned the requirement that age be a "determining factor," in favor of the following: "A factor, upon which a differentiation is based, is not a valid defense, however, <u>if age discrimination com-</u>

---

[77] (Footnote Continued)

or employee benefit plan shall require or permit the involuntary retirement of any individual specified by Section 12(a) of this Act because of the age of such individual." 29 U.S.C. 623(f)(2).

[78] <u>See</u> note 8, <u>supra</u>.

[79] 29 CFR 1625, 46 Fed. Reg. 47724 (Sept. 29, 1981).

[80] 44 Fed. Reg. 68858 (Nov. 30, 1979).

prises any element of the employment decision adverse to the applicant or employee, either expressly or by implication."[81]

However, in the final version of the regulations promulgated in 1981, neither the "determining factor" language of the original administrator's interpretation, nor the above-quoted language appears. The "final" interpretation simply states that the defense of "reasonable factor other than age" is not available if age was used as a criterion.[82] This avoided the issue of the extent to which age considerations must be involved in a decision prior to it becoming illegal.

On the crucial issue of whether the "effect" test applies under the ADEA, the final regulations have the same meaning as the proposed regulations.[83] Paragraph 1625.7(d) of the regulations as adopted states:

> When an employment practice, including a test, is claimed as a basis for different treatment of employees or applicants for employment on the grounds that it is a "factor other than" age, and such a practice has an adverse impact on individuals within the protected age group, it can only be justified as a business necessity. Tests which are asserted as "reasonable factors other than age" will be scrutinized in accordance with the standards set forth at Part 1607 of this Title.

The reference to Part 1607 is to the Uniform Guidelines on Employee Selection Procedures, which apply the "adverse effect" standard in connection with race, sex and na-

---

[81] 44 F.R. 68858, Sec. 1625.7(c) (Nov. 30, 1979).

[82] Note 80, Sec. 1625.7(c).

[83] The EEOC proposed rule sought to apply the adverse impact principle overtly as follows "When an employment practice, including a test, is claimed as a basis for different treatment of employees or applicants for employment on the grounds that it is a 'factor other than age,' and such practice has an adverse impact on persons in the protected age group and cannot be shown to be related to job performance, such a practice is unlawful." Note 81, supra, Sec. 1625.7(d).

tional origin cases under Title VII.[84] This interpretation is at sharp variance with the original interpretation by the Wage-Hour administrator which said: ". . . situations in which an employee test is used as the sole tool or the controlling factor in the employee selection procedure will be carefully scrutinized to insure that the test is for a possible _purpose_ and not for purposes prohibited by the statute."[85]

The question is whether the original interpretations of the administrator or the later interpretations of the EEOC should prevail. The basic principle which the Supreme Court has applied a number of times in Title VII cases is that the administrative construction of the statute contemporaneous with its adoption is entitled to greater deference than subsequent interpretations.[86] One could argue that the agency gradually acquires expertise in its subject matter and therefore that interpretations based on accumulated awareness of problems not well understood earlier should be given equal or greater deference. But this argument is valid only if the later interpretation is within the zone of permissible interpretation of the statute. Whether the Commission's effort to apply Title VII principles to the ADEA is within the zone which Congress left to administrative interpretation is a matter for the courts to decide.

IV. THE QUESTION OF POLICY

In deciding whether to utilize the "adverse effect" test, or to restrict the ADEA to an "intent" standard, the courts should compare the policies of Title VII and the ADEA. While such policy comparisons are difficult, and of necessity leave room for the play of unarticulated assumptions, the effort is nevertheless required,[87] and, I think, is rewarding in this situation.

Title VII was part of a comprehensive legislative program which primarily addressed the problems of racial

---

[84] 29 CFR S 1607. See Blumrosen, The Bottom Line in Equal Employment Guidelines: Administering a Polycentric Problem, 33 Ad. L. Rev. 323 (1981).

[85] Op. cit. supra note 65, Sec. 860:104(b).

[86] See Hardison v. Trans World Airlines, 432 U.S. 63 (1977) Gilbert v. General Electric Corp., 429 U.S. 125 (1976).

[87] See Note 11, _supra_.

- 34 -

minorities. The Civil Rights Act of 1964 encompassed not only discrimination in employment but also in voting, public accommodations, public facilities, education and federally funded programs. It was accompanied in short order by legislation concerning housing opportunities. By 1968 the Congress had adopted a battery of laws addressing the subordinate position of minorities in society. Title VII was but one part of this comprehensive program.[88] The placement of Title VII in a part of the United States Code dealing with employment should not obscure the fact that it was one aspect of a massive civil rights "legislative package."[89]

In Griggs, the court interpreted Title VII as part of the broad sweep of the entire Civil Rights Act. An employer had restricted employment opportunities of blacks by reliance on educational standards which relatively few blacks could meet because of the history of discrimination in education. The employer could show that his "intent" in establishing these educational standards related to the capacity of his employees, not their race. Thus, the "intent" test of discrimination would have permitted the employer to use the results of discrimination in education to deny employment opportunities to blacks. The Supreme Court viewed the different areas of discrimination as interrelated, just as Congress had done in passing the Civil Rights Act. The Court adopted the "effect test" in order to prevent discrimination against blacks in one area -- education -- from unnecessarily influencing opportunities in another area -- employment.[90] Thus, the definition of discrimination in Griggs reflected the legislative concern for the status of minorities as expressed in the totality of the Civil Rights Act of 1964. A similar concern infused the decision in United Steelworkers v. Weber upholding affirmative action programs against a reverse discrimination claim.[91]

Race, national origin and sex discrimination have ancient roots in slavery and cultural subordination. The

---

[88] Senator Muskie summed up the objective of the Civil Rights Act: "it seeks to do nothing more than to lift the Negro from the status of inequality to one of equality of treatment." 110 Cong. Rec. 14328 (1964).

[89] See Warner v. Goltra, 293 U.S. 155, 159-60 (1934).

[90] See text at Note 70, supra, note 88, supra, Strangers in Paradise, note 2, supra.

[91] 443 U.S. 193 (1979).

status of minorities and women is the result of the cumulative burdens which history has imposed upon the present generation. The lifting of those burdens, insofar as this can be accomplished by law, has been the objective of the Civil Rights Acts including Title VII. The "effect" or "impact" test is an important handmaiden in pursuit of this policy. The improvement in the status of one minority or female person can be presumed to benefit others in the group; there is a "ripple effect" in this area because membership in the "affected group" is fixed at birth, and continues through life.

Age discrimination is different in historical roots, as well as in the consequence of benefitting "aged persons". There is no long history of subordination of aged persons. As Secretary Wirtz noted, the problem is largely a new one, created by increasing longevity of our time.[92] The result is that support and benefit programs have been viewed as the dominant need of the older worker, with legal recognition of their claims largely in the area of employment. Furthermore, because membership in the group is "transient", recognition of the rights of one "aged person" may not benefit other members of the group as is the case in race or sex discrimination. The attempt to define "aged persons" as all persons over 40 makes sense as an effort to wipe out specific age limits, but not as creating a "protected class" like race or sex, precisely because of the transient composition of the group. The fact that membership in the "over 40" class is determined not by birth, but by living, is the underlying phenomena which should infuse the interpretation of the statute.

"Age discrimination" in employment is oppressive. The stereotypes of the abilities of persons over 40 should be shattered. All this can be done within a conventional definition of age discrimination, which focuses on the abolition of intentionally imposed age barriers based on assumptions of incapacity. A broader interpretation of the ADEA, which is not necessary to achieve this objective, may create quixotic and patchwork results which Congress did not intend.[93] In many situations, a principle or policy which has adverse effect on one aged person or group will have a beneficial effect on other older workers. This is true of seniority, promotion within and "step" increases in wages. Thus the "adverse impact" test is likely to have a "two sided" effect

---

[92] See text *supra* at note 18.

[93] See text infra, Part V.

on older workers. This is true even in the cases which are clearly covered by the statute. A requirement of termination at 60 benefits those below that age, in opening promotional opportunity; a maximum age on hiring protects incumbents against outside competition from the "over age group." Even though "fixed" age limits may have this "double edged" effect on older workers, Congress has struck a balance in favor of that group of workers who would be excluded from employment opportunities. Beyond these specific age limits, Congress has struck no balance whatsoever.

Race and sex cases are different. There Congress struck the balance, both in 1964 and 1972, in favor of improving employment opportunities for minorities and women. In pursuit of this policy, the "adverse impact" test is a useful tool. The "adverse impact" test does not have a "two sided" effect in race or sex cases because the practices it condemns rarely benefit minorities or women. Its use is unnecessary in the age discrimination field, and its attempted application is fraught with difficulties, uncertainties and incongruities not present in race or sex cases.

There is one additional concern; the potential for a conflict between the principles of Title VII and the principles of the ADEA.[94] This potential, as we have seen, was minimized by Senator Javits during the Senate debates, in part because the statutes would be administered by different agencies.[95] Now that EEOC has jurisdiction over age discrimination cases, this "safeguard" no longer exists. One might expect that an agency charged with interpreting two statutes would do so in a manner which would make them harmonious.

Affirmative action programs for minorities and women are likely to be most effective at the hiring level. The more vacancies, the greater likelihood that affirmative action will benefit minorities and women coming into the work force. Restrictions on termination of senior employees, beyond those necessary to avoid the rigid age limits and stereotyped judgments, will inevitably reduce the scope for affirmative action for minorities and women. This is evident when one examines the typical beneficiaries of the Age Discrimination Act. They appear frequently to be middle

---

[94] McKenry, Enforcement of Age Discrimination in Employment Legislation, 32 Hastings L. Jour. 1157, at 1172, (1981) considers this a "potential conflict of interest" for the EEOC.

[95] See text at note 51, supra.

or upper class white collar workers who are white males. An examination of the District Court and Court of Appeals opinions indexed in the Fair Employment Practice cases between 1975-1979 under the category "in general," identified the plaintiffs as having the following occupations: security officer, research scientist, supervisor of airline departures, secretary to chairman of board of brewing company, insurance claims adjustor, check pilot and instructor, industrial engineer, plant foreman, shipping supervisor, department foreman, assistant fire chief, landscape architect, staff accountant, test pilot, TV newscast anchorman, warehouse supervisor, automotive plant manager, field engineer.

The entry level jobs in these areas are precisely the ones which have traditionally been difficult for minorities and women to secure. Thus, a broad interpretation of the ADEA will limit the scope for possible affirmative action for minorities and women. It is thus incumbent on the agencies and, ultimately, the courts to harmonize the two statutes so as to fairly achieve their respective policies, and reduce or eliminate conflicts between them. Why then has the EEOC proposed regulations which would exacerbate this conflict? One can only speculate that interest group pressures, coupled with the EEOC's own tradition of using the "impact test," produced the proposed interpretations. But it is, finally, for the judiciary to strike this balance, to be faithful to the legislative intent so clearly delineated by the Secretary of Labor's Report with respect to the age Act while maintaining the "adverse effect" standard under Title VII.

V. GELLER V. MARKHAM EXAMINED

The case of Geller v. Markham[96] demonstrates some of the problems involved in use of "adverse impact" discrimination under the ADEA. Ms. Geller alleged that she was denied a teaching position because of an employer policy which provided that, where possible, "teachers needed in West Hartford next year will be recruited at levels below the sixth step of the salary schedule." The salary schedule apparently provided for annual step increases based on years of experience in teaching. The policy was likely to bear "more strongly" on persons over forty than on those under, because a higher proportion of those over 40 were likely to have had more than five years experience. Statistics in the case suggest that 92% of the teachers over 40 would have the requisite teaching time to be disqualified, while

---

96   Note 10, supra.

only 60% of those under 40 would have put in more than five years. The Court of Appeals rejected the "cost defense" because, in its view, the defense was directly related to the age distinction which was implicit in the policy.

The Board of Education of West Hartford did not consider that Ms. Geller was less competent than the younger person who was hired later. They did consider her to be more "expensive," because the school board had a policy of increasing pay based on experience: a policy which directly favored the more senior and likely older employees.[97]

West Hartford teachers are covered by Connecticut teacher tenure laws, which provide that continuous service for more than 3 years gives a teacher a right to continue so long as his or her performance is satisfactory and a position is available.[98] This is, indeed, the principle of protecting incumbent employees as they age. The policy invalidated in Geller complements the teacher tenure laws by encouraging the employment of younger teachers, in order to maintain some kind of "age balance" in employment. This is precisely the situation considered to be appropriate in the Committee reports.[99] To conclude that the employer discriminated because of age because it (1) provided job security for incumbent employees as they grew older, (2) adopted a salary structure which favored longer service and hence older employees, and (3) sought to hire new employees toward the bottom of the scale to maintain an "age balance", is to demonstrate that the adverse impact concept produces results in age discrimination cases which are contrary to congressional intention. It penalizes the employer whose wage policies favor experienced workers and prevents the maintenance of an age balance which Congress permitted.

---

[97] Strangely, the "cost defense" has been asserted in relatively few cases. Compare Geller, note 10, supra with Mastie v. Great Lakes Steel Corp. 424 F. Supp. 1299 (E.D. Mich. 1976). This paper does not address costs which are associated with pensions.

[98] CGSA S 10-151(b).

[99] See text and note 45, supra.

VI.

SOME PRACTICAL CONSEQUENCES OF CONFINING THE ADEA TO THE "INTENT" STANDARDS.

Some of the problems which have been encountered in administering the ADEA will be profoundly affected by the adoption of the "intent" standard, others will not. I will outline a few areas which may be substantially affected by the adoption of the intent standard.

1. Burden of Persuasion

Treating the ADEA as requiring proof of intent to discriminate will clarify questions of burden of persuasion and burden of going forward with the evidence. The complexities of the burden of persuasion issue in Title VII cases arise because there are different proof processes in "intent" and "impact" cases. In "impact" cases, the burden of persuasion shifts to the employer to demonstrate business necessity once adverse impact is shown. In "intent" cases, the burden of persuasion remains throughout with the plaintiff.[100] Under an ADEA interpreted to require proof of intent, the burden of persuasion would remain on the plaintiff at all times to establish that the employment decision in question was "because of" age. The plaintiff may array statistics as well as live evidence, addressed to the issue of the intent of the employer or its agents.

The defendant would bear burdens of persuasion only if it asserted an affirmative defense under the statute. Of the affirmative defenses recognized in the act, there is only one, the "bona fide occupational qualification" which the employer might wish to assert.[101] That defense is available where the employer has a policy which avowedly utilizes age in the employment decision. The other so-called defenses, "good cause" and "reasonable factors other than age" should not be viewed as defenses at all. Rather, the employer may utilize the evidence concerning "good cause" and "reasonable factors other than age" as a direct denial of plaintiff's claim that age was the basis of the decision which is complained of.[102] The employer will treat evidence on these points as a denial of plaintiff's case rather than as an affirmative defense because the burden of persuasion on such issues is on the plaintiff. If the tryer of fact is uncer-

---

100 Teamsters v. United States 431 U.S. 324, n. 15 (1977).

101 See 29 U.S.C. S623 (f).

102 See Laugesen, note 46 supra; Mastie, note 97 supra.

tain, it must find for the defendant. On the other hand, if the employer asserts the same material as an affirmative defense, then it bears the burden of persuasion, and, in cases of uncertainty, will lose on the issues. It is only where the employer's policy is overtly based on race that an affirmative defense becomes important.

2. Burden of going forward with Evidence: The Prima Facie Case

The burden of going forward with evidence may "shift" to the employer if the plaintiff has introduced sufficient evidence to survive a motion to dismiss at the close of his or her case. The sufficiency of such evidence has been the subject of two Supreme Court decisions in the Title VII context.[103] The underlying question is whether the plaintiff has presented sufficient evidence to require the defendant to justify or explain its conduct. A decision on this issue requires some understanding of what the plaintiff must prove.[104] If the plaintiff ultimately must establish that the employer intended to discriminate, then the question is whether plaintiff's evidence is suggestive of that intent. In the Title VII context, the Supreme Court's most useful statement on the point is found in Texas Community Development Agency v. Burdine that "the burden of establishing a prima facie case of disparate treatment is not onerous."[105]

In Title VII cases, the Supreme Court has articulated the rationale for determining whether there is a "prima facie case," requiring the employer to justify. In "disparate treatment" or "intent" cases, a prima facie case consists of evidence that a minority or woman was presumptively qualified, applied and was rejected for an existing position. These facts create an inference of discrimination because, "we presume these acts, if otherwise unexplained are more likely than not based on the consideration of impermissible factors."[106] The elimination of the two most common reasons for rejection,

---

[103] McDonald Douglas, note 70, supra; Texas Department of Community Affairs v. Burdine, 101 S. Ct. 1089 (1981). See Blumrosen, Strangers no More: All Workers are Entitled to "lost cause" protection under Title VII, 2 Industrial Rel. L. J. 519 (1979).

[104] See Williams v. General Motors Corp., 26 FEP 1381 (5th Cir. 1981).

[105] 101 S. Ct. at 1089 (1981).

[106] Furnco Construction Co. v. Waters, 438 U.S. 567 at 577 (1978).

no qualifications or no vacancy, creates an inference of discrimination.[107]

In Hazelwood School District v. United States,[108] a rationale for the proof of intentional discrimination through statistics was presented. "Absent explanation, it is ordinarily to be expected that nondiscriminatory hiring practices will in time result in a work force more or less representative of the racial and ethnic composition of the population in the community from which the employees are hired."

The underlying problem in applying these methods of demonstrating intentional discrimination to the ADEA is that the predicates stated above are inapplicable. The rejection of a qualified person between 40-70 does not of itself create an inference of age discrimination.[109] Similarly, the predicate for the use of statistics to establish intentional discrimination outlined in Hazelwood is absent in ADEA cases. Can it be said that, absent discrimination, the work force of an employer will over time reflect the "age balance" in the labor force from which the workers are drawn? There are too many variables to permit this assumption. Therefore, statistics showing a deviation from such a "norm" would not prove anything in the ADEA context, nor would statistics showing some "lowering" of the average age of the work force on termination of the complainant.[110]

I believe that most "statistical" cases under the ADEA can be kept relatively simple, avoiding the bog of statistics into which Title VII law has stumbled.[111] An ADEA case which seeks to infer discrimination based on numbers of employees must involve a "before" and an "after." The "before" in a refusal to hire case, is the applicant pool. The "after" is the group hired. In a termination case, the

---

[107] Teamsters v. United States, 431. U.S. 324, 358 n.44 (1977).

[108] 433 U.S. 299, 307 (1977).

[109] Marshall v. Goodyear Tire & Rubber Co., 554 F.2d 730, 736 (5th Cir. 1977). See Schickman, The Strengths and Weaknesses of the McDonnell Douglas Formula in Jury Actions under the ADEA, 32 Hastings L. Jour. 1239 (1981) 229 See Laugesen, note 46, supra.

[110] Laugesen, note 46, supra.

[111] See, for a different view, Harper, Statistics as Evidence of Age Discrimination, 32 Hastings L. Jour. 1347 (1981).

"before" is the pool of employees available for termination, and the "after" is the group actually terminated.

If the distribution of ages in the two pools, "before" and "after", is more or less the same, there is no inference of discrimination. If, however, it is apparent that those hired were the younger workers, or that those terminated were the older workers, then the employer should be required to explain the basis on which the decisions were made. The statistics suggest intentional discrimination. This approach enforces the underlying policy of the ADEA that decisions should be based on "qualifications," not on "age" because it compels the suspect employer to produce evidence that the decisions were individually tailored to the applicant or employee, and were not based on the stereotypes which the act proscribes.

3. <u>The "cost" justification</u>.

The question of whether an employer may take account the costs of hiring or retaining an older person as an employee as compared to a younger person is somewhat clarified by the analysis of the ADEA as requiring an "intent" to discriminate on the basis of age. The clarification takes the following form:

a. An employer who assumes that an older worker will be lower in productivity because of age and thereby will "cost" more, violates the act if action is taken on that assumption. Such an employer has relied on the stereotyped assumption that an older worker is less productive and therefore more expensive.

b. An employer who assumes that older workers are not "worth" their keep without examining the qualifications which they bring to the job, likewise violates the ADEA.

c. An employer who has analyzed costs of employment, and who knows that, as a result of internal policies which provide higher incomes and perhaps fringe benefits, to employees who have remained with the employer for a long time, workers with greater experience are more costly, is not required to disregard that fact in making personnel decisions. That is because the employer is not operating on a stereotyped assumption about higher costs of longer service employees, but upon a reality which is applicable to the particular employees in question.[112]

---

[112] See Mastie, note 97, <u>supra</u>.

d. An employer who is aware of the higher costs of more senior and hence older employees may take reasonable action based on that knowledge. One problem is the definition of reasonable action. An "overreaction" to the cost issue may create a situation where an employee may establish that the "cost" question was only a "pretext" for age discrimination. For example, assume an employer who believes that it can get the same productivity from a $20,000 new employee that it now gets from an incumbent $45,000 employee, who is competent; does that employer have an obligation to offer to retain the $45,000 per year person at a lower salary as an alternative to discharge?

I have found no cases on this point, probably because employers do not believe that retaining an employee at a lower salary is good personnel practice.[113] I am not sure that these beliefs fit the realities of a shrinking economy. I suspect that many older workers would prefer to retain jobs at a lower rate of pay rather than being terminated and might function productively because the "hot breath" of discharge was at hand. Furthermore, many older employees have satisfied their basic familial obligations so that their level of need for the higher wages we have traditionally associated with longer service may be less than in earlier years.

e. An employer may consider the "pay out" which it can expect from the expenditure on training of an employee as one of the considerations in the decision to provide such training. The closer an employee to lawful retirement age, the less economic sense it makes for the employer to invest in further training. Yet the absence of training, or of job rotation which provides for further upward mobility because of broadened experience may then be the alleged nondiscrimi-

---

[113] See Note: The Cost of Growing Old; Business Necessity and the Age Discrimination in Employment Act, 88 Yale L. Jour. 565, 587 (1979). Levine v. Fairleigh Dickenson University, 646 F.2d 825 (3rd Cir. 1981) comes close to addressing this problem. The University had a three year "phase out program" for emeritus professors who had reached mandatory retirement. Levine was included in that program shortly before the ADEA was amended to increase the mandatory retirement age to 70. He applied the program to the plaintiff. The court held, "An involuntary reduction of teaching load, with its concomitant reduction in pay, based solely on age patently falls within the statutory prescription."

natory basis for denial of employment opportunities.[114]

It is unreasonable to expect an employer to treat a 69 year old employee in the same manner as a 30 year old with respect to preparation for continued service with the employer.[115] While it may be speculative whether the 30 year old in whom the employer invests will remain, it is not speculative that that 65 year old will leave, even though the exact time of leaving may depend on the preferences and performance of the employee, the value of various retirement options, and state law concerning mandatory retirement.

The question remains, however, as to what actions the employer may take based on "foreknowledge" that an older employee has a relatively short future as compared to a younger worker. Several preliminary comments may be offered.

First, it is lawful for the employer to seek to have the employee participate in planning his or her own future, including the question of job assignments and retirement options. Such planning is not evidence of violation of the Act.[116]

---

[114] See Coates v. National Cash Register Co., 433 F. Supp. 655 (D. Va. 1977).

[115] Marshall v. Bd. of Ed. of Salt Lake City, 15 FEP 368 (D. Utah) appears to be the contrary. Airline decisions to impose maximum hiring age for flight officers may be based on the factor discussed in the text. Compare Murnane v. American Airlines, Inc., 26 FEP 1537 (D.C. Cir. 1981) (airline upheld) with Smallwood v. United Airlines, Inc. 26 FEP 1655 (4th Cir. 1981) (airline held to have violated the ADEA.) The functional difference apparent in the two cases was that American, which prevailed, had an "up or out" policy concerning the qualifications to become a captain, whereas United apparently permitted persons to remain as co-pilots throughout their career. If this is an accurate reading of factual differences noted by the courts, the result is ironic. American, with a more draconian policy toward its employees is not liable under the ADEA while United, which took greater account of the capacities of its workers, is liable. The other difference in the cases is the manner in which the safety issue was tried. American argued that long term employees were safer; United argued that older employees were higher risk.

[116] Stanojev v. Ebasco Services, Inc., 643 F.2d 914, 922
(Footnote Continued)

Secondly, the employer is entitled to act upon the results of such planning in determining opportunities to be made available to the employee in question and to other employees. Thus, if an employee, as a result of such a planning process, were to decide to retire in a year, the employer would be justified in preparing another employee for the position and in not giving further training opportunities to the employee who is about to retire.[117]

Thirdly, "phasing out" options made available to the employee as a result of such planning, such as leaves of absence to prepare for future activity at a lower salary, or other reductions in responsibilities accompanied by salary reductions, which relate to the impending retirement might not violate the ADEA. The ADEA does not write into law the practices of increasing wages with length of service which has become common, nor does it require an employer to maintain an employee in a specific job and salary level.[118] However, the Act would be violated if, for example, an employer discharged an employee at 69 because he would be around for no more than an additional year. Therefore, an employer would be well advised to pursue voluntary arrangements of the sort suggested here as long as the law remains in flux.[119]

VII. CONCLUSION

Congress used the same words to prohibit age discrimination as it used to prohibit race and sex discrimination. Common sense suggests that those words should have the same meaning in both statutes unless there is evidence of legislative intent to the contrary. The legislative history of the ADEA is clear. The ADEA is based on a report

---

[116] (Footnote Continued)

(2d Cir. 1981). The risks of misinterpretation of such efforts by the employee are substantial. It might be well to accompany a proposal for planning retirement with a written recognition by the employer of the employee's rights under the ADEA.

[117] See EEOC v. Home Insurance Co., 25 EPD ¶ 31,566 (S.D.N.Y. 1981).

[118] Compare Williams v. General Motors Corp., 26 FEP Cas. 1381 (5th Cir. 1981).

[119] See Levine, note 113, supra.

prepared by Secretary of Labor W. Willard Wirtz, a law professor and labor arbitrator, known for both the clarity of his thought and the depth of his concern for the human condition.[120] The Report clearly and unambiguously recommended a prohibition on rigid age limits based on stereotypes of aging. It went no further. In fact, it made clear that practices which affected older workers "more strongly" than younger workers should not be prohibited by law. Congress intended to implement the conclusions in the Report. The Courts should respect this intention by interpreting the ADEA, to prohibit only those actions based on an intent to discriminate because of age.

---

[120] Wirtz, The Boundless Resource (1975).

THE ADEA PLAINTIFF'S PRE-TRIAL TACTICS

Ronald M. Gaswirth[*]

---

[*] Member, Gardere & Wynne, Dallas, Texas. Formerly Trial Attorney, Office of the Solicitor, U.S. Department of Labor, 1968-75; and Regional Solicitor of Labor, 1975-78. Mr. Gaswirth received his B.A. and J.D. degrees from the University of Houston and his LL.M. in Labor Law with honors from Southern Methodist University. He is a member of the Bars of Texas and Georgia and the American Bar Association Section on Labor and Employment Relations Law.

TABLE OF CONTENTS

```
I.    INTRODUCTION..............................................1
      A.  Procedural Overview..................................1
      B.  Tactics before the Administrative Agencies...........2
      C.  Disclosure of the EEOC file..........................3

II.   PLEADINGS.................................................4
      A.  Jury Demand..........................................4
      B.  Willful vs. Unwillful................................4
      C.  Pendent state claims.................................5

III.  CLASS ACTION..............................................8

IV.   DISCOVERY.................................................9
      A.  General..............................................9
      B.  Request and use of statistical evidence.............10

          1.  How the data may be used........................10
          2.  Form of disclosure..............................11
          3.  Hiring an expert................................11
          4.  Legal principles................................12
```

I. Introduction

Thank you for this opportunity to share with you my views on the Age Discrimination in Employment Act. My talk today will focus on the basic tactics available to the private plaintiff in the pre-trial setting.

The Age Discrimination in Employment Act, which I will refer to as the Age Act, was enacted by Congress in 1967. The purpose of the Act, as stated in section two, is to promote employment of older persons based on their ability rather than age, to prohibit arbitrary age discrimination in employment, and to help employers and workers find ways of meeting problems arising from the impact of age of employment.

A. Procedural Requirements of the ADEA[1]

In an ADEA action, the plaintiff must make an initial inquiry involving the existence of applicable state law and the agencies dealing with age discrimination. The procedures vary, depending upon whether the potential plaintiff's state has an age discrimination law that allows a state agency to seek or grant relief for discriminatory practices. If a state agency does not have such authority, the plaintiff must file a charge of age discrimination with the EEOC within 180 days "after the alleged unlawful practice occurred," and then wait at least sixty days before filing a lawsuit in order to give the Commission a chance to remedy the practice by "informal methods of conciliation, conference, and persuasion."

Procedure is more complicated if a state agency is involved. Section 14(b) of the ADEA, 29 U.S.C. 633(b), provides that if the alleged age discrimination occurred in a state that has a law prohibiting discrimination in employment because of age and a state agency authorized to seek or grant relief (a "deferral state") no suit may be brought under the ADEA "before the expiration of sixty days after proceedings have been commenced under the state law, unless such proceedings have been earlier terminated...." The Supreme Court has determined that the ADEA's deferral requirement is mandatory.[2] The plaintiff must file a charge with the EEOC within thirty days after he is notified that the state proceedings have ended, but in no case more than 300 days after the alleged discriminatory practice occurred.

---

[1] The procedural complexities and the resulting judicial controversies stemming from ADEA Section 14(b) and Section 7(d)(1) filing requirements were more fully discussed in the presentations yesterday morning.

[2] Oscar Mayer & Co. v. Evans, 441 U.S. 750 (1979).

Whether in a deferral state or not, the plaintiff must wait 60 days after filing the discrimination charge to give the state and federal agencies a chance to settle the dispute before the commencing of a private action in federal court. These requirements cannot be over emphasized. In 1977 an analysis of the case law under the ADEA during its first ten years showed that 21% of all reported cases were lost because the plaintiff failed to abide by procedural prerequisites or time limits.[3]

B. Tactics before the Administrative Agencies

If the client consults counsel before he or she goes to the EEOC, counsel should submit a notice of representation to the EEOC at the time charges are filed or as soon thereafter as possible. This puts the EEOC on notice that it should contact the attorney and not the charging party directly. The drafting of the charge of discrimination should also be carefully reviewed. Often, the EEOC agent assisting the uncounseled employee in drafting the charge, unduly restricts the scope of the charge. The charge should always be drawn to preserve potential claims for the discriminatee and others similarly situated which may not be anticipated initially.

If the charge has already been filed, counsel should review this charge and if appropriate file an amended charge which establishes the proper scope. Once the charge has been filed the responsibility for investigating it is turned over to the EEOC. The EEOC will attempt to engage in a "fact finding/conciliation" conference between the charging party and representatives of the employer. This meeting combines a discussion of possible settlement of the charge with an exploration of the facts of the charge and the position of both parties. Counsel is permitted to attend this meeting but according to EEOC rules must remain mute. The EEOC will ordinarily not allow counsel to speak for his client. As a practical matter, however, since counsel may still advise his client, he can speak indirectly through the discriminatee. I have also found that most EEOC fact finders will allow counsel to indirectly question the employer by "suggesting" questions to the fact finder.

The fact finding conference affords the plaintiff an opportunity to do some informal and very cost effective discovery. While statements made at the fact finding conference are not under oath, they can be significant strategically as an early indication of the employer's case. Furthermore, any statements against interest may be admissible at trial. The attorney is well advised to carefully prepare the charging party and come equipped with

---

[3] Reed, *First Ten Years of the ADEA*, 4 *Ohio N.L. Review.* 748, 759 (1977).

questions for the employer representatives. The attorney should also suggest a list of employer witnesses/representatives, so the EEOC can request their presence at the fact finding conference.

C. Disclosure of the EEOC Files

After the EEOC has completed its investigation, plaintiff's lawyer should seek access to and carefully review the full EEOC investigatory file. The EEOC and the courts have vacillated on the availability of EEOC investigative files for pre-litigation discovery by the potential plaintiff.[4] Until recently, the EEOC has been forced to disclose in accordance with the rule of the Circuit in which the investigation took place. In some jurisdictions the EEOC disclosed case files only to complainants who had filed suit. In other jurisdictions the EEOC disclosed case files to charging parties prior to initiating suit. 1 EEOC Compliance Manual (BNA) p. 83 at 9-12 (1979). This situation should change as a result of the recent Supreme Court decision, EEOC v. Associated Dry Goods Corp.[5] In a five-two ruling the Court resolved the controversy by holding that the EEOC could release investigative files to the charging party prior to initiation of litigation. Access to the file is helpful in focusing the lawsuit and some courts have even held that EEOC determinations are admissible evidence.[6] Courts have, however, refused to admit underlying documentation which appears in the EEOC file.[7]

---

[4] Compare H. Kessler & Co. v. EEOC, 472 F.2d 1147 (5th Cir.) (en banc), cert. den., 412 U.S. 939 (1973); with Sears, Roebuck & Co. v. EEOC, 581 F.2d 941 (D.C. Cir. 1978).

[5] 449 U.S. 590, 101 S.Ct. 817 (1981).

[6] Compare Bradshaw v. Zoological Soc. of San Diego, 569 F.2d 1066, 1069 (9th Cir. 1978) [disapproved Jepsen v. Flordia Board of Regents, 610 F.2d 1379 (5th Cir. 1980)]; Johnson v. University of Pittsburgh, 435 F. Supp. 1328, 1363 (W.D. Pa. 1977); and Stebbins v. Continental Ins. Cos., 12 FEP Cases 219 (D.D.C. 1976) aff'd without op (D.C.C. 1976) 543 F.2d 1390, cert. den. 429 U.S. 1107 (1977); with Angelo v. Bacharach Instrument Co., 555 F.2d 1164, 1166 (3d Cir. 1977).

[7] Watford v. Birmingham Stove & Range Co., 14 FEP Cases 626, 629 (N.D. Ala. 1976).

II. Pleadings

   A. Jury Demand

In 1978 the United States Supreme Court in Lorillard, Div. of Loew's Theatres, Inc. v. Pons[8] held that in a private action under the ADEA a trial by jury would be available when sought by either party. In so holding the Court resolved the conflict in the Circuits as to the right to trial by jury under the ADEA.[9]

Despite the increased cost and time involved, there are few circumstances under which the plaintiff in an ADEA action would opt not to exercise his right to demand a trial by jury. A jury will often be more sympathetic to the aged plaintiff than to the corporate giant that either employs him or has taken away his livelihood. It is also a generally accepted theory that a jury is more likely to make a larger award. For these reasons the plaintiff should timely exercise his right to a jury trial.[10] This election can normally be waived at a later time.

   B. Willful v. Unwillful

The ADEA provides that liquidated damages can be awarded for willful violations.[11] Three standards have emerged for

---

[8] 434 U.S. 575 (1978).

[9] Pons v. Lorillard, 549 F.2d 950 (4th Cir. 1977) (right to jury trial); Morelock v. NCR Corp., 546 F.2d 682 (6th Cir. 1976) (no right to jury trial); Rogers v. Exxon Research & Engineering Co., 550 F.2d 834 (3rd Cir. 1977) (right to jury trial), cert. denied, 434 U.S. 1022, 98 S.Ct. 749. The 1978 amendments to the ADEA specifically address the right to trial by jury, providing "a person shall be entitled to a trial by jury of any issue of fact in any such action for recovery of amounts owing as a result of a violation of this chapter, regardless of whether equitable relief is sought by any party in such action." 23 U.S.C.A. 626(c)(2) (Supp. 1981).

[10] Under Rule 38(b) of the Federal Rules of Civil Procedure a party who does not make a timely demand for a jury trial waives his right. Under Rule 39(b) the court may in its discretion grant a party's motion for a jury trial notwithstanding the failure of a party to demand a jury.

[11] 29 U.S.C. §626(b) (1976). In addition to making liquidated damages possible, "willfulness" is relevant to the ADEA lawsuits in another aspect. §626(e) of the ADEA specifically incorporates §255 of the Portal to Portal Pay Act. Under §255 the two year statute of limitations is extended to three years when the cause of action has arisen from a willful violation. See Goodman v. Heublein, Inc., 645 F.2d 127, 192 n.1 (2d Cir. 1981) for a discussion of how the courts have defined "willful" for the purpose of extending the statute of limitations.

defining willfulness. Approximately half of the reported cases have defined the term to mean any violation that is intentional, knowing, or voluntary as opposed to accidental.[12] To illustrate, an employer would be guilty of a willful violation if he intended to discharge the employee, even if he did not mean to violate the Act. Under this construction, virtually every violation would be willful. Other courts have adopted a more limited view, requiring proof that the employer intended to take the action and that it knew or should have known that the decision was prohibited by the ADEA.[13] The Seventh Circuit is the latest to adopt this view in Syrock v. Milwaukee Boiler Manufacturing Co., Inc.[14]

Yet another standard was recently expressed by the Fifth Circuit in Hedrick v. Hercules, Inc.[15] According to the court, to establish a willful violation it is not necessary to show that the employer knew his actions were violative of the ADEA; it is sufficient that the employer was aware that his actions were governed by the Act. Id. at 1096. See Spagnuolo v. Whirlpool Corp.[16] ("An employer acts willfully...if he knows, or has reason to know, that his conduct is governed by the...Act").

Given the propensity of the courts to find willfulness, the plaintiff should always allege willfulness and make a request for liquidated damages in the pleadings. Once the trier of fact has decided that the employer acted willfully, the court has no discretion to withdraw or reduce an award of liquidated damages.[17]

C. Pendent state claims

Plaintiffs should consider whether they have other related

---

[12] Hays v. Republic Steel Corp., 531 F.2d 1307 (5th Cir. 1976); Rogers v. Exxon Research and Engineering Co., 404 F.Supp. 324 (D.N.J. 1975), reversed on other grounds, 550 F.2d 834 (3rd Cir. 1977), cert. denied, 434 U.S. 1022 (1978); Hodgson v. Ideal Corrugated Box Co., 8 CCH EPD ¶9805 (N.D. W. Va. 1974).

[13] Loeb v. Textron, Inc., 600 F.2d 1003 (1st. Cir. 1979); Coates v. National Cash Register Co., 433 F.Supp. 655 (W.D. Va. 1977); Bishop v. Jelleff Associates, 398 F.Supp. 579 (D.D.C. 1974).

[14] ___ F.2d ___ (7th Cir. 1981), DLR No. 233, p.D-1 (BNA, December 4, 1981).

[15] 658 F.2d 1088 (5th Cir. 1981).

[16] 641 F.2d 1109, 1114 (4th Cir. 1981) cert den., 26 FEP Cases 1688 (U.S. 1981).

[17] Lorillard v. Pons, 434 U.S. 575, 581 n.8 (1971).

claims against the employer in addition to the age bias charge. Under certain circumstances these claims can be tried along with the age discrimination allegations in federal court. The factors a court will consider in deciding whether or not to exercise pendent jurisdiction were laid out by the United States Supreme Court in United Mine Workers of America v. Gibbs.[18] Pendent jurisdiction is appropriate when (1) there is a federal claim with sufficient substance to confer subject matter jurisdiction on the court, (2) the state and federal claims derive from a common nucleus of operative fact, and (3) the plaintiff's claims are such that he would ordinarily be expected to try them in a single judicial proceeding.[19] The court also considers whether pendent jurisdiction will result in judicial economy, convenience and fairness to the litigants.[20]

Pendent jurisdiction of state claims has been exercised by the courts in cases involving the ADEA. Plaintiffs have asked the courts, with varying results, to exercise jurisdiction over: (1) state age discrimination claims, Sussman v. Vornado, Inc.;[21] (2) breach of contract claims, Morris v. Frank IX & Sons, Inc.;[22] Kennedy v. Mountain States Tel. & Tel. Co.;[23] Rechsteiner v. Madison Fund, Inc.;[24] (3) claims of intentional infliction of emotional distress, Morris;[25] Kennedy;[26] Hannan v. Continental National Bank;[27] (4) claims of loss of reputation in the community, Hannan;[28] and (5) defamation claims, Douglas v. American Cyanamid Co.[29] Whether or not the courts will exercise pendent jurisdiction

---

[18] 383 U.S. 715 (1966).

[19] Id. at 725.

[20] Id. at 726.

[21] 26 FEP Cases 335, 341-342, 90 FRD 680 (B.N.J. 1981).

[22] 486 F. Supp. 728, 735 (W.D. Va. 1980).

[23] 449 F. Supp. 1008, 1011 (D. Colo. 1978).

[24] 75 FRD 499, 505-06 (D. Del. 1977).

[25] 486 F. Supp. at 735.

[26] 449 F. Supp. at 1011.

[27] 427 F. Supp. 215, 218 (D. Colo. 1977).

[28] 427 F. Supp. at 218.

[29] 472 F. Supp. 298, 304 (D. Conn. 1979).

will turn on the facts of the particular case and the extent to which the factors enunciated in Gibbs are present.[30]

A relatively new option to a discharged employee is to bring an action against the employer for "abusive" discharge. Under certain circumstances the ADEA plaintiff may have such a claim. In the last few years many jurisdictions have rendered decisions eroding the long established "termination at will" doctrine. States have been especially prone to make exception to the doctrine where it is in the public policy interest:

> "The rule giving the employer the absolute right to discharge an 'at will' employee must be tempered by the further principle that where the employer's motivation for the discharge contravenes some substantial public policy principle, then the employer may be liable to the employee for damages occasioned by the discharge." Harless v. First Nat. Bank, 246 S.E.2d 270, 275 (W. Va. 1978)

Courts have found public policy exceptions to the general rule of termination at will where the discharge is for such things as serving on a jury, Nees v. Hocks;[31] for seeking and receiving workers compensation benefits, Kelsay v. Motorola, Inc.;[32] Frampton v. Central Indiana Gas Co.,[33] and for refusal to take part in a price fixing scheme, Tameny v. Atlantic Richfield Co.[34]

Federal Courts hearing ADEA claims have both allowed and disallowed pendent claims. In Hovey v. Lutheran Medical Center,[35] a New York Federal Court trying an ADEA suit exercised pendent jurisdiction over a state claim of tortious, abusive discharge.[36]

---

[30] A private plaintiff in an ADEA action who does not timely raise applicable pendent state claims may lose the right to litigate these claims. See Cemer v. Marathon Oil Company, 583 F.2d 830, 832 (6th Cir. 1978).

[31] 536 P.2d 512 (Ore. 1975).

[32] 384 N.E.2d 353 (Ill. 1978).

[33] 297 N.E.2d 425 (Ind. 1973).

[34] 610 P.2d 1330 (Calif. 1980).

[35] 25 FEP Cases 1773 (E.D. N.Y. 1981).

[36] In an earlier case New York recognized the tort of abusive discharge in a case involving the integrity of state pension plans. Savodnik v. Korvettes, 482 F. Supp. 822, 826 (E.D. N.Y. 1980).

In <u>Wehr v. Burroughs Corp.</u>,[37] a Pennsylvania district court did not allow the plaintiff to supplement his ADEA discharge claim with a count asserting a breach of contract and violation of public policy.

> "A finding that certain conduct contravenes public policy is not enough by itself to warrant the creation of a contract remedy for wrongful dismissal by employer. The cases which have established a tort or contract remedy for employees discharged for reasons violative of public policy have relied on the fact that in the context of their case the employee was otherwise without remedy and that permitting the discharge to go unredressed would leave a valuable social policy to go unvindicated." <u>Id</u>. at 1054.

III. Class Actions

Rule 23 Class Actions are not available under the ADEA. Class actions may, however, be brought pursuant to the procedures incorporated by Section 16(b) of the Fair Labor Standards Act.[38] Class actions under the ADEA are different from class actions brought under Rule 23.[39] In the ADEA class action, there are no notice provisions and only named plaintiffs are bound by a judgment. An individual who wants to become a party plaintiff to an ADEA class action must "opt in" by filing with the court written consent to becoming such a party a reasonable time before the

---

[37] 438 F. Supp. 1052 (E.D. Pa. 1977) <u>aff. as modified</u>, 619 F.2d 276 (3rd Cir. 1980).

[38] 29 USC 626(b) (1975) incorporates 29 USC (216(b)) (1980 Supp.) which provides in part:

> "An action to recover the liability prescribed in either of the preceding sentences may be maintained against any employer (including a public agency) in any Federal or State court of competent jurisdiction by any one or more employees for and in behalf of himself or themselves and other employees similarly situated. No employee shall be a party plaintiff to any such action unless he gives his consent in writing to become such a party and such consent is filed in the court in which action is brought."

[39] <u>See</u>, <u>Mistretti v. Sandia Corp.</u>, 21 FEP Cases 1671 (D.N.M. 1978), <u>aff'd in part, reversed in part</u>, and remanded in part on other grounds, 639 F.2d 588 (10th Cir. 1980).

trial begins.[40] Some courts have allowed an employee to solicit fellow employees to join in the action.[41] The most extensive discussion of the procedural requirements under Section 16 are contained in Donovan v. University of Texas at El Paso.[42]

IV. Discovery

   A. General

As in most employment discrimination cases, the age plaintiff must make extensive use of discovery procedures to prepare for trial. The plain fact is that almost all evidence of discrimination is in the custody of the defendant. This is especially true where the plaintiff's case relies primarily on statistical data.

There are no standard procedures in discovery. Each case presents its own factual circumstances which ultimately control tactical and strategic decisions. The common practice is to begin discovery by combined use of a Rule 33 set of interrogatories and the Rule 34 notice to produce. Early use of these devices is helpful in collecting basic data. This is the time to request basic statistical data and specify the form in which the data should be organized. An answer listing all employees by date of hire and specifying position, salary, promotions, and age is much more useful than random data that requires extensive reorganization. In large cases, the plaintiff should seek the computer tape in lieu of manually gathered data (see discussion below).

The initial set of interrogatories is generally followed by additional interrogatories and depositions. Depositions permit the attorney to follow up on new lines of inquiry, determining what a witness will testify to in court, and provide a basis for impeaching later testimony that varies from the statements in the deposition.

---

[40] Gebhard v. GAP Corp., 5 FEP Cases 1043 59 FRD 504 (D.D.C. 1973); La Chapelle v. Owens-Illinois, Inc., 513 F.2d 286 (5th Cir. 1975) (per curiam).

[41] Joyce v. Sandia Laboratories, 22 FEP Cases, 1727 (N.D. Calif. 1980); Franci v. Avco Corp., 460 F.Supp. 389 (D. Conn. 1980); Price v. Maryland Casualty Co., 561 F.2d 609 (5th Cir. 1977); Osborne v. United Technologies Corp., 16 FEP Cases 586 (D. Conn. 1977).

[42] 643 F.2d 1201 (5th Cir. 1981).

B. Request and use of statistical evidence

1. How the data may be used

In the preparation and prosecution of major age cases it frequently becomes necessary to prove or attempt to prove the employer's discriminatory action in discharge, reduction, hiring, promotion or demotion cases by statistical evidence demonstrating the employer's action or lack thereof and its effects on workers in the protected age group or subgroup. I have constructed an example for today's presentation based on an actual case involving a major employer who laid off several hundred employees. Because these cases typically do not involve "smoking guns" (i.e., direct evidence of discriminatory intent), it becomes necessary to evaluate the employer's action and potential liability by evaluating the statistical impact of his acts. To do that we must examine the population of employees usually by unit, group, classification or other relevant subpopulation and by age group both before and after the employer's action to determine what happened to who and in what age group. (See Table I in Appendix.) We then examine statistically what the expected terminations would be by age group, based on a statistical spread of terminations in each age group. (See Table II.) As you can see in Table II, the expected number of terminees in the 60-64 group was about 6 and the observed number of terminations were 49; in the 55-59 age group the expected number were 14 or 15 and observed number 118; in the 50-54 age group the expected number was 45 and observed number 372. This statistical disparity, presented to the Court through an expert statistician, is probative of whether the employer's action constituted age discrimination.

These calculations are then further refined by calculating a standard deviation and confidence interval. (See Table 3 and Table 4.) The purpose of this calculation is to determine statistical probability of the results achieved by the employer occurring by chance. As you can see from Table 4, the chances of the observed terminations occurring by chance are infinitesimal. Thus, the expert is able to conclude that a reason for the distribution of laid off employees occurring in the manner in which this example sets forth was, in his opinion, age.

Oftentimes, it becomes necessary to statistically evaluate employee performance ratings when the employer relies on these ratings as a defense to the charge that his method of selection for lay-off was biased on account of age. It is then necessary to examine the often subjectively-based rating system for inherent age bias.

The first thing to do in looking at the ratings is to see whether a pattern of age discrimination in the assignment of the ratings can be graphed. In this case, such a graph was prepared. The performance ratings graphed by age yielded a "bell" curve. In other words, employees started on the low end of the curve at age 20 and reached the top of the bell in terms of performance ratings at some point in their early or mid 40's. Thereafter, performance ratings decreased as age increased. This type of analysis introduced during the trial through an expert statistician helps to rebut the employer's suggestion that his method of selection was based upon valid performance evaluations, ratings, etc.

2. Form of disclosures

When the defendant is a larger corporation, the majority of items sought in discovery are probably entered on computer tapes or cards. As a result, the production of the material, though requiring considerable effort, is not the mammoth task that it was prior to computerization of business records. Plaintiff's counsel should demand production of the cards or tapes rather than a print out of some of the data in the files. With the raw material in hand, the plaintiff can create and run programs to draw on whatever material may be useable.[43] Data that can be read by computer are easier to analyze and are not considered duplicative of the massive records from which the same data could be sensitized.[44]

3. Hiring an expert

It is difficult to try a large scale class discrimination suit without the aid of computerized information and statistical analysis of the data produced during discovery. Since much of the proof adduced by plaintiff and defendant is statistical in nature, the plaintiff's attorney should obtain the services of a statistician and a computer analysist early in the litigation. These experts can educate the attorneys as to the type of data needed and methods available for analysis, and can testify at trial as to the methods used and the import of results of statistical analysis. Problems of admissability of statistical evidence at trial may be avoided by early careful, accurate

---

[43] See *Donaldson v. Pillsbury Co.*, 554 F.2d 825 (8th Cir.), cert. denied, 434 U.S. 856 (1977); *Adams v. Dan Rivers Mills, Inc.*, 4 FEP Cases 523, 54 FRD 220 (W.D. Va. 1972)

[44] See *Donaldson v. Pillsbury Co.*, supra; *United States v. Davey*, 404 F.Supp. 1283 (S.D.N.Y. 1975), aff. as modified, 543 F.2d 996 (2nd Cir. 1976); *Adams v. Dan Rivers Mills, Inc.*, supra.

record keeping and by adopting a systematic method of data storage, retrieval, and analysis at the outset of discovery.[45]

4. Legal principles

Statistics may be used either to support an individual's claim of disparate treatment or to establish an employer's liability to a class of older employees. In EEOC v. Sandia Corp.,[46] the court discussed statistics and the need to validate the results to obtain probative evidence. In that case, statistics were used to establish that a performance evaluation procedure was a pretext for unlawful age discrimination. To isolate the impact of age on any particular employment decision, a coefficient or regression analysis is commonly used.

The courts scrutinize the use of statistics very carefully especially where the sample size is not large.[47] Thus, in certain cases it may be appropriate for the plaintiff to forego use of statistics in favor of proof of discriminatory intent in some other manner.

Statistics may, however, be useful to support many different inferences. Statistical data must be derived from an appropriate group of comparable employees.[48] Statistics must be beyond what a surface review might indicate. The widespread use of employment statistics in Title VII claims may not be transported without modification to the ADEA area. On the other hand, it may be appropriate to apply statistical analysis in novel ways based on the

---

[45] See Manual for Complex Litigation 99-118, Sections 2.70-2.717 (1977) for guidelines on the management of original data, discovery procedures and the use of the summaries in a complex case. For an explanation of available computer techniques and methods of statistical analysis useful in cases involving volumninous, complex data, see the Computer Framework for Complex Litigation, N.Y.; Practicing Law Institute (1976).

[46] 639 F.2d 600, 23 FEP Cases 799 (10th Cir. 1980). A good summary of a plaintiff's use of statistics in an ADEA case is found in Moore v. Sears, Roebuck & Co., 464 F.Supp. 357 (N.D. Ga. 1979). See also, Vuyanich v. Republic National Bank, 24 FEP Cases 128 (N.D. Tex. 1980).

[47] Kephart v. Institute of Gas Technology, 630 F.2d 1217 (7th Cir. 1980) cert. den. 450 U.S. 959 (1981).

[48] Houghton v. MacDonald Douglas Corp., 553 F.2d 561 (8th Cir.), cert. denied, 434 U.S. 966 (1977); Polstorff v. Fletcher, 430 F.Supp. 592 (N.D. Ala. 1978); Robb v. Chemetron Corp., 17 FEP Cases 1535 (S.D. Tex. 1978).

facts unique to age cases. In EEOC v. Sandia Corp.,[49] the trial court findings of age discrimination resulted from cutbacks in government programs which required that 800 persons be terminated. Each of the employer's vice presidents was assigned a quota for terminations. Supervisors at various levels nominated candidates for termination. These candidates were reviewed by two committees. Performance evaluations for each candidate were considered. Ages were considered, the employer testified, "only for humanitarian reasons." The statistics showed that the percentage of those terminated who fell within the older age categories was substantially higher than the percentage of the pre-determination work force within such categories. The plaintiff produced memoranda which indicated that the company was focusing on "new blood" and on young Ph.D's because of the rapidly changing technological climate. The plaintiff's statistical expert testified that the chances of age being independent with respect to the lay off analysis was less than one percent. The defense evidence statistically tied terminations to performance evaluation. The court rejected this defense because it found the performance evaluations to be age biased. The trial court found that the defendant's statistics were insufficient to defeat the plaintiff's statistically based prima facia case with respect to terminations in individuals between the ages of 52 and 64.

---

[49] 639 F.2d 600, 23 FEP Cases 799 (10th Cir. 1980), later app. Mistretta v. Sandia Corp. 639 F.2d 588 (10th Cir. 1980), reh. granted in part, den. in part, 26 FEP Cases 218 (10th Cir. 1980).

Appendix

Age Discrimination:
Statistical Analysis

A hypothetical example below depicts the reduction in force (RIF) of some 353 employees in a firm having initially 2940 employees. The first table shows the number of employees and terminees in age group categories.

Table I

Age Group	Number of Employees Before RIF	Number of Employees After RIF	Number of Employees Terminated
20-29	285	236	49
30-34	714	653	61
35-39	489	454	35
40-44	513	477	36
45-49	400	370	30
50-54	372	291	81
55-59	118	81	37
60-64	49	25	24
	2940	2587	353

One may easily determine that 208 of the 353, or 58.9% of those terminated were in the protected age category of 40-64 years. This percentage is meaningless until compared to the percentage of employees in the protected age category. That figure is 1452/2490 or 49.5%. To determine whether the number of percentage of persons terminated differs for various age groups, the first step is to determine the expected or theoretical frequencies that would have occurred if there were no difference by age. Since 353 of 2940, or 12.01% of the total work force was terminated, it would seem that if there were in fact no discrimination by age then 12.01% of the employees in each age group would have been terminated. Table II shows the expected number of employees in each age group that would have been terminated

Table II

Age Group	Number of Employees n	Expected Number Terminated n x 12.01%
20-29	285	34.2
30-34	714	85.7
35-39	489	58.7
40-44	513	61.6
45-49	400	48.0
50-54	372	44.7
55-59	118	14.2
60-64	49	5.9
	2940	353.0

if the percentage terminated, 12.01%, were the same for each age category. If in fact, there were no age discrimination then there would be an equal percentage of persons terminated in each age group. In reality, one would not expect the observed frequencies to match exactly the theoretical or expected number in each age group. With the decimal numbers, it would be impossible. But the observed values should be close.

If the observed values differ from the expected values by large amounts, then the differences cannot be attributed to random chance occurrence and the differences become meaningful and significant. The interpretation of significance and the determination of what constitutes a significant versus an insignificant difference is the sphere of statistical inference. Probability theory and sheer random sampling variation are used to determine the significance of observed differences.

Confidence intervals may be calculated showing the ranges within which sample values could fall by sheer chance assuming no age discrimination. Commonly used levels of confidence are 95% and 99% levels. An example follows showing the range within which sample values would fall 95% and 99% of the time by sheer chance if there were no age discrimination. While it is true that a sample value might fall outside of the interval, the probability of such an event occurring by sheer chance is small, 5% and 1% respectively.

n = number of employees
n = 285
p = percent terminated
p = .1201

mean = expected number terminated
mean = np
mean = $285 \times .1201 = 34.2$

S = standard deviation
S = $\sqrt{npq}$
S = $\sqrt{285 \times .1201 \times .8799} = 5.488$

95% confidence interval for sample value:

X = mean $\pm$ 2(S)
X = 34.2 ± 11.0
$23.2 \leq X \leq 45.2$ 95% of the time

99% confidence interval for sample value:

X = mean $\pm$ 2.58(S)
X = 34.2 ± 14.2
$20.0 \leq X \leq 48.4$ 99% of the time

Confidence intervals may similarly be constructed on the percentage of employees terminated that could occur in samples

Table III

Age Group	Expected Number Terminated	Expected Percent Terminated (95% Confidence)	Actually Terminated (Number)	(Percent)
20-29	34.2	.0816 to .1586	49	17.19
30-34	85.7	.0958 to .1444	61	8.54
35-39	58.7	.0907 to .1495	35	7.16
40-44	61.6	.0914 to .1488	36	7.02
45-49	48.0	.0876 to .1526	30	7.50
50-54	44.7	.0864 to .1538	81	21.77
55-59	14.2	.0602 to .1800	37	31.36
60-64	5.9	.0272 to .2130	24	48.98
	353.0		353	

assuming no discrimination by age. Table III shows the expected number and percentage (95% confidence interval) of terminees assuming there were no difference by age groups, compared with the actual number and percentage of employees terminated in each age group. The expected percentage interval is a 95% confidence interval using the relationship below. If there were no age discrimination 95% of sample percentages would fall within the interval $.1201 + 2\sqrt{(.1201 \times .8799)/n}$, where n is the number employed in the age group.

The differences between the observed number of employees and the number expected under conditions of no age discrimination may be analyzed further. One may calculate the probability that such could occur by sheer chance assuming no age discrimination. This involves the calculation of a standard normal deviate value (Z to T value) and then the determination of the probability that such a value (or larger) could occur. If the so determined probability, that the results could occur by chance and be a part of a non-age discrimination distribution, is high (usually greater than 5% or 10%) then the conclusion reached is that the difference occurred by chance and therefore there is no age discrimination. If the so calculated probability is low (usually smaller than 5% or 1%) then the conclusion reached is that the difference did not occur by chance. Since something caused it to occur, it is highly unlikely that no age discrimination occurred. One would reject the hypothesis that there was no age discrimination. Table IV shows the differences between expected and actual number of terminees. The probability that such differences could have occurred by sheer chance (assuming no differences among different age categories) is also shown. It should be noted that all probabilities are less than 1%.

Table IV
Differences Between Observed & Expected Terminees

Age Group	Number Terminated Actual	Number Terminated Expected	Difference Actual-Expected	Standard Normal Deviate (Z)*	Chi-square Component (Act. Expected/Exp.)	Prob. that Difference Happened by Sheer Chance
20-29	49	34.2	14.8	2.69	6.40	.004
30-34	61	85.7	-24.7	2.85	7.12	.003
35-39	35	58.7	-23.7	3.30	9.57	.001
40-44	36	61.6	-25.6	3.48	10.26	.0003
45-49	30	48.0	-28.0	2.77	6.75	.003
50-54	81	44.7	36.3	5.79	29.48	$.0^71$**
55-59	37	14.2	22.8	6.47	36.61	$.0^93$
60-64	24	5.9	18.1	7.96	55.53	$.0^{11}2$
	353	353.0			162.10	less than .001

*Z = (sample percent - .1201)/ $\sqrt{(.1201 \times .8799/\text{number in age group})}$

** $.0^71$ is compact notation for .00000001

Table IV may be analyzed by stating that:

    1.   A significantly high number of 20-29 year olds were terminated; 49 is significantly higher than 34.2 (12.01%).

    2.   In age groups 30-34, 35-39, 40-44, and 45-49 the number of employees terminated was significantly less than what was expected, (61 less than 85.7; 35 less than 58.7; 36 less than 61.6; and 30 less than 48.0).

    3.   In age groups 50-54, 55-59, and 60-64 a very significantly high number of employees were terminated. The percentage terminated was so high that it could have happened by chance (and still have come from a distribution with no age discrimination) less than one time in one hundred million. To call it insignificant, or a chance occurrence (i.e. to say there is no pattern of age discrimination) is ignoring the results altogether.

    4.   The overall pattern is that the persons terminated predominately came from the very young (under 30) and from the older (50 and over) age groups. Those ages 30-49 were retained more so than those in the extreme age groups.

    Some graphs are included to visualize the differences. The first two show the pattern more than the latter one.

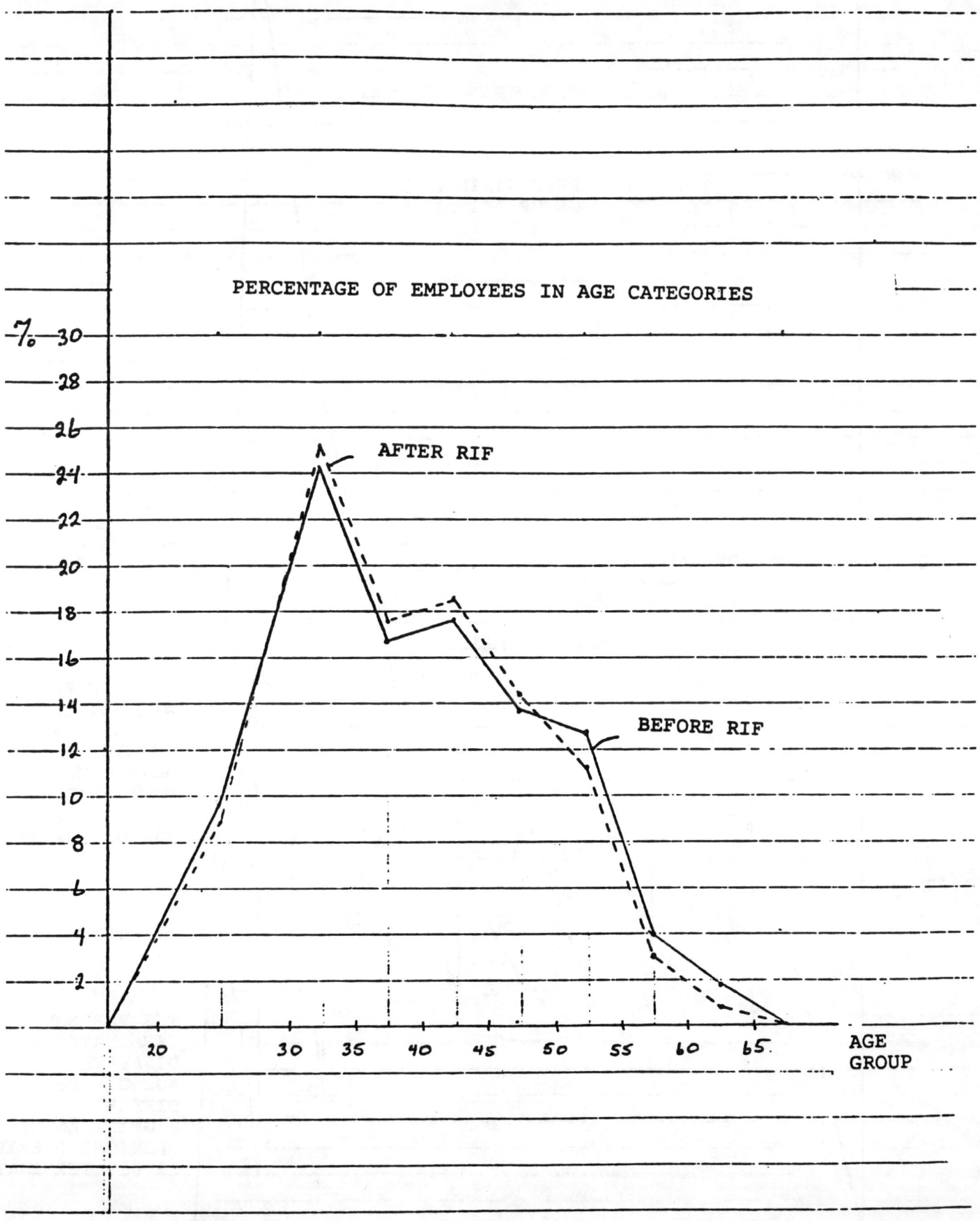

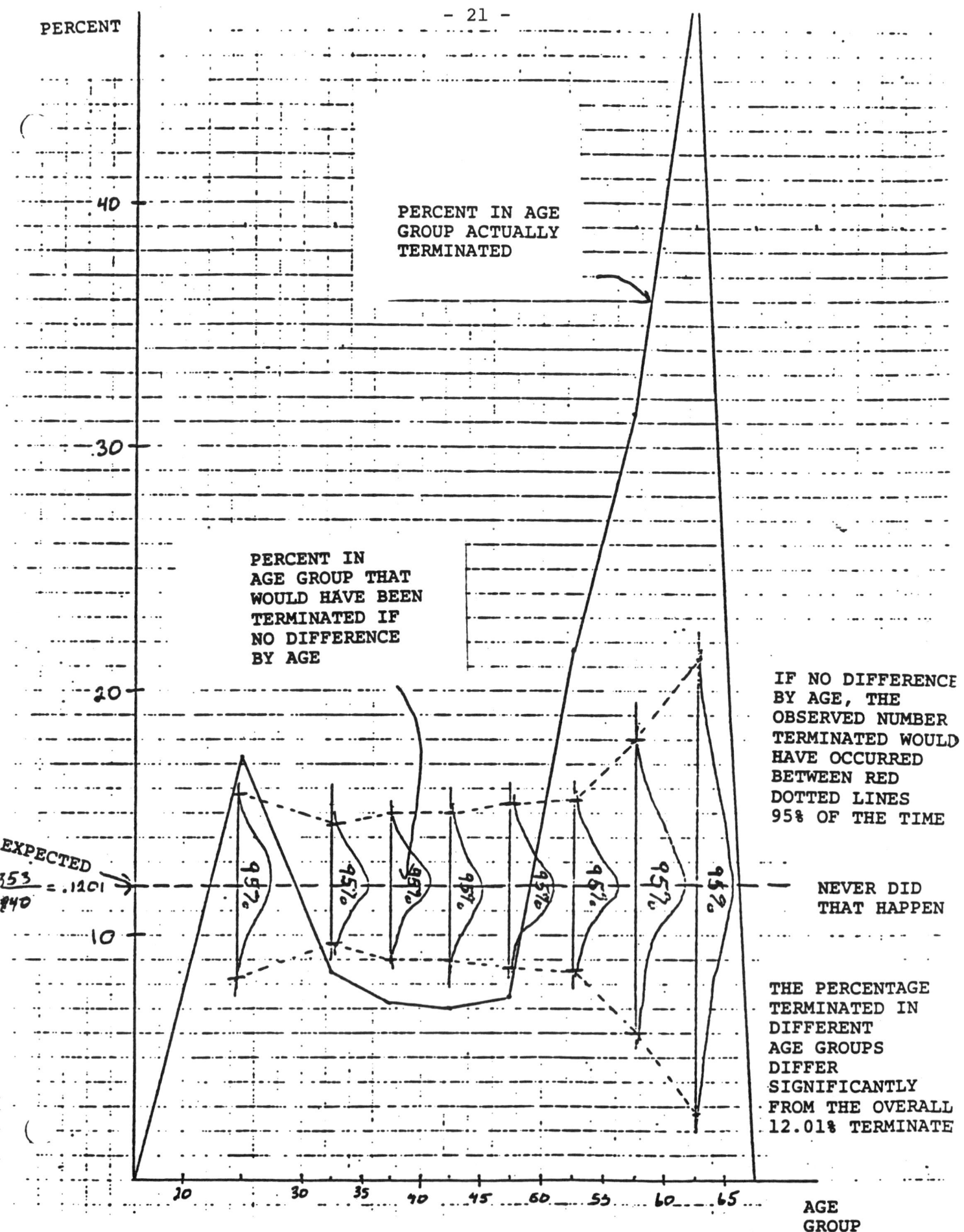

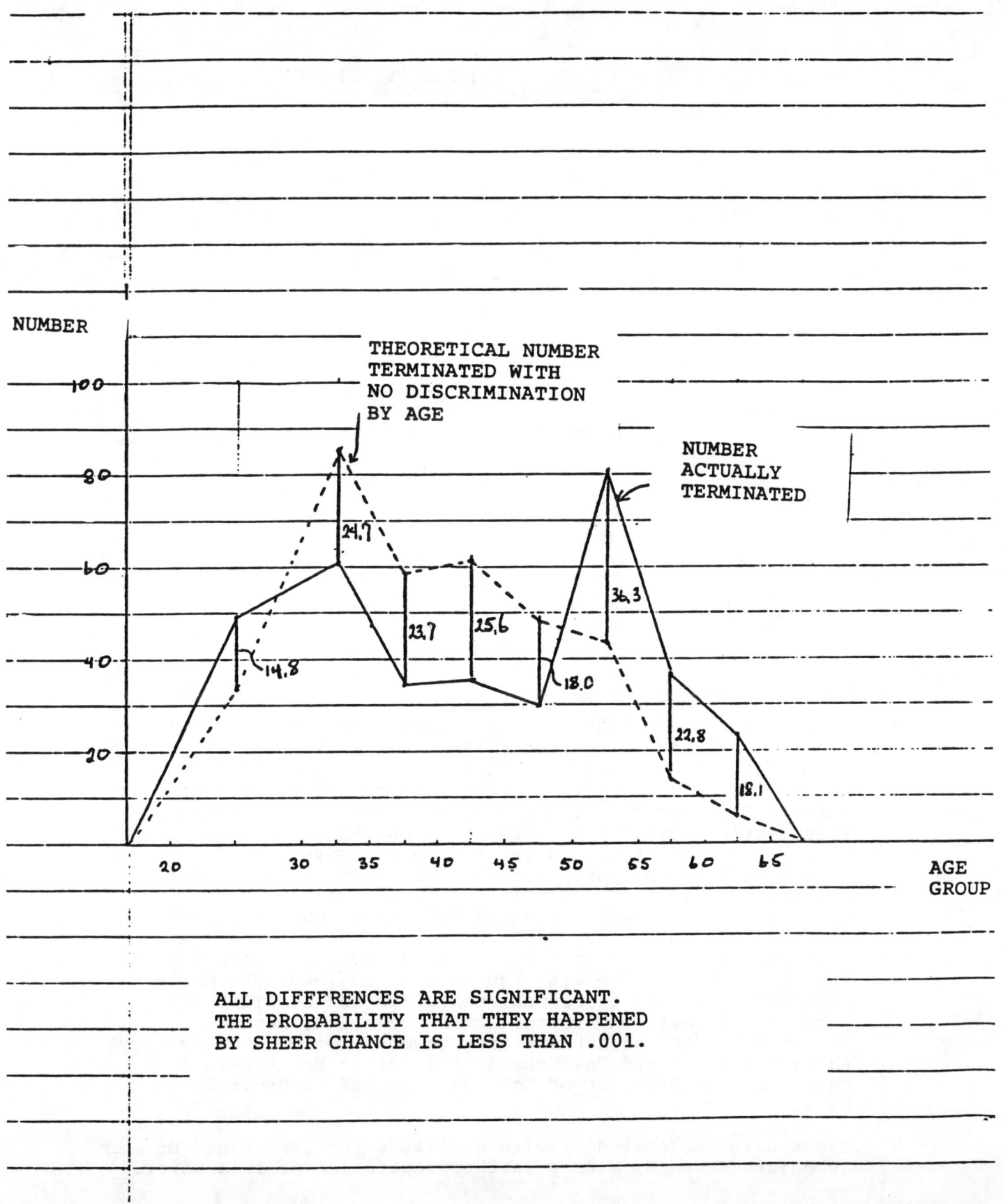

PRETRIAL TACTICS FROM THE PERSPECTIVE
OF DEFENDANT'S COUNSEL

By Thompson Powers [*]

---

[*] Member, Steptoe & Johnson Chartered; formerly Assistant to the Under Secretary of Labor, 1961-62; Deputy Solicitor of Labor, 1962-63; Executive Assistant to the Secretary of Labor, 1964-65; Consultant, International Labor Affairs Bureau, Department of Labor, 1965-66; Executive Secretary, President's Advisory Committee on Labor-Management Policy, 1963-64; Member, Presidential Emergency Board #170 for Long Island Railroad Dispute, 1967 and Chairman, 1969; Special Counsel, President's Committee on Equal Employment Opportunity, 1962-65; Executive Director, Equal Employment Opportunity Commission, 1965; Special Counsel, Interagency Committee on Mexican Affairs, 1966-68; Adjunct Professor of Law, Georgetown University Law Center (1967-80) and Member, Arbitration Panels of Federal Mediation and Conciliation Service and American Arbitration Association; Member, National Academy of Arbitrators; graduate of Duke University, AB 1951 and Harvard Law School, LLB 1954. Mr. Powers is a member of the District of Columbia and U.S. Supreme Court Bars.

The speaker acknowledges with gratitude the assistance of his associate Susan E. Murphy in the preparation of this paper.

TABLE OF CONTENTS

INTRODUCTION..1

I. HAVE THE PROCEDURAL PREREQUISITES TO SUIT
   BEEN SATISFIED...2

   A. Overview of Enforcement Provisions
      of ADEA...2

   B. Prerequisites to Private Suit..........................4

      1. Filing of charge with EEOC.........................4

         a. Has the plaintiff
            filed a charge?.................................4

         b. Is the charge sufficient?.......................6

         c. Was the charge timely filed?...................7

         d. Can the plaintiff claim that
            an untimely charge should be
            excused on equitable grounds?...................8

      2. Conciliation by EEOC..............................10

      3. Commencement of state proceedings.................11

   C. Prerequisites to Action by EEOC.......................12

II. CAN THE SCOPE OF THE ACTION BE NARROWED?................14

   A. Multi-Party Private Actions..........................14

      1. Does the action include
         individuals who are not
         properly in the suit?.............................15

         a. Has any individual
            failed to opt-in?..............................15

         b. Has every claimant met the
            procedural prerequisites to suit?..............16

         c. Are there individuals included
            who are not similarly situated?................18

         d. Are any claims time barred?....................19

141

                    (1) Continuing Violations.............19
                        (a) Terminations..................19
                        (b) Demotions.....................22
                        (c) Failure to promote...........23
                        (d) Refusal to hire..............26
                    (2) Willful versus nonwillful
                        violations........................26

            e. Are any claims exempted by
                section 4(f)(2) as originally
                enacted?..............................29

            f. Is the defendant entitled to
                summary judgment on the merits?.......31

        2. Are individuals who are proper parties
            to the action asserting claims
            that are subject to dismissal?..............32

            a. Claims that were not the
                subject of an administrative
                charge or conciliation.................32

            b. Claims that are time barred...........34

            c. Claims for compensatory damages
                for pain and suffering.................34

            d. Claims that are improperly
                based on pendent jurisdiction..........35

    B. Actions by EEOC....................................39

        1. Did the EEOC investigate and seek
            to conciliate all matters that it
            is seeking to litigate?.....................39

        2. Does the EEOC have a basis for any
            "pattern or practice" claims it
            is asserting?...............................42

        3. Are any of the claims EEOC is
            asserting time barred?......................46

            a. Section 16(c) claims...................46

            b. Section 17 claims......................47

III. JURY TRIAL CONSIDERATIONS..............................48

    A. Is it in Defendant's
       Interest to Have a Jury Trial?...................48

       1. Who is the judge?...........................48

       2. What is the likely
          composition of the jury?....................49

       3. What are the nature and
          number of the claims?.......................49

       4. What are the facts?........................50

    B. If the Plaintiff has Demanded a Jury can
       the Demand be Defeated or Limited?...............51

       1. Private action.............................51

          a. Timely demand..........................51

          b. Scope of jury trial....................52

       2. Action by EEOC.............................53

IV. DISCOVERY..55

    A. Discovery by the Defendant.......................55

       1. Deposition of the plaintiff................56

       2. Interrogatories, document requests
          and requests for admission.................56

          a. Private action.........................56

          b. Action by EEOC.........................57

       3. Discovery of expert witnesses
          and other witnesses........................59

       4. Offer of judgment..........................59

    B. Discovery by the Plaintiff.......................60

       1. Limiting the scope of responses to
          the plaintiff's interrogatories
          and document requests......................60

       2. Use of Rule 33(c)..........................61

       3. Claims of privilege
          and work product...........................62

		a.	Attorney-client privilege..............62
		b.	Work product doctrine..................62

V. PRETRIAL ORDER 63

    A. Narrowing the Issues................................63

    B. Limiting Witnesses.................................64

    C. Preliminary Hearings...............................65

    D. Order of Proof in Multi-Party Suits 66

    E. Bifurcated Section 16(c)/17 Trials................66

    F. Bifurcation of Liability
       and Damages Determinations........................66

PRETRIAL TACTICS FROM THE PERSPECTIVE
OF DEFENDANT'S COUNSEL

By Thompson Powers

INTRODUCTION

This paper explores some of the major issues that may arise in the pretrial stages of a lawsuit under the Age Discrimination in Employment Act ("ADEA"). 1/ It addresses the following issues that defense counsel would ordinarily confront in an effort to defeat or limit the plaintiff's case prior to trial: (1) Have the procedural prerequisites to suit been satisfied? (2) Can the scope of the action be narrowed? (3) Is a jury trial advisable? (4) Can discovery by the plaintiff be limited? (5) How can discovery by the defendant be used most advantageously? and (6) What proposals for the pretrial order may promote the defendant's interests at trial?

Because of its complexity, the Age Discrimination Act has engendered much litigation on pretrial issues. The Act imposes on plaintiffs a number of special procedural requirements and time limits that must be satisfied prior to trial. It also precludes the use of class actions under Rule 23 of the Federal Rules of Civil Procedure, which has been frequently used by plaintiffs litigating under Title VII of the Civil Rights Act of 1964. From the defendant's perspective, each of these elements of the ADEA may present opportunities for motions to dismiss some or all of the claims or parties. Moreover, the fact that the Act allows jury trials introduces another special set of tactical considerations that must be weighed at the beginning of the case.

Increasingly, both private plaintiffs and the EEOC are seeking to test the limits of the ADEA in areas in which the law is not yet fully developed. For example, a "pattern or practice" suit brought by the EEOC may challenge numerous employment decisions and seek relief for unnamed individuals on a much broader basis than may be justifiable. In private suits, despite the ADEA's special rules, some plaintiffs continue to attempt to use traditional class action concepts to expand the extent of multi-party suits. Also, it is becoming more and more common for plaintiffs to join state law claims for wrongful discharge with their ADEA claims. If the defendant does not succeed in having the state claims dismissed or carefully circumscribed, their presence may prejudice the jury or provide the basis for an award of compensatory and punitive damages, which are not available under the ADEA.

1/   29 U.S.C. §§ 621-634 (1976 & Supp. III 1979).

As these points suggest, failure to limit the scope of the suit at the outset can be very damaging to the defendant's case. Careful and exhaustive pretrial preparation is thus essential.

I.   HAVE THE PROCEDURAL PREREQUISITES TO SUIT BEEN SATISFIED?

As in most litigation, the defendant's initial objective in an ADEA case should be to narrow the scope of the action as much as possible, or even to have the suit dismissed prior to trial. Therefore this section and the next are devoted to a review of the procedural and substantive grounds that may serve as the basis for pretrial motions to dismiss some or all of the claims or parties.

    A.   Overview of Enforcement Provisions of ADEA

The Age Discrimination Act is a composite statute. Its substantive prohibitions are modeled after Title VII of the Civil Rights Act of 1964 2/ and its enforcement scheme is derived from the Fair Labor Standards Act ("FLSA"). 3/ In addition, the ADEA requires compliance with certain administrative prerequisites to suit which are borrowed directly from Title VII but which have no counterpart in the FLSA enforcement scheme. The plaintiff's failure to meet the requirements of the FLSA provisions or to comply with any of the ADEA's pretrial procedural hurdles may provide the basis for a dispositive motion by the defendant.

The ADEA essentially authorizes three types of lawsuits, which are briefly described below:

(1) _Action by an individual_. Section 7(c) of the ADEA provides that "[a]ny person aggrieved may bring a civil action in any court of competent jurisdiction for such legal or equitable relief as will effectuate the purposes of this [Act]." 4/

(2) _Multi-party action_. Section 7(b) of the ADEA 5/ incorporates section 16(b) of the FLSA. 6/ The FLSA provision

---

2/   42 U.S.C. §§ 2000e-2000e-17 (1976 & Supp. III 1979).

3/   29 U.S.C. §§ 201-219 (1976 & Supp. III 1979).

4/   29 U.S.C. § 626(c)(1) (Supp. III 1979). A successful plaintiff is entitled to liquidated or double damages if the violation was "willful." 29 U.S.C. §§ 216(b), 626(b). See pp. 26-29 below.

5/   29 U.S.C. § 626(b).

6/   29 U.S.C. § 216(b) (Supp. III 1979).

allows suit to be brought by "any one or more employees for and in behalf of himself or themselves and other employees similarly situated." This section further provides that "no employee may be a party plaintiff to any such action unless he gives his consent in writing to become such a party and such consent is filed in the court in which such action is brought." 7/ Thus, the ADEA does not permit class actions under Rule 23 of the Federal Rules of Civil Procedure but instead limits actions to those persons who have "opted in" by filing written consents to suit. 8/

(3) **Action by EEOC.** 9/ The EEOC is authorized to bring suit for alleged age discrimination under sections 16(c) and 17 of the FLSA, 10/ which are incorporated by section 7(b) of the ADEA. The right of an individual to bring suit terminates if the EEOC commences an action on his behalf. 11/

(i) **Section 16(c) suits.** Section 16(c) of the FLSA authorizes the Secretary of Labor to bring suit on behalf of aggrieved employees to recover unpaid minimum wages or overtime compensation and an additional equal amount as liquidated damages. To recover damages in a section 16(c) suit, an individual claimant must be named as a party plaintiff in the Secretary's complaint. 12/ Thus, in ADEA cases, the EEOC may bring suit under section 16(c) to recover monetary damages 13/ on behalf of named individuals.

(ii) **Section 17 suits.** Section 17 of the FLSA authorizes the Secretary to seek injunctive relief to restrain

---

7/ Id.

8/ See discussion at p. 14 below.

9/ As originally enacted, the ADEA, like the FLSA, vested enforcement authority in the Secretary of Labor. On July 1, 1979 responsibility for enforcing the ADEA was transferred to the EEOC by Executive Order.

10/ 29 U.S.C. §§ 216(c), 217 (Supp. III 1979).

11/ 29 U.S.C. § 626(c)(1) (Supp. III 1979).

12/ Section 16(c) provides that for purposes of the statute of limitations, an action by the Secretary under section 16(c) is considered to be commenced in the case of any individual claimant on the date when the complaint is filed "if he is specifically named as a party plaintiff in the complaint, or if his name did not so appear, on the subsequent date on which his name is added as a party plaintiff in such action." 29 U.S.C. § 216(c). See pp. 46-48 below.

13/ Actions under the ADEA to recover "amounts owing" as a result of a violation are treated as actions for unpaid minimum wages or overtime compensation for purposes of utilizing the FLSA's enforcement procedures. 29 U.S.C. § 626(b). As in individual suits, liquidated damages are available only in the case of "willful" violations. Id.

violations of the FLSA, including "the restraint of any withholding of payment of minimum wages or overtime compensation." 14/ In contrast to section 16(c), such relief may be sought for all affected individuals without any requirement that they be specifically named in the complaint. 15/

Particular questions relating to the scope of multi-party suits and EEOC suits under sections 16(c) and 17 will be discussed in section II. In the remainder of this section, the administrative prerequisites to suit will be reviewed with respect to single-plaintiff private suits and actions by the EEOC.

B. Prerequisites to Private Suit

1. Filing of charge with EEOC

Section 7(d) of the ADEA 16/ provides that "[n]o civil action may be commenced by an individual . . . until 60 days after a charge alleging unlawful discrimination has been filed" with the EEOC. This notice must be filed within 180 days after the alleged unlawful practice occurred, or, if the practice occurred in a state having a state agency authorized to grant relief from discrimination on the basis of age (a so-called "deferral state"), within 300 days after the alleged unlawful practice occurred. 17/

This requirement raises several questions that defense counsel should ask in the early stages of an ADEA case:

a. Has the plaintiff filed a charge?

The filing of a charge with the EEOC has consistently been viewed as a jurisdictional prerequisite to suit. 18/ Thus, a court cannot entertain an ADEA action until a charge has been filed.

14/ 29 U.S.C. § 217. Liquidated damages are not available in a section 17 suit. EEOC v. Gilbarco, Inc., 615 F.2d 985, 991 (4th Cir. 1980).

15/ See Hodgson v. Brookhaven Gen. Hosp., 436 F.2d 719 (5th Cir. 1970).

16/ 29 U.S.C. § 626(d) (Supp. III 1979).

17/ Id. § 626(d)(1) and (2). In deferral states, if the state proceeding is terminated before the end of the 300-day period, the charge must be filed with the EEOC within 30 days after receipt of notice of the state proceeding's termination. Id.

18/ See Wright v. Tennessee, 628 F.2d 949, 953 (6th Cir. 1980) (en banc); Ewald v. Great Atl. & Pac. Tea Co., 620 F.2d

The reason for this requirement is apparent from the statute itself. Section 7(d) requires that upon receipt of a charge the EEOC "promptly notify" all prospective defendants and "promptly seek to eliminate any alleged unlawful practice by informal methods of conciliation, conference, and persuasion." [19] As is the case under Title VII, informal resolution of age discrimination complaints is "patently encouraged and preferred" to private lawsuits. [20]

When no administrative charge is filed, the defendant is deprived of early notice of the claim and the opportunity to engage in informal conciliation. Therefore, if the plaintiff has bypassed the EEOC entirely, the defendant has clear grounds to move for dismissal of the suit. [21]

1183, 1187-88 (6th Cir. 1980), cert. denied, 101 S. Ct. 2319 (1981); Newcomer v. International Business Mach. Corp., 598 F.2d 968, 969 (5th Cir.) (per curiam), cert. denied, 444 U.S. 984 (1979); Dartt v. Shell Oil Co., 539 F.2d 1256, 1260-61 (10th Cir. 1976), aff'd by an equally divided court, 434 U.S. 99 (1977); Fulton v. NCR Corp., 472 F. Supp. 377, 380 (W.D. Va. 1979); Bengochea v. Norcross, Inc., 464 F. Supp. 709, 712 (E.D. Pa. 1979); see also H.R. Rep. No. 805, 90th Cong., 1st Sess., reprinted in [1967] U.S. Code Cong. & Ad. News 2213, 2223.

[19] 29 U.S.C. § 626(d) (Supp. III 1979). The requirement that conciliation be undertaken is discussed below at pp. 10-11.

[20] Dean v. American Sec. Ins. Co., 559 F.2d 1036, 1038 (5th Cir. 1977), cert. denied, 434 U.S. 1066 (1978).

[21] However, one caveat must be noted. If time remains under the statute of limitations, a court may choose to dismiss the case without prejudice to permit the plaintiff to belatedly pursue administrative remedies and then file suit anew. This was the procedure the court followed in Bengochea, supra note 18. The court first reasoned that the enforcement scheme of the ADEA makes it clear that conciliation is intended to take place "before the parties assumed the formal adversary posture of litigants." 464 F. Supp. at 712 (emphasis in original). Therefore because the plaintiff had not yet brought an administrative charge, his complaint should be dismissed, rather than held in abeyance, so that the conciliation process would not be "hampered by the pendency of federal-court litigation." Id. "Dismissal of the complaint . . .," the court noted, ". . . would not by itself preclude a subsequent civil action arising from the same alleged unlawful practice." Id. Cf. Oscar Mayer & Co. v. Evans, 441 U.S. 750, 764-65 (1979) (action should be held in abeyance while plaintiff is given opportunity to satisfy prerequisite of filing charge with state).

b. **Is the charge sufficient?**

As originally enacted, section 7(d) of the ADEA required that a "notice of intent to sue," rather than a charge, be filed. This led some courts to require that the notice formally and unequivocally express an intention to file suit, rather than simply complain of an allegedly unlawful practice. 22/ Other courts, on the other hand, held that the notice need not be so explicit, and could even be an oral communication to the Department of Labor. 23/

In 1978 section 7(d) was amended to require that a "charge" be filed. The Conference Committee approving the amendment reported that the change in language was not intended to alter the basic purposes of the notice requirement, and that the "charge" requirement would "be satisfied by the filing of a written statement which identifies the potential defendant and generally describes the action believed to be discriminatory."24/

Despite this easing of the notice requirement, the defendant may still contest the sufficiency of the plaintiff's charge by raising the following questions: (1) Was a written charge filed? (2) Does the complainant's statement clearly indicate a belief that he has been discriminated against on the basis of age? 25/ (3) Is each defendant to the suit properly identified in

---

22/ E.g., Powell v. Southwestern Bell Tel. Co., 494 F.2d 485, 489 (5th Cir. 1974); Reich v. Dow Badische Co., 575 F.2d 363, 368 (2d Cir.), cert. denied, 439 U.S. 1006 (1978), and cases cited therein.

23/ Noto v. JFD Elec. Corp., 446 F. Supp. 92 (E.D.N.C. 1978); Woodford v. Kinney Shoe Corp., 369 F. Supp. 911 (N.D. Ga. 1973).

24/ H. Conf. Rep. No. 95-950, 95th Cong., 2d Sess. 12, reprinted in [1978] U.S. Code Cong. & Ad. News 528, 534.

25/ See Fulton v. NCR Corp., 472 F. Supp. 377, 381 (W.D. Va. 1979) (response to Labor Department's form questionnaire may be insufficient to indicate plaintiff was filing a charge of discrimination). Note that with respect to actions filed before 1978, courts continue to impose the requirement that the complainant convey an express intention to file suit. See Hageman v. Philips Roxane Laboratories, Inc., 623 F.2d 1381, 1384 (9th Cir. 1980) (where plaintiff knew of the notice of intent to sue requirement and of his failure to have satisfied it, submission of Labor Department's "Employment Information Form" was insufficient and summary judgment must be granted; 1978 amendment applies only to actions brought after April 6, 1978); Newcomer v. IBM Corp., 598 F.2d 968, 969 (5th Cir.) (percuriam), cert. denied, 444 U.S. 984 (1979); Tonka v. American Tel. & Tel. Co., 22 Empl. Prac. Dec. ¶ 30,885 (N.D. Ga. 1980).

the charge? 26/ and (4) Does the charge include all claims of discrimination that the plaintiff is seeking to litigate in his judicial complaint? 27/

c. <u>Was the charge timely filed?</u>

As noted previously, the ADEA requires that the charge be filed within 180 or 300 days of the alleged unlawful employment practice. The Act also requires that the complainant wait at least 60 days after filing the charge before bringing suit. 28/ These time limits raise several questions that defendants should answer at the outset of the case: (1) When does the 180/300-day period begin to run, <u>i.e.</u>, when did the alleged unlawful practice occur? 29/ (2) Is the complainant entitled to the 180- or the 300-day period? 30/ and (3) Is the plaintiff's suit premature? 31/

26/ <u>Compare</u> Travers v. Corning Glass Works, 76 F.R.D. 431 (S.D.N.Y. 1977) (defendant dismissed because not named in notice), <u>and</u> Hannon v. Continental Nat'l Bank, 427 F. Supp. 215, 217 (D. Colo. 1977), <u>with</u> Goodman v. Board of Trustees, 498 F. Supp. 1329 (N.D. Ill. 1980).

27/ <u>See</u> Scaramuzzo v. Glenmore Distilleries Co., 501 F. Supp. 727, 730-32 (N.D. Ill. 1980) (judicial complaint properly encompasses any discrimination like or reasonably related to the allegations of the charge filed with the Department of Labor). The consequences of failing to include all claims in the charge are discussed in more detail below at pp. 32-33.

28/ 29 U.S.C. § 626(d) (Supp. III 1979).

29/ <u>See</u> Chardon v. Fernandez, 102 S. Ct. 28 (1981) (in a discharge case, alleged unlawful employment practice occurs on date plaintiffs were notified that a final decision had been made to terminate their employment, rather than on their last day of work). The question of when an alleged unlawful employment practice can be considered to have occurred is explored in more detail below at pp. 19-26 with respect to various types of employment actions.

30/ The defendant should ascertain whether the state is a deferral state. <u>See</u> 29 U.S.C. § 633 <u>and</u> discussion below at p. 11. In deferral states, it is generally held that the complainant has the benefit of the 300-day period for filing with the EEOC even though he did not resort to state administrative remedies within 180 days. <u>See</u> Ciccone v. Textron, Inc., 651 F.2d 1 (1st Cir. 1981); Davis v. Calgon Corp., 627 F.2d 674 (3d Cir. 1980); Bean v. Crocker Nat'l Bank, 600 F.2d 754 (9th Cir. 1979); <u>cf.</u> Mohasco Corp. v. Silver, 447 U.S. 807 (1980) (implied holding that Title VII plaintiff need not file within 180 days in a deferral state).

31/ Courts have dismissed actions when the plaintiff has not complied with the 60-day waiting period. <u>E.g.</u>, Rucker v. Great Scott Supermarkets, 528 F.2d 393 (6th Cir. 1976).

d. Can the plaintiff claim that an
untimely charge should be excused
on equitable grounds?

Initially, a number of courts refused to recognize any exceptions to the time limits for filing an ADEA charge, holding that failure to file a timely charge deprived the court of jurisdiction to hear the case. 32/ Now, however, it is generally agreed that the time limits in section 7(d) are analogous to statutes of limitation and may be equitably modified. 33/ The courts have done so by application of the doctrines of equitable tolling and equitable estoppel.

Equitable tolling focuses on factors such as: (1) the plaintiff's lack of actual notice of his rights and obligations under the ADEA; (2) his lack of constructive knowledge, i.e., through an attorney; (3) his diligence in pursuing his rights; (4) the absence of prejudice to the defendant; and (5) the plaintiff's reasonableness in remaining ignorant of the filing requirement. 34/ In particular, the employer's failure to post the informational notice required by the ADEA 35/ will toll the 180-day period, according to a number of courts, at least until the plaintiff consults with an attorney or acquires actual

---

32/ E.g., Powell v. Southwestern Bell Tel. Co., 494 F.2d 485 (5th Cir. 1974).

33/ See Coke v. General Adjustment Bureau, Inc., 640 F.2d 584 (5th Cir. 1981) (en banc), and Title VII and ADEA cases cited therein; Naton v. Bank of California, 649 F.2d 691 (9th Cir. 1981); Wright v. Tennessee, 628 F.2d 949 (6th Cir. 1980) (en banc); Nielsen v. Western Elec. Co., 603 F.2d 741 (8th Cir. 1979); Kephart v. Institute of Gas Technology, 581 F.2d 1287 (7th Cir. 1978); Bonham v. Dresser Indus., Inc., 569 F.2d 187 (3d Cir. 1977), cert. denied, 439 U.S. 821 (1978); Dartt v. Shell Oil Co., 539 F.2d 1256 (10th Cir. 1976), aff'd by an equally divided court, 434 U.S. 99 (1977).

34/ Abbott v. Moore Business Forms, Inc., 439 F. Supp. 643, 646 (D.N.H. 1977), cited with approval in, e.g., Wright, supra note 33, 628 F.2d at 953; Naton, supra note 33, 649 F.2d at 696. See also Volk v. Multi-Media, Inc., 516 F. Supp. 157 (S.D. Ohio 1981) (attorney's error justifies tolling, where plaintiff was as diligent as he could be expected to be, and defendant suffered no prejudice).

35/ 29 U.S.C. § 627.

knowledge of his rights. 36/ Also of importance is whether the purposes of the charge-filing requirement--early notification to the defendant and prompt conciliation--have been substantially satisfied. 37/

Equitable estoppel is applied to prevent the defendant from profiting from his own wrongful conduct when he has induced the plaintiff to forebear filing a charge until the limitations period has expired. 38/ Courts have also held that a defendant who has concealed or misrepresented the facts giving rise to an ADEA claim is estopped from pleading that the plaintiff's charge is untimely. 39/ The plaintiff must show actual and reasonable reliance on the defendant's conduct or representations; there must also be evidence of the defendant's knowledge of the deceptive nature of its conduct. 40/

Although these equitable concepts have gained widespread acceptance, that does not mean that they are "an escape valve through which jurisdictional requirements will evaporate." 41/ Thus, just as frequently courts have dismissed suits because the

---

36/ E.g., Kephart, supra note 33, 581 F.2d at 1289; Bonham, supra note 33, 569 F.2d at 193; Pirone v. Home Ins. Co., 507 F. Supp. 1281, 1287-88 (S.D.N.Y. 1981).

37/ E.g., Dartt, supra note 33, 539 F.2d at 1261; Pirone, supra note 36, 507 F. Supp. at 1288.

38/ The principles of equitable estoppel and tolling also apply to the ADEA's statute of limitations (see p. 19 below) as well as to the charge-filing period. Thus, in Ott v. Midland-Ross Corp., 523 F.2d 1367 (6th Cir. 1975), the defendant induced the plaintiff to forebear filing suit by promising he would be rehired. When the defendant failed to carry out this promise, the plaintiff filed suit. The court held that the defendant was estopped from pleading that the suit was untimely under the ADEA's statute of limitations. 523 F.2d at 1370.

39/ E.g., Wilkerson v. Siegfried Ins. Agency, Inc., 621 F.2d 1042, 1045 (10th Cir. 1980) (employer lied to plaintiff, saying her position was being eliminated, when in fact it was filled by a younger person).

40/ Naton, supra note 33, 649 F.2d at 696.

41/ Brown v. Mead Corp., 646 F.2d 1163, 1165 (6th Cir. 1981) (Title VII case). See also Barber v. Commercial Union Ins. Co., 27 Fair Empl. Prac. Cas. 703, 705 (E.D. Pa. 1981) (the tolling exception does not permit a court to ignore the legislative intent to grant the defendant a period of repose after the limitations period has expired).

plaintiff's charge was untimely and no reason existed to justify equitable tolling or estoppel. 42/

2. Conciliation by EEOC

When a charge is submitted, the EEOC is required to engage in informal conciliation with the employer in an effort to resolve the charging party's allegations without resort to litigation. Although this requirement is a statutory directive, 43/ courts have refused to dismiss individual suits simply because the EEOC has failed to conciliate. 44/

Nonetheless, the fact that conciliation has been inadequate or nonexistent may be used by the defendant to bolster other pretrial arguments, for example, that it was prejudiced by lack of timely notice of the plaintiff's claim. Courts are generally not disposed to grant plaintiffs' requests for equitable tolling of the charge-filing period when the purposes of that short time limit have not been substantially satisfied. 45/ The Tenth Circuit has described those purposes as two-fold:

42/ E.g., Phillips v. Southern Bell Tel. & Tel. Co., 650 F.2d 655 (5th Cir. 1981) (no evidence that defendant induced delay); Hageman v. Philips Roxane Laboratories, Inc., 623 F.2d 1381, 1385-86 (9th Cir. 1980) (plaintiff knew of the ADEA violation and his rights and responsibilities); Nielsen v. Western Elec. Co., 603 F.2d 741, 743 (8th Cir. 1979); Hrzenak v. White-Westinghouse Appliance Co., 510 F. Supp. 1086, 1091-92 (W.D. Mo. 1981) (plaintiff's assertion he did not see posted notices cannot justify tolling). See also Ott v. Midland-Ross Corp., 600 F.2d 24, 34 (6th Cir. 1979) (plaintiff has burden of proof to establish facts necessary to avoid statute of limitations).

43/ 29 U.S.C. § 626(d) (Supp. III 1979).

44/ See, e.g., Woerner v. Bell Helicopter, 16 Fair Empl. Prac. Cas. 480, 482 (N.D. Tex. 1977) (action or inaction of government agency cannot affect grievant's substantive rights); Lundgren v. Continental Indus., Inc., 14 Fair Empl. Prac. Cas. 58, 61 (N.D. Okla. 1976); cf. Russell v. American Tobacco Co., 528 F.2d 357, 365 (4th Cir. 1975), cert. denied, 425 U.S. 935 (1976) (EEOC's failure to attempt conciliation will not bar suit by a private party under Title VII). Note, however, that in suits in which the EEOC is the plaintiff, inadequate conciliation of some or all of the claims may preclude litigation of those claims by the agency. See discussion below at pp. 39-42. Also, the scope of the plaintiff's judicial complaint will be limited by the scope of his EEOC charge and the ensuing conciliation. See pp. 32-33 below.

45/ See cases cited in note 37 above.

(1) To provide the Labor Department with an opportunity to achieve a conciliation of the complaint while the complaint is still fresh, and (2) to give early notice to the employer of a possible lawsuit, the latter promoting both the preservation of evidence and good faith negotiating on the part of the employer during the conciliation period. 46/

Thus, if the defendant has been deprived of the protections afforded by the notice requirement, that fact should weigh heavily in favor of dismissal of an untimely claim. 47/

Finally, it should be noted that the pendency of conciliation efforts does not toll the statute of limitations for private suits, as it does with respect to suits by the EEOC. 48/

3. Commencement of state proceedings

Section 14(b) 49/ of the ADEA requires that an aggrieved individual resort to appropriate state remedies before bringing suit under the Act. In Oscar Mayer & Co. v. Evans, 50/ the Supreme Court ruled that commencement of state proceedings in deferral states is mandatory, not optional. The Court reasoned that section 14(b), like its counterpart in the Title VII enforcement scheme, 51/ "is intended to screen from the federal courts those discrimination complaints that might be settled to the satisfaction of the grievant in state proceedings." 52/

46/ Dartt v. Shell Oil Co., 539 F.2d 1256, 1261 (10th Cir. 1976), aff'd by an equally divided court, 434 U.S. 99 (1977). See also Bonham v. Dresser Indus., Inc., 569 F.2d 187, 192 (3d Cir. 1977), cert. denied, 439 U.S. 821 (1978).

47/ In Fulton v. NCR Corp., 472 F. Supp. 377 (W.D. Va. 1979), for example, the court granted the employer's motion to dismiss because neither the plaintiff's charge nor his lawsuit was timely, and no grounds for equitable tolling were shown with respect to either time period. Significantly, the court noted, no investigation was made by the Labor Department of the plaintiff's particular case. 472 F. Supp. at 385.

48/ Hovey v. Lutheran Medical Center, 516 F. Supp. 554, 556 (E.D.N.Y. 1981); cf. Aguilar v. Clayton, 452 F. Supp. 896 (E.D. Okla. 1978) (FLSA case). See p. 12 below.

49/ 29 U.S.C. § 633(b).

50/ 441 U.S. 750 (1979).

51/ 42 U.S.C. § 2000e-5(c).

52/ 441 U.S. at 756.

The Court went on to hold, however, that the plaintiff's right to bring suit in federal court could not be defeated by his failure to commence a state proceeding within the time limit prescribed by state law. "[S]tate procedural defaults cannot foreclose federal relief and . . . state limitations periods cannot govern the efficacy of the federal remedy." 53/ Section 14(b) of the ADEA does not require that state remedies be exhausted, the Court emphasized. 54/

Finally, softening the effect of its view that compliance with section 14(b) is mandatory, the Court made it clear that a plaintiff's failure to comply should not bar his federal suit. In such a case the complaint should not be dismissed, the Court said; rather, the federal suit should be "held in abeyance" while the plaintiff is given an opportunity to file a complaint with the state. 55/

C. Prerequisites to Action by EEOC

The only prerequisite to an action by the EEOC is that the agency must "attempt to eliminate the discriminatory practice or practices alleged, and to effect voluntary compliance with the requirements of this [Act] through informal methods of conciliation, conference, and persuasion." 56/ As with private suits, this provision reflects the intention of Congress to make conciliation and mediation "the most favored method of enforcement." 57/ In aid of this purpose, the Act also provides that the statute of limitations is tolled for up to a year while the EEOC and the employer are engaging in conciliation pursuant to section 7(b) of the Act. 58/

The conciliation provision requires that the EEOC make affirmative efforts to resolve controversies before resorting to formal litigation. 59/ At a minimum, the EEOC must inform the employer of the nature of the charges against him, identify the

---

53/ Id. at 762.

54/ Id.

55/ Id. at 764-65.

56/ 29 U.S.C. § 626(b).

57/ Rogers v. Exxon Research & Eng'r Co., 550 F.2d 834, 841 (3d Cir. 1977), cert. denied, 434 U.S. 1022 (1978).

58/ 29 U.S.C. § 626(e)(2) (Supp. III 1979).

59/ See, e.g., Brennan v. Ace Hardware Corp., 495 F.2d 368, 374 (8th Cir. 1974); Usery v. Gilbarco, Inc., 14 Empl. Prac. Dec. ¶ 7625 (M.D.N.C. 1977).

alleged discriminatory action and reveal the basis for the charges, specify the actions necessary to remedy the alleged discrimination, and provide the employer with an opportunity to respond to the charges. 60/ Both the scope of the EEOC's investigation and the specificity of its conciliation efforts may be significant in this regard. 61/

    The EEOC's right to enforce the Age Act is not conditioned on the filing of a complaint by an individual. 62/ Nor is the EEOC required to resort to state age discrimination remedies under section 14(b) as a precondition to filing suit. 63/ Finally, a suit by the EEOC under section 17 of the FLSA is not a class action and therefore is not governed by Rule 23 of the Federal Rules of Civil Procedure. 64/ Consequently, the EEOC need not meet the class action prerequisites of numerosity, commonality, typicality, and adequacy of representation imposed by Rule 23. 65/

60/ See, e.g., Marshall v. Hartford Fire Ins. Co., 78 F.R.D. 97, 103-07 (D. Conn. 1978). Some courts have held that the Act's conciliation requirement is not jurisdictional, and that district courts have equitable discretion to stay lawsuits pending before them in order to permit conciliation to be completed before the lawsuit continues. Marshall v. Sun Oil Co. (Delaware), 605 F.2d 1331, 1337-39 n.8 (5th Cir. 1979); Marshall v. Sun Oil Co. (Pa.), 592 F.2d 563, 566 (10th Cir. 1979); Brennan v. Ace Hardware Corp., 495 F.2d 368 (8th Cir. 1974) (district court did not abuse its discretion in failing to grant a stay); H.R. Conf. Rep. No. 95-950, 95th Cong. 2d Sess. 13, reprinted in [1978] U.S. Code Cong. & Ad. News 528, 534.

61/ This issue is discussed below at pp. 39-42.

62/ See EEOC v. Gilbarco, Inc., 615 F.2d 985, 989 n.3 (4th Cir. 1980) (noting that the 1974 amendments to the FLSA removed the requirement that written request of employees be made as prerequisite to an action by the Secretary under section 16(c)); Hodgson v. Wheaton Glass Co., 446 F.2d 527, 532 (3d Cir. 1971) (FLSA action under § 17); Wirtz v. Jones, 340 F.2d 901, 903 (5th Cir. 1965) (same).

63/ Marshall v. Chamberlain Mfg. Corp., 601 F.2d 100 (3d Cir. 1979); Marshall v. American Motors Corp., 475 F. Supp. 875, 881-83 (E.D. Mich. 1979); Dunlop v. Crown Cork & Seal Co., 405 F. Supp. 774, 776 (D. Md. 1976); cf. Marshall v. West Essex Gen. Hosp., 575 F.2d 1079 (3d Cir. 1978) (state filing by aggrieved employees not a prerequisite to suit by EEOC under section 17).

64/ Donovan v. University of Texas, 643 F.2d 1201 (5th Cir. 1981) (Equal Pay Act suit under section 17).

65/ See General Tel. Co. v. EEOC, 446 U.S. 318 (1980) (Title VII suit by EEOC).

II. CAN THE SCOPE OF THE ACTION BE NARROWED?

This section deals with issues that arise primarily in multi-party suits by private plaintiffs and suits by the EEOC under sections 16(c) and 17 of the FLSA. In such suits pretrial motions may be essential to eliminate overly broad claims of age discrimination. A variety of grounds for dispositive motions are discussed in the following pages. Of course, certain of these issues will also be relevant to single-plaintiff suits as well--for example, compliance with the statute of limitations, the sufficiency of the plaintiff's prima facie case, and the propriety of pendent state law claims.

A. Multi-Party Private Actions

As mentioned earlier, the Age Act has unique rules for multi-party suits. Such suits must proceed under section 16(b) of the FLSA, which provides that each person who participates in the action as a party plaintiff must file a written consent with the court. 66/ This procedure is radically different from the type of class action provided for by Rule 23 of the Federal Rules of Civil Procedure and widely used under Title VII. As the Fifth Circuit explained in LaChapelle v. Owens-Illinois,

> There is a fundamental, irreconcilable difference between the class action described by Rule 23 and that provided for by FLSA § 16(b). In a Rule 23 proceeding a class is described; if the action is maintainable as a class action, each person within the description is considered to be a class member, and, as such, is bound by judgment, whether favorable or unfavorable, unless he has "opted out" of the suit. Under § 16(b) of FLSA, on the other hand, no person can become a party plaintiff and no person will be bound by or may benefit from judgment unless he has affirmatively "opted into" the class; that is, given his written filed consent. 67/

Other courts have uniformly endorsed this conclusion that representative or multi-party suits under the ADEA are not governed by the standards of Rule 23. 68/

66/ 29 U.S.C. § 216(b) (Supp. III 1979). See pp. 2-3 above.

67/ 513 F.2d 286, 288 (5th Cir. 1975) (per curiam).

68/ E.g., Naton v. Bank of California, 649 F.2d 691 (9th Cir. 1981); McCorstin v. United States Steel Corp., 621 F.2d 749 (5th Cir. 1980); Price v. Maryland Cas. Co., 561 F.2d 609 (5th Cir. 1977); McGinley v. Burroughs Corp., 407 F. Supp.

Starting from this premise, the defendant should attempt to limit any multi-party ADEA action with the following questions in mind: (1) Does the action include individuals who are not properly in the suit? and (2) Are individuals who are properly parties to the action asserting claims that are subject to dismissal?

1. Does the action include individuals who are not properly in the suit?

The defendant can seek to narrow the scope of the suit on both procedural and substantive grounds:

a. Has any individual failed to opt in?

In light of the clear dictates of section 16(b) of the FLSA, broad allegations in the complaint that the plaintiff represents, for example, "all other similarly situated employees over 40 years of age who were terminated at the same time as plaintiff" are susceptible to a motion to strike. The defendant should further argue that the suit is confined to those persons who have already filed written consents with the court along with the complaint. However, some courts have allowed additional consents to be filed for a specified period of time after the complaint is filed. 69/ In no event, though, should "opting in" be permitted after the statute of limitations has run. 70/

---

903 (E.D. Pa. 1975); Sanders v. National Cash Register Corp., 21 Fair Empl. Prac. Cas. 1643 (N.D. Ala. 1979); Montalto v. Morgan Guar. Trust Co., 83 F.R.D. 150 (S.D.N.Y. 1979); Hill v. Western Elec. Co., 76 F.R.D. 4, 5-6 (M.D.N.C. 1976); cf. Kinney Shoe Corp. v. Vorhes, 564 F.2d 859, 862 (9th Cir. 1977) (FLSA suit); Schmidt v. Fuller Brush Co., 527 F.2d 532, 536 (8th Cir. 1975) (FLSA suit); Sims v. Parke Davis & Co., 334 F. Supp. 774, 780-81 (E.D. Mich.) aff'd on basis of district court opinion, 453 F.2d 1259 (6th Cir. 1971), cert. denied, 405 U.S. 978 (1972) (FLSA suit). See generally Annot., 44 A.L.R. Fed. 118 (1979).

69/ E.g., Montalto v. Morgan Guar. Trust Co., 83 F.R.D. 150, 152 (S.D.N.Y. 1979) (90 days after court's decision that action was not maintainable under Rule 23); Wagner v. Loew's Theatres, Inc., 76 F.R.D. 23, 24 (M.D.N.C. 1977) (opportunity to opt in continues at least until a reasonable time prior to trial); Roshto v. Chrysler Corp., 67 F.R.D. 28, 30 (E.D. La. 1975) (cut-off date for opt-ins set at 30 days prior to trial).

70/ Section 7 of the FLSA, 29 U.S.C. § 256, provides that a multi-party action is considered to be commenced for purposes of the statute of limitations in the case of any individual claimant

b. Has every claimant met the
procedural prerequisites to suit?

Although it is undisputed that each claimant must "opt in" by filing a consent to suit, the law is unsettled on the question of whether the named plaintiff may represent individuals who have not themselves complied with the procedural prerequisites to suit.

Defendants should argue that any claimant who has failed either to file a timely charge with the EEOC or to commence state administrative proceedings should be dismissed from the suit. Supporting this view, the Fifth Circuit has held that the notice/charge-filing requirement of section 7(d) of the ADEA is "a prerequisite to and complement of the class action mechanism" of section 16(b) of the FLSA. 71/ The claim of one plaintiff who had failed to file the required notice was accordingly dismissed. 72/

Other cases take the contrary position: that the representative plaintiff's notice or charge satisfies the requirement with respect to "opt-ins" who have not themselves filed notices or charges. 73/ These decisions rely primarily on the fact that

---

> (a) on the date when the complaint is filed, if he is specifically named as a party plaintiff in the complaint and his written consent to become a party plaintiff is filed on such date . . . or
>
> (b) if such written consent was not so filed or if his name did not so appear – on the subsequent date on which such written consent is filed . . . .

However, this section of the FLSA is not incorporated into the ADEA. Defendants should nonetheless argue that the filing of a complaint does not toll the limitations period for individuals who subsequently opt in. Rather, a person's claim must be timely as of the date the consent is filed. For a discussion of statute of limitations questions, see below at pp. 19-29.

71/ McCorstin v. United States Steel Corp., 621 F.2d 749, 755 (5th Cir. 1980).

72/ Accord, Price v. Maryland Cas. Co., 561 F.2d 609 (5th Cir. 1977); Hays v. Republic Steel Corp., 12 Fair Empl. Prac. Cas. 1637 (N.D. Ala. 1974); Oshiro v. Pan American World Airways, Inc., 378 F. Supp. 80 (D. Hawaii 1974).

73/ Mistretta v. Sandia Corp., 639 F.2d 588, 593-94 (10th Cir. 1980) (requirements of both sections 7(d) and 14(b) met with respect to opt-ins by named plaintiff's notice which alleges class-based discrimination); Bean v. Crocker Nat'l Bank, 600 F.2d 754, 760 (9th Cir. 1979); Sussman v. Vornado, Inc., 26

- 17 -

this is the well-established rule in Title VII class actions under Rule 23. 74/

In a recent case, the Ninth Circuit attempted to reconcile this conflicting authority. 75/ The case upheld dismissal of the claims of the non-filing "opt-ins" because the named plaintiff's charge "expressed no intention to sue on behalf of anyone other than himself." 76/ Unlike those cases in which the representative party's notice was deemed to suffice for the class, this notice failed to satisfy the purposes of section 7(d) because it did not alert the Secretary of Labor and the employer "'that the discrimination charges encompassed a pattern of unlawful conduct transcending an isolated individual claim and that they should act accordingly.'" 77/

This view will obviously aid defendants in cases in which the charge filed by the named plaintiff is devoid of class-type allegations. However, regardless of the contents of the charge, defendants should still insist that the statute requires each plaintiff who intends to opt in to give timely pre-suit notice, so that conciliation can be undertaken with respect to each individual. The fact that one claimant has thought to include class allegations in his charge does not guarantee that other individuals' claims will be conciliated, nor does it mean that the filing of a charge by others would necessarily be a repetitive or futile effort. Furthermore, Congress' conscious choice of the special FLSA "opt in" requirement over the Rule 23 "opt out" procedure strongly implies that principles from Title VII class actions are inapplicable to ADEA actions. 78/ An ADEA

Fair Empl. Prac. Cas. 335, 339 (D.N.J. 1981); Pandis v. Sikorsky Aircraft Div. of United Tech. Corp., 431 F. Supp. 793 (D. Conn. 1977); Locascio v. Teletype Corp., 74 F.R.D. 108 (N.D. Ill. 1977); Burgett v. Cudahy Co., 361 F. Supp. 617 (D. Kan. 1973).

74/ Under Title VII, the class is not limited to those persons who have filed a charge with the EEOC, because "[i]t would be wasteful, if not vain, for numerous employees, all with the same grievance, to have to process many identical complaints with the EEOC." Pandis, supra note 73, 431 F. Supp. at 797, quoting Oatis v. Crown Zellerbach Corp., 398 F.2d 496, 498-99 (5th Cir. 1968).

75/ Naton v. Bank of California, 649 F.2d 691 (9th Cir. 1981).

76/ Id. at 697.

77/ Id., quoting Bean, supra note 73, 600 F.2d at 760.

78/ Cf. Lorillard v. Pons, 434 U.S. 575, 582 (1978) (the selectivity that Congress exhibited in incorporating and modifying provisions from the FLSA "strongly suggests that

multi-party action is not a true class action but rather is a form of permissive joinder, and each plaintiff should be required to meet the prerequisites to suit as he would if he were suing independently.

Even if the court permits individuals who have not filed charges to participate in the case, it should recognize, as most courts have, two important limitations: the claims in the case will be "limited to the category of claims fairly raised by the notice given by the representative class member," and claims that were time barred on the date the plaintiff filed his charge will not be revived by the filing of the suit as multi-party action. 79/

    c.   Are there individuals included who are not similarly situated?

Section 16(b) requires that those persons who consent to be represented by the named plaintiff be "similarly situated" to the named plaintiff. 80/ Defendants can rely on this statutory restriction to argue for the exclusion of any plaintiff who is not similarly situated to the named plaintiff with respect to: (1) the type of claim asserted, e.g., demotion, termination, failure to promote, etc.; (2) the type of job held, e.g., managerial or non-managerial; (3) the time when the disputed employment decision occurred; (4) the location of employment, e.g., different departments or facilities; and (5) the persons who made the employment decisions at issue. 81/

---

    but for those changes Congress expressly made, it intended to incorporate fully the remedies and procedures of the FLSA," in this case the right to a jury trial).

79/   Pandis v. Sikorsky Aircraft Div. of United Tech. Corp., 431 F. Supp. 793, 798 (D. Conn. 1977); Cavanaugh v. Texas Instruments, Inc., 440 F. Supp. 1124 (S.D. Tex. 1977).

80/   29 U.S.C. § 216(b) (Supp. III 1979).

81/   The few ADEA cases that have construed the term "similarly situated" have had little trouble finding that it correctly characterized the particular plaintiffs in the suit. E.g., Locascio v. Teletype Corp., 74 F.R.D. 108 (N.D. Ill. 1977) (employees had same date of termination, and employer's application of uniform rules to reduction in force overrides the fact that they worked in different departments); Cavanaugh v. Texas Instruments, Inc., 440 F. Supp. 1124, 1126 (S.D. Tex. 1977) (employees occupying non-managerial engineering positions, terminated in same two-year period, and complaining of same pattern of discrimination); Burgett v. Cudahy, 316 F. Supp. 617 (D. Kan. 1973) (all plaintiffs were ages 60-65, long-time supervisory personnel at one plant, fired at the same time for ostensibly the same reasons, complaining of the same discriminatory behavior, and all seeking the same relief).

d. Are any claims time barred?

The Age Discrimination Act applies the statute of limitations found in the Portal-to-Portal Act of 1947, which was enacted as an amendment to the FLSA. 82/ Section 6(a) of the Portal-to-Portal Act provides that:

> [T]he cause of action . . . shall be forever barred unless commenced within two years after the cause of action accrued, except that a cause of action arising out of a willful violation may be commenced within three years after the cause of action accrued. 83/

Thus, a plaintiff whose claim arises outside of the two-year period cannot recover if the violation was not "willful."

Statute of limitations questions under the ADEA involve two types of issues: (1) when is recovery for an alleged discriminatory act time barred? and (2) what constitutes a willful violation?

(1) Continuing violations

The Supreme Court has recently issued a definitive ruling on the question of when the cause of action for an alleged unlawful termination accrues. Other issues relating to timeliness remain unsettled, however. In particular, litigation will no doubt continue unabated on the question of whether the plaintiff can prolong the life of a cause of action by alleging a "continuing violation." The current state of the law on these issues is surveyed briefly below:

(a) Terminations

In Chardon v. Fernandez, the Supreme Court considered the claims of several plaintiffs who alleged that they had been terminated from non-tenured positions in the Puerto Rico Department of Education for political reasons in violation of the First Amendment. 84/ The plaintiffs had filed suit less than a year after their final day of employment, but more than a year after they received notice that a final decision had been made to terminate their appointments. The Court held that the claims

---

82/ Section 7(e) of the ADEA, 29 U.S.C. § 626(e), incorporates section 6 of the Portal-to-Portal Act, 29 U.S.C. § 255.

83/ 29 U.S.C. § 255(a).

84/ 102 S. Ct. 28 (1981) (per curiam). Suit was brought under 42 U.S.C. § 1983.

were barred by the applicable one-year statute of limitations. The cause of action accrued, the Court said, on the date notice of termination was given, not on the last day of employment.

The Court regarded its decision as controlled by Delaware State College v. Ricks, a case decided the previous term, which involved a claim by a college teacher that he had been denied tenure in violation of Title VII. 85/ There the Court ruled that the cause of action accrued when the plaintiff was denied tenure, rather than on the date his employment actually ended a year later.

In Chardon, a per curiam decision with three justices dissenting, the Court held that the facts were indistinguishable from Ricks. As in Ricks, "the proper focus is on the time of the discriminatory act, not the point at which the consequences of the act become painful." 86/

By establishing the rule that the date of notice of termination controls, Chardon and Ricks have apparently superseded a number of ADEA cases identifying different dates as the date when a cause of action for termination accrues. 87/ The decisions

---

85/ 449 U.S. 250 (1980).

86/ Chardon, 102 S. Ct. at 29 (emphasis in original).

87/ Compare Bonham v. Dresser Indus., Inc., 569 F.2d 187, 191-92 (3d Cir. 1977), cert. denied, 439 U.S. 821 (1978) (alleged unlawful act occurs when unequivocal notice of termination and last day of work coincide, notwithstanding employee's continued receipt of severance pay or insurance coverage; if dates do not coincide, court suggests that cause of action accrues when employee ceases to render further services); and Payne v. Crane Co., 570 F.2d 198, 199 (5th Cir. 1977) (discharge occurs at the latest as of the date after which the employee's services are no longer accepted), with Moses v. Falstaff Brewing Corp., 525 F.2d 92 (8th Cir. 1975) (company's official termination date, on which all benefits end, is controlling). The choice of the final date of employment had itself led to some difficulties of interpretation. See Marshall v. Kimberly-Clark Corp., 625 F.2d 1300 (5th Cir. 1980).
   In a case decided after Ricks but before Chardon, the Ninth Circuit applied the rationale of Ricks to an ADEA claim. In Aronsen v. Crown Zellerbach, 27 Fair Empl. Prac. Cas. 518, 526 (9th Cir. 1981), the court rejected the Bonham and Moses tests and held that "the applicable limitations period is activated once the employee knows or should know that an unlawful employment practice has been committed." The court reversed the district court's grant of summary judgment for the employer because a factual dispute existed on the issue of when the plaintiff knew or should have known

also will put to rest attempts by plaintiffs to argue that a discharge is a "continuing violation." Courts consistently treat most terminations and layoffs as discrete events that start the statute of limitations running. 88/ The fact that the employee has requested and been denied reinstatement does not usually convert the alleged discriminatory discharge into a continuing violation. 89/

The starting point for the employer's defense of a continuing violation claim (whether with respect to discharge, demotion, or failure to promote or hire) is the Supreme Court's decision in United Air Lines, Inc. v. Evans. In that case the Court held that a continuing violation does not exist simply because an employee may continue to suffer from the effects of a discriminatory act. Rather, as stressed by the Court, "the emphasis should not be placed on mere continuity; the critical question is whether any present violation exists." 90/

The plaintiff in the Evans case had been dismissed because of a company policy subsequently held to be in violation of Title VII. She was later reinstated, but was not given seniority credit for the intervening years during which the illegal policy kept

---

"that he was being terminated or that he was being subjected to an unlawful practice." Id. at 527 (footnote omitted).

88/ See, e.g., United Air Lines, Inc. v. Evans, 431 U.S. 553 (1977) (Title VII case), discussed below; Roberts v. North American Rockwell Corp., 650 F.2d 823, 826 (6th Cir. 1981) (Title VII case); Hart v. J.T. Baker Chemical Corp., 598 F.2d 829 (3d Cir. 1979) (Title VII case); Prophet v. Armco Steel, Inc., 575 F.2d 579 (5th Cir. 1978) (Title VII case); Olson v. Rembrandt Printing Co., 511 F.2d 1228 (8th Cir. 1975) (Title VII case).

89/ See, e.g., Woodburn v. LTV Aerospace Corp., 531 F.2d 750 (5th Cir. 1976) (in ADEA case, failure to reemploy plaintiff did not constitute continuing violation, although hiring and firing in jobs similar to plaintiff's continued after his discharge, when there was no evidence of overt, documented company policies that discriminated on the basis of age, and employer had no contractual obligation to rehire the plaintiff); Collins v. United Air Lines, Inc., 514 F.2d 594 (9th Cir. 1975) (Title VII case); Norton v. Tallahassee Memorial Hosp., 25 Fair Empl. Prac. Cas. 1706 (N.D. Fla. 1979) (Title VII case); Wagner v. Sperry Univac, Div. of Sperry Rand Corp., 458 F. Supp. 505, 512 (E.D. Pa. 1978), aff'd mem., 624 F.2d 1092 (3d Cir. 1980) (cause of action under ADEA accrues when employee is laid off although he remains eligible for rehire).

90/ United Air Lines, Inc. v. Evans, 431 U.S. 553, 558 (1977) (emphasis in original).

her from working. The Supreme Court conceded that "the seniority system gives present effect to a past act of discrimination," in that the plaintiff's pay and fringe benefits were lower than they would have been absent the discriminatory act. However, the court held that her claim was time barred:

> A discriminatory act which is not made the basis for a timely charge is the legal equivalent of a discriminatory act which occurred before the statute was passed. It may constitute relevant background evidence in a proceeding in which the status of a current practice is at issue, but separately considered, it is merely an unfortunate event in history which has no present legal consequences. 91/

The continuing impact of the past violation did not extend the limitations period, and the plaintiff could not allege that a present violation existed. The defendant's present seniority system treated former employees who were discharged for a discriminatory reason no differently than those who resigned or were discharged for a non-discriminatory reason. 92/

(b) Demotions

Like terminations, demotions are usually considered to be completed events from which the limitations period is measured. 93/ As the Supreme Court has repeatedly emphasized, "[m]ere continuity in employment, without more, is insufficient to prolong the life of a cause of action for employment discrimination." 94/

Relying on Evans, courts have held that a demotion or job reclassification does not constitute a continuing violation even

---

91/ Id.

92/ Id.

93/ E.g., Coke v. General Adjustment Bureau, Inc., 616 F.2d 785, 788 (5th Cir. 1980), aff'd on other grounds on rehearing en banc, 640 F.2d 584 (1981) (ADEA case) (alleged unlawful demotion occurs on date of demotion notwithstanding employee's uncertainty over whether his employer will reinstate him); Trabucco v. Delta Airlines, 590 F.2d 315, 316 (6th Cir. 1979) (Title VII case) (job reclassification is discrete event, not continuing violation); Hoggs v. Bethlehem Steel Corp., 25 Fair Empl. Prac. Cas. 1568, 1570 (D. Md. 1979) (Title VII case) (demotion is a discrete event).

94/ Chardon, 102 S. Ct. at 29; Ricks, 449 U.S. at 257; Evans, 431 U.S. at 558.

- 23 -

though it has a continuing adverse effect on the plaintiff's pay and benefits. 95/ Nor can a plaintiff state a continuing violation by alleging that he continued to protest his demotion, and that the employer refused to rectify the alleged violation. 96/ As in Evans, the plaintiff's claim fails if he alleges nothing to indicate that the later refusals were themselves "motivated by a discriminatory animus." 97/

(c) Failure to promote

When the suit challenges the employer's promotion system, plaintiffs have been somewhat more successful in arguing that a continuing violation exists. Courts have found continuing violations when plaintiffs allege an ongoing pattern or practice of discrimination, or a present, identifiable policy that is discriminatory in purpose or effect. 98/ Thus, in a case

---

95/ Downey v. Southern Natural Gas Co., 649 F.2d 302 (5th Cir. 1981) (ADEA case); Trabucco, supra note 93; Macellaro v. Goldman, 643 F.2d 813 (D.C. Cir. 1980) (ADEA case); Goldman v. Sears, Roebuck & Co., 607 F.2d 1014, 1018 (1st Cir. 1979), cert. denied, 445 U.S. 929 (1980) (ADEA and Title VII case) (plaintiff's transfer and subsequent repeated requests to be transferred back to old department did not constitute continuing violation; "a complaint must indicate that not only the injury, but the discrimination, is in fact ongoing").

96/ Gonzalez v. Firestone Tire & Rubber Co., 610 F.2d 241, 249 (5th Cir. 1980) (Title VII case); Goldman, supra note 95, 607 F.2d at 1019 (Congress did not intend limitations period to be circumvented by mere allegation that plaintiff continued to protest demotion). But see Thomas v. E.I. DuPont deNemours & Co., 574 F.2d 1324, 1330-32 (5th Cir. 1978) (a plaintiff who was demoted should be allowed to amend his complaint to allege a separate Age Act violation occurring within the limitations period when the employer turned down his transfer requests and filled an opening, for which the plaintiff was qualified, with a younger man; the plaintiff must prove that these actions were impermissibly tainted by age considerations).

97/ Goldman, supra note 95, 607 F.2d at 1018-19.

98/ Reed v. Lockheed Aircraft Corp., 613 F.2d 757, 759-60 (9th Cir. 1980) (Title VII case); Gonzalez, supra note 96, 610 F.2d at 249 (discriminatory testing system challenged under Title VII); Morelock v. NCR Corp., 586 F.2d 1096 (6th Cir. 1978), cert. denied, 441 U.S. 906 (1979) (under the ADEA a seniority system is a continuing violation); Patterson v. American Tobacco Co., 586 F.2d 300, 304 (4th Cir. 1978) (Title VII case); Acha v. Beame, 570 F.2d 57, 65 (2d Cir.

alleging sex discrimination, the violation was found to be
continuing because "each day without promotion constituted a new
violation of Title VII, assuming that similarly situated males
were promoted with more regularity." 99/ This may be realistic
where promotion is not dependent on vacancies or in regard to
subsequent vacancies for which the claimant is qualified.
However, I do not believe that even in such situations there is
justification for litigating the lawfulness of earlier discrete
events that are time barred when viewed separately or for basing
the award of back pay on such earlier events as some courts have
done:

> A continuously maintained illegal employment
> policy may be the subject of a valid com-
> plaint until a specified number of days
> after the last occurrence of an instance of
> that policy. . . . Furthermore, where an
> illegal policy is so maintained, relief for
> injuries sustained even before the beginning
> of the limitations period is appropriate. 100/

Notwithstanding this case law, the principles set forth by the
Supreme Court in Evans, Ricks, and Chardon do impose important
limitations on a plaintiff's ability to allege a continuing
violation.

Unquestionably, "mere continuity in employment" does not
extend the limitations period for a claim of refusal to
promote. 101/ It is also clearly insufficient for a plaintiff to
allege only that he continues to suffer from the adverse effects
of the denied promotion. The plaintiff must show that a present,
ongoing violation exists. 102/ Moreover, a bare allegation of a

---

1978) (Title VII case challenging broad "policy of
exclusion"); Clark v. Olinkraft, 556 F.2d 1219 (5th Cir.
1977) (Title VII case), cert. denied, 434 U.S. 1069 (1978);
Cedeck v. Hamiltonian Federal Savings & Loan Ass'n, 551 F.2d
1136 (8th Cir. 1977) (Title VII case); Rich v. Martin
Marietta Corp., 522 F.2d 333, 348 (10th Cir. 1975) (Title
VII case) ("[p]laintiffs here challenge the entire promotion
system maintaining that it continually operated so as to
hold them in lower echelons").

99/ Reed, supra note 98.

100/ Acha, supra note 98, 570 F.2d at 65 (citations omitted;
emphasis in original).

101/ Chardon, 102 S. Ct. at 29; Ricks, 449 U.S. at 257; Evans,
431 U.S. at 558.

102/ Id. See also Jewett v. International Tel. & Tel. Corp.,
653 F.2d 89 (3d Cir. 1981) (failure to promote was not a
continuing violation because whatever discriminatory

"present policy of age discrimination" does not meet this requirement; the plaintiff must adduce some evidence of ongoing discrimination. 103/

     Sometimes a plaintiff will argue that a series of events constitutes a continuing pattern of discrimination. For example, the employer may have demoted the plaintiff and then repeatedly refused requests for promotion or transfer, or the plaintiff may have been discharged or laid off, then rejected for reemployment. Under this theory the plaintiff claims to be entitled to relief for the entire series of discriminatory acts, not just those occurring within the limitations period.

     Defendants should oppose such allegations on the ground that the present acts are unrelated to the prior time barred events. It is clear that more than "a series of unrelated and isolated instances of discrimination" must be shown; the violations must be part of "an organized scheme leading to a present violation." 104/ The essential element, as one court has said, is the "interrelatedness of the past and present acts and not simply any similarity between them." 105/ Where different positions involving different qualifications and different selecting officials were involved, this element of interrelatedness was found lacking. 106/ The absence of any evidence of an ongoing policy or practice of discrimination also will require exclusion of the untimely claims from a series of events. 107/

---

        pattern or practice that may have existed ended long before the actionable period).

103/ See Phillips v. Southern Bell Tel. & Tel. Co., 650 F.2d 655, 658 (5th Cir. 1981) (ADEA case).

104/ Nelson v. Williams, 25 Fair Empl. Prac. Cas. 1214, 1215 (D.D.C. 1981) (Title VII and ADEA case).

105/ Scott v. Claytor, 469 F. Supp. 22, 25 (D.D.C. 1978) (Title VII case).

106/ Id. at 26.

107/ Aikens v. United States Postal Serv., 642 F.2d 514, 516 n.1 (D.C. Cir. 1980) (Title VII case); Goldman, supra note 95; Stout v. Amoco Production Co., 508 F. Supp. 30, 33 (D. Wyo. 1980) (failure to promote and failure to give a wage increase were separate and distinct, and not a continuing violation of the Age Act). Cf. Jenkins v. Home Ins. Co., 635 F.2d 310, 312 (4th Cir. 1980) (the plaintiff's allegation that she was paid less than her male counterparts in violation of Title VII and the Equal Pay Act stated a continuing violation, because the violation occurred in a "series of separate but related acts" throughout the course of the plaintiff's employment).

(d) Refusal to hire

Generally, a refusal to hire is a separate discriminatory act. 108/ A series of rejected job applications, without more, does not constitute a continuous violation. 109/ However, as with promotions, if the court finds evidence of an ongoing policy of discrimination, then it is more likely to find a continuing violation. Thus, in a recent case in the Sixth Circuit, the plaintiff sought to apply for a job but was repeatedly told that the company did not hire women. The court concluded that this was a continuing violation, "since each time the company hires, it violates Title VII so long as its discriminatory policy is in effect." 110/ Again, while there is justification for letting plaintiffs challenge the current application of practices that have been in effect for some time, I see no basis for considering discrete events that are time barred.

(2) Willful versus non willful violations

The second major question of timeliness is what conduct constitutes a "willful" violation for purposes of the statute of limitations in section 6(a) of the Portal-to-Portal Act. 111/ Courts have applied standards of varying restrictiveness to define this term.

108/ Smith v. Office of Economic Opportunity, 538 F.2d 226, 229 (8th Cir. 1976); Molybdenum Corp. v. EEOC, 457 F.2d 935 (10th Cir. 1972).

109/ DeMedina v. Reinhardt, 444 F. Supp. 573, 577 (D.D.C. 1978) (rejections of thirteen job applications by the plaintiff were "'isolated and completed acts against a particular individual'"); but see Kohn v. Royall, Koegel & Wells, 59 F.R.D. 515 (S.D.N.Y. 1973), appeal dism'd on other grounds, 496 F.2d 1094 (2d Cir. 1974).

110/ Roberts v. North American Rockwell Corp., 650 F.2d 823, 827 (6th Cir. 1981). The Sixth Circuit said that its decision was not affected by the Supreme Court's holding in Evans, supra note 90, which it regarded as "a narrow case, which should be limited to instances of past discrimination perpetuated by bona-fide seniority systems." 650 F.2d at 827.

111/ The term "willful" is also used in the ADEA to describe the type of violation for which the defendant is liable for liquidated or double damages, 29 U.S.C. § 626(b). Although some courts apply the same "willfulness" standard in both contexts, at least one court has said that more is required to establish willfulness for liquidated damages than for timeliness. See Kelly v. American Standard, Inc., 640 F.2d 974, 979 (9th Cir. 1981).

The most lenient standard of "willfulness" and the one for which plaintiffs will invariably argue is that expressed by the court in <u>Coleman v. Jiffy June Farms, Inc.</u>, 112/ an FLSA case. The court said that an action could be considered willful for purposes of section 6(a) although taken in good faith and upon the advice of counsel. The employer acts willfully if he:

> knew or suspected that his actions might violate the FLSA. Stated most simply . . . the test should be: Did the employer know the FLSA was in the picture? 113/

However, by making virtually every violation willful, the <u>Jiffy June</u> standard allows the three-year "exception" to obliterate the two-year "rule" of section 6(a). 114/ For this reason, defendants should argue for one of the alternatives to the <u>Jiffy June</u> standard.

Some courts have said that the employer's conduct is willful if it is "intentional, knowing, or voluntary, as distinguished from accidental," and involves conduct displaying a "careless disregard whether or not one has the right so to act." 115/ Defendants should press for a narrow construction of

---

112/ 458 F.2d 1139, 1142 (5th Cir. 1971), <u>cert</u>. <u>denied</u>, 409 U.S. 948 (1972).

113/ <u>Id</u>. <u>See</u> Hedrick v. Hercules, Inc. 658 F.2d 1088, 1096 (5th Cir. 1981) (ADEA case applying the <u>Jiffy June</u> standard in liquidated damages context); Brennan v. Heard, 491 F.2d 1, 3 (5th Cir. 1974) (FLSA case); Hicks v. Communications Counselors Network, Inc., 451 F. Supp. 575 (N.D. Ga. 1978) (ADEA case). <u>See also</u> Kelly v. American Standard, Inc., 640 F.2d 974 (9th Cir. 1981) (liquidated damages); Wehr v. Burroughs Corp., 619 F.2d 276, 283 (3d Cir. 1980) (to recover liquidated damages, it is sufficient for the plaintiff to show that his discharge was "voluntary and not accidental, mistaken, or inadvertent" or that the discharge "was precipitated in reckless disregard of consequences"); <u>cf</u>. Laffey v. Northwest Airlines, Inc., 567 F.2d 429, 462 (D.C. Cir. 1976), <u>cert</u>. <u>denied</u>, 434 U.S. 1086 (1978) (in Equal Pay Act case, employer's conduct is willful if he is "cognizant of an appreciable possibility that he may be subject to the statutory requirements and fails to take steps reasonably calculated to resolve the doubt").

114/ <u>See</u> Hodgson v. Heard, 69 Lab. Cas. ¶ 32,776 at 45,600 (N.D. Ga. 1972) (the <u>Jiffy June</u> standard "subjects all but the most ignorant unsophisticated businessmen to the three-year statute").

115/ United States v. Illinois Central Railroad, 303 U.S. 239, 243 (1938); Marshall v. J.C. Penney Co., 464 F. Supp. 1166

the "intentional, knowing or voluntary" standard. For example, some courts have required proof of an actual intent to violate the ADEA. Indeed, one court has used a jury instruction that "willfulness" means "with bad purpose either to disobey or to disregard the law." 116/

Plaintiffs can be expected to criticize the "bad purpose" test as an inappropriately high standard for civil as opposed to criminal violations. A less stringent alternative but one defendants will still prefer to Jiffy June is illustrated by a recent holding of the Seventh Circuit (in the context of the liquidated damages provision) that to prove a willful violation the plaintiff must show:

> that the defendant's actions were knowing and voluntary and that he knew or reasonably should have known that those actions violated the ADEA. 117/

The defendant's "knowledge of the illegality of his actions" 118/ requires proof greater than that necessary for the initial liability finding and

> sufficient to indicate that the defendant's discrimination was not unconscious. In a disparate treatment case, a finding of willfulness will generally require some direct evidence of discriminatory intent toward the plaintiff or a showing that, at the time of the alleged discriminatory action, the employer was motivated to discriminate or engaged in a pattern of discriminating against older employees. 119/

(N.D. Ohio 1979) (FLSA case); Brennan v. Westinghouse Credit Corp., 75 Lab. Cas. ¶ 33,159 (E.D. Tenn. 1973), aff'd on other grounds, 509 F.2d 81 (6th Cir. 1975) (FLSA case); Hodgson v. Hyatt, 318 F. Supp. 390 (N.D. Fla. 1970) (FLSA case).

116/ Loeb v. Textron, Inc., 600 F.2d 1003, 1020 n.27 (1st Cir. 1979) (ADEA case), quoting E. Devitt & C. Blackmar, Federal Jury Practice & Instructions, § 14.06 at 384 (3d ed. 1977). See also Westinghouse, supra note 115, 75 Lab. Cas. at 46,746; Bishop v. Jelleff Assoc., 398 F. Supp. 579, 593 (D.D.C. 1974) (ADEA case) ("bad faith evasion of the Act and definite knowledge of its applicability").

117/ Syvock v. Milwaukee Boiler Mfg Co., 27 Fair Empl. Prac. Cas. 610, 615 (7th Cir. 1981) (footnote omitted).

118/ Id.

119/ Id. at 615-16 n.10.

Other courts have said that while intent to violate the law is unnecessary, "[not] every act consciously done is done willfully. The 'extra ingredient' needed for willfulness is either the element of intentional disregard or plain indifference." 120/

It is certainly appropriate for defendants to insist on the application of one of these higher standards. Requiring a knowing violation would read meaning into the statute's two-tier limitations period and best serve the Congressional goal of deterring violations.

As a practical matter, the issue of whether the two- or the three-year limitations period applies would generally not be suitable for resolution on a pretrial motion, because "willfulness" is easily disputable and is inherently a factual question of motivation. Nevertheless, defendants should determine early in the case whether arguments exist for the shorter time period. Especially in a suit with many parties, the extra year may create significant additional liability, and so determining whether or not a "willful" violation has occurred will be important in calculating potential exposure and preparing pretrial settlement offers.

e. Are any claims exempted by section 4(f)(2) as originally enacted?

Section 4(f)(2) of the ADEA provides that it is not unlawful for an employer "to observe the terms of a bona fide seniority system or any bona fide employee benefit plan such as a retirement, pension, or insurance plan, which is not a subterfuge to evade the purposes of this [Act]." 121/ A number of courts, including the Supreme Court, interpreted this to mean that a pension plan that predated the ADEA could require mandatory retirement of employees within the protected age group, because such a plan could not be a "subterfuge." 122/

120/ Georgia Elec. Co. v. Marshall, 595 F.2d 309, 318 n.22 (5th Cir. 1979) (Occupational Safety and Health Act case). See also Marshall v. Liggett & Myers, Inc., 22 Empl. Prac. Dec. ¶ 30,591 (M.D.N.C. 1979) (Equal Pay Act case); Rogers v. Exxon Research & Eng'r Co., 404 F. Supp. 324, 334 (D.N.J. 1975), rev'd on other grounds, 550 F.2d 834 (3d Cir. 1977), cert. denied, 434 U.S. 1022 (1978) ("careless disregard" whether employer had a right to act as it did) (ADEA case).

121/ 29 U.S.C. § 623(f)(2) (Supp. III 1979).

122/ See, e.g., United Air Lines, Inc. v. McMann, 434 U.S. 192 (1977); Marshall v. Hawaiian Tel. Co., 575 F.2d 763 (9th Cir. 1978); Minton v. Whirlpool Corp., 569 F.2d 1012 (7th Cir. 1978); Zinger v. Blanchette, 549 F.2d 901 (3d Cir.

Congress disagreed with this view, and in 1978 it added a proviso to section 4(f)(2) that "no such seniority system or employee benefit plan shall require or permit the involuntary retirement of any individual [within the protected age group] because of the age of such individual." 123/ As a result of the 1978 amendment, the Act now prohibits the involuntary retirement of persons between the ages of 40 and 70 on account of age.

However, the courts have virtually all held that the 1978 amendment to section 4(f)(2) does not apply retroactively to retirements that occurred before its effective date. 124/ Thus, defendants should ascertain whether any plaintiffs are asserting a claim based on involuntary retirement pursuant to a pension plan exempted by section 4(f)(2) as originally enacted. If there is no dispute about the terms of the plan or that it is bona fide and not a subterfuge, 125/ then the defendant should move for summary judgment. This issue, of course, will arise with decreasing frequency because the statute of limitations has now

---

1977), cert. denied, 434 U.S. 1008 (1978) (early retirement pursuant to an optional early retirement provision is lawful under section 4(f)(2) even if age is the sole basis for retirement); Brennan v. Taft Broadcasting Co., 500 F.2d 212 (5th Cir. 1974).

123/ 29 U.S.C. § 623(f)(2) (Supp. III 1979).

124/ See, e.g., Aldendifer v. Continental Air Lines, Inc., 650 F.2d 171 (9th Cir. 1981); EEOC v. Shell Oil Co., 637 F.2d 683 (9th Cir. 1981); Carpenter v. Continental Trailways, 635 F.2d 578 (6th Cir. 1980), cert. denied, 101 S. Ct. 2320 (1981); Jensen v. Gulf Oil Ref. & Mkt'g Co., 623 F.2d 406 (5th Cir. 1980); Sikora v. American Can Co., 622 F.2d 1116 (3d Cir. 1980). Despite this line of cases, EEOC continues to assert that the amendment does apply retroactively, unless, "as determined on a case-by-case basis, . . . the application of the amendment would result in 'manifest injustice.'" See Final Interpretations: Age Discrimination in Employment Act, 46 Fed. Reg. 47724, 47725-26, 47728 (Sept. 29, 1981), to be codified at 29 C.F.R. § 1625.9.

125/ One issue on which the courts are split is whether a "post Act" plan will be considered a subterfuge unless there are independent business justifications for it. The Third Circuit found no need for such justification in Zinger, supra note 122, and the Sixth Circuit found the desirability of establishing a plan to be a sufficient justification in Carpenter, supra note 124. But cf. EEOC v. Eastern Airlines, Inc., 474 F. Supp. 364 (S.D. Fla. 1979), aff'd mem., 645 F.2d 69 (5th Cir. 1981), cert. denied, 50 U.S.L.W. 3245 (1981); EEOC v. Baltimore and O. R. Co., 632 F.2d 1107 (4th Cir. 1980), cert. denied, 50 U.S.L.W. 3245 (1981).

- 31 -

run on most claims based on retirements prior to the 1978 amendment. That amendment took effect as of the date of enactment (April 6, 1978) except with respect to certain collective bargaining agreements, as to which the amendment became effective no later than January 1, 1980. 126/

f. Is the defendant entitled to summary judgment on the merits?

If the plaintiff has asserted a baseless claim or cannot make a prima facie showing of age discrimination, then the defendant should move for dismissal or summary judgment on the merits. As a general rule courts are hesitant to decide discrimination claims without a full factual hearing because questions of motivation and pretext are usually involved. Nevertheless, some cases may present facts so clear that summary judgment is appropriate.

The plaintiff's patent inability to establish each element of a prima facie case would be one such situation. Thus, summary judgment should be sought when there is undisputed evidence that the plaintiff was not discharged by the employer but rather resigned. 127/ Summary judgment should also be sought if the plaintiff was replaced by an older employee, thereby negating any inference of age discrimination. 128/

In some cases, if the undisputed facts convincingly favor the defendant, a summary judgment motion may succeed regardless of whether the plaintiff has made out a prima facie case. For example, in one case summary judgment was upheld because the

---

126/ See Pub. L. No. 95-256, § 2(b) (1978).

127/ See Sills v. Fort Pitt Steel Casting Co., 24 Fair Empl. Prac. Cas. 927 (W.D. Pa. 1979), aff'd mem., 633 F.2d 211 (3d Cir. 1980).

128/ See Kephart v. Institute of Gas Tech., 630 F.2d 1217, 1223-24 (7th Cir. 1980) (per curiam), cert. denied, 101 S. Ct. 1418 (1981); cf. Stanojev v. Ebasco Services, Inc., 643 F.2d 914, 920-21 (2d Cir. 1981) (directed verdict for employer should have been granted when plaintiff was unable to establish a prima facie case because he was not replaced by a younger employee; plaintiff also lacked any direct, statistical, or circumstantial proof of age discrimination); Sahadi v. Reynolds Chemical, 636 F.2d 1116 (6th Cir. 1980) (directed verdict affirmed when plaintiff failed to establish a prima facie case; it is insufficient for a plaintiff terminated during an economic cutback to show that a younger person was retained in a position which the plaintiff was capable of performing where the plaintiff would have had to be relocated to perform that position and where the employer had not relocated others).

plaintiff's case was "wholly empty" and lacked any indications of discriminatory motive and intent; indeed, the plaintiff could not dispute the fact that his performance was unsatisfactory. 129/ In other cases defendants should consider moving for summary judgment when the reason for the challenged employment decision is manifestly non-discriminatory. 130/

    2. Are individuals who are proper parties to the action asserting claims that are subject to dismissal?

  Although each individual claimant may have satisfied the procedural prerequisites to suit in a timely manner and may have set forth a prima facie case of age discrimination, not every claim asserted by each individual should necessarily be tried in the suit. Motions to dismiss may be appropriate with respect to claims that are: (1) beyond the scope of the EEOC charge or conciliation; (2) time barred; (3) not compensable under the ADEA; or (4) improperly based on pendent jurisdiction.

    a. Claims that were not the subject of an administrative charge or conciliation

  As a general rule, the scope of the plaintiff's lawsuit is limited by the scope of his EEOC charge; however, this standard is often interpreted liberally, resulting in rulings that the suit "may encompass any acts of discrimination similar to, or reasonably related to the allegations made in the charge." 131/

129/ Kephart, supra note 128, 643 F.2d at 1218. See also Brennan v. Reynolds & Co., 367 F. Supp. 440 (N.D. Ill. 1973) (summary judgment for defendant where affidavits showed that plaintiff was discharged for a legitimate reason, tardiness).

130/ See Carter v. Maloney Trucking & Storage Inc., 631 F.2d 40 (5th Cir. 1980) (affirming a trial court finding that the employer's refusal to rehire former employee was due to the fact that the former employee had murdered a co-worker and that rehiring him would cause deep animosity among the victim's friends at work); Houser v. Sears, Roebuck & Co., 627 F.2d 756 (5th Cir. 1980) (the employer's motion for judgment notwithstanding the verdict was properly granted where evidence showed that the plaintiff had intentionally misapplied customers' funds, and no evidence existed that this reason for discharging the plaintiff was pretextual); Peterson v. Colonial Stores, Inc., 19 Empl. Prac. Dec. ¶ 8992 (N.D. Ga. 1979) (summary judgment for employer granted when evidence was uncontradicted that the plaintiff, a pilot, was dismissed for drinking on the job).

131/ Scaramuzzo v. Glenmore Distilleries Co., 501 F. Supp. 727, 730 (N.D. Ill. 1980), citing Jenkins v. Blue Cross Mut. Hosp.

Indeed, one court has held that the plaintiff could litigate claims of illegal demotion and retaliation although his notice to the Secretary of Labor said only that "one of the bases" of his lawsuit was his termination. 132/ As in Title VII cases, "the court may infer the existence of other discriminatory acts from the allegations contained in the administrative charges." 133/ In contrast, another court has more narrowly construed a notice of intent to sue; because the notice mentioned only a termination claim, that court dismissed the plaintiff's claims relating to alleged retaliation and discriminatory terms and conditions of employment. 134/

A corollary of the "scope of the charge" rule is that the charge acts merely as a "starting point" for a reasonable investigation by the EEOC. 135/ Therefore the lawsuit may also properly include matters that the EEOC actually investigated and conciliated during a reasonable investigation of the original charge. 136/

This rule can act as an important limitation to prevent the plaintiff from raising claims for the first time in the judicial complaint. When faced with such new allegations, the defendant should move to dismiss them from the suit because "the statutory scheme of conciliation would be nullified" if a private plaintiff could surprise the defendant with new claims long after the charge-filing period and the opportunity for conciliation have expired. 137/

Ins., Inc., 538 F.2d 164, 167 (7th Cir.) (en banc), cert. denied, 429 U.S. 986 (1976) (Title VII case).

132/ Scaramuzzo, 501 F. Supp. at 729-32.

133/ Id. at 730.

134/ Looney v. Commercial Union Assur. Cos., 428 F. Supp. 533 (E.D. Mich. 1977).

135/ EEOC v. General Elec. Co., 532 F.2d 359, 364 (4th Cir. 1976) (citation omitted) (Title VII case).

136/ Id. at 366.

137/ Stubbs v. Bendix Field Eng'r Corp., 21 Fair Empl. Prac. Cas. 804, 806 (D. Md. 1977) (Title VII case). See also, e.g., Clements v. H. Goodman & Sons, 25 Fair Empl. Prac. Cas. 511 (N.D. Ga. 1981) (Title VII case); Abraham v. Field Enterprises, 511 F. Supp. 91 (N.D. Ill. 1980) (Title VII case); Hubbard v. Rubbermaid, Inc., 436 F. Supp. 1184 (D. Md. 1977) (Title VII case). For a discussion of the effect of failure to conciliate issues prior to suit by the EEOC, see below at pp. 39-42.

b. Claims that are time barred

Needless to say, defendants should move for dismissal of or summary judgment on any claims based on acts occurring outside the limitations period. As discussed previously, 138/ the principal statute of limitations problems will involve the question of whether a continuing violation exists. Defendants should oppose attempts to characterize alleged discriminatory acts as "continuing" and should insist that only events occurring within the limitations period may be litigated.

c. Claims for compensatory damages for pain and suffering

Defendants should move to strike requests for damages for pain and suffering or emotional distress. The five circuit courts that have addressed this issue to date have all held that such damages are not available under the Age Act. 139/ These courts reason that neither the Act nor its legislative history evidences an intention to allow damages for emotional or mental distress. Moreover, allowing such damages would interfere with the conciliation process and discourage out-of-court settlements, because it would introduce "a volatile ingredient into the tripartite negotiations involving the Secretary, the employer and the employee which might well be calculated to frustrate rather than to 'effectuate the purposes' of the Act." 140/

Most district courts also hold that damages for pain and suffering are not recoverable. 141/ However, some district

---

138/ See pp. 19-26 above.

139/ Ford v. General Motors, 656 F.2d 117 (5th Cir. 1981); Naton v. Bank of California, 649 F.2d 691 (9th Cir. 1981); Walker v. Pettit Constr. Co., 605 F.2d 128 (4th Cir. 1979); Slatin v. Stanford Research Inst., 590 F.2d 1292 (4th Cir. 1979); Vazquez v. Eastern Air Lines, Inc., 579 F.2d 107 (1st Cir. 1978); Dean v. American Security Ins. Co., 559 F.2d 1036 (5th Cir. 1977), cert. denied, 434 U.S. 1066 (1978); Rogers v. Exxon Research & Eng'r Co., 550 F.2d 834 (3d Cir. 1977), cert. denied, 434 U.S. 1022 (1978).

140/ Dean, supra note 139, 559 F.2d at 1039, quoting 29 U.S.C. § 626(b).

141/ E.g., Reade v. Delta Calif. Indus., 25 Fair Empl. Prac. Cas. 687 (N.D. Cal. 1980); Ayres v. Federated Dept. Stores, 24 Fair Empl. Prac. Cas. 528 (S.D.N.Y. 1980); Douglas v. American Cyanamid Co., 472 F. Supp. 298 (D. Conn. 1979); Knerr v. Norge Co., 476 F. Supp. 1352 (S.D. Ill. 1979); Riddle v. Getty Ref. & Mkt'g Co., 460 F. Supp. 678 (N.D. Okla. 1978); Postemski v. Pratt & Whitney Aircraft, 443 F. Supp. 101 (D. Conn. 1977).

courts have awarded such damages, reasoning that they are authorized by the ADEA's language allowing "such legal or equitable relief as may be appropriate to effectuate the purposes of this [Act] . . . without limitation . . . ." 142/ These courts are located within circuits in which there has been no appellate ruling on this issue.

A very few courts even permit recovery of punitive damages as well as compensatory damages for pain and suffering. 143/ The prevailing view, however, is that punitive damages are not available. Courts reason that the Act's provision for liquidated or double damages is a substitute for punitive damages and adequately deters intentional violations. 144/ Therefore in all but a few jurisdictions defendants should have no trouble striking requests for pain and suffering and punitive damages under the ADEA.

d. Claims that are improperly based on pendent jurisdiction

In contrast to the ADEA, many state anti-discrimination laws authorize damages for emotional distress. Also, in a significant new trend, a number of state courts now reject the traditional rule that the employment relationship is generally terminable at will, and recognize the right of a discharged employee to sue for damages based on common law principles of tort or contract law under appropriate circumstances.

Because these state law alternatives may offer more extensive relief than ADEA, it is not surprising that many plaintiffs are now pleading state law claims along with their ADEA claims in suits brought in federal court. From the

---

142/ 29 U.S.C. § 626(b). See, e.g., Wise v. Olan Mills, Inc., 485 F. Supp. 542 (D. Colo. 1980); Flynn v. Morgan Guar. Trust Co., 463 F. Supp. 676 (E.D.N.Y. 1978); Gifford v. B.D. Diagnostics, 458 F. Supp. 462 (N.D. Ohio 1978); Buchholz v. Symons Mfg. Co., 445 F. Supp. 706 (E.D. Wis. 1978); Bertrand v. Orkin Exterminating Co., 419 F. Supp. 1123 (N.D. Ill. 1976), aff'd on rehearing, 432 F. Supp. 952 (N.D. Ill. 1977).

143/ Wise, supra note 142; Kennedy v. Mountain States Tel. & Tel. Co., 449 F. Supp. 1008 (D. Colo. 1978); Karijolic v. Illinois Bell Tel. Co., 19 Fair Empl. Prac. Cas. 447 (N.D. Ill. 1977).

144/ Kelly v. American Standard, Inc., 640 F.2d 974 (9th Cir. 1981); Walker, supra note 139; Murphy v. American Motors Sales Corp., 570 F.2d 1226 (5th Cir. 1978); Dean, supra note 139; Stevenson v. J.C. Penney Co., 464 F. Supp. 945 (N.D. Ill. 1979); Hannon v. Continental Nat'l Bank, 427 F. Supp. 215 (D. Colo. 1977).

defendant's point of view, such additional claims complicate the trial and may possibly impair the defense of the ADEA claim. Therefore defendants should usually urge the court to refuse to exercise pendent jurisdiction over the state claims. 145/

State law claims may include: (1) a claim based on a state statute that prohibits discrimination on the basis of age; (2) a claim alleging the tort of "wrongful discharge"; (3) a tort claim for intentional infliction of emotional distress; (4) a contract claim alleging breach of an implied agreement not to discharge an employee without just cause.

The tort theory centers on the concept that certain public policies limit the employer's right to terminate an employee. For example, the California Supreme Court recently held that an employer was liable for the tort of "wrongful discharge" when it terminated an employee for refusing to take part in an illegal scheme to fix prices. 146/ The California courts have also been in the forefront of development of the implied contract theory. In a recent case, a lower state court held that an employer's conduct may give rise to an implied promise that it will not arbitrarily discharge an employee. 147/ As evidence of an implied promise in that case, the court took note of "the duration of [the employee's] employment [32 years], the commendations and promotions he received, the apparent lack of any direct criticism of his work, the assurances he was given, and the employer's acknowledged policies." 148/ Finally, in extreme

---

145/ However, defendants should balance these considerations against the burden of defending a second lawsuit, if one is brought, in the state forum.

146/ Tameny v. Atlantic Richfield Co., 27 Cal. 3d 167, 610 P.2d 1330 (1980). See also, e.g., Savodnik v. Korvettes, Inc., 488 F. Supp. 822 (E.D.N.Y. 1980) (tort claim for "abusive discharge" stated by employee who was terminated after 13 years of service in order to prevent his pension from vesting); Kelsay v. Motorola, Inc., 74 Ill. 2d 172, 384 N.E.2d 353 (1978) (employee who was fired for filing workers' compensation claim states cause of action for tort of "retaliatory discharge"); Nees v. Hocks, 272 Or. 210, 536 P.2d 512 (1975) (employer liable in tort for discharging employee for serving on a jury).

147/ Pugh v. See's Candies, Inc., 116 Cal. App. 3d 311, 171 Cal. Rptr. 917 (1981).

148/ 116 Cal. App. 3d at 329. For other similar cases, see, e.g., Toussaint v. Blue Cross & Blue Shield of Mich., 408 Mich. 579, 292 N.W.2d 880 (1980) (employee's legitimate expectations arising out of employer's policy statements may give rise to implied contract not to discharge employee except for cause); Monge v. Beebe Rubber Co., 114 N.H. 130,

circumstances, courts have permitted suits by employees for the tort of intentional infliction of emotional distress in conjunction with an alleged act of discrimination. 149/

These emerging concepts are being utilized in suits by older, long-term employees who believe that they were terminated unfairly, perhaps because of age. In suits under the ADEA, attempts to join state claims with the federal cause of action have been accepted by some courts 150/ and rejected by others. 151/

---

316 A.2d 549 (1974). See generally Note, Protecting At Will Employees Against Wrongful Discharge: The Duty to Terminate Only in Good Faith, 93 Harv. L. Rev. 1816 (1980).

149/ See Alcorn v. Anbro Eng'r Co., 2 Cal. 3d 493, 468 P.2d 216 (1970) (racial discrimination).

150/ E.g., Kelly v. American Standard, Inc., 640 F.2d 974, 983-84 (9th Cir. 1981) (awarding $15,000 damages for emotional distress under state anti-discrimination statute, without discussion of propriety of pendent jurisdiction over state claim); Fellows v. Medford Corp., 431 F. Supp. 199, 202 (D. Or. 1977) (allowing jury trial on claim for compensatory and punitive damages based on "tort of employee discharge based on a socially undesirable motive"); Rechsteiner v. Madison Fund, Inc., 75 F.R.D. 499 (D. Del. 1977) (accepting pendent claim based on contract of employment); McGinley v. Burroughs Corp., 407 F. Supp. 903, 910 (E.D. Pa. 1975) (breach of contract claim allowed for termination contrary to public policy against age discrimination).

151/ E.g., Mazzare v. Burroughs Corp., 473 F. Supp. 234 (E.D. Pa. 1979) (declining jurisdiction over tort claim for intentional infliction of emotional distress); Douglas v. American Cyanamid Co., 472 F. Supp. 298 (D. Conn. 1979) (declining jurisdiction over tort claim for defamation); Kennedy v. Mountain States Tel. & Tel. Co., 449 F. Supp. 1008 (D. Colo. 1978) (declining jurisdiction over tort and contract claims); Seider v. Canada Dry Corp., 17 Empl. Prac. Dec. ¶ 8369 (S.D.N.Y. 1978) (dismissing state claims for compensatory and punitive damages for mental distress because adjudication of such claims would subvert policy of excluding damages for emotional distress under ADEA); Hannon v. Continental Nat'l Bank, 427 F. Supp. 215 (D. Colo. 1977) (declining to accept jurisdiction of state tort action for intentional infliction of emotional distress because to do so would subvert policy of ADEA); Looney v. Commercial Union Assur. Cos., 428 F. Supp. 533 (E.D. Mich. 1977) (declining pendent state claim because law unclear); Pandis v. Sikorsky Aircraft, 431 F. Supp. 793 (D. Conn. 1977) (declining pendent state claim under state age discrimination act because federal action under ADEA supersedes state action pursuant to 29 U.S.C. § 633(a), indicating that federal remedy is meant to take precedence).

If the plaintiff couples state law claims with an ADEA claim, the defendant should usually argue that pendent jurisdiction is improper or ill-advised. A federal court has power to accept and try pendent state claims only if the state and federal claims "derive from a common nucleus of operative fact." 152/ Even if that is the case, it is within the court's discretion to decline to hear the state claims because of considerations such as judicial economy, convenience and fairness to the litigants, and the likelihood of jury confusion. 153/

Defendants can thus argue that the court should refuse to exercise pendent jurisdiction if: (1) judicial economy and convenience and fairness to the litigants would not be promoted by trying the claims together, because proof of each claim would involve largely distinct factual and legal issues; 154/ (2) joinder of divergent legal theories would tend to confuse the jury; 155/ (3) the state claim presents an unsettled question of state law, which federal courts should refrain from deciding; 156/ (4) the state claim "constitutes the real body of [the] case, to which the federal claim is only an appendage"; 157/ or (5) the state claim seeks broader relief than does the ADEA count, and allowing it to be joined would subvert the policies of limiting the scope of the remedies under the federal statute. 158/

152/ United Mine Workers v. Gibbs, 383 U.S. 715, 725-26 (1966).

153/ Id.

154/ See, e.g., Mazzare, supra note 151, 473 F. Supp. at 241 (proof of tort of intentional infliction of emotional distress would require additional medical testimony and proof of outrageous conduct, thus enlarging entire scope of trial); Douglas, supra note 151, 472 F. Supp. at 304-06 (defamation claim involves post-termination events); Kennedy, supra note 151, 449 F. Supp. at 1011 (breach of contract claim insufficiently related to ADEA claim and would cloud issues).

155/ See, e.g., United Mine Workers, supra note 152, 383 U.S. at 726; Mazzare, supra note 151, 473 F. Supp. at 241.

156/ See, e.g., United Mine Workers, supra note 152, 383 U.S. at 726; Mazzare, supra note 151, 473 F. Supp. at 241; Grogg v. General Motors Corp., 444 F. Supp. 1215, 1221 (S.D.N.Y. 1978) (Title VII case).

157/ United Mine Workers, supra note 152, 383 U.S. at 727.

158/ See, e.g., Lim v. International Inst. of Metropolitan Detroit, 510 F. Supp. 722 (E.D. Mich. 1981) (inclusion of state contract and civil rights law claims, under which compensatory and punitive damages are available, would conflict

B. **Actions by EEOC**

The Age Act empowers the EEOC to bring suit under sections 16(c) and 17 of the FLSA. 159/ As explained above, the two provisions authorize suits that are different in character: a section 16(c) suit seeks monetary damages on behalf of specific named individuals, while a section 17 suit seeks broad injunctive relief. In a section 17 suit individual claimants need not be named, and the recovery of back wages is incidental to the goal of eliminating discriminatory practices. 160/ A section 17 suit is thus not a representative action but rather "is brought primarily in the public interest despite the fact that employees may be the ultimate beneficiaries of the actions." 161/

These differences are often significant for purposes of defense counsel's efforts to limit the government's suit, as will be seen below. The following section examines possible motions based on: (1) the EEOC's failure to conciliate all claims that it is seeking to litigate; (2) the EEOC's inability to establish a "pattern or practice" of age discrimination under section 17; and (3) the existence of time-barred claims under sections 16(c) or 17.

1. Did the EEOC investigate and seek to conciliate all matters that it is seeking to litigate?

The Age Discrimination Act requires the EEOC, as a prerequisite to bringing suit, to attempt to eliminate the alleged discriminatory practice and "to effect voluntary compliance . . . through informal methods of conciliation, conference, and persuasion." 162/ To satisfy this requirement, the EEOC must make "strong, affirmative attempts" to achieve voluntary compliance before resorting to legal action. 163/ Effective conciliation must be based on an investigation of the alleged violation. To that end the ADEA grants the government broad investigatory powers; 164/ the only

---

with Congressional intent to provide more limited relief under Title VII); Seider, supra note 151, 17 Empl. Prac. Dec. at 5911; Hannon, supra note 151, 427 F. Supp. at 218.

159/ 29 U.S.C. § 626(b), incorporating 29 U.S.C. §§ 216(c), 217.

160/ Donovan v. University of Texas, 643 F.2d 1201, 1206 (5th Cir. 1981) (Equal Pay Act case under section 17).

161/ Id. at 1208.

162/ 29 U.S.C. § 626(b). See pp. 12-13 above.

163/ Brennan v. Ace Hardware Corp., 495 F.2d 368, 374 (8th Cir. 1974); Marshall v. Hartford Fire Ins. Co., 78 F.R.D. 97, 103-07 (D. Conn. 1978). See p. 12 above.

164/ 29 U.S.C. §§ 209, 211 and 626(a).

restrictions on the government's investigation are those it chooses for itself. Through investigation, the EEOC must determine whether there is reason to believe a violation exists and assess the nature and extent of the violation. 165/ The investigation thus establishes the "framework for conciliation." 166/

The scope of the EEOC's investigation and conciliation efforts operates as an important limitation on the scope of its judicial action. As is the rule under Title VII, which contains a similar conciliation requirement, the scope of a suit brought by the EEOC is limited to those issues that it has investigated and conciliated. 167/ Therefore defendants should move to dismiss any portions of the EEOC's complaint that were not the subject of conciliation. 168/ Such issues might fall into one of the following categories:

(1) _Employment practices_. Courts in numerous cases have dismissed allegations relating to employment practices that had not been investigated or conciliated. 169/ The EEOC is required

---

165/ Hartford Fire Ins. Co., supra note 163, 78 F.R.D. at 103-04.

166/ EEOC v. Allegheny Airlines, 436 F. Supp. 1300, 1306 (W.D. Pa. 1977) (Title VII case).

167/ See, e.g., EEOC v. Bailey Co., 563 F.2d 439 (6th Cir. 1977), cert. denied, 435 U.S. 915 (1978); EEOC v. General Electric Co., 532 F.2d 359 (4th Cir. 1976); EEOC v. American Nat'l Bank, 21 Fair Empl. Prac. Cas. 1532 (E.D. Va. 1979); Allegheny Airlines, supra note 166; EEOC v. E.I. duPont de Nemours & Co., 373 F. Supp. 1321 (D. Del. 1974), aff'd, 516 F.2d 1297 (3d Cir. 1975).

168/ Defendants should insist that efforts to investigate new allegations during discovery do not compensate for a lack of investigation prior to filing suit. See EEOC v. Mallinckrodt, Inc., 22 Empl. Prac. Dec. ¶ 30,842 (E.D. Mo. 1980) (Title VII case); Allegheny Airlines, supra note 166; Dunlop v. Resource Sciences Corp., 410 F. Supp. 836 (N.D. Okla. 1976). Dismissal of any claims that have not been investigated is thus appropriate. Mallinckrodt, supra; EEOC v. Sherwood Medical Indus., Inc., 452 F. Supp. 678 (M.D. Fla. 1978). To do otherwise, defendants should argue, would ignore the Congressional policies behind the conciliation requirement--encouraging voluntary settlements, affording the employer a fair opportunity to respond to charges prior to suit, and relieving the courts of unnecessary litigation.

169/ See, e.g., Clements v. H. Goodman & Sons, 25 Fair Empl. Prac. Cas. 511 (N.D. Ga. 1981) (Title VII case); Abraham v. Field Enterprises, 511 F. Supp. 91 (N.D. Ill. 1980) (Title VII case); Stubbs v. Bendix Field Eng'r Corp., 21 Fair Empl. Prac. Cas. 804 (D. Md. 1977) (Title VII case); EEOC

to "'make a genuine effort to conciliate with respect to <u>each and every employment practice complained of</u> . . . .'" 170/ Therefore if the investigation dealt with only claims of discriminatory discharge, for example, any other claims, such as claims of promotion or pay violations, are beyond the scope of the EEOC's suit.

(2) <u>Departments or organizational units</u>. Courts have likewise restricted the scope of an EEOC suit to those departments or branches of the defendant's organization that were actually investigated during the conciliation period. 171/

(3) <u>Job classifications</u>. It is also clear that the EEOC is precluded from litigating claims of employees in job classifications that never were the subject of conciliation. For example, one court limited an EEOC suit to hourly workers, when no investigation was made of salaried employees. 172/ In another case the court restricted the suit to the job category of flight attendants and eliminated allegations relating to managerial, professional and technical employees because no investigation or conciliation had been attempted beyond the flight attendant category. 173/

(4) <u>Individual claims</u>. If the EEOC has investigated only an individual claim, it cannot maintain a pattern or practice suit. Courts have recognized that the investigation required to support a pattern or practice claim is significantly different in nature from that required in an individual case. 174/ Conversely, unless a <u>prima facie</u> showing of a pattern or practice of age discrimination is made, the EEOC must investigate and conciliate

---

    v. Federated Mutual Ins. Co., 16 Fair Empl. Prac. Cas. 820 (N.D. Ga. 1977) (Title VII case; allegations of discrimination in terms and conditions of employment dismissed where EEOC investigated hiring practices only); EEOC v. National Cash Register Co., 405 F. Supp. 562 (N.D. Ga. 1975) (Title VII action is limited to wage disparity and termination claims, which were the only claims investigated; other claims relating to other employment practices must be dismissed as beyond the proper scope of the suit).

170/ EEOC v. Sears, Roebuck & Co., 650 F.2d 14, 19 (2d Cir. 1981), quoting EEOC v. Sherwood Medical Indus., 452 F. Supp. 678, 683-84 (M.D. Fla. 1978) (emphasis added).

171/ <u>See, e.g., Sears, supra</u> note 170; <u>American Nat'l Bank, supra</u> note 167.

172/ EEOC v. Honeywell, Inc., 73 F.R.D. 496 (N.D. Ill. 1977) (Title VII case).

173/ <u>Allegheny Airlines, supra</u> note 166.

174/ <u>Mallinckrodt, supra</u> note 168; EEOC v. Stroh Brewery Co., 83 F.R.D. 17, 30 (E.D. Mich. 1979) (Title VII case); <u>National Cash Register, supra</u> note 169.

claims individually. 175/ It must likewise conciliate with respect to each named claimant in a section 16(c) suit. 176/

2. Does the EEOC have a basis for any "pattern or practice" claims it is asserting?

The term "pattern or practice" is found in section 707 of Title VII, which authorizes the EEOC to bring suit alleging a "pattern or practice of discrimination." 177/ The Age Discrimination Act does not mention the term. Nevertheless, where systemic age discrimination or an identifiable, discriminatory policy is alleged, the EEOC is likely to characterize a suit under section 17 as a "pattern or practice" suit. 178/ Indeed, this characterization seems appropriate in view of the statutory scheme. The distinctive feature of a section 17 suit is the availability of injunctive relief, which appropriately would operate to halt application of an ongoing practice or policy, such as an age restriction. Section 16(c), in contrast, provides a different avenue of relief specifically geared to individualized claims.

Defendants should insist that this distinction between the two types of suits be observed. When confronted by a pattern or practice claim under section 17 (which may also be coupled with individual claims under section 16(c)), defendants should determine whether the pattern or practice allegations have any substance. If

---

175/ See, e.g., Sears, Roebuck & Co., supra note 170; Marshall v. Sun Oil Co. (Del.), 605 F.2d 1331 (5th Cir. 1979); Marshall v. American Motors Corp., 475 F. Supp. 875, 878 (E.D. Mich. 1979) (if the Secretary seeks only prospective relief, then a period of conciliation dedicated to generalized discriminatory practices would be adequate; however, if the Secretary seeks retrospective relief, such as back pay, then the merits of individual cases must be discussed).

176/ See, e.g., Marshall v. Sun Oil Co. (Pa.), 592 F.2d 563 (10th Cir.), cert. denied, 444 U.S. 826 (1979); Sun Oil Co. (Del.), supra note 175; Brennan v. Ace Hardware Corp., 495 F.2d 368 (8th Cir. 1974); Marshall v. Hartford Fire Ins. Co., 78 F.R.D. 97, 103-07 (D. Conn. 1978).

177/ 42 U.S.C. § 2000e-6.

178/ See, e.g., EEOC v. Sandia Corp., 639 F.2d 600 (10th Cir. 1980); Marshall v. Sun Oil Co. (Del.), 605 F.2d 1331, 1336 n.2 (5th Cir. 1979). Courts have also noted the similarity of purpose between section 707 of Title VII and section 17 of the FLSA: suits under both provisions primarily serve to redress a "public wrong." Donovan v. University of Texas, 643 F.2d 1201, 1204, 1208 (5th Cir. 1981); Marshall v. West Essex Gen. Hosp., 575 F.2d 1079, 1084-85 (3d Cir. 1978)(Gibbons, J., concurring).

they do not, then defendants should move for summary judgment on the section 17 claim, arguing that individualized relief is properly the subject of a section 16(c) action. Permitting the case to proceed under section 17 would simply allow the EEOC to circumvent the section 16(c) requirement of identifying individual claimants and attempting individual conciliation. 179/

It should be noted that Age Act cases have generally not addressed the distinction between section 16(c) and section 17 suits in terms of individual versus systemic claims. However, given the appropriate case, there are persuasive reasons to believe that defendants can succeed in preventing the EEOC from suing under section 17 when no pattern or practice of discrimination exists.

The standard for establishing a pattern or practice violation under Title VII was articulated by the Supreme Court in International Brotherhood of Teamsters v. United States. 180/ It is necessary, the Court said, for the government to prove "more than the mere occurrence of isolated or 'accidental' or sporadic discriminatory acts." There must be proof that "discrimination was the company's standard operating procedure--the regular rather than the unusual practice." 181/ A pattern or practice is present only when the denial of rights is "repeated, routine, or of a generalized nature." 182/

Using the Title VII standard, defendants should determine whether claims of a pattern or practice of age discrimination are factually unjustifiable:

(1) Has the EEOC failed to identify a discriminatory policy, practice or procedure? Clearly, a policy such as a mandatory retirement age or a maximum hiring age affects a broad class of employees and thus is an appropriate subject of a pattern or practice suit under section 17, because injunctive relief to halt application of the policy would be the EEOC's primary

---

179/ See above note 176.

180/ 431 U.S. 324 (1977).

181/ Id. at 336.

182/ Id. at 336 n.16, quoting remarks of Sen. Humphrey, 110 Cong. Rec. 14270 (1964). See also, e.g., Chrisner v. Complete Auto Transit, Inc., 645 F.2d 1251, 1257 (6th Cir. 1981) (the essential element is "an identifiable employment practice or policy that demonstrably affects all members of a class in a substantially similar, if not an identical manner. . . ."); EEOC v. Moore Group, Inc., 11 Empl. Prac. Dec. ¶ 10,886 (N.D. Ga. 1976).

aim. 183/ However, if a discriminatory policy has not been alleged, then a section 17 suit is not necessarily proper.

(2) <u>Are the claims individualized</u>? A group of factually diverse individual claims should appropriately proceed under section 16(c) rather than as a pattern or practice suit. For example, if the case involves a reduction in force, the defendant might argue that the circumstances of the individual terminations are very different, and the claimants in the suit are too few in number to provide a basis for inferring that the overall reduction was characterized by a pattern of age discrimination. 184/

183/ An open question under the ADEA is whether a facially <u>neutral</u> criterion or policy is illegal if it has a "disparate impact" on members of the protected age group. Under Title VII it is well established that a neutral employment criterion that has a disparate impact on minorities or women violates the law unless the employer can meet the heavy burden of showing that the policy is justified by "business necessity." <u>See</u> Griggs v. Duke Power Co., 401 U.S. 424 (1971). The EEOC takes the position that the same theory applies to the Age Act. <u>See</u> Final Interpretations: Age Discrimination in Employment Act, 46 Fed. Reg. 47724, 47725, 47727 (Sept. 29, 1981), to be codified at 29 C.F.R. § 1625.7(d).

To date only one reported ADEA case has upheld a <u>Griggs</u>-type disparate impact analysis. In that case, Geller v. Markham, 635 F.2d 1027 (2d Cir. 1980), <u>cert. denied</u>, 101 S. Ct. 2028 (1981), the Second Circuit held that a school board's cost-cutting policy of not hiring teachers with more than five years' experience had a disparate impact on older teachers and thus violated the ADEA. When the Supreme Court denied certiorari, Justice Rehnquist wrote a sharp dissent questioning the applicability of the disparate impact approach to ADEA cases.

The issue is certain to provoke more litigation, because the EEOC has filed a number of pattern or practice cases challenging cost-saving policies that have an adverse impact on older employees. <u>See</u> BNA Daily Labor Report, No. 193 at A-1, E-1 (Oct. 6, 1981). There are a number of persuasive legal arguments why disparate impact should not constitute a violation of the Age Act, and defendants should not hesitate to challenge the legal sufficiency of an EEOC pattern or practice case when the identified practice or policy is an age-neutral one.

184/ <u>See</u> Marshall v. Hills Bros., 432 F. Supp. 1320, 1325 (N.D. Cal. 1977) (evidence based on only 9 of 341 terminations not probative of legality of force reorganization).

(3) *Are the statistics favorable?* Usually, the EEOC will attempt to establish its pattern or practice case by using statistical evidence to infer a pattern of intentional age discrimination. 185/ Defense counsel should counter this evidence by preparing statistical analyses of its own. Statistics "come in infinite variety" 186/ and their appropriate use in age discrimination cases is not yet as well understood or well developed as it is under Title VII. 187/ Thorough analysis of the data using various accepted statistical methods may demonstrate that there has been no statistically significant age discrimination. 188/ Such a conclusion would substantially

---

185/ See Teamsters, supra note 180, 431 U.S. at 337-40. Statistics might also be used to show the "disparate impact" of an age-neutral policy, see supra note 183; however, as noted above, the legal applicability of this approach to ADEA cases is open to serious question.

186/ Teamsters, supra note 180, 431 U.S. at 340.

187/ See generally Harper, *Statistics as Evidence of Age Discrimination*, 32 Hastings L.J. 1347 (1981).

188/ Some courts have cautioned against placing excessive weight on statistical evidence in age discrimination cases. Unlike race or sex, age is not an immutable characteristic, but rather falls along a continuum. As the Sixth Circuit observed in Laugesen v. Anaconda Co.:

> The progression of age is a universal human process. In the very nature of the problem, it is apparent that in the usual case, absent any discriminatory intent, discharged employees will more often than not be replaced by those younger than they, for older employees are constantly moving out of the labor market, while younger ones move in.

510 F.2d 307, 312-13 n.4 (6th Cir. 1975).

For examples of cases in which statistical evidence was found probative of age discrimination, see EEOC v. Sandia Corp. 639 F.2d 600, 609-10 (10th Cir. 1980) (affirming district court finding that the evidence established a *prima facie* case that a pattern and practice of age discrimination begins to appear at age 52 in its influence on layoff decisions, and that the inference becomes stronger for ages 55 to 64); Laugesen, supra, 510 F.2d at 311 (evidence was introduced that the employer's reduction in force had the effect of lowering the average age in the plaintiff's job category from 43 to 37 years); Hodgson v. First Fed. Sav. & Loan Ass'n, 455 F.2d 818, 823 (5th Cir. 1972) ("Of thirty five persons hired as

- 46 -

undercut the EEOC's allegation of an overall pattern or practice of age discrimination.

       3.   Are any of the claims the EEOC is asserting time barred?

As in suits by private plaintiffs, it is critical for defendants in EEOC suits to identify and move for summary judgment on any individual claims that are barred by the statute of limitations. Questions regarding continuing violations will of course present the same kinds of complications in measuring the appropriate time periods as in individual suits. 189/ There are different rules, however, under sections 16(c) and 17 for determining when the action is commenced for purposes of tolling the statute of limitations.

       a.   Section 16(c) claims

Section 16(c) of the FLSA explicitly provides that the statute of limitations is not tolled for any given claimant until that individual is named in the EEOC's complaint:

---

tellers or teller trainees during that period all were younger than forty and all but three were under thirty"); Polstorff v. Fletcher, 452 F. Supp. 17, 22 (N.D. Ala. 1978) (30 percent of those 55 years and older were adversely affected in reduction in force while only 3.5 percent of those below age 55 were adversely affected); Schulz v. Hickok Mfg. Co., 358 F. Supp. 1208, 1213 (N.D. Ga. 1973) (average age had declined almost 13 years).

    Cases in which statistical evidence was found to be not probative of age discrimination include the following: Trinidad v. Pan American World Airways, Inc., 575 F.2d 983, 985 (1st Cir. 1978) (evidence showed that out of 518 terminations between 1968 and 1977, 66.93 percent were of non-protected group employees, and that average age after reduction in force was 50.3 years); Lindsey v. Southwestern Bell Tel. Co., 546 F.2d 1123, 1124 (5th Cir. 1977) (per curiam); Peterson v. Colonial Stores, Inc., 19 Empl. Prac. Dec. ¶ 8992 at 6153 n.1 (N.D. Ga. 1979) (percentage of employees within protected age group compared favorably with the work force percentage, and discharges from the protected group were proportionately fewer than for other employees); Hughes v. Black Hills Power & Light Co., 18 Fair Empl. Prac. Cas. 1365, 1367 (D.S.D. 1978), aff'd, 585 F.2d 918, 920 (8th Cir. 1978) (statistics showing decrease in average age of some 340 employees from 39.42 to 39.06 years did not indicate a pattern of age discrimination); Mastie v. Great Lakes Steel Corp., 424 F. Supp. 1299, 1319-21 (E.D. Mich. 1976) (decline in average age of foremen of 1.29 years was not a substantial enough discrepancy to indicate age discrimination); Stringfellow v. Monsanto Co., 320 F. Supp. 1175 (W.D. Ark. 1970).

189/   See pp. 19-26 above.

> In determining when an action is commenced
> by the Secretary of Labor under this sub-
> section for the purposes of the statutes of
> limitations provided in section 255(a) of
> this title [the two- or three-year limita-
> tions period of the Portal-to-Portal Act],
> it shall be considered to be commenced in
> the case of any individual claimant on the
> date when the complaint is filed if he is
> specifically named as a party plaintiff in
> the complaint, or if his name did not so
> appear, on the subsequent date on which his
> name is added as a party plaintiff in such
> action. 190/

Thus, defendants should move to exclude any individual claimant whose cause of action accrued more than three years before the date when his name was added to the complaint.

    b.   Section 17 claims

In contrast, section 17 is silent on tolling. It provides only that back wages are recoverable with the exception of "sums which employees are barred from recovering, at the time of the commencement of the action to restrain the violations, by virtue of the provisions of section 255 [the statute of limitations]." 191/

In the only case to construe this provision, EEOC v. Gilbarco, Inc., the Fourth Circuit ruled that the special definition of "commencement" found in section 16(c)--the naming of a claimant in the complaint--did not apply to a section 17 action. 192/ Rather, the court held, a section 17 action "is effectively commenced for all purposes with the filing of the complaint, regardless of whether the complaint names the aggrieved individuals." 193/ Any uncertainty as to which employees are included within the EEOC's suit could be resolved through the use of discovery procedures, the court added. 194/

Under this interpretation a section 17 suit may include individuals who become known to the EEOC only after their causes of action could no longer be asserted under section 16(c). For this reason defendants have an added incentive to seek summary

---

190/   29 U.S.C. § 216(c) (Supp. III 1979).

191/   29 U.S.C. § 217 (emphasis added).

192/   615 F.2d 985 (4th Cir. 1980).

193/   Id. at 990.

194/   Id.

judgment on the EEOC's section 17 claim, as described above. 195/ Defendants should also keep in mind that liquidated damages are not recoverable for individuals whose claims proceed only under section 17. 196/

III. JURY TRIAL CONSIDERATIONS

The Age Discrimination Act, unlike Title VII, grants the parties the right to demand a trial by jury. Section 7(c)(2) provides that

> In an action brought under [section 7(c)(1)], a person shall be entitled to a trial by jury of any issue of fact in any such action for recovery of amounts owing as a result of a violation of this chapter, regardless of whether equitable relief is sought by any party in such action. 197/

The availability of a jury trial gives rise to several strategic considerations:

A. Is it in the Defendant's Interest to Have a Jury Trial?

Whether the defendant should demand a jury trial is a decision that essentially depends on whether it seems advantageous to the defendant to have a jury rather than the judge decide the facts and determine damages, if any. In making this assessment, the defendant should consider the known propensities of the judge, the likely composition of the jury, the abilities of opposing counsel, and the particular facts of the case.

1. Who is the judge?

The first step should be to investigate the judge assigned to the case in an effort to determine if he or she may be

---

195/ See pp. 42-46 above.

196/ 29 U.S.C. §§ 216(c), 217; Gilbarco, supra note 192, 615 F.2d at 990-91.

197/ 29 U.S.C. § 626(c)(2) (Supp. III 1979). This provision was enacted in 1978 shortly after the Supreme Court in Lorillard v. Pons, 434 U.S. 575 (1978), had construed the ADEA as providing for a right to a jury trial in private actions. It has been held to apply retroactively to a cause of action arising before its enactment. Scarboro v. First American Nat'l Bank, 619 F.2d 621 (6th Cir.), cert. denied, 449 U.S. 1014 (1980).

expected to be particularly sympathetic or unsympathetic to the defense. As in any case, the defendant should research the judge's past decisions, in age discrimination and related types of cases. For example, it is important to determine whether the judge is one who has deviated from the majority position and considers that compensatory damages for emotional distress are recoverable under the ADEA. 198/ If that is the case, it would seem best to avoid a jury, because the judge would be less likely to make an award out of proportion to the actual evidence of "pain and suffering." 199/

Aside from the judge's position on ADEA issues, the defendant should also investigate whether the judge generally takes an assertive role in selecting and instructing juries, reserving issues for judgment, and granting judgments notwithstanding the verdict when the verdict is contrary to the law.

2. What is the likely composition of the jury?

As a general matter, jury panels will have a higher average age than does the surrounding population, because older or retired persons will be more likely to be available and willing to serve than will those who are younger and are still working or have family responsibilities. Rightly or not, the defendant may feel that a jury composed of older persons may display an instinctive sympathy for age discrimination plaintiffs. Consideration should therefore be given to the likely age composition of the panel from which a jury would be selected.

In addition, the defendant should carefully review the facts of the case to determine if there is anything that may be expected to adversely influence a jury more so than it would a judge. Some considerations are suggested below.

3. What are the nature and number of the claims?

To take an extreme example, the case of a 41-year-old plaintiff claiming a discriminatory demotion would present little if any risk of the jury being swayed by emotional rather than logical concerns. Such a risk would be more likely if the case involved a 61-year-old employee who, after rendering many years

---

198/ See cases cited above in notes 142-143.

199/ Cf. Rogers v. Exxon Research & Eng'r Co., 550 F.2d 834, 840 (3d Cir. 1977), cert. denied, 434 U.S. 1022 (1978) ("the jury's excessive award of $750,000 for 'pain and suffering' is more a condemnation of the defendant's activity than a measurement of the actual distress fairly attributable to the plaintiff's treatment by the company").

of satisfactory service, had been terminated in an abrupt manner because of recently identified deficiencies in performance. Similarly, the number of claimants is also a factor to be weighed. The cumulative effect of testimony by plaintiff after plaintiff in a multi-party case may confuse, if not unduly prejudice, a jury with respect to any given claim. In such types of cases, trial to the bench would be preferable because the judge would probably be better able to make a fair evaluation of the evidence in light of the appropriate legal principles.

Another very significant consideration is whether the suit involves an ADEA claim alone, or has pendent state law causes of action as well. As described previously, such causes of action might consist of claims for violation of a state law against age discrimination, a state common law doctrine against unjust discharge, and an express or implied employment contract. For defendants, the commingling of such claims would make the case a poor candidate for jury trial. It is likely that the claims would involve different limitations periods, different evidence, different burdens of proof, and different types of allowable damages. Even if jury confusion could be avoided by careful instructions, trial to a jury rather than to the court would probably take longer.

4. <u>What are the facts?</u>

If the evidence points strongly to the conclusion that the plaintiff's age did not "in fact make a difference" [200] in the employment decision at issue, then the case would be appropriate for either a judge or a jury. Other sets of facts or types of defenses, however, may suggest a preference for one type of fact-finder over the other. For example, if the employer can show that age is a bona fide occupational qualification necessary to the safety of the public in the operation of its business, then the jury's sympathies might particularly be expected to lie with the defendant. On the other hand, the risk of an adverse verdict would be greater in a jury trial if the defendant's conduct, though free of illegal age discrimination, could be characterized as unfair, callous or arbitrary.

Other factors should also be taken into account: for example, the demeanor and personality of the plaintiff and key witnesses; the significance and understandability of statistical proof; and the absence or presence of what may appear to be direct, damaging evidence of age discrimination which may be of little relevance but which may unduly influence a jury.

Whatever the facts of the case, defendants should recognize that the presentation of a case to a jury is inherently more

---

[200] See Laugesen v. Anaconda Co., 510 F.2d 307, 317 (6th Cir. 1975).

complicated than a bench trial. Trial exhibits, for example, will have to be carefully prepared in terms of eye appeal. But if the evidence can be presented in the form of charts or visual aids that will have a persuasive impact on the jury, then a jury trial could be turned to the defendant's advantage.

As a final matter, if the plaintiff's lawyer has had little or no jury trial experience, competent defense counsel might gain some tactical advantage by trying the case to a jury.

B. If the Plaintiff Has Demanded a Jury, Can the Demand be Defeated or Limited?

If the defendant decides it would not be in its interest to have a jury trial, then steps may be taken to oppose or to limit the plaintiff's demand.

1. Private action

a. Timely demand

The governing standard for jury demands is Rule 38 of the Federal Rules of Civil Procedure. Subsection (b) of that rule provides that a jury demand must be served "in writing," "not later than 10 days after service of the last pleading directed" to a jury question. Subsection (d), in turn, states that "the failure of a party to serve a demand as required by this rule and to file it . . . constitutes a waiver by him of trial by jury." 201/

A waiver under Rule 38 is not irreversible. Rule 39(b) provides that "[n]otwithstanding the failure of a party to demand a jury . . . the court in its discretion may order a trial by jury of any or all issues." However, despite the discretion afforded the court under this rule, courts generally "have been extremely reluctant to exercise this discretion in favor of jury trial." 202/ Motions are generally considered on a case-by-case basis, without any preconception that they are normally denied. 203/ Thus it is difficult to state a controlling standard for the rule's application.

Nevertheless, defendants opposing Rule 39(b) motions can make a number of points to convince the court to deny the plaintiff relief from the consequences of failing to file a timely

---

201/ See Sutton v. Atlantic Richfield Co., 20 Fair Empl. Prac. Cas. 1292 (C.D. Cal. 1978) (age discrimination plaintiff's failure to demand jury within 10 days constitutes waiver).

202/ 9 C. Wright & A. Miller, Federal Practice & Procedure: Civil, § 2321 at 102.

203/ Id. § 2334 at 116.

jury demand. First, "mere inadvertence" in neglecting to comply with Rule 38 usually does not warrant the granting of a Rule 39(b) motion. 204/ Second, the motion should be denied if the plaintiff has delayed in requesting relief from waiver of a jury, and the defendant has been prejudiced thereby. 205/ Third, when the plaintiff has made a deliberate and intentional waiver, defendants should strenuously resist a Rule 39(b) motion based on the plaintiff's "belated change of strategy." 206/ Fourth, and of particular significance in ADEA cases, Rule 39(b) motions should be denied when the issues are complicated, there are "complex and interrelated considerations of federal and state law," and both legal and equitable relief is sought. 207/

b. Scope of jury trial

As noted above, the ADEA permits a jury trial "of any issue of fact," regardless of whether equitable relief is also sought in the action. The courts have designated certain issues as triable by the jury and others for decision by the judge depending on whether the issues are characterized as legal or equitable:

(1) The basic questions of liability and damages in the form of back wages and other items of pecuniary relief are of course legal in nature, and a party is entitled to have these

---

204/ E.g., Rhodes v. Amarillo Hospital Dist., 654 F.2d 1148 (5th Cir. 1981); Bush v. Allstate Ins. Co., 425 F.2d 393, 396 (5th Cir.), cert. denied, 400 U.S. 833 (1970); Noonan v. Cunard Steamship Co., 375 F.2d 69, 70 (2d Cir. 1967).

205/ E.g., Littlefield v. Fort Dodge Messenger, 614 F.2d 581, 585 (8th Cir.), cert. denied, 445 U.S. 945 (1980); Mardesich v. Marciel, 538 F.2d 848, 849 (9th Cir. 1976).

206/ Reefer Express Lines v. Arkwright-Boston Manufacturers Ins. Co., 87 F.R.D. 133, 135 (S.D.N.Y. 1980). See also William Goldman Theatres v. Kirkpatrick, 154 F.2d 66, 69 (3d Cir. 1946); Interstate Cigar v. Sterling Drug, 88 F.R.D. 110, 111 (S.D.N.Y. 1980).

207/ Hawkinson v. Blandin Paper Co., 54 F.R.D. 517, 519 (D. Minn. 1972). See also General Tire & Rubber Co. v. Watkins, 331 F.2d 192, 197-98 (4th Cir.), cert. denied, 377 U.S. 952 (1964); but see Hoffman v. Alside, Inc., 596 F.2d 822, 823 (8th Cir. 1979) (in ADEA case, district court did not abuse its discretion in denying an untimely jury request but allowing the plaintiff leave to dismiss without prejudice and without condition that plaintiff agree not to seek jury trial in any subsequent suit).

issues decided by a jury. 208/ The issue of whether the defendant's violation of the Act was willful, thus supporting an award of liquidated damages, 209/ is also a question for the jury. 210/

(2) Judgments compelling reinstatement, employment or promotion are equitable in nature, and thus are issues for the court. 211/

(3) Compensation for lost pension benefits has been considered to be equitable if the plaintiff seeks an order restoring his pension status and requiring the employer to make appropriate payments into a pension fund. 212/ In other cases, courts have allowed the jury to assess pension benefits as an element of legal damages, awarding relief in the form of a monetary payment. 213/

(4) Attorneys' fees are awardable only by the court, as explicitly provided in the statute. 214/

(5) One court has held that issues of fact relating to whether the defendant should be equitably estopped from relying on the statute of limitations are to be decided by the jury. 215/

2. Action by EEOC

Although the ADEA as amended unquestionably provides the right to a jury trial in individual actions, it is not clear

---

208/ See Lorillard v. Pons, 434 U.S. 575, 583 n.11 (1978); H. Conf. Rep. No. 95-950, 95th Cong., 2d Sess. 13-14, reprinted in [1978] U.S. Code Cong. & Ad. News 528, 535.

209/ 29 U.S.C. § 626(b).

210/ Goodman v. Heublein, Inc., 646 F.2d 560 (2d Cir. 1980); Cleverly v. Western Elec. Co., 594 F.2d 638, 640 (8th Cir. 1979); H. Conf. Rep. No. 95-950, 95th Cong., 2d Sess. 13-14, reprinted in [1978] U.S. Code Cong. Ad. News 504, 535.

211/ E.g., Geller v. Markham, 635 F.2d 1027, 1036 (2d Cir. 1980); Cleverly, supra note 210, 594 F.2d at 640; Quinn v. Bowmar Publishing Co., 445 F. Supp. 780, 788 (D. Md. 1978).

212/ E.g., Geller, Quinn, supra note 211; Cleverly, supra note 210.

213/ E.g., Fellows v. Medford Corp., 431 F. Supp. 199, 201 (D. Or. 1977); cf. Kelly v. American Standard, Inc., 640 F.2d 974, 986 n.20 (9th Cir. 1981).

214/ 29 U.S.C. § 216(b) (Supp. III 1979). See Quinn, supra note 211; Fellows, supra note 213.

215/ Ott v. Midland-Ross Corp., 600 F.2d 24, 34 (6th Cir. 1979).

whether that right extends to actions brought by the EEOC under sections 16(c) and 17. The EEOC takes the position that it does. However, a number of good arguments can be made by defendants that the EEOC is not entitled to demand a jury trial.

First, the statute does not explicitly provide for a jury trial right in EEOC actions. The section that was amended in 1978 to provide for jury trials is section 7(c) of the ADEA, the section authorizing individual actions. 216/ Section 7(c)(2) states that a jury trial is available in actions brought under section 7(c)(1), which are actions brought by "any person aggrieved." EEOC does not appear to be a "person aggrieved" as that term is defined in the statute. 217/ Furthermore, suits by the EEOC are brought not under section 7(c), but under section 7(b), which was not amended by Congress to provide a jury trial right. 218/ Thus, on its face the statute does not provide for jury trials in suits by the EEOC. 219/

Second, even if the EEOC is deemed to have a jury trial right, that right extends only to section 16(c) actions. Courts have unanimously held that an ADEA or FLSA action brought pursuant to section 17 is equitable in nature and no jury trial right exists, even if monetary relief is sought incident to such injunctive relief. 220/

216/ 29 U.S.C. § 626(c) (Supp. III 1979).

217/ See 29 U.S.C. § 630(a).

218/ Cf. Lehman v. Nakshian, 101 S. Ct. 2698 (1981) (federal employees have no right to trial by jury in ADEA actions against the government; absence of express language providing for jury trial in section authorizing suits by federal employees, 29 U.S.C. § 633a, indicates that Congress did not intend to confer such a right).

219/ The only reported decisions that have considered this question since the enactment of the 1978 amendment have held to the contrary, however. In EEOC v. Western Elec. Co., 25 Empl. Prac. Dec. ¶ 31,711 (E.D. Mich. 1981), and EEOC v. Blue Star Foods, Inc., 22 Fair Empl. Prac. Cas. 504 (S.D. Iowa 1980), the district courts held that the EEOC is entitled to a jury trial in actions under section 16(c). However, neither case is particularly persuasive, because in each the court misreads or fails to notice sections of the ADEA that contradict its reasoning.

220/ See, e.g., Lorillard v. Pons, 434 U.S. 575, 580 n.7 (1978); Sullivan v. Wirtz, 359 F.2d 426 (5th Cir.), cert. denied, 385 U.S. 852 (1966); Wirtz v. Jones, 340 F.2d 901, 904 (5th Cir. 1965) (the purpose of an injunction under section 17 is "not to collect a debt owed by an employer to his employee but to correct a continuing offense against the

Thus, if the 1978 amendment to section 7(c) is construed to apply to EEOC actions, defendants should argue that it provides for jury trial only on factual issues underlying individual claims, not on equitable claims under section 17. Defendants should then insist that a bifurcated trial is necessary. Only the facts underlying the section 16(c) claims or common to both claims should be tried to a jury, and any facts related solely to the equitable claims under section 17 should be tried to the court after the jury is dismissed. If the defendant is faced with an EEOC action that involves both highly individualized claims under section 16(c) and broad "pattern or practice" allegations under section 17, bifurcation of the trial can be critical, because it would remove from the jury's consideration any evidence relating solely to pattern or practice issues that might unduly influence its judgment on individual claims.

IV. DISCOVERY

Up to this point the discussion of pretrial tactics has focused on the types of motions that may limit or defeat the plaintiff's case. This section turns to a second major pretrial activity, discovery. Following this, the last section of the paper discusses final trial preparations centering on the drafting of the pretrial order.

These three major activities are closely interrelated. For example, the extent to which the defendant must submit to discovery will be more limited if pretrial motions to narrow the scope of the action have succeeded. The defendant's ability to raise motions challenging jurisdictional defects will in turn depend upon whether the necessary facts have been developed through discovery. And while discovery is underway, defense counsel of course should be investigating and developing the facts on its own through interviews with management and review of records.

Discovery in an age discrimination case operates under the same basic principles that govern discovery in any civil case. Because relatively few ADEA decisions deal specifically with discovery, reference must usually be made to Title VII cases for appropriate precedents. Therefore this section will not attempt to set forth all pertinent discovery rules but rather will suggest some strategic considerations relating to discovery by both plaintiffs and defendants in age discrimination cases.

A. Discovery by the Defendant

Before taking discovery, the defendant should identify the objectives that discovery is expected to serve in the particular case. Usually, the defendant will be seeking: (1) to learn as

---

public interest"); Marshall v. Kreten Char-Broil, Inc., 507 F. Supp. 445 (E.D.N.Y. 1980); Marshall v. Holland Hitch Co., 24 Fair Empl. Prac. Cas. 1337 (W.D. Mich. 1978).

much as possible about the plaintiff's case; (2) to gain information to support preliminary motions; and (3) to lock the plaintiff into a position on his claims.

To prepare for discovery, it is essential for defense counsel to investigate and analyze the strengths and weaknesses of his own case. Questions of timing should also be considered. In most cases defendants will want to depose the plaintiff at the earliest opportunity. Then, other forms of discovery--interrogatories, document requests, and requests for admission--can be used to pin the plaintiff further down on the details of his claim.

1. Deposition of the plaintiff

The deposition is the defendant's central discovery device. It enjoys several advantages over other methods of discovery because it allows defense counsel to seek direct, spontaneous responses from the plaintiff and to move into a new line of questioning if new issues become apparent. Therefore, much care should be put into preparing for and taking the depositions of the plaintiff in a section 7(c) suit, of each named plaintiff and those who have "opted in" to a multi-party suit under section 7(b), or of the individual claimants in a section 16(c) suit by EEOC.

The defendant should explore the specifics of the claims of such individuals--the facts relied on, the particular incidents, practices or policies alleged to be discriminatory, and the witnesses to the events referred to. The goal should be to narrow the scope of the individual's allegations and to elicit admissions whenever possible. In a multi-party suit under section 7(b), it is particularly critical for the defendant to develop facts that demonstrate the individualized nature of the named plaintiff's claim, in order to argue that a representative suit cannot be maintained because the plaintiffs are not "similarly situated." 221/ The defendant should also go over the plaintiff's background, work history, and qualifications. Finally, the defendant should question the plaintiff on whether all prerequisites to suit have been met in a timely manner.

2. Interrogatories, document requests, and requests for admission

a. Private action

Interrogatories and document requests should generally be used as a follow-up to the deposition, to obtain additional details on the claims, to clarify vague answers, and to request information on damages. All relevant documents should be sought. Even though some might already be in the defendant's

---

221/ See p. 18 above.

possession, it is important to identify those documents on which the plaintiff is relying. The defendant should also make the standard requests for the identity of the plaintiff's witnesses and expert witnesses, as well as for the substance of their testimony. Although the witnesses may not yet be known, the plaintiff is nevertheless under a duty to supplement his responses when the information becomes available. 222/ In a multi-party suit under section 16(b), the defendant should not fail to serve discovery requests on the "opt-in" plaintiffs as well as on the named plaintiffs. Because such persons are referred to as "parties" in the statute, they would appear to be subject to interrogatories under Rule 33 of the Federal Rules of Civil Procedure.

Once the facts have been fairly well developed, the defendant should consider serving requests for admission under Rule 36. This could help narrow the issues for trial, and may induce the plaintiff to settle. On the other hand, the defendant may wish to forego admissions or stipulations on some issues if testimony on those issues would be a more effective means of presenting defendant's case.

b. Action by EEOC

Discovery served on the EEOC should seek to obtain factual support for motions that may limit the agency's suit. 223/ The defendant should determine the extent of the EEOC's investigation and conciliation, as well as the bases for a charge of a pattern or practice of age discrimination.

Discovery of the details of the underlying individual claims in an EEOC suit is also essential. 224/ In a section 17 suit, the discovery process presents the defendant's first opportunity to learn the identity of those persons who are within the scope of the EEOC's suit. 225/ In a section 16(c) suit, the defendant is entitled to serve interrogatories on any individual claimant who is named in the EEOC's complaint. 226/ In a large suit

---

222/ Fed. R. Civ. P. 26(e).

223/ See pp. 39-48 above.

224/ See General Tel. Co. v. EEOC, 100 S. Ct. 1698, 1708 (1980) (in a Title VII suit by the EEOC, the defendant is entitled to discovery to determine the nature and extent of the claims the EEOC intends to pursue against it).

225/ See EEOC v. Gilbarco, Inc., 615 F.2d 985, 990 (4th Cir. 1980); Donovan v. University of Texas, 643 F.2d 1201, 1208 (5th Cir. 1981); see pp. 46-48 above.

226/ As does section 16(b), section 16(c) refers to an individual claimant as a "party plaintiff," 29 U.S.C. § 216(c),

interrogatories would be the most economical means of discovery, and would be useful to determine the intensity of interest in the suit and the potential extent of damages. Taking the depositions of the individual claimants in either a section 16(c) or section 17 suit is also advisable, to the extent resources permit.

A special issue that arises in EEOC suits is the applicability of the so-called "informer's privilege." The EEOC will invoke this privilege to shield from discovery any information provided to it by employees during the investigation. Fearing that the identification of employee-informers would leave those persons vulnerable to retaliation, the EEOC goes to great lengths to avoid turning over information such as questionnaires or statements taken during its investigation. This information, of course, is essential to the defense. Defense counsel should respond by insisting on production of the documents but agreeing to do so under a protective order. Such an order would restrict disclosure of the materials to outside counsel only, and would prohibit disclosure to managerial employees of the defendant. 227/ Thus, the offer of a protective order should allay concerns regarding reprisals and remove any legitimate reason for the EEOC to withhold the documents.

---

thereby apparently subjecting each person to Rule 33 of the Federal Rules of Civil Procedure, which authorizes service of interrogatories on "parties," as well as to other discovery provisions. Cf. Brennan v. Midwestern United Life Ins. Co., 450 F.2d 999 (7th Cir. 1971), cert. denied, 405 U.S. 921 (1972) (in a Rule 23 class action under Title VII, unnamed class members are required to respond to interrogatories).

227/ See, e.g., EEOC v. Consolidated Edison Co., 26 Empl. Prac. Dec. ¶ 31,975 (S.D.N.Y. 1981). In this ADEA case the court ordered discovery of questionnaires and documents concerning 163 employees named in the EEOC's complaint, under a protective order limiting disclosure to counsel. The court held that the applicability of the informer's privilege is "determined by a balancing test, weighing the Government's interest in protecting the identities of its informants against the defendant's need for the materials in question." Id. at 21,394. It would be unfair, the court concluded, for the EEOC to rely at trial on the information provided by the 163 employees while denying that information to the defendant.

The court also held that the EEOC's investigative files were discoverable. Although they were covered by the qualified work product privilege, the defendant had shown substantial need for the files and undue hardship in attempting to obtain their equivalent elsewhere. Id. at 21,396. See pp. 62-63 below.

3. Discovery of expert witnesses and other witnesses

The testimony of experts is indispensable to both parties in any ADEA case that relies on statistical evidence. 228/ It will also be critical in cases in which the employer asserts that an age-based restriction is a bona fide occupational qualification. 229/ In such cases experts would appropriately testify regarding, for example, the medical basis for believing that the restriction is essential to safe performance of the job.

Discovery of expert witnesses is governed by Rule 26(b)(4) of the Federal Rules of Civil Procedure. That rule makes a distinction between experts who are expected to be called as trial witnesses, and experts who have been retained in anticipation of litigation or preparation for trial but who are not expected to be called at trial. Only the former type, the trial expert, is generally subject to discovery; the non-witness expert is shielded from discovery unless the party seeking discovery can show "exceptional circumstances" justifying discovery. 230/

Before taking the deposition of the plaintiff's expert, defense counsel should prepare thoroughly in consultation with his own expert. The deposition also should be preceded by interrogatories seeking information about the expert's qualifications, writings, previous testimony and previous opinions given, as well as the substance of the expert's opinion in the case at hand. 231/

Aside from experts, the testimony of non-party witnesses may be taken by deposition; however, interrogatories may not be utilized. 232/

4. Offer of judgment

Rule 68 of the Federal Rules of Civil Procedure permits the defendant to make an "offer of judgment" to the plaintiff. The offer is for a specific sum of money in settlement; if the plaintiff does not accept the offer and obtains a final judgment

---

228/ See pp. 45-46 above.

229/ 29 U.S.C. § 623(f)(1).

230/ Fed. R. Civ. P. 26(b)(4)(B).

231/ See Fed. R. Civ. P. 26(b)(4)(A)(i) and (ii).

232/ Fed. R. Civ. P. 30, 33.

that is not more favorable than the offer, 233/ he is liable for the defendant's costs incurred after the making of the offer.

A Rule 68 offer of judgment is an important tactic for defendants in age discrimination cases, because it puts pressure on the plaintiff to accept a reasonable settlement of his claims. This incentive may be otherwise lacking under the Age Discrimination Act because, like Title VII, the Act provides for payment of attorneys' fees to the prevailing plaintiff. 234/

B. Discovery by the Plaintiff

In employment discrimination cases the courts generally permit broad discovery by plaintiffs. 235/ Nevertheless, defendants can insist that certain limits be observed. The principal types of objections that defendants will have are: (1) that the discovery sought is unduly burdensome or overbroad; (2) that it covers irrelevant matters; and (3) that it seeks information protected by the attorney-client privilege or the work product rule.

1. Limiting the scope of responses to the plaintiff's interrogatories and document requests

Limitations on the scope of discovery will generally parallel the limitations on the scope of the plaintiff's suit. 236/ Any issues that are beyond the scope of the EEOC charge and conciliation are not properly in the suit, and therefore discovery as to those issues is not relevant. 237/

(1) Geographical/departmental limitations. Defendants should usually object to discovery at any facilities other than the one at which the plaintiff was employed. 238/ In appropriate

---

233/ Cf. Delta Air Lines v. August, 101 S. Ct. 1146 (1981) (Rule 68 does not apply to a case in which judgment is entered against the plaintiff-offeree and in favor of the defendant-offeror).

234/ 29 U.S.C. § 216(b).

235/ See, e.g., Rich v. Martin Marietta Corp., 522 F.2d 333 (10th Cir. 1975) (Title VII case).

236/ See pp. 32-33 and 39-42 above.

237/ See, e.g., EEOC v. Honeywell, Inc., 73 F.R.D. 496 (N.D. Ill. 1977); EEOC v. Prestolite Battery Div. of Eltra Corp., 14 Fair Empl. Prac. Cas. 1634 (W.D. Okla. 1976).

238/ See Marshall v. Westinghouse Elec. Corp., 576 F.2d 588 (5th Cir. 1978); Prestolite, supra note 237.

cases arguments can also be made to confine discovery responses to the plaintiff's department or job category. To support such objections it would be helpful to have evidence that decision-making is localized, and that the other departments are sufficiently different so that information about them would not be relevant.

(2) <u>Temporal limitations</u>. Defendants should generally object to discovery requests that ask for information beyond a five-year period. 239/ The facts of the case, however, may dictate a shorter or longer period; for example, the defendant may wish to include information on earlier major reorganizations or changes in policy that are material to the defense.

(3) <u>Limitation by issues</u>. Discovery should also be limited to those employment practices that are properly part of the suit. If the plaintiff's claim challenges only a discriminatory termination, for example, the defendant should object to discovery relating to hiring, promotion and other practices. 240/

2. Use of Rule 33(c)

Rule 33(c) of the Federal Rules of Civil Procedure gives defendants the option, in lieu of answering an interrogatory, to produce business records from which the plaintiff can derive the answer to the interrogatory. Rule 33(c) may be invoked only when "the burden of deriving or ascertaining the answer is substantially the same for the party serving the interrogatory as for the party served." 241/ The defendant must specify the records in sufficient detail to permit the plaintiff to locate and identify the records from which the answer may be obtained. 242/

A Rule 33(c) tender of documents is thus a valuable means for the defendant in an employment discrimination case to shift some of the burden of discovery onto the plaintiff. Before providing the plaintiff the opportunity to inspect records, the defendant should review the documents to ensure that they are responsive to the interrogatory and do not contain privileged material.

239/ See, e.g., Stevenson v. General Elec. Co., 18 Empl. Prac. Dec. ¶ 8777 (S.D. Ohio 1978).

240/ See, e.g., McClain v. Mack Trucks, Inc., 85 F.R.D. 53 (E.D. Pa. 1979).

241/ Fed. R. Civ. P. 33(c).

242/ Id.

3. Claims of privilege and work product

   a. Attorney-client privilege

The attorney-client privilege affords absolute protection from disclosure of the confidential communications between an attorney and a client seeking legal advice. The Supreme Court's recent decision in Upjohn Co. v. United States 243/ sets forth the broad scope of the privilege as between an attorney and a corporate client. In Upjohn, the Court held that the attorney-client privilege protected communications between the general counsel and the employees of Upjohn that were made during an internal investigation of questionable foreign payments. For a communication to be privileged, the Court said, there must be:

- a communication,

- by a corporate employee,

- to corporate counsel acting as such,

- made at the direction of corporate superiors,

- in order to secure legal advice from counsel,

- concerning matters within the scope of the employee's corporate duties,

- made with awareness by the employees that they were being questioned in order that the corporation could obtain legal advice, and

- considered confidential when made and kept confidential thereafter. 244/

Using these explicit criteria, defense counsel should take steps to ensure that all communications in the pretrial stage of the case remain protected by the privilege. The Court's opinion in the Upjohn case also gives impetus to the growing recognition of a privilege of "self-evaluation." Thus, whether in litigation or not, an employer who wants to make a confidential evaluation of the age-impact of a policy or decision would be well advised to involve corporate counsel in the process and to observe the Upjohn criteria.

   b. Work product doctrine

The work product doctrine gives a qualified privilege against disclosure of documents, notes, memoranda, and other

---

243/ 101 S. Ct. 677 (1981).

244/ Id. at 685.

materials prepared in anticipation of litigation by a party or a party's representative or attorney. The doctrine is incorporated in Rule 26(b)(3) of the Federal Rules of Civil Procedure. The work product protection is not absolute, because the opposing party may obtain discovery of work product upon a showing of "substantial need" and inability "without undue hardship to obtain the substantial equivalent of the materials by other means." 245/ Even if a court orders disclosure upon such a showing, it must still protect "the mental impressions, conclusions, opinions, or legal theories of an attorney or other representative of a party concerning the litigation." 246/

V. PRETRIAL ORDER

In many jurisdictions, a pretrial conference is used to decide preliminary issues and encourage agreements on as many issues as possible. 247/ Agreements and decisions reached at the conference are embodied in a pretrial order, which controls the subsequent course of the action. Usually the litigants are directed to exchange proposed pretrial orders and reach agreement on as many issues as possible before the pretrial conference.

A. Narrowing the Issues

The form of the pretrial order will usually be governed by local rule or the preferences of the judge. The elements typically will include: (1) uncontested facts; (2) contested factual issues; (3) legal issues; (4) witnesses; (5) expert witnesses; and (6) documentary evidence. In a jury case the parties may be asked to prepare proposed voir dire questions and jury instructions; in a non-jury case the parties would draft proposed findings of fact and conclusions of law.

The purpose of the pretrial order is to narrow the scope of the issues to be tried. The defendant should draft proposed uncontested findings of fact in a succinct, neutral style, with each factual point isolated in a separate paragraph. The issues should be organized by topic. In a multi-party action or a section 16(c) suit by the EEOC, the facts pertinent to each individual plaintiff should be set out separately. When considering potential stipulations of fact, defendants should assess the relative effectiveness of stipulations and testimony. 248/

245/ Fed. R. Civ. P. 26(b)(3).

246/ Id.

247/ See Fed. R. Civ. P. 16.

248/ See p. 57 above.

The pretrial conference gives the defendant a final opportunity to move to eliminate claims on any of the grounds discussed in the foregoing sections of this paper. Last-minute attempts by the plaintiff or the EEOC to add new claims or claimants should be resisted.

B. Limiting Witnesses

Evidentiary issues should also be resolved at the pretrial conference. Of particular concern to the defendant is the plaintiff's proposed witness list. Often, the private plaintiff or the EEOC will seek to introduce the testimony of other employees or employee-plaintiffs concerning personal claims of age discrimination against the employer. These witnesses' claims may have been raised in other lawsuits, or previously dismissed from the case. The defendant should move to prevent the plaintiff from calling such witnesses, arguing that the probative value of their testimony would be outweighed by the danger of confusion and prejudice.

The clearest case for doing so is illustrated by Moorhouse v. Boeing Co. 249/ There, six plaintiffs brought suit against the employer, but because the court ruled that a consolidated trial of the claims would be impractical and confusing, only the claim of plaintiff Moorhouse was before the court at the time. The trial court held that the testimony of the five other employee-plaintiffs should be excluded from consideration by the jury. The court relied on Rule 403 of the Federal Rules of Evidence, which provides that the court may exclude evidence "if its probative value is substantially outweighed by the danger of unfair prejudice, confusion of the issues, or misleading the jury, or by considerations of undue delay, waste of time, or needless presentation of cumulative evidence."

To allow the other employees to testify, the court reasoned, would place the defendant in the position of having to either justify each witness' layoff, or leave the testimony unrebutted. The latter alternative would have an obviously prejudicial impact on the jury, while the former option would force the defendant in effect to try all six cases together "with the attendant confusion and prejudice inherent in that situation." 250/ The court emphasized that "even the strongest jury instructions could not have dulled the impact of a parade of witnesses, each recounting his contention that the defendant had laid him off because of his age." 251/

249/ 501 F. Supp. 390 (E.D. Pa.), aff'd mem., 639 F.2d 774 (3d Cir. 1980).

250/ Id. at 393.

251/ Id. at 393 n.4. Similarly, in Harpring v. Continental Oil Co., 628 F.2d 406 (5th Cir. 1980), cert. denied, 50

As *Moorhouse* suggests, defendants are most likely to succeed in excluding witnesses when the case is a jury trial. Other courts have allowed testimony concerning other employees' alleged discriminatory experiences, but those cases were not jury trials. 252/ Aside from reasons of jury confusion and cumulative presentation of evidence under Rule 403, defendants can also assert that testimony by other employees is irrelevant and inadmissible under Rule 401 of the Federal Rules of Evidence, particularly so when the testimony relates to time-barred events. 253/ However, the chances that the testimony will be admitted are much greater if the suit is a pattern or practice action by the EEOC under section 17. 254/

C. Preliminary Hearings

Preliminary hearings serve a useful function in simplifying the issues for trial, particularly in jury trials. Defendants should suggest that the court hold such a hearing to resolve as many evidentiary disputes as possible before trial. In a jury case, frequent objections by defense counsel during the trial itself would be disruptive and may turn the jury against

---

U.S.L.W. 3245 (1981), the Fifth Circuit held that the district court had not abused its discretion in refusing to allow the plaintiff to introduce the testimony of two other employees to prove a pattern of age discrimination. The appellate court said that the testimony was correctly excluded under Rule 403, because its introduction would have necessitated "trying another lawsuit within the existing lawsuit." *Id.* at 409-10.

252/ Buchholz v. Symons Mfg. Co., 445 F. Supp. 706 (E.D. Wis. 1978); Schulz v. Hickok Mfg. Co., 358 F. Supp. 1208 (N.D. Ga. 1973).

253/ See *Moorhouse*, *supra* note 249 (testimony of other employees irrelevant if it does not aim at establishing a pattern or practice of age discrimination); Wilson v. Sealtest Foods Div. of Kraftco Corp., 501 F.2d 84, 87 (5th Cir. 1974) (testimony of witnesses excluded because one witness was employed in a totally different capacity than was the plaintiff, and another witness' testimony related only to company practices fifteen years earlier).

Rule 408 of the Federal Rules of Evidence may also provide grounds for exclusion of evidence. In Scaramuzzo v. Glenmore Distilleries Co., 501 F. Supp. 727, 732-34 (N.D. Ill. 1980), the court granted the employer's motion in limine to prevent the plaintiff from referring to or introducing testimony on the filing of other charges of age discrimination, the settlement of such charges, and the terms of such settlements.

254/ See *Schulz*, *supra* note 252.

the defendant, or give rise to adverse inferences in the minds of the jurors.

Rule 16 of the Federal Rules of Civil Procedure also permits the court to refer issues to a master for findings to be used as evidence when the trial is by jury. Defendants should urge the court to order such fact-finding with respect to issues that are complex and would require a lengthy presentation to the jury, as well as issues that might unduly prejudice the jury.

D. Order of Proof in Multi-Party Suits

Another strategic consideration is the order of proof in an EEOC suit or a private suit with multiple plaintiffs. The defendant should seek to reach agreement with the plaintiff that testimony should be heard first on any plaintiffs' claims that involve issues that are dispositive with respect to other plaintiffs. In that way the defendant would have an early opportunity to move for summary judgment if the plaintiffs' proof fails. The defendant might also attempt to have presented first those claims on which its rebuttal is strongest. This could put the defendant in a better position to negotiate a settlement mid-trial.

E. Bifurcated Section 16(c)/17 Trials

As discussed in the section on jury trials, the EEOC is not entitled to a jury trial under section 17, and arguably is not entitled to a jury trial on section 16(c) claims as well. [255]/ If the court rules otherwise and the case involves both types of claims, the defendant should insist that the jury trial right does not extend to the section 17 claim for injunctive relief. It will probably be advisable for the defendant to urge the court to bifurcate the trial, with the section 16(c) individual claims tried first to the jury, and the section 17 claim then tried to the court. The factual issues common to both claims would have to be tried first along with factual issues specific to the individual section 16(c) claims. [256]/ Nevertheless, bifurcation would keep from the jury evidence pertaining only to the section 17 pattern or practice claim. Such evidence, like the testimony of other aggrieved employees, presents a substantial risk of jury confusion and prejudice to the defense of individual claims.

F. Bifurcation of Liability and Damages Determinations

In private class actions and EEOC pattern or practice suits under Title VII, bifurcation of the liability and damages

---

[255]/ See pp. 53-55 above.

[256]/ Beacon Theatres, Inc. v. Westover, 359 U.S. 500 (1959); Dairy Queen, Inc. v. Wood, 369 U.S. 469 (1962).

determinations is usually required. The procedural rules and presumptions to be applied in such cases were established by the Supreme Court in International Brotherhood of Teamsters v. United States. 257/ At the initial or "liability" stage the plaintiff has the burden to demonstrate "that unlawful discrimination has been a regular procedure or policy" followed by the employer. 258/ If the court concludes that a violation has occurred, it then must conduct additional proceedings to determine the scope of individual relief. 259/

In the damages stage the court first must identify actual victims of discrimination:

> Initially, the court will have to make a substantial number of individual determinations in deciding which of the minority employees were actual victims of the company's discriminatory practices. 260/

The second step is to determine the amount of back pay to which the identified victims are entitled. To do this the court must, "as nearly as possible, 'recreate the conditions and relationships that would have been had there been no' unlawful discrimination." 261/

The only major ADEA case to have applied these principles is EEOC v. Sandia Corp., 262/ a pattern or practice suit by the EEOC. There does not appear to be any reason why the Teamsters rules should not continue to be used in age discrimination litigation. From the defendant's perspective, Teamsters stands for the important proposition that only identified, actual victims of discrimination are entitled to back pay relief. The decision also guarantees the defendant the right to rebut individual entitlement to back pay on a case-by-case basis. For these reasons defendants generally should urge the court to bifurcate the liability and damages stages in EEOC actions as well as large multi-party private actions under the ADEA.

257/ 431 U.S. 324 (1977).

258/ Id. at 360.

259/ Id. at 361.

260/ Id. at 371-72.

261/ Id. at 372, quoting Franks v. Bowman Transp. Co., 424 U.S. 747, 769 (1976).

262/ 639 F.2d 600 (10th Cir. 1980). See note 188 above.

AGE DISCRIMINATION LITIGATION: HOW
DEFENSE COUNSEL HANDLES THE JURY TRIAL

Ronald M. Green *

---

* Member, Epstein Becker Borsody & Green, P.C., New York, New York, where he is actively engaged in the private practice of labor law on behalf of management. Mr. Green has served as the Department of Labor's Counsel for Civil Rights. He is on the adjunct faculty of Cornell University School of Industrial and Labor Relations and has authored various publications concerning equal employment opportunity law. Mr. Green received his Juris Doctor degree from Brooklyn Law School and earned an LL.M. degree in Labor Law from George Washington University School of Law.

TABLE OF CONTENTS

		Page
I.	SELECTION OF JURORS	1
II.	SELECTION AND PREPARATION OF EXPERTS AND NON-EXPERT WITNESS	3
III.	PRESENTATION OF THE CASE	5
	A. The Opening Statement	6
	B. The Closing Statement	6
IV.	SELECTING APPROPRIATE JURY INSTRUCTIONS	7
V.	PRESENTATION OF THE CASE SO AS TO MINIMIZE DAMAGES	12

AGE DISCRIMINATION LITIGATION: HOW DEFENSE COUNSEL HANDLES THE JURY TRIAL

I. SELECTION OF JURORS

First, I will focus on the ideal jury composition from the perspective of an attorney defending a client charged with age discrimination.

The attorney first meets potential jurors during pre-trial voir dire examination. The federal courts, and most state courts, permit attorneys to examine potential jurors by voir dire. In some states, only the judge may examine potential jurors, however, it is hoped that the judge's questions would be as probing as those posed by counsel for the respective parties. In any case where defense counsel controls voir dire, counsel is aware that it serves two essential purposes. First, voir dire enables defense counsel to uncover bias, prejudice, and hostility on the part of the potential juror, which may indicate that he is unable or unwilling to vote in favor of the defendant, even before he hears the relevant testimony. Second, voir dire examination is used by experienced counsel to educate the juror as to the issues presented by the case and, more important, to extract from the juror a commitment that he will set aside his prejudices and vote fairly, based on the evidence presented.

With respect to the first function of voir dire -- uncovering the juror's biases -- defense counsel in an age discrimination case will attempt to eliminate certain types of jurors who may be expected to be predisposed to render an unfavorable verdict. From the defendant's standpoint, certain types of jurors are typically avoided.

The most difficult problem is whether older persons should be eliminated from the jury. Older working persons and retirees constitute a large proportion of the population and retirees generally have more time to spend on jury duty than persons in other age groups. For this reason, defense counsel is often faced with a large number of potential jurors who are approximately the same age as plaintiff. Should counsel attempt to eliminate such persons from the jury? As a general matter, defense counsel often finds the older jurors may be more tolerant of a plaintiff's shortcomings and so may be sympathetic to a plaintiff even if the employer presents strong evidence of, for example, poor job performance. However, in both age discrimination and other cases, I have observed that, because older jurors may be predisposed to be sympathetic to the plaintiff, they become plaintiff's opponent simply because they wish to appear impartial. Thus, if there is one older person on the jury, he or she may be less inclined than other, younger jurors to find in favor of plaintiff. The same reasoning applies if there are two older persons on the jury. And, an older person who is independent and cantankerous may be predisposed to cast his vote against a plaintiff who he views as not having been strong enough to deal with the corporate defendant. However, defense counsel should generally avoid having more than two older persons on the jury, because, finding strength in numbers, three or more older jurors may throw aside the cloak of impartiality and, based on their sympathy for plaintiff, attempt to convince their counterparts that the plaintiff was not at fault, no matter how egregious his conduct.

There are a few other types of jurors that defendant's counsel will typically seek to eliminate. As you might suspect, we routinely challenge jurors who have a history of employment problems, nor do we look with favor upon employees who have themselves filed employment discrimination cases against their companies, or who have otherwise been involved in litigation as plaintiffs or on behalf of plaintiffs. In addition, union members may be more sympathetic to the plaintiff who is battling a corporation than other jurors. Jurors who appear prejudiced against corporations should also be challenged. And, a juror who is infirm, even if not aged, may be predisposed to vote against the defendant. Careful questioning by defense counsel should expose the juror's biases and provide the basis for a challenge.

By comparison, defense counsel *will* attempt to have certain types of jurors impanelled. These may include younger workers (who may be predisposed to believe that plaintiff was unable to properly perform his or her job duties); lower-income workers (who may be less likely to render a substantial award of damages); and, as noted, the fiercely independent older person who may not wish to be identified with his other, aging counterparts. Defense counsel may also welcome jurors employed as nurses (who are, by training, not swayed by recitals of pain and suffering, even by the elderly), claims adjusters (who regularly handle inflated if not untruthful claims against corporations), and other persons such as accountants, scientists, and technicians, who counsel has reason to believe will assess the facts logically without permitting sympathy for the aged plaintiff to influence their decision. Moreover, defense counsel usually favors jurors who are well-educated, can identify with management, and are cognizant of the difficulties inherent in reaching any business decision. Such jurors may more readily accept defendant's proferred reason for discharging a plaintiff, which can be crucial to a defendant whose case rests upon the defense of business justification. By the same token, such jurors will also be less likely to find defendant guilty simply because, in the same circumstances, they would have made a different decision.

Every defense attorney is keenly aware that the elimination of jurors who are sympathetic to plaintiff may also serve to reduce the amount of damages awarded even in the event of an unfavorable verdict.

Of course, the only way for defense counsel to ascertain potential biases is to pose direct questions to the potential juror during voir dire. This is not time to be polite, or to pose questions in a roundabout or circumspect manner, as it is defense counsel's only opportunity to ensure that the triers of fact are not predisposed to vote against his client. Only careful, probing examination by counsel can uncover whether, for example, the juror harbors a bias against corporations, or whether his or her spouse is a union member who has, over the years, inculcated the juror with his or her views. By the same token, effective voir dire can uncover the fact that although the juror himself is aged, he subconsciously views his age as indicative of weakness, and will for that reason be predisposed to believe that the plaintiff was in fact unable to perform his job.

The second function of voir dire -- education of the jury -- is also of paramount importance in an age discrimination case. Here, defense counsel will attempt to extract from the juror a promise that he will decide the case fairly, based on the evidence presented, and not according to any preconceived notions, biases, or hostilities. In this way, defense counsel can protect his client even if, for some reason, he elects not to challenge the juror. The potential juror must be asked, point blank, if he can reach an equitable decision. Few persons would answer such a question in the negative, and therefore each juror will, through the course of the trial, remember and be guided by his promise to be impartial. Having made such a promise, it is unlikely that the juror will be controlled by his biases when he enters the jury room to discuss the case and his verdict.

II. SELECTION AND PREPARATION OF EXPERT AND NON-EXPERT WITNESS

In every case, whether or not based upon age discrimination, defense counsel's most important task is to discredit the testimony offered by plaintiff and his witnesses. This task is more difficult in any age case, because the plaintiff may appear to be a helpless victim. For this reason, defense counsel must choose those witnesses who will have the greatest persuasive effect on the jury, which will ultimately decide whether to accept or reject the witnesses' testimony.

The expert witness, on the other hand, must be able to convince the jury that certain inferences should be drawn from the facts, and counsel's case will be weakened to the extent that the expert is unable to convince the jurors to draw the desired inferences.

One source of expert witnesses is specialists with whom the corporate personnel department interfaces on a regular basis. Such persons might include, for example, industrial psychologists. However, when it comes time to prepare for trial, the strengths of the expert must be carefully assessed, and a different expert witness sought if it appears that the one most familiar to you will not be a convincing witness.

In an age discrimination case, the age of the expert witness is of extreme importance. Jurors generally tend to give greater weight to the testimony of older witnesses and, in an age case, the expert may be one of few defense witnesses who is approximately the same age as plaintiff. Therefore, it is even more likely that experienced counsel can use the expert's testimony to discredit that offered by plaintiff.

Even if the expert is not an older person, the defense will attempt to establish that his credentials, background, and experience dictate that his opinions be seriously considered by the jury. Thus, defense counsel will often call an expert witness who is a recognized specialist in his field, or who has taught others in his field. These factors, together with the expert's demeanor and mature appearance, are as important as his chronological age.

Defense counsel will have had an opportunity to assess the expert's value as a witness during the course of preparation for trial. Here, it should be noted that evidence gathered by an expert who has been retained by defendant to prepare for litigation, but is not to be used at trial, can be discovered by plaintiff only upon a showing of exceptional circumstances, 1/ and at least one court has held that not even the expert's name need be divulged absent such a showing. 2/ In addition, neither the name nor the opinion of an expert witness who has been only informally consulted can be discovered. For these reasons, defense counsel must make judicious use of expert witnesses. For trial purposes, his foremost task is to identify those experts who are most likely to favorably impress the jury. Other experts, including those not chosen as witnesses, can be called

---

1/ Fed. R. Civ. Proc. 26(b)(4)(B). The rule incorporates an additional exception set forth in Fed. R. Civ. Proc. 35(b), relating to physical and mental examinations.

2/ Perry v. W.S. Darley & Co., 54 F.R.D. 278 (E.D. Wis. 1971). But see Baki v. B. F. Diamond Constr. Co., 71 F.R.D. 179 (D. Md. 1976) (names and addresses of experts retained in preparation for trial but who were not expected to testify were held discoverable without any special showing of exceptional circumstances in the absence of some indication that the information was irrelevant, privileged, or for some other reason should not be disclosed); Sea Colony, Inc. v. Continental Ins. Co., 63 F.R.D. 113 (D. Del. 1974) (where only the identity of an expert witness not intended to be used at trial is sought, exceptional circumstances need not be shown.).

upon to assist in the preparation for trial, and the material they gather may not be discoverable.

With respect to non-expert witnesses, defense counsel often has a choice among the many persons involved in the action taken against plaintiff, usually personal representatives, various management officials, and perhaps plaintiff's co-workers. Clearly, counsel will seek those witnesses who are best able to present the corporate defendant in its best light, namely, those who can most clearly articulate the non-discriminatory rationale for the action taken. To the extent that these witnesses are younger employees, counsel may have no choice but to call them. In all age cases, however, counsel must attempt to present mature witnesses. The advantages of this approach are threefold. First, such witnesses make clear to the jury that the defendant employs older persons in responsible positions. Second, such witnesses may evoke as much or more sympathy from the jury than the plaintiff. Finally, mature, seasoned witnesses may be better able to articulate the reasons for the actions taken against plaintiff, and for that reason their testimony is more likely to be credited by the jury.

I'd like to make one final note that concerns the preparation of non-expert witnesses that is especially relevant to age cases. In any jury trial, counsel cautions his witnesses not to exaggerate or overstate their case because such testimony is easily discredited upon cross examination and the jury will readily surmise that if the witness has exaggerated on one point, he has exaggerated others. In an age case, this will increase the jury's suspicion of the defendant and increase the likelihood that it will view the plaintiff's claims sympathetically. Thus, for example, if it is alleged that the plaintiff was discharged for poor work performance, defendant should stick to the justification clearly supported by documentary evidence and the testimony presented by its witnesses. Any puffery will indelibly harm defendant's case.

III. PRESENTATION OF THE CASE

One problem faced by every defendant is the fact that plaintiff usually opens and closes the case. Thus, plaintiff has the first and last opportunity to impress the jury with his analysis of the facts and to answer the arguments put forth by defendant. Moreover, as every defendant's counsel is keenly aware, once the jurors come to understand the basis of plaintiff's case, they may be reluctant to give any thought to defendant's point of view. And, jurors may resent what they view as defendant's attempt to confuse them.

For these reasons, in an age case, defendant's counsel must take advantage of every opportunity to clearly explain the theories upon which he relies, and to point out the weaknesses in his opponent's case.

A. The Opening Statement

Counsel's opening statement is extremely important in any case tried before a jury, perhaps more so in an action under the ADEA. A successful opening statement sets the stage for the remainder of counsel's case. This is counsel's first opportunity to acquaint the jury with his client's position, the issues involved, and the proof that must be established if either party is to prevail. Defense counsel will use his opening statement to succinctly advise the jury that the burden of proof is always with the plaintiff and, if the plaintiff fails to establish a prima facie case, that is, if he does not carry his burden, the jury cannot render a verdict in plaintiff's favor, even if the plaintiff has given sympathy-evoking testimony and even if the jury does not agree with management's decision concerning plaintiff. Moreover, defense counsel can use the opening statement as an opportunity to introduce the jury to the corporate decision-making process and thereby increase the chances that the jury will lend credence to the reason given by the employer in support of the action taken against the plaintiff.

At the same time, defense counsel can, if he chooses, use the opening statement to introduce the jury to the employer's witnesses. Particularly if counsel's intended witnesses are mature persons, this early introduction will impress the jurors with the fact that the corporation employs older people in responsible positions.

At the end of his opening statement, then, counsel will have outlined the intent of the statute, explained plaintiff's burden of proof as it relates to the facts at hand, and reviewed defendant's position and made clear why the defenses offered will prevent plaintiff from establishing a prima facie case. Defense counsel may also use the opening statement to make the jurors more comfortable with his own witnesses and, in this way, make them more willing to credit their testimony.

B. The Closing Statement

When defense counsel makes his closing argument, he will take advantage of his last opportunity before the jury retires to present his client's case. Thus, counsel will redefine the issues involved -- a tactic of great importance in an age discrimination case, where the jury may remain unfamiliar with the legal issues involved even after all of the evidence is in. Counsel may also summarize the testimony given by his witnesses and attempt to persuade the jury that their testimony is credible. At the same time, defense counsel will explain how his witnesses' testimony undermines plaintiff's case. In this way defense counsel can reiterate and reinforce the intent of the statute in the minds of the jurors. The defense can also use its closing argument to remind the jurors that his witnesses testified to legitimate, non-discriminatory reasons for the action taken against plaintiff. It is important to note that, even if the employer is adjudged guilty, the jury will not levy punitive damages if it is convinced that the employer's actions were not willful or in reckless disregard of plaintiff's rights. A convincing closing argument (combined, of course, with credible and persuasive testimony) may, therefore, prevent the imposition of an award of liquidated damages.

If the jurors have been asked to answer specific interrogatories, defense counsel, in his closing argument, should address the issues that are the subject of these interrogatories. Here, again, defense counsel will take this opportunity to convince the jurors that his point of view warrants their serious consideration.

Finally, in an age discrimination case, counsel must, in making his closing argument, consider whether, and to what extent, he should vigorously attack the plaintiff himself. Counsel may find that a more effective tactic is to emphasize the strength of his own case, rather than to attack a plaintiff who may be viewed by the jurors as the victim of corporate policy-making. Of course, counsel's decision in this regard will be based upon his assessment of plaintiff's demeanor and the jurors' reactions to his testimony.

IV. SELECTING APPROPRIATE JURY INSTRUCTIONS

In any jury case, the court's instructions to the jurors will normally include an explanation of the nature of the action, the issues involved, and what plaintiff and defendant must prove in order to prevail. The judge will also explain the purpose of the statute under which the case arises. Such explanation is of extreme importance in a case under the ADEA, for its must be made clear to the jurors that that statute is not designed to give older workers greater rights than their younger counterparts, rather, its purpose is to insure that older workers are not denied employment or advancement solely because of their age. 3/ In addition, the judge will cover the application of the law to the facts of the case, and explain the court's role (making findings of law), as compared to that of the jury, (making findings of fact). The judge will also highlight for the jury the facts that are not in dispute, for, to the extent that the parties have been able to stipulate to material facts (or where it is clear from the testimony that there are no issues with respect to a particular element of the case), the jury's job is

---

3/ Cova v. Coca-Cola Bottling Co., 574 F.2d 958, 960 (8th Cir. 1978) ("The [ADEA] does not require that advanced age and substantial length of service entitle employees to special favorable consideration"); EEOC v. Air Line Pilots Ass'n., 489 F. Supp. 1003, 1005 (D. Minn. 1980) ("ADEA does not require that older employees receive preferential treatment over younger employees").

made easier and it can focus on the issues in dispute, which are likely to be dispositive of the case.

Finally, the court's charge to the jurors will also include an explanation of the burden of proof, a matter which we'll discuss in a moment, inferences which may be drawn by the jury, which I'll also return to, weight of the evidence, witness credibility, and damages.

Under Rule 51 of the Federal Rules of Civil Procedure, counsel may file a written request for certain jury instructions at or prior to the close of the evidence. Prior to the closing argument, the court will inform counsel of its ruling on proper instructions. Any objections to the court's instructions must be made before the jury retires, or the objections to the claimed error are waived.

With respect to the jury instructions that defense counsel in an age case will seek, I will focus on the case where plaintiff claims to have been discharged because of his or her age. In such cases, the central question which must be put to the jurors is whether plaintiff was discharged because of his age. No matter how sympathetic the jury may be to plaintiff's situation, and even if the jurors themselves would have taken a different course of action, unless it can find that the employer terminated him because of his age, it must find for the defendant. 4/

The jury instruction must also take into account the parties' respective burdens of proof, and defense counsel should propose an instruction that clearly sets forth the relative burdens. Let's take the "classic" age case in which plaintiff has proven that he is in the protected category, competently performed his work, was fired, and was replaced by a younger worker. 5/ We will assume that defendant has attempted to disprove plaintiff's case by showing that the discharge was for a reason other than age. The jury must be instructed that defendant is not required to prove that its actions were motivated by a factor other than age. Rather, the employer

---

4/ See, e.g., Spagnuolo v. Whirlpool Corp., 641 F.2d 1109, 1112 (4th Cir.), cert. denied, 50 U.S.L.W. 3248 (1981); Kelly v. American Standard, Inc., 640 F.2d 974, 984 (9th Cir. 1981); Bentley v. Stromberg-Carlson Corp., 638 F.2d 9, 11-12 (2d Cir. 1981); Loeb v. Textron, Inc., 600 F.2d 1003, 1019 (1st Cir. 1979).

5/ See, e.g., Douglas v. Anderson, 27 FEP Cases 47 (9th Cir. 1981); Price v. Maryland Cas. Co., 561 F.2d 609 (5th Cir. 1977); Erwin v. Bank of Mississippi, 512 F. Supp. 545 (N.D. Miss. 1981); Sills v. Fort Pitt Steel Casting Co., 24 FEP Cases 927 (W.D. Pa. 1979).

satisfies its burden by simply articulating a legitimate, nondiscriminatory reason for the discharge. 6/ Once the employer has stated a valid reason, plaintiff may then attempt to show that the proferred reason is pretextual. 7/ However, the point remains that the jury must understand that the employer's stated justification, if credible and supported by other relevant evidence, is sufficient to sustain the employer's burden of proof and destroy plaintiff's case.

If there is any dispute as to what facts each party must prove, counsel should suggest to the court that the jurors be required to answer separately whether that fact has been proven, in order to minimize the need for a new trial if, on appeal, it is found that proof of such fact is essential.

Moreover, if the employer offers a business justification for the discharge, the jury must be instructed that the *sole* focus of its inquiry is whether the employer's decision was unlawfully motivated. The jury need not agree with the employer's decision, but it cannot find discrimination simply because it feels that the employer's decision was incorrect. 8/ Such an instruction is especially important in a case where the

---

6/ See, e.g., Smith v. Farah Mfg. Co., 650 F.2d 64, 67 (5th Cir. 1981); Goodman v. Heublein, Inc., 645 F.2d 127, 130 (2d Cir. 1981); Smith v. University of North Carolina, 632 F.2d 316, 332-33 (4th Cir. 1980); Marshall v. Westinghouse Elec. Corp., 576 F.2d 588, 592 (5th Cir. 1978); Price v. Maryland Cas. Co., 561 F.2d at 612; Marshall v. Arlene Knitwear, Inc., 454 F. Supp. 715, 728-29 (E.D.N.Y. 1978), modified, 608 F.2d 1369 (2d Cir. 1979). Accord (under Title VII): Texas Dept. of Community Affairs v. Burdine, 450 U.S. 248, 253-56 (1981); Board of Trustees of Keene State College v. Sweeney, 439 U.S. 24, 25 n. 2 (1978).

7/ See, e.g., Smith v. Farah Mfg. Co., 650 F.2d at 68; Loeb v. Textron, Inc., 600 F.2d at 1012. Accord (under Title VII): Texas Dept. of Community Affairs v. Burdine, 450 U.S. at 256; McDonnell Douglas Corp. v. Green, 411 U.S. 792, 804-05 (1973).

8/ In Loeb v. Textron, Inc., 600 F.2d at 1012 n. 6, the court noted:
> The employer's stated legitimate reason must be reasonably articulated and nondiscriminatory, but does not have to be a reason that the judge or jurors would act on or approve. . . . An employer is entitled to make his own policy and business judgments, and may, for example, fire an adequate employee if his reason is to hire one who will be even better, as long as this is not a pretext for discrimination.

plaintiff is able to show that the employer incorrectly assessed his competence but there is no evidence that the employer did so because of plaintiff's age. This problem typically arises where, for example, the employer's records are incomplete and supervisor's testimony fails to establish plaintiff's incompetence. Here, the jury must be instructed that, unless it finds unlawful motivation, the employer cannot be found guilty simply because its business judgment was incorrect. Of course, the reasonableness of the employer's action may be probative of whether the reason it offers is pretextual, and defense counsel will endeavor to clearly explain its actions in a way that the jury will understand. However, the jury must receive clear instructions that it may not, in assessing the reason for discharge offered by the employer, substitute its judgment for the business judgment of the employer. These considerations are especially pertinent if the plaintiff held a managerial position, where his performance was judged by a number of objective, subjective, and perhaps technical criteria best assessed by those who have actual experience in plaintiff's field.

Similar principles apply where the defense contends that age is a bona fide occupational qualification for the position in question. 9/ This defense is often employed in cases where the plaintiff's job is one involving the safety of third parties. Thus, in one case involving bus drivers, the employer, to establish a BFOQ, relied primarily on a federal agency finding, reached after a full hearing, that it was not possible to rely on facts other than age to predict the onset of physical ailments that could endanger passengers. The court in this case noted that, where the safety of third parties is involved, the jury should not be permitted to speculate on the sufficiency of medical evidence as to the reasonable necessity of the employer's rule. The court reasoned that, if permitted to so speculate, different juries could reach different conclusions, and third

---

9/ However, the establishment of an age-related BFOQ has been treated by the courts as an affirmative defense, thereby requiring the employer to carry the burden of persuasion on that issue. See, e.g., Marshall v. Westinghouse Elec. Corp., 576 F.2d at 591; Arritt v. Grisell, 567 F.2d 1267, 1271 (4th Cir. 1977); Houghton v. McDonnell Douglas Corp., 553 F.2d 561, 564 (8th Cir.), cert. denied, 434 U.S. 966 (1977); Laugesen v. Anaconda Co., 510 F.2d 307, 313 (6th Cir. 1975). The other defenses available under the Age Discrimination in Employment Act, such as discipline or discharge for good cause and differentiations based on reasonable factors other than age or a bona fide seniority or benefit plan, merely require that the employer produce some evidence. Smith v. Farah Mfg. Co., 650 F.2d at 67. See also Marshall v. Westinghouse Elec. Corp., 576 F.2d at 591-92; Marshall v. Goodyear Tire & Rubber Co., 554 F.2d 730, 736 (5th Cir. 1977).

party interests would not be adequately protected. Thus, in safety cases, as well, the court must limit the jury's ability to substitute its own judgment for that of the employer, and defense counsel must seek an instruction to that effect.

In a "mixed motive" case where the plaintiff establishes that age was one of a number of factors that lead to his discharge, the court must inform the jury that, unless age was the proximate cause of plaintiff's discharge, the employer has not violated the ADEA. In "mixed motive" cases, unless the plaintiff can show that age was the determinative factor, he cannot prevail, and the jury must understand that, if other legitimate factors predominated, the employer is not liable. 10/ Defense counsel must seek such an instruction, otherwise the jury may not weight the other factors involved in the employer's determination, and find the defendant guilty even if age played but a small part in the discharge.

I'd like to focus for a moment on another problem that defense counsel often face -- the non-production of relevant records or necessary witnesses. The defense often finds that employer records have been destroyed or not adequately or consistently compiled, or that witnesses whose testimony is relevant to the case have left the defendant's employ, and would be unwilling (and perhaps hostile) witnesses, even if subpoenaed.

In this case, plaintiff will seek an instruction under which the jury is told that certain inferences may be drawn from defendant's failure to produce. Here, the defense must make sure that the jury is adequately instructed as to what inferences it may draw.

First, an appropriate instruction must include the fact that the jurors can, but need not, draw any inferences from defendant's failure to produce records, made in the ordinary course of business, over which it has custody.

Next, the jury must be instructed to consider the reasons for non-production. If the employer has shown that a particular witness is, for example, disabled or senile or left defendant's employ under questionable circumstances not relevant to the case and would be a hostile witness because he is biased against the defendant, the jurors must be instructed to take this into account before deciding whether to draw an inference against the employer. Thus, in a case where the defense showed that certain

---

10/ See Spagnuolo v. Whirlpool Corp., 641 F.2d at 1112; Kelly v. American Standard, Inc., 640 F.2d at 984; Bentley v. Stromberg-Carlson Corp., 638 F.2d at 12; Smithers v. Bailar, 629 F.2d 892, 897-98 (3d Cir. 1980); Loeb v. Textron, Inc., 600 F.2d at 1019-20; and Cleverly v. Western Elec. Co., 594 F.2d 638, 641 (8th Cir. 1979).

records had been destroyed in a move to new corporate headquarters and were only tangentially relevant to plaintiff's claim, no negative inferences were drawn from defendant's failure to produce those records.

Finally, defense counsel will request that the court explain what inferences may be drawn. In the absence of direct evidence, the jurors cannot speculate as to what the missing document or witness would have said. Rather, the jury must be told that it can give strong weight to evidence already in the case in favor of the other side.

As concerns inferences, one other point is important. Defense counsel must seek an instruction to the effect that no inference of discrimination can be drawn from the fact that plaintiff was replaced by a younger worker. Such an inference could easily be drawn in a Title VII case where a black worker is replaced by a white employee. In age cases, however, defense counsel can argue that the nature of the job market is such that older workers are constantly being replaced by younger ones, therefore, plaintiff cannot prove discrimination simply upon a showing that his replacement is younger than plaintiff or not within the protected category. This view has been approved by the courts and is clearly an appropriate jury instruction. 11/ As concerns the jury, such an instruction not only helps defendant to negate a charge of improper motive, but also puts the fact of a younger replacement in its proper perspective, as the jury will understand that, even if plaintiff had voluntarily left his job, he probably would have been replaced by a younger person.

V. PRESENTATION OF THE CASE SO AS TO MINIMIZE DAMAGES

First, I will discuss a matter that is also relevant to appropriate jury instructions. As you are aware, the ADEA authorizes the award of liquidate damages in an amount equal to lost wages _if_ the violation was found to have been "willful." The courts have held that, to establish the willfulness of a violation, a plaintiff does not have to show that the defendant knowingly acted in violation of the ADEA. Rather, the plaintiff need only establish that defendant knew or had reason to know that his conduct was governed by that statute. Moreover, a finding of willfulness is not restricted to a case where defendant intentionally violated the statute; it is enough to show that plaintiff was discharged because of his age _and_ that this action was not accidental, mistaken, or inadvertent. In

---

11/ See, e.g., Laugesen v. Anaconda Co., 510 F.2d at 313 ("in the usual case, absent any discriminatory intent, discharged employees will more often than not be replaced by those younger than they, for older employees are constantly moving out of the labor market, while younger ones move in").

most cases, it will probably be futile to attempt to persuade the jury that the employer was unaware of the existence of a statute protecting workers in the 40-70 age category. Thus, to avoid an award of liquidated damages, the defense must attempt to establish that the employer did not willfully violate the statute. This can be accomplished only if defense counsel makes sure that the jury is given an appropriate definition of "willful" by the court. 12/

In order to avoid a liquidated damages award, the defense must show that the employer's actions, even if found to have been discriminatory, were not so arbitrary, or taken with such callous disregard of plaintiff's rights that liquidated damages should be awarded. In a recent case tried in the federal court in New York, the jury was so impressed with the unfairness of the employer's performance review procedures that it awarded liquidated damages even though the defendant arguably acted more out of ignorance than malice. The point here is that, even if the defense is unable to prove that it did not discriminate, counsel must present witnesses who can clearly explain the reasons underlying the action taken against plaintiff *and* counsel must introduce the documents on which it relies in a manner calculated to convince the jury that personnel actions were taken based upon uniform standards evenhandedly applied to all employees.

With respect to jury instructions, the defense should request that jurors be told that a "willful" violation is made out only where the conduct complained of was intentional, knowing, and voluntary or in negligent disregard of plaintiff's rights. A charge defining "willful" based on any lesser standard increases the possibility that defendant will be found to have willfully violated the statute and thus be liable for liquidated damages. To this end, defense counsel may also request that the jurors answer a special interrogatory concerning the definition of "willfulness" to ensure that the jurors fully understand that term.

I will also touch briefly on reinstatement as a remedy under the ADEA. The employer will often ask the court to deny reinstatement, even to a successful plaintiff, particularly where defendant feels that to do so would jeopardize employee morale or otherwise adversely affect its business. If the defense intends

---

12/ For definitions of "willful," see Syvock v. Milwaukee Boiler Mfg. Co., 233 Daily Lab. Rep. D-1, D-2 to D-3 (7th Cir. 1981); Hedrick v. Hercules, Inc., 658 F.2d 1088, 1095-96 (5th Cir. 1981); Spagnuolo v. Whirlpool Corp., 641 F.2d 1109, 1114 (4th Cir.), cert. denied, 50 U.S.L.W. 3248 (1981); Loeb v. Textron, Inc., 600 F.2d 1003, 1020 (1st Cir. 1979); Coates v. National Cash Register Co., 433 F. Supp. 655, 664 (W.D. Va. 1977).

to argue against reinstatement, it must tailor its proof accordingly. Thus, in a recent case, the employer put on no evidence concerning the employee's lack of qualifications, nor did it show that tensions between the parties were so high that they could not work together. Plaintiff, on the other hand, showed that he was discharged because of his age and not for any other reason. Under these facts, it was found that plaintiff was entitled to reinstatement. To be sure, even if counsel cannot prove that his client has not discriminated against plaintiff, this case suggests that, to lessen the breadth of damages levied against his client, counsel must introduce evidence tending to negate plaintiff's claim that reinstatement is an appropriate remedy.

HANDLING AGE DISCRIMINATION LITIGATION:
TRIAL TACTICS FROM THE PERSPECTIVE OF PLAINTIFF'S COUNSEL

Joseph Guerrieri, Jr., Esquire*

---

*   Member, Highsaw & Mahoney, P.C.; formerly Assistant United States Attorney for the District of Columbia, serving in the Criminal, Appellate and Civil Divisions; Attorney General's Advocacy Institute, Trial Advocate Program; Mr. Guerrieri received a Bachelor of Arts degree from the University of Michigan in 1969 and a Juris Doctor degree with honors from the National Law Center of George Washington University in 1972. He served as law clerk to the Hon. Nicholas S. Nunzio, Associate Judge, Superior Court of the District of Columbia.

TABLE OF CONTENTS

		Page
I.	INTRODUCTION	1
II.	RIGHT TO A JURY TRIAL	1
	A. The Jury Demand	2
	B. Selection of Federal Jury Panels	2
III.	VOIR DIRE EXAMINATION AND CHALLENGES	3
	A. Challenges for Favor or Cause	6
	B. Peremptory Challenges	6
	C. The Impaneling Process	7
	D. Voir Dire Tactics and Strategy	7
IV.	PRELIMINARY MATTERS	9
	A. Swearing and Preliminary Instructions	9
	B. Invocation of the Rule on Witnesses	9
V.	EVIDENTIARY REQUIREMENTS: THE PRIMA FACIE CASE AND THE RESPECTIVE BURDENS OF PROOF AND PERSUASION UNDER THE ADEA	10
VI.	OPENING STATEMENT	11
VII.	PREPARING A WITNESS	13
VIII.	THE USE OF STATISTICS IN AGE DISCRIMINATION CLAIMS	14
IX.	EXPERT WITNESS	17
X.	DAMAGES AND REMEDIES	18
	A. Back Pay	18
	B. Liquidated Damages	20
	C. Damages for Pain and Suffering	20
	D. Punitive Damages	21
	E. Affirmative and Injunctive Relief	21
XI.	SUMMATION	22
	A. Structuring of the Final Argument	23
	B. Selecting a Theme for the Case	23
	C. Simplifying Issues	24
	D. Preparation for Summation in Voir Dire	24
	E. Preparation for Summation During Direct and Cross-Examination	24
	F. Arguing Damages	25
XII.	JURY INSTRUCTIONS AND INTERROGATORIES	26

HANDLING AGE DISCRIMINATION LITIGATION:
TRIAL TACTICS FROM THE PERSPECTIVE OF PLAINTIFF'S COUNSEL

I. INTRODUCTION

This paper is intended to assist plaintiff's counsel in the trial of cases brought pursuant to the Age Discrimination in Employment Act of 1967, as amended. 1/ While its focus is on jury trial tactics and procedures from a plaintiff's perspective, many of the observations apply with equal force to cases tried to the court alone.

II. RIGHT TO A JURY TRIAL

Unlike plaintiffs in Title VII suits, a private Age Discrimination in Employment Act (ADEA) litigant is entitled to a jury trial. Next to the passage of the Act itself, perhaps the greatest boon to older Americans has been the right to a jury trial in age discrimination cases. As a general rule, the right to a jury trial in age discrimination cases benefits the plaintiff. This is so because jurors in age cases tend to empathize with the plaintiff and draw upon their own experiences in aging in employment. A jury of one's peers is more apt to be moved by the humiliation and genuine human suffering that is incurred by an individual who has been deprived of his livelihood because of his age. Accordingly, juries are more amenable to finding a willful violation of the Act thus entitling the plaintiff to liquidated damages in addition to back pay and benefits.

Even prior to the 1978 amendments to the Act 2/ specifically authorizing a right to a jury trial in age discrimination cases, the Supreme Court held that the reference to "legal" relief entitled the plaintiff to a jury trial in an ADEA case as contrasted with a Title VII litigant who is only entitled to "equitable" relief which must be determined by the court alone. 3/ However, the right to a jury trial does not exist for federal employees in age discrimination cases. 4/ The Court's holding is not surprising for it has been long settled that the Seventh Amendment right to a jury trial does not apply to actions against the federal government. When the federal government

---

1/ 29 U.S.C. § 621-634.

2/ 29 U.S.C. § 626(c) (Supp. II, 1978).

3/ See Lorrilard v. Pons, 434 U.S. 575 (1978).

4/ Lehman v. Makshian, ___ U.S. ___, 26 FEP Cases ___ (1981).

waived its immunity from suit as it did in the ADEA, 6/ it did not specifically submit to trial by jury. 7/

While private plaintiffs in age cases should generally demand a trial by jury, this should by no means be a mechanical approach to litigating ADEA claims. One must consider the composition of the community from which the jury will be drawn. There are a number of instances in which one might be better off trying a case to the court alone. It may be that a particular plaintiff simply does not have jury appeal. A manager of an adult book store may not fare well before a jury in some communities. A supervisor who himself or herself was responsible for the termination of employees may not gain the sympathy of the jury. It may be prudent to waive a jury trial and hope that the court will view your client more dispassionately. Moreover, the track record in age discrimination cases of the particular United States District Court judge to whom your case has been assigned will be of substantial interest to you when determining whether to exercise your right to a jury trial.

A. The Jury Demand

It is critical that if a plaintiff decides to exercise the right to a jury trial counsel serve a demand therefor upon the other parties in the action. 8/ The demand must be written and should be "endorsed upon a pleading." It is the better practice to interpose the demand at the conclusion of the pleading or on a separate form. It is important to consult the local rules in the District Court in which you are planning to file your civil action to determine how the jury demand must be put forth. To be effective under the Federal Rules, the demand must be served upon the other parties "at any time after the commencement of the action and not later than ten days after the service of the last pleading directed to such issues." Additional time is provided for service by mail. Failure to serve a timely demand in the mode required by Civil Rule 38(b) will result in a waiver of the right to have any issue so neglected tried to a jury.

B. Selection of Federal Jury Panels

The selection of persons to serve as jurors in the federal courts is governed exclusively by federal law. The Jury Selection and Service Act of 1968 had as its fundamental purpose the elimination of discrimination in federal jury selection and

---

6/   29 U.S.C. § 633(a).

7/   Lehman v. Makshian, ___ U.S. ___, 26 FEP Cases ____ (1981).

8/   See Rule 38(b), Fed. R. Civ. P.

service. The Act implemented a random selection of jurors in such a manner as to produce a jury venire which constitutes a fair cross section of the community in the district or division wherein the court sits. 9/ There is no requirement that every jury panel proportionately represent every recognized group in the district or division wherein the court is held. It is sufficient that each qualified citizen has the "opportunity to be considered for service" on grand or petit juries. 10/ The names of prospective jurors are to be selected from voter registration lists or lists of actual voters or other official lists of eligible voters for the political subdivision within the district or division. In those districts or divisions where voter lists do not constitute a fair cross section of the community, the Act authorizes the use of other lists in addition to the voter lists to ensure the representative cross section. The plan may specify occupational classes or groups whose members shall be exempt from jury service. Such exemption must be based on a finding by the district court that it is in the public interest and would not be inconsistent with the Act. Generally, persons over the age of 70 are exempted from jury service. However, such persons are not automatically excluded but rather, may be excluded upon request.

While the jury selection process would seem to produce jury panels which represent a true cross section of the community, such is not always the case. In some communities, excusal from jury service such as in the case of women with young children, persons in the military service or in certain other occupations, or those excused for other reasons, tends to cause the average age of prospective jurors who actually serve to be generally older. There also tends to be a disproportionate number of retired persons who serve as jurors.

III. VOIR DIRE EXAMINATION AND CHALLENGES

In the federal courts, wide discretion is vested in the trial judge as to the method of examination of jurors. Rule 47 of the Federal Rules of Civil Procedure authorizes the court "(a) to conduct the examination of prospective jurors, or (b) to permit the parties or their attorneys to supplement it by such further inquiry as it deems proper, or submit to the prospective jurors such additional questions of the parties or their attorneys as it deems proper." It is important to note that the availability before trial of the list of veniremen or prospective jurors varies widely. In many of the United States District Courts, the lists of veniremen are available to attorneys and to the public before trial, but in some districts they are provided by rule of court but the names of veniremen are not to be made

---

9/ 28 U.S.C. § 1861.

10/ Id.

public except upon order of the court. Obviously, if one has the lists of the veniremen substantially in advance of the trial, one may be able to determine that juror's voting record on other juries, juror's occupation and age, and other relevant data about his or her background that might have impact on their decision. In many jurisdictions, the list itself will indicate the prospective juror's name, address, age, and occupation. This information alone is of substantial assistance in determining which jurors to strike from the panel.

A study by the Judicial Conference Committee on the operation of the jury system indicates that a substantial majority of federal district judges personally conduct the voir dire. However, an opportunity is given to counsel to submit supplemental questions. Some judges require that such questions be submitted before the voir dire, but most who employ this method allow counsel to suggest questions before the examination begins and immediately after the judge has completed his questioning. A fair number of courts, and many here in the District of Columbia, allow counsel to address supplemental questions directly to the jurors after the court has done so. In other jurisdictions, voir dires are handled exclusively by the judge or exclusively by counsel. It generally takes about one hour to impanel a jury in a civil case.

The scope of the voir dire examination is largely within the discretion of the trial judge. The trial judge should conduct the examination as extensively as possible to determine if a cause for challenge exists and to advise counsel as to the best exercise of their peremptory challenges. Courts are generally solicitous of the reasonable requests of counsel for questions to the jurors. The failure to ask a question cannot serve as a basis for claim of error in the absence of a request, but a court subjects itself to possible reversal on appeal if it refuses to ask questions which had been properly requested. It has been held that questions about racial prejudice, prior service on certain types of cases, and membership in certain organizations should be asked if proper request is made.

In preparing questions for voir dire, counsel's primary objective is the impaneling of a fair and impartial jury that will reach a decision free from bias or prejudice against his/her client. Additionally, counsel must be cognizant of the fact that an advance favorable portrayal of your case can be made during voir dire. Moreover, answers given in voir dire may be effectively utilized in summation as will be discussed in greater detail later.

Whether the court conducts the voir dire or whether counsel for the parties are permitted to ask questions, plaintiff's counsel may wish to have questions like the following posed to the jury:

(1) Whether any of the prospective jurors know any of the parties, witnesses, or attorneys in the case?

(2) Whether any of the prospective jurors could not fairly and impartially sit on a case involving age discrimination?

(3) Whether any of the prospective jurors has himself or herself been involved in the termination of an employee?

(4) Whether any of the prospective jurors own their own business or are self-employed?

(5) Whether any of the prospective jurors feel that younger employees generally perform better than older employees?

(6) Whether members of the prospective jury panel believe that it is within management's prerogative to terminate, fail to promote, or fail to hire an individual because of his or her age?

(7) Whether any members of the prospective jury panel, their relatives or close friends have themselves been accused of discrimination or have been witnesses in a discrimination case or been the victims of discrimination?

(8) Whether any members of the prospective jury panel feel that they could not follow the law concerning age discrimination as the court instructs them?

(9) Whether any of the prospective jurors would give greater weight to the statements of the employer simply because he/she is the employer?

(10) Whether any of the prospective jurors knowing that the ADEA protects the age group 40-70 feel that a plaintiff in his forties deserves any less protection than anyone else?

(11) Whether any of the prospective jurors feel that they would have difficulty awarding a large money damages award if the evidence warranted such an award?

(12) Whether any of the prospective jurors feel that they would have difficulty awarding liquidated damages entitling plaintiff to a doubling of his damages if the evidence showed that defendant willfully violated the ADEA?

Remember that if there is no response to a particular voir dire question, you should state "I take by your silence your answer is 'no.'" The court reporter will thus be able to transcribe the negative response to your question.

Challenges may be made either to the array or to individual jurors. Challenges to the array go to the manner of making up the whole venire and relate to the legality of drawing, summoning, selecting, or impaneling the federal petit jury. As a practical matter, you should concern yourself with the selection of individual jurors.

A. Challenges for Favor or Cause

Each party has the right to challenge individual jurors for favor or for cause, or by peremptory challenge. If upon examination a prospective juror demonstrates some actual or implied bias or prejudice against your client or your client's case or type of case, he/she may be challenged "for favor." If a juror is absolutely disqualified as where he/she is incompetent, that juror may be challenged by either party "for cause." The term "for cause" generally encompasses both for favor and for cause.

Failure to make objections to individual jurors before their impaneling results in a conclusive waiver of the right to challenge. Challenges for favor or cause should be supported by distinct evidence so the court can properly determine the objection. The court has a broad discretion in its ruling on challenges. It is common for the trial judge *sua sponte* to excuse jurors who he/she believes are not fully qualified or may be biased. As a practical matter, federal judges are generally quite liberal in excusing prospective jurors as against whom any plausible ground for objection can be stated. Any juror who admits to possible prejudice should certainly be excused. The court is generally on firmer ground in sustaining challenges for cause which may have some merit, for there is almost never a reversal for excusing jurors for asserted cause. On the other hand, a refusal to sustain a meritorious challenge can lead to a reversal.

B. Peremptory Challenges

In civil cases, each side is entitled to three (3) peremptory challenges and several defendants or several plaintiffs may be considered as a single party for the purpose of making challenges. The court may allow additional challenges and permit them to be exercised separately or jointly. 28 U.S.C. § 1870. A peremptory challenge is a challenge to be exercised without a reason stated without inquiry and without being subject to the court's control.

C. The Impaneling Process

The mechanics of placing jurors in the box and the sequence in which the parties exercise their peremptory challenge varies. In almost all districts, the juries are impaneled in the courtroom. Where this practice prevails, the jurors are sometimes challenged directly and sometimes against the jury list. In some districts, jurors are challenged directly by the attorneys. The jurors then, of course, know who has challenged them. This practice may occasion some embarrassment to counsel and counsel should request the court to allow challenges to be done at the bench out of the hearing of the jury. In other districts where the challenge is exercised by striking the names from a list of eighteen (18) jurors in a civil case, the jurors do not know who has challenged them since the names of all jurors stricken are read off at the same time. Generally speaking, the parties exercise their challenges alternatively. In a few districts one party first exercises all his challenges then the other party exhausts his. It is thus important to know what the local practice is well in advance of trial. It is a simple matter to acquire a copy of the local rules or to inquire of the clerk in the jurisdiction in which you are practicing. In many instances, the method of impaneling jurors and the sequence in which peremptory challenges are exercised and other mechanics of jury selection are those which prevail in the courts and state in which the federal court is sitting.

D. Voir Dire Tactics and Strategy

The prospective jury panel or venire's first impression of you and your client is made, of course, when they first enter the courtroom. It is essential that you be seen sitting next to or consulting with your client or addressing the court when in view of the jury. From the perspective of many laymen, it is suspicious activity for plaintiff's counsel to be seen seated with or talking in a friendly manner with defendant's counsel prior to the trial.

If the court should allow counsel to conduct _voir dire_ in whole or in part, it becomes an excellent opportunity for you to become acquainted with the prospective jury and for the jury to get its first and perhaps most important impression of you, your client, and your case. This is your first opportunity to appear knowledgeable, sincere, and committed to your client's cause. That is not to say that the _voir dire_ permits argument of the case or any more than a rudimentary recitation of the allegations in the case.

If, as plaintiff's counsel, you are conducting _voir dire_, you may be permitted to introduce yourself, your client, and hopefully opposing counsel, and the defendant in the case. You should leave the impression that next to the judge himself, you are in control of the litigation and are the most knowledgeable about your case.

It is the plaintiff's counsel's burden to convince each and every one of the jurors that his client has been discriminated against on the basis of his age, and if liquidated damages are to be obtained, that such discrimination was willful. It is the plaintiff who must have a unanimous verdict to recover anything, unless there is an agreement between the parties that a majority verdict will suffice. Because it is the plaintiff's burden to obtain a unanimous verdict, in selecting jurors and utilizing your peremptory challenges it is important to keep in mind that what you hope to achieve is a jury as homogenous as possible to improve the chances of agreement on a verdict. While individuals from similar walks of life and similar socioeconomic background may not universally agree on all things, uniformity of such characteristics among the jurors generally enhances the possibility that they will reach a unanimous conclusion in your case. Because of the unique nature of an age discrimination case, young people who may benefit or who may have benefited from age discrimination are to be avoided. Generally, older jurors who have not themselves been involved in a decision to terminate an employee are preferred.

In one age discrimination case tried before a jury in the District of Columbia, the average age of the jury was 67 1/2 years old. This was so because many of those initially summoned to jury duty in the jurisdiction were excused for occupational reasons, or because in the case of younger women, they cared for small children, or for a variety of other reasons. That jury found that the plaintiff's termination was as a result of age discrimination and that such discrimination was willful. The plaintiff was thus entitled to back pay and liquidated damages of $200,000.

Obviously, in a civil trial with only three (3) peremptory strikes, the parties are limited in the amount of selection that they can do. To the extent that you can do so, it is helpful to determine your opponent's strategy in jury selection. It may well be that the type of jury defense counsel wishes to have is not dissimilar from the one that you consider ideal. For instance, in the case in which the jury panel averaged 67 1/2 years old, counsel for the defendant thought that an older jury would benefit defendant because the plaintiff in that case was only 47 years old. Thus, defendant's counsel reasoned that older jurors would be less inclined to think that a person in his/her forties had been discriminated against on the basis of his/her age. Obviously, these are judgment calls based in part on experience and in large part on intuition.

The information that you have obtained from the list of veniremen including age, occupation, and address, as well as those questions asked on _voir dire_ plus your intuition should guide your decision in selecting a jury panel. Assuming the system of selection involving alternating between counsel is adhered to, remember the juror you strike may be replaced by one that is even less favorably disposed to your client.

It should be noted that an alternate juror or two may also be impaneled by the court within its discretion. From a plaintiff's point of view, this is extremely important. It may well be that during the course of a trial lasting several days or several weeks one or more jurors may become ill or unavailable. To avoid having to retry the entire case, alternates are selected by the court and listen as jurors do to the entire case until it is submitted to the jury when the alternates, if not needed, are excused. Rule 47(b) of the Federal Rules of Civil Procedure permits the court in its discretion to impanel alternate jurors and to substitute them in the order in which they are called for jurors who, prior to the time the jury retires to consider its verdict, become unable or disqualified to discharge their duties. In civil cases, up to six alternate jurors may be called. Additional peremptory challenges which may be exercised only against the alternate jurors are allowed if alternates are impaneled. Generally if one or two alternate jurors are impaneled, then each side is entitled to one additional challenge. If three or four alternates are impaneled, each side is entitled to two additional challenges. In some districts, alternate jurors are seldom impaneled but the parties through counsel stipulate to accepting the verdict of less than six of the jurors in the event of the illness or incapacity of one or more of the jurors. This practice prevails quite generally in those states where a provision is made in the state statutes or rules for less than a unanimous verdict, _e.g._ a 5/6 verdict.

IV. PRELIMINARY MATTERS

    A. <u>Swearing and Preliminary Instructions</u>

Once the jury has been impaneled and the jurors who have been selected have taken their oath to uphold the law, the trial has officially begun.

In some districts, the foreperson is designated by the court immediately after the oath is administered. In most other jurisdictions, the foreperson is elected by the jury members upon retiring to consider the verdict. This is governed by rule or local practice.

    B. <u>Invocation of the Rule on Witnesses</u>

The rule of exclusion of witnesses is of ancient origin and is based on the observation that a witness who hears prior testimony might modify his testimony to avoid inconsistencies. Inasmuch as the plaintiff puts on its case first, plaintiff's counsel should be diligent in invoking the rule so that all witnesses, especially defendant's witnesses, are excluded from the courtroom. Federal Rules of Evidence No. 615 provides that the court shall order witnesses excluded so they cannot hear the testimony of other witnesses. The plaintiff or any party to the case is specifically permitted by the rule to be present. A corporation is entitled to have a representative, an officer or an employee of the corporation, who it designates to be present. The term of the rule appears to be mandatory and the request, once made, is invariably granted by the court. There is authority in the language of the rule to continue exceptions such as for expert witnesses who will not have seen or heard matters testified to by other witnesses but who may base their expert testimony on facts testified to by other witnesses. Often considerable time may be saved if such experts are allowed to hear the testimony of other witnesses instead of being required to answer hypothetical questions. The normal sanction for violation of the rule is rejection of testimony from the offending witness. It would be unusual to reject the testimony of a witness called only in rebuttal for violating "the rule" especially since he/she would be expected to take direct issue with the testimony of another witness.

V. EVIDENTIARY REQUIREMENTS: THE PRIMA FACIE CASE AND THE RESPECTIVE BURDENS OF PROOF AND PERSUASION UNDER THE ADEA

While the elements of the _prima facie_ case and the respective burdens of proof and persuasion will be discussed in greater detail elsewhere in this collection, it is important for the trial advocate to know and for the jury to understand exactly who has what burden in an ADEA case. The plaintiff has the initial burden of production, and the ultimate burden of proof in establishing a _prima facie_ case under the ADEA. In discriminatory discharge cases, the courts generally require the plaintiff to show that (1) the plaintiff was within the protected age group; (2) plaintiff was discharged; and (3) defendant sought to replace plaintiff with a younger worker. 11/ If the plaintiff does not introduce some evidence in his case-in-chief on each and every element of the _prima facie_ case, the defendant can move the court for a directed verdict pursuant to Rule 41(b), Fed. R. Civ. P. which, if granted, would dismiss the case with prejudice against the plaintiff's claim.

Once the plaintiff has established a _prima facie_ case, the burden of production, that is, the burden of going forward with some credible evidence, shifts to the defendant. 12/ The defendant must show, but need not persuade, that the alleged discriminatory action was taken for either a legitimate non-discriminatory business purpose or for some reason other than age. 13/ After the defense is raised, the burden of persuasion

---

11/ _Marshall v. Goodyear Tire & Rubber Company_, 554 F.2d 735 (5th Cir. 1977).

12/ _Texas Department of Community Affairs v. Burdine_, 450 U.S. 248 (1981).

13/ See, e.g., _Loeb v. Textron, Inc._, 600 F.2d 1003, 1011-12 (1st Cir. 1979); _Bittar v. Air Canada_, 512 F.2d 582 (5th Cir. 1975).

remains with the plaintiff who must then prove in rebuttal that the stated business reason is pretextual, or that age was the real reason for the employer's actions. The plaintiff must make these showings by a preponderance of the evidence. 14/ If the plaintiff successfully rebuts the employer's defenses to the charge of discriminatory conduct, the employer may allege that age is a bona fide occupational qualification. In so doing, the employer has both the burden of production and the ultimate burden of persuasion in proving that age is a bona fide occupational qualification under 29 U.S.C. § 623(f)(1).

VI. OPENING STATEMENT

Perhaps the most underutilized weapon in plaintiff's counsel's arsenal is the opening statement. There is a school of thought based on a University of Chicago study that 80 percent of the jurors make up their minds regarding liability after the opening statement. Whether that conclusion is accurate or not is open to debate, but it is certainly true that first impressions are lasting.

Because the plaintiff has the burden of proof, plaintiff's counsel speaks first. It is critical in your opening statement to leave the jury with an impression which persists throughout the course of the trial until you have an opportunity to speak to them again in your closing statement.

To be effective, the opening statement must be well organized and must be stated in such positive terms so as to sell validity of the plaintiff's case to the jury. If this is not done, the greatest summation in the world will not reverse the opinion of those who have made up their minds to find for the defendant on liability. Making up one's mind is a difficult process for most people, and once having done so, they seldom wish to repeat the whole process and change their mind. Thus, liability is often won or lost in the opening statement.

The opening statement is not an argument to the jury, but rather, a statement of what one expects to prove. However, that is not to say that your opening staement cannot be forceful or impassioned.

The opening statement sets a theme and picks the issues upon which the lawsuit is going to be tried. Because the plaintiff goes first, plaintiff's counsel has a key advantage in the opening statement. During opening, he/she is talking to the jury when the jurors' attention spans are at their highest level and

---

14/ See, e.g., Loeb v. Textron, Inc., supra; Bittar v. Air Canada, 512 F.2d at 582-83; Mastie v. Great Lake Steel Corp., 424 F. Supp. 1299, 1308 (E.D. Mich 1978).

their minds are most receptive. It is at this point that counsel must convey a theme which he/she knows is psychologically readily acceptable to the jurors. He can then effectively return to his theme in summation.

Even more important, as plaintiff's counsel you should pick issues in the opening statement that you know you can win on. Pick such key issues and themes as it is unfair to fire someone who is doing a good job; it is unfair to fire someone who has devoted his entire adult life to a company; to summarily deprive someone of their livelihood is to deprive him of human dignity. Human beings are not material goods to be used up and thrown away. One can then try the entire case on the tone set in the opening statement and effectively return to the same issue and theme in the closing argument.

There may be key statements in the depositions or in the testimony that can be quite useful in setting the tone in your statement. For instance, such statements attributed to the decision maker and made about the plaintiff or other older workers such as "the chemistry wasn't right," "tired, senile, and gutless," "my senior citizen," "you can't teach an old dog new tricks," can have a substantial impact on the jury which will be reinforced when the actual testimony is adduced.

It is the obligation of plaintiff's counsel in his opening statement to allege facts sufficient to support a claim of statutory violation of the Age Discrimination in Employment Act. However, if the violation was committed in a particularly shabby, cavalier, or insensitive manner, the jury should be made aware of it in the opening statement. It is your obligation to create sympathy for your client and to show that basic notions of fairness were not complied with in your client's case. The fact that the notice of termination arrived on Christmas Eve, the fact that the termination meant a discontinuance of hospitalization coverage during the illness of the plaintiff or a family member or that the plaintiff was told to "clear out" upon being notified of his termination can have a substantial impact on the jury.

The opening statement is a preview of coming attractions, a road map to the case. It must be kept in mind that you must be able to prove that which you allege in your opening statement. If not, defendant may be entitled to a curative instruction from the court advising the jury that while you stated something would be testified to, such evidence was never adduced. Or if such statement rises to the level of being prejudicial to the defendant beyond being remedied by a curative instruction, you face the possibility of a mistrial. Thus, you must be sure the facts that you are asserting in your opening statement can be proven and that you are commenting on admissible evidence. Thus, in opening statements especially before a jury, counsel must walk a tight rope between two opposing possibilities: (1) that he/she will lose a possible influential opportunity to explain why his side should prevail at a time when the mind of the tribunal is most open; and (2) that he/she will claim more than will actually be delivered by evidence, the content of which is still necessarily subject to surprises and uncertainties. These pitfalls can be somewhat minimized by phrasing such as "plaintiff will introduce evidence which we expect to show that . . . ." In the case of potentially inflammatory or questionably relevant material, an advance ruling from the court should be obtained.

VII. PREPARING A WITNESS

Preparing a witness, especially the plaintiff, for direct and cross-examination, is vital. A case may be won or lost because a witness was not properly prepared. Preparation for direct examination consists chiefly in counsel learning everything the witness knows about the case. The witness must be advised of which questions to expect on direct and which to expect on cross-examination. In preparing a witness, a fear of cross-examination can be overcome by simulating the kind of cross-examination to be expected. If this is done properly, the actual examination will seem easy by comparison. An unprepared witness may be mislead on cross-examination and leave a false impression. The witness must be made to understand that his primary task is to simply answer the examiner's questions and to assiduously avoid becoming involved with the personality of the examiner and attempt to placate, retaliate against, try to convince, or attempt to argue with the examiner.

The witness should have a mental picture of that which he/she is testifying about so that the witness can recreate this picture for the jury. This brings immediacy and accuracy to the testimony. The witness' answers are primarily intended for the judge and jury and should be directed to them. If the court asks questions, the witness should be advised to answer fully and respectfully. This generally impresses the jury as well as the court.

Some witnesses become confused to the point of panic when they cannot remember the details of what happened in full and think that they are required to do so. This problem can be solved by making it clear that the witness can testify to recollection of the substance of a conversation even if not the exact words and dates.

The witness must be cautioned to resist giving conclusions and to concentrate on the facts. A statement like "he drinks too much" is fine in everyday conversation but will be objected to during a trial.

The witness must also be prepared for questions which intentionally or otherwise cause anger. The court can control questioning to some extent, however, and such questions can boomerang and create an adverse impression on the questioner as opposed to the witness. Heavy-handed examination can create sympathy for your client if the plaintiff responds with the proper amount of righteous indignation. For instance,

>Question: Isn't it a fact that you haven't worked a day since you were terminated by the Acme Corporation?
>Answer: Yes.
>Question: So you have been sitting home collecting your unemployment check since you left the corporation.
>Answer: I have been pounding the pavement attempting to find work to only have doors slammed in my face because of my age.

The witness must be prepared to give complete yet succinct answers. While some answers may be supplemented through redirect examination, it is no substitute for having responded fully when initially asked the question. Some witnesses believe they can discern from the context of the questioning what the examiner really wants to find out and then provide the answer to it. This creates problems and may unduly assist your adversary. Equally dangerous is the tendency exhibited by some witnesses to contradict implications the examiners may seek to draw but which have not yet been mentioned.

>Question: Were you in charge of the department?
>Answer: Yes, but I could not possibly be aware of what everyone was doing.

A witness should be repeatedly advised that his role is merely to convince the jury and not the cross-examiner.

In cross examination, as in everyday conversation, the same words frequently mean different things to different people. It can be deliberately exploited by a cross-examiner for the purpose of creating a false impression.

>Question: Did you have any income which you did not report?

If a witness answers "No," this lays the groundwork for possible contradiction later giving the impression that the witness was trying to hide something. If the witness answers "Yes," it may given the impression that he has done something illegal. The witness can be prepared in advance to give the best answer. "No, not as I define income."

VIII. THE USE OF STATISTICS IN AGE DISCRIMINATION CLAIMS

While the Congress in enacting the 1967 ADEA specifically declined to amend Title VII of the 1964 Civil Rights Act to include age as a protected classification, the courts have been quick to utilize their Title VII experience in their judicial enforcement of the ADEA. In support of this trend, the First Circuit in Loeb v. Textron, supra, stated that:

> One naturally might expect to use the same methods and burdens of proof under the ADEA as under Title VII. Nothing in either the ADEA or its legislative history indicates a different conclusion.
>
> The mere fact that Congress chose to pass a separate statute rather than to amend Title VII does not imply that age discrimination was intended to be subject to different standards and methods of proof than race or sex discrimination.

Id. at 1015. Courts have relied on Title VII case law in ADEA cases in determining the standard for a prima facie case, 15/ causation, evaluating motions for a directed verdict, 16/ and resolving disputes relating to notice and time limitations. 17/ While courts have been initially reluctant to utilize statistical evidence in age discrimination cases, the trend has been toward greater reliance on statistical evidence in certain instances. 18/

While the use of statistics is a valuable tool in employment discrimination litigation, the use of statistical evidence in ADEA cases poses some unique problems for the trial advocate. Because of the availability of jury trials in ADEA actions, the advocate is confronted with the problem of presenting the results of an inherently complex statistical analysis in a meaningful fashion to a trier of fact with little or no experience in the world of statistics. Since the statistical evidence will customarily be introduced through expert witnesses, the examination, cross-examination, and utilization, where appropriate, of rebuttal experts takes on added importance. If in preparing for trial plaintiff's attorney determines that his case relies exclusively, or even primarily, on statistical evidence, the plaintiff might be wise to reconsider the request for a jury trial.

15/ Marshall v. Sun Oil Company, 605 F.2d 1331 (5th Cir. 1979).

16/ Laugeson v. Anaconda Company, 510 F.2d 307 (6th Cir. 1975).

17/ Reich v. Dow Badische Company, 575 F.2d 363, 367 (2nd Cir.), cert. denied, 439 U.S. 1006 (1978).

18/ Price v. Maryland Gas Company, 561 F.2d 609, 612 (5th Cir. 1977); Moore v. Sears Roebuck & Company, 464 F. Supp. 357, 363-64 (N.D. Ga. 1979).

Another problem with the use of statistics in ADEA cases is the construction of an appropriate statistical model that accurately reflects the actual discrimination on the basis of age experienced by the plaintiff. The character of discrimination on the basis of race or sex, the traditional subjects of statistical models in employment discrimination, differs in several respects from discrimination on the basis of age. While the prima facie case under the ADEA is most commonly established by showing that a member of the protected class has been denied a benefit of employment while a similarly qualified non-class member has received a benefit, some courts have held that a prima facie case under the ADEA can be established by showing that the employer has denied a job benefit to the older members of the protected class while extending the benefit to the younger members of the class. [19] While traditional employment discrimination statistical models may be successfully employed by the plaintiff in a class vs. non-class ADEA case, they are not helpful, and in certain cases may be utilized by the defendant in rebuttal, in cases alleging intra-class age discrimination.

The statistical model for analysis in employment discrimination on the basis of age shares several essential characteristics with the model employed in cases alleging discrimination on the basis of race or sex in violation of Title VII. Both models are founded on the assumption, often unarticulated by the courts, that the composition with respect to the suspect classification of the group of employees in question should be roughly equivalent to the population that possesses the bona fide or legitimate qualifications for the job or benefit in question. If there is a statistically significant disparity between the population and the holders of the job benefit in question on the basis of membership in the protected class, this result raises the presumption of unlawful discrimination.

In International Brotherhood of Teamsters v. United States [20] the Supreme Court in a Title VII context categorized the two forms that this kind of discrimination would take and defined the role to be played by statistical evidence in each. In a disparate treatment case, the plaintiff must allege that because of his membership in the protected class, the employer has intentionally treated him differently from other employees. A disparate treatment case ultimately requires proof of a discriminatory motive (intent) and such statistical evidence can only raise an inference of discrimination. In a disparate impact case, however, the plaintiff must allege that the employer

---

[19] Moore v. Sears Roebuck & Co., supra; Marshall v. Baltimore & Ohio Railway Co., 461 F. Supp. 362 (D. Md. 1978), modified, 632 F.2d 1107 (4th Cir. 1980), cert. denied, 50 U.S.L.W. 3245 (1981); Polstorff v. Fletcher, 452 F. Supp. 17 (D. Ala. 1978).

[20] 431 U.S. 324 (1977).

has unnecessarily utilized a facially neutral employment practice that unintentionally has had an adverse impact on the protected class. In Griggs v. Duke Power Company, 401 U.S. 424 (1971), the Supreme Court in a disparate impact case found that statistical evidence alone was determinative of the issue of employment discrimination.

Since the plaintiff's burden under the ADEA does not require a showing of intent, statistical evidence could be of particular importance in establishing the prima facie case (disparate impact). Statistical evidence could also be used to support the plaintiff's showing of willfulness on the part of his employer in support of the claim for liquidated damages under the Act (disparate treatment).

IX. EXPERT WITNESSES

It is unfortunately true that some expert witnesses are simply paid advocates who will testify to whatever conclusions the party calling them and paying them wants them to make. Such experts can be effectively cross-examined on their bias. However, when it appears that the expert is seeking to testify truthfully, an unsuccessful attack aimed at exposing bias on the part of the expert can backfire. It may well serve to strengthen the persuasiveness of the opposing expert. However, even a sincere expert may be mistaken for a number of other reasons, including adequacy of facts presented by the party calling the expert, or theoretical errors made in the expert's analysis.

An appeal to the impartiality of the expert may be helpful. "Dr. X you have no interest in helping either side in this case, but you are simply giving your best opinion about the facts, is that so?" Or another question--"And if you were shown evidence that would convince you of the contentions of the cross-examiner, you would have no hesitation to say so, is that true?"

A truthful opposing expert can be turned into a witness in favor of the cross-examiner in a number of circumstances. The most common arises where the party calling the expert has failed to call the expert's attention to important facts in the case. Thus, the expert simply knows facts favoring the examiner and is simply without knowledge of facts favorable to your case.

The expert's qualifications in a subspecialty may also be questioned even if the expert is basically truthful and legitimate: "Have you performed studies in the past involving this particular industry?"

It is of critical importance for the cross-examiner to consult an expert who can evaluate the opinion to be given by the expert witness. This is so whether or not an opposing expert will be called. Such assistance is invaluable in cross-examining the expert on impressive sounding conclusions. It is important to have an expert available for analysis of the testimony and to prepare an attack upon the conclusion. Advance information about opposing experts and their contemplated testimony may be available under Rule 26(b)(4) of the Federal Rules of Civil Procedure.

X. DAMAGES AND REMEDIES

Section 626(b) of the ADEA provides for "such legal or equitable relief as may be appropriate to effectuate the purposes of this chapter." Reinstatement, promotion, back pay, liquidated damages, attorneys' fees, and costs are the only specifically enumerated, although not necessarily the exclusive, forms of relief provided by the Act. [21] The focus of a jury trial is on legal relief which includes the award of back pay benefits and liquidated damages. Other equitable relief such as reinstatement and attorneys' fees is strictly within the province of the court.

A. Back Pay

The measure of back pay which is a standard form of relief under the ADEA varies in discharge, refusal to hire, and refusal to refer cases. In discharge cases, it is defined as the amount which the discriminatee would have earned but for the discriminatory discharge, offset by compensation and benefits received from other sources. [22] The amount includes wages and other forms of compensation accrued on the date of discharge. [23]

Back pay is measured from the date of the discriminatory discharge to when either the affected employee accepts or rejects a genuine offer of reinstatement, [24] or, if reinstatement is part of relief, the court makes a judgment. [25] The back pay award is offset by compensation received during the measuring period for damages. Most cases indicate this compensation includes all salary from other employment held during the measuring period, severance pay and unemployment compensation

---

[21] 29 U.S.C. § 626(b) (1975); See also 29 U.S.C. § 626(c)(1) (Supp. 1979).

[22] Brennan v. Ace Hardware Corp., 495 F.2d 368 (8th Cir. 1974).

[23] Coates v. Nat'l. Cash Register Co., 433 F. Supp. 658 (W.D. Va. 1977).

[24] Bishop v. Jelleff Assocs., Inc., 398 F. Supp. 579 (D.D.C. 1974).

[25] Monroe v. Penn-Dixie Cement Corp., 335 F. Supp. 231 (W.D. Ga. 1971).

received as a result of discharge. 26/ A few courts also impose an affirmative duty to mitigate damages on the plaintiff. They use Title VII's mitigation standard: back pay awards . . . reduced by interim earnings or amounts earnable with "reasonable diligence." 27/ It is important to note that the reasonable diligence standard does not force the discharged employee to pursue every possible avenue of reemployment, 28/ or to relocate within three (3) years of retirement. 29/ The employee need not look for nor accept employment unless it is comparable with the former position with respect to pay, status, duties, working environment and advancement opportunities. 30/ Should the plaintiff accept a lessor paying position, the back pay award will be offset by those interim earnings. 31/ Furthermore, where the defendant employer offers reinstatement, the plaintiff's back pay award will not be limited by the reinstatement offer unless it is a good faith offer of a comparable job (made in specific terms and conditions so the person can make an intelligent decision thereon). 32/

Back pay in a refusal to hire case is defined as the amount which the rejected job applicant would have earned but for the discrimination, minus wages earned at other employment which could not have been performed simultaneously with the job for which he/she applied. 33/ Damages accrue from the day of the discriminatory refusal to hire until either the date of judicial relief, 34/ placement in the desired or a comparable position, 35/ or the end of the contract period for the desired job. 36/ Where the plaintiff is "reasonably certain" of the

---

26/ Marshall v. Arlene Knitwear Co., 454 F. Supp. 715 (E.D.N.Y. 1979), modified, 608 F.2d 1369 (2d Cir. 1979).

27/ Coates v. Nat'l Cash Register Co., supra at 661.

28/ Marshall v. Arlene Knitwear, Inc., supra at 730-31.

29/ Buchholz v. Symons Mfg. Co., 445 F. Supp. 706 (E.D. Wis. 1978).

30/ Marshall v. Arlene Knitwear, Inc., supra at 662.

31/ Coates v. Nat'l Cash Register Co., 433 F. Supp. at 662.

32/ Id. at 662-63, n. 2.

33/ Rodriquez v. Taylor, 569 F.2d 1231, 1243 (3d Cir. 1977).

34/ Id. at 1240-41.

35/ Jones v. Cleland, 466 F. Supp. 39 (W.D. Ala. 1978).

36/ Geller v. Markham, 481 F. Supp. 835 (D. Conn. 1979), modified, 635 F.2d 1027 (2d Cir. 1980), cert. denied, 101 S. Ct. 2028 (1981).

employer's age discrimination violation and hence "deterred from seeking interim or more permanent employment lest it interfere with his opportunity to gain the preferred job from which he/she was unlawfully rejected" there is no affirmative obligation to mitigate damages. In many cases the task of the parties and the court can be simplified by a stipulation as to the precise amount of back pay and damages to which the plaintiff would be entitled upon a verdict of age discrimination.

B. Liquidated Damages

Liquidated damages are available under the Act "in cases of willful violations." 29 U.S.C. § 626(b), incorporating 29 U.S.C. § 216(b)-(c). Aggrieved individuals may recover an amount equal to the award of back pay as liquidated damages. Bad faith is not generally held to be an element of "willful violations", nor good faith a viable affirmative defense. 37/ The majority of courts hold that to be "willful" the defendant need only have violated the Act with an awareness of the potential applicability of the ADEA or that the violation must be "intentional, knowing and voluntary" rather than "accidental or unknowing." 38/ Seldom will a decisionmaker acknowledge that he/she was unaware of the ADEA.

C. Damages for Pain and Suffering

Damages for pain and suffering generally are not available under the ADEA. In Rogers v. Exxon Research and Engineering Company, 39/ a district court in the Third Circuit found that the ADEA created a new statutory tort and hence made damages for mental pain and suffering available to make the plaintiff whole. 40/ The decision was reversed by the United States Court of Appeals for the Third Circuit. 41/

The Third Circuit found that the statute expressly provided for only liquidated damages and that the legislative history contains no specific authorization for damages for pain and suffering. Moreover, the recovery of such damages, the court found, could impair the mediation and conciliation efforts which

---

37/ Wehr v. Burroughs Corp., 22 FEP Cases 994 (3d Cir. 1980).

38/ Kelley v. American Standard Inc., 25 FEP Cases 94 (9th Cir. 1981).

39/ 404 F. Supp. 324 (D.N.J. 1975), rev'd 550 F.2d 834 (3d Cir. 1977), cert. denied, 434 U.S. 1022 (1978).

40/ Id. at 327.

41/ 550 F.2d at 839-42.

the court believed Congress felt was "the most favored method of enforcement," 42/ The Third Circuit's rationale has been followed by the First Circuit in Vasquez v. E. Airlines, Inc., 43/ the Third Circuit in Rodriquez v. Taylor, 44/ the Fourth Circuit in Slatin v. Stanford Research Inst., 45/ and the Fifth Circuit in Dean v. Am. Security Ins. Co., 46/ and many district courts. However, it is nevertheless important to convey your client's pain and suffering, emotional distress, and the hardship he/she has suffered in the course of presenting a plaintiff's case for back pay and liquidated damages.

D. Punitive Damages

Punitive damages are excluded specifically as a remedy for post amendment violations by the House Conference Report on the 1978 amendments to the ADEA. Most courts have denied punitive damages on the basis of this Conference Report, the presence of liquidated damages as a remedy for "willful violations" and the negative effect of such damages on conciliation efforts.

Where liquidated damages are not awarded, the court should grant prejudgment interest on any monies due. 47/

E. Affirmative and Injunctive Relief

Affirmative relief is available to ADEA litigants and includes reinstatement, promotion, and compelled employment. 48/ Injunctive relief is also available by the ADEA's incorporation by reference of 29 U.S.C. § 217 of the FLSA. In a wrongful discharge case, the court can order reinstatement. 49/ If the desired position is filled prior to the time of the judgment, the order compelling employment might require the employer to "red-

---

42/ Id. at 841.

43/ 579 F.2d 107 (1st Cir. 1978).

44/ 569 F.2d at 1241.

45/ 590 F.2d 1292 (4th Cir. 1979).

46/ 559 F.2d 1036 (5th Cir. 1977), cert. denied, 434 U.S. 1036 (1978).

47/ Combs v. Griffin Television, Inc., 421 F. Supp. 841 (W.D. Okla. 1976).

48/ 29 U.S.C. § 626(b).

49/ 29 U.S.C. § 626(b).

circle" the plaintiff and give him/her the next comparable position to be filled. 50/ Presumably that position would be comparable in pay, responsibility, and advancement opportunities. If the individual was denied the opportunity to apply for a position, the court can grant the right to apply but cannot compel employment unless the applicant meets current job qualifications. 51/ Injunctive and affirmative relief as well as attorneys' fees are within the province of the court to grant and are not jury issues.

XI. SUMMATION

Like the construction of a building, a summation to a jury can only be successful if a proper foundation preceded it. During summation, attention is focused on the advocate, he is the center of attention until that attention is forfeited by losing the interest of the jury. The following are important points to keep in mind in preparing an effective summation:

(1) Counsel's arguments should take into account the law, the instructions of the court to the jury, and how the case ought to be decided according to basic notions of fairness;

(2) The advocate must convey his belief in the argument. Counsel's firm belief in his client's cause is infectious and can be conveyed forcefully in summation;

(3) The advocate must appear believable. The arguments of the advocate must agree with the evidence. Since the tribunal is not likely to remember everything, a critical question is which advocate (if either) can be relied upon as supplying a truthful picture of what happened. Competency and easy familiarity with the evidence carries credibility. Being able to find exhibits immediately, for example, has a tremendous advantage in persuasion as well as in conservation of time; and

(4) The argument must be succinct and complete.

The summary of facts should paint a verbal picture so that

50/ Jones v. Cleland, 466 F. Supp. 34 (N.D. Ala. 1978).

51/ Rodriquez v. Taylor, 569 F.2d 1231 (3d Cir. 1977).

the jury can visualize what happened, convinced that the occurrences are believable. One must remember that visualizing a traumatic occurrence like a termination from employment after loyal service might not be easy for all jurors. While attorneys may become accustomed to the depth of misery modern civilization can inflict upon its own, many jurors may not fully appreciate the reasons and circumstances which occasioned the plaintiff's suffering. In summation, each juror must be made to stand in the plaintiff's shoes.

A. Structuring of Final Argument

A good speech, like a good summation, must have a beginning, a middle, and an end. Your first remarks must capture the attention of the jury when its attention is at its highest. The best opening lines command the jury's attention and also effectively sum up the key points one wants to make regarding the case. Counsel then turns to the evidence and argues its meaning both in terms of liability and damages.

At the close of the summation counsel again has a high degree of attention from the jury. This is the time to appeal to the emotions and remind the jury of the seriousness of the case and weight of their responsibility.

The advocate cannot testify in closing argument. On the other hand, counsel may argue proper inferences which can be drawn from the evidence. Do not say, "I believe the evidence showed" or even worse "I may be wrong but I think the evidence showed" or "in my opinion." You may say, "I submit the evidence showed" or "the evidence clearly demonstrated that."

It is counsel's function in summation to reason with the jury and to show them what is significant about the facts. The facts have already been proven from the witness stand. It is not effective to restate the testimony of each and every witness or to quarrel with each detail of the defendant's testimony. During summation it is the advocate's duty to convince the members of the jury that his client has been wronged and that the wrong has caused a significant damage which must be remedied.

B. Selecting a Theme for the Case

A central theme and issue should be selected and utilized in the case from _voir dire_ through summation. The theme can involve such concepts as the community's interest in a corporation treating its employees fairly. The jury can be reminded that through its verdict it can send a clear message to the corporation that illegal discriminatory behavior will not be tolerated in the community. Similar themes can be used in almost every case. For example, it can be argued that there is a key relationship between a sense of one human's dignity and one's job; stripping a man of his employment without good cause is humiliating; a corporate profit and loss statement should not include human suffering as an asset; an employee who gives years of loyal service should not be put out on the street without good reason; a person is not a material good to be used up and thrown away because he/she is old.

A case theme is a central thought or idea to which counsel can repeatedly return. He can use the theme as a solid consistent thread to weave together the entire summation. The theme must be a thought which is readily acceptable to the jury and which motivates the jury to find for your client.

C. Simplifying Issues

Since the plaintiff has the ultimate burden of proving all the elements of the prima facie case, a defendant can sometimes win because the case is perceived by the jury as too complex or by the creation of confusion. It is plaintiff's counsel's duty to simplify the case and prevent confusion. You must boil the case down succinctly to the major arguments that the plaintiff is making. Do not fall into the trap and play directly into the defense counsel's hands by attempting to elucidate all the complicating factors. Often in age discrimination cases points are lost in piles of documents and a plethora of organizational charts. If you try in summation to answer every defense argument on each technical issue, you and the jury will become bogged down in the mire of detail. The effectiveness of plaintiff's argument will be destroyed. Simplify the facts. State them your way and make the defendants face the simple issues for which he/she has no direct answer. Bring the defendant onto your turf.

D. Preparation for Summation in Voir Dire

Many good summations include references to questions asked on voir dire. A standard question on voir dire, which can lay a foundation for summation, is the question regarding the jury's ability to return a verdict for liquidated damages if willfulness is proven. It is entirely appropriate to remind the jury that they each were asked on voir dire if they could return such a verdict if the evidence showed willfulness and they each answered in the affirmative at that time. In light of the evidence, they must act in accordance with their legal duty and their answer on voir dire. In effect you are calling in a "promissory note" from each juror during the summation.

E. Preparation for Summation During Direct and Cross-Examination

Statements made in summation must be based on the evidence adduced at trial and permissible inferences that can be drawn therefrom. Plaintiff's counsel can prepare the jury for that evidence on voir dire, outline it in opening statement, and produce it on direct examination. Contrary to popular belief, a case is seldom won or lost on cross-examination. Very rarely in a real life trial does the defendant break down under cross-examination and admit guilt. However, one can neutralize adverse testimony on cross-examination and counsel can make a witness for the defense appear to agree with his side as much as with the other side. Occasionally, effective cross-examination reveals a major inconsistency, a vital admission or raises substantial credibility questions. This information can then be effectively argued to the jury in summation.

F. Arguing Damages

Unless liability is a close question, more of your time in summation ought to be spent on damages than on liability. The psychological effects of the termination, failure to hire or failure to promote, must be stressed. What has happened to this man or woman? How has his or her life changed because of the termination? Talk about unemployability in the future; loss of wages in the past; the fact that he/she is no longer a respected member of the community as a result of unemployment; he/she cannot enjoy life as before. While pain and suffering cannot be specifically compensated in an age discrimination case, the pain and anguish that the plaintiff suffered must be analyzed. Usually this can be done by quoting short passages of the plaintiff's testimony. Jurors can become callous with over-exposure to suffering thus an excess of rhetoric about suffering can be counter-productive. Often times understatement is more effective for this reason.

Lastly, assuming there has not been a stipulation as to the amount of damages, you must justify the demand for money damages. In the usual personal injury case, plaintiff's counsel determines how much damages would be adequate and doubles that amount. This is done in the belief that juries usually begin discussing damages at about half what the plaintiff's counsel has requested. In an age discrimination case, however, damages are specifically limited by statute to back pay and benefits and liquidated damages. It is always important that the jury be made to understand the precise amount of money damages and that an award of money damages is the only means we have to do justice. The law authorizes such awards, and they are bound to follow the law and have sworn to do so in their oaths as jurors.

Arguments should also be made in anticipation of the defendant's closing. If mitigation of damages is an important issue in the case, an effective summation by the plaintiff's attorney should make reference to the plaintiff's struggle to find employment and the problems faced by an elderly job applicant in the labor market. It can be effectively argued that the plaintiff's failure to find a job is as a result of his age. Indeed, it is because older persons have greater difficulty finding alternative employment that the Act was passed.

XII. JURY INSTRUCTIONS AND INTERROGATORIES

There are a substantial number of pattern jury instructions which are read by the court to the jury in every civil case to apprise the jury of the law they are to apply to the evidence. In addition, the parties are permitted to propose additional special instructions. Unfortunately, even the most dramatic reading of them by the court cannot cure the juror's boredom. Even those jurors who remain attentive are often confused by the time they retire to begin their deliberations. Plaintiff's counsel is well advised to attempt to keep the instructions as simple and straightforward as possible.

In addition to apprising the jury of the law it is to apply in reaching its verdict, instructions perform a second important function. Instructions provide guidance to counsel in summation. Thus, the court hears argument on instructions and announces which instructions it will give in advance of summation.

In summation it is effective to highlight certain instructions that the court will give. It is appropriate to preface an argument to the jury with "As the court will instruct you later . . . ." Your argument is given added force when the jury hears the judge give the promised instruction. For instance, when arguing that the jury reject defendant's expert witness' testimony, you may state "As the court will instruct you later, you may disregard an expert witness' opinion if you conclude that the reasons given in support of the opinion are not sound."

In an age discrimination case, special instructions should be proposed on what constitutes age discrimination and plaintiff's burden in establishing entitlement to liquidated damages. The instructions should be personalized by referring to the contentions of the party as developed during the trial. However, again it is in plaintiff's interest to keep them as simple as possible.

Interrogatories to the jury or verdict forms are often used by federal courts. The number of questions posed to the jury should be kept to a minimum and require simple yes or no answers. It again bears emphasis that it is critical for plaintiff's counsel to make every effort to avoid jury confusion which may result in a "hung jury" or a defendant's verdict.

EEOC'S ADEA ENFORCEMENT POLICIES AND PROCEDURES

Daniel M. Williams, Jr.[*]

---

[*] Trial Counsel for ADEA Office of General Counsel, Trial Division, Equal Employment Opportunity Commission.

TABLE OF CONTENTS

			Page
I.	INTRODUCTION		1
II.	CHARGE PROCESSING		3
	A.	ADEA Settlement and Fact Finding Processes	3
	B.	Procedures in States Which Have Age Discrimination Laws	4
	C.	Differences Between the Handling of Charges and Complaints	5
	D.	Expansion of Title VII Charges and Equal Pay Act Investigations to Include Age Discrimination	5
	E.	Scope of Investigation and Factfinding	5
		1. Application of Early Litigation Identification (ELI) to ADEA Claims	6
	F.	Charge Settlement Practices	7
	G.	Complaint and Other Investigations	7
	H.	File Closing and Commmission Lawsuits	8
		1. File Closing	8
		2. Commission Lawsuits	8
		3. Suits and Intervention by the Commission	9
	I.	Employee Benefit Plans and Substantive Regulations	9

I. INTRODUCTION

The Age Discrimination in Employment Act (ADEA), 29 U.S.C. 621 et seq., gives the Equal Employment Opportunity Commission (EEOC) broad investigative and litigative authority coupled with two administrative responsibilities.

The power to make investigations and to require the keeping of records in accordance with the powers and procedures provided in Sections 9 and 11 of the Fair Labor Standards Act (FLSA), 1/ and to enforce the ADEA in accordance with the powers, remedies and procedures provided in Sections 11(b) and (c), and 17 of the FLSA, 2/ is the foundation of enforcement of the ADEA.

The powers, remedies and procedures are:

(1) Right to require attendance of witnesses and the production of books and documents. Section 9.
(2) Right to investigate and gather data in any industry subject to the Act. Section 11(a).
(3) Right to enter and inspect places of business and records, question "employees, and investigate such facts, conditions, practices, or matters as it may deem necessary or appropriate to determine whether any person has violated any provision of this Act, or which may aid in the enforcement of the provisions of this Act." Section 11(a).
(4) Right to contract with State and local agencies. Section 11(b).
(5) Right to make substantive record-keeping regulations. Section 11(c).
(6) Private right of action, liquidated damages, and attorney fees. Section 16(b)
(7) Right of EEOC to supervise private settlements. Section 16(c).
(8) Right of EEOC to institute action for named persons and obtain liquidated damages on their behalf. Section 16(c).
(9) Right of EEOC to institute action to restrain violations of the Act, including obtaining an injunction ordering the payment of money found due by the court. Sections 17 and 11(a).

1/ 29 U.S.C. 209 and 211.

2/ 29 U.S.C. 211(b) and (c), and 217.

In the case of Lorillard v. Pons, 3/ the Supreme Court pointed out that the ADEA follows the FLSA procedures except as they were expressly modified in the ADEA. The major changes in FLSA procedures are: (a) Injunctive relief is available to private parties, but jury trial is available on all issues of fact; 4/ (b) No criminal action for violations of the Act 5/ which expressly does not incorporate Section 16(a) of FLSA; (c) Before an individual may file a court action, a charge must be filed, and a waiting period of 60 days observed while the Commission attempts to conciliate; 6/ (d) Where there is a state law prohibiting discrimination on account of age, the state must have 60 days to attempt conciliation, 7/ but this rule does not apply to the Commission; 8/ (e) No liquidated damages except upon the proof of willful violation 9/ but note that the good faith defense and court discretion in the awarding of liquidated damages contained in Section 11 of the Portal-to-Portal Act 10/ is not incorporated by reference in Section 7(e), 11/ (f) Before instituting any action, the EEOC shall attempt to eliminate the discriminatory practice through informal methods of conciliation, conference and persuasion 12/ and (g) The running of the statute of limitations is tolled for a period of up to one year 13/ while the Commission conciliates for itself under Section 7(b) but not while it is conciliating for private parties under 7(d) of the Act.

3/ 434 U.S. 575 (1978).

4/ Sections 7(b) and (c)(2), 29 U.S.C. 626(b) and 626(c)(2).

5/ See Section 7(b), 29 U.S.C. 626(b).

6/ Section 7(d), 29 U.S.C. 626(d).

7/ Section 14(b), 29 U.S.C. 633(b); see Oscar Mayer & Co. v. Evans, 441 U.S. 750 (1979).

8/ See Marshall v. Chamberlain Manufacturing Corp., 601 F.2d 100 (3d Cir. 1979).

9/ Section 7(b), 29 U.S.C. 626(b).

10/ 29 U.S.C. 260.

11/ 29 U.S.C. 626(e).

12/ Section 7(b), 29 U.S.C. 626(b).

13/ Section 7(e)(2), 29 U.S.C. 626(e)(2).

II. CHARGE PROCESSING

Because ADEA charges have been dramatically increasing in both numbers and total overall percentage of the Commission's workload, much of the resources dedicated to the enforcement of the ADEA have been directed toward promptly notifying "all persons named in such charge as prospective defendants in the action and promptly seek[ing] to eliminate any alleged unlawful practice by informal methods of conciliation, conference, and persuasion." 14/ There has been a gradual shifting from the methodology used by the Department of Labor to a system of charge processing similar to that used by EEOC under Title VII of the Civil Rights Act of 1962, 42 U.S.C. 2000e et. seq. The current method of charge processing is set forth in detail in a recently approved Age Discrimination Compliance Manual.

The filing of a charge of age discrimination is a statutory prerequisite to private suit for violations of the ADEA. After the statutory 60-day waiting period both the charging party, and other similarly situated aggrieved individuals, as to whom the charge was timely, may exercise their rights to sue under Section 16(b) of the FLSA. 15/

A. ADEA Settlement and Fact Finding Processes

The purpose of the ADEA fact finding process is to determine if an investigation is warranted and to obtain settlement of the charge for the charging party and, in appropriate caes, other affected individuals. In one form or another, it is the process for handling all ADEA charges. The basic elements of the fact finding and settlement processes are the notification to respondents of the charge, requests for information, opportunity to settle.

The Commission does not make "reasonable cause" determinations under the ADEA as it does in Title VII charges, and it may stop processing the charge at any time. Normally the fact finding and settlement processes are stopped upon an informal determination that the charge has no merit, the likelihood of settlement is remote, the issues raised are unclear or unsettled, the number of persons or amount of money involved are of such size that the around-the-table fact finding or settlement discussions are likely to be nonproductive, or any other reason that indicates either a broader investigation or private action is the most efficient use of Commission resources.

14/ Section 7(b), 29 U.S.C. 626(d).

15/ See Mistretta v. Sandia Corp., 639 F.2d 588 (10th Cir. 1980).

Charges outside the 180- or 300-day timeliness requirement of Section 7(d) of the Act are received and processed in the same manner as are charges filed within the time requirements. The reasons are that the Commission's actions are not bound by the timeliness requirements of Section 7(d), [16]/ and the fact finding process frequently results in an amicable settlement of differences. An administrative decision has been made not to process charges where the event complained of occurred more than two years before the filing of the charge, because equitable tolling of the 180- and 300-day requirements are unlikely to be for such an extended period of time. The chance of a successful private action is minimal, and the combination of being required to prove willful violations to extend the statute of limitations to three years, together with the necessity to complete an investigation and toll the statute of limitations pursuant to Section 7(e)(2) [17]/ before the expiration of three years, creates an undue burden on the Commission.

The goal of the fact finding process is to obtain settlements where possible or close charge files where settlement is not possible and further investigation is unlikely to result in either settlement or suit by the Commission.

B. Procedures in States Which Have Age Discrimination Laws

Unlike Title VII, the ADEA does not require deferral to State agencies but instead merely referral. To protect the rights of charging parties who file with State agencies, the EEOC has requested that all such agencies file copies of ADEA charges with the Commission. The Commission notifies the respondent of receipt of the charge, that the individual's rights under the ADEA have been protected, and requests the respondent to cooperate with the agency. The charging party is also notified of the protection of rights, the statute of limitations requirements of the ADEA, and that the Commission does not contemplate any further action.

Where the charge is filed with the EEOC, a copy is sent to the appropriate State agency. This is done so that the Charging Party will not be required to go through a "time-out-for-conciliation" by the State agency in the event suit is filed under the ADEA. [18]/

Some State agencies, by contract with the EEOC, are performing all conciliation functions of the EEOC relative to all

---

[16]/ 29 U.S.C. 226(d).

[17]/ 29 U.S.C. 626(e)(2).

[18]/ See Oscar Mayer & Co. v. Evans, supra, 441 U.S. 750.

ADEA charges they receive and are from time to time performing the same function for charges received initially by the Commission pursuant to the authority of Section 7(b) [19]/ of the Act which specifically incorporates Section 11(b) [20]/ of the FLSA. The State agencies are by contract required to perform both Section 7(d) conciliation for the Commission and whatever their own Age Act requires.

C. Differences Between the Handling of Charges and Complaints

Complaints do not lend themselves to the fact finding, sit-down-at-the-table method of resolution because, by their very nature, complaints are any confidential information that may be used to initiate an investigation.

D. Expansion of Title VII Charges and Equal Pay Act Investigations to Include Age Discrimination.

Information obtained during a Title VII or Equal Pay Act (EPA) [21]/ investigation may be treated by the Commission the same as information from any source. It may be used as the basis for scheduling an investigation and expanding the on-going investigation to include ADEA issues. The affected individuals may be advised about their individual rights and the necessity of filing a charge to protect their right to file suit.

It is also true that an Age investigation may be expanded to include EPA issues where information relative to violations of that Act are uncovered during an Age or Title VII investigation. The EPA has no charge provisions and injured parties may exercise their rights to file suit at any time. Before an Age investigation may be expanded to cover Title VII issues, a charge must be filed under Title VII.

E. Scope of Investigation and Factfinding.

The Commission has general investigative authority, and the scope of the investigation or factfinding process is determined by a number of factors not the least of which is the amount of resources of the Commission that are, or can be, dedicated to enforcement of the ADEA.

Charges falling outside the 180- or 300-day charge filing requirement are in a sense non-confidential complaints where there is no equitable tolling of this statutory period for

---

[19]/   29 U.S.C. 626(b).

[20]/   29 U.S.C. 211(b).

[21]/   29 U.S.C. 206(d).

filing. Since it is unnecessary for Commission jurisdictional purposes to determine the equitable tolling issue, they are for processing purposes treated as charges, and are normally appropriate for the factfinding conference method of resolution.

The factfinding and settlement process is best adapted to those charges which allege individual harm. Contracting with State agencies for the handling of factfinding and settlement in those states which have Age Acts in individual harm cases is likewise a resource efficient method of fulfilling the requirements of Section 7(d) 22/ of the Act.

Factfinding can also be useful to determine the nature of violations and defenses in many charges in which the charging party has alleged that the violations complained of were applicable to a class of people. Information gathered during factfinding may be used to determine the scope of the investigation. Based on such informtion the EEOC may elect to close the file, continue to attempt settlement for the charging party only, continue the factfinding process for a defined group of people, or conduct a broad scale investigation.

(1) Application of Early Litigation Identification (ELI) to ADEA Claims.

ELI in the ADEA field is an internal method for selecting which investigations to conduct on a broad scale basis. The selection process is one that requires concurrence of the top management in each EEOC district office. It is nothing more than a resource management tool based on the premise that it is an unwise use of available resources to expend large blocks of investigative time developing issues, determining the victims of supposed discrimination, and accumulating large quantities of information if in the long run the Commission is unwilling or unable to litigate the issues involved. In the ADEA field, ELI identification may be made at any time from the filing of the charge to the decision to issue a letter of violation.

There is a great deal of misunderstanding about the ELI process under the ADEA and the Compliance Manual sets forth a generalized list of issues that may be litigable for guidance to the various district offices. This does not mean that all charges involving those issues will be selected for ELI treatment.

From time to time, based on information received from many sources, an employer may be placed on an ELI employer list. This likewise is an administrative control mechanism to be utilized in determining the type of treatment to be given charges or complaints received by the Commission or State agencies with con-

---

22/   29 U.S.C. 626(d).

tracts to process age charges. The Respondents list is made up of employers where there are ongoing or scheduled investigations and employers who have been identified for investigation. New charges or complaints may have a part to play in determining the timing of the investigation. It is not a wise use of available resources to put a charge through the factfinding process of the Commission or a contract State agency when there is an ongoing investigation or an investigation is scheduled or contemplated.

F. Charge Settlement Practices.

The purpose of Section 7(d) 23/ is to give the respondent an opportunity to settle ADEA allegations with the charging party instead of, or before, going to court. The EEOC is primarily a mediator given the responsibility to attempt an amicable resolution of their differences. This role is to be played in both a factfinding context and an investigation format. The Commission must be careful not to trade the rights of other people to obtain a favorable settlement for the charging party or complainants. For this reason, the respondent must be advised that a settlement with the charging party has nothing to do with an investigation relative to other persons who may be victims of a pattern or practice of age discrimination.

If an investigation of the class aspects of a charge has been scheduled, the scheduled investigation will take place. The settlement for a charging party is not used to influence a decision to direct an investigation of the practice which precipitated the charge. Resource availability, together with the nature of the overall information in the possession of the EEOC, are the primary factors that must be considered when scheduling, or continuing, an investigation after settlement with the charging party.

G. Complaint and Other Investigations.

Investigations may be initiated by any information available to the Commission, and that may be in the form of a confidential complaint, news stories, advertisements, etc. Where the information is received from an individual who is in a position to know the facts, such as an adversely affected employee, it will generally be scheduled for some type of investigation. The complainant is advised that the complaint may or may not be investigated because of the Commission's limited resources, and that if a charge is filed it will be the subject of factfinding. Investigations may be limited to a specific location, job, event, department, etc., or they may be of a broad scope covering the entire business and all issues, such as hiring, promotion, retention, firings, benefits, retirement, etc. The nature and extent of the investigation is largely dictated by the

---

23/ 29 U.S.C. 626(d).

available resources. To date, the volume of charges and complaints has been so far in excess of resources that most investigations have been of limited scope and issues.

Investigations have been largely confined to complaints, charges, and a few instances of matters so flagrant that they could not be ignored, such as newspaper advertisements for employees between the ages of 25 to 40, news stories that the new officer of a business replaced management with a new, young, vigorous team, etc.

All investigations which require the allocation of substantial resources are first screened by district office top management (ELI process).

H. File Closing and Commission Lawsuits

1. File Closing

Any file may be closed at any time, and the respondent will be notified that the file has been closed. The charging party and complainant will also be notified that the Commission has closed its file and contemplates no further action in the matter. All individuals whose rights have been preserved by the filing of a charge are also to be notified. This method of closing does not indicate, and should not be taken to indicate, the views of the Commission on the merits of the charge or complaint. It means nothing more than the Commission has expended as much of its resources on the file as it desires to spend, including informal attempts to eliminate the discriminatory practice by means of conciliation, persuasion, etc. under Section 7(d) [24] of the ADEA.

2. Commission Lawsuits

If the office of the EEOC's regional attorney has reviewed the file and determined that the file is litigation worthy, a letter of violation requesting conciliation under Section 7(b) [25] of the ADEA is sent to the respondent. This letter of violation also notifies the respondent of the tolling provision of Section 7(e)(2) [26] of the Act and invokes this tolling provision.

A determination by the regional attorney that the file is litigation worthy means that his or her office has reviewed the file and determined, based on the contents of the file, that the claim has sufficient merit to warrant litigation. It is not a

---

[24] 29 U.S.C. 626(d).

[25] 29 U.S.C. 626(b).

[26] 29 U.S.C. 62(e)(2).

decision to file suit. The fact that a file was closed without a letter of violation being issued does not mean that the file was determined to be not litigation worthy.

The letter of violation is the first step toward fulfilling the requirements of Section 7(b) to attempt conciliation before a suit by the Commission. Upon failure of this conciliation, or a refusal by the Respondent to pursue further conciliation, the file will be referred to the regional attorney for consideration of suit by the Commission.

3. Suits and Intervention by the Commission

The first and primary consideration in suits brought by the Commission is, "Can this case be won given the facts and the status of the law?" There are many other subsidiary questions that enter into the ultimate decision to litigate or not, among them are: the number of persons affected or potentially affected by the conduct to be complained of in the action; the status of private rights of action by aggrieved persons and are they in a position to exercise those rights; are the issues involved likely to be litigated by the private bar given the restrictions on class actions; 27/ Commission resources available; number of Commission actions pending involving the same or similar issues; attitude of the respondent; and the need for decisions on undecided issues.

These same criteria are used for determining to intervene in suits brought by private parties with two additional considerations which are: the ability to expand the suit beyond the private parties to include others who for one reason or another have not or cannot opt into the existing action, and the extent of the private parties' need for help. Interventions are not done except on consent of the private parties' attorney.

I. <u>Employee Benefit Plans and Substantive Regulations</u>.

The May 25, 1979, Interpretive Bulletin published in Volume 44, No. 103, page 30648, and codified in 29 C.F.R. 860.120, was issued by the Department of Labor with the concurrence of the EEOC. Thereafter certain proposed changes in this provision have been published by the EEOC for comment but, to date, no amendments or changes have been made. The substantive regulations recently issued by EEOC did not reissue these Department of Labor interpretations and specifically reserved the employee benefits section.

It is clear from the legislative history of the 1978 amendments to the ADEA that benefit plans should not discriminate against older workers except to the extent that it is necessary

---

27/ See Section 16(b), 29 U.S.C. 216(b).

to avoid extremely high cost of providing the same benefit level to older employees or as Congressman Waxman (124 Cong. Rec. H 2277) put it: "In the absence of actuarial data, which clearly demonstrates that the costs of this service are uniquely burdensome to the employer, such a policy (terminating older workers from benefit plans because of age) constitutes discrimination and a conscious effort to evade the purposes of the act." This, together with Senator Javits statement (124 Cong. Rec. S 4450 - S 4451) and Senator Williams concurrence (S 4451), are the guiding principles of any interpretations.

The purpose of section 4(f)(2) is to take account of the increased cost of providing certain benefits to older workers as compared to younger workers.

> Welfare benefit levels for older workers may be reduced only to the extent necessary to achieve approximate equivalency in contributions for older and younger workers. Thus a retirement, pension, or insurance plan will be considered in compliance with the statute where the actual amount of payment made, or cost incurred in behalf of an older worker is equal to that made or incurred in behalf of a younger worker, even though the older worker may thereby receive lesser amount of pension or retirement benefits, or insurance coverage. This is consistent with the following statement I made during the November 6, 1967 floor consideration of the original act:
>
> The amendment relating to *** employee benefit plans is particularly significant: Because of it an employer will not be compelled to afford older workers exactly the same pension, retirement, or insurance benefits as younger workers and thus employers will not, because of the often extremely high cost of providing certain types of benefits to older workers, actually be discouraged from hiring older workers. At the same time, it should be clear that this amendment only relates to the observance of bona fide plans. No such plan will help an employer if it is adopted merely as a subterfuge for discriminating against older workers.

The only exceptions to the above stated principles are those in the letter from Donald Elisburg, Assistant Secretary of Labor to Senator Williams appended to the Senate Report, 95th Congress 1st Session Report No. 95-493.

Even though many people view the May 25 interpretations as giving a too narrow view to the legislative intent or too great an exception based on the Elisburg letter, the EEOC is currently bound by it.

The guiding principle is that benefit levels may be reduced for older employees if, and only if, the reductions are based on significant actuarial cost considerations. The most important word is reduced. A benefit may not be completely eliminated. For instance if disability coverage is provided for employees up to age 60, it must be provided thereafter. If it is significantly more expensive then it is permissible to reduce the amount of coverage or the term of coverage. It is not permissible to eliminate the coverage.

The other important element is "significant actuarial cost consideration" which is a matter of proof. The interpretations set forth a number of "safe harbor" guidelines which may be used by employers in lieu of producing cost data. Variance with these guidelines requires the production of data to substantiate the benefit reduction.

Very few cases have been filed, and even fewer tried, pursuant to the May 25, 1979, interpretations so there is little additional guidance that can be given.

The remainder of the substantive regulation has no real variation with the pre-transfer of Department of Labor interpretations found in 29 C.F.R. 860, but is really a change in sytle rather than a change in substance.

RESOLVING AGE CLAIMS THROUGH INTERNAL
CORPORATE MEDIATION SYSTEMS AND ARBITRATION

Robert Coulson*

---

*   President of the American Arbitration Association; member of the New York and Massachusetts Bars and a Certified Association Executive (CAE) of the American and New York Societies of Association Executives; member, Board of Directors of the Institute for Mediation and Conflict Resolution, Center for Community Justice, Federation of Protestant Welfare Agencies, Fund for Modern Courts, Edwin Gould Foundation for Children and National Resource Center for Consumers of Legal Services; Fellow of the New York Bar Foundation; formerly Secretary of the Association of the Bar of the City of New York, 1961-1963; member, International Council for Commercial Arbitration; the London Panel of International Arbitrators and an Honorary Fellow, Arbitrators' Institute of Canada; and Honorary Member, American Society of Appraisers. Mr. Coulson is the author of <u>Business Arbitration--What You Need to Know</u>, <u>Labor Arbitration--What You Need to Know</u> and <u>How to Stay Out of Court</u>, and has written and lectured extensively on the settlement of disputes. He is a graduate of Yale University and Harvard Law School.

RESOLVING AGE CLAIMS THROUGH INTERNAL CORPORATE MEDIATION SYSTEMS AND ARBITRATION

As our symposium program candidly states, and as every speaker will emphasize in refrain, "Litigation under the Age Discrimination in Employment Act is the fastest growing area of employment discrimination activity." This statement may come as glad tidings to trial lawyers who specialize in employment problems. It underlines the bleak prospects facing the many older workers who are trying to maintain their footing in the deteriorating employment market of the present recession. These are threatening times. Now that the holiday season is over, private and public employers, facing demands for cost reduction, are making cruel decisions about who must go and who may stay.

The older worker often qualifies as the leading candidate for the corporate chopping block. In a recent Harris poll, ninety percent of the workers who responded believed that there is "serious discrimination in employment against older workers." In an employment climate where people are viewed as production machinery, the older worker is a fully depreciated tool that modern management can effectively do without. Educated many years ago, the older worker can be difficult to train, costly to maintain and redundant. Unless protected by an iron-clad seniority clause, encased in a collective bargaining contract or civil service regulations, the older employee is at risk.

This symposium will explore the nuances of ADEA. Speakers will provide practical advice for those of you who plan to engage in age discrimination litigation. For your diversion, I intend to explore a more compassionate way to cope with the confrontation that faces many older workers and their employers. How can litigation be avoided? How can the parties resolve their problems without going to court for a decision?

There are good reasons why employees and employers should prefer to resolve age claims internally. In the conversations that I had with workers and employers while writing <u>The Termination Handbook</u>, I came to realize that our national preference for litigation has distorted our perception of the employment relationship. If a worker must be fired, it is not long before the boss begins to regard his former associate as his present enemy. The conversion takes place automatically. Even when an older worker has been with the firm for many years, the first mention of statutory rights will set the employer to worrying about defending an ADEA lawsuit.

Eleanor Holmes Norton is quoted as saying that age claims are "in a period of perhaps the greatest fertility." We suffer from an adversarial astigmatism if we think that the growth of litigation is some indication of positive growth. It is not. It is a blight on the productive relationships that ought to exist between workers and employers.

There are valid moral reasons for employers to exercise restraint in dealing with older employees, even those that seem obsolete. There also are practical reasons for restraint. Corporations want to be known as good employers. Employees watch to see how employers treat older employees who may have given loyal service to the enterprise.

Some employers have decided that it is good business to be fair and generous. Recent studies of corporate grievance procedures indicate a trend towards the strengthening and formalization of such arrangements. Increasingly, employees may go over the head of their immediate supervisor, to seek review from higher levels in management, perhaps at the highest level through an open-door policy. Some companies have provided impartial review by a neutral third party.

One can be cynical about this. Skeptics say that employers are motivated by a desire to avoid union organization. Some experts tell us that justice in the workplace is a child of good times, which will melt away like April snow during a recession. Perhaps. But formal grievance procedures, fairly administered, reflect an enlightened respect for the workers and for their contribution to the success of the enterprise.

You will not be surprised that I favor fair grievance procedures. The mission of the American Arbitration Association is to encourage the voluntary resolution of disputes. Few areas of controversy are more important than employee grievances. Our society places great importance on jobs. Our work is what we are. In America, most of us are not assigned a job by some remote governmental board. We seek out work. We must persuade personnel departments and potential employers to hire us. We win our jobs in a free market. In many cases, our job gives us our main source of identity. This is even more true of older workers than of others. But every employee maintains an emotional and practical hold on his individual job rights. Job security is a primary personal concern for most workers; but again, particularly for older workers.

An employer who announces that employees are terminable at will is hacking away at the core of their value system. This can be dangerous, if not foolhardy. Would it not be better to announce a policy of restraint, a recognition that drastic personnel decisions are subject to review? This is not a revolutionary concept; many corporations have designed effective review procedures because they recognize the value of providing a fair working climate for employees.

Many corporations have recently established some form of "open door" policy. International Business Machines, for example, believes that each employee should be given an opportunity to have grievances reviewed by top management. IBM takes this pledge seriously. I have spoken to senior IBM executives who have flown across the country to interview a single worker in a faraway plant. Such a policy transmits a message: IBM cares about the fairness of its personnel decisions.

Other so-called "open door" programs have enjoyed less credibility. In some cases, employees become convinced that the open door leads directly to the back door. Executives review decisions in a perfunctory way, without an independent investigation and without providing a fair hearing to the employee involved. Few complaints are filed. The system is held in ill repute.

So too, some ombudsmen systems, sometimes touted as an innovative way to handle employee complaints, fall into disuse when employees discover that an ombudsman can wear out his welcome in the executive suite. Ombudsmen, unlike Eveready batteries, can lose their sparkle.

Theoretically, impartial arbitration provides an attractive alternative for employers who would prefer to resolve grievances privately and conveniently. Arbitration promises impartial review, in a convenient package. In practice, serious technical problems arise in the design and administration of such programs. I have investigated several major companies that use voluntary arbitration systems for their nonunion employees. Each of these schemes is different. Some systems are modeled on conventional grievance arbitration, as found in collective bargaining contracts. They provide for meetings between the employee and ascending levels of management. The personnel department is usually involved at an early stage. Then, for final review, the employee is given an opportunity to present the grievance to an impartial arbitrator. Immediate questions arise:

How to find an impartial expert? Generally, the arbitrator is appointed by a neutral agency such as the American Arbitration Association. The arbitrator should not be selected independently by the employer.

Who will present the employee's case? In labor arbitration, a union is available at every step of the grievance procedure, including the arbitration. The union is obligated by law to represent its members. In nonunion systems, the individual grievant is left to his own resources, unless the employer lets him designate some co-worker as advocate or retain a lawyer at his own expense. In any arbitration where the employee is not represented by a competent advocate, the employer should exercise restraint. In some systems, the personnel department or the corporate ombudsman is expected to represent the employee. One program provides that the personnel department will help the employee prepare his case, leaving the supervisor to represent the employer. These may be somewhat artificial and inadequate solutions.

Another concern is whether any award rendered under such a system will be upheld in subsequent litigation. The case of <u>Alexander v. Gardner-Denver</u> 1/ is not strictly relevant. There, the discharged black grievant was represented by his union which processed the claim under a collective bargaining contract. The union lost the case before an arbitrator and abandoned the grievance. The employee then retained an attorney, filed a claim of race discrimination and was given the right to sue the employer in Federal district court. The case finally came before the Supreme Court of the United States which decided that the adverse award was not binding on the trial court. The plaintiff was asserting his personal statutory rights in the district court; the arbitrator's decision dealt with collective bargaining rights. The trial judge could give whatever weight was deemed appropriate to the arbitrator's award. Guidelines to district courts were suggested in footnote 21 of the opinion. The <u>Alexander</u> decision is not relevant because it deals with a situation where the individual grievant was a mere beneficiary under a collective bargaining contract.

In a nonunion situation, where an employee has accepted the company's offer to arbitrate his statutory rights on a two-party basis, under the Age Discrimination and Employment Act or some similar protective law, <u>Alexander</u> is not applicable. Courts enforce agreements to arbitrate existing disputes. Even in the few states where arbitration clauses in contracts are not enforced as to future disputes, agreements to arbitrate existing disputes have been honored and enforced by the courts.

If the facts suggest that an individual is not competent to enter into such an agreement, or is fraudulently induced to do so, or if the arbitration scheme is patently unfair because the individual was not competent or was deprived of adequate representation, there may be strong arguments why such an award should not be enforced. Such arguments are not based on <u>Alexander v. Gardner-Denver</u>. They would be based on considerations of incapacity or unjust inducement or various other doctrines that protect individuals from their own foolishness.

I am not sure that the question of legal enforcement is critical. Employers should ask themselves whether impartial review procedures will help to resolve employee complaints fairly and without subsequent litigation.

Arbitration may be offered to all employees or it can be offered selectively. For example, one issue that will arise under the Age Act is whether a particular executive may be retired at 65. Such questions turn on questions of fact, or on an interpretation of the statutory language. Does the executive fall within the exempt category? That issue seems particularly

---

<u>1</u>/   415 U.S. 36 (1974).

appropriate for arbitration. Questions of statutory definition are often resolved by arbitrators. If the executive is willing to enter into arbitration under procedures that provide a fair opportunity to be heard, it is unlikely that an arbitrator's decision would be overturned. In the real world employers know that terminated executives have a pressing need to find subsequent employment. By offering private arbitration, the employer can resolve such disputes without destroying the reputation of the executive. An informal commitment to provide good references, whatever the outcome, may be part of the parties' submission to arbitration.

Just because an employee has a wrong-headed opinion as to his rights, does not mean that individual is necessarily an enemy of the enterprise. Nor will the people who continue to work in the firm necessarily sever their long-term concerns for the welfare of a terminated employee.

Many responsible corporations retain out-placement consultants for executives who are being terminated. This practice shows concern for people who must leave the corporation. Providing an impartial review procedure in situations where the terminated employee has a good-faith difference of opinion about the termination or about the benefits that should be paid, is a somewhat similar indication of fair dealing on the part of the corporate employer.

Where layoffs or across-the-board reductions are taking place, older workers are likely to be involved. A class action may be in the wind. Then, an employer may not want to handle claims on a case-by-case basis. Class litigation is expensive, results in bad publicity and serves as a rallying point for employees who might not otherwise persist in challenging their termination. If an employer believes that such a movement is developing, the early complaints can be processed together in arbitration. The criteria for recovery can first be determined by a panel of arbitrators; then, individual claims can be processed. In arbitration, dirty linen is not flaunted in the public press or in the law reports, no small advantage in the present climate of personnel relations.

Because of recent notoriety that liberal law professors have given to the termination-at-will doctrine, state legislatures may be asked to extend protection against unjust dismissal, particularly for the elderly. Such legislation may encapsulate emerging legal doctrines of "unjust dismissal" or "implied contract of employment." One has only to look at the labor laws of other "civilized" countries to see models for such protective legislation. Indeed, Puerto Rico and various provinces in Canada already have such statutes protecting workers against dismissal.

Notorious cases of abuse by employers may increase the likelihood of such laws. I believe that voluntary fair grievance procedures are good business for most corporations, particularly when the firm's employees provide unique and valuable skills. Whether or not corporations will decide to offer arbitration to their nonunion employees may depend upon questions of employee morale, the general fairness of management's personnel decisions, the applicable law and the style and ideology of the chief executive. Some enlightened corporations will follow the lead of the IBMs and Xeroxs. Less idealistic managers will continue to treat workers like machines.

Corporate employee grievance systems are usually the same for the older members of the work force as for other workers. But the willingness of corporations to give extra consideration to long-term employees may be more acute. During the two days of this program, some management lawyers may recommend exactly the opposite attitude. Perhaps their clients will welcome such advice and will view their older employees as the enemy. Speaking from the catbird seat of impartiality, I can encourage employers to be fair to older employees. If you snatch away an older person's job, you may be taking his life as well as his livelihood. Employability melts away with age. Employees know this; so do the courts. If you fail to resolve age claims internally, you may find yourself before the suspicious eyes of a jury. Think about that! I wonder if any alternative would not be preferable, better for your client, better for the employee. The prospect of lengthy litigation, with all the problems of obtaining a competent lawyer, of trial tactics, coping with the strategy that you will learn tomorrow morning, is hardly very appetizing. Many of your older employees would be delighted to resolve their disagreements in a private forum. Problems with most employees can be resolved through face-to-face bargaining, sometimes with the assistance of a mediator or with the intervention of an impartial arbitrator. By offering such options to your employers, you can resolve most problems with older workers.

Thank you for your attention. I hope that I have provided some ideas that will prove useful in dealing with the problems of older persons in the workplace. This subject must concern each and every one of us, not only as professionals, but because we too will become older workers. We too will suffer a dilution of our employment value. We too will become insecure and can expect to be treated unfairly by our employers, or by our partners, or by our clients, or by our spouses, or by our children, or by our nursing-home attendants. Our career may have some temporary ups, but, finally, it leads down. We ought to do what we can, consistent with the requirements of the Age Discrimination in Employment Act, subject to our own conscience, to act with compassion towards the older worker. Is it too much to ask that corporate employers offer a system of impartial review?

DEFENSE OF AGE DISCRIMINATION IN EMPLOYMENT ACT
CHARGES RELATING TO PROMOTION ISSUES

Arthur E. Joyce [*]

---

[*] Labor Arbitration & Litigation Counsel, Corporate Legal Operations, General Electric Company. Prior to joining General Electric, Mr. Joyce was a Legal Assistant at the National Labor Relations Board in Washington, D.C. Mr. Joyce received his bachelor's degree from Brown University and his juris doctor degree cum laude from Boston University.

TABLE OF CONTENTS

		Page
I.	INTRODUCTION	1
	A. The Prima Facie Case of Age Discrimination in a Promotion Context	2
	B. Articulating a Non-discriminatory Reason for the Failure to Promote the Plaintiff	5
II.	CONCLUSION	11

DEFENSE OF AGE DISCRIMINATION IN EMPLOYMENT ACT
CHARGES RELATING TO PROMOTION ISSUES

I. INTRODUCTION

Most of the litigation under the Age Discrimination in Employment Act (ADEA) has dealt primarily with termination or lack of work issues. Few have dealt with issues affecting present employees such as the denial of a promotion. There have been some exceptions, of course, such as the Goodman v. Heublein, Inc. case 1/ which has gained much notoriety. However, for one reason or another, employees who still have jobs seem less likely to file ADEA charges than employees who were discharged or laid off. Perhaps the reason for the reluctance of present employees to file charges involving promotion issues is the tendency of employees not to rock the boat -- a latent fear that if they file a charge it could adversely affect them even though ADEA protects them against retaliation.

Despite the relative paucity of ADEA cases involving issues other than termination, it is likely that employers will see more ADEA litigation involving promotion issues. Employees are becoming aware of their ADEA rights and there has been a lot of publicity concerning the rewards for militancy. Goodman, for example, was successful in obtaining a highly publicized award of $452,400 including compensatory and liquidated damages against Heublein in an ADEA suit involving the claim that Heublein failed to promote him because of his age, and then discharged him for pressing his age discrimination claim. We also hear a lot about the midlife crisis. Is an employee who has not attained his or her career goals likely to place the blame on himself or herself or is it more likely that the person will look for a scapegoat? And for a person who does not fit readily into another protected group, age discrimination litigation may be psychologically more apppealing than a candid appraisal that one's failure lies solely with oneself. Moreover, EEOC intake specialists seem to be adding age to claims of promotion discrimination under Title VII or adding promotion issues to ADEA charges which have as their primary thrust the termination of employees whether it be layoff or discharge. What this adds up to is an increase in ADEA charges and litigation involving promotion issues.

This paper will address the defense of the ADEA promotion case. Specifically how does a plaintiff establish a prima facie case, how is that case rebutted, and what types of practices will make the case easier to defend from the employer's viewpoint?

1/   Goodman v. Heublein, 645 F.2d 127 (2d Cir. 1981).

A. The Prima Facie Case of Age Discrimination in a Promotion Context

The proof of a _prima facie_ case of age discrimination with respect to promotion is likely to follow the proof model for disparate treatment cases that has been adopted by the Supreme Court in Title VII cases.[2] Under this model, the plaintiff has the initial burden of showing actions taken by the employer from which one can infer, if such actions remain unexplained, that it is more likely than not that such actions were based on a discriminatory criterion. If the plaintiff is successful in establishing a _prima facie_ case, the employer has the burden of articulating some nondiscriminatory explanation for its conduct. If the employer meets this burden, the burden shifts back to the plaintiff to show that the supposedly legitimate nondiscriminatory explanation was in fact pretextual. The ultimate burden of persuasion always rests with the plaintiff. This three tiered proof model has been applied to ADEA cases by a number of courts.[3]

In a promotion case the initial burden on the plaintiff to establish a _prima facie_ case will consist of establishing the following:

1) The plaintiff was in the protected class (between 40 and 70 years old)
2) The plaintiff applied for and was qualified for the position in question
3) He or she was not appointed to the position despite his or her qualifications
4) The position was ultimately filled by an employee who was younger than the plaintiff[4]

---

[2] _Texas Dep't of Community Affairs v. Burdine_, 49 U.S.L.W. 4215 (U.S. Mar. 4, 1981), 25 F.E.P. Cases 113; _Board of Trustees of Keene State College v. Sweeney_, 439 U.S. 24 (1978); _Furnco Constr. Corp. v. Waters_, 438 U.S. 567 (1978); _McDonnell Douglas Corp. v. Green_, 411 U.S. 792 (1973).

[3] E.g. _Houser v. Sears & Roebuck & Co._, 627 F.2d 756 (5th Cir. 1980); _Smith v. University of N.C._, 632 F.2d 316 (4th Cir. 1980); _Smithers v. Bailar_, 629 F.2d 892 (3rd Cir. 1980); _Loeb v. Textron, Inc._, 600 F.2d 1003 (1st Cir. 1979); _Schwager v. Sun Oil Co. of Pa._, 591 F.2d 58 (10th Cir. 1978). _Cova v. Coca-Cola Bottling Co. of St. Louis_, 574 F.2d 958 (8th Cir. 1978).

[4] _Smithers v. Bailar_, 629 F.2d 892 (3d Cir. 1980).

Simply showing that a younger employee got a vacant job which the plaintiff wanted is not enough.5/ Obviously, if the plaintiff has direct or circumstantial evidence of age discrimination such as where the supervisor tells the plaintiff that he or she is too old for the job, a *prima facie* case can be established without strict adherence to this formulation.6/

In the typical promotion case, the plaintiff will usually have no difficulty establishing the first and the last two elements of the *prima facie* case. The plaintiff's main difficulty will probably occur in showing that he or she applied for the promotion and was qualified for the promotion.

One of the more helpful employer practices in dealing with promotion issues in the Title VII area is also helpful in ADEA cases, that is, job posting systems. In a typical job posting system, employees are notified of the open position and the minimum qualifications for the job. They then have a certain amount of time to express their interest in the job. If they do not express their interest in a timely manner, they will be precluded from consideration. Such a system does two things. First, it definitively establishes whether or not the plaintiff applied for the job. Second, it establishes the minimum qualifications for the job before the candidate slate is compiled rather than after, and thus is helpful in rebutting the contention that the employer's job qualifications were designed to eliminate the plaintiff.

While most large companies now have job posting for many jobs, there is usually a cut off with respect to a certain level of exempt job. Where there is no job posting procedure, the employer is open to a claim that the plaintiff was interested in all higher openings for which he arguably was qualified. A way to meet this is to have some formal means for employees at these levels to express their interest in promotions. For example, career development forms may be filled out by employees expressing their job interests. This type of procedure may be helpful in demonstrating the plaintiff's lack of interest in certain positions.

Assuming that the plaintiff can establish that he or she applied for or expressed an interest in a particular job, he or she must also establish that he or she was qualified for the job. A point to note here is that satisfactory performance on one job does not necessarily qualify a person for another job.7/

5/ *LaRue v. General Tel. Co. of Southwest*, 545 F.2d 546 (5th Cir. 1977).

6/ *Loeb v. Textron, Inc.*, 600 F.2d 1003 (1st Cir. 1979).

7/ *Lindsey v. Southwestern Bell Telephone Co.*, 546 F.2d 1123 (5th Cir. 1977); *Braswell v. Kobelinski*, 428 F. Supp. 324 (D.D.C. 1976).

A highly competent engineer doesn't necessarily make the best salesperson.8/ Each job has its own requirements and demands. The ability to demonstrate that the plaintiff lacks a key qualification of the job in question may be critical in preventing the plaintiff from establishing a prima facie case.

In cases which involve job requirements which are objective, such as education or experience requirements, the plaintiff's qualifications or lack thereof will be apparent. In cases where the plaintiff does not meet some objective job qualification, the plaintiff's only hope is to switch from a theory of disparate treatment to one of disparate impact. Under the disparate impact theory which has been applied to cases under Title VII, the plaintiff need only establish that a particular employment requirement has an adverse impact on the protected group. The burden then shifts to the defendant to establish that the requirement is job related or justified by business necessity.9/ Although the Second Circuit has held that the disparate impact theory can be applied to ADEA cases, the issue is still in doubt.10/

In cases which involve more subjective job requirements like the ability to supervise, leadership, writing ability, etc., supervisor appraisals relating to the ability in question may become important. Some of the litigated ADEA promotion cases have turned on supervisor appraisals.11/ The employer's judgment as to the

---

8/ Davis v. Bolger, 496 F. Supp. 599 (D.D.C. 1980).

9/ Griggs v. Duke Power Co., 401 U.S. 424 (1971).

10/ Geller v. Markham, 635 F.2d 1027 (2d Cir. 1980), cert. denied, 49 U.S.L.W. 3803 (U.S. Apr. 27, 1981), 25 F.E.P. Cases 847. In dissenting to the court's denial of certiorari in this case, Justice Rehnquist stated that the Supreme Court has never held that proof of discriminatory impact can establish a violation of the ADEA. Rehnquist would apparently not apply the disparate impact doctrine to an otherwise neutral employment criterion because the statute provides an affirmative defense to the employer where its actions are based on "factors other than age." The Supreme Court's recent decision in County of Washington v. Gunther, 49 U.S.L.W. 4623 (U.S. June 8, 1981), 25 F.E.P. Cases 1521, involving the application of the Bennett Amendment to Title VII sex-based wage discrimination claims supports Rehnquist's position. In Gunther, the majority opinion seems to indicate that the Griggs disparate impact doctrine would not be applicable to sex-based wage discrimination claims because of the Bennett Amendment's inclusion of the Equal Pay Act's affirmative defense involving a wage differential based on "factors other than sex."

11/ These cases generally have found the plaintiff not to be qualified for the promotion based on written appraisals or oral testimony as to the plaintiff's ability by his

ability or performance of the employee ordinarily will not be second guessed by a court.12/ The plaintiff's only recourse in such a case will be to establish pretext by establishing that the performance appraisals were tainted by age discrimination.13/

B. Articulating a Non-discriminatory Reason for the Failure to Promote the Plaintiff

If the Plaintiff is able to establish a *prima facie* case, the employer will have to articulate a non-discriminatory reason for its decision. In the promotion case, the reason which will be articulated in the vast majority of cases will be that the plaintiff did not get the job because a more suitable or better qualified candidate was selected. The employer's burden in such cases will be to establish a legitimate reason for picking the successful candidate over the plaintiff.

Pretext

Once the employer has articulated a non-discriminatory reason for not selecting the plaintiff, the burden swings back to the plaintiff to establish that the reason articulated by the defendant for selecting another employee was pretextual.14/ The plaintiff

---

supervisors. *Lindsey v. Southwestern Bell Telephone Co.*, 546 F.2d 1123 (5th Cir. 1977); *Davis v. Bolger*, 496 F. Supp. 559 (D.D.C. 1980); *Zell v. United States*, 472 F. Supp. 356 (E.D. Pa. 1979); *Johnson v. Adams*, 20 F.E.P. Cases 1534 (D.D.C. 1979); *Braswell v. Kobelinski*, 428 F. Supp. 324 (D.D.C. 1976). One case, however, relied on the employer's favorable appraisals as evidence of age discrimination. *DeFries v. Haarhues*, 488 F. Supp. 1037 (C.D. Ill. 1980). Another case finding discrimination under ADEA relied on letters of commendation and a supervisory recommendation for promotion which had been changed at the urging of another of the employer's officials. *Snead v. Harris*, 22 F.E.P. Cases 1434 (D.D.C. 1980).

12/ *Kephart v. Institute of Gas Technology*, 630 F.2d 1217 (7th Cir. 1980), *cert. denied* 49 U.S.L.W. 3619 (U.S. Feb. 23, 1981), 24 F.E.P. Cases 1827. See also *Kerwood v. Mortgage Bankers Ass'n.*, 494 F. Supp. 1298 (D.D.C. 1980).

13 *EEOC v. Sandia Corp.*, 639 F.2d 600 (10th Cir. 1980).

14/ One case involving an employer defense of selecting a better qualified applicant seemed to require more than an articulation of this defense. In *Jones v. Cleland*, 466 F. Supp. 34 (N.D. Ala. 1978), the Court held that the reason that the successful candidate was chosen over the plaintiff was because the plaintiff's application failed to accurately reflect her experience. Finding that this deficiency was due primarily to a lack of assistance and guidance from the

may attempt to do this by either direct or circumstantial evidence. Direct evidence of age discrimination such as where the plaintiff claims his supervisor told him he would not be promoted because of his age will generally raise credibility issues to be resolved by the fact finder. Indirect evidence of pretext may take the form of proof that the plaintiff was in fact more qualified than the successful candidate15/ or that the defendant was age conscious.16/ It may also take the form of statistical evidence.

Evidence of age consciousness will usually create a factual issue for the finder of fact. However, in some cases it may be excluded or disregarded as untimely.17/ General age conscious statements may be even explained away as truisms.18/ In addition,

---

defendant in the preparation of her application and that such assistance and guidance was the result of the failure of the defendant to implement its affirmative action plan, the court held that the defendant violated both ADEA and Title VII. Query whether this case is good law in light of the Supreme Court's ruling in Texas Dep't of Community Affairs v. Burdine, 49 U.S.L.W. 4215 (U.S. Mar. 4, 1981), 25 F.E.P. Cases 113.

15/ DeFries v. Haarhues, 488 F. Supp. 1037 (C.D Ill. 1980).

16/ See EEOC v. Sandia Corp., 639 F.2d 600 (10th Cir. 1980) (layoff context).

17/ Wilson v. Sealtest Foods Div. of Kraftco Corp., 501 F.2d 84 (5th Cir. 1974). See also Meyer v. California & Hawaiian Sugar Co., 20 Empl. Prac. Dec. 30, 152 (N.D. Cal. 1979) (Title VII case).

18/ The Fourth Circuit made some interesting observations on this point:

> "There was testimony that Bureau and others had made statements such as that the Division's future lay in its young Ph.Ds and that all employees at some time reached the peak in efficiency. Rather than indicating a discriminatory purpose, however, such statements seem only truisms. In any enterprise, today's juniors will be tomorrow's seniors. Today's seniors can help create foundation for tomorrow's growth and prosperity, but future realization of the potential of an enterprise lies principally with those who will be in positions of leadership and responsibility in the future. So, too, every individual at sometime reaches a peak in efficiency. The peak may be relatively flat over a considerable period of time, but surely it will begin to wane if the individual lives long enough."

they may be explained as not reflecting a discriminatory animus.[19]

The plaintiff may also seek to introduce statistical evidence in a promotion case to show pretext. While statistical analysis is becoming increasingly important in age discrimination cases, there are some possible differences in the use of statistics in age cases as a result of the natural aging process which may preclude a strict application of a Title VII statistical analysis to age cases.[20]

Where the promotion allegation involved jobs that were posted, applicant flow information for promotions may be readily available. A comparison between the promotion success rates of employees in

---

Smith v. Flax, 618 F.2d 1062, 1066 (4th Cir. 1980).

Contrast EEOC v. Sandia Corp., 639 F.2d 600 (10th Cir. 1980), where evidence that management was convinced that "new blood" or young Ph.Ds were the Company's future due to the rapidity of technological changes and that management arbitrarily generalized that older employees could not keep pace with new technology and were becoming technologically obsolete was instrumental along with statistical evidence in a finding of age discrimination.

[19] See e.g., Sutton v. Atlantic Richfield Co., 26 Empl. Prac. Dec. 31, 897 (9th Cir. 1981) (Comment made to the plaintiff by his superior, "I would suggest you find a well qualified, younger man, someone I can replace you with," could be properly found by the trial court to not indicate a discriminatory animus, but rather to be an admonition that the plaintiff was not meeting his responsibility to develop younger executives to succeed himself or other employees approaching retirement age); Trinidad v. Pan American World Airways, 575 F.2d 983 (1st Cir. 1978) (A statement by a supervisor that rejected transferees were "older people . . . a bunch of Social Security people" does not vitiate directed verdict for defendant: "a scintilla of evidence is not enough to warrant submission to the jury"); Simmons v. McGuffey Nursing Home, Inc., 619 F.2d 369 (5th Cir. 1980) (Statement by Board members that Board wanted "a younger man this time" as plaintiff's replacement does not create question of fact that plaintiff was terminated because of his age). See also Ford v. South Cent. Bell Tel. Co., No. 79-0490-L (B) (W.D. Ky. Jul. 20, 1981); Haynes v. Yellow Freight Sys., Inc., 487 F. Supp. 1325 (N.D. Ga. 1980); Olsen v. Southern Pac. Transp. Co., 480 F. Supp. 773 (N.D. Cal. 1979).

[20] Williams v. City & Cty. of San Francisco, 483 F. Supp. 335 (N.D. Cal. 1979). See also Laugesen v. Anaconda, 510 F.2d 307 (6th Cir. 1975).

the protected age class and those that are not21/ when compared to the qualified applicant pool22/ might be used as an indicator of discrimination or lack thereof.23/ Statistically significant disparities between the promotion rates for the different groups may raise a rebuttable inference of discrimination.24/

21/ It should be noted that a plaintiff may attempt to gerrymander the statistical analysis. Instead of comparing promotion rates of employees 40 and older with the promotion rates of employees under 40, the plaintiff's comparison might be those employees 50 and over to those employees under 50 or those employees 55 and over to those under 55. The theory behind allowing such alternative comparisons is that statistics comparing employees under the age of 40 to those 40 and over may arguably hide statistical disparities involving employees in upper age levels. Unlike race and sex discrimination, age discrimination is a relative concept. Discrimination at the higher age levels may not be present at the lower levels of the protected class. Some courts have allowed this approach. See e.g., EEOC v. Sandia Corp., 639 F.2d 600 (10th Cir. 1980); Polstorff v. Fletcher, 452 F. Supp. 17 (N.D. Ala. 1978).

22/ The Supreme Court has held that a statistical comparison must be to the available pool of qualified persons or qualified applicants to be probative under Title VII. Hazelwood School Dist. v. United States, 433 U.S., 299 (1977). This principle would seem to be applicable to age discrimination cases as well. Lindsey v. Southwestern Bell Tel. Co., 546 F.2d 1123 (5th Cir. 1977). This means that applicants who are not qualified should be eliminated from the applicant pool for the purpose of a valid statistical comparison. Of course, if a job qualification has an adverse impact on older employees, the plaintiff may attack the requirement under a disparate impact analysis.

23/ See Davis v. Bolger, 496 F. Supp. 559 (D.D.C. 1980).

24/ Statistical inferences are always rebuttable. As the Supreme Court has stated:

> "Statistics are. . .competent in proving employment discrimination. We caution only that statistics are not irrefutable: they come in infinite variety and, like any other kind of evidence, they may be rebutted. In short, their usefulness depends on all the surrounding facts and circumstances."

International Bhd. of Teamsters v. United States, 431 U.S. 324, 339-340 (1977).

In situations where jobs are not posted, the plaintiff may want to make certain assumptions such as that the qualified pool of candidates for a certain position level in a certain function consists of all employees in the next lowest position in the particular function. The premise of this analysis is that the average age of those promoted into a certain level should be approximately the same as the average age of those employees in the lower level. The underlying assumption, however, is not valid since it fails to reflect the reality of the aging process. Many older employees in the level below may not be qualified for promotion to the next level of management.[25]/ While the quick reply to this fact is that the proportion of qualified older employees should be the same as the proportion of younger employees, this does not necessarily follow.

All employees eventually reach a peak in their career paths depending on their own ability and the competition inherent in a pyramid structured hierarchy. Employees generally rise in the organization to a level at which they are barely able to perform. While their performance may be satisfactory at this level, they are not capable of performing at the next highest level of the organization.[26]/ The end result of this topping out phenomenon is that at any point in time, a given job level will consist of two groups: 1) those that have reached their level of competence and have gone as far as they can and 2) those who still have potential for further growth. The first group will remain in their positions growing older. Such employees are not really viable candidates for higher level positions yet they significantly impact on the average age of the alleged potential candidate pool. The second group of employees is just passing through the level and is constantly being replaced by generally younger employees.[27]/ This group is obviously going to be significantly younger than the first group. It will also have, by necessity, a lower mean age than the combination of the two groups.

The absurdity of the assumption that all persons in the level below constitute the qualified applicant pool for the next higher level can also be graphically demonstrated by construction of a computer model. By making certain assumptions on additions and

---

[25]/ _Lindsey v. Southwestern Bell Tel. Co._, 546 F.2d 1123 (5th Cir. 1977).

[26]/ One court has recognized as a "truism" the fact that all employees at some time will reach a peak in efficiency. _Smith v. Flax_, 618 F.2d 1062 (4th Cir. 1980).

[27]/ In _Laugesen v. Anaconda_, 510 F.2d 307 (6th Cir. 1975), the Sixth Circuit recognized that the "progression of age is a universal human process" and that employees will more often than not be replaced by younger employees absent any discrimination.

removals from actual past data, the average age of each level in the employer's pay structure can be constructed. By assuming that all persons going into an entry level position are age 21, an average age can be calculated for the level when the level reaches a steady state.28/ The average age of this level at steady state now becomes the average age of the input into the next level and the average age at the higher level is then computed. This process is continued until the average age for the highest level is reached.

Calculations done in accordance with the above procedure on some sample data in my Company resulted in an average age in the higher levels well in excess of a 100 years. This model proves by *reducto ad absurdim* the absurdity of the assumption that the average age of those promoted into a given level should be the average age of the level below. It also supports the topping out or plateau theory that there are essentially two groups of employees in each level -- those that have reached their level of competence and those that have the potential for future growth with the average age of those in the former group necessarily being greater than in the later group.

A better measure of whether or not there is any discrimination might be the average age in a given position level over time. A statistically significant decrease in the average age for a

---

28/ The dynamics of this steady state concept are fairly simple. Suppose an employer has 100 people in the entry level position, it promotes out 20 and hires 20 new employees each year. The first year the average age of employees in this level would be 21 (100 employees hired at age 21). The next year all employees will have aged 1 year for a net gain of 100 man years. You will lose 20 employees who are now 22 and gain 20 new employees at age 21 for a net loss of 20 man years. The new average age will be 21.8.

$$\frac{(20 \times 21 + 80 \times 22)}{100}$$

The next year the 80 employees at age 22 will now be 23, the 20 at 21 will be 22. 20 of the age 23 employees are promoted and replaced by 20 employees age 21. The average age now will be 22.4.

$$\frac{(20 \times 21 + 60 \times 23 + 20 \times 22)}{100}$$

The average age will continue to increase until it reaches a balance where the net loss in years from promotions and replacements will be equal to the next gain of age resulting from the present incumbents aging one year. This balance is the steady state for the level.

particular level over a representative time period might create an inference of a youth movement with respect to promotions. A lack of any statistically significant deviation in the mean age over time may be relevant evidence that no youth movement is taking place. However, it should be noted that a significant increase or decrease in the workforce may result in an increase or decrease in the mean age without creating any inference relating to age discrimination with respect to promotions or hiring into the level. In one case a court disregarded statistics showing a decrease in the mean age of an employer's work force from 1969 - 1976 where the employer submitted evidence that during the same period its exempt employee population increased from 258 to 419. The court stated:

> "Such a drop in the average age of the exempt employees can be explained by the natural tendency of the newly hired employee to be younger."[29]

An alternative to mean age comparison over time is to build a computer model based on the steady state concept which will construct the average age of replacements needed to keep the mean age in a certain level or position from rising over time. Comparison of the mean age of actual replacements versus the calculated mean could give a rough indication of any age bias. The model could also predict the eventual mean age of the level if the mean age of the replacements remains the same. A sample of the data from such a model would look like this:

Position Level	Mean age of position level	Mean age of inflow necessary to hold average age of level constant	Mean age of promotions	Predicted average age of level if mean age of promotions remains constant
10	49.87	39.86	44.39	65.50

II. Conclusion

While not many of the litigated ADEA cases have involved promotion issues, it is likely that the promotion issue will be raised in a number of future ADEA cases. Employers should be prepared to deal with these cases. Employers that have job posting or self nominated systems in place for promotions will be better able to deal with amorphous claims by employees that they were passed over for promotions because of their age. Sound performance evaluation procedures will also help establish employee qualifications or lack thereof for promotion. Finally, the

---

[29] *Paxton v. Lanvin - Charles of the Ritz*, 19 F.E.P. Cases 194, 196 (S.D.N.Y. 1978).

employer should be prepared to deal with statistical analysis showing a pattern or practice with respect to its promotions.

THE USE OF EFFECTIVE PERSONNEL SYSTEMS TO OBVIATE
UNDERUTILIZATION AND LEGAL PROBLEMS OF OLDER WORKERS:
A PRACTICAL GUIDE FOR EMPLOYERS

Karl R. Kunze [*]

---

[*] President, Kunze Associates, Oxnard, California; retired Manager of Training and Development, Lockheed-California Company; Chairman, Advisory Committee of the National Institute on Work, Retirement and Income; and Executive Board Member, The National Council on the Aging, Inc. Mr. Kunze is a consultant specializing in manpower, industrial relations, employee assessment and development, and equal employment opportunity. He is also an instructor in human factors and systems management, University of Southern California and has published a number of papers. Mr. Kunze received his masters degree in Psychology from Boston University and did graduate work in psychology at Harvard Graduate School of the Arts and Sciences.

TABLE OF CONTENTS

I. INTRODUCTION..1

II. ADEA-EMPLOYER BACKGROUND.....................................1

III. SUBJECT MATTER COVERED 2

    A. Policies...3
    B. Accession Practices....................................3

        1. Recruitment and Selection......................3
        2. Bona Fide Occupational Qualification...........6

    C. Workforce Maintenance..................................7

        1. Age Bias in Management.........................7
        2. Training and Career Development................7
        3. Performance Evaluation........................10
        4. Downgrades, Promotions and Layoffs............11

    D. Manpower Planning.....................................12

        1. Age Audits....................................12

IV. SUMMARIZING STATEMENT.......................................13

I. INTRODUCTION

Personnel policies and systems, including those having to do with employee selection, classification, promotion, training, evaluation, and separation, can aid in preventing age complaints and lawsuits if effectively designed and implemented. Further, they can help integrate the talents and potential of age 40 plus workers with the goals of the organization for mutual benefit. Lastly, attorneys bent on discovering employer strengths and weaknesses in legal suits can benefit from a knowledge of the inner workings of these systems.

The presence, absence, or misuse of any of the above processes does not prove or even imply older worker inequity or adverse impact, but differential or inconsistent applications would certainly warrant further attention from companies and complainants. A plaintiff's attorney can examine any of the aspects of these systems in looking for inequitable treatment of a client. As an aside, the author has found no conflict between federal age legislation and good personnel practices.

II. ADEA-EMPLOYER BACKGROUND

With the exception of larger firms with legal offices, the private sector hardly noticed the passage of the Age Discrimination in Employment Act (ADEA). When the Act was passed, employees and employers were preoccupied with other forms of discrimination. Age cases finally trickled down through the time-consuming processes of conciliation, conference, persuasion, discovery, and adjudication -- the latter step reached attention-getting proportions during the mid-Seventies.

Although the ADEA 1978 Amendments received the attention of the private sector, the impact was softened by delays of the Department of Labor (DOL) and the Equal Employment Opportunity Commission (EEOC) in issuing final interpretations of the Act. Despite valiant efforts of these organizations, hampered by circumstances (an absence of trained attorneys, the transfer of the age function to EEOC), the delays were substantial and caused employers to assume a wait and see attitude. After two preliminary interpretations by DOL and a proposed interpretation by EEOC, the final document was issued 9/28/81, over 3 1/2 years after the ADEA Amendments were signed into law.

The release of the Uniform Guidelines on Employee Selection Procedures, in the judgment of the author, helped to keep the age issue on firms' back burners. The document, produced by the EEOC, the Civil Service Commission, the Departments of Labor and Justice, was published 11 years after ADEA, and at a time when the age amendments were a hot issue on Capitol Hill. 1/

1/ 43 Fed. Reg. No. 166 (Aug. 25, 1978).

The procedures were designed "to establish a uniform federal position in the area of prohibiting discrimination in employment practices on grounds of race, color, religion, sex, or national origin." Age is missing in the listing of protected groups, yet the subject matter has to do with adverse impact, test validation, job analysis, selection procedures for hire and promotion, disparate treatment, etc. -- subjects as vital to age discrimination as to any other form of discrimination. And as potentially illegal. There appears to be a growing interest in the aging field in private sector and government circles. This may be because of an awareness of the ethical and economic issues involved, the volume and costs of recent court cases, and because of the superlative work of professional organizations such as those sponsoring this symposium in bringing the message of older worker problems to the nation.

III. SUBJECT MATTER COVERED

So much for the personal observations of someone on the inside looking out. Subjects addressed in this paper will be:

A. Policy as a basis for age-neutral treatment of employees
B. Accession practices
   1. Recruitment and selection
   2. The bona fide occupational qualification (bfoq)
C. Workforce maintenance
   1. Age bias in management
   2. Training and career development
   3. Performance evaluation
   4. Selection for promotion, layoffs and other separations
D. Manpower planning
   1. Age audits, records, and reports
   2. Planning to reduce employment cycles

Emphasis herein will be placed on employer internal operations rather than the law and correlative court cases. For an excellent treatment of ADEA and the private sector, read Patrick Clelland's AGE DISCRIMINATION LAW: Rights and Responsibilities of Employers and Individuals. 2/ For comments on initial effects of the 1978 Amendments, read Edward Howard's ADEA Update. 3/

2/ Clelland, P.G., Age Discrimination: Rights and Responsibilities of Employers and Individuals, Industrial Gerontology, Summer 1973, No. 18, pp. 53-64.

3/ Howard E., ADEA Update, Aging and Work, Vol 4, No. 2, Spring 1981.

A. Policies

Many organizations have overlooked the value of policy declarations on the issue of age discrimination. There are notable exceptions however. The General Electric Company has included the age factor in its affirmative action policy: "It is the policy of the General Electric Company to provide employment, training, compensation, promotion, and other conditions of employment without regard to race, color, religion, national origin, sex or age." 4/ In 1976, the Lockheed Aircraft Corporation issued a Corporate Industrial Relations Operating Statement titled COMPLIANCE WITH THE AGE DISCRIMINATION IN EMPLOYMENT ACT in which it covered hiring, promotion, layoff or termination, and involuntary retirement. The document cautioned about the use of the bfoq. 5/

Firms composing such policies might well consider placing implementation responsibility with the line organization. Industrial relations may be given accountability for monitoring results of the policy, and for keeping management informed of changes in federal and state legislation. The topical outline on page 2 can serve as a guideline for a policy statement, along with pensions and other fringe benefit considerations treated in other papers in this seminar. Feedback and compliance with affirmative action and similar non-discriminatory programs can be obtained by requiring an annual reporting of progress and present status by top management, such as functional vice presidents, division or branch heads, to the chief executive officer.

B. Accession Practices

1. Recruitment and Selection

An age policy statement is of utmost importance for guidance in a firm's recruitment and hiring operations. Absence of such a policy leads to guesswork on the part of interviewers about the company's position in this regard. Now with the increasing number of professional and technical people hired, employment interviewers often perform a screening function, referring those with required qualifications to requisitioners. This procedure can result in disparities from one line manager to another in the selection for openings in the same or comparable openings--much to the glee of plaintiffs' attorneys.

4/ Albright, L.E., Staffing Policies and Strategies, ASPA Handbook of Personnel and Industrial Relations, Eds. Yoder, D., and Henemon, H.G., BNA, Inc., Washington, D.C., 1974, pp. 4-15, 4-18.

5/ Unpublished internal document, Lockheed Aircraft Corporation, Corporate Industrial Relations Operating Statement, No. 29, 1976.

As far back as the author can remember, industrial firms were quick to react to changes in labor market supply and demand. During the last three wars engaged in by the United States, experienced workers in their sixties were welcomed with open arms. In between wars, with different job market dynamics operating, practices changed. Help wanted advertisements contained age restrictions, training programs flourished for young people with potential, and promotable people were those with the punch and vinegar to show enthusiasm, run through hallways, and work endless hours to get a job done. Up to ADEA, the hiring and separation of older workers was, to a great extent, a matter of company convenience.

Under present-day legislation, firms have less latitude in their recruitment and hiring practices. There are manpower advantages to this. The 40 plus labor market is steadily improving in terms of overall competency, potentiality, and availability. Some of the changing characteristics concerning this group are as follows:

* A progressively higher educational age;
* Improved health and longevity and longer employment tenure;
* Inflation (1969-70=6%, now about double) necessitating older people to remain in the work force longer; and
* A continuing practice of involuntary retirement.

Regarding the capabilities of older workers, an abundance of good research is now available indicating that primary mental abilities important in most work today (verbal and numerical ability, reasoning, etc.) either remain stable or trend upward until the late sixties or early seventies. Moreover, studies point out that the total environment in which people work is an important determiner of productivity of all employees. [6]

Inspections of help wanted advertisements in the larger communities reveal that ADEA has aided in removing phrases in these ads referring to age, i.e., recent college graduate, messenger boy, retired person, etc. With an excellent 40 plus labor market in the United States, age specific ads are unwise because they delimit the recruiting span and the number of applicants per job opening. The practice obviously is now also illegal. Use of the phrase "state age" is not illegal per se, but should be avoided because it tends to deter older applicants; and the use of such information may well be subject to EEOC scrutiny. [7]

---

[6] For an overall reference, see Birren, J.E. and Schaei (Eds.) Handbook of the Psychology of Aging, New York, NY, Von Nostrand Reinhold Co., 1977.

[7] 46 Fed. Reg. 47726 (Sept. 29, 1981).

Further, less obvious age restrictive statements are receiving the attention of attorneys and the courts. In a well-known case of a weapons research facility accused by plaintiffs of age discrimination in a layoff, the U.S. District Judge's Interlocutory Opinion referred to the practice of screening those who received their Ph.D. degrees after 30 years of age. In some cases interviewers noted applicants who received their degrees later than the company established norms and made such statements as "we should overlook his age," or "age should not be considered a detriment."

Application blanks are best either devoid of age items or containing a question such as, "Are you under 18 or 70 or over?" Important in the selection process is the employment requisition, prepared by some person within the organization having manpower decision-making authority. Employment interviewers should examine requisitions for assurance that they reflect up-to-date position descriptions and contain no reference to age unless a bfoq is involved. If a requisition does not meet company policy or ADEA requirements, good procedure dictates that an employment department official return the requisition to the sender in person, explaining his reason for rejection. Obviously, in legal suits, attorneys should review requisitions as well as other employment documents.

The use of tests in selection (for hire, classification, promotion, performance evaluation, etc.) is covered in the Uniform Guidelines. As stated earlier, the Guidelines did not include age in its coverage of protected groups. However, the document is definitive and specific in its treatment of selection standards in such aspects as job relatedness, criterion measures, fairness and evidence, so that if tests of any sort are used, employers should use Guidelines standards. Arvey and Mussio, in a study of civil service clerical workers, found that in one test battery, some subtests discriminated against older workers (produced a situation in which older persons with an equal probability of success would have had unequal chances of selection on the basis of tests) whereas others discriminated against younger workers. [8] Test development is a sophisticated and tricky business and should only be attempted by fully-qualified psychometrists and in accordance with American Psychological Association and Uniform Selection Guidelines standards.

2. Bona Fide Occupational Qualifications

Frequent reasons for using bfoq's have been: business necessity, inability to perform, and public safety. Apparently cognizant of the past employer successes in such cases, the Equal

---

[8] Arvey, R.D. and Mussio, S.J., Test Discrimintion, Job Performance and Age, Industrial Gerontology, No. 16, Winter 1973.

Employment Opportunity Commission has set more stringent standards to be met for this kind of exception and has declared its intention to construe narrowly this exception. 9/

Bfoq's should be used sparingly and only when justified. A litmus test for their use can be phrased in the form of questions:

* Is the age limit unequivocally necessary in the operation of the business? (To photograph young people in advertisements for young peoples' clothes, for example.)
* Are all or substantially all excluded workers in fact disqualified? It is most difficult to provide supporting evidence that this is the case. There are certain occupations, with intensive tasks, necessitating great physical strength and/or sensor-motor coordination, that may be unsuitable for many 40 plus persons. On the other hand, each such case is different, and many factors must be considered before the initial question can be answered, e.g., can it be shown with statistical significance that older workers are poorer performers, and that it is unreasonable to expect employers to single out older persons possessing adequate competence? The author expects EEOC to pay increasing attention to bfoq's. In a recent case, a federal district judge determined that Los Angeles County unlawfully discriminated against 35 plus applicants by rejecting them as sheriff's deputies and fire department helicopter pilots. The judge explained the overlapping of age groups by saying "many over 40 can out-perform many who are under 35". 10/
* Are individuals excluded because of a disqualifying trait that cannot be ascertained except by reference to age (state or federal laws, for instance)?
* Have considerations been given to altering the work environment to improve worker effectiveness and control labor costs? Over the last several decades, factory jobs have been made less strenuous and hazardous with the use of forklifts, overhead cranes, other conveyor mechanisms; automatic machinery, and safety devices. Further, the cost of recruitment, selection, training,

---

9/ 46 Fed. Reg. 47727 (Sept. 29, 1981). For an excellent examination of early cases, read James, R.J. and Alaimo, M.A., BFOQ: An Exception Becoming the Rule? Industrial Gerontology, Vol. 4, No. 4, Fall 1971. Miller, Stanley, Aircraft Accidents and Age, Vol. 4, No. 1, Winter 1981, p. 57.

10/ Los Angeles Times, Part II, p. 2, Court Rejects County Hiring Limits on Age, 11/21/81.

and lowered production of new hires is ballooning. Albert Angrisani, Assistant Secretary of Labor for Employment and Training, with reference to a Chamber of Commerce study, recently said: "A new entrant costs an employer approximately $50,000." 11/
* Cost-benefit analyses may favor work environment changes and/or retraining of 40 plus workers over the acquisition of new entrants.

C. Workforce Maintenance

1. Age Bias in Management

As is the case in the general population, age bias or age stereotypes exist in employer management. Researchers have discovered that the presence of these negative attitudes among managers is now a supportable generalization and can have detrimental effects on employment aspects of older people. Rosen and Jerdee, in their well-designed research study, were able to determine that the use of the age criterion in management decisions was frequent and often unconscious; and in fact, contrary to the expressed belief of the same managers who participated in the study that older people were not treated fairly in employment matters. 12/

Stereotypes about older workers and their capabilities took decades to filter into our subconscious and will not be excised overnight. This symposium will have a salutary effect on participants, including presenters who have looked into subjects more deeply than before. A central question is: "What changes will occur when conferees return to their work places?" One change agent is a firm's training and development activity, which as we shall see, has been underutilized by 40 plus people for a number of reasons.

2. Training and Career Development

There appears to be at least four major problems in the training and career development areas:

* The notion that older people are less trainable than others.
* The causes and effects of older worker obsolescence.

11/ Significant Segment: CETA and the Mature Worker, Nov., 1981, No. 3, a publication of the N.C.O.A., Dorothy Bauer, Project Staff Director.

12/ Rosen, B., and Jerdee, T. H., Too Old or Not Too Old? Harvard Business Review, November-December 1977, pp. 97-106.

* The tendency, because of occupational structure and job progressions of most organizations, for employees to become specialized in short order.
* The absence of capable career counselors in organizations.

Enlightening information on older worker trainability can be found in the results of the Aer Lingus or Irish Airlines project. Technology and competition required extensive changes in work methods and job requirements in the headquarters warehouse. Those selected for the transition were men of long tenure who had customarily performed their work using a forklift method of warehousing. The new method consisted of an electronically controlled storage and retrieval system with an associated computerized documentation system. The carefully designed retraining program was characterized by:

* Group participation by trainees in the plans for conversion to the new system and in the content of the training program.
* Use of the "Discovery Method" in which the trainee arrives at an understanding of the program's content on his own, in contrast with learning this content passively from an instructor.
* Use of simulations, including models, and concrete objects rather than charts, graphs, and other abstract learning devices.

The program, designed especially for older persons of long tenure, was immensely successful. 13/

The generalization can be made that, with few exceptions, younger and older participants respond about equally to the various training programs; and that the quality put into the programs is more important than the ages of those in attendance. One modifying statement is in order. Studies suggest that approaches characterized by high trainee involvement, open communicating, and flexible rather than rigid scheduling are effective for the elderly (e.g., discussion, case T [team] group methods). Programmed instruction, including teaching machines, is a method that appears to be especially applicable to the training of 40 plus employees. It is a self-instructional and self-paced process and the training content can easily be made job relevant. In project Transportation Opportunity Program, a joint government, university, and union effort, basic literacy skills, in addition to work training, were taught through job functions requiring the reading of bills of lading, manifests,

---

13/ Mullan, C. and Gorman, L. Middle Aged and Older Workers at Aer Lingus, Industrial Gerontology, Fall 1972.

and driver examinations. In other words, learning became meaningful. 14/

Skills obsolescence, a subject of increasing concern to industry, is often attributed erroneously to the aging process. Unfortunately this is the case even though those who have given this subject serious thought would have to admit that skills obsolescence of someone 30 years of age could be greater than another 50 years old. It is easy to assume that because age and obsolescence are associated in a general way, one causes the other, i.e., that correlation means causation.

In one comprehensive study of obsolescence, Kaufman 15/ names three personal characteristics possessed by those having a low rate of obsolescence: high intellectual ability, self-motivation and personal flexibility. He reasons that obsolescence can be minimized by good personnel practices and effective organizational environments to permit these worker characteristics to develop. Kaufman lists among environmental conditions: Challenging initial jobs, frequent job changes, rewards for performance, participative leadership, and matrix structures.

Dubin, in his studies of the obsolescence of scientists and technicians in several companies, suggests that companies become obsolete, causing employees to follow. 16/ An earlier study 17/ found that supervisors generally do not actively encourage older workers to take update training. In this study, 64% of 2000 engineers reported that their supervisors assumed a non-committal attitude toward their further training. The researchers' conclusion: company reimbursement is insufficient, subordinates need encouragement. Career obsolescence is serious, but not mysterious. Company initiative and planning can prevent much of it.

14/ Schmidt, F. H., A Repair Shop for Unemployables, Industrial Relations, Vol. 8, No. 3, May 1969, pp. 280-285.

15/ Super, D. and Hall, D.T., Career Development and Planning: Exploration and Planning, Annual Review of Psychology, 1978, 29: 333-372.

16/ Dubin, S. S., Updating and Midcareer Development and Change. A paper presented at the American Psychologic Association annual meeting, Montreal.

17/ Dubin. S. S., Defining Obsolescence and Updating, Maintaining Professional and Technical Competence of the Older Engineer, Dubin, S. S., Shelton, H., and McConnell, J. Eds., American Soc. Engineering Education, 1974.

Some employers have learned that job rotation, well-timed training exposures, "assistant to" assignments, task force participation, and effective organizational design can compensate for the detrimental effects of employee specialization. Specialization is good and necessary, and will be intensified as products, services, and developing disciplines call for it. So the question becomes: how can we foster necessary specialization while helping those being funneled into it by giving a broad base on which to operate? One company that has achieved substantial success in this objective is TRW, Inc. [18]

In TRW's matrix organization, a person may be assigned to one project, or many, depending on his/her expected contribution to a project. Multi-disciplinary task forces are used, creating an exchange of background. In this process, specialized expertise becomes built on a broad rather than a narrow infrastructure. In counseling at TRW, career development rather than organizational development is stressed so that the individual becomes the focus of attention.

There is a deficiency in most companies to provide in-depth career counseling to employees. Employees have uncertainties, fears, lack of confidence and information about what can be in store for them in the future. Some have "had it" with their former jobs, others need help in answering the question, "can I do it all over again?" or "am I really wanted?"

At the beginning of career counseling sessions, analysis, understanding, thoroughness, patience, and honest communicating are necessary. Then, a collaborative search for career objectives is essential. If the latter effort leads to out-of-company possibilities, then these should be given every consideration.

3. Performance Evaluation

During the last decade, severe criticisms have been lodged against the usual performance ratings used by employers. [19] It has been contended that most plans in present use invite rater subjectivity, lack job relatedness and are generally inaccurate when compared with measurable job performance criteria. To minimize rater-biasing influences, Smith and Kendall [20] designed a

---

[18] The Systems Group of TRW, Inc., Behavioral Science Concepts and Management Application, National Industrial Conference Board, New York, New York, 1969, pp. 157-174.

[19] MacGregor, D., An Uneasy Look at Performance Appraisal, Harvard Business Review, September-October 1972, Vol. 50.

[20] Smith, P. and Kendall, L. M., Retranslations of Expectations: An Approach to the Construction of Unambiguous Anchors for Rating Scales, Journal of Applied Psychology, 1963, 47, 149-155.

behaviorally-anchored rating scale (BARS). Since this original effort, variants have been introduced to improve its application. 21/ The new method is described adequately in the literature. Suffice it to say here, the method is based on scaled expectations of job performance, progressing from highly ineffective behavior at the low end of the scale, to highly effective behavior at the other end. Critical job factors are determined by those who are to conduct the ratings and, in some instances, with the help of ratees. Similarly, the points or anchors on the scales are defined by the users of the method. With this new approach, a rater does not make an abstract rating of above or below average or whatever, but matches an aspect of observed performance with the described behaviors on a continuum having to do with a work related critical factor.

Recently, Fred G. Buenger, Chief Executive Officer of Coast Chandlery Enterprises, a marine sales and services organization covering the West Coast, and the author designed a Performance Growth Analysis system with the help of many other employees. The plan's objective is to assist employees in improving work performance and promotability for their and the company's benefit. Findings generated by the plan will be influential in determining promotions, training opportunities, compensation, and so on. As an example of the BARS design, two factors of the eleven used in the Coast Chandlery form can be found in Exhibit A at the end of this paper.

4. Downgrades, Promotions and Layoffs

Many employers do not realize that selection for various forms of reassignment is no less suspect in age bias cases than any other kind of selection. Age bias suits involving promotion, downgrade, and layoff are becoming more frequent, and many employers are not prepared for investigations into these procedures and actions. In such status changes, all non-age factors can be given consideration: education, related training, past and present work performance, physical and psychological tests, etc. However, an employer may be required to prove the job relatedness of any of the factors utilized in the selection.

The use of committees for selection for any form of reassignment in sophisticated or technical positions is becoming customary. Such committees usually consist of the person possessing the opening or surplus, some of his peers, his boss, and a representative of the personnel department. In good practice, recorders prepare a detailed report on why one was selected and others rejected. Copies of the minutes are placed in the folders

---

21/ Campbell, J.P., Dunnette, M.D. Lawler, E.E. and Weick, K.E., Managerial Behavior, Performance and Effectiveness, McGraw-Hill, New York, New York, 1970.

of all candidates. It is acceptable practice that all candidates are interviewed for the purposes of informing them that they were considered, and if not selected, of discussing how they can improve their probability of later selection, if it happens to be a promotion involved.

D. Manpower Planning

Manpower planning is the process of applying organizational planning, based on the goals and objectives of the enterprise, to present and future manpower requirements. It consists essentially of determining numbers and characteristics of people now in the organization's workforce, and of predicting future labor requirements. A beneficial result of such planning is that selection, training, promotion, and other employment functions can be planned in advance to reduce labor costs, improve operating efficiency, and minimize employee dislocation. The planning of manpower can accomplish a leveling off of high and low points in production and services by the use of normal turnover ahead of slack periods (to avoid layoffs), and by the acquisition of retirees and other experienced workers during peak periods. To an increasing extent, companies are making use of former employees now retired, who because of their job knowledge, are in need of little or no training. A serendipitous benefit goes, of course, to the retiree who may want only temporary or part-time work.

1. Age Audits

One aspect of manpower planning is the age audit. Information from such an audit can be especially significant to employers at the present time because the projected age composition of the nation's population shows a labor force that is growing older and living longer. The age 20-24 population will build up until 1985, reflecting the high birth rates of the 1950's and 60's. During the late 1960's, birth rates began to decline sharply and this decline will be reflected in the shrinkage of the 20-24 year old population from the mid-1980's on. As a result, firms must know about their present 40 plus employees, and how well they are being groomed and utilized.

A well-designed age audit can reveal:

* The extent of utilization of 40 plus workers;
* Instances of under- and over-representation of people in certain age categories by occupations;
* New placement possibilities for older workers;
* Personnel problems when still remediable; and
* The changing age composition of the workforce;

An age audit is a review and analysis of an organization's employment policies, procedures, and practices with regard to the age of its employees. All information generated by such an audit is entirely confidential to the initiating company and is performed only for that organization's benefit. Recommended steps for an age audit are:

* Interviews with personnel, labor relations, supervision, etc. on subjects of labor utilization, age and work, state and federal age legislation, and work problems in the area of the interviewee's jurisdiction.
* A determination of the presence and adequacy of policy statements regarding the company's compliance with ADEA and its intention to employ all persons on an age-neutral basis.
* An examination of personnel data reports on training, compensation, promotions, layoffs, etc.
* An inspection of a random sampling of requisitions, employment interviewer comments, employer jackets or folders, etc. If in such material age-biased comments are found, these should not be removed but the writers of such statements should be interviewed and informed of company policy and existing law. The results of such interviews should then be recorded and placed with the document containing the age comment to serve as evidence of affirmative corrective action by the company.
* Tabulations of occupational age distributions by hires, promotions, and retirements. Tabulations of age distributions by training programs, and performance ratings, etc.
* Comparisons of age distributions obtained above with reference populations. Reference populations may be the local labor market, all employees qualified for a training program or promotion, or all employees who should have been considered for downgrade or layoff. Reference populations are compared with the results of company-initiated actions (employment decisions) to ascertain whether significant age discrepancies exist.

For a statistical treatment of age audits, refer to Spalding's article in Aging & Work. [22]

IV. SUMMARIZING STATEMENT

The escalating number of EEOC age cases (from 3097 in fiscal 1979 to 8779 in fiscal 1981), and the burgeoning suits in the employment maintenance areas (training and development, promotion, reassignment, etc.) all suggest that employers, the EEOC, and attorneys in this field should be busy preparing for much more activity as a result of discrimination. As is the case with the general population, age discrimination is pervasive in management. That it is often not deliberate and sometimes even subconscious elevates the seriousness of the problem. Further,

---

[22] Spalding, J.B. Self-Inventory Methods to Prepare for ADEA Suits, Aging and Work, Vol. 2, No. 4, Fall 1979.

the usual industrial relations systems tend to be inherently biasing because of the absence of policy guidelines, the acceptance of incomplete reporting, the subjectivity of performance ratings, the existence of inadequate job descriptions, and a host of other conditions that can make for emotionally-loaded or whimsical attitudes about personnel decisions. True, many progressive companies cannot be accused of many of the conditions cited above. Yet, many can be, and in the opinion of the author, most employers can benefit from a critical look at their personnel policies, procedures, and practices.

Innovation is needed now, when this country's gross national product is tapering off, when we are losing ground in competition with foreign business and industry, when our younger workforce is about to reduce in relative size, and when our 40 plus workers are being overlooked as a potentially valuable source of labor. Underutilization of manpower is a luxury this nation cannot afford.

EXHIBIT A

Levels

Service Effectiveness. Consider initiative and perseverance in satisfying customer needs, friendliness and diplomacy, technical knowledge and experience in repair and overhaul		Inventory Control Performance. Consider scrutinizing all inventory items for disposition of superannuated, slow moving merchandise; identifying for purchase new, high potential items, and establishing optimal lead times for inventory stock purchases.
Performs simple assembly and disassembly operations under close supervision	1	Not familiar with most inventory items. Needs close supervision when carrying out most assignments.
Performs more common assembly and disassembly operations under supervision	2	Somewhat familiar with more common items. Carries out some assignments on own initiative.
	3	Specializes in some inventory items. Has good knowledge of limited area.
Is able to diagnose and repair most instruments/equipment in his field.	4	Knows the stock or where to get information about it. Satisfactory control of inventory items.
Diagnoses and repairs nearly all instruments and equipment in this field and has working knowledge of related fields.	5	
	6	
Top-notch technician in all or most service areas. Knows references. High familiarity with service supply sources	7	Assumes initiative in administering inventory control, shipping, receiving, etc. Has installed improved methods, minimized costs.

THE ADEA AND EMPLOYEE BENEFIT PLANS

Bernard T. King, Esq. *

---

* Partner, Blitman and King, Syracuse, New York. Mr. King is a graduate of LeMoyne College with a Bachelor of Science in Industrial and Labor Relations and a cum laude graduate of Syracuse University College of Law. His firm represents a wide array of union and employee benefit fund clients in the Northeast. Mr. King is an Executive Committee member and immediate past president of the Labor and Employment Section of the New York State Bar Association. He is a Council Member of the Labor and Employment Law Section of the American Bar Association, having also served as a Co-Chairman of that Section's Committee on the Development of the Law under the NLRA. He is also the Section's Council Liaison to its Committee on Employee Benefits and to its Committee on the Development of the Law under the NLRA and a committee member of the ABA's Joint Committee on Employee Benefits.

The author gratefully acknowledges the participation of his associate, David A. Kline, in the researching, analyzing and writing of this paper.

TABLE OF CONTENTS

			Page
I.	INTRODUCTION		1
II.	CURRENT ADMINISTRATIVE INTERPRETATIONS OF THE ACT		4
	A.	The DOL Interpretations	4
		1. The Benefit-by-Benefit Approach	6
		2. The Benefit Package Approach	9
	B.	The EEOC Interpretations	10
	C.	Internal Revenue Service Guidelines	12
III.	PROPOSED LEGISLATION		13
	A.	Five Year Vesting	14
	B.	Participation Requirements	15
	C.	Benefit Accrual Beyond Normal Retirement Age	16
	D.	Proposed Changes to the ADEA	16
IV.	COMMENT		16

THE ADEA AND EMPLOYEE BENEFIT PLANS

I. INTRODUCTION

The purpose of this Article is to examine the impact of the Age Discrimination in Employment Act 1/ on employee benefit plans. The Act itself, as well as pertinent administrative interpretations and guidelines, will be discussed. And, some of the options available to plans seeking compliance with the law will be presented. Comment will also be made upon some of the proposed legislation in this area.

It can be said generally that the ADEA has created substantial new rights for older workers, including rights as they relate specifically to employee benefit plans. On the other hand, the Act has not created significant direct costs for employers or benefit plans. Rather, the ADEA, as will be explained later, largely leaves to the collective bargaining process (in unionized industries) the extent to which these older employees will receive benefits on a parity with younger workers.

The Act applies to employers, employment agencies and labor organizations and prohibits age discrimination in employment, compensation, referral for employment and membership in unions. The original 1967 Act covered individuals in the 40 to 65 age group. The Act's protection was expanded by the 1978 amendments to cover persons at least 40 but less than 70 years of age. All employers in commerce with twenty or more employees are covered by the Act. 2/

While the current ADEA condemns employment discrimination against persons within the protected age group, Section 4(f)(2) of the Act 3/ provides a major exception for actions undertaken

---

1/ 29 U.S.C. § 621 et seq., hereafter "ADEA" or "the Act."

2/ An employer not covered by ADEA should determine whether he is subject to a similar state statute, since many states have legislation prohibiting age discrimination. Many of those states do not require a minimum number of employees to trigger coverage; when there is such a requirement, the specified minimum number varies widely.

3/ 29 U.S.C. § 623(f)(2). That section provides:

> It shall not be unlawful for an employer, employment agency, or labor organization -
> * * *
> to observe the terms of a . . . bona fide employee benefit plan, which is not a subterfuge to evade the purposes of this chapter, except that no such employee benefit plan

pursuant to the terms of bona fide employee benefit plans. Thus, actions which would otherwise seem to constitute illegal discrimination under the Act are in fact legal if undertaken in compliance with the terms of a bona fide employee benefit plan. An analysis, then, of the breadth and scope of this Section 4(f)(2) exception shall be the principal subject matter of this paper.

The Act's original Section 4(f)(2) had been held to permit the mandatory retirement of employees irrespective of age if retirement was called for by the terms of an employee benefit plan. 4/ The Act's 1978 amendments, however, make it clear that such involuntary retirement of employees within the protected age group will no longer be permitted. 5/

The statute itself does not specify in any detail what will be permitted under the Section 4(f)(2) exception. For instance, it does not clarify what benefit level employee benefit plans will be permitted or required to maintain for older workers. Administrative interpretations and guidelines are intended to fill the void. There has been a certain amount of confusion in this regard created by a change in agencies charged with administering the statute.

The administration and enforcement of ADEA was transferred in 1979 from the Department of Labor 6/ to the Equal Employment Opportunity Commission. 7/ Before this change the DOL had issued guidelines interpreting the Act. 8/ The EEOC's final Interpretations issued in 1981 replace most of those guidelines. However, the EEOC expressly left standing the DOL's

---

shall excuse the failure to hire any individual and no such . . . employee benefit plan shall require or permit the involuntary retirement of any individual . . . [covered by the Act] because of the age of such individual. . . .

4/ See United Air Lines, Inc. v. McMann, 434 U.S. 192 (1977).

5/ See the Age Discrimination in Employment Act Amendments of 1978, P.L. 95-256, 92 Stat. 189 (1978). The individuals covered by the Act are referred to in this article as "older workers."

6/ Hereafter "DOL." See 29 U.S.C. § 626.

7/ Hereafter "EEOC." See, Reorg. Plan No. 1 of 1978, 43 Fed. Reg. 19,807 (1978); Exec. Order No. 12144 of June 22, 1979, 44 Fed. Reg. 37,193 (1979).

8/ See, generally, Interpretive Bulletin On Costs and Benefits Under Employee Benefit Plans, 29 C.F.R. part 860 (1979).

Interpretations as they relate to employee benefit plans. 9/ Portions of the 1981 EEOC Interpretations do have a bearing on benefit plans, but, for those seeking to determine the law in this area, the principal authority still remains the 1979 DOL Interpretations.

Adding to the earlier confusion were EEOC draft proposals circulated prior to its 1981 Interpretations which would have substantially changed the DOL guidelines as they related to benefit plans. Those draft proposals were never incorporated into the EEOC's 1981 Interpretations, however, that agency having decided to retain the earlier DOL guidelines in this area until it could later complete a full substantive review. 10/

The discussion which follows will generally focus on the DOL's 1979 Interpretive Bulletin on Costs and Benefits Under Employee Benefit Plans. 11/ To the extent that EEOC's 1981 guidelines deal with benefit plans they will also be treated. 12/

9/ In its September 29, 1981 Interpretations, 29 C.F.R. § 1625, the EEOC states:

> These final interpretations are not intended to rescind the Department of Labor's Interpretive Bulletin on employee benefit plans . . . . That interpretive bulletin will remain in effect . . . . Upon completion of its substantive review of that interpretation, the Commission will publish any proposed modifications as to that document for notice and comment in the Federal Register.

10/ Id.

11/ 29 C.F.R. § 860.120. Hereafter "DOL Interpretations," or "Interpretations."

12/ 29 C.F.R. § 1625 et seq. It should be noted that the DOL and EEOC interpretations are guidelines, not substantive regulations with the force of law. There is no statutory standard which governs the deference which must be afforded such interpretations by the courts. The Supreme Court has indicated that such interpretations,

> while not controlling upon the courts by reason of their authority, do constitute a body of experience and informed judgment to which courts and litigants may properly resort for guidance. The weight of such a judgment . . . will depend upon . . . all those factors which give it power to persuade, if lacking power to control.

Additionally, certain caveats will be mentioned as to IRS's guidelines in this area. 13/

II. CURRENT ADMINISTRATIVE INTERPRETATIONS OF THE ACT

   A.   The DOL Interpretations.

The 1979 Department of Labor Interpretation provides general guidelines for applying the Section 4(f)(2) exception from ADEA to employee plans and specifically establishes rules governing the way in which employers and plans will be permitted to reduce employee benefits without running afoul of ADEA.

Although the DOL Interpretations do not so state, it should be noted that there are a wide variety of different types of plans and benefits to which these Interpretations would apply. Employee benefit plans might be broadly categorized according to (1) the manner in which the plan is established or maintained and (2) the type of benefits provided. Plans which are established as a result of collective bargaining between a union and an employer are called "collectively-bargained" plans. If only one employer is involved it is a "single employer" plan. If more than one employer is obligated to contribute to the plan, it is called a "Multiemployer" plan. Non collectively-bargained plans may likewise be maintained by a single employer or by a group of employers.

Employee plans provide two basic categories of benefits: (1) "retirement" benefits and, (2) a wide variety of related benefits commonly referred to as "welfare" benefits. Retirement benefits represent some form of deferred compensation such as is provided by a pension, profit-sharing, or employee stock ownership plan. Welfare benefits, on the other hand, are generally designed to protect against unexpected contingencies such as those covered by health insurance, life insurance, disability insurance, supplemental unemployment, accident, death, and sick leave benefits. Welfare benefits may also include benefits such as vacation benefits, disability benefits, holiday benefits, apprenticeship training, or prepaid legal services. 14/

Generally, under the DOL Interpretations, older employees are guaranteed only a minimum level of benefit protection. Benefit plans may reduce benefit levels for older workers but no

---

   See, General Electric v. Gilbert, 429 U.S. 125, 141, (1976).

13/ Rev. Rul. 81-210, I.R.B. 1981-36, 7.

14/ See the Employee Retirement Income Security Act of 1974, [hereafter "ERISA") Section 3(1), 29 U.S.C. § 1002(1), defining the term "welfare benefit plan."

more than is necessary to achieve approximate equivalency in employer or plan cost as between older and younger workers. 15/ A benefit plan is not in compliance with the statute unless the actual cost incurred on behalf of an older worker is at least equal to that incurred on behalf of a younger worker. Under these Interpretations, the older worker may indeed receive a smaller benefit but the cost of providing that benefit for the employer or plan must remain the same. And, the older worker's benefits may not be reduced unless the plan contains an express provision, communicated to the employees, setting forth each such reduction. 16/

The Section 4(f)(2) exemption is an exception to the general prohibitions of the Act and must be narrowly construed. The burden is on the plan to show that all reductions are justified by significant cost considerations. This burden must be met by data showing the actual cost of providing the benefit in question to the employees involved over a representative period of years, or data for a larger group of similarly situated employees.

The Interpretations permit only two basic methods by which an employer or a plan may reduce the benefits of older workers without running afoul of the Act: (1) The "Benefit-by-Benefit" approach, which requires that each specific benefit reduction be justified by the increased cost of providing that specific benefit for the older worker, 17/ and (2) the "Benefit Package" approach which permits a reduction in one specific type of benefit in excess of what would be justified by the increased

---

15/ Such a plan in order to avail itself of the Section 4(f)(2) exception must be "bona fide" and must not be a "subterfuge to evade the purposes of the Act." 29 U.S.C. § 623(f). The Interpretation provides that a plan is "bona fide" if its terms have been accurately described in writing to all employees and if it actually provides the benefits specified in the plan. A plan is not a "subterfuge" if the lower benefits provided older workers are justified by age-related cost considerations. 29 C.F.R. § 860.120(b) and (d).

16/ 29 C.F.R. § 860.120(c). The Interpretation explains that this requirement is important because it assures that employees will have an opportunity to learn about the reductions and, consequently, have an opportunity to protest. With respect to collectively bargained plans, this requirement brings the issue of benefit reduction to the attention of the union and its membership and may well result in a bargaining issue. Disclosure of such provisions to employees in a document which satisfies the disclosure requirements of ERISA, such as a Summary Plan Description, satisfies this communication requirement.

17/ 29 C.F.R. § 860.120(d)(2).

cost of that benefit but only if the excess reduction is offset by an equivalent increase in another benefit. 18/

1. The Benefit-by-Benefit Approach

This approach must be looked at in relation to the two types of benefit plans referred to in the DOL Interpretations, namely, employee welfare plans, 19/ and employee retirement plans.

(a) <u>Employee Welfare Plans</u>. Welfare benefit plans may reduce benefits under the benefit-by-benefit approach so long as each reduction is not greater than that which is necessary to make the cost of providing the benefit the same for older as for younger workers. 20/ It must be understood, however, that the language of the Interpretation is permissive only. Employers and plans may well continue the same level of benefits for older workers as they do for the younger workers. In fact, collective bargaining may compel the maintenance of higher benefits for older workers. But, the Interpretations do permit a reduction of benefits under this Benefit-by-Benefit approach. And, the DOL Interpretations, in this regard, apply specifically to life insurance, health insurance, and long term disability insurance. The same principles apply to other welfare benefits even though not individually dealt with in the Interpretations.

<u>Life Insurance</u>

The amount of life insurance coverage for older workers may be decreased only as the cost of providing each dollar of coverage rises with the workers' increasing age. Employees may be grouped in five-year age brackets for purposes of the reduction so that, for example, all employees between age 60 and 65 receive the same coverage, while all employees between age 65 and 69 receive lower coverage. Under the Interpretation, however, no employees may be totally denied life insurance coverage on the basis of age. 21/

18/ 29 C.F.R. § 860.120(f)(2). The total cost to the Plan must remain the same. Also, the Benefit Package approach must be used for the overall benefit of older workers.

19/ As used herein, the term "welfare plan" refers to an employee plan which provides benefits other than retirement benefits. <u>See</u> the discussion in the text at note 14, <u>supra</u>. The Interpretations indicate that because there are no significant cost considerations for providing paid vacations and uninsured sick leave to older employees, no reductions in such benefits are permitted.

20/ 29 C.F.R. §860.120.

21/ <u>Id</u>.

Health Insurance

Health insurance benefits may be reduced for older workers according to the same increased-cost principles. The reductions may not be concentrated, however, on specific items which would have the effect of making coverage less attractive to older workers.

Health insurance plans are not required to duplicate benefits provided to older workers by Medicare. Under the DOL Interpretations, such benefits may be "carved out" of the health insurance plan. This means that Medicare will provide primary health care coverage for eligible employees, with the health insurance plan paying only those expenses not covered by Medicare. If the plan wants to make use of this Medicare "carve out," it must inform each employee eligible for Medicare of the need to apply for coverage and must provide assistance in the Medicare application process. The plan or employer must pay the employee's Medicare premium costs so that the total benefits provided these older workers are as favorable as for those who are not eligible for Medicare. [22]

Long Term Disability

It is no longer permissible for a plan to cut off long term disability benefits at age 65. [23] If such protection is provided for younger employees, it must also be continued for older workers. However, a plan may avoid age related cost increases by reducing the amount of benefits available to such older employees, or by reducing the duration of such benefits. The Interpretations set forth two representative situations in which the Act permits a reduction in the duration of benefits so long as the amount is not reduced: (1) with respect to disabilities which occur at age 60 or less, benefits may cease at age 65, and (2) for disabilities occurring after age 60, benefits may cease five years after disablement or at age 70, which ever occurs first. [24]

---

[22] Id. As an alternative to the "carve out," employees eligible for Medicare may be placed in a separate plan which supplements Medicare benefits. The cost of providing the supplemental plan must be at least as great as the cost of incuding the Medicare employees in the regular plan under the "carve-out" approach, and the supplemental plan must provide benefits equal to those which a Medicare employee would receive under the regular plan.

[23] Id. It has been customary to cut off such coverage at age 65. However, this is no longer permissible because the ADEA now extends protection to employees until age 70.

[24] Id.

(b) _Employee Retirement Plans_. The benefit-by-benefit approach generally permits benefit reductions for older workers with respect to both defined benefit and defined contribution retirement plans. A defined benefit plan is a plan which promises an employee a particular benefit on retirement based on a formula such as years of service multiplied by a dollar amount per year, or based on average compensation. The benefits are paid for ("funded") through employer contributions and the plan's investment earnings.

A defined contribution plan is a plan which calls for specific contributions to be made for each employee based on dollars per hour, or upon a percentage of compensation each year. Accumulated contributions plus a pro-rata share of plan earnings are maintained in an individual account for each employee. No specific benefit is promised. Upon retirement, the employee receives the value of his individual account.

In most circumstances 25/ neither type of retirement plan is required, under the Act, to add to a participant's accumulated pension benefits for employment after a participant reaches normal retirement age. 26/ Where an employer has only a defined contribution plan, this means that the employer need not make contributions on behalf of a person who reaches normal retirement age. 27/ Similarly, a defined benefit plan may stop crediting a

---

25/ See, note 27, infra, for a discussion of the exceptions.

26/ Usually, normal retirement age will be age 65. However, a plan may specify an earlier normal retirement age. Section 411(a)(8) of the Internal Revenue Code, 26 U.S.C. § 411(a)(8) requires that normal retirement age be the earlier of

    (A) the time a plan participant attains normal retirement age under the plan, or
    (B) the later of --
        (i) the time a plan participant attains age 65, or
        (ii) the 10th anniversary of the time a plan participant commenced participation in the plan.

In no event may normal retirement age be later than the mandatory retirement age, if a mandatory retirement age is specified in the plan.

27/ If the defined contribution plan is deemed to be "supplemental," contributions must be made to employees after normal retirement age. A plan is "supplemental" if the employees are also covered by a defined benefit plan. If there is no defined benefit plan, but more than one defined contribution plan, the employer must designate one plan as

participant for service, and the employer may cease making contributions, after that age.

Both defined benefit and "non-supplemental" defined contribution plans 28/ may exclude from participation an employee who is hired after he reaches normal retirement age. A defined benefit plan may also exclude an employee who is hired less than five years prior to normal retirement age. 29/ A plan may provide that no pension payments will begin until the employee actually retires. 30/ And, although involuntary retirement is prohibited before age 70, the guidelines make it clear that plans may continue to provide for voluntary early retirement.

Of course, as with welfare plans, any reduction of benefits is merely permissive. An employer or plan may continue to credit service after the normal retirement age, or the collective bargaining process may require that such service be credited.

(2) The Benefit Package Approach.

The benefit package approach is intended to permit greater flexibility than the benefit-by-benefit approach. It permits a plan to balance off reductions in one benefit by an increase in a different benefit. For example, benefits which are less desirable for older workers may be reduced further than would be justified by the increased cost of such benefits provided the cost savings are used to increase other benefits which are more desirable for such workers. Under this approach, a welfare plan might reduce life insurance benefits for older workers to a greater extent than would otherwise be justified under the benefit-by-benefit approach, if this reduction is offset by a comparable increase in health insurance coverage.

---

non-supplemental. Only the non-supplemental plan could then provide for the cessation of contributions after normal retirement age. See 29 C.F.R. § 860.120(f)(1)(iv).

28/ See note 27, supra.

29/ 29 C.F.R. § 860.120(f)(1)(iv). This interpretation of the Act is consistent with ERISA and the regulations issued thereunder which contain extensive provisions pertaining to retirement and other employee benefit plans. Neither ERISA nor ADEA require a plan to exclude persons hired during this period.

30/ 29 C.F.R. § 860.120. Salary increases and benefit improvements which take place under the plan after an employee reaches his normal retirement age need not be applied to employees working beyond normal retirement age. Such employees must, however, be afforded the benefit improvements afforded retirees.

The Benefit Package approach has limited utility for most employee plans, however, because of the restrictions that go with it. It expressly may not be used to justify reductions in health benefits greater than would be permitted under the Benefit-by-Benefit approach, even if such reductions are balanced off by other increases. Furthermore, it cannot be used at all with retirement plans. And, the examples cited by DOL to show how benefit cost trade-offs are to occur leave the impression that it would be difficult to achieve and maintain a satisfactory balancing of reductions against increases. 31/

B. The EEOC Interpretations.

EEOC's 1981 Interpretations have a pertinent, although limited, impact on employee plans. 32/ Under the Interpretations, bona fide apprenticeship programs may continue to impose age limits for participation which restrict training benefits to youths. This exception to the general prohibitions

---

31/ See the examples in 29 C.F.R. § 860.120(f)(2)(v). This section requires the production of data to justify the reductions. Even if a proper balancing were initially achieved, rising costs of various benefits might quickly upset it.

32/ EEOC has at least temporarily adopted the DOL's 1979 Interpretive Bulletin. See note 9, supra. Prior to its 1981 Interpretive Bulletin, the EEOC had circulated a draft revision to the DOL's Interpretive Bulletin for review by the DOL, IRS, and the President's Commission on Pension Policy. The draft would have: (1) required defined benefit plans to cover employees hired even after normal retirement age; (2) required defined benefit plans to accrue benefits beyond normal retirement age unless a participant is entitled to a fully accrued benefit at normal retirement age; (3) required defined benefit plans to adjust accrued benefits for employment after normal retirement age by augmenting the benefits with either interest earned or by taking into account all salary increases and benefit improvements occurring after normal retirement age; (4) permitted the application of a "benefit package" approach to retirement plans; and (5) effected changes to the concept of "supplemental plans" described in the DOL Interpretive Bulletin. After DOL review of the EEOC draft, Secretary of Labor Ray Marshall wrote a detailed letter to EEOC Chair Eleanor Holmes Norton criticizing the EEOC approach in these areas. See Letter from Secretary Ray Marshall, reprinted in [1980] Pension Reptr. No. 315 (BNA), at R-1. The letter pointed out various conflicts between the EEOC proposals and provisions of ERISA and the Internal Revenue Code. Subsequently the EEOC withdrew its draft pending further study.

of the Act against age discrimination was made in recognition of the fact that apprenticeship programs are an extension of the educational process designed to prepare young men and women for skilled employment. 33/

The Interpretations also provide that the Bona Fide Executive and High Policymaking Exemption which was added by the 1978 ADEA amendments and which permits the mandatory retirement of such employees at age 65 if a certain level of retirement benefits is paid, will be narrowly construed so as to apply to only a very few top level employees. 34/ Thus, the exemption will probably have little impact on most employee plans.

Detailed rules are set forth in the Interpretations which describe the general requirements for keeping records under the ADEA. These rules require that employers keep copies of employee benefit plans and related documents on file while the plan is in effect and for at least one year after the plan terminates.

The final EEOC Interpretations also make it clear that the 1978 amendment prohibiting involuntary retirement prior to age 70 applies to all employee plans regardless of whether that plan predates the 1967 Act or the 1978 amendments. The EEOC also provides that the amendment applies to lawsuits pending on the date of enactment (April 6, 1978) or filed thereafter, challenging involuntary retirements occurring either before or after

---

33/ 29 C.F.R. § 1625.13. Such programs must meet the standards set forth in 29 C.F.R. § 521.2 and 621.3.

34/ 29 C.F.R. § 1625.12. The provision permits the compulsory retirement of executives or employees in high policymaking positions who are 65 years of age or older if such persons have occupied such positions for 2 years immediately preceding retirement and are entitled to an annual retirement benefit of at least $27,000.

The "high policy making position" exemption applies to those individuals who have little or no line authority but whose position and responsibilities are such that they play a significant role in the development of corporate policy and effectively recommend the implementation of that corporate policy.

The $27,000 annual retirement benefit required by the exemption may include amounts payable from the employer's pension, profit sharing, savings, or other deferred compensation plan. Detailed methods of calculating these benefits are described in the Interpretation.

the date of enactment. 35/ The courts, however, have not upheld the EEOC position on this latter point. 36/

C. *Internal Revenue Service Guidelines*.

Recently issued I.R.S. guidelines caution employers and employee plans that they must be cognizant of the indirect effects which amendments designed to comply with ADEA may have on a plan's tax-qualified status. 37/ Plan amendments adopted to comply with ADEA, and lawful on their face, might interact with other plan provisions to jeopardize a plan's tax exemption.

For example, a plan amendment increasing the mandatory retirement age in certain defined benefit plans from 65 to 70 could result in a participant being entitled to a pension benefit in excess of that permitted by the tax laws. 38/ In such a situation, another amendment would have to be added to limit the maximum possible benefit under the plan. Several examples of how

---

35/ 29 C.F.R. § 1625.9.

36/ *EEOC v. Shell Oil Co.*, 637 F.2d 683 (9th Cir. 1981); *Jensen v. Gulf Oil Refining & Marketing Co.*, 623 F.2d 406 (5th Cir. 1980); *Smart v. Porter Paint Co.*, 630 F.2d 490 (7th Cir. 1980); and *Sikora v. American Can Co.*, 622 F.2d 1116, (3d Cir. 1981).

37/ Rev. Rul. 81-210, I.R.B. 1981-36,7.

38/ Section 415 of the Internal Revenue Code, 26 U.S.C. § 415, provides for limits on pension benefits payable from a qualified plan. Generally, the highest annual benefit which can be paid is the lesser of $75,000 or 100% of the participant's average compensation for the highest three consecutive calendar years during which he was an active participant in the plan. In order to satisfy these requirements, the plan must preclude the possibility that any annual benefit exceeding the limitations will be payable at any time. A plan could thus fail to satisfy the § 415 limitations even though no participant has in fact accrued a benefit in excess of the limitations. See Reg. § 1.415.1(d) and 1.415-3(a).

A plan amendment increasing the mandatory retirement age in a defined benefit plan which bases the benefit on years of participation or service may result in a violation of the maximum limitations of Section 415. Such an amendment might result in a participant who works past age 65 accruing benefits in excess of 100% of average compensation, in violation of the Section. In that event, the plan would have to be further amended to limit the maximum benefit to 100% of average compensation.

amendments intended to comply with ADEA may affect the tax-status of retirement plans are set forth in the guidelines. 39/

Amendments adopted to comply with ADEA will not cause tax qualification problems for most plans, but any such amendment should be reviewed by plan consultants and attorneys to assure IRS compliance.

III. PROPOSED LEGISLATION

Two new bills have been introduced in the House which would require retirement plans to grant older workers substantial additional rights. 40/ These bills would expand vesting, participation, and benefit accrual rights, and would remove the upper age limit for coverage under ADEA. Many of the provisions in the bills are similar to the provisions of the early EEOC draft interpretations of the Act which were never finalized. 41/ The major provisions of the bills are discussed below.

39/ According to the guidelines, problems may arise which would affect vesting, accrual of benefits, and coverage. The situations described are extremely technical, and would probably arise very infrequently. However, the possible effect of any amendment on a plan's tax qualification should always be considered.

40/ H.R. 3396, the "Retirement Security Portability Non-Discrimination Act" and H.R. 3397, the "Older Worker Employment Incentives Act" were introduced in May, 1981. It is expected that these bills will not be enacted during the first session of the 97th Congress, but that they will be reintroduced in the second session. Many of the provisions contained in the bills have received strong support from those interested in the problems of older Americans, and it is likely that pressure to enact these provisions will continue in the future.

41/ See note 32, supra for an outline of the EEOC draft proposals. One criticism of the EEOC proposals which cannot be directed against the bills is that they conflicted with portions of ERISA and the Internal Revenue Code. The bills amend those provisions of ERISA and the Code which conflicted with the EEOC proposals. Moreover, the bills contain a provision which requires the I.R.S. to submit to Congress a draft of any technical amendments which may be required to give effect to the substantive provisions of the legislation.

A. *Five Year Vesting*

The bills would change the vesting provisions of ERISA and the Internal Revenue Code to require full vesting in five years. 42/ The provision would make it easier for older workers to become fully vested in a retirement benefit in situations where they change jobs as they near retirement age. This could result in many such persons receiving larger benefits than is required under the currently permissible vesting provisions. 43/

42/ An employee is vested in his pension benefits when, under the plan, he has a nonforfeitable right to receive the benefits. Current provisions of the law allow the vesting of benefits to occur in steps over periods as long as 15 years. The bills would replace those provisions with a requirement that vesting be complete in five years.

43/ Under current law, an employee must have ten years of service to become 100% vested upon reaching normal retirement age. Under the bill he would be 100% vested after only 5 years; thus the provision could result in such persons receiving larger pensions at normal retirement age. Section 203(a)(2) of ERISA, 29 U.S.C. § 1053(a)(2), provides that a plan satisfies the vesting requirements if an employee with 10 years of service is 100% vested, or if it meets the requirements of either of the two following vesting schedules:

(1) Years of Service	Nonforfeitable Percentage of Accrued Benefit
5	25
6	30
7	35
8	40
9	45
10	50
11	60
12	70
13	80
14	90
15 or more	100

(2) If years of service equal or exceed--	and sum of age and service equals or exceeds--	then the nonforfeitable percentage is--
5	45	50
6	47	60
7	49	70
8	51	80
9	53	90
10	55	100

The proposal would, of course, also benefit younger workers who change jobs before becoming vested under current law. Under the proposed legislation, they would become 100% vested in a benefit after only five years.

B. Participation Requirements

The bills would amend ERISA and the Internal Revenue Code to prohibit defined benefit retirement plans from excluding persons from the plan if they begin employment before they reach normal retirement age. Current law permits a plan to exclude from participation those persons who begin employment five years or less before normal retirement age. 44/

This proposal would allow employees beginning work as late as normal retirement age (65 in many plans) to participate in a defined benefit plan. Older employees commencing new occupations could obtain vested benefits in situations where, under present law, such employees could be totally excluded from the plan. For example, under the proposed legislation, a 64 year old who entered a plan with a normal retirement age of 65 could be eligible for a pension at age 69. 45/

It is evident that if either of these two vesting schedules is used, a worker who has only five years of service in a plan at normal retirement age would be entitled to less than 50 percent of the benefit he had accrued under the plan. In order to become 100% vested, he would need 5 more years of service. The proposed 5-year vesting would thus require full vesting much sooner than the currently permissible rules, and would result in increased benefits for older workers who have relatively few years of service at normal retirement age.

44/ § 202(a)(2) of ERISA, 29 U.S.C. § 1052(a)(2), provides:
No Pension plan may exclude from participation (on the basis of age) employees who have attained a specified age, unless --

   (a) the plan is a --
      (i) defined benefit plan, or
      (ii) target benefit plan (as defined under regulations prescribed by the Secretary of Treasury), and
   (b) such employees begin employment with the employer after they have attained a specific age which is not more than 5 years before the normal retirement age under the plan.

45/ The amount of the pension might not be very large compared to other pensions paid by the plan because such an employee would have few years of service.

C. **Benefit Accrual Beyond Normal Retirement Age**

The bills would add a new provision to the Code and to ERISA which would require plans to credit service beyond normal retirement age for those employees who have not accrued the maximum normal retirement benefit. The intent of the proposed legislation is to entitle an employee who continues to work beyond the plan's normal retirement age to a benefit greater than he would have had if he had ceased work at normal retirement age.

This would clearly be the result with a defined contribution plan to which post-normal retirement age contributions are made, since the participant's benefit in such a plan constitutes the accumulated contributions and accrued interest to his credit in the plan. It is not clear because of the way the present legislation is drafted, however, whether the proposal in its present form would have an equivalent effect on defined benefit plans. 46/

D. **Proposed Changes to the ADEA**

The proposed legislation would also remove the upper age limit for ADEA coverage, thus providing protection for all persons 40 years of age or older. It would also remove the Bona Fide Executive and High Policymaking exemption from the Act.

Removal of the upper age limit in the Act, along with the expansion of vesting, participation, and accrual rights, would obviously make it easier for some older employees to remain in the work force. The proposed deletion of the Bona Fide Executive Exemption would probably have no substantial effect on the work force because the present exemption is limited to so few top level employees.

COMMENT

Unquestionably the ADEA has a significant impact on employee benefit plans. New rights are created for older workers. They may not be compulsorily retired under the Act prior to age 70. If older workers continue working, their welfare plan benefits may not be reduced beyond the age-related cost of providing them such benefits. On the other hand, by virtue of the Act's Section 4(f)(2) exemption, the level of protection afforded such workers with respect to employee benefit plans is minimal. Older

---

46/ Two of the three methods of accruing benefits for defined benefit plans (the 133-1/3% method and fractional rule method) result in the participant being 100% accrued in his normal retirement benefit, by definition, when he reaches normal retirement age. The language in the proposal would seem to have no effect on benefit accrual in such plans. The methods of benefit accrual are set forth in Section 411(b) of the Internal Revenue Code, 26 U.S.C. § 411(b).

workers' welfare benefits need not be maintained on a parity with those of younger workers. Furthermore, the exemption, as interpreted by the DOL, means that most retirement benefits cease to be enriched for older workers if they elect to work past normal retirement age, because employers and plans are permitted but not required to improve most retirement benefits for such workers.

From the employer and/or the benefit plan's point of view, the cost of providing benefits for older workers need not exceed the cost of providing benefits for younger workers. In fact, the employer may actually profit from continuing these older workers because, unlike younger workers, no added contribution or credit to the retirement plan on their behalf is required. Furthermore, older workers who continue working past normal retirement age will reduce the retirement plan's liability by reason of their shortened number of retirement years.

On the other hand, from the older worker's standpoint, he benefits from the Act because he cannot be forced from his job prior to age 70. He benefits also by the floor which is placed under any reduction in his welfare benefits. Furthermore he may be able to correct any felt inequities in the level of his welfare or retirement benfits through the collective bargaining process. His union is free to negotiate benefits to a level of parity with younger workers. Employees not covered by a union contract are, of course, free to bargain individually with their employer for benefits above the minimal level protected by the statute.

There are many technical requirements for employers, unions and benefit plans to consider in conforming with the Act. The rather detailed requirements of the statute, the DOL Interpretation, the EEOC Interpretation and the IRS ruling have already been referred to. As already suggested, further requirements may yet emerge from the EEOC after its substantive review of the DOL Interpretations. Proposed legislation may also be enacted which would create new obligations. But, in an area already extensively regulated by ERISA and MPPAA, 47/ the DOL, and the IRS, these new and potential elements of compliance are of manageable proportions.

Organized labor's attitude toward the current state of the law in this regard, and of the interpretations of that law, is unlikely to be singular. Generally, unions will favor the strongest possible protection for older workers. Union concern for the older worker has been clearly demonstrated by the history of collective bargaining in this country. The entire development

---

47/ The Multiemployer Pension Plan Amendments Act of 1980, P.L. 96-254, 94 Stat. 1208 (1980), amended numerous provisions of ERISA and the Internal Revenue Code as they relate to retirement plans.

of collectively-bargained retirement plans is a reflection of that union concern. Furthermore, no provisions are found more uniformly in collective bargaining agreements than those creating seniority rights. Seniority clauses are primarily a protection of the older worker vis-a-vis the younger. Collectively-bargained health and life insurance plans are commonplace and are, of course, even more important to the older than to the younger worker. Collectively-bargained vacations based on seniority are found in most agreements and decidely favor the older worker. And, organized labor's legislative efforts to increase social security benefits and to expand the Social Security Act's coverage amply confirms its concern for older persons.

However, unions also represent younger workers. To the extent that added employment costs must come out of the negotiated wage package, added employment costs specifically attributable to older workers will be subject to competitive considerations within the membership of any particular labor union. How the fruits of collective bargaining will be allocated amongst the differing special interests within the union will be influenced by many factors. The extent to which a substantial percentage of the membership is in fact older or younger will influence how much of the total wage package will be allocated to improve retirement benefits. The type of industry involved may also have a substantial impact on the union's attitude. For instance, the construction industry makes heavy physical demands on its workers. In this industry the union can be expected to tailor the negotiated package to improve early and disability retirement rather than emphasizing added pension credits for the work beyond age 65. Unions in declining industries will want to maintain jobs for younger workers while protecting the security of older workers. To achieve this goal, such unions might favor earlier retirements and/or increased early retirement benefits rather than favoring added incentives to encourage older workers to continue working beyond normal retirement age.

Organized labor's attitude towards increased benefits for older workers may often vary with the union's particular relationship to the benefit plan. If the plan is funded and administered solely by the employer, the union may well more aggressively seek higher benefits for older workers than those required by ADEA. In this instance it is the employer who will appear more singularly to bear the cost of such benefits. If the plan is, however, a jointly administered (union-management) plan, only the overall funding is customarily negotiated and the union must share the responsibility to allocate these funds to satisfy the needs of both its older and younger members. Experience with multiemployer, jointly administered, funds suggests, however, that most of these funds would not simply provide the minimum protection afforded by ADEA. Most such funds would probably grant older workers the same welfare benefits as provided to younger workers and most such funds would continue granting retirement credits for older workers, even beyond normal retirement age regardless of the law.

The proposed legislation referred to above contains many proposals benefiting older workers. Some of these proposals would benefit workers generally. They would improve the condition of working people beyond that required under ADEA as it is currently being interpreted. The proposed legislation would, however, create substantial added costs for employers and/or benefit plans by reason of the increased benefits which are mandated and because of some of the added administrative costs which would result. The proposed legislation would also have the effect of removing the options now available to employers, unions and employee plans at the bargaining table. In this respect, the current legislation is preferable to that being proposed because it allows more flexibility thus permitting the parties to tailor benefits to meet the needs of particular industries and particular economic conditions. On the other hand, not all workers are beneficiaries of the collective bargaining process and it can well be expected that especially those older workers who are not represented by unions will see the legislative process as the only vehicle by which they can improve their conditions.

STRUCTURING EMPLOYEE BENEFIT PLANS TO COMPLY
WITH THE 1978 AMENDMENTS TO THE ADEA

George J. Pantos*
Jonathan A. Cohen**

---

*   Partner, Vedder, Price, Kaufman, Kammholz and Day, Washington, D.C. specializing in employee benefits law. Mr. Pantos formerly was Deputy Under Secretary of Commerce, U.S. Department of Commerce. He came to government service from the Chamber of Commerce of the United States where he was a senior staff member and an attorney, specializing in employee benefits and labor relations. Mr. Pantos graduated from Syracuse University in 1952 and received an LL.B. from George Washington University Law School in 1958. He was admitted to the practice of law in the District of Columbia in 1959.

** Member, Vedder, Price, Kaufman, Kammholz and Day in Washington, D.C. Mr. Cohen is a graduate of Brandeis University and received a J.D. from Georgetown University in 1976 and an LL.M. in Labor Law from George Washington University in 1979.

TABLE OF CONTENTS

	Page
I. INTRODUCTION	1
II. DOL REGULATIONS -- THE INTERPRETATIVE BULLETIN	2
A. Coverage of Section 4(f)(2)	2
B. Cost Considerations and Cost Data	4
C. "Cost Data" Requirements	5
D. Methods of Cost Comparison	6
1. Benefit-by-Benefit Method	6
2. Benefit Package Method	6
E. Cost Comparison in Specific Types of Benefit Plans	8
1. Life Insurance	8
2. Health Insurance	9
3. Long-Term Disability Plans	10
4. Retirement Plans	11
a. Participation	11
b. Benefits	11
III. PROPOSED MODIFICATIONS TO THE I.B.	13
A. EEOC's Recommended Changes	13
B. EEOC Recommendations: Conflict with Relevant ADEA Legislative History	14
C. Legislative Proposals	19

STRUCTURING EMPLOYEE BENEFIT PLANS TO COMPLY WITH THE 1978 AMENDMENTS TO THE ADEA

I. INTRODUCTION

In 1978, Congress amended the Age Discrimination in Employment Act (ADEA) (29 U.S.C. §§ 621, et seq.), to raise the upper age limit from 65 to 70 and to prohibit mandatory retirement for employees between ages 40 and 70. In May, 1979, the Department of Labor (DOL), which at the time had jurisdiction over enforcement of the ADEA, issued a final Interpretative Bulletin (I.B.) concerning the effect of the 1978 Amendments on employee benefit plans. 29 C.F.R. § 860.120. The I.B. focuses primarily on Section 4(f)(2) of the ADEA, which permits employers to discriminate on the basis of age if such discrimination is in observance of "the terms of ... any bona fide employee benefit plan, such as a pension, retirement or insurance plan, which is not a subterfuge to avoid the purposes of this chapter...." [1] One of the more significant features of the I.B. is its interpretation of § 4(f)(2) to the effect that an employer does not violate the ADEA, as amended, when it reduces benefits for employees over 65 if such reductions can be justified on the basis of "actuarially significant cost considerations." [2] Moreover, with regard to retirement plans, employers may eliminate contributions and accruals for older workers under certain circumstances which are not tied directly to "actuarially significant cost considerations." [3]

In July, 1979, ADEA enforcement responsibility was transferred from DOL to the Equal Employment Opportunity Commission (EEOC). [4] The EEOC circulated proposed staff modifications to the I.B. which would have reversed DOL's I.B. which permits defined benefit plans to stop accruing benefits for employees who work beyond normal retirement age. [5] This proposal has been subjected to considerable criticism, most notably from officials at DOL, and has been temporarily withdrawn. Thus, when the EEOC issued final interpretations of the ADEA in September, 1981, it did not deal with the issue of costs

---

[1] See 29 C.F.R. § 860.120(a)(1). This list of types of plans is illustrative and not exhaustive. Brennan v. Taft Broadcasting Co., 500 F.2d 212, 215-16 (5th Cir. 1974). Opinion Letter, Wage-Hour Administrator, WH-207, April 29, 1974.

[2] 29 C.F.R. § 860.120(a)(1).

[3] 29 C.F.R. § 860.120(f)(1)(iv).

[4] E.O. 12114 (44 Fed. Reg. 37193), July 1, 1979.

[5] BNA Pension Reporter, No. 289, May 5, 1980.

and benefits for older workers under employee benefit plans. The preamble to these guidelines does state that the DOL's I.B. on the subject is under review by the EEOC, but is, for the present, applicable. 6/ Thus, at least for now, employers may continue to rely on the I.B. which was published in final form in May, 1979. In addition, two bills were introduced in the 97th Congress which would require continued pension benefit accruals for employees who work beyond normal retirement age. 7/

Below, we discuss, in detail, the provisions of the I.B. as they relate to various employee benefit plans. We also discuss how the changes supported by EEOC would conflict with the legislative history of the 1978 ADEA Amendments, as well as with ERISA and the Internal Revenue Code. In addition, we note the economic consequences which could result from adoption of the EEOC proposal and/or enactment of the pending legislative proposals.

II. DOL REGULATIONS--THE INTERPRETATIVE BULLETIN

A. Coverage of Section 4(f)(2)

Section 4(f)(2) of the ADEA, by its own terms, provides an exception to the non-discrimination provisions of the ADEA for benefit plans which meet the following prerequisites:

1. The plan and its provisions must be "bona fide."
2. The discriminatory action taken must be in "observance" of the terms of that plan.
3. The particular terms of the plan must not be a "subterfuge to evade the purposes" of the ADEA. 8/

The I.B. interprets this exception to allow age-based reductions in benefits. Under the I.B., the exception is "narrowly construed"; an employer must prove that every element of the exception "has been clearly and unmistakenly met." 9/ The

---

6/ See EEOC Final Interpretation Under ADEA, 29 C.F.R. § 1625.10, 46 Fed. Reg. 47726, September 29, 1981.

7/ See H.R. 3396, 97th Cong. 1st Session (May 1, 1981); H.R. 3397, 97th Cong. 1st Session (May 1, 1981).

8/ Section 4(f)(2) also provides that the terms of such a plan cannot excuse a refusal to hire any individual on the basis of age, nor can it require involuntary retirement of individuals between the ages of 40 and 70. Regulations pertaining to this aspect of § 4(f)(2) appear at 29 C.F.R. § 860.110, which is not part of the I.B.

9/ 29 C.F.R. § 860.120(a)(1).

I.B. interprets these elements as follows:

"Bona fide employee benefit plan" requirement -- Under the I.B., a plan is "bona fide" only if its terms, including those providing for age-based reductions, have been accurately described in writing to all employees, and if the plan actually provides benefits in accordance with its terms. Moreover, an employer must notify employees promptly of the provisions and any changes in its benefit plans so that employees will know how the plan affects them and will have the opportunity to act accordingly. 10/

The I.B. interprets "employee benefit plan" under Section 4(f)(2) to encompass plans which provide "fringe benefits." Thus the term (and hence, the exception to the non-discrimination requirement) does not apply to wages or salary in cash. Reductions in wages or salary on the basis of age are never excused. 11/

Requirement that discrimination be "in observance" of terms of the plan -- In order for a bona fide employee benefit plan which provides lower benefits to older employees on account of age to be lawful under the § 4(f)(2) exception, the lower benefits must be specifically provided for in the terms of the plan. According to the I.B., the purposes for this requirement are two-fold: (1) where a discriminatory policy is an express term of a benefit plan, employees have an opportunity to become aware of the policy and to plan, or protest accordingly; and (2) requiring that the age-based discrimination actually be prescribed by the plan helps assure that it will be uniformly and fairly applied. 12/

Requirement that plant not be "subterfuge" -- According to the I.B., a bona fide employee benefit plan which provides lower benefits on the basis of age will not be deemed a "subterfuge" to evade the ADEA, and thus will come within the § 4(f)(2) exception if "the lower level of benefit is justified by age related cost considerations." The only exception to this general rule is with respect to certain retirement plans which, as will be discussed

---

10/ 29 C.F.R. § 860.120(b). The I.B. provides that this notice requirement is satisfied by compliance with the disclosure regulations under ERISA.

11/ 29 C.F.R. § 860.120(b). The I.B. also states that § 4(f)(2) does not apply to benefits such as paid vacations and uninsured paid sick leave, since reductions in these "would not be justified by significant cost considerations."

12/ 29 C.F.R. § 860.120(c)-(d).

below, are governed by rules not tied to acturial cost considerations. 13/

B. Cost Considerations and Cost Data

As mentioned, the I.B. interprets the ADEA to allow benefit reductions for older workers when such reductions are cost-justified. The I.B. states, further, that benefit levels may be reduced only to the extent necessary to achieve approximate equivalency in cost for older and younger workers. Thus, an employer will not violate the ADEA if actual benefit payments made under the plan or costs incurred on behalf of older workers are equal to payments or costs for younger workers, even though older workers receive a lesser amount of benefits or insurance coverage. 14/

The I.B. sets forth several rules as to the circumstances under which older employees may or may not be required to make greater contributions to benefit plans to offset the increased costs associated with older employees:

a. An employer may _not_ require, _as a condition of employment_, that employees protected under the ADEA make greater contributions than younger employees to support an employee benefit plan since such a requirement would constitute a mandatory reduction in wages based on age -- which would not fall within the § 4(f)(2) exception. 15/

b. However, protected employees may be required as a condition of participation in a _voluntary_ employee benefit plan to make greater contributions than younger employees, provided that older employees are not required to fund a greater proportion of the total premium cost than younger employees. This rule is applicable to three categories of plans: employee-pay-all plans, contributory plans, and non-contributory plans ("employer-pay-all"). Thus, in a plan in which employees pay all of the cost, an older employee may be required to contribute the full premium needed to provide his or her benefit, even if it is more than younger employees pay, as long as the younger employees also pay the entire premium cost for their benefit. In plans where the employer and employees share the cost, older employees may be required to increase their contributions so long as the proportion of the total premium paid by them (_i.e._, their share vis a vis the employer's share) does not increase with age. If a non-contributory or employer-pay-all plan is in effect, older employees may not be required to contribute any portion of the

---

13/ See _infra_, pp. 11-13.

14/ 29 C.F.R. § 860.120(a)(1)

15/ 29 C.F.R. § 860.120(d)(4)(i).

total premium cost since younger employees are not so required. 16/

    c. The I.B. also provides that it is not a violation of the ADEA to give older employees the option of making an additional contribution to receive the same, unreduced benefits as younger employees. 17/

    C.   "Cost Data" Requirements

    In order for a benefit plan not to be a "subterfuge" under § 4(f)(2), the I.B. requires that cost data used to justify lower benefits for older workers in such a plan be "valid and reasonable." 18/ The I.B. gives flexible though somewhat vague guidance as to the kinds of data that will meet this criterion. It permits employers to rely on data which show the actual cost to it of providing the particular benefit over "a representative period of years." 19/ The I.B. provides no explanation as to what constitutes a "representative period." As an alternative to relying on cost data for its own employees, the I.B. allows an employer to rely on data for "similarly situated" employees of other employers unless the employer "incurs costs that differ significantly" from costs for the group of similarly situated employees and reliance on such data would result in significantly lower benefits for the employer's older employees. Again, there is little guidance as to the meaning of the term "similarly situated employee" or as to what constitutes "costs that differ significantly."

    The I.B. also provides that where reliable cost information is not yet available to an employer (such as for some benefits after age 65), reasonable _projections_ may be made from existing cost data (such as data for younger ages). 20/

    Under the I.B., cost comparisons and adjustments may be made on the basis of age brackets of up to five years. Thus, an employer may reduce a particular benefit for employees who are protected under the ADEA, by the amount attributable to the additional cost of providing those employees with the same level of the benefit as younger employees within the five year age group immediately preceding that of the protected employees. 21/ The

---

16/ 29 C.F.R. § 860.120(d)(4)(ii)(A)-(C).

17/ 29 C.F.R. § 860.120(d)(4)(iii).

18/ 29 C.F.R. § 860.120(d)(1).

19/ Id.

20/ 29 C.F.R. § 860.120(d)(i); Preamble to I.B., 44 Fed. Reg. 30650 (May 25, 1979).

I.B. discusses the example of an employer who chooses to provide unreduced group life insurance benefits until age 60. He may reduce benefits for employees between ages 60 and 65 only to the extent necessary to achieve approximate equivalency in costs with employees who are 55-60 years old. [22]

D. Methods of Cost Comparison

1. Benefit-by-Benefit Method

Comparison of benefit costs for older versus younger employees may be made on a benefit-by-benefit basis. Adjustments made on a benefit-by-benefit basis must be made with regard to a specific benefit based on increased costs associated with that benefit only. In other words, the higher costs of providing one benefit would not justify a decrease in any other benefit. For example, an increase in group term life insurance costs for older workers would justify a corresponding reduction in the amount of group term life insurance for such workers, but it would not permit a reduction in any other benefit. Moreover, the I.B. provides that under the benefit-by-benefit approach, increased costs associated with one benefit will not justify reductions in another benefit, even if both benefits are designed to serve the same contingency or event, such as death. [23]

2. Benefit Package Method

In a substantial departure from the I.B. as originally proposed, the final I.B. permits employers to make cost comparisons by a "benefit-package" approach, under certain circumstances. Under this approach cost comparisons and adjustments can be made, with respect to benefit plans, in the aggregate.

---

[21] 29 C.F.R. § 860.120(d)(3).

[22] The basis for the maximum five-year bracket is the widespread practice in the insurance industry of pricing insurance based on average costs for five-year age brackets. See Preamble, supra, n. 16, 44 Fed. Reg. 30650 (May 25, 1979).

[23] 29 C.F.R. § 860.120(d)(2)(i). In the Preamble to the I.B., see supra, n. 16, it is stated:

> The Department therefore now takes a strict view of a "benefit" under the benefit-by-benefit approach. The Department specifically rejects the suggestion that the benefit-by-benefit approach should be understood as an "event-by-event" approach which would ignore differences in the forms of benefits available for a particular event. 44 Fed. Reg. 30651 (May 25, 1979).

The purpose in permitting this alternative method is to provide greater flexibility than is afforded by the benefit-by-benefit approach so as to achieve the legislative purpose behind § 4(f)(2) "to help employers and workers find ways of meeting problems arising from the impact of age on employment." 24/

Although this alternative approach offers an employer greater flexibility than a benefit-by-benefit approach, it is subject to the following limitations, which are intended to make sure that the approach helps rather than hurts older workers:

1. The benefit package approach may not be used to reduce the cost of providing benefits for older employees (as compared to the benefit-by-benefit approach), or to reduce the favorability to the employees of overall benefits for older employees. 25/

2. The benefit package approach cannot be applied to retirement or pension plans. As will be seen in greater detail later, 26/ the I.B. sets forth specific and comprehensive rules regarding such plans. Unlike the general principles with respect to other plans under Section 4(f)(2), these rules are not tied to actuarially significant cost considerations but are intended to deal with the special funding arrangements of retirement or pension plans, which were of concern to Congress. Therefore, the drafters of the I.B. determined that it would be a departure both from the general principles of Section 4(f)(2) and from the specific legislative history to apply a benefit package approach, which is based on general cost principles, to a retirement or pension plan, which is specifically governed by other rules. Thus, the I.B. takes the position that a reduction in retirement benefits will not be justified by an increase in some other benefit for older workers. Conversely, an increase in retirement benefits over what is required by the specific rules of the I.B., will not justify a decrease in some other benefit. For example, an employer who does not make an age-based reduction in group term life insurance which could be justified under a benefit-by-benefit approach may not justify on that basis an age-based reduction in employees' annual accrual of pension benefits prior to normal retirement age. On the other hand, an employer who does not cease pension accrual at normal retirement age (as benefit-by-benefit approach would permit) may not justify on that basis a reduction in group term life insurance benefits greater than would be justified under a benefit-by-benefit approach. 27/

24/ 29 C.F.R. § 860.120(d)(2)(ii).

25/ 29 C.F.R. § 860.120(d)(2)(ii).

26/ See infra at pp. 11-13.

27/ Preamble, see supra, n. 16, 44 Fed. Reg. at 20656.

3. Since health benefits are of particular importance to older workers, the benefit package approach may not be used to justify reductions in such benefits greater than would be justified under a benefit-by-benefit approach, and any greater reduction constitutes a subterfuge to evade the purposes of the ADEA.

4. Any benefit reduction greater than that which would be justified under a benefit-by-benefit approach must be offset by another benefit available to the same employees. 28/

The I.B. provides the following example to illlustrate operation of the benefit package approach and its limitations:

> Assume two employee benefit plans, providing Benefit "A" and Benefit "B." Both plans fall within section 4(f)(2) and neither is a retirement or pension plan subject to special rules. Both benefits are available to all employees. Age-based cost increases would justify a 10% decrease in both benefits on a benefit-by-benefit basis. The affected employees would, however, find it more favorable - that is, more consistent with meeting their needs - for no reduction to be made in Benefit "A" and a greater reduction to be made in Benefit "B." This "trade-off" would not result in a reduction in health benefits. If the data show that Benefit "A" and Benefit "B" cost the same, Benefit "B" may be reduced up to 20% if Benefit "A" is unreduced. If the data show that Benefit "A" costs only half as much as Benefit "B," however, Benefit "B" may be reduced up to only 15% if Benefit "A" is unreduced, since a greater reduction in Benefit "B" would result in an impermissible reduction in total benefit costs. 29/

E. Cost Comparison in Specific Types of Benefit Plans

The I.B. discusses in detail how the cost comparison justification for reduced benefits derived from § 4(f)(2) is applied to several common types of benefit plans, under the benefit-by-benefit approach.

1. *Life Insurance* -- Under the I.B., an employer will not violate the ADEA by following the common practice of maintaining

---

28/ 29 C.F.R. § 860.120(f)(2)(iv).

29/ 29 C.F.R. § 860.120(f)(2)(v).

a constant level of group term life insurance coverage until age 65 and then reducing the benefit in direct correlation to age-based increases in its cost. Such reductions may be made on the basis of average costs over a period of up to five years, but no longer. 30/ However, where the level of group term life insurance benefits is based on the employees' wages or salary (e.g., 2 x base pay) increases in wages or salary will not be considered the type of increased cost that justifies a reduction in benefits. The reason for this is that such increases are not directly related to age. 31/

It should be noted that complete elimination of life insurance benefits prior to age 70 is not permitted under the I.B. 32/

2. <u>Health Insurance</u> -- The I.B. states that given the many various types of health insurance plans, it is "difficult to offer a general guideline" as to when reductions in health insurance benefits are justified based on age-related cost increases. The I.B. does however furnish one general guideline: reductions based on increased costs may not "be concentrated on certain items so as to make coverage less attractive to older workers." 33/

The I.B. permits health insurance benefits to be coordinated with Medicare, under two different approaches: the "carve-out" approach and the "supplemental" approach. Under the "carve-out" approach an employer carves out of his own health plan those benefits which are provided by Medicare. Thus, Medicare would be the primary source for health coverage and the employer's health plan would pay only those expenses which are insurable under the plan and which are not actually paid by Medicare. In other words, regular health plan benefits are directly offset by benefits paid under Medicare; employees over 65 receive the same benefits as those under 65.

Under the "supplemental" approach, the employer creates a separate health plan for those employees eligible for Medicare which "supplements" Medicare coverage by covering those types of expenses which Medicare does not. Under this type of arrangement employees over 65 do not necessarily receive the same total health benefits as employees under 65. For example, Medicare may pay for professional services, but not as much as the employer's regular plan. This shortfall would not be made up under the

---

30/ 29 C.F.R. § 860.120(f)(1)(i).

31/ Preamble, 44 Fed. Reg. at 30653.

32/ 29 C.F.R. § 860.120(f)(1)(i).

33/ 29 C.F.R. § 860.120(f)1)(ii)

"supplement" approach. On the other hand, prescription drugs, not covered by Medicare would be covered by the supplemental plan. If, as is likely, the employer's regular plan, also does not cover drugs, older employees would be receiving a greater benefit than younger employees. 34/

Under the I.B., "supplement" plans are a permissible alternative to "carve-out" plans only if: (1) their cost to the employer is no less than a "carve-out" plan would be, and (2) taken together with Medicare benefits, the "supplement" plan provides no less favorable benefits on an overall basis than a "carve-out" plan.

Under either approach, an employer must inform employees eligible for Medicare of the need to apply for Medicare and must provide assistance in the application process. Thus, employers may not assume that employees have taken advantage of available Medicare coverage. Moreover, if a plan requires no employee contributions or a contribution less than the cost of "Part B" of Medicare, the employer must pay or contribute to the "Part B" cost. 35/

3. *Long-Term Disability Plans* -- Since the 1978 Amendments to the ADEA extended ADEA protection to age 70, employers may no longer engage in the common practice of completely cutting off long-term disability benefits for all disabled employees and long-term disability coverage for all active employees at age 65. However, employers may lawfully reduce long-term disability benefits for older employees who are under 70 when such reductions are cost justified. 36/ The I.B. envisions several ways for employers to accomplish such reductions, and discusses two methods specifically. One way is by reducing the level of benefits to offset increased costs. Another approach is to reduce the duration of benefits available to employees who become disabled at older ages without reducing the level of benefits. The I.B. gives an example of how this "duration approach" can be applied, stating that no violation of the ADEA would be found with regard to reduction of the duration of long term disability coverage as follows: (a) with respect to disabilities which occur at age 60 or less, benefits cease at age 65; (b) with respect to disabilities occurring after age 60, benefits cease five years after disablement or at age 70, whichever occurs first. 37/ This example is meant to be illustrative and not exclusive; the I.B. states that cost data which support other patterns of reduction

---

34/ Preamble, 44 Fed. Reg. at 30653.

35/ 29 C.F.R. § 860.120(f)(1)(ii)(A)-(B).

36/ 29 C.F.R. § 860.120(f)(1)(iii).

37/ 29 C.F.R. § 860.120(f)(1)(iii)(A)-(B).

will also be acceptable. It should be noted, however, that since most plans before 1978 did not provide any coverage beyond age 65, data to support cost reductions is rare.

4. <u>Retirement Plans</u> -- In addition to the general rules regarding cost justification which apply to all benefit plans under § 4(f)(2), the I.B. sets forth special rules governing treatment of older employees with regard to participating in and funding of retirement plans. Underlying these rules are two considerations: (1) the need to accommodate the ADEA to existing ERISA requirements; and (2) the intent of Congress to limit the costs of funding pension plans after the 1978 Amendments.

Under the rules, defined benefit plans and defined contribution plans are treated somewhat differently.

a. <u>Participation</u>

A pension plan which provides for a defined benefit (such as a flat monthly payment after retirement or an amount determined by a formula based on salary and years of service), may <u>exclude</u> older workers hired <u>less</u> than five years <u>prior</u> to the stated normal retirement age of the plan. 38/ The purpose of this rule is to allow employers to avoid the substantial cost of funding a specific level of benefits in a relatively short amount of time. On ther other hand, an employee hired prior to normal retirement age may <u>not</u> be excluded from a defined contribution plan, because for such plans an employer does not have to fund a specific level of benefits and the benefit received by the employee at retirement equals only the value of the contributions which have been made. 39/ This particular distinction between defined benefit and defined contribution plans is based on § 202 of ERISA. 40/ The I.B. extends the ERISA prohibition against exclusion from defined benefit plans of employees hired more than five years prior to normal retirement age to retirement plans not covered by ERISA, except that such exclusion may be justified on the basis of cost considerations. 41/

b. <u>Benefits</u>

Under the I.B., a defined benefit plan is not required to credit, for purposes of benefit accrual, service which occurs after an employee's normal retirement age. 42/ Nor must such a

---

38/ 29 C.F.R. § 860.120(f)(1)(iv)(A).

39/ 29 C.F.R. § 860.120(f)(i)(iv)(A). <u>See also</u> Opinion Letter of Wage-Hour Administrator, No. 406, March 2, 1977.

40/ ERISA § 202(a)(2), 29 U.S.C. § 1052(a)(2).

41/ 29 C.F.R. § 860.120(f)(1)(iv)(A).

plan adjust actuarially the benefit accrued as of normal retirement age for an employee who continues to work beyond that age. 43/ Furthermore, a defined benefit plan need not provide for the accrual of benefits for an employee who continues to work after normal retirement age. 44/ Finally, a defined benefit plan need not take into account salary increases or benefit improvements under the plan which are granted to employees with respect to an employee who works beyond normal retirement age. However, benefit improvements for <u>retirees</u> may not be denied to employees who work beyond normal retirement age and who do not receive benefit accruals and improvements given younger employees. 45/

With regard to defined contribution plans, the I.B. distinguishes between plans that are supplemental and those that are non-supplemental. A defined contribution plan is deemed supplemental with respect to any employee who is a participant in both the defined contribution plan and a defined benefit plan. 46/ Under the I.B., a defined contribution plan which is non-supplemental may provide for the cessation of employer contributions after the normal retirement age; it may also provide that no contributions will be made by the employer on behalf of any employee hired after normal retirement age. 47/ On the other hand, a supplemental plan -- one which is in addition to a principal plan -- may not provide for the cessation of contributions after normal retirement age.

The I.B. provides that if an employer has no defined benefit plans, but has two or more defined contribution plans, all but one of the plans are deemed "supplemental." The one defined contribution plan which is not "supplemental" may provide for the cessation of employer contributions after normal retirement age, and an employer may designate which one of the defined contribution plans is not "supplemental." 48/

The I.B. regulations regarding retirement plans were interpreted and applied in a recent district court case in California. In <u>Criswell v. Western Airlines</u>, 49/ the jury found

---

43/ 29 C.F.R. § 860.120(f)(1)(iv)(B)(4).

44/ 29 C.F.R. § 860.120(f)(1)(iv)(B)(5).

45/ 29 C.F.R. § 860.120(f)(1)(iv)(B)(7).

46/ 29 C.F.R. § 860.120(f)(1)(iv)(B)(1).

47/ <u>Id</u>.

48/ <u>Id</u>.

49/ 514 F. Supp. 384 (C.D. Cal. 1981).

that the airline had violated the ADEA by involuntarily retiring several pilots. The jury assessed damages and the court ordered reinstatement. The pilots contended that their reinstatement should be with full pension benefits under the Pilot Pension Plans. With respect to the Pilots Variable Pension Plan, a defined contribution plan which was supplementary to the Pilots Fixed Pension Plan (a defined benefit plan), the court ordered the airline to make contributions to this plan on behalf of the pilots as if they had continued as officers after their normal retirement dates. However, with regard to the Fixed Plan, the defined benefit plan, the court cited the I.B. and concluded that the reinstated pilots were <u>not</u> entitled to any increases in their Fixed Plan pensions which resulted from benefit accruals based on additional years of service after the normal retirement date.

The pilots also contended that they were entitled to any increase in the "Minimum Normal Pilot Pension" which would become effective between their normal retirement dates and their ultimate actual retirement dates. In fact, one such increase had already been granted. The court rejected this contention citing the I.B. provision (§ 860.120(f)(1)(iv)(B)(7)) which provides that <u>employees</u> who work past normal retirement age are not entitled to benefit improvements which take place between their normal retirement date and their actual retirement date. The court rejected the plaintiffs' argument that they were covered by the I.B. provision which states that benefit improvements for retirees may not be denied to such employees who do not receive the advantage of benefit accruals and increases given to younger employees, holding that since the plaintiffs would be employees after reinstatement, rather than retirees, they were not entitled to the benefit improvements granted after their normal retirement date.

III. PROPOSED MODIFICATIONS TO THE I.B.

    A. <u>EEOC's Recommended Changes</u>

On April 25, 1980, the Equal Employment Opportunity Commission (EEOC) submitted for comment to the Department of Labor, Internal Revenue Service, and the President's Commission on Pension Policy certain staff proposals which would revise the current I.B. on employee benefits. 50/ The major changes suggested by the EEOC were that pension or retirement plans be required to: (i) credit service, for the purpose of benefit accrual, after normal retirement age if the employee is not already entitled to a full actuarially unreduced benefit at normal retirement age; (ii) actuarially increase the normal retirement benefit or recalculate the normal retirement benefit to include compensation increases and benefit improvements which

---

50/ BNA Pension Reporter, No. 289, May 5, 1980.

occur prior to the postponed retirement date; and (iii) include in pension coverage, contrary to ERISA, those employees hired within five years of normal retirement age. 51/

The EEOC's recommendations were severely criticized by employers and by the Department of Labor, 52/ and did not become part of the EEOC's final guidelines pertaining to the ADEA which were issued on September 29, 1981. The EEOC final interpretations do not deal with the issue of costs and benefits for older workers under employee benefit plans. In particular, they are silent about providing pension benefits for employees over age 65. In fact, the final EEOC guidelines specifically state that while the current I.B. issued by DOL is still in effect, it is being subjected to subsantive review and a new I.B., possibly with modifications, will eventually be issued for comment by the EEOC. 53/ Until and unless EEOC indicates otherwise, the DOL's 1979 interpretations on costs and benefits under employee benefit plans will remain in effect.

The crux of the criticism of the EEOC's proposals has been the argument that they conflict with the legislative history of the 1978 Amendments to the ADEA as well as with certain provision of ERISA and the Internal Revenue Code.

B. EEOC Recommendations: Conflict With Relevant ADEA Legislative History

On July 25, 1977, the U.S. House of Representatives Committee on Education and Labor submitted its report on the Age Discrimination in Employment Act Amendments of 1977. In this report the Committee gave assurances that no additional benefit accruals or actuarial adjustments would have to be made other than those required by ERISA.

> Nothing in these amendments would change the provisions of the Employee Retirement Income Security Act of 1974, and no additional requirements would be made of pension plan programs under these amendments.

51/ The EEOC proposal would also change the definition of what constitutes a "supplemental" defined contribution benefit plan and allow reductions in retirement benefits on a benefit package as well as a benefit-by-benefit basis. These proposals have received less critical attention than the others.

52/ Letter of October 17, 1980 from Ray Marshall to Eleanor Holmes Norton.

53/ 46 Fed. Reg. 47726 (September 29, 1981).

> The Employee Retirement Income Security Act of 1974 (ERISA) now defines normal retirement age; this is usually age 65 or before, but may be later for persons beginning participation in the plan after age 55. Normal retirement is the age at which a worker receives full benefits, that is, benefits that are now actuarially reduced on account of early retirement. This bill would not change the definition of normal retirement age. <u>These amendments do not require that any additional benefits, benefit accruals or actuarial adjustments be provided other than those required under ERISA.</u> (Emphasis added). 54/

This Congressional intent was specifically reiterated in the additional views of Congressman Ted Weiss, which are included in the report:

> Some members questioned whether this provision is in conflict with the Employment, Retirement, and Security Income Act (ERISA) (sic).
>
> ERISA added certain funding, vesting, and insurance obligations to most pension plans. The amendment to section 4(f)(2) does not effect the cost or structure of bona fide pension plans which conform to ERISA or other IRS regulations. <u>Further, it should be noted that ERISA does not require increased actuarial adjustments if an employee chooses to work beyond the ERISA-defined retirement age of 65.</u> (Emphasis added.) 55/

On October 12, 1977, the U.S. Senate submitted its report on the Age Discrimination in Employment Act Amendments. This report included a letter dated August 29, 1977, from Senator Williams to Assistant Secretary of Labor for Employment Standards Donald Elisburg and Mr. Elisburg's subsequent response which reiterates the previously articulated intent of the House of Representatives concerning benefit accruals and actuarial adjustments for employment time worked beyond normal retirement age. Mr. Ellisburg also clearly enunciated to Senators Williams and Javits the cost impact that an increase in the upper age limit of ADEA would produce on the funding of private pension plans.

54/ House Report No. 95-527, Part 1, 95th Cong., 1st Session (July 5, 1977) at p. 9.

55/ <u>Id</u>. at p. 29.

> An increase in the upper age limit of the ADEA would not increase the funding costs for private pension plans. As a matter of fact, financial pressure on private pension plans could be alleviated. Requiring an employer to permit a qualified employee to work until the Act's upper age limit, regardless of the pension plan's normal retirement age, would result in cost savings to plans rather than increases. As an actuarial matter, the longer an employee works, the shorter the period retirement payments will have to be made, thus lowering the funding assumptions of the plan. Savings would of course come from the added years of accumulated interest on the fund. Savings would also stem from the fact that, as indicated above, a plan need not provide for further accrual of benefits after the participant has reached the plan's normal retirement age, and thus the added years of service do not increase the ultimate retirement benefit or the cost of providing it. (Emphasis added). 56/

The Senate Report indicates that Congress specifically adopted the remarks on these subjects made by Mr. Elisburg as the Congressional intent concerning the 1978 Amendment of ADEA.

> The argument that pension and other employees benefit plan costs would increase if the act's upper age limit is increased has not been substantiated. At the hearings on this legislation, Donald Elisburg, Assistant Secretary of Labor for Employment Standards, assured this committee that officials in the Department of Labor who administer ERISA are in complete agreement that "there would be no interference with the relevant provisions of the 1974 pension law if the upper age limit were raised ***"

> This legislation would not change the definition of normal retirement age under ERISA. It does not require the accrual of additional benefits or the payment of the actuarial equivalent of normal retirement benefits to employees who choose to work beyond the plan's normal retirement date.

56/ Senate Report No. 95-493, 95th Cong., 1st Session (1977) at pp. 15-16.

- 17 -

> Included in this report is a letter from
> Assistant Secretary Elisburg responding in
> detail to questions from the Chairman and
> ranking minority member of the committee on
> the relationship between ERISA and the
> proposed amendments to the ADEA <u>which
> reaffirms the committee's intent in this
> regard</u>. (Emphasis added.) 57/

In the Senate and House floor debates upon passage of the ADEA amendments, the Congressional intent to adopt Mr. Elilsburg's remarks, embodied in his 1977 letter to Senator Williams, concerning additional benefit accruals and contributions required by the ADEA amendments is quite clear. On March 21, 1978, Congressman Hawkins answered Congressman Dent's question concerning continued employer contributions past normal retirement age:

> MR. DENT. Mr. Speaker, in order that there be
> no question about the committee handling of
> pension legislation, I have arranged with the
> gentleman from California to make the record
> very clear. I would like to put this question
> to the gentleman:
>
> Is it the intention of the conferees that an
> employer will be permitted, under the Age
> Discrimination in Employment Act of 1967 as
> amended, to maintain a defined contribution
> plan - other than a plan which is merely
> supplemental to a defined benefit or defined
> contribution plan maintained by the employer -
> which precludes employer and, if applicable,
> employee contributions to such a plan
> subsequent to an employee's attainment of the
> normal retirement age contained in the plan?
>
> MR. HAWKINS. Yes. The answer to the
> gentleman's question is "Yes." The conferees
> intend that an employer will not violate the
> Age Discrimination in Employment Act by
> maintaining such a defined contribution
> plan. <u>This position is in keeping with the
> general view of the House and the Department
> of Labor with regard to prohibited age
> discrimination in the context of pension plans
> covering employees who continue employment
> beyond the normal retirement age</u>, as expressed
> in a letter of September 8, 1977, from
> Assistant Secretary Elisburg to me which

57/ <u>Id</u>. at p. 5.

<u>appears in the Congressional Record of
September 23, 1977, at page H9977.</u> (Emphasis
added.) 58/

On March 23, 1978, Senator Javits asked Senator Williams for clarification of certain issues surrounding the amendments:

> Mr. President, if I may have the attention of the chairman of our committee and manager of the conference report on the floor, I wish to clarify a number of issues involving employee benefit plans and the Age Discrimination in Employment Act of 1967, as modified by the 1978 amendments. I want to ask our distinguished committee chairman whether he agrees that an employer will be permitted under the act, as amended, to maintain a defined contribution plan - other than a plan which is merely supplemental to a defined benefit or defined contribution plan maintained by the employer - which precludes employer and, if applicable, employee contributions to such a plan subsequent to an employee's attainment of the plan's normal retirement age.
>
> MR. WILLIAMS. The answer is "yes." I completely agree with the statement of the distinguished Senator from New York. Your statements are consistent with the position taken by the Department of Labor regarding these matters. <u>As Assistant Secretary Elisburg's letter, which appears in the Senate committee report, makes clear, employers will not be required to continue contributions to either defined benefit or defined contribution plans for employees who continue working beyond a plan's normal retirement age.</u> Cong. Rec. at S4450. (Emphasis added.) 59/

Thus, it appears that critics of the EEOC's proposals are correct in arguing that the legislative history of the passage of the ADEA Amendments indicates that the Congressional intent was to adopt the Department of Labor's interpretation of the relationship between ERISA and ADEA, as embodied in Assistant Secretary Elisburg's letter to Senator Williams, which allows the cessation of crediting of years of service, for benefit accrual purposes, once an employee has reached normal retirement age and

---

58/ Congressional Record, March 21, 1978, p. H 2271.

59/ Congressional Record, March 23, 1978, p. S 4450.

does not require employers to actuarially adjust an employee's benefit if that employee continues in employment beyond normal retirement age.

C. Legislative Proposals

On May 1, 1981, Rep. Claude Pepper, Chairman of the House Select Committee on Aging, introduced a package of five bills aimed, in part, at "beefing up the private pension system." 60/ One of the bills, the proposed Retirement Security Portability Non-Discrimination Act (H.R. 3396), would, among other things, amend ERISA and the Internal Revenue Code to require continued pension benefit accruals for individuals who work beyond normal retirement age.

Another of Rep. Pepper's bills, the proposed Older Worker Employment Incentives Act (H.R. 3397), would also, among other things, amend ERISA, the Internal Revenue Code, and the ADEA to require continued pension accruals for older workers.

Enactment of these amendments would constitute a total about-face for Congress; it would be a major departure from the understanding of Congress when it enacted the 1978 ADEA Amendments, as well as provisions of the Internal Revenue Code and ERISA. Moreover, the legislation would require substantial amendment of existing pension plans and would impose on employers higher costs in funding and administering their retirement programs.

60/ BNA Pension Reporter, May 4, 1981, at A-4.

JOB OPTIONS FOR OLDER CITIZENS:
AN IDEA WHOSE TIME HAS COME

Matthew M. Lind *

---

*   Vice President, Corporate Planning and Research, The
    Travelers Insurance Companies. Prior to joining Travelers in
    July 1979, Mr. Lind was the Executive Director of the Pension
    Benefit Guaranty Corporation. Mr. Lind had been with the
    PBGC since its inception in 1974. Previously, Mr. Lind was a
    Management Associate at the Office of Management and
    Budget. He also worked for the Mitre Corporation and for the
    Addressograph-Multigraph Corporation. Mr. Lind attended the
    Massachusetts Institute of Technology where he received S.B.
    and S.M. degrees in Electrical Engineering, and Harvard
    University where he received his M.A. and Ph.D. degrees in
    Applied Mathematics.

JOB OPTIONS FOR OLDER CITIZENS:
AN IDEA WHOSE TIME HAS COME

Thank you. It's a privilege to be part of your program today to address the topic of creating employment opportunities for the older worker.

In particular, I want to shed some light today on practical efforts that are already underway in the business world; programs designed to use the skills and energies of older workers, to increase their incomes and their sense of usefulness--while at the same time directly advancing the business interest of the companies involved.

My thesis is simple: I believe that expanded job opportunities for older people is an idea whose time has come.

Let me begin by focusing on the older individual, the man or woman who has worked for years and is now retired.

For millions, full-time retirement is a long-awaited blessing, filled with rewards.

But retirement may also present a different, darker picture. One retiree I know went back to work as a secretary when her children reached their teens; after several years, she switched to a job in personnel management. She always enjoyed her work. Work filled her time--especially after her husband died and her children grew up; work accounted for much of her social life and her sense of self-worth. But now she is retired. She enjoys her old friends, but friendships can't fill her life: her friends, after all, have lives of their own. She feels dull and boring. She has abundant energy, but not enough outlets for it. Worst of all, she worries about money. Social Security increases periodically with rises in the cost of living, but inflation eats into her pension and her modest savings. She would like to go back to work part-time, but that seems an impossible dream. She knows that opportunities for part-time work are scarce for everybody--especially for people over 65. And even if she did find work, her part-time income might threaten her retired status, her pension benefits and her Social Security income. So she faces a long stretch of existence in a kind of gray exile: too much time, too little to do--and not enough money.

I believe this to be the case in millions of situations. I also believe that this woman, for psychic and economic reasons, needs an opportunity to work; needs a choice between the polar extremes of full-time work and full-time retirement.

I believe it is time for a national effort by business to create job options--with the help and encouragement of government. To succeed in this effort would be good for the nation's older citizens. It would be good for business. And it would be good for our national economy.

Consider the wellbeing of the nation's 24 million people age 65 or older--and the additional 21 million between 55 and 65 who are approaching retirement age.

We know, first of all, that millions of them want to work even after they reach age 65. America's older people, to be sure, have by no means given up their dream of leisure in retirement. But growing numbers of them seem to be rejecting the notion of being totally sidelined. A substantial number are willing, even eager to work--especially part-time.

For example, a Harris poll just published surveyed attitudes toward work and retirement. Despite the fact that 46% of the labor force, ages 55-64, today looks forward to retiring completely, a larger proportion--59%--says that when they do "retire," they want to have some type of paid part-time job. The study also showed that for the entire labor force, of all ages, three-fourths would prefer some kind of part-time paid work after "retirement."

These findings support our own survey at The Travelers. We polled our employees aged 55 and over in 1980: we were impressed by how strongly they felt about work after retirement. Fully 85 percent of them expressed an interest in some form of paid employment after retirement; most expressed a preference for part-time work with our company.

And millions of older people are not only willing, but perfectly able to work--successfully and productively. This century's spectacular advances in health care and living standards have lengthened the span of active life in America. Today men who reach age 65 can expect, on the average, to live beyond age 79 and women to live beyond age 83. The experts predict that life expectancy will continue to increase in the future, though at a slower pace. And meanwhile, advances in treating disorders of aging promise that life beyond age 65 will not only be longer, but healthier and more active.

Today's older people, moreover, are better educated than any previous generation--for this century has seen major advances in educational status as well as health. And the educational levels of older people will continue to improve as more and more people complete high school and go on to college.

For millions of older people, then, the opportunity to work beyond the traditional retirement age, or the option to work during retirement, means a chance to remain active, alert, useful and in touch with other people.

And the opportunity to work means something else: extra income. Automatic cost-of-living increases in Social Security payments have helped millions of retired people. But inflation continues to erode private pensions and retirement savings.

A major expansion of economic opportunity for older citizens would help reassure millions that they need not fear old age: that if they should choose to supplement their incomes with earnings from employment, they would have a good chance to do so.

But there are other reasons.

One is that creating work opportunities for older people will be good for business.

What do lengthening life spans, the aging of the "baby boom" generation and falling birth rates mean for corporate America?

These demographic facts of life mean, among other things, that the composition of the work force in America is changing dramatically. Because of falling birth rates and the passing of the boom-babies into later life, the Census Bureau projects that the number of new entrants into the labor force--workers age 18 to 24--will drop by 16 percent over the next twenty years. The labor force, which grew by almost 2 1/2 percent each year in the Seventies, will grow only 1 1/2 percent annually in the Eighties-- and less than one percent a year in the Nineties. Meanwhile, the over-65 segment of the population will grow by 28 percent between now and the year 2000.

In short, the supply of younger workers will be contracting, while the supply of older workers will be growing more abundant. Demographic reality will make it simple common sense for businesses seeking employees to find them where the potential supply is greatest.

Fortunately, this growing cohort of older citizens represents a vast repository of skill, knowledge, experience, and potential productivity.

More than this, what promises to be good for older individuals and good for business promises also to be good for the nation and our national economy.

Last year I was staff director on a committee of the White House Conference on Aging which sought to measure the probable impact of several national policy changes on the future economy. Our technical Committee on the Economy engaged Data Resources, Incorporated, to study several questions among them this one: What would happen to our economy over the next 25 years if older people, instead of continuing to leave the work force in ever-increasing numbers, should gradually return to work at the level prevailing in 1970?

The economic analysis of this question yielded some highly interesting results:

*First of all, it was estimated that the economy would show significant longterm improvement as a result of increased work by older people. There would be a significant increase in the available pool of workers--enough to offset the shrinking supply of younger workers by the late 1980s. Opportunities would expand for older workers without closing off opportunities for younger workers. Real economic growth would be stimulated--with our Gross National Product growing 3.9 percent more by the year 2005 than it would without the stimulating effect of older employment. And this growth would be accomplished without inflation; in fact, by the mid-1980s and thereafter, annual inflation would average two-tenths of a percent lower each year.

*Second, and perhaps most significantly, our analysis suggests that increases in employment for older people can create a major increase in Federal tax revenues at $40 billion by the year 2005--a fiscal dividend large enough to expand considerably our programs to aid the neediest elderly people without raising taxes--or, alternatively, to allow for a significant tax cut.

Given all these enormous potential benefits--benefits to older people themselves, benefits to business, benefits to the nation--and given the passage of the Age Discrimination in Employment amendments in 1978, one would expect a strong national trend toward expanded employment of older people.

Yet this is not the case. In fact, only 21 percent of men and 18 percent of women over 65 to 69 worked last year.

Indeed, since World War II, no social trend in America has been more pronounced than the decline in labor-force participation by older people. In 1950, for example, more than 40 percent of men over 65 were in the labor force; by last year, the proportion of older men in the work force had been cut by more than half.

But even as we have built a system which allows more and more people to enjoy retirement, we have unwittingly created a structure which severely limits choice for older people. In reality, most people over 65, whatever they may wish to do, face two stark alternatives: either full-time work or full-time retirement, with few options in between. We have, with the best intentions in the world, created a kind of economic Catch-22 for the elderly: a system of economic disincentives, public and private, which penalize older people seeking to earn extra income.

You are familiar with the public side of this Catch-22, the Social Security earnings test. Although this feature of Social Security has repeatedly been liberalized in recent years, it still confronts a retired person with the prospect of losing benefits if he or she earns wages beyond a certain level.

Most private pensions systems work in a similar way--and most of them define retirement so rigorously that an older person's pension benefits are jeopardized even if the retiree works a relatively short time in a given month.

Consider the dilemma of the retiree I mentioned earlier. She would like to work part-time and she needs the extra income. She gets a call from her old supervisor. The office needs an extra person to fill in for absent employees, to handle an increasing workload, and to help train less experienced employees in the procedures of the personnel office. She would be perfect for the assignment. Her supervisor can offer her full-time work at her old salary of $20,000--but he will take her part-time, also, if she prefers part-time work. Can she do it?

What are her choices? In full-time retirement, her pension and Social Security income give her over $11,000 in income. And her Federal taxes are zero.

If she returns to work full-time, she will forfeit her private pension entirely. Her Social Security income will decrease. She will pay Federal taxes, plus Social Security taxes. By returning to work, she will incur the equivalent of an average tax rate of about 75 percent.

What about the half-time option? Here, too, she will forfeit her private pension entirely. Her Social Security income will drop. She will pay Federal taxes and contribute to Social Security. Her average tax rate will become <u>73 percent</u>. Again, not a very attractive proposition.

Quite logically--and sadly--she concludes that even part-time work just isn't worth the effort.

These figures are real. They are based on salary and pension scales of my own company, The Travelers, which were in effect until we changed our pension policies last January. And they are based on the Social Security earnings test now in effect.

So we face a paradox. Many older people want to work and need the income. The potential benefits, as we have seen, are considerable. Yet our system of work and retirement, of pension and employment policies, features too many barriers and too few choices.

What should we do?

In my judgment, we should enlist American business in a great effort to expand job options for older workers.

We should boldly reassess public and corporate policies that present barriers to work by older people--from mandatory retirement policies to pension restrictions to the Social Security earnings test. Do such policies create more problems than they solve? If so, they should be phased out.

Above all, we should begin experimenting, on a much larger scale than at present, with a whole range of work options for older people: part-time jobs, job sharing, flextime and flexiplace, job transfers and retraining, and the rehiring of retirees.

At the company I know best, The Travelers, we have been exploring what we can do to help older workers and retirees. We began by eliminating all mandatory retirement ages--even the 70-year age still permitted by Federal law. We did this not just in Connecticut, where required by state law, but throughout our company, nationwide. Today, hiring and work at The Travelers are based on skill, ability, aptitude and performance--not on age.

Earlier this year, after months of testing, we launched a retirement counseling program, which was developed by NCOA, for employees 55 and older. This program is designed to help our employees set financial goals and plan for the future. An important aspect of the program is a review of employment and retirement options for older workers.

In view of the fact that so many of our older employees expressed interest in some form of paid employment after retirement, we hit upon another idea: Why not make it possible for our retirees to fill temporary jobs in our home office? Such jobs traditionally have been filled by workers from temporary service agencies--an average of 63 workers each day. Hiring our own retirees to do such jobs appeared to make good sense for everyone. Our retirees, after all, know our company and its systems. And establishing our own temporary agency of retirees promised to save money--making it possible to pay our retirees more than they could earn by working for an outside agency.

This led to another idea: to create job opportunities for retirees who want more than occasional part-time work. We surveyed all our home-office departments and found more than 300 fulltime jobs that could possibly be performed on a jobsharing basis by retirees. We have begun offering such jobs to our retired workers who want them.

To turn these ideas into reality, we created The Travelers Retirees Job Bank. Through the Job Bank, our retirees can register to fill temporary positions with the company. And as permanent, shared-job opportunities open up, retirees can find these also through the Job Bank. The Job Bank, by the way, is run by two retirees sharing a full-time position--one of whom is 71 years old.

The only obstacle to our new Job Bank was a long-standing company policy: a policy which specified a complete loss of pension benefits in any month for any retiree who worked more than 40 hours for the company. We decided to change that policy. Early this year, our Board approved a new policy increasing the number of work hours allowed and eliminating the monthly restriction. Since last March, it has been company policy that any retiree can work for the company 960 hours a year--roughly halftime--with no loss of pension from the company.

Today, at Travelers, 60 percent of our daily temporary jobs are filled by retirees.

How have people fared under this new policy?

Take the former woman employee I mentioned. By working half-time, she will now be able to keep her company pension. Her total income while working half-time under the new policy will be more than her full-time work income would have been under the old policy. Her effective "tax" rate will be reduced to 43 percent--and it is this high only because of the Social Security earnings test.

This is powerful incentive for her to do what she actually wants to do--return to work part-time.

All business, of course, will not find it possible or feasible to launch such efforts. In heavy industry, for example, it is logical to assume that older workers will not be as effective as younger ones in physically demanding jobs. But as our economy shifts more toward service jobs, I would expect that more and more jobs would be appropriate for older workers.

We at The Travelers, of course, are not alone in our efforts. Other companies have made their commitments and launched their programs to create job options for older workers. I will mention only a few of many.

*Bankers Life and Casualty, Atlantic Richfield and Polaroid, among others, have ended mandatory retirement.

*The Wrigley Company of Chicago and Towle Silver Company offer their employees phased retirement.

*Tektronix, an instrument maker in Oregon, has a "job redesign" program which allows aging workers to change their responsibilities.

*The Sun Oil Company and the Bank of America hire retirees for temporary and part-time jobs.

I am convinced that many employers could expand job opportunities for their older workers and retirees just as we have done. I am also convinced that if they do, the results will be truly impressive. They will find that older workers are highly productive. They will find that helping older workers continue working is profitable. They will find, in short, that it works.

Thank You.

THE FUTURE OF THE ADEA

Malcolm H. Morrison, Ph.D.*

---

*   Acting Chief, Research Support Staff, Employment Standards
    Administration, U.S. Department of Labor. Dr. Morrison
    directs the Department's preparation of major national
    studies which will be used in reporting to the President and
    Congress the consequences of the Age Discrimination in
    Employment Act, as amended. Dr. Morrison is the Department's
    representative for the 1982 United Nations World Assembly on
    Aging and, in 1980, was the government's Technical Advisor on
    Older Workers at the 66th Session of the ILO Conference in
    Geneva. Dr. Morrison is the editor of Economics of Aging:
    The Future of Retirement to be published by Van Nostrand
    Reinhold Publishers. He also serves on the faculty of Johns
    Hopkins and George Washington Universities. Dr. Morrison
    received his doctoral degree from The Florence Heller
    Graduate School for Advanced Studies in Social Welfare at
    Brandeis University.

TABLE OF CONTENTS

I. INTRODUCTION..1

II. RESPONSE OF EMPLOYERS AND EMPLOYEES TO CONCERN
    WITH THE AGING OF THE WORKFORCE............................2

III. RESEARCH FINDINGS FROM THE NATIONAL STUDY OF
     MANDATORY RETIREMENT (U.S. DEPARTMENT OF LABOR)...........5

   A. The Short-Run Impact of the ADEA Amendments..........5
   B. The Long-Run Impact Impact of the ADEA Amendments....7
   C. Summary of Major Findings--National Survey of
      Employer/Employee Response to the 1978 ADEA
      Amendments...9

   D. Conclusion..10

IV. THE CONSEQUENCES OF MANDATORY RETIREMENT ON
    OLDER WORKER LABOR FORCE PARTICIPATION....................10

   A. Major Conclusions of Labor Supply Research..........11

   B. Other Estimates of the Responses of Older Workers
      to the Change in Mandatory Retirement Age...........12

V. EFFECTS OF MANDATORY RETIREMENT ON
   YOUNGER WORKERS..14

VI. IMPACT OF THE EXEMPT EXECUTIVE PROVISION
    IN THE 1978 ADEA AMENDMENTS...............................15

VII. EFFECTS OF THE TENURED FACULTY EXEMPTION IN THE
     1978 ADEA AMENDMENTS.....................................16

VIII. FUTURE LABOR FORCE CHANGES..............................18

IX. CONSEQUENCES OF ALTERNATIVE MANDATORY RETIREMENT
    AGE POLICIES..19

   A. Long-term Effects of the 1978 Increase in
      Mandatory Retirement Age to 70......................19
   B. Effects of Eliminating Mandatory Retirements........20

X. THE ADEA AND NATIONAL RETIREMENT POLICY...................21

THE FUTURE OF THE ADEA

I. INTRODUCTION

The 1978 Amendments to the Age Discrimination in Employment Act have contributed significantly to raising the level of corporate attention to older employees. Since passage of the Amendments there has been a significant increase in litigation under the ADEA and a substantial increase in employer concern with personnel policies related to older workers.

The purpose of this presentation is to examine the consequences of the present and likely future ADEA law on several broad employer concerns including employee retirement patterns, corporate manpower needs and public policy related to retirement. While available research findings make it possible to be quite definite regarding current employer policies and perceptions and the retirement age choices of their employees, future developments in these areas remain uncertain. This is largely a consequence of being unable to accurately predict the future course of public policy related to retirement benefit programs. Despite the difficulty of precise prognostication, we can be sure that future policies will seek to alter the present early retirement trend and that this will bring about increasing labor force participation by older workers. This trend will develop relatively slowly and will be enhanced by implementation of more flexible retirement policies by employers.

Discussion of these issues will proceed as follows. First, an overview will be presented highlighting the current employer concern with the aging workforce in terms of attitudes and actual policy changes. Second, a discussion of the major findings from the recent Department of Labor Interim Report on studies conducted to evaluate the consequences of the 1978 ADEA Amendments will be presented. Third, probable labor force effects of upcoming demographic changes will be discussed. Fourth, the findings concerning the consequences of removing the mandatory retirement age will be considered. Finally, a conclusion will evaluate the effects of the ADEA as related to the multiple factors which influence retirement policies and retirement age choices of employees.

II. RESPONSE OF EMPLOYERS AND EMPLOYEES TO CONCERN WITH THE AGING OF THE WORKFORCE

Recent surveys [1]/ have clearly documented the increasing concern of employers with the changing composition of the workforce and specifically with the gradual aging of the population. In addition, surveys continue to indicate that a majority of older persons expect to continue to work after "retirement" and prefer flexible work arrangements for such employment.

A major change has occurred with reference to employer perceptions of older workers. Senior corporate officers no longer necessarily view older employees as having reduced capabilities or of having "peaked" in terms of their contributions to the firm. In fact, often older workers are now viewed as more valuable than younger employees. In conjunction with this change, employers now generally believe that older workers are discriminated against in employment and that as their number and proportion increases more legislation protecting their interests will be enacted.

Employers seem to be divided on the question of whether the mandatory retirement age should be abolished but at the same time believe that no one should be forced to retire because of age alone. This contradiction is indicative of the conflict between "what is right" and "what is practical" from the employer standpoint. We will see that factual information (such as the results of the ADEA studies) can sometimes resolve such ambivalence.

In contrast to the ambivalence about mandatory retirement, most employers favor raising the Social Security retirement age, reducing early retirement benefits and liberalizing or eliminating restrictions on earned income in the Social Security system. While these objectives appear to be consistent, many employers also suggest that if these types of policies were enacted, they would liberalize private pension programs to provide benefits to "supplement" those available from Social Security. Such provisions, depending upon how they were structured, would encourage retirement at ages below the increased Social Security age. Most policy proposals for raising

---

[1]/ Harris, Louis and Associates. "Aging in the Eighties: America in Transition," National Council on the Aging, Washington, D.C., November 1981; Mercer, William M. "Employer Attitudes: Implications of an Aging Workforce," William M. Mercer, Incorporated, New York, New York, November 1981; U.S. Department of Labor, "Interim Report on Studies Required by Public Law 95-256, The Age Discrimination in Employment Act Amendments of 1978," Washington, D.C., December 1981.

the Social Security retirement age refer to age 68 with early retirement permitted at age 65. If such a policy were enacted it is extremely likely that over time the usual retirement age would increase to age 65 which would replace age 62 as the most frequent retirement age. At present, very little attention has been given to developing a more flexible Social Security retirement system which would involve a sliding benefit scale and partial benefit payments when employment continues.

About one third of employers have examined the idea of flexible benefits for employees and about half feel that the problems of an aging workforce will be a low priority in the next few years. However, almost three fifths either are already planning to adjust to a smaller, younger labor pool or expect to adjust to this problem in the next five years. Finally, a majority of employers believe that in ten years: (a) a larger proportion of their employees will be older workers; (b) more workers will postpone retirement due to inflation; (c) current "early retirement" policies will have to be reversed because of the shortage of younger workers; (d) benefit plans will have to be modified to attract and retain older workers; and (e) flexible work arrangements will have to increase to accommodate the growing number of older workers.

Overall, these findings indicate that employers are becoming accustomed to the aging of the workforce and are beginning to think more seriously about the likelihood that they will employ more older workers in the future. Most say they have reviewed personnel policies recently to make sure they contain no de facto age discrimination elements; however, only a small minority plan to modify their performance appraisal programs believing that these are presently age neutral. The substantial majority of employers have seen little change in the average retirement age of employees since the enactment of the ADEA Amendments and are evenly split as to the likelihood of an increase in the average age in the next five years. The most important continuing concerns related to older workers remain productivity-related issues, pension/benefit issues and promotional blockage issues. However, employers do not view any of these concerns as particularly problematic at present.

There is little evidence indicating any significant change in the early retirement trend. While it has been suggested that the rate of increase in early retirements may be slowing, 1981 labor force participation figures indicate a further reduction in labor force participation of men over age 65 to a new low of about 18.5 percent. Of course, the present business slowdown and consequent unemployment has adversely affected all employment and unfortunately has resulted in increasing early retirements. (The perverse effects of this trend are felt in increased claims for unemployment, disability and retirement benefits, just at the time when revenues for such benefits are reduced.) There is now fairly uniform agreement that the early retirement trend is becoming dysfunctional particularly for economic reasons and that continuing increases in life expectancy and future labor shortages will require increased labor force participation by older workers and later retirement ages. The reversal of the early retirement trend will be gradual and involve changes in private and public sector policies. At present, employers perceive that government policies are being designed to keep workers employed longer while business policies are still oriented toward encouragement of early retirement. In fact, in general, neither public nor private sector policies currently have the objective of encouraging later retirement. Therefore, it is not surprising that the early retirement trend is persisting.

Over the past 7 years, the proportion of older workers aged 55-64 who plan to retire no sooner than age 65 has grown from 57 to 67 percent. About 60 percent of these employees say they would prefer to continue working part-time after retirement. For the entire labor force about 75 percent suggest they would prefer some type of part-time paid work after retirement. By a two-thirds majority, younger persons disapprove of the idea that older people should retire to make room for younger workers (a significant change in attitude over the past seven years) and most people of all ages agree that employers discriminate against older people.

In light of continuing early retirement, how should these findings be interpreted? It is clear that public attitudes now reflect considerable appreciation of the problems of inflation and their probable consequences on lengthening working life. Most older and younger workers anticipate somewhat later retirement _and_ continued post-retirement employment. The entire population therefore anticipates many more persons continuing to work at older ages. To an extent, these views also represent a recognition of the "civil rights" of older persons in terms of protection from arbitrary age discrimination in employment. More than 90 percent of the American people believe that no one should be forced to retire because of age.

These findings strongly suggest that if public and private retirement policies were changed to permit more flexibility in retirement age policy (particularly as influenced by availability and structure of public and private pensions), the labor force response of older workers would be substantial. While only 3-4 million older persons work today, estimates suggest that 2-3 times this number might work if the disincentives to employment contained in pension and personnel policies were removed. Thus, while the number of older persons desiring part-time employment after retirement is increasing significantly, public and private policy to encourage and enhance this objective have been slow in developing.

III. RESEARCH FINDINGS FROM THE NATIONAL STUDY OF MANDATORY RETIREMENT (U.S. DEPARTMENT OF LABOR)

The National Studies of Mandatory Retirement were undertaken by the U.S. Department of Labor pursuant to research requirements of the Age Discrimination in Employment Act Amendments of 1978. The law mandated a study of the consequences of raising the mandatory retirement age to 70, the feasibility of extending or eliminating the age limit, and the effects of exemptions for business executives and tenured faculty members at universities. Key issues for the study were the impact of the increased mandatory retirement age on employment of youth, minority and women employees, effects on promotional opportunities, increased administrative burdens for employers (including performance evaluations) and effects on pension plans. Two reports on this research were required by law--an Interim Report in 1981 and a Final Report including recommendations of the Secretary of Labor, in 1982.

The Department of Labor has conducted three major studies in meeting the requirements of the 1978 ADEA Amendments:

1. The National Survey of Employer/Employee Response to the 1978 ADEA Amendments,
2. Effects of Raising the Age Limit for Mandatory Retirement in the ADEA (Analytical Studies),
3. The Academic Retirement Study.

In addition, several smaller studies examined characteristics of older workers, alternative employment approaches for older workers and the legal application of the Bona Fide Occupational Qualification provision in the ADEA law.

Reported here are summary findings from the major studies that have been conducted. Further detailed analysis is available from the Department of Labor. In conducting these studies, the Department of Labor was concerned with both the impact of mandatory retirement on individuals and the administrative and financial consequences of the ADEA Amendments for employers. In addition, the Department recognized that the retirement decision is simultaneously influenced by mandatory retirement policies, public and private pension policies and personnel policies. The study findings in this report examine the consequence of mandatory retirement policies in the context of these other major factors influencing retirement behavior.

A. The Short-Run Impact of the ADEA Amendments

In assessing the impact of the ADEA Amendments, it is useful to separate the short-run and long-run effects. In the short run, the Amendments had their most direct impact on the behavior of firms--particularly firms' mandatory retirement policies--and a much smaller impact on the plans of employees. In the long run, this balance may be reversed.

We estimate that in the mid-1970's, about 60 percent <u>of persons surveyed</u> had faced <u>some</u> mandatory retirement age. By the time of the survey itself (early 1980), 51 percent of the sample faced a mandatory retirement age of 70 or more while 45 percent of the sample faced no mandatory retirement age whatsoever.

Fifty-three percent of employees sampled in the survey worked for firms that had changed their retirement policies 'in the last few years.' In almost all cases, (82 percent) these changes have arisen in whole or in part from the ADEA Amendments. Most of these recent changes attributed to the Amendments involved moving from one mandatory retirement age to a higher one, while relatively few changes involved abandoning a mandatory retirement age altogether. This reaction suggests that by the late 1970's, most employers who retained mandatory retirement policies did so by conscious choice.

The Amendment's short-run impact on other aspects of firm behavior was relatively weak. For example, it has often been asserted that a relaxation of mandatory retirement age would result in a more widespread use of performance evaluations as an alternative way of removing people from jobs. The survey suggests, to the contrary, that the incidence of performance evaluations was already highest in firms that have mandatory retirement rules, those with such rules were no more likely to have stricter evaluations in the future. Thus, the two policies serve as complements, rather than substitutes, for each other.

It was also anticipated that firms might discontinue pension accruals for workers over age 65. However, only a very small percentage (6 percent) of the more than 50 percent of employers currently permitting accruals have considered such a change.

Although at least half the short-run changes in employer policy had been made by the time of the survey, the results suggest that nearly all the employer response has been, and will be, in the direction of providing more encouragement for employees to retire by liberalizing existing benefits, adding types of benefits, and shifting costs more toward the company.

The ADEA Amendments' short-run impact on employee retirement plans was very weak, a conclusion that arises from several pieces of data. First, only 15 percent of the survey respondents could correctly identify the Amendments' barring of mandatory retirement before age 70. By itself, this data means little since the ADEA Amendments might be affecting persons indirectly through changes in firm policy. But in practice, only 11 percent of the sample report having made a recent change in their retirement plans for any reason. About one-third of these actually decreased their retirement age and only one-tenth of these increased their retirement age explicitly because of the ADEA Amendments.

Finally, the survey contained an "experiment" to see whether people would change their planned retirement age upon being informed of the ADEA Amendments' details. In this experiment, about 8 percent of the respondents did increase their retirement age from 65 or less to 66 or more. But an equal proportion of the sample decreased their retirement age. And individuals' increases or decreases in planned retirement age had nothing to do with whether the person thought he faced mandatory retirement at 65, mandatory retirement at 70, or no mandatory retirement whatsoever.

These data are consistent with the idea that most people have devoted at least some prior thought to retirement and their plans are based on their understanding of their employers' policies. While these plans may change in the long run, they will not be changed immediately by being informed of the new age 70 mandatory retirement provision.

In summary, the ADEA Amendments had a significant impact on increasing the mandatory retirement age of some firms, but it had relatively small impact on other aspects of firm behavior, and it had very little impact on employees' retirement plans.

B. The Long-Run Impact of the ADEA Amendments

In the long run, the impact of the ADEA Amendments on employee plans may be somewhat larger and this, in turn, may induce employers to change their policies. Our analysis of the retirement plans of men showed significant differences in retirement behavior between men who believed they were covered by an age-65 retirement rule and men who faced a retirement rule at age 70 or above. On average, the second group retired two years later than the first with one quarter of the group wanting to retire at age 66 or age 67. Over time, as all men became aware that they can work to age 70, we would expect retirement dates to be delayed. (A parallel pattern for married women can be expected to affect them at lower age levels since their retirement decisions appear to be planned jointly with their husbands and these women are, on average, two years younger than their husbands).

Employees were found to be retiring relatively early, on average, particularly if they were subject to an age limit (usually age 70). Among those subject to an age limit, employers reported that 43 percent of persons in the sampled employee occupations had been retiring by age 61, 63 percent by age 62, and 79 percent by age 64, on average. Few changes were expected in that pattern over the near term and only 7 percent of the older workers subject to an age limit were expected to retire at ages older than 65. The relatively early retirements were in response to substantial financial incentives to early retirement offered by employers, including pension plans with young normal retirement ages, payment of full accrued early retirement benefits, and continuation of company-paid insurance after retirement. There appeared to be little reason for employers to alter their policies in the short term.

One argument against raising the age limit mandatory retirement was that age limits were needed to assure jobs and promotional opportunities for younger workers. Employer personnel respondents representing workers subject to an age limit did believe that mandatory retirement rules were more important in this regard than as a simple way to remove unproductive older workers.

Although approximately 50 percent of workers' employers believed the cost of labor would increase if significant numbers of older workers postponed retirement to age 70, the employers of workers subject to an age limit were four times more likely to believe costs would _decrease_ as other employers. Twenty-one percent of workers in manufacturing firms subject to an age limit, and 34 percent in the largest firms, had employers believing costs would decrease.

Given the relatively young current retirement ages, little expectation that retirement ages will change, continued offerings of incentives to early retirement, and policy changes already accomplished, relatively few older workers can expect additional changes in their pension or health and welfare benefits in the near future. The short-term impact of ADEA Amendments on employee benefits thus appears to have been quite limited.

C. Summary of Major Findings--National Survey of Employer/Employee Response to the 1978 ADEA Amendments

In terms of the number of older workers affected, the greatest impact of the ADEA Amendments was on employers' mandatory retirement rules. Forty-four percent of the employees surveyed were subject to new mandatory retirement policies as a result of the Amendments, and an additional 9 percent had policies changed for other reasons. The great majority (87 percent) of the changes attributed to ADEA involved retaining mandatory retirement with an older age limit. Only 6 percent of all surveyed workers had their age limit removed as a result of ADEA. Nearly all employers responded to the legal mandatory retirement age permitted by the Amendments. Most of the employees experiencing no recent change in employer policy had been subject to no age limit since 1976, and nearly all of the remainder had been subject to age limits of 70 or older prior to the Amendments. Although the impact on employers' mandatory retirement policies was found to be quite large, the corresponding impact on other retirement-related benefits and policies was found to be of a much smaller order of magnitude.

Many employers, especially those retaining an age limit, were offering their workers continuing incentives to encourage retirement before the normal retirement age, including full accrued early retirement benefits, continuation of health, life and disability insurance after retirement, and retirement counseling.

Employers were asked whether the average retirement age was expected to change in the next few years. Sixty-four percent expected no change in the average age. When change was expected, twice as many employers expected workers to delay retirement as retire earlier, but only 7 percent expected the average retirement age to exceed 65. Thus, a small minority of employers believed that a later retirement age might occur--but this age would still not be later than 65.

When pension plan sponsors' recommendations were compared to the reason why policy changes were being actively considered or planned, ADEA was found to be responsible, even in part, for very few of the likely benefit adjustments in the near future. Consequently, the impact of ADEA on employee's retirement benefits in the near future is expected to be quite limited.

When employers and pension plan sponsors were asked what policy change they might recommend that their organizations consider should a large number of older workers postpone retirement to age 70, the response was again overwhelmingly in the direction of providing more generous benefits. While it was feared that employers would discontinue pension accruals for workers over age 65 in response to the Amendments, the results did not confirm this expectation.

Despite inducements offered to encourage early retirement, relatively young retirement ages and an anticipation that very few employees would postpone retirement beyond age 65, the employers retaining their age limits believed that mandatory retirement rules were important. However, these employers believed age limits were more important as a way to assure promotional opportunities than as a simple way to remove unproductive older workers.

D. Conclusion

The major short-term impact of 1978 ADEA Amendments was to force employers to raise their mandatory retirement age limits. There has been relatively little change in other retirement related policies, and there will probably be little in the near future due to ADEA. Most changes were being made in response to other factors. Rather than attempting to mitigate the potential effect of the Amendments, most employers appeared to be waiting to see whether, and how, employees' retirement behavior will change before they alter policies.

If retirement ages increase precipitously, employers might be faced with the choice of making major structural changes in their system of personnel management, or spending large sums of money to pay retiring workers supplemental benefits until they are old enough to qualify for Social Security benefits.

If retirement ages increase more slowly, the outcome is more likely to be determined by other factors such as the rate of growth in the economy, and the unemployment rate. The total long-term impact of the Amendments on employee behavior and employer policies will likely be determined largely by the degree to which employees respond to the extended ADEA protection they now have in the context of potential changes in other Federal retirement policies and future economic performance.

IV. THE CONSEQUENCES OF MANDATORY RETIREMENT ON OLDER WORKER LABOR FORCE PARTICIPATION

This section presents an analysis of the labor market effects on older workers of raising the mandatory retirement age limit. Two types of analysis are reported: (a) an examination of the effects of raising the mandatory retirement age, availability of pension benefits and other variables on the retirement decisions of workers who were subject to the former mandatory retirement age of 65; and (b) a review of estimates of overall labor supply effects of raising the mandatory retirement age based on the above analysis and other major estimates.

A. <u>Major Conclusions of Labor Supply Research</u>

Our study has found that the prior existence of age-65 mandatory retirement rules had a significant impact on the likelihood that workers reaching that age would withdraw from the labor force. For example, men aged 62-64 who were wage or salary workers in 1973 had their probability of continuing to work at any job over a two-year period diminished by about 28 percentage points due to facing an age-65 mandatory retirement rule. Women age 58-61 were estimated to have a decline in their probability of continued work of about 8 percentage points associated with the prospects of the <u>future</u> imposition of mandatory retirement by their employers.

Had the 1978 ADEA Amendments become effective during 1973-75, the result of raising the mandatory retirement age from 65 to 70 would have been that at most 200,000 older workers would have been working in 1975 instead of retired. The level of the permitted mandatory retirement age was, of course, of great significance to individual workers approaching age 65 who wanted to continue working and were unlikely to have much opportunity at that age to move to other jobs. This increase is less important in the degree of impact it had in the measurable increment to the total number of such workers; for example, this maximum figure (200,000) implied a 3-percent labor force increase for men aged 64-6 in 1975. However, viewed in the context of the <u>national economy</u>, this change in labor supply would be a miniscule increase in the total workforce (less than two-tenths of one percent).

This study also estimates that relative importance of Social Security and pension benefit entitlements to the retirement decision, both in terms of the current year tradeoff (loss of a year's wages vs. loss of retirement benefits) and the wealth effect (the present asset value of a lifetime of future benefits). The current trade-off of benefits vs. wages was found to be especially important, reflecting the fact that Social Security and the bulk of pension plans are designed to facilitate retirement.

Since mandatory retirement provisions are closely tied to private pensions, this research indicates that the incentives inherent in pension plans are most important determinants of behavior--people do respond to these incentives. Therefore, the eventual impact of changes in mandatory retirement legislation in terms of the degree to which people will actually avail themselves of the legal opportunity to continue working, depends critically on how pension characteristics change. If employers cannot dismiss employees at age 65 on the basis of age but are permitted to structure fringe benefits to make it very expensive for workers to forego retirement benefits beyond this point, changes in mandatory retirement rules will have only a modest aggregate impact. On the other hand, if employers were to remove these financial disincentives to work, the impact of the ADEA Amendments will be more pronounced.

B. Other Estimates of the Responses of Older Workers to the Change in Mandatory Retirement Age

The various studies examined in this analysis present evidence that mandatory retirement age policies have significant effects on the labor force participation of older workers.

The Department of Labor Estimate. One of the earliest and most frequently cited estimates of the number of older workers projected to remain on their jobs in response to the change in mandatory retirement age was made by the U.S. Department of Labor. The Department estimated that between 150,000 to 200,000 workers aged 65 to 69 were not in the 1976 labor force because of enforced mandatory retirement.

Halpern's Estimate. Halpern (1978) suggests that the short and long-run effects of raising the mandatory retirement age may be quite different. Halpern projects out six years beyond the change in mandatory retirement age (1984) and predicts that the labor force may have an additional 375,000 older workers as a result of the change. Since her estimate assumes that everyone who wants to work past the old mandatory retirement age of 65 will continue to work until forced to retire at age 70, it is overstated. Taking the over estimation problem into account, Halpern suggests a more realistic estimate would be around 200,000 additional workers, which is consistent with the Department of Labor estimate.

Clerk, Barker and Cantrell's Estimate. Clark, Barker and Cantrell (1979) use three estimation procedures to predict the increase in labor force participation due to the change in mandatory retirement age. Results of all three procedures are approximately the same. The removal of mandatory retirement is projected to increase the labor force participation of the age-64 group by 5 to 6 percentage points--slightly higher than the Department of Labor estimate.

<u>Wertheimer and Zedlewski's Estimate</u>. In a study for the Administration on Aging and further refined under this study, Wertheimer and Zedlewski analyzed the impact of mandatory retirement on the labor market behavior of men and single women in the 1969-1975 waves of the Social Security Administration Retirement History Survey. This study found that mandatory retirement had significant negative effects on the labor supply of older workers, even when controlling for other strong retirement incentives. The most significant impact of mandatory retirement was on the probability of participating in the labor force. For 65-year-olds, the average reduction estimated for the three observation periods was 20 percentage points. For 66-69-year-olds, the average reduction found was smaller (13 percentage points for the 66-67-year-olds and 11 percentage points for the 68-69-year-olds). This anticipatory effect reduced their participation rate by about 9 percentage points.

These results were used to make a projection of the impact of raising the mandatory retirement age to 70. It was estimated that in 1985 there will be approximately 250,000 more workers aged 62-69 as a result of the change in the law. This represents an 8 percent projected increase in the number of workers aged 65-69 and about a 3 percent projected increase in the number of workers aged 62-64. The authors also point out that while these increases are significant for the older population, they result in very small changes in the labor force as a whole.

Thus, the results of this study are generally in agreement with those presented earlier.

<u>The various studies combined present evidence that mandatory retirement age policies have significant effects on reducing the labor force participation of the older population.</u>

Although these estimates of additional older workers represent a substantial increase in the number of older workers in the labor force, and a modest increase in the proportion in the work force, they represent a very small portion of the entire labor force.

V. EFFECTS OF MANDATORY RETIREMENT ON YOUNGER WORKERS

An analysis of census survey data was undertaken to assess the maximum immediate impact on younger workers resulting from any direct competition for jobs held by age-64 workers who might elect to remain in the labor force past 65 due to the increase in the mandatory retirement age. The possible job competition was assessed for youth, women and black workers who hold full-time, full-year jobs at wage levels comparable to the older workers. The logic behind the analysis was that any short-term effect on these groups will result from a substantial number of older workers (holding jobs comparable to younger workers) continuing to work longer than they otherwise would have because of the increase in the mandatory retirement age.

The immediate effect of the 1978 Amendments on younger, female, and minority workers based on estimates of the direct effect on older workers was found to be small. The estimated additional number of comparable age-65 workers are potential competition for less than one quarter of one-percent of all full-time workers ages 16-24; less than one half of one percent of all full-time black workers ages 16-59; and one tenth of one percent of all full-time women workers ages 16-59.

In all three comparisons (younger workers, black workers, and women workers) with older workers, the wage-comparable younger workers were concentrated in manufacturing, professional services, and wholesale and retail trade, while the wage-comparable older workers expected to work past 65 were concentrated in manufacturing, professional services, and public administration. When these wage-comparable workers were compared, the potential for significant job slot competition within specific industries did not materialize. The general pattern was that apparent high levels of potential competition within certain industries tended to result, on closer scrutiny, from potential competition between workers <u>in only a few particular occupations</u>. The greatest potential for job slot competition was not in occupations with the greatest number of wage-comparable younger workers but in the occupations with the highest ratio of wage-comparable older to younger workers, such as: craft workers for all younger workers; managers, craft workers and laborers for younger black workers; and transportation operatives, laborers and craft workers for younger female workers. However, the magnitude of the competition is still very small, representing no more than four percent of the pool of comparable younger workers in any occupation.

VI. IMPACT OF THE EXEMPT EXECUTIVE PROVISION IN THE 1978 ADEA AMENDMENTS

Two years after the 1978 ADEA Amendments became effective, a survey of the personnel officers of nearly 3,000 firms and an in-depth case study of 50 of the firms revealed a great deal of indecision and confusion surrounding firms' use of the authority left them by Congress to exempt executives from the increased mandatory retirement age. Although 20 percent of all personnel officers indicated that their firms either were using the exemption or were planning to apply it within a year, nearly 30 percent said their firms' executives must retire before reaching age 70. About a fifth of the larger sample and a third of the case study firms had not made final decisions about whether to apply the exemption.

Larger firms and those engaged in manufacturing were more likely to use the exemption than other firms. Seventy-five percent of the executives who could be mandatorily retired under the exemption work for firms already using the exemption and personnel officers expected only a 3 percent increase in the numbers of officers who could be mandatorily retired at ages 65-69 over the next 5 years.

The main reason given by nearly half of the <u>case study respondents</u> for using the exemption was the need to assure promotional opportunities for younger workers; cost savings were also frequently cited.

<u>Although the majority of firms (60 percent of the case study sample and 80 percent of the larger sample) were not using the exemption at the time of the survey</u>, case study responses indicate that executive retirement age was not an issue for these firms. The firms either had no older executives, their executives were retiring by age 65, or there was no policy encouraging retirement at a specific age.

In general, the effect of the exemption has been to permit a partial retention of the old age 65 mandatory retirement age policy for those firms that have the organizational capability to administer a complex policy (the larger firms) that have executives in the age bracket affected, and that have the least growth in executive positions (the manufacturing firms) and thus the greatest pressure for turnover in jobs. Large firms and the manufacturing sector have traditionally been more likely to apply mandatory retirement and pension incentives to their older employees as a part of personnel policy. However, the great majority of firms are not using the exemption at the present time and may not use it in the future.

VI. EFFECTS OF THE TENURED FACULTY EXEMPTION IN THE 1978 ADEA AMENDMENTS

The effects of the 1978 ADEA Amendments with the special exemption for tenured faculty members are diverse. These effects differ in the short and long run and vary in quantitative and qualitative dimensions.

The immediate effects of the expiration of the exemption will be limited. As of 1980, only 46 percent of institutions, employing 32 percent of all faculty members still had a mandatory retirement age of 65, and of these only a limited number have the older age structures that our simulations indicated are especially vulnerable to a change of the mandatory retirement age to 70.

Expiration of the exemption will have both short-run and long-run effects, some quantitative and others qualitative. The impact of a one-time change in the mandatory retirement age will bring about almost immediate changes in the age distribution of faculty members, institutional costs, and hiring rates, but this will be followed by a relatively smooth adjustment to the situation. In other words, the short-run effects are significant; the long-run effects are barely perceptible. On the other hand, some of the qualitative effects of the expiration of the exemption will take longer to manifest themselves and will necessarily be more nebulous though nonetheless important. For example, the impact of having considerably larger proportions of faculty members over age 60 or of being required to devise more formal systems for evaluating the performance of faculty members may produce changes in higher education.

The immediate effects of a change in mandatory retirement age in higher education are likely to be greater than in the economy in general. In contrast to findings of other studies on the national labor force, faculty members are generally not expecting to retire well before mandatory retirement age. The results indicate that with the expiration of the exemption, the expected average age of retirement in higher education will rise by 1.4 years (from age 65.6 to 67.0). For private institutions, in which an average retirement occurs almost two years later than in public institutions and for which institutional age structures are most likely to be unfavorable, the effect of a change in the mandatory retirement age from 65 to 70 will be larger than is indicated by overall averages.

The findings indicate clearly that for those subject to mandatory retirement of 65, this age is an effective employment constraint. This is apparently so because as faculty members age they appear to be less responsive to financial incentives in determining the timing or age of their actual retirement even though these financial variables entered into their earlier retirement planning. Apparently, the attractiveness of employment in institutions of higher education and the good health of faculty members encourage them to extend their appointments well past "normal" retirement age. The study further indicates that even though a mandatory retirement age of 65 is a constraint on employment it operates not to force retirement age at 65 but to discourage faculty members or their administrators from extending employment to age 70 and beyond. Although higher education has in general historically adopted a late age of mandatory retirement (between 65 and 70), these policies have been applied flexibly in that extensions have been allowed and retirements on the average have occurred later than 65. Thus, the effect of a legislated change in the minimum allowed age of mandatory retirement may be to reduce the discretionary ability of institutions to apply extension and retirement policies flexibly between ages 65 and 70.

The impact of the expiration will be reflected in higher compensation costs for those older and more highly paid faculty members who opt to continue teaching past age 65 and up to age 70. The cost increases will over the period 1982-87 rise about 3 percent, and in some unusual cases may reach as high as 7-8 percent, depending upon the age structures of individual institutions, their age-earnings structure, and the preferences of faculty members to continue teaching.

The stronger are the desires and pressures on faculty members to continue teaching, the more limited will be the numbers of new Ph.Ds who can be hired.

Despite these potential effects (some of which may be already occurring) changes in the policies of higher education institutions have already resulted in (1) more than half of all institutions with a mandatory retirement age of 70 and (2) about two-thirds of all faculty now subject to this higher mandatory age. Thus, for most institutions and faculty, the expiration of the tenured faculty exemption will have no immediate effect. Also, since enrollments are not declining at present, initial institutional adjustment to the expiration of the exemption to the age 70 mandatory retirement criterion is possible with only relatively moderate budgetary and personnel consequences; however, a removal of any mandatory retirement age would pose more serious problems for higher education.

VIII. FUTURE LABOR FORCE CHANGES

Today, the median age of the population is 30 and the civilian labor force is about 104 million. In the decade of the 1970's, the labor force grew by 2.25 percent per year--a very high rate of growth. As a result, 19 million additional workers were added to the labor force (11 million women, 8 million men). Today, young persons (16-24) comprise 23 percent of the labor force, prime age workers (25-44) represent 46 percent, and older workers (65 and over) comprise just 3 percent of the labor force. Statistics for 1981 indicate that labor force participation by older persons is continuing to decline (particularly for men) possibly influenced by the recession. Nevertheless, despite all of the opinion polls demonstrating changing attitudes by older employees, personnel managers, younger workers, etc., and discussion of "flexible retirement" alternatives, current retirement policies continue to result in encouraging older persons to leave the labor force.

While recognizing present circumstances, it is extremely important to consider demographic trends already in progress which will significantly alter the future labor force. In addition, it is certain that retirement policies in this country will be changing because of the growing financial support requirements for an increased retired population, the need for more older workers and individual preferences for employment at older ages.

What will be happening in the years ahead is as follows. First, the labor force growth will slow considerably and employment will grow at rates of only 1.3 to 1.8 percent annually. Moderate growth will lead to a labor force of about 120 million in 1990 and 130 million by 2000. Second, contrary to trends in the 1970's, the decrease in births beginning in the late 1960's will result in reducing labor force entrants aged 16-24 in the 1980's. The proportion of younger labor force entrants will decrease by 8 percent or about 2 million persons by 1990. Another loss of about the same magnitude will occur between 1990 and 2000, and thus about 4 million younger workers will simply not be available over the next 20 years. While some have suggested that this change is significant it is not in itself a cause for alarm. What is of importance is that this reduction will exacerbate the problems of skill shortages which are already apparent and will grow in the future.

In 1990, the median age of the population will be 33; more than half the labor force will be composed of persons aged 25-44 and by 2000 these workers will age to 35-55 years old and the median population age will be 36. These facts, of course, lead to the inevitable conclusion that the problems of the workforce in the near term will primarily be the problems of middle-aged employees as they approach normal retirement age. We should note, however, that if national retirement policies begin to change, extensions of worklife may become much more common as the large middle-aged cohort approaches retirement.

What about older workers—now commonly considered persons aged 65 or more? We all know that the population is aging rapidly, that in 1980 older persons will represent 12 percent of our national population (or more if persons aged 60 and over are included) and that life expectancy at older ages still increasing. The key question is whether labor force participation of older workers will continue to decline, will stabilize or will increase in the near-term future? Most informed observers agree with the experts that despite the current early retirement trend which is really a direct consequence of current public and private pension policies, it is likely that there will be a stabilization of labor force participation in the future, followed by actual increases in participation. This will occur for a number of reasons, including personal preferences of employees, changes in corporate personnel and employee benefit policies brought about by the need to retain older employees, and changes in national Social Security policies. While it is difficult to predict the exact timing of these developments related to older workers, some evidence of increased labor force participation will certainly be available by the mid- to late 1980's and the lessened availability of younger workers and growing skill shortages will certainly result in greater numbers of older workers in the 1990's. It is for these reasons that employers are well advised to perform workforce analyses and develop plans for altering personnel and employee benefit policies to accommodate an aging workforce in the years ahead.

IX. CONSEQUENCES OF ALTERNATIVE MANDATORY RETIREMENT AGE POLICIES

The Department of Labor National Studies of Mandatory Retirement included a specific analysis of the labor force participation consequences of eliminating the mandatory retirement age. The results from this analysis are as follows.

   A. <u>Long-term Effects of the 1978 Increase in Mandatory Retirement Age to 70</u>.

The estimates indicate that labor force participation of older men 2/ should rise as a result of the 1978 ADEA Amendments

---

2/ The effects in this summary apply to older men. Underlying problems with the data used in this retirement decision model for women preclude attributing the same degree of validity to estimated effects on women.

prohibiting mandatory retirement before age 70. Slight increases in the participation rate were forecast for older men under age 65. The most significant impacts on older workers remaining in the labor force were found for those age 65 and over. In all three years projected (1985, 1990, 2000), men age 65-67 were estimated to experience a participation rate increase from about 33 percent to about 40 percent. For men age 68-70, a significant increase was also found, although the pattern was not as uniform. In 1985 the participation rate is estimated to rise from 17.6 to 22.0 percent. In 2000, however, the rise is is only by about five percent, from 18.9 to 19.8 percent. This difference over time results from the interaction of mandatory retirement policies with trends in Social Security and pension income for this age group, with the retirement benefit effects becoming stronger than mandatory retirement for 68-70-year-olds.

Other factors being equal, the change from age-65 to age-70 mandatory retirement will result in approximately 217,200 more older men being in the labor force in 2000, <u>or approximately 5 percent of all male workers age 60-70 estimated for that year.</u> The bulk of this increase is in the 65 to 67 age range.

B. Effects of Eliminating Mandatory Retirement.

As in the policy changes described above moving from the current age-70 mandatory retirement policy to a situation in which mandatory retirement is prohibited affects, but only modestly, older men who are not yet at the mandatory age. However, for the age bracket that includes age 70 (the 68-70-year-old men), the participation rate rises sharply, from 22.0 to 27.8 percent in 1985, a 26 percent increase in participation, and from 19.8 to 23.9 percent in 2000, a 21 percent increase in participation.

Compared to the age-70 policy, elimination of mandatory retirement would result in 195,100 additional older men being in the labor force in 2000. Almost half (90,300) would be in the 68-70 age group. If added to the 217,200 estimated rise in the labor force size caused by the increase in the mandatory retirement age from 65 to 70, eliminating any mandatory retirement age would induce 412,300 men to remain in the labor force in 2000. This number constitutes about <u>10 percent of all male workers age 60-70 estimated for that year.</u>

Several important conclusions may be drawn from these projections of the labor supply effects of alternative mandatory retirement policies. First, the rate of increase of the downward trend in the labor force participation of older men that has prevailed for two decades should be reversed, at least temporarily, by the 1978 ADEA Amendments unless other more powerful economic forces offset the effects attributable to the new age-70 mandatory retirement policy. However, the long-term decline in older men's labor force participation can be expected to resume in the mid-to late-1980's absent other significant policy change or economic trends that depart sharply from previous long-run experience. (Available data do not indicate that the recent relatively high inflation experience has resulted in any significant delayed retirement trend). Elimination of mandatory retirement would constitute such a policy change, and in this case the projections found that older men's labor force participation would rise not only immediately after enactment of such a policy but would also continue to rise slightly over the longer run.

A second conclusion is that the order of magnitude of the increase in the workforce that should result from the age-70 policy (a 5 percent increase in labor force participation by older workers) found in other studies conducted by the Department was confirmed here and found to apply even when viewed over a long period of time.

Third, the total elimination of mandatory retirement would have a similar impact (an additional 5 percent increase in labor force participation) on the male workforce when compared to the labor force participation expected under the age-70 policy. Taken together, assuming a continuation of current retirement policies, the 1978 Amendments and further Congressional action to eliminate mandatory retirement would add 412,300 men age 60-70 to the labor force by the year 2000. Thus, elimination of mandatory retirement, while helpful to employment aspirations in thousands of individual cases, would be expected to have a marginal impact on the overall labor force that is no greater than the impact of setting the age at 70 vs. 65.

VII. THE ADEA AND NATIONAL RETIREMENT POLICY

In the recent book, Economics of Aging: The Future of Retirement 3/ I comment

> While it is clear that we do not presently have one uniform national retirement policy, it is also evident that most of our current uncoordinated policies result in the major trend of early retirement. This trend is beginning to be perceived as dysfunctional mainly because of increasing pension costs. Of course, it may also be dysfunctional because it limits the human potential of millions of persons who could contribute to productivity if provided with the opportunity. . . . A major question that confronts our society is whether we will consciously act to develop and implement a retirement policy which emphasizes more balance in utilizing the capacities of the available work-

---

3/ Morrison, Malcolm H., Ph.D., Ed., Economics of Aging: The Future of Retirement, Van Nostrand Reinhold Company, New York, 1981.

> force, or continue our present approach of
> reacting to limited aspects of the problem with
> stop-gap measures designed to temporarily remedy
> the most immediate problems? . . . Although an
> overall multifaceted retirement policy is not
> available at present, a conceptual understanding
> of the linkages between pension, employment and
> retirement policy is clearly a necessity if a
> new retirement policy is to be developed on an
> incremental basis.

There are at least two ways of viewing national policy related to age discrimination in employment. First, arbitrary discrimination based on age is a clear violation of the principle of equal protection of the laws upon which our Constitution is based. There is virtually no basis for assuming that older persons who benefit from public and private pension programs desire that such programs restrict them from being employed. The law should not, therefore, permit such restrictions and should be designed to protect older persons against employment discrimination based upon irrational beliefs not based upon evaluation of performance. Second, it has now been demonstrated that the existence of legal mandatory retirement ages does in fact reduce the employment opportunities of older persons--albeit modestly. While there are many other factors which also result in inducing older persons out of the workforce, the mandatory retirement age has been shown to be a barrier to continued employment. There is widespread agreement that this restriction should be eliminated since it constitutes an arbitrary limit on employment.

In recognizing these issues, and in light of the findings from the National Studies of Mandatory Retirement, we know that the elimination of the mandatory retirement age will not result in major changes in labor force participation by older workers. For this to occur major changes in the retirement age provisions of public and private pension systems would be required. There is substantial reason to believe that changing demographic and economic circumstances will result in the development of more flexible employment and retirement policies in the future. These new policies will permit our economy to <u>gradually adjust</u> to an aging workforce and a reduction in younger labor force entrants. In many ways, therefore, the Age Discrimination in Employment Act represents not only an affirmation of the basic rights of middle-aged and older persons but is also an assertion and re-definition of the potential of the older population to contribute to society.

THE FUTURE OF THE ADEA:
PRESSURE BUILDS TO ABOLISH MANDATORY RETIREMENT

Charles H. Edwards *
and
Stephen R. McConnell **

---

*   Staff Director and General Counsel, House Select Committee on Aging, serving as chief administrative and legal officer since November, 1979; formerly attorney with Haley, Bader & Potts, Washington, D.C.; Regional Director of State Government Relations, Pharmaceutical Manufacturers Association; professional staff member for U.S. Senate Committee on Human Resources, Subcommittee on Labor; and staff assistant, U.S. Senate Committee on Labor and Public Welfare; legislative and legal research assistant, National Retired Teachers Association/American Association of Retired Persons; legal education, Georgetown University Law Center, 1977; B.A. cum laude, Duke University, 1973.

** Industrial Gerontologist, House Select Committee on Aging; formerly Research Associate at the Andrus Gerontology Center, University of Southern California, where he received his Ph.D. in the Sociology of Aging in 1976.

TABLE OF CONTENTS

		Page
I.	INTRODUCTION	1
II.	EFFECTS OF THE 1978 ADEA AMENDMENTS	2
	A. Small Number of Older Workers Affected	3
	B. Minimal Effects on Youth, Minorities and Women	3
	C. Loopholes in the ADEA Lack Support	5
	1. Professor exemption	5
	2. Executive exemption	6
	3. Employee benefits	6
III.	CLIMATE FOR NEW CHANGES IN THE ADEA	7
	A. Public Opinion Strongly Opposes Mandatory Retirement	7
	B. Business Attitudes Improving Toward Older Workers	8
	C. Demographic Trends Favor the Older Worker	9
	1. Improved health of older population	10
	2. No increase in insurance risks	11
	D. Congress Favors Prolonged Worklives	12
	1. Social Security bills encourage employment	12
	2. Bills introduced to amend the ADEA	13
	3. Key Congressional Committees are cautious	13
	4. Critical factors influencing Congressional action	14
IV.	ISSUES TO BE ADDRESSED IN FUTURE ADEA AMENDMENTS	15
	A. Raising the Upper Age Limit	15
	B. Eliminating the Professor and Executive Exemptions	16
	C. Requiring Continued Pension Accrual	17
	D. Modifying the BFOQ Provision	18
	E. Amending Title VII of the Civil Rights Act to Include Age	20
	1. Advantages of including age in Title VII	20
	2. Disadvantages of repealing the ADEA	22
V.	CONCLUSION	24

Appendix
    Table 1
    Chart 1

THE FUTURE OF THE ADEA:
PRESSURE BUILDS TO ABOLISH MANDATORY RETIREMENT

I. INTRODUCTION

America is undergoing an aging explosion, having entered a period in which the ranks of its older population will swell and in which public consciousness regarding the needs and rights of older Americans will continue to increase. Statistics amply demonstrate that the demographic revolution has already begun. Today there are 24 million Americans age 65 and over, and by the year 2000 this number will grow by one-third to 32 million. Similarly, a dramatic change in public attitudes toward the elderly has already taken place in conjunction with this "graying of America." In contrast to the intergenerational warfare which some doomsdayers had predicted, the aging of the population has brought with it a strengthening of support on the part of the young and the middle aged for improving the quality of life of the elderly. A recent Harris poll commissioned by the National Council on the Aging, for example, found that Americans of all ages are overwhelmingly opposed to mandatory retirement.

Developments in public opinion have been paralleled by remarkable changes in the attitude of the business community toward the aged. Employers have a heightened sense of the value of older workers, as well as the inequities of age discrimination in employment. Predicted labor shortages in the future, together with business concern about retirement income funding problems will no doubt enhance the attractiveness of retaining older workers in the labor force. Business's changing attitude toward the aged as an important reservoir of productive potential is paralleled by new views regarding the aged as an important consumer market. Conventional products are being marketed to appeal to an older population, and new products are being introduced specifically to capture a share of this burgeoning market. The importance of this market to the American economy will increase as the population ages; the role of income earned by the aged through employment thus takes on added significance.

Another measure of the revolution in aging which is taking place is the sharp increase in litigation brought by older workers under the Age Discrimination in Employment Act. In FY 1980, the Equal Employment Opportunity Commission received 8,779 charges alleging violations of the Age Discrimination in Employment Act, a 60 percent increase over FY 1979. Age discrimination cases may prove to be the fastest growing area of employment discrimination litigation during the next two decades and beyond.

Congressional action to expand the ADEA's protections can be anticipated to occur in the relatively near future in response to social and economic conditions, present and expected, and the political appeal of freeing those older workers who would like to remain active in the labor force from the continued obstacles posed by employment discrimination on account of age.

II. EFFECTS OF THE 1978 ADEA AMENDMENTS

Prior to enactment of the 1978 Amendments to the ADEA, many employers vehemently argued that any change in mandatory retirement practices would be extremely disruptive. At the time the 1978 ADEA Amendments were enacted, a Fortune magazine article warned that, "few legislative initiatives will create more new problems than the recently enacted Amendments to the Age Discrimination in Employment Act . . . for it overturns the cornerstone of the nation's retirement policy." 1/ This proclamation was fueled by unsubstantiated fears that overwhelming numbers of older workers would remain on the job past 65, thereby creating blocked promotional opportunities for younger workers, lowering rates of productivity and increasing the overall costs of labor. Sears, Roebuck and Co., for example, offered the "Chicken-Little" scenario that one-third of its employees would continue to work after age 65 and that this would hinder their efforts to comply with other laws requiring hiring of minorities and women.

According to recent Labor Department data, none of these doomsday projections have been realized; moreover, most employers have by now adapted quite easily to the recent statutory changes. 2/ Most employers have simply raised their mandatory retirement age to the new upper limit of 70 without encountering difficulties. Six percent of firms actually abolished mandatory retirement in response to the Amendments, but 51 percent of the workforce still

---

1/ Fortune Magazine, 1978.

2/ The 1978 ADEA Amendments included as one provision a requirement that the Secretary of Labor conduct, an extensive study of the consequences of these Amendments, including: a) an examination of raising the upper age limit to 70; b) a determination of the feasibility of further extending or eliminating the age 70 limit, and c) an examination of the effects of the exemptions for tenured faculty of institutions of higher education and high policymaking executives. The interim study results were to be released to Congress on January 1, 1981, to be followed by final results and recommendations on January 1, 1982, but as of this writing no official results have been released. The data in this paper are based on findings reported in a draft document, believed to be a close facsimile to the official interim report, released by Chairman Claude Pepper of the House Select Committee on Aging.

faces formalized employer-imposed mandatory retirement ages. 3/ Other employer responses have been less significant steps, such as implementing pre-retirement counseling programs; 29 percent of firms in a recent survey by William M. Mercer, Inc. have implemented a formal pre-retirement education program. 4/ Thus, most employers now expect only minor short-term repercussions from the Amendments but are taking a "wait and see" attitude toward the future, rather than making drastic modifications in personnel and benefits policies.

A. Small Number of Older Workers Affected

The full impact of the increase in the permissible mandatory retirement age is largely dependent on the number of workers who are expected to alter their retirement plans and remain in jobs where they would have been previously forced to retire at age 65. At the time the ADEA Amendments were being debated in Congress, its proponents estimated that only 200,000 workers would be affected by the legislation. While these estimates were little more than paper and pencil guesses, they proved to be remarkably accurate. The Labor Department's calculations project that the law change will result in 217,200 more older men in the labor force in the year 2000, most of whom will be in the 65-67 age range. 5/ (See Table 1 attached.) Only minor changes are expected in the labor force rates of older women.

Eliminating mandatory retirement altogether would produce an additional 195,100 older men in the labor force, over and above the 217,200 added by raising the age limit to 70. These increases of roughly 400,000 older workers are not insignificant in themselves, but they represent only .04 of 1 percent of the 104.7 million workers age 16 and over who are now in the labor force. Therefore, their residual impact on employment policies and nonelderly groups in the workforce is expected to be minor.

B. Minimal Effects on Youth, Minorities and Women

Fears are unfounded that raising the mandatory retirement age would restrict employment opportunities for youth and other groups. The small number of older workers who will remain employed after age 65, coupled with the absence of direct job

---

3/ Select Committee on Aging, U.S. House of Representatives, Abolishing Mandatory Retirement: Implications for America and Social Security of Eliminating Age Discrimination in Employment, August, 1981. Comm. Pub. No. 97-283.

4/ Mercer, William M. "Employer Attitudes: Implications of an Aging Workforce." William M. Mercer, Inc. 1211 Avenue of the Americas, New York, N.Y. 10036, November 1981.

5/ Select Committee on Aging, Rept. No. 97-283, p. 19.

competition among age groups in most occupations, means that a rise in the mandatory retirement age will have no significant negative impact on these groups. The Labor Department found that direct job slot competition created by older workers would occur among less than 1/4 of 1 percent of young workers age 16-24. 6/ These effects are miniscule and are not likely to disrupt the present hiring and promotion mechanisms established by employers. Furthermore, impending declines in the youth population over the next two decades will virtually eliminate any remaining job competition among the generations.

The effects of the ADEA Amendments on women and minority workers are also expected to be slight. Among black workers age 16-59, only .4 of 1 percent are in direct job competition with older workers who will stay on their jobs longer due to the new protections of Federal law. 7/ Similarly, the additional older workers are potential competition for only .11 of 1 percent of female workers age 16-59. 8/ The minimal impact on women and minorities is further mitigated by the fact that the older members of both groups will benefit by the ADEA Amendments. Not only is it likely that women and minorities will face as great or greater age discrimination in the future than white males, but it would be ironic if these groups, having gained greater access to employment opportunities, were to be deprived of continued individual opportunity on account of their age.

The virtual absence of heightened job competition among age groups is similarly reflected in an absence of ill-feeling toward older workers by the young. According to a nationwide Lou Harris Survey in 1981, younger workers (ages 18-54) disagree by two to one with the statement, "Older people should retire when they can to give younger people more of a chance on the job." 9/ It is even more significant that sentiment for pushing older workers out to make room for the young has dropped off by 25 percent since 1974. 10/ Thus, contrary to predictions of

---

6/ Select Committee on Aging, Rept. No. 97-283, p. 137-173. Some industries would exhibit higher levels of job slot competition. Mining and recreation are the only occupations where 1 percent or more younger women would be in direct competition with older women for jobs.

7/ Select Committee on Aging, Rept. No. 97-283, p. 158.

8/ Select Committee on Aging, Rept. No. 97-283, p. 162.

9/ Harris, Louis and Associates, "Aging in the Eighties: America in Transition." Conducted for the National Council on the Aging, Inc., November 1981, Available from National Council on the Aging, 600 Maryland Avenue, S.W., Washington, D.C. 20024.

intergenerational warfare, the 1978 ADEA Amendments have added to neither perceived nor actual job competition among the generations.

C. Loopholes in the ADEA Lack Support

Congress, in an attempt to accommodate powerful lobby groups, incorporated several loopholes into the 1978 ADEA Amendments. Today, however, these gaps in the law are unevenly applied and appear to have only minimal support among the employer community.

Two such exemptions in the law allow age-65 forced retirement for both tenured faculty of institutions of higher education (the "professor exemption") and certain executives who upon retirement would receive annual pension benefits of $27,000 or more (the "executive exemption"). A third major loophole allows differential benefit treatment for workers over age 65. Each of these exemptions is not widely used and could be abolished without causing undue hardship to employers.

1. Professor exemption.

Due to expire on July 1, 1982, the professor exemption is being used by a minority of academic institutions. Prior to the 1978 Amendments, 8 of 10 colleges and universities had a mandatory retirement age, in most cases age 65. [11] Following the ADEA Amendments nearly 30 percent of these institutions made a change in their mandatory retirement policy, such that today, only 27 percent of all private institutions and 55 percent of public institutions have a retirement age below 70. The number of faculty subject to a mandatory retirement age lower than 70 has fallen from 69 percent to 35 percent since passage of the Amendments. [12]

The exemption also has very little support among faculty. A Labor Department survey found that 70 percent of faculty oppose continuation of the exemption and 60 percent favor complete elimination of mandatory retirement. [13] Thus, with strong opposition to the professor exemption among faculty and its waning use among academic institutions, the expiration of this exemption in July will likely enter quietly into history with little fanfare.

---

[10] Harris, Louis and Associates, "The Myth and Reality of Aging in America," conducted for the National Council on the Aging, Inc., 1974, available from the National Council on the Aging, 600 Maryland Ave., S.W., Washington, D.C. 20024.

[11] Select Committee on Aging, Rept. No. 97-283, p. 27.

[12] Select Committee on Aging, Rept. No. 97-283, p. 28.

[13] Select Committee on Aging, Rept. No. 97-283, p. 30.

2. Executive exemption.

The executive exemption, much like its academic counterpart, is not widely used. In the Labor Department's survey of nearly 3,000 firms, only 20 percent were using the exemption or planned to use it in the near future. 14/ In contrast, 60 percent were not using it and had no plans to use it. Even among those firms using the exemption, only half expected to continue using it in the future. The exemption was most widely used among large manufacturing firms.

Ostensibly, the reasons supporting the executive exemption are that it opens channels for promotion of younger employees and it is a cost-saving measure. Most employers, however, offer ample pension benefits to induce executives to retire by age 65, thereby rendering the exemption obsolete. Some firms surveyed in the Labor Department study also reported that so few executives would be affected that it was administratively infeasible to implement the exemption. 15/ Since the vast majority of firms are functioning without the exemption, its continuation in law is of doubtful value.

3. Employee benefits.

The 1978 ADEA Amendments have been interpreted to permit employers to offer lower benefits for older workers where it could be demonstrated that the cost of such benefits for older workers exceeded that of younger workers. The most critical benefit is pension accrual, which, according to a Labor Department Interpretive Bulletin (29 CFR Part 860), can be frozen at age 65. The Labor Department study found that 36 percent of workers were covered by plans that continued to accrue benefits after age 65. An additional 22 percent would receive benefit increases if they do not exceed age or service limits. Thus, 58 percent of employees are unaffected by the pension accrual exemption. In contrast, 42 percent will receive no benefit increases for work after age 65. 16/

The pension accrual exemption should be abolished: it applies to fewer than half of the workforce; it unnecessarily discourages continued employment, and evidence from pension actuaries suggests that it is an irrational policy.

14/ Select Committee on Aging, Rept. No. 97-283, p. 221.

15/ Select Committee on Aging, Rept. No. 97-283, p. 221.

16/ Select Committee on Aging, Rept. No. 97-283, 206-211.

III. CLIMATE FOR NEW CHANGES IN THE ADEA

The climate is ripe for further amendments to the ADEA. Public opinion now more strongly favors the elimination of mandatory retirement than prior to the 1978 ADEA Amendments. Business leaders, in the face of impending labor shortages as well as the increased incidence of ADEA lawsuits, have become more receptive toward older workers. Demographic shifts, fueled by increased longevity and decreased morbidity, make the older worker a more desirable labor force participant. Also, the Congress is receptive to encouraging voluntarily delayed retirements and prolonged worklives in order to help refinance the troubled Social Security system. When these public opinion, business, demographic and congressional factors are combined with the earlier evidence that the 1978 ADEA Amendments had no appreciable negative effects, the net result is a very favorable climate for amending the ADEA further to abolish mandatory retirement altogether and to close many of the remaining loopholes in the law which allow age discrimination on the job.

A. Public Opinion Strongly Opposes Mandatory Retirement

In 1977, just prior to the 1978 ADEA Amendments, a nationwide CBS News/New York Times poll found only a bare majority (52 percent) in favor of raising the mandatory retirement age. [17] In contrast, a Louis Harris poll released recently reported that 9 out of 10 Americans agree, "Nobody should be forced to retire because of age, if he wants to continue working and is still able to do a good job." [18] Not only are more people now opposed to mandatory retirement, but they feel more strongly about the issue than a few years ago: According to the Harris poll 78 percent are "strongly" opposed to mandatory retirement, compared with 66 percent in a comparable poll taken in 1974. [19]

The 1978 Amendments went a long way toward eliminating age discrimination in employment, but most Americans feel the problem still exists. According to the 1981 Harris Poll, Americans, by a margin of 4 to 1, believe that, "most employers discriminate against older people and make it difficult for them to find work." [20] It is interesting that this 4 to 1 margin had not

---

[17] CBS News, Press release on CBS News/New York Times poll dealing with affirmative action, mandatory retirement and other topics. CBS, Inc. 524 W. 57th St., N.Y., N.Y., October 1977.

[18] Harris, L. and Associates, 1981.

[19] Harris, L. and Associates, 1981.

[20] Harris, L. and Associates, 1981.

changed between 1974 and 1981, despite legislative changes in the ADEA.

The pressure to amend the ADEA stems not only from the widely held belief that mandatory retirement and age discrimination are unjust, but also because the vast majority (75 percent) of Americans look forward to working, at least part-time, in their old age. 21/ Even current retirees report that they would like to be working: 46 percent of retirees in a 1979 Harris poll said they would prefer to be working, in large part because they feared inflation. 22/

In sum, public opinion is solidly behind the complete elimination of mandatory retirement, both because it is perceived to be an unjust policy and because it may someday affect individual employment plans.

B. Business Attitudes Improving Toward Older Workers

Business attitudes about the older worker have been steadily improving, and although there are some unenlightened segments of the business community that remain staunchly opposed to any further strengthening of the ADEA, a growing majority views the increase in older worker rights as an inevitable fact of business life.

According to a 1981 survey of employers by William M. Mercer, Inc., most employers believe age discrimination does not exist in their firm, but more than half believe older workers are discriminated against in the employment market, presumably by other firms. 23/ Negative stereotypes about older employees have long been a problem among business managers and executives, but according to the Mercer study these appear to be subsiding. Nine out of ten business leaders surveyed believe that "Older workers can perform as well on the job as younger workers." 24/ Nearly as many (87 percent) also agreed that, "Older workers are more committed to company objectives than younger workers." 25/ In line with these changing perceptions, a

---

21/ Harris, L. and Associates 1981.

22/ Harris, L. and Associates, "American Attitudes Toward Pensions and Retirement." Conducted for Johnson and Higgins, February 1979.

23/ Mercer, W. 1981.

24/ Mercer, W., 1981.

25/ Mercer, W. 1981.

majority of business leaders now favor abolishing mandatory retirement by the end of the decade. 26/

Attitude changes in America's corporate boardrooms are paralleled by changes in corporate policies toward older workers. Widespread hiring and retention of older workers is occurring in the aerospace, defense, banking, insurance and fast food industries. 27/ In most cases, these practices are the direct result of declining labor supplies among younger workers. The Mercer study found that 59 percent of employers already are, or will be in the next 5 years, taking into account the smaller young labor pool. 28/ As a result nearly half (45 percent) expect the average retirement age to _increase_ over the next 5 years, both because employers will be attempting to retain their mature workers and because continued inflation is expected to force delayed retirements.

American business is not a monolith and there are widely varying opinions on the impact of an aging workforce. (For example, 74 percent believe, "Allowing older workers to extend their worklife will hinder advancement among younger workers for several years to come.") 29/ Nonetheless, most business leaders are beginning to accept the weight of evidence endorsing the virtues of older workers and the inevitability of a demographic shift toward an older population, and are, in turn, beginning to adjust personnel practices accordingly. The "knee-jerk" opposition to raising the mandatory retirement age so evident among business leaders in 1978 has all but subsided, in favor of a more balanced and reasoned approach toward older worker issues.

C. _Demographic Trends Favor the Older Worker_

Two important demographic factors are contributing to the renewed attention being paid to older workers: 1) low birth rates and a general decline in the younger working-age population, and 2) increased longevity and overall health among the older population. Both factors are improving the employment outlook for older workers and further argue for amendments to the ADEA to remove the remaining obstacles to prolonged employment lives among the older population.

26/ Mercer, W. 1981.

27/ Select Committee on Aging, U.S. House of Representatives, "New Business Perspectives on Older Workers" Hearing, October 28, 1981.

28/ Mercer, W. 1981.

29/ Mercer, W. 1981.

Despite current high rates of unemployment, a general decline in the youth population is already generating labor shortages in some industries -- most notably, skilled crafts, fast food restaurants and computer programming -- and the situation will continue to worsen over the next two decades. Census Bureau statistics project that the number of 18-24 year olds will decline by more than 4 million by the year 1990. 30/ Thus, the segment of the population that typically fills entry level and part-time jobs will be reduced to 25.1 million from its peak of 29.5 million last year. The baby boom of the 1950s is over, leaving in its wake a baby bust and an increasingly older population. (See Chart I.)

As noted earlier, the decline in young workers is causing a shift toward hiring the over 55 worker. This shift in hiring practices is appropriate not only because the over 55 population will grow by nearly 10 percent this decade and by another 9 percent in the 1990s, but also because the older population is increasingly healthy, able and productive.

1. Improved Health of Older Population

The increased health of older persons is especially significant. In a recent article published in the New England Journal of Medicine, Dr. James Fries notes that the most significant development in human aging in this century is the gradual but consistent postponement of debilitating diseases until later in life. 31/ Average life expectancy has increased from 47 years at the turn of the century to 73 years today. Although most of this increase is due to the reduction of "premature death" (infant mortality), there has been an increase of 2 to 3 years in life expectancy at age 65. But the most striking finding is that older people maintain their health much longer than their counterparts 50 years ago.

On a practical level, these healthier old people are much more capable of performing at work than the old of previous eras. Research shows that older workers are as productive as younger workers, they have lower absenteeism, higher reliability and, in many cases, better decision-making ability. 32/ The slow

---

30/ U.S. Bureau of the Census, Current Population Report, Series P-25 #704.

31/ Fries, James F., M.D. "Aging, Natural Death, and the Compression of Morbidity." The New England Journal of Medicine, July 17, 1980, pp. 130-135.

32/ Green, R. F. "Age Intelligence and Learning." Industrial Gerontology, 1972, 12 (winter); Meier, E.L. and Kerr, E.A. "Capabilities of Middle-Aged and Older Workers." Industrial Gerontology, 1976, 3(1-4), 147-156; Baugher, Dan "Is the

but consistent decline in strength and stamina associated with age introduces some limitations on the older worker's ability to perform heavy physical labor, but the physical requirements for most jobs are so low that workers of any age are not overly taxed. More importantly, Dr. Fries points out that between age 30 and 70 "the age-related decrement in maximal performance is only 1 percent per year. Variation between healthy persons of the same age is far greater than the variation due to age; age is a relatively unimportant variable." 33/

    2. No increase in insurance risks.

Older workers have often been assumed to be more expensive because of a greater risk of accident. This is a false assumption, according to Labor Department data and experts in the risk assessment consulting field. Labor Department data show a consistent decline in on-the-job accident rates with age, indicating that a 20-24 year old is more than 3 times as likely to suffer an accident as a 65 year old. 34/ As a result, the overall costs of insuring older workers is or should be actually lower. According to one risk assessment expert, "An older, more experienced workforce would lead to fewer product liability claims and fewer workers compensation claims (with probably no pregnancy-related insurance claims), than a relatively younger workforce. Though health insurance claims might be higher with more aging workers . . . health insurance is one of the least expensive portions of corporate coverage, while workers compensation and pregnancy claims are usually the most costly." 35/

The increased health, longevity, productivity and reliability of older workers, then, makes them an increasingly sought after labor pool and, for the most part, refutes the oft-cited stereotypes about the aged which in the past have inhibited the enactment of legislation expanding their employment rights further.

D. Congress Favors Prolonged Worklives

The 97th Congress may find good reasons to encourage older workers to remain active in the labor force. Ultimately, a sense of compassion and concern for civil rights may prove less significant factors than the search for solutions to budget deficits

---

    Older Woman Inherently Incompetent?" *Aging and Work*, 1 (4) Fall, 1978: 243-249.

33/ Fries, p. 134.

34/ Root, Norman, "Injuries at Work are fewer among older employees." *Monthly Labor Review*, March, 1981: 30-34.

35/ Coole, Daniel D., "Older Workers: A Resource We'll Need." *Industry Week*, 206, July 7, 1980, p. 43.

and a projected shortfall in the Social Security trust funds, as well as a sluggish national economy. Nonetheless, the support for prolonging worklives and increasing employment among the elderly is real. Furthermore, it is bipartisan in nature.

   1. Social Security bills encourage employment.

All of the major Social Security refinancing bills introduced or proposed in the 97th Congress have profound implications for older workers. Most notably, President Reagan's 13 proposals for Social Security reform included a 30 percent reduction in early retirement benefits, which would, in the words of Health and Human Services Secretary Schweiker, "encourage older workers to remain in the labor force longer." 36/ Similarly, the legislation (H.R. 3207) championed by Congressman Pickle, Chairman of the House Ways and Means Subcommittee on Social Security, would raise the Social Security entitlement age to 68, thereby requiring older persons to work an average of 3 years longer to acquire the same benefits they would now receive at age 65. Thus, both the Reagan and Pickle proposals would coerce older workers into delaying retirement.

In stark contrast to these coercive proposals is an extensive package of bills (H.R. 3393-3397) introduced by Claude Pepper, Chairman of the House Select Committee on Aging. This package would refinance Social Security using partial general revenues and would at the same time offer _incentives_, rather than cuts in benefits, to foster delayed retirement. These incentives include an increase in Social Security delayed retirement credits, liberalization of the Social Security earnings test, equitable pension treatment for workers after age 65, and tax credits for employers who hire older workers. The centerpiece of this legislation is a bill that would amend the ADEA and eliminate all remaining vestiges of age discrimination, including mandatory retirement at any age.

The emphasis on employment as a solution to Social Security's problems is not unfounded. According to a Data Resources, Inc. study released at a House Select Committee on Aging hearing in September, an increase to 1970 levels in labor force participation rates among older workers would add $10 billion annually to the Social Security fund. 37/ One step toward such an increase in workforce rates would be to eliminate mandatory retirement and other age-based employment obstacles.

36/ Schweiker, Richard S. "Provision of the Social Security Proposal," U.S. Department of Health and Human Services, May 12, 1981.

37/ Olson, Lawrence before the House Select Committee on Aging, Testimony September 8, 1981.

2. Bills Introduced to Eliminate Mandatory Retirement.

To date, five bills have been introduced in the 97th Congress to amend the ADEA and eliminate mandatory retirement. [38] Three of these bills (S. 484, H.R. 4683, and H.R. 1666) would merely strike the ADEA's upper age limit of 70 with no further amendments. A fourth bill (H.R. 70) would eliminate the upper age limit, abolish the professor and executive exemptions, and amend other statutes to eliminate maximum hiring ages and mandatory retirement ages for many Federal or D.C. employees, including: air traffic controllers, U.S. Park Police, law enforcement officers, firefighters, Alaska Railroad employees and Panama Canal employees.

The fifth and most comprehensive bill (H.R. 3397) would accomplish all of the above changes (except it would allow the professor exemption to expire unchanged), but in addition it would eliminate the BFOQ provision (discussed later) and would amend still other statutes to abolish mandatory retirement for federal court judges, the Director of the Federal Judicial Center, U.S. District Court judges, lighthouse service employees, coast and geodetic survey employees, Comptroller General, CIA employees and Foreign Service officers. The bill also offers incentives to both employers and older employees to further promote an increase in labor force participation rates among older persons.

3. Key congressional committees are cautious.

Before amendments to the ADEA affecting the private sector can be enacted they must first be reported out of both the House Committee on Education and Labor and the Senate Labor and Human Resources Committee. Neither Committee expressed overwhelming interest in amending the ADEA during the first session of the 97th Congress, but interest is increasing. On the House side, Augustus Hawkins, Chairman of the Education and Labor Committee's Subcommittee on Equal Employment Opportunities, expressed reluctance to open up the ADEA early in 1981 for two reasons: 1) the 1978 Amendments were passed only recently, leaving a sense among many members of Congress that the issue was settled and could not possibly need attention again so soon; and 2) the Labor Department studies mandated by the 1978 ADEA Amendments were not due to be completed until January 1, 1982. In 1982, these concerns will be less important: four years will have passed since the 1978 Amendments, and the Labor Department study will be completed. As well, Chairman Hawkins' additional duties as the new House Administration Committee Chairman will have become more

---

[38] S. 484 (Mr. Chiles); H.R. 70 (Mr. Findley and 88 cosponsors); H.R. 1666 (Mr. Young of Florida); H.R. 3397 (Mr. Pepper and 20 cosponsors); H.R. 4683 (Mr. Mottl).

institutionalized, affording him additional time to devote to his Employment Opportunities Subcommittee.

On the Senate side the picture is less clear. Early in 1981 an informal proposal was circulated among members of the Senate Labor Committee calling for fundamental changes in the enforcement mechanisms for the Civil Rights Act and the ADEA. In effect, these changes would have lessened EEOC's ability to enforce anti-discrimination laws. Although the proposals were never formally introduced, they suggested by their very tone that the Senate Labor Committee was seeking to reduce rather than expand the scope and effectiveness of employment discrimination laws. If this is the case, it is unlikely that amendments improving the ADEA would be forthcoming from the Senate.

4. Critical factors influencing congressional action.

Four key factors will play an important role in determining when, or if, amendments to the ADEA will be forthcoming. These are:

Factor #1: President Reagan - To date, President Reagan has alluded to the virtues of older workers, and is himself in the age group that could be mandatorily retired if he were working in the private sector. But since assuming the Presidency he has offered no public support for the elimination of mandatory retirement or other age-based employment obstacles. If he were to call for an end to mandatory retirement he would likely meet with almost no opposition, and his endorsement would be applauded by most Members of Congress. It should be pointed out that the President's campaign platform called for abolition of mandatory retirement.

Factor #2: Labor organizations, civil rights groups and women's organizations - In the past these groups have remained almost silent on issues pertaining to older workers. With high unemployment, labor and civil rights groups have not been strong proponents of an end to mandatory retirement. Support from any of the major labor unions, civil rights or women's organizations would lend important impetus to legislation eliminating mandatory retirement. It may prove significant that women's rights groups such as the National Organization for Women are devoting increasing attention to the problems of older women in the job market. It is also worth noting that the National Caucus and Center on the Black Aged recently took the position that the ADEA needs expansion and strengthening.

Factor #3: Labor Department study - The interim report of the Labor Department study, which was released in draft form by the House Select Committee on Aging, presents evidence that clearly supports the elimination of mandatory retirement, as well as abolishing the discriminatory loopholes in the ADEA. If the final report, due January 1, 1982, offers strong recommendations in line with the interim report findings, this could be a critical factor for initiating action in Congress.

Factor #4: Economy and budget considerations - Much of Congress' time and attention during the first session of the 97th Congress was taken up with budget cuts. If the economy continues to worsen and major budget cutting efforts resume, there may not be adequate time for dealing with ADEA amendments. On the other hand, the pressure to solve the Social Security financing problems will become more intense under weakening economic conditions, which, in turn, will hasten the need for eliminating mandatory retirement.

IV. ISSUES TO BE ADDRESSESD IN FUTURE ADEA AMENDMENTS

The 1978 ADEA Amendments made significant substantive and procedural improvements in the ADEA as originally enacted in 1967. Numerous gaps and inconsistencies remain, however, most of which can only be addressed through additional legislation. Substantive proposals that might be addressed by future ADEA amendments are: raising the upper age limit; eliminating the professor and executive exemptions; requiring continued pension accrual; and modifying the bona fide occupational qualification. On the procedural side, one major proposal has been made to incorporate age into Title VII of the Civil Rights Act and abolish the ADEA. The pros and cons of each of these proposals are discussed below.

A. Raising the Upper Age Limit

The most visible and widely supported amendment to the ADEA would be the removal of the upper age limit of 70, thus making the Act's protections against discrimination and forced retirement applicable to all persons age 40 and over. According to the Labor Department's analyses, such a change would not have major implications: it would result in an additional 195,000 older persons remaining employed than would have retired under present law. Since the number affected is so small, there is expected to be no negative effect on employers, youth, women or minorities.

It could be argued that removing the upper age limit is largely a symbolic gesture, but there is evidence that it would have major implications beyond allowing continued employment for the few hundred thousand individuals directly affected by it. One spin-off of removing the upper age limit would be the further demise, initiated by the 1978 Amendments, of the unfounded attitude that age 65 automatically ushers in senility and decline. Having no specific upper age limit with which to label a person "retired" or "over the hill" will contribute to the decline of age-based negative stereotypes. Furthermore, it is likely to initiate improvements in self-concept among the elderly and near elderly, thereby encouraging some retired and near retired persons to seek employment opportunities more actively.

A further benefit of eliminating the upper age limit would come in the form of improved personnel policies and practices based on objective individual assessments rather than chronological age. There is evidence that the 1978 Amendments have already had this effect on some employers. Among employers who say their attitudes toward older workers have changed recently, 60 percent claim the change was the direct result of government action, presumably the ADEA Amendments. 39/

B. Eliminating the Professor and Executive Exemptions

The exemptions contained in Sections 12(c) and (d) of the ADEA, allowing age 65 mandatory retirement for tenured professors and high policymaking executives, were originally included in the 1978 ADEA Amendments in order to "permit employers to replace certain key employees and to keep promotional channels open for younger employees." 40/ Some business leaders claimed to be concerned that top executives would remain in their posts until they died, blocking the upward mobility of younger employees and causing morale problems for the entire organization. The apprehension of college and university administrators had a slightly different basis. Faced with the problem of declining enrollments and diminishing revenues, college administrators feared that an increase in the mandatory retirement age would prevent them from hiring "younger professors, particularly women and minorities," and would increase "the financial burden on already hard-pressed institutions of higher learning . . . because it may require the retention of highly paid senior employees for additional years." 41/

Amending the ADEA to eliminate the professor exemption will be moot as of July 1, 1982, the date on which it is scheduled to expire. To date, there is no organized opposition to this automatic expiration. Thus, it is probably wise politically to allow the exemption to expire as scheduled.

The executive exemption is more complex. Despite its infrequent use by most corporations, there still appears to be some degree of interest in retaining it. Corporate officers who support continuation of the exemption do so because they wish to

---

39/ Mercer, W. 1981.

40/ "Amending the Age Discrimination in Employment Act of 1977," Report of the Committee on Human Resources, U.S. Senate, Rept. No. 95-493, October 12, 1977, p. 7-8.

41/ U.S. Senate, Report No. 95-493, p. 9.

"retain the option" of creating executive turnover when it is deemed necessary. While a case can be made for turnover among the leadership of an organization, it is curious why this turnover must be accomplished via forced retirement. Lateral transfers, special emeritus positions and even downgrading would appear to be a more rational management policy, and, according to one study, would be preferred by most executives. 42/ Furthermore, the demand for older executives is on the rise, according to a recent study of executive recruiting firms presented to the House Committee on Aging, which may cause employers to encourage retention rather than retirement for their older executives.

In sum, the executive exemption should be abolished or modified to protect the rights of older executives, while still allowing flexibility for the employer.

C. Requiring Continued Pension Accrual

The most controversial loophole in the 1978 ADEA Amendments is Section 4(f)(2) which has been interpreted by the Labor Department as allowing pension benefits to be frozen when an employee reaches the "normal retirement age," usually age 65. 43/ Recently, the EEOC proposed a new interpretation of Section 4(f)(2) that would require continued pension accrual for workers between the ages of 65 and 70. 44/ These proposed interpretations were circulated to various Federal agencies for comment, and the day before the EEOC was to vote on them the Labor Department submitted a comment that effectively killed the proposal for the foreseeable future. As a result, the only way this issue can be addressed is through legislation, since on this issue the legislative history of the 1978 ADEA Amendments is vague at best.

The rationale used to support freezing of pension accrual at age 65 is that requiring such accrual would substantially increase the costs to employers of hiring older workers, thereby diminishing the likelihood that they would be hired. Upon careful analysis, however, this argument is unsupported. According to a study done for the University of Southern

---

42/ Hedda, Laurids, "Danish Survey Suggests Demotion of 'Obsolete' Managers; Finds Executives Prefer Lesser Jobs to Retirement" in World of Work Report, vol. 3 (11) November 1978. Published by Work in America Institute, 700 White Plains Road, Scarsdale, N.Y. 10583

43/ Sec. 44 Fed. Reg. 30648, May 25, 1979.

44/ Huffman, Diana, "Stopping Pension Accruals at 65 May Become Illegal." Legal Times of Washington, Monday, April 28, 1980, p. 4.

California's Andrus Gerontology Center by William M. Mercer, Inc., and soon to be released by the House Aging Committee, "There is no actuarial (or cost) reason to justify freezing of pension accruals at age 65." 45/ The evidence is clear that the costs for providing pension accrual after age 65 are not greater than for those between age 60 and 65. Thus, there is no cost justification to support the pension accrual exemption.

Without a cost justification to support its continuation, the pension accrual exemption could be overturned by Congress. The only complication is that changing the present ruling on frozen pension accruals would contravene existing provisions of the Employee Retirement Income Security Act (ERISA). If such an amendment is viewed as tampering with the "normal retirement" age provision of ERISA, it may generate a cacophony of criticism from the pension consulting industry. It is not necessary, however, to alter ERISA's normal retirement provision. Rather, ERISA need only be amended to require that benefit accruals cannot be reduced or stopped based on age. 46/ With the cost arguments no longer applicable, such an amendment should be possible.

D. Modifying the BFOQ Provision

Section 4(f)(1) of the ADEA states that an employer is free to discriminate based on age, "where age is a bona fide occupational qualification necessary to the normal operation of the particular business, or where the differentiation is based on reasonable factors other than age." 47/ This provision, known simply as the "BFOQ," has been successfully used to uphold mandatory retirement and age-based hiring practices for bus drivers, airline pilots, police officers and firefighters. 48/

45/ Rappaport, Ann, "An Analysis of the Cost of Pension Accrual After Age 65." Forthcoming from the House Select Committee on Aging.

46/ The specific language of such an amendment is incorporated into H.R. 3397, introduced by Rep. Pepper on May 1, 1981.

47/ The Age Discrimination in Employment Act of 1967, as Amended (29 U.S.C. 621, et. seq.).

48/ Selected cases involving the BFOQ include: Hodgson v. Greyhound Lines, Inc., 499 F.2d 859 (7th Cir. 1974), cert. denied 419 U.S. 1122 (1975); Murnane v. American Airlines, Inc., 26 FEP Cases 1537 (D.C. Cir. 1981) Arritt v. Grisell, 421 F. Supp. 800 (N.D. W. Va. 1976); Usery v. Tamiami Trial Tours, Inc., 531 F.2d 224 (5th Cir. 1974); Houghton v. McDonnell-Douglas Corp., 553 F.2d 561 (8th Cir. 1977); EEOC v. City of St. Paul, 500 F. Supp. 1135 (D. Minn. 1980); EEOC v. City of Janesville, 630 F.2d 1254 (7th Cir. 1980).

A careful review of 14 years of judicial decisions involving the BFOQ defense suggests that the provision has been abused. 49/ The assertion of a BFOQ defense where "public safety" is involved seems to have almost automatically resulted in the judicial approval of the discrimination, regardless of the weight of the evidence. Thus, legislative language should be introduced to restrict the BFOQ.

Several alternatives for amending the BFOQ have been suggested. These include:

<u>Abolish the BFOQ defense altogether</u> 50/ - The rationale supporting this change is that enough is now known about the process of aging such that individual assessment is fully within the capability of any employer. Furthermore, studies of the so-called "public safety" occupations (police, firefighters and airline pilots) suggest that age is not a good indicator of ability to perform. 51/

<u>Restrict the BFOQ to non-cost-related factors</u> - In an analysis of the BFOQ prepared for the Labor Department, Charles Edelman argues that the BFOQ has not been too widely interpreted. 52/ Edelman was concerned, however, that courts have been too liberal in permitting use of "cost differences" between young and old employees as a justifiable defense for age discrimination. Thus, he would add language to Section 4(f)(1) to the effect that cost differences shall not be a bona fide occupational qualification or a reasonable factor other than age. 53/

<u>Restrict the BFOQ to situations in which assessments of individual performance are not possible</u> - The courts

---

49/ See, Select Committee on Aging, U.S. House of Representatives, "An Analysis of the BFOQ Provisions in the ADEA," unpublished document available upon request from the Committee.

50/ H.R. 3397 would abolish the BFOQ.

51/ "Report of the National Institute on Aging Panel on The Experienced Pilots Study," U.S. Department of Health and Human Services, August 1981.

52/ Edelman, Charles. "The Bona Fide Occupational Qualification and Reasonable Factors Other Than Age Exceptions to the Federal Age Discrimination in Employment Act of 1967: The Rule Proved," unpublished paper (1980) available from the Employment Stds. Div., U.S. Department of Labor.

53/ Edelman, 1980, p. 55.

have too often allowed the BFOQ to be applied to groups without sufficient proof that individual assessments were impossible. Adding language to the ADEA that limits the BFOQ only to those situations where individual assessments could not have been successfully carried out could prevent further abuses of the intent of the Act and would, in turn, encourage employers to develop assessment mechanisms.

Amending the ADEA in any one of the above three ways will depend on the political reaction to proposals which would impose further restrictions on employers' freedom. It will also depend on close examination through the Congressional hearing process of the adequacy of performance and skills assessment, and the availability of examples of successful individual assessments on various critical occupations.

E. Amending Title VII of The Civil Rights Act to Include Age

When the Civil Rights Act of 1964 was enacted, age was not included as a protected category, pending a study by the Department of Labor to determine the extent and seriousness of age discrimination in American society. 54/ Following the completion of that study, the ADEA was enacted in 1967 in response to the study's conclusions regarding the desirability of a Federal age discrimination statute. Since that time there have been arguments presented for and against amending Title VII of the Civil Rights Act of 1964 to include age as a protected category.

Presented below are the advantages and disadvantages of amending Title VII of the Civil Rights Act to include age. 55/ The arguments, for the most part, hinge on procedural and enforcement matters, and, on balance, support retention of the ADEA as an alternative to amendment of Title VII.

1. Advantages of Including Age in Title VII

EEOC's overall administration could be more efficient and economical. EEOC would have one process for all charges instead of the separate processes for each that it now has. Charge processing would be simpler because employment opportunity specialists (EOS) and attorneys

---

54/ U.S. Equal Employment Opportunity Commission, "Legislative History of the Age Discrimination in Employment Act." USGPO, 1981.

55/ Special thanks are extended to Mr. Endel Kaseoru of the General Accounting Office, Division on Human Resources, for preparation of these pro and con arguments.

would have only one set of legal requirements to contend with and the problems caused by dual charges (ADEA/Title VII) would be eliminated. Also, some cost savings would result from the elimination of the separate facilities, staff, charge processing materials (e.g. intake forms, "standard" letters, manuals), and training materials and courses.

Class action litigation would be more easily utilized. Title VII allows class suits on the basis of a single complaint or charge, without the specific identification of all class members; ADEA requires class members to be identified.

Discrimination in employee benefits would be disallowed. The 1978 ADEA amendments relieve employers from having to accrue pension benefits for those employees who continue working after age 65. This is unfair to such employees and would not be allowed under Title VII if age was to be included as a protected category without exceptions.

The number of employers covered by age discrimination prohibitions would increase. ADEA applies to employers with 20 or more employees while Title VII applies to employers with 15 or more employees.

Enforcement jurisdiction would be less ambiguous. The ADEA authorizes the Labor Department (now EEOC) to administratively enforce its provisions. However, it does not state which Federal agencies may sue. Since the Department of Justice is the Government's legal representative, the Department of Labor (now EEOC) had an agreement with Justice under which Labor brought ADEA suits on behalf of the Government. In contrast, Title VII specifically authorizes EEOC to sue to enforce its provisions. Therefore, the need for an agreement with Justice would be eliminated.

Conciliation efforts would not be subject to court review. Under ADEA, the matter of what conciliation attempts are made by the Government on a complaint is subject to court review and in some instances the courts have held against the Government when they felt that conciliation attempts were inadequate. Under Title VII, the adequacy of conciliation on a charge is not subject to court review.

The statute of limitations would be extended. The ADEA has a basic two-year statute of limitations for suit on a complaint (pursuant to the Portal-to-Portal Act) while Title VII has no such provision. The two-year limitation has been a problem in cases of Fair Employment

Practices agencies (FEPs) performing inadequate investigations of deferred age charges.

Courts would have greater discretion in determining relief. Under Title VII, the Federal courts have great discretion in determining what relief to award and whether attorneys' fees will be assessed. Under ADEA the courts have substantially less discretion.

Temporary relief would be more easily obtained. Obtaining temporary relief (e.g., a temporary restraining order) is a simpler process under Title VII than under ADEA.

EEOC's enforcement efforts would be expanded. Under ADEA, agency action in processing a case may be limited to as little as a telephone call to the employer, whereas Title VII requires a more substantive investigative effort. The almost unlimited discretion under ADEA can be easily abused, and complaint processing is more readily subject to the whims of the individual EOS. This discretion has been of such concern to EEOC top management that it is now applying Title VII charge processing procedures to age complaints, within the limits of ADEA. Incorporating age into Title VII, then, would be a possible advantage to the extent that it brings certain aspects of age discrimination charge processing more closely in line with Title VII charge processing.

Resources for enforcement could increase. Age charge processing would have full access to Title VII resources, in contrast to the present situation in which age has a separate and smaller budget. This would be a possible advantage to the extent that ADEA resources have been insufficient in the past.

2. Disadvantages of Repealing the ADEA

EEOC would be unable to file suit against State and local governments. Title VII specifically provides that the Department of Justice, rather than the EEOC, is to bring Title VII suits against State and local governments. The ADEA contains no such requirement. (Note: In its April 9, 1981 EEOC report (HRD-81-29), GAO recommended that the Congress amend Title VII to allow EEOC to sue State and local governments.)

Jury trials would be unavailable. ADEA provides for jury trials but Title VII does not. (Note: The issue here is the extent to which the threat of a jury trial per se - which is not available under Title VII - promotes efforts to settle age complaints. For example, an employer may agree to an administrative settlement or a consent order because he feels that he could not win a jury trial since the jury is likely to be sympathetic to the complainant.)

Damage awards could be reduced. The ADEA provision for liquidated damages by the courts would be lost; Title VII only provides for equitable relief remedies. (Note: The issue here is similar to that for jury trial: i.e., to what extent is the threat of a trial and double damages a factor in administratively settling ADEA complaints, or in getting recalcitrant employers to agree to a consent order.)

EEOC would lose the authority to do self-initiated age discrimination investigations. Under the ADEA, an EOS can literally just walk into an employer's place of business and demand to review employment records for ADEA violations. Title VII, however, limits EEOC's investigation to charges - i.e., EEOC must have a charge on file against an employer before it can inspect employment records. (Note: Title VII authorizes the EEOC Commissioners to issue charges against employers suspected of Title VII violations and such charges are currently the basis of EEOC's systematic program. EEOC has made the process of getting a Commissioner's charge issued very rigorous. However, the process could be changed if or as needed.)

Charging parties would lose right to anonymity. ADEA requires that the anonymity of complainants be protected if requested, but Title VII requires that EEOC notify the employer within ten days after the charge has been filed. (Note: EEOC's Title VII charge processing procedures provide that if a complainant's identity has to be kept from the employer, then a Commissioner's charge can be obtained against the employer.)

Charge processing could be slowed. The Title VII charge process is replete with technical requirements, compared to ADEA, and age charges could take longer to process under Title VII. Also, Title VII requires charge deferral to FEPs, whereas ADEA only permits it. If age is incorporated into Title VII, then age charges would have to be deferred, which could result in a longer processing period and inadequate FEP resolutions.

Case law could be nullified. Substantive case law developed under ADEA could be lost because the courts might view age under Title VII differently than under ADEA.

Class-based investigations would be curtailed. ADEA complaints can be investigated on a class basis, while Title VII charges are investigated on an individual complainant basis. (Note: EEOC has an Early Litigation Identification program (ELI) under which Title VII charges which appear to have class potential are investigated on a class basis if the complainant agrees. Also, the Federal courts have held that EEOC may expand an individual Title VII charge investigation to include "like and related isues."

Discharging non-meritorious charges would be more difficult. Under ADEA, EEOC has a great deal of discretion for dealing with charges, and it can readily cease processing charges it feels have no merit. However, under Title VII a no-merit age charge would have to be substantively investigated and a no-reasonable-cause finding would have to be made on it before it could be dismissed. This would be wasteful of EEOC resources. (Note: EEOC's Title VII processing procedures provide for quick dismissal/no cause decisions on charges lacking merit.)

V. CONCLUSION

Various factors such as public attitudes, increasing business enlightenment, and crises in retirement income financing make it extremely likely that liberalization of the Age Discrimination in Employment Act will be undertaken by the Congress within the foreseeable future. At this point, no significant organized constituency is vigorously opposing strengthening the ADEA's provisions. At the same time, a consensus regarding the desirability of encouraging older workers to remain active in the labor force is developing. At the recent White House Conference on Aging, no other issue emerged with stronger support; 6 of the 14 working committees approved resolutions calling for an end to mandatory retirement. Even the President and the Republican Senate may soon come to the realization that their support for eliminating mandatory retirement and expanding the ADEA makes both good political and economic sense. On the one hand, it is unlikely that the Republicans will be able to carry out other mandates from the White House Conference on Aging, most of which would result in additional federal expenditures, but they are aware that they will need to have taken some symbolic actions on behalf of older Americans to benefit during the 1982 and, particularly, the 1984 elections. On the other hand, Republicans and Democrats alike should have an interest in increasing national productivity and lessening the strains on the Social Security and private pension systems through encouraging older workers to remain active in the labor force voluntarily and protecting the right of capable and healthy older workers to do so free from discrimination on account of their age.

Table 1. Number of Older Males in the Labor Force in the Year 2000 Under Alternative Mandatory Retirement Policies */

Age Group	Age Mandatory Retirement Total Male Workforce (000)	Increase in Labor Force for Mandatory Retirement Policy Change from:	
		Age 65 to Age 70 (000)	Age 70 to No Mandatory Retirement (000)
60-61	1491	12.4	12.2
62-64	1458	30.0	27.9
65-67	772	155.5	64.7
68-70	417	19.3	90.3
Total	4138	217.2	195.1

---

*/ Adopted from table in Select Committee on Aging, Rept. No. 97-283, p. 203.

CHART 1. POPULATION PROJECTIONS FOR YOUNGER & OLDER AGE GROUPS

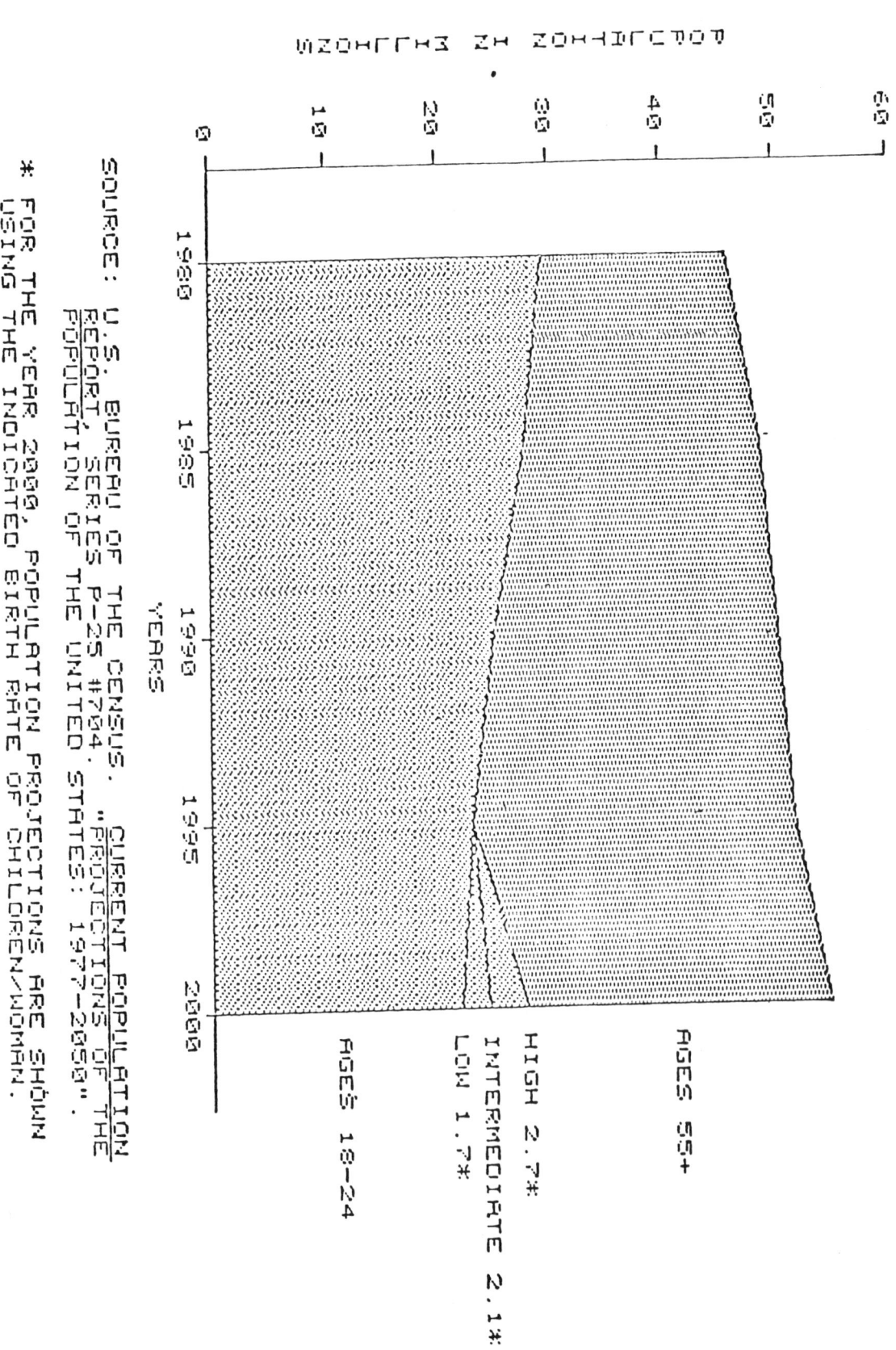

SOURCE: U.S. BUREAU OF THE CENSUS. CURRENT POPULATION REPORT, SERIES P-25 #704. "PROJECTIONS OF THE POPULATION OF THE UNITED STATES: 1977-2050".

* FOR THE YEAR 2000, POPULATION PROJECTIONS ARE SHOWN USING THE INDICATED BIRTH RATE OF CHILDREN/WOMAN.

THE AGE DISCRIMINATION IN EMPLOYMENT ACT OF 1967, AS AMENDED* (29 U.S.C. 621, et seq.)

An Act
To prohibit age discrimination in employment

Be it enacted by the Senate and House of Representatives of the United States of American in Congress assembled, that this Act may be cited as the "Age Discrimination in Employment Act of 1967".

STATEMENT OF FINDINGS AND PURPOSE

SEC. 2. (a) The Congress hereby finds and declares that—

(1) in the face of rising productivity and affluence, older workers find themselves disadvantaged in their efforts to retain employment, and especially to regain employment when displaced from jobs;

(2) the setting of arbitrary age limits regardless of potential for job performance has become a common practice, and certain otherwise desirable practices may work to the disadvantage of older persons;

(3) the incidence of unemployment, especially longterm unemployment with resultant deterioration of skill, morale, and employer acceptability is, relative to the younger ages, high among older workers; their numbers are great and growing; and their employment problems grave;

(4) the existence in industries affecting commerce, of arbitrary discrimination in employment because of age, burdens commerce and the free flow of goods in commerce.

(b) It is therefore the purpose of this Act to promote employment of older persons based on their ability rather than age; to prohibit arbitrary age discrimination in the employment; to help employers and workers find ways of meeting problems arising from the impact of age on employment.

EDUCATION AND RESEARCH PROGRAM

SEC. 3. (a) The Secretary of Labor shall undertake studies and provide information to labor unions, management, and the general public concerning the needs and abilities of older workers, and their potentials for continued employment and contribution to the economy. In order to achieve the purposes of this Act, the Secretary of Labor shall carry on a continuing program of education and information, under which he may, among other measures—

(1) undertake research, and promote research, with a view to reducing barriers to the employment of older persons, and the promotion of measures for utilizing their skills;

(2) publish and otherwise make available to employers, professional societies, the various media of communication, and other interested persons the findings of studies and other materials for the promotion of employment;

(3) foster through the public employment service system and through cooperative effort the development of facilities of public and private agencies for expanding the opportunities and potentials of older persons;

(4) sponsor and assist State and community informational and educational programs.

(b) Not later than six months after the effective date of this Act, the Secretary shall recommend to the Congress any measures he may deem desirable to change the lower or upper age limits set forth in section 12.

PROHIBITION OF AGE DISCRIMINATION

SEC. 4. (a) It shall be unlawful for an employer—

(1) to fail or refuse to hire or to discharge any individual or otherwise discriminate against any individual with respect to his compensation, terms, conditions, or privileges of employment, because of such individual's age;

(2) to limit, segregate, or classify his employees in any way which would deprive or tend to deprive any individual of employment opportunities or otherwise adversely affect his status as an employee, because of such individual's age; or

(3) to reduce the wage rate of any employee in order to comply with this Act.

(b) It shall be unlawful for an employment agency to fail or refuse to refer for employment, or otherwise to discriminate against, any individual because of such individual's age, or to classify or refer for employment any individual on the basis of such individual's age.

---

*The original text of the Age Discrimination in Employment Act of 1967 is set in the "Century" typeface. Added or amended language as enacted by subsequent amendments is represented by other typefaces as indicated below.

Amendments	Typeface Used	Public Law	Date Enacted	Statute Citation
Original	Century	90-202	12/15/67	81 Stat. 602
1974	Century Boldface	93-259	4/8/74	88 Stat. 55
1978	*Century Italics*	95-256	4/6/78	*92 Stat. 189*

(c) it shall be unlawful for a labor organization—

(1) to exclude or to expel from its membership, or otherwise to discriminate against, any individual because of his age,

(2) to limit, segregate, or classify its membership, or to classify or fail or refuse to refer for employment any individual, in any way which would deprive or tend to deprive any individual of employment opportunities, or would limit such employment opportunities or otherwise adversely affect his status as an employee or as an applicant for employment, because of such individual's age;

(3) to cause or attempt to cause an employer to discriminate against an individual in violation of this section.

(d) It shall be unlawful for an employer to discriminate against any of his employees or applicants for employment, for an employment agency to discriminate against any individual, or for a labor organization to discriminate against any member thereof or applicant for membership because such individual, member or applicant for membership has opposed any practice made unlawful by this section, or because such individual, member or applicant for membership has made a charge, testified, assisted, or participated in any manner in an investigation, proceeding, or litigation under this Act.

(e) It shall be unlawful for an employer, labor organization, or employment agency to print or publish, or cause to be printed or published, any notice or advertisement relating to employment by such an employer or membership in or any classification or referral for employment by such a labor organization, or relating to any classification or referral for employment by such an employment agency, indicating any preference, limitation, specification, or discrimination, based on age.

(f) It shall not be unlawful for an employer, employment agency, or labor organization—

(1) to take any action otherwise prohibited under subsections (a), (b), (c), or (e) of this section where age is a bona fide occupational qualification reasonably necessary to the normal operation of the particular business, or where the differentiation is based on reasonable factors other than age;

(2) to observe the terms of a bona fide seniority system or any bona fide employee benefit plan such as a retirement, pension, or insurance plan, which is not a subterfuge to evade the purposes of this Act, except that no such employee benefit plan shall excuse the failure to hire any individual, *and no such seniority system or employee benefit plan shall require or permit the involuntary retirement of any individual specified by section 12(a) of this Act because of the age of such individual;* [1] or

(3) to discharge or otherwise discipline an individual for good cause.

STUDY BY SECRETARY OF LABOR

SEC. 5. *(a)(1) The Secretary of Labor is directed to undertake an appropriate study of institutional and other arrangements giving rise to involuntary retirement, and report his findings and any appropriate legislative recommendations to the President and to the Congress. Such study shall include—*

(A) an examination of the effect of the amendment made by section 3(a) of the Age Discrimination in Employment Act Amendments of 1978 in raising the upper age limitation established by section 12(a) of this Act to 70 years of age;

(B) a determination of the feasibility of eliminating such limitations;

(C) a determination of the feasibility of raising such limitation above 70 years of age; and

(D) an examination of the effect of the exemption contained in section 12(c), relating to certain executive employees, and the exemption contained in section 12(d), relating to tenured teaching personnel.

(2) The Secretary may undertake the study required by paragraph (1) of this subsection directly or by contract or other arrangement.

(b) The report required by subsection (a) of this section shall be transmitted to the President and Congress as an interim report not later than January 1, 1981, and in final form not later than January 1, 1982.

ADMINISTRATION

SEC. 6. The Secretary shall have the power—

(a) to make delegations, to appoint such agents and employees, and to pay for technical assistance on a fee for service basis, as he deems

---

[1] As amended by section 2(a) of the Age Discrimination in Employment Act Amendments of 1978. The effective date of this amendment is set forth in section 2(b) of the 1978 amendments: "The amendment made by subsection (a) of this section shall take effect the date of enactment of this Act, except that, in the case of employees covered by collective bargaining agreement which is in effect on September 1, 1977, which is entered into by a labor organization (as defined by section 6(d)(4) of the Fair Labor Standards Act of 1938), and which would otherwise be prohibited by the amendment made by section 3(a) of this Act, the amendment made by subsection (a) of this section shall take effect upon the termination of such agreement or on January 1, 1980, whichever occurs first." The revision of section 12 of the ADEA is the "amendment made by section 3(a) of this Act" referred to in the previous sentence.

THE AGE DISCRIMINATION IN EMPLOYMENT ACT OF 1967, AS AMENDED

necessary to assist him in the performance of his functions under this Act;

(b) to cooperate with regional, State, local, and other agencies, and to cooperate with and furnish technical assistance to employers, labor organizations, and employment agencies to aid in effectuating the purposes of this Act.

RECORDKEEPING, INVESTIGATION, AND ENFORCEMENT

SEC. 7. (a) The Secretary shall have the power to make investigations and require the keeping of records necessary or appropriate for the administration of this Act in accordance with the powers and procedures provided in sections 9 and 11 of the Fair Labor Standards Act of 1938, as amended (29 U.S.C. 209 and 211).

(b) The provisions of this Act shall be enforced in accordance with the powers, remedies, and procedures provided in sections 11(b), 16 (except for subsection (a) thereof), and 17 of the Fair Labor Standards Act of 1938, as amended (29 U.S.C. 211(b), 216, 217), and subsection (c) of this section. Any act prohibited under section 4 of this Act shall be deemed to be a prohibited act under section 15 of the Fair Labor Standards Act of 1938, as amended (29 U.S.C. 215). Amounts owing to a person as a result of a violation of this Act shall be deemed to be unpaid minimum wages or unpaid overtime compensation for purposes of sections 16 and 17 of the Fair Labor Standards Act of 1938, as amended (29 U.S.C. 216, 217): *Provided,* That liquidated damages shall be payable only in cases of willful violations of this Act. In any action brought to enforce this Act the court shall have jurisdiction to grant such legal or equitable relief as may be appropriate to effectuate the purposes of this Act, including without limitation judgments compelling employment, reinstatement or promotion, or enforcing the liability for amounts deemed to be unpaid minimum wages or unpaid overtime compensation under this section. Before instituting any action under this section, the Secretary shall attempt to eliminate the discriminatory practice or practices alleged, and to effect voluntary compliance with requirements of this Act through informal methods of conciliation, conference, and persuasion.

(c)(1) Any person aggrieved may bring a civil action in any court of competent jurisdiction for such legal or equitable relief as will effectuate the purposes of this Act: *Provided,* That the right of any person to bring such action shall terminate upon the commencement of an action by the Secretary to enforce the right of such employee under this Act.

(2) In an action brought under paragraph (1), a person shall be entitled to a trial by jury of any issue of fact in any such action for recovery of amounts owing as a result of a violation of this Act, regardless of whether equitable relief is sought by any party in such action.[2]

(d) No civil action may be commenced by an individual under this section until 60 days after a charge alleging unlawful discrimination has been filed with the Secretary. Such a charge shall be filed—

(1) within 180 days after the alleged unlawful practice occurred; or

(2) in a case to which section 14(b) applies, within 300 days after the alleged unlawful practice occurred, or within 30 days after receipt by the individual of notice of termination of proceedings under State law, whichever is earlier.

Upon receiving such a charge, the Secretary shall promptly notify all persons named in such charge as prospective defendants in the action and shall promptly seek to eliminate any alleged unlawful practice by informal methods of conciliation, conference, and persuasion.[3]

(e)(1) Sections 6 and 10 of the Portal-to-Portal Act of 1947 shall apply to actions under this Act.

(2) For the period during which the Secretary is attempting to effect voluntary compliance with requirements of this Act through informal methods of conciliation, conference, and persuasion pursuant to subsection (b), the statute of limitations as provided in section 6 of the Portal-to-Portal Act of 1947 shall be tolled, but in no event for a period in excess of one year.[4]

NOTICE TO BE POSTED

SEC. 8. Every employer, employment agency, and labor organization shall post and keep posted in conspicuous places upon its premises a notice to be prepared or approved by the Secretary setting forth information as the Secretary deems appropriate to effectuate the purposes of this Act.

RULES AND REGULATIONS

SEC. 9. In accordance with the provisions of subchapter II of chapter 5 of title 5, United States Code, the Secretary of Labor may issue such rules and regulations as he may consider necessary or appropriate for carrying out this Act, and may establish

---

[2] Effective with respect to civil actions brought after April 6, 1978.

[3] Effective with respect to civil actions brought after April 6, 1978. Prior to the Age Discrimination in Employment Act Amendments of 1978, section 7(d) read as it does now, except that it required a "notice of intent to sue" rather than a "charge alleging unlawful discrimination."

[4] Effective with respect to conciliations commenced by the Secretary of Labor after April 6, 1978.

such reasonable exemptions to and from any or all provisions of this Act as he may find necessary and proper in the public interest.

CRIMINAL PENALTIES

Sec. 10. Whoever shall forcibly resist, oppose, impede, intimidate or interfere with a duly authorized representative of the Secretary while he is engaged in the performance of duties under this Act shall be punished by a fine of not more than $500 or by imprisonment for not more than one year, or both: *Provided, however,* That no person shall be imprisoned under this section except when there has been a prior conviction hereunder.

DEFINITIONS

Sec. 11. for the purposes of this Act—

(a) The term "person" means one or more individuals, partnerships, associations, labor organizations, corporations, business trusts, legal representatives, or any organized groups of persons.

(b) The term "employer" means a person engaged in an industry affecting commerce who has **twenty**[5] or more employees for each working day in each of twenty or more calendar weeks in the current or preceding calendar year: *Provided,* That prior to June 30, 1968, employers having fewer than fifty employees shall not be considered employers. **The term also means (1) any agent of such a person, and (2) a State or political subdivision of a State and any agency or instrumentality of a State or a political subdivision of a State, and any interstate agency, but such term does not include the United States, or a corporation wholly owned by the Government of the United States.**

(c) The term "employment agency" means any person regularly undertaking with or without compensation to procure employees for an employer and includes an agent of such a person; but shall not include an agency of the United States.[6]

(d) The term "labor organization" means a labor organization engaged in an industry affecting commerce, and any agent of such an organization, and includes any organization of any kind, any agency, or employee representation committee, group, association, or plan so engaged in which employees participate and which exists for the purpose, in whole or in part, of dealing with employers concerning grievances, labor disputes, wages, rates of pay, hours, or other terms or conditions of employment, and any conference, general committee, joint or system board, or joint council so engaged which is subordinate to a national or international labor organization.

(e) A labor organization shall be deemed to be engaged in an industry affecting commerce if (1) it maintains or operates a hiring hall or hiring office which procures employees for an employer or procures for employees opportunities to work for an employer, or (2) the number of its members (or, where it is a labor organization composed of other labor organizations or their representatives, if the aggregate number of the members of such other labor organization) is fifty or more prior to July 1, 1968, or twenty-five or more on or after July 1, 1968, and such labor organization—

(1) is the certified representative of employees under the provisions of the National Labor Relations Act, as amended, or the Railway Labor as amended; or

(2) although not certified, is a national or international labor organization or a local labor organization recognized or acting as the representative or employees of an employer or employers engaged in an industry affecting commerce; or

(3) has chartered a local labor organization or subsidiary body which is representing or actively seeking to represent employees of employers within the meaning of paragraph (1) or (2); or

(4) has been chartered by a labor organization representing or actively seeking to represent employees within the meaning of paragraph (1) or (2) as the local or subordinate body through which such employees may enjoy membership or become affiliated with such labor organization; or

(5) is a conference, general committee, joint or system board, or joint council subordinate to a national or international labor organization, which includes a labor organization engaged in an industry affecting commerce within the meaning of any of the preceding paragraphs of this subsection.

(f) The term "employee" means an individual employed by any employer except that the term "employee" **shall not include any person elected to public office in any State or political subdivision of any State by the qualified voters thereof, or any person chosen by such officer to be on such officer's**

---

[5] Section 28(a)(1) of the Fair Labor Standards Amendments of 1974 substituted "twenty" for "twenty-five," effective May 1, 1974.

[6] Prior to the Fair Labor Standards Amendments of 1974, the Act's definition of an "employment agency" excluded "an agency of a State or political subdivision of a State, except that such term shall include the United States Employment Service and the system of State and local employment services receiving Federal assistance."

THE AGE DISCRIMINATION IN EMPLOYMENT ACT OF 1967, AS AMENDED

personal staff, or an appointee on the policymaking level or an immediate adviser with respect to the exercise of the constitutional or legal powers of the office. The exemption set forth in the preceding sentence shall not include employees subject to the civil service laws of a State government, governmental agency, or political subdivision.

(g) The term "commerce" means trade, traffic, commerce, transportation, transmission, or communication among the several States; or between a State and any place outside thereof; or within the District of Columbia, or a possession of the United States; or between points in the same State but through a point outside thereof.

(h) The term "industry affecting commerce" means any activity, business, or industry in commerce or in which a labor dispute would hinder or obstruct commerce or the free flow of commerce and includes any activity or industry "affecting commerce" within the meaning of the Labor-Management Reporting and Disclosure Act of 1959.

(i) The term "State" includes a State of the United States, the District of Columbia, Puerto Rico, the Virgin Islands, American Samoa, Guam, Wake Island, the Canal Zone, and Outer Continental Shelf lands defined in the Outer Continental Shelf Lands Act.

AGE LIMITATION

SEC. 12. *(a)*[7] *The prohibitions in this Act shall be limited to individuals who are at least 40 years of age but less than 70 years of age.*

(b)[8] *In the case of any personnel action affecting employees or applicants for employment which is subject to the provisions of section 15 of this Act, the prohibitions established in section 15 of this Act shall be limited to individuals who are at least 40 years of age.*

(c)[9] *(1) Nothing in this Act shall be construed to prohibit compulsory retirement of any employee who has attained 65 years of age but not 70 years of age, and who, for the 2-year period immediately before retirement, is employed in a bona fide executive or a high policymaking position, if such employee is entitled to an immediate nonforfeitable annual retirement benefit from a pension, profit-sharing, savings, or deferred compensation plan, or any combination of such plans, of the employer of such employee, which equals, in the aggregate, at least $27,000.*

(2) In applying the retirement benefit test of paragraph (1) of this subsection, if any such retirement benefit is in a form other than a straight life annuity (with no ancillary benefits), or if employees contribute to any such plan or make rollover contributions, such benefit shall be adjusted in accordance with regulations prescribed by the Secretary, after consultation with the Secretary of the Treasury, so that the benefit is the equivalent of a straight life annuity (with no ancillary benefits) under a plan to which employees do not contribute and under which no rollover contributions are made.

(d)[10] *Nothing in this Act shall be construed to prohibit compulsory retirement of any employee who has attained 65 years of age but not 70 years of age, and who is serving under a contract of unlimited tenure (or similar arrangement providing for unlimited tenure) at an institution of higher education (as defined by section 1201(a) of the Higher Education Act of 1965).*

ANNUAL REPORT

SEC. 13. The Secretary shall submit annually in January a report to the Congress covering his activities for the preceding year and including such information, data, and recommendations for further legislation in connection with the matters covered by this act as he may find advisable. Such report shall contain an evaluation and appraisal by the Secretary of the effect of the minimum and maximum ages established by this Act, together with his recommendations to the Congress. In making such evaluation and appraisal, the Secretary shall take into consideration any changes which may have occurred in the general age level of the population, the effect of the Act upon workers not covered by its provisions, and such other factors as he may deem pertinent.

FEDERAL-STATE RELATIONSHIP

SEC. 14. (a) Nothing in this Act shall affect the jurisdiction of any agency of any State performing like functions with regard to discriminatory employment practices on account of age except that upon commencement of action under this Act such action shall supersede any State action.

(b) In the case of an alleged unlawful practice occuring in a State which has a law prohibiting

---

[7] Subsection 12(a) takes effect on January 1, 1979. Prior to the Age Discrimination in Employment Act Amendments of 1978, section 12 provided in its entirety: "The prohibitions in this Act shall be limited to individuals who are at least forty years of age but less than sixty-five years of age."

[8] Subsection 12(b), which was added by the 1978 Amendments, takes effect on September 30, 1978.

[9] Subsection 12(c), which was added by the 1978 Amendments, takes effect on January 1, 1979.

[10] Subsection 12(d), which was added by the 1978 Amendments, takes effect on January 1, 1979. It is repealed on July 1, 1982.

discrimination in employment because of age and establishing or authorizing a State authority to grant or seek relief from such discriminatory practice, no suit may be brought under section 7 of this Act before the expiration of sixty days after proceedings have been commenced under the State law, unless such proceedings have been earlier terminated: *Provided,* That such sixty-day period shall be extended to one hundred and twenty days during the first year after the effective date of such State law. If any requirement for the commencement of such proceedings is imposed by a State authority other than a requirement of the filing of a written and signed statement of the facts upon which the proceeding is based, the proceeding shall be deemed to have been commenced for the purposes of this subsection at the time such statement is sent by registered mail to the appropriate State authority.

NONDISCRIMINATION ON ACCOUNT OF AGE IN FEDERAL GOVERNMENT EMPLOYMENT

Sec. 15. (a) All personnel actions affecting employees or applicants for employment *who are at least 40 years of age* (except *personnel actions* with regard to aliens employed outside the limits of the United States) in military departments as defined in section 102 of title 5, United States Code, in executive agencies as defined in section 105 of title 5, United States Code (including employees and applicants for employment who are paid from nonappropriated funds), in the United States Postal Service and the Postal Rate Commission, in those units in the government of the District of Columbia having positions in the competitive service, and in those units of the legislative and judicial branches of the Federal Government having positions in the competitive service, and in the Library of Congress shall be made free from any discrimination based on age.

(b) Except as otherwise provided in this subsection, the Civil Service Commission is authorized to enforce the provisions of subsection (a) through appropriate remedies, including reinstatement or hiring of employees with or without backpay, as will effectuate the policies of this section. The Civil Service Commission shall issue such rules, regulations, orders and instructions as it deems necessary and appropriate to carry out its responsibilities under this section. The Civil Service Commission shall—

(1) be responsible for the review and evaluation of the operation of all agency programs designed to carry out the policy of this section, periodically obtaining and publishing (on at least a semiannual basis) progress reports from each department, agency, or unit referred to in subsection (a);

(2) consult with and solicit the recommendations of interested individuals, groups, and organizations relating to nondiscrimination in employment on account of age; and

(3) provide for the acceptance and processing of complaints of discrimination in Federal employment on account of age.

The head of each such department, agency, or unit shall comply with such rules, regulations, orders, and instructions of the Civil Service Commission which shall include a provision that an employee or applicant for employment shall be notified of any final action taken on any complaint of discrimination filed by him thereunder. Reasonable exemptions to the provisions of this section may be established by the Commission but only when the Commission has established a maximum age requirement on the basis of a determination that is a bona fide occupational qualification necessary to the performance of the duties of the position. With respect to employment in the Library of Congress, authorities granted in this subsection to the Civil Service Commission shall be exercised by the Librarian of Congress.

(c) Any person aggrieved may bring a civil action in any Federal district court of competent jurisdiction for such legal or equitable relief as will effectuate the purposes of this Act.

(d) When the individual has not filed a complaint concerning age discrimination with the Commission, no civil action may be commenced by an individual under this section until the individual has given the Commission not less that thirty days' notice of an intent to file such action. Such notice shall be filed within one hundred and eighty days after the alleged unlawful practice occurred. Upon receiving a notice of intent to sue, the Commission shall promptly notify all persons named therein as prospective defendants in the action and take any appropriate action to assure the elimination of any unlawful practice.

(e) Nothing contained in this section shall relieve any Government agency or official of the responsibility to assure nondiscrimination on account of age in employment as required under any provision Federal law.

(f) [11] *Any personnel action of any department, agen-*

---
[11] Effective September 30, 1978.

THE AGE DISCRIMINATION IN EMPLOYMENT ACT OF 1967, AS AMENDED

cy, or other entity referred to in subsection (a) of this section shall not be subject to or affected by, any provision of this Act, other than the provisions of section 12(b) of this Act and the provisions of this section.

(g)[12] (1) The Civil Service Commission shall undertake a study relating to the effects of the amendments made to this section by the Age Discrimination in Employment Act Amendments of 1978, and the effects of section 12(b) of this Act, as added by the Age Discrimination in Employment Act Amendments of 1978.

(2) The Civil Service Commission shall transmit a report to the President and to the Congress containing the findings of the Commission resulting from the study of the Commission under paragraph (1) of this subsection. Such report shall be transmitted no later than January 1, 1980.

EFFECTIVE DATE [13]

SEC. 16. This Act shall become effective one hundred and eighty days after enactment, except (a) that the Secretary of Labor may extend the delay in effective date of any provision of this Act up to an additional ninety days thereafter if he finds that such time is necessary in permitting adjustments to the provisions hereof, and (b) that on or after the date of enactment the Secretary of Labor is authorized to issue such rules and regulations as may be necessary to carry out its provisions.

APPROPRIATIONS

SEC. 17. There are hereby authorized to be appropriated such sums as may be necessary to carry out this Act.[14]

Approved December 15, 1967.

---

[12] Effective April 6, 1978.
[13] The effective date of the provisions added by the Fair Labor Standards Amendments of 1974, which are shown in bold face type, was May 1, 1974. See section 29(a) of the Fair Labor Standards Amendments of 1974. The effective dates of the provisions added by the Age Discrimination in Employment Act Amendments of 1978, which are shown in italic type, are indicated in footnotes to each provision.

[14] Section 7 of the Age Discrimination in Employment Act Amendments of 1978 amended this section by eliminating the $5 million authorization ceiling on appropriations.

ADDITIONAL PROVISIONS OF THE AGE DISCRIMINATION IN EMPLOYMENT ACT AMENDMENTS OF 1978 (92 Stat. 189)

[PUBLIC LAW 95-256]
[95TH CONGRESS, 2D SESSION]

An Act

To amend the Age Discrimination in Employment Act of 1967 to extend the age group of employees who are protected by the provisions of such Act, and for other purposes.

Be it enacted by the Senate and House of Representatives of the United States of America in Congress assembled, That this Act may be cited as the "Age Discrimination in Employment Act Amendments of 1978".

[Sections 2 through 4, 5(a), 6 and 7 of the Age Discrimination in Employment Act Amendments of 1978 amend the Age Discrimination in Employment Act of 1967, and are incorporated in their proper place in the Act. Where the effective dates of these amendments are not part of the Act proper, they are noted in footnotes. Section 5(b), (c) and (d) of the 1978 Amendments amend title 5 of the United States Code, and are set forth below.]

FEDERAL GOVERNMENT EMPLOYMENT

SEC. 5.[15] * * *

(b)(1) Section 3322 of title 5, United States Code, relating to temporary appointments after age 70, is repealed.

(2) The analysis for chapter 33 of title 5, United States Code, is amended by striking out the item relating to section 3322.

---
[15] The amendments in Section 5(b), (c) and (d) take effect on September 30, 1978.

(c) Section 8335 of title 5, United States Code, relating to mandatory separation, is amended—

(1) by striking out subsections (a), (b), (c), (d), and (e) thereof;

(2) by redesignating subsections (f) and (g) as subsections (a) and (b), respectively; and

(3) by adding after subsection (b), as so redesignated, the following new subsections:

"(c) An employee of the Alaska Railroad in Alaska and an employee who is a citizen of the United States employed on the Isthmus of Panama by the Panama Canal Company or the Canal Zone Government, who becomes 62 years of age and completes 15 years of service in Alaska or on the Isthmus of Panama shall be automatically separated from the service. The separation is effective on the last day of the month in which the employee becomes age 62 or completes 15 years of service in Alaska or on the Isthmus of Panama if then over that age. The employing office shall notify the employee in writing of the date of separation at least 60 days in advance thereof. Ac to separate the employee is not effective, without consent of the employee, until the last day of the month in which the 60-day notice expires.

"(d) The President, by Executive order, may exempt an employee from automatic separation under this section when he determines the public interest so requires".

(d) Section 8339(d) of title 5, United States Code, relating to computation of annuity, is amended by striking out "section 8335(g)" and inserting in lieu thereof "section 8335(b)".

PERTINENT PROVISIONS OF THE FAIR LABOR STANDARDS ACT WHICH AFFECT THE AGE DISCRIMINATION IN EMPLOYMENT ACT
(29 U.S.C. §§211, 216 and 217)

Investigations, Inspections, Records, and Homework Regulations

SEC. 11. (a) The Secretary of Labor or his designated representatives may investigate and gather data regarding the wages, hours, and other conditions and practices of employment in any industry subject to this Act, and may enter and inspect such places and such records (and make such transcriptions thereof), question such employees, and investigate such facts, conditions, practices, or matters as he may deem necessary or appropriate to determine whether any person has violated any provision of this Act, or which may aid in the enforcement of the provisions of this Act. Except as provided in section 12 and in subsection (b) of this section, the Secretary shall utilize the bureaus and divisions of the Department of Labor for all the investigations and inspections necessary under this section. Except as provided in section 12, the Secretary shall b   all actions under section 17 to restrain violations of this Act.

(b) With the consent and cooperation of State agencies charged with the administration of State labor laws, the Secretary of Labor may, for the purpose of carrying out his functions and duties under this Act, utilize the services of State and local agencies and their employees and, notwithstanding any other provision of law, may reimburse such State and local agencies and their employees for services rendered for such purposes.

(c) Every employer subject to any provision of this Act or of any order issued under this Act shall make, keep, and preserve such records of the persons employed by him and of the wages, hours, and other conditions and practices of employment maintained by him, and shall preserve such records for such periods of time, and shall make such reports therefrom to the Secretary as he shall prescribe by regulation or order as necessary or appropriate for the enforcement of the provisions of this Act or the regulations or orders thereunder.

(d) The Secretary is authorized to make such regulations and orders regulating, restricting, or prohibiting   strial homework as are necessary or appropriate to prevent the circumvention or evasion of and to safeguard the minimum wage rate prescribed in this Act, and all existing regulations or orders of the Administrator relating to industrial homework are hereby continued in full force and effect.

Penalties

SEC. 16. (a) Any person who willfully violates any of the provisions of section 15 shall upon conviction thereof be subject to a fine of not more than $10,000, or to imprisonment for not more than six months, or both. No person shall be imprisoned under this subsection except for an offense committed after the conviction of such person for a prior offense under this subsection.

(b) Any employer who violates the provisions of section 6 or section 7 of this Act shall be liable to the employee or employees affected in the amount of their unpaid minimum wages, or their unpaid overtime compensation, as the case may be, and in an additional equal amount as liquidated damages. Any employer who violates the provisions of section 15(a)(3) of this Act shall be liable for such legal or equitable relief as may be appropriate to effectuate the purposes of section 15(a)(3), including without limitation employment, reinstatement, promotion, and the payment of wages lost and an additional equal amount as liquidated damages. An action to recover the liability prescribed in either of the preceding sentences may be maintained *against any employer (including a public agency)* in any *Federal or State* court of competent jurisdiction by any one or more employees for and in behalf of himself or themselves and other employees similarly situated. No employee shall be a party plaintiff to any such action unless he gives his consent in writing to become such a party and such consent is filed in the court in which such action is brought. The court in such action shall, in addition to any judgment awarded to the plaintiff or plaintiffs, allow a reasonable attorney's fee to be paid by the defendent, and costs of the action. **The right provided by this subsection to bring an action by or on behalf of any employee, and the right of any employee to become a party plaintiff to any such action, shall terminate upon the filing of a complaint by the Secretary of Labor in an action under section 17 in which (1) restraint is sought of any further delay in the payment of unpaid minimum wages, or the amount of unpaid overtime compensation as the case may be, owing to such employee under section 6 or section 7 of this Act by an employer liable therefor under the provisions of this subsection** or (2) legal or equitable relief is sought as a result of alleged violations of section 15(a)(3).

(c) The Secretary is authorized to supervise the payment of the unpaid minimum wages or the unpaid overtime compensation owing to any employee or employees under section 6 or 7 of this Act, and the agreement of any employee to accept such payment shall upon payment in full constitute a waiver by such employee of any right he may have under subsection (b) of this section to such unpaid minimum wages or unpaid overtime compensation and an additional equal amount as liquidated damages. The Secretary may bring an action in any court of competent jurisdiction to recover the amount of *the unpaid minimum wages or overtime compensation and an equal amount as liquidated damages. The right provided by subsection (b) to bring an action by or on behalf of any employee* to recover the liability specified in the first sentence of such subsection *and of any employee to become a party plaintiff to any such action shall terminate upon the filing of a complaint by the Secretary in an action under this subsection in which a recovery is sought of unpaid minimum wages or unpaid overtime compensation under sections 6 and 7 or liquidated or other damages provided by this subsection owing to such employee by an employer liable under the provisions of subsection (b), unless such action is dismissed without prejudice on motion of the Secretary.* Any sums thus recovered by the Secretary on behalf of an employee pursuant to this subsection shall be held in a special deposit account and shall be paid, on order of the Secretary, directly to the employee or employees affected. Any such sums not paid to an employee because of inability to do so within a period of three years shall be covered into the Treasury of the United States as miscellaneous receipts. In determining when an action is commenced by the Secretary under this subsection for the purposes of the *statutes* of limitations provided in section 6(a) of the Portal-to-Portal Act of 1947, it shall be considered to be commenced in the case of any individual claimant on the date when the complaint is filed if he is specifically named as a party plaintiff in the complaint, or if his name did not so appear, on the subsequent date on which his name is added as a party plaintiff in such action.

(d) In any action or proceeding commenced prior to, on, or after the date of enactment of this subsection, no employer shall be subject to any liability or punishment under this Act or the Portal-to-Portal Act of 1947 on account of his failure to comply with any provision or provisions of such Acts (1) with respect to work heretofore or hereafter performed in a workplace to which the exemption in section 13(f) is applicable, (2) with respect to work performed in Guam, the Canal Zone or Wake Island before the effective date of this amendment of subsection (d), or (3) with respect to work performed in a possession named in section 6(a) (3) at any time prior to the establishment by the Secretary, as provided therein, of a minimum wage applicable to such work.

(e) Any person who violates the provisions of section 12, relating to child labor, or any regulation issued under that section, shall be subject to a civil penalty of not to exceed $1,000 for each such violation. In determining the amount of such penalty, the appropriateness of such penalty to the size of the business of the person charged and the gravity of the violation shall be considered. The amount of such penalty, when finally determined, may be—

(1) deducted from any sums owing by the United States to the person charged;

(2) recovered in a civil action brought by the Secretary in any court of competent jurisdiction, in which litigation the Secretary shall be represented by the Solicitor of Labor; or

(3) ordered by the court, in an action brought for a violation of section 15(a)(4), to be paid to the Secretary.

Any administrative determination by the Secretary of the amount of such penalty shall be final, unless within fifteen days after receipt of notice thereof by certified mail the person charged with the violation takes exception to the determination that the violations for w the penalty is imposed occurred, in which event final determination of the penalty shall be made in an adm istrative proceeding after opportunity for hearing in accordance with section 554 of title 5, United States Code, and regulations to be promulgated by the Secretary. Sums collected as penalties pursuant to this section shall be applied toward reimbursement of the costs of determining the violations and assessing and collecting such penalties, in accordance with the provision of section 2 of an Act entitled "An Act to authorize the Department of Labor to make special statistical studies upon payment of the cost thereof, and for other purposes" (29 U.S.C. 9a).

Injunction Proceedings

SEC. 17. The district courts, together with the United States District Court for the District of the Canal Zone, the District Court of the Virgin Islands, and the District Court of Guam shall have jurisdiction, for cause shown, to restrain violations of section 15, including in the case of violations of section 15(a)(2) the restraint of any withholding of payment of minimum wages or overtime compensation found by the court to be due to employees under this Act (except which employees are barred from recovering, at the time of the commencement of the action to restrain the violations, by virtue of the provisions of section 6 of the Portal-to-Portal Act of 1947).

PERTINENT PROVISIONS OF THE PORTAL-TO-PORTAL ACT WHICH AFFECT THE AGE DISCRIMINATION IN EMPLOYMENT ACT
(29 U.S.C. §§255 and 258)

* * * * *

SEC. 6. STATUTE OF LIMITATIONS.—Any action commenced on or after the date of the enactment of this Act to enforce any cause of action for unpaid minimum wages, unpaid overtime compensation, or liquidated damages, under the Fair Labor Standards Act of 1938, as amended, the Walsh-Healey Act, or the Bacon-Davis Act—

(a) if the cause of action accrues on or after the date of the enactment of this Act—may be commenced within two years after the cause of action accrued, and every such action shall be forever barred unless commenced within two years after the cause of action accrued, *except that a cause of action arising out of a willful violation may be commenced within three years after the cause of action accrued;*

* * * * *

(d) with respect to any cause of action brought under section 16(b) of the Fair Labor Standards Act of 1938 against a State or a political subdivision of a State in a district court of the United States on or before April 18, 1973, the running of the statutory periods of limitation shall be deemed suspended during the period beginning with the commencement of any such action and ending one hundred and eighty days after the effective date of the Fair Labor Standards Amendments of 1974, except that such suspension shall not be applicable if in such action judgment has been entered for the defendant on the grounds other than State immunity from Federal jurisdiction.

* * * * *

SEC. 10. RELIANCE IN FUTURE ON ADMINISTRATIVE RULINGS, ETC.—

(a) In any action or proceeding based on any act or omission on or after the date of the enactment of this Act, no employer shall be subject to any liability or punishment for or on account of the failure of the employer to pay minimum wages or overtime compensation under the Fair Labor Standards Act of 1938, as amended, the Walsh-Healey Act, or the Bacon-Davis Act, if he pleads and proves that the act or omission complained of was in good faith in conformity with and in reliance on any written administrative regulation, order, ruling, approval, or interpretation, of the agency of the United States specified in subsection (b) of this section, or any administrative practice or enforcement policy of such agency with respect to the class of employers to which he belonged. Such a defense, if established, shall be a bar to the action or proceeding, notwithstanding that after such act or omission, such administrative regulation, order, ruling, approval, interpretation, practice, or enforcement policy is modified or rescinded or is determined by judicial authority to be invalid or of no legal effect.

EQUAL EMPLOYMENT OPPORTUNITY COMMISSION

29 CFR Part 1626

Proposed Procedural Regulations

AGENCY: Equal Employment Opportunity Commission.

ACTION: Proposed Regulations; request for comments.

SUMMARY: The Equal Employment Opportunity Commission is publishing for comment proposed procedural regulations (29 CFR Part 1626). These regulations advise the public as to the procedures the Commission proposes to follow in processing charges and issuing interpretations and opinions under the Age Discrimination in Employment Act. These regulations will complement the Commission's existing procedural regulations under Title VII of the Civil Rights Act of 1964.

DATES: Comments must be submitted on or before March 31, 1981.

ADDRESS: Comments should be addressed to the Office of the Executive Secretariat, Room 4096, Equal Employment Opportunity Commission, 2401 E Street, N.W., Washington, D.C. 20506.

FOR FURTHER INFORMATION CONTACT:
John J. Pagano, Legal Counsel Division, Office of the General Counsel, Equal Employment Opportunity Commission, 2401 E Street, N.W., Washington, D.C. 20506, (202) 634-6505.

SUPPLEMENTARY INFORMATION: On July 1, 1979, pursuant to Reorganization Plan No. 1 of 1978, 43 FR 19807 (May 9, 1978) responsibility and authority for enforcement of the Age Discrimination in Employment Act of 1967, as amended, 29 USC 621 *et seq.*, (ADEA), was transferred from the Department of Labor to the Equal Employment Opportunity Commission. Procedural regulations under the ADEA did not exist when authority for the Act was with the Department of Labor. In addition to the ADEA the EEOC is responsible for enforcement of Title VII of the Civil Rights Act of 1964, as amended, 42 USC 2000e *et seq.* and has published procedural regulations under that statute at 29 CFR 1601.

With the desire to provide continuity, to the extent possible, in the processing of charges under the ADEA and Title VII the Commission is publishing its procedural regulations under the ADEA. In those areas where the statutory provisions of the two Acts allow, the proposed procedural regulations under the ADEA conform to the Title VII procedural regulations.

It is the intention of the EEOC to publish these proposed regulations and to receive comments from interested members of the public for 60 days. The proposed procedural regulations appear below.

Signed at Washington, D.C. this 9th day of January 1981.

For the Commission.

Eleanor Holmes Norton,
Chair, Equal Employment Opportunity Commission.

29 CFR Part 1626 is proposed to be added as follows:

PART 1626—PROCEDURES AGE DISCRIMINATION IN EMPLOYMENT ACT

Sec.
1626.1 Purpose.
1626.2 Terms defined in the Age Discrimination in Employment Act of 1967, as amended.
1626.3 Other definitions.
1626.4 Information concerning alleged violations of the Act.
1626.5 Where to submit complaints and charges.
1626.6 Form of charge.
1626.7 Timeliness of charge.
1626.8 Contents of charge; amendment of charge.
1626.9 Referrals to State agencies.
1626.10 Referral States.
1626.11 Notice of charge.
1626.12 Conciliation Efforts Pursuant to section 7(d) of the Act.
1626.13 Withdrawal of charge.
1626.14 Right to inspect or copy data.
1626.15 Commission enforcement.
1626.16 Subpoenas.
1626.17 Procedure for requesting an opinion letter.
1626.18 Interpretations by the Commission.
1626.19 Rules to be liberally construed.

Authority: Sec. 9, 81 Stat. 605; (29 USC 628); sec. 2 Reorg. Plan No. 1 of 1978, (43 FR 18907)

§ 1626.1 Purpose.

The regulations set forth in this Part contain the procedures established by the Equal Employment Opportunity Commission for carrying out its responsibilities in the administration and enforcement of the Age Discrimination in Employment Act of 1967, as amended.

§ 1626.2 Terms defined in the Age Discrimination in Employment Act of 1967, as amended.

The terms "person," "employer," "employment agency," "labor organization," "employee," "commerce," "industry affecting commerce," and "State" as used herein shall have the meanings set forth in section 11 of the Age Discrimination in Employment Act, as amended.

§ 1626.3 Other definitions.

For purpose of this Part, the term "the Act" shall mean the Age Discrimination in Employment Act of 1967, as amended; the "Commission" shall mean the Equal Employment Opportunity Commission or any of its designated representatives; "charge" shall mean a written statement filed with the Commission by or on behalf of an aggrieved person which alleges that the named prospective defendant has engaged in or will engage in actions in violation of the Act; "complaint" shall mean a confidential statement filed with the Commission, which alleges that a named prospective defendant has engaged in or will engage in actions in violation of the Act; "charging party" means the person by whom or on whose behalf a charge is filed; "complainant" means the person filing a complaint; and "respondent" means the person named as a prospective defendant in a charge or complaint, or as a result of a Commission-initiated investigation.

§ 1626.4 Information concerning alleged violations of the Act.

The Commission may, on its own initiative, conduct investigations of employers, employment agencies and labor organizations, in accordance with the powers vested in it pursuant to sections 6 and 7 of the Act. The Commission shall also receive information concerning alleged violations of the Act, including charges and complaints, from any source. Where the information discloses a possible violation, the appropriate Commission office shall render assistance in the filing of a charge. The identity of a complainant shall not be disclosed without the prior written consent of the complainant, unless necessary in a court proceeding.

§ 1626.5 Where to submit complaints and charges.

Complaints and charges may be submitted in person or by mail to any of the District or Area Office of the Commission, or at the Headquarters of the Commission at Washington, D.C. or with any designated representative of the Commisssion. The addresses of the Commission's District Offices appears at § 1610.4.

§ 1626.6 Form of charge.

A charge shall be in writing and shall name the prospective respondent and shall generally allege the discriminatory act(s).

§ 1626.7 Timeliness of charge.

(a) Charges will not be rejected as untimely provided that they are not barred by the statute of limitations as stated in section 6 of the Portal to Portal Act of 1947.

(b) Potential charging parties will be advised that, pursuant to section 7(d)(1) and (2) of the Act, any person who wishes to bring a civil action alleging a violation of the Act must file a charge with the Commission within 180 days of the alleged discriminatory action, or, in a case where the alleged discriminatory action occurs in a state which has its own age discrimination law and authority administering that law, within 300 days of the alleged discriminatory action, or 30 days after receipt of notice of termination of State proceedings, whichever is earlier.

(c) For purposes of determining the date of filing with the Commission, the following applies:

(1) Charges received by mail: (i) Date of postmark, if legible, (ii) Date of letter, if postmark is illegible, (iii) Date of receipt by Commission, if postmark and letter date are illegible and/or cannot be accurately affixed;

(2) Written charges received in person: Date of receipt;

(3) Oral charges delivered in person or by telephone, date of communication.

§ 1626.8 Contents of charge; amendment of charge.

(a) In addition to the requirements of 1626.6, each charge should contain the following:

(1) The full name, address and telephone number of the person making the charge;

(2) The full name and address of the person against whom the charge is made;

(3) A clear and concise statement of the facts, including pertinent dates, constituting the alleged unlawful employment practices;

(4) If known, the approximate number of employees of the prospective defendant employer or members of the prospective defendant labor organization.

(5) A statement disclosing whether proceedings involving the alleged unlawful employment practice have been commenced before a State agency charged with the enforcement of fair employment practice laws and, if so, the date of such commencement and the name of the agency.

(b) Notwithstanding the provisions of paragraph (a) of this section, a charge is sufficient when the Commission receives from the person making the charge either a written statement or information reduced to writing by the Commission that conforms to the requirements of Section 1626.6.

(c) A charge may be amended to clarify or amplify allegations made therein. Such amendments and amendments alleging additional acts which constitute unlawful employment practices related to or growing out of the subject matter of the original charge will relate back to the date the charge was first received. A charge that has been so amended shall not again be referred to the appropriate State agency.

§ 1626.9 Referral to State agencies.

The Commission shall refer all charges to any appropriate State agency, in order to assure that the jurisdictional prerequisites for private law suits, as set forth in § 14(b) of the Act, are met. Charges so referred shall be deemed filed with the Commission in accordance with the specifications contained in 1626.7(b) above. The Commission may begin processing of any charge immediately upon filing, notwithstanding the requirement of referral to appropriate State agencies.

§ 1626.10 Referral States.

(a) States to which all ADEA charges are referred: Alaska, California, Connecticut, Delaware, District of Columbia, Florida, Georgia, Hawaii, Idaho, Illinois, Iowa, Kentucky, Maryland, Massachusetts, Michigan, Minnesota, Montana, Nebraska, Nevada, New Hampshire, New Jersey, New Mexico, New York, Oregon, Pennsylvania, South Carolina, Utah, West Virginia, and Wisconsin.

(b) States to which only specified classes of charges are referred: Arizona, Colorado, Kansas, Maine, Ohio, Rhode Island, South Dakota, and Washington.

§ 1626.11 Notice of charge.

Upon receipt of a charge, the Commission shall promptly notify the respondent that a charge has been filed.

§ 1626.12 Conciliation efforts pursuant to section 7(d) of the Act.

Upon receipt of a charge, the Commission shall promptly attempt to eliminate any alleged unlawful practice by informal methods of conciliation, conference and persuasion.

§ 1626.13 Withdrawal of charge.

Charging parties may request withdrawal of a charge. Because the Commission has independent investigative authority, see 1626.4 above, it may continue any investigation and may secure relief for all affected persons notwithstanding a request by a charging party to withdraw a charge.

§ 1626.14 Right to inspect or copy data.

A person who submits data or evidence to the Commission may retain or, on payment of lawfully prescribed costs, procure a copy or transcript thereof, except that a witness may for good cause be limited to inspection of the official transcript of his or her testimony.

§ 1626.15 Commission enforcement.

(a) As provided in Sections 9, 11, 16 and 17 of the Fair Labor Standards Act of 1938, as amended (29 U.S.C. 209, 211, 216 and 217) (FLSA) and Sections 6 and 7 of this Act, the Commission and its authorized representatives may (1) investigate and gather data; (2) enter and inspect establishments and records and make transcripts thereof; (3) interview employees; (4) impose on persons subject to the Act appropriate recordkeeping and reporting requirements; (5) advise employers, employment agencies and labor organizations with regard to their obligations under the Act and any changes necessary in their policies, practices and procedures to assure compliance with the Act; (6) subpoena witnesses and require the production of documents and other evidence; and (7) supervise the payment of amounts owing pursuant to section 16(c) of the FLSA.

(b) The Commission may conduct its own investigations to determine whether violations of the Act have occurred and investigate alleged discriminatory practices forming the basis of charges and complaints. When, on the basis of the evidence, the Commission believes that a violation of the Act has occurred or will occur, it may issue a written violation letter to that effect; provided, however, that failure to issue a written violation letter shall in no instance be construed as a finding of no violation. The Commission shall notify the respondent and charging party of its written determination. In the process of conducting investigations and/or issuing written violation letters, the identity of a complainant shall not be disclosed, except in accordance with § 1626.4.

(c) Pursuant to section 7 (b) and (d) of the Act, the Commission shall attempt to remedy any violations by informal methods of conciliation, conference and persuasion. Any agreement reached as a result of efforts undertaken pursuant to this section shall, as far as practicable, require the respondent to eliminate the unlawful practice(s) and provide appropriate affirmative relief. Such agreement shall be reduced to writing and shall be signed by the Commission's delegated representative and the parties. A copy of the signed agreement shall be sent to all the signatories thereto; provided, however, that if the agreement contains provisions or information relating to complainants who wish their identities to remain confidential, their names and other identifying data shall be deleted from the copies sent to all the signatories to whom the complainant's identity has not previously been disclosed.

(d) If the Commission determines that its efforts at informal conciliation, conference and persuasion have failed, it shall so notify the respondent and the charging party.

(e) Upon the failure of informal conciliation, conference and persuasion, the Commission may, pursuant to the Act, initiate and conduct litigation.

(f) The District Directors, the Director of the Office of Field Services and the Director of the Office of Systemic Programs, or their designees, are hereby delegated authority to exercise the powers enumerated in 1626.15(a)–(d). The General Counsel or his/her designee is hereby delegated the authority to exercise the powers in paragraph (a) of this section and at the direction of the Commission to initiate and conduct litigation.

§ 1626.16 Subpoenas.

(a) To effectuate the purposes of the Act the Commission shall have the authority to issue a subpoena requiring:

(1) The attendance and testimony of witnesses;

(2) The production of evidence including, but not limited to, books, records, correspondence, or documents, in the possession or under the control of the person subpoenaed; and

(3) Access to evidence for the purpose of examination and the right to copy.

The power to issue subpoenas has been delegated by the Commission to the General Counsel, the District Directors, the Director of the Office of Field Services, and the Director of the Office of Systemic Programs, or their designees. The subpoena shall state the name, address and title of the issuer, identify the person or evidence subpoenaed, the name of the person to whom the subpoena is returnable, the date, time and place that testimony is to be given or that documents are to be provided or access provided.

(b) A subpoena issued by the Commission or its designee pursuant to the Act is not subject to review or appeal.

(c) Upon the failure of any person to comply with a subpoena issued under this section, the Commission may utilize the provisions of sections 9 and 10 of the Federal Trade Commission Act, 15 U.S.C. 49 and 50, to compel compliance with the subpoena.

(d) Persons subpoenaed shall be entitled to the same fees and mileage that are paid witnesses in the courts of the United States.

§ 1626.17 Procedure for requesting an opinion letter.

(a) A request for an opinion letter should be submitted in writing to the Chair, Equal Employment Opportunity Commission, 2401 E Street, N.W., Washington, D.C. 20506, and shall contain:

(1) A concise statement of the issues on which an opinion is requested;

(2) As full a statement as possible of relevant facts and law; and

(3) The names and addresses of the person making the request and other interested persons.

(b) Issuance of an opinion letter by the Commission is discretionary.

(c) Informal Advice: When the Commission, at its discretion, determines that it will not issue an opinion letter as defined in § 1626.18, the Commission may provide informal advice or guidance to the requestor. An informal letter of advice does not represent the formal position of the Commission and does not commit the Commission to the views expressed therein. Any letter other than that defined in § 1626.18(a) will be considered a letter of advice and may not be relied upon by any employer within the meaning of section 10 of the Portal to Portal Act of 1947, incorporated into the Age Discrimination in Employment Act of 1967 through section 7(e)(1) of the Act.

§ 1626.18 Interpretations of the Commission.

(a) Section 10 of the Portal to Portal Act of 1947, incorporated into the Age Discrimination in Employment Act of 1967 through section 7(e)(1) of the Act, provides that:

In any action or proceeding based on any act or omission on or after the date of the enactment of this Act, no employer shall be subject to any liability or punishment . . . if he pleads and proves that the act or omission complained of was in good faith in conformity with and in reliance on any written administrative regulations, order, ruling, approval or interpretation, . . . or any administrative practice or enforcement policy of [the Commission.]

The Commission has determined that only (1) a written document, entitled "opinion letter" and signed by the General Counsel on behalf of the Commission or (2) a matter published and specifically designated as such in the **Federal Register** may be relied upon by any employer as a "written regulation, order, ruling, approval or interpretation" or "evidence of any administrative practice or enforcement policy" of the Commission "with respect to the class of employers to which he belongs," within the meaning of the statutory provisions quoted above.

(b) An opinion letter issued pursuant to § 1626.18(a) above, when issued to the specific addressee has no effect upon situations other than that of the specific addressee.

(c) When an opinion letter, as defined in § 1626.18(a), is requested, the procedure stated in § 1626.17 shall be followed.

§ 1626.19 Rules to be liberally construed.

(a) These rules and regulations shall be liberally construed to effectuate the purposes and provisions of this Act and any other acts administered by the Commission.

(b) Whenever the Commission receives a charge or obtains information relating to possible violations of one of the statutes which it administers and the charge or information reveals possible violations of one or more of the other statutes which it administers, the Commission will treat such charges or information in accordance with all such relevant statutes.

[FR Doc. 81-3576 Filed 1-29-81: 8:45 am]
BILLING CODE 6570-06-M

PART 1625—INTERPRETATIONS; AGE DISCRIMINATION IN EMPLOYMENT ACT

29 CFR Part 1625 is amended as follows:

1. In Part 1625, the table of contents is amended by adding the following sections:

Sec.
1625.1 Definitions.
1625.2 Discrimination between individuals protected by the Act.
1625.3 Employment agency.
1625.4 Help wanted notices or advertisements.
1625.5 Employment applications.
1625.6 Bona fide occupational qualifications.
1625.7 Differentiations based on reasonable factors other than age.
1625.8 Bona fide seniority systems.
1625.9 Prohibition of involuntary retirement.
1625.10 Costs and benefits under employee benefit plans.

* * * * *

1625.13 Apprenticeship programs.

2. The authority citation for Part 1625 is revised to read as follows:

Authority: 81 Stat. 602; 29 U.S.C. 621, 5 U.S.C. 301, Secretary's Order No. 10–68; Secretary's Order No. 11–68, and sec. 2; Reorg. Plan No. 1 of 1978, 43 FR 19807.

3. Sections 1625.1 through 1625.10 and 1625.13 are added to read as follows:

§ 1625.1 Definitions.

The Equal Employment Opportunity Commission is hereinafter referred to as the "Commission". The terms "person", "employer", "employment agency", "labor organization", and "employee" shall have the meanings set forth in Section 11 of the Age Discrimination in Employment Act of 1967, as amended, 29 U.S.C. 621 et seq., hereinafter referred to as the "Act". References to "employers" in this part state principles that are applicable not only to employers but also to labor organizations and to employment agencies.

§ 1625.2 Discrimination between individuals protected by the Act.

(a) It is unlawful in situations where this Act applies, for an employer to discriminate in hiring or in any other way by giving preference because of age between individuals within the 40–70 age bracket. Thus, if two people apply for the same position, and one is 42 and the other 52, the employer may not lawfully turn down either one on the basis of age, but must make such decision on the basis of some other factor.

(b) The extension of additional benefits, such as increased severance pay, to older employees within the protected age bracket may be lawful if an employer has a reasonable basis to conclude that those benefits will counteract problems related to age discrimination. The extension of those additional benefits may not be used as a means to accomplish practices otherwise prohibited by the Act.

§ 1625.3 Employment agency.

(a) As long as an employment agency regularly procures employees for at least one covered employer, it qualifies under section 11(c) of the Act as an employment agency with respect to all of its activities whether or not such activities are for employers covered by the act.

(b) The prohibitions of section 4(b) of the Act apply not only to the referral activities of a covered employment agency but also to the agency's own employment practices, regardless of the number of employees the agency may have.

§ 1625.4 Help wanted notices or advertisements.

(a) When help wanted notices or advertisements contain terms and phrases such as "age 25 to 35," "young," "college student," "recent college graduate," "boy," "girl," or others of a similar nature, such a term or phrase deters the employment of older persons and is a violation of the Act, unless one of the exceptions applies. Such phrases as "age 40 to 50," "age over 65," "retired person," or "supplement your pension" discriminate against others within the protected group and, therefore, are prohibited unless one of the exceptions applies.

(b) The use of the phrase "state age" in help wanted notices or advertisements is not, in itself, a violation of the Act. But because the request that an applicant state his age may tend to deter older applicants or otherwise indicate discrimination based on age, employment notices or advertisements which include the phrase "state age," or any similar term, will be closely scrutinized to assure that the request is for a lawful purpose.

§ 1625.5 Employment applications.

A request on the part of an employer for information such as "Date of Birth" or "State Age" on an employment application form is not, in itself, a violation of the Act. But because the request that an applicant state his age may tend to deter older applicants or otherwise indicate discrimination based on age, employment application forms which request such information will be closely scrutinized to assure that the request is for a permissible purpose and not for purposes proscribed by the Act. That the purpose is not one proscribed by the statute should be made known to the applicant, either by a reference on the application form to the statutory prohibition in language to the following effect: "The Age Discrimination in Employment Act of 1967 prohibits discrimination on the basis of age with respect to individuals who are at least 40 but less than 70 years of age," or by other means. The term "employment applications," refers to all written inquiries about employment or applications for employment or promotion including, but not limited to, résumés or other summaries of the applicant's background. It relates not only to written preemployment inquiries, but to inquiries by employees concerning terms, conditions, or privileges of employment as specified in section 4 of the Act.

§ 1625.6 Bona fide occupational qualifications.

(a) Whether occupational qualifications will be deemed to be "bona fide" to a specific job and "reasonably necessary to the normal operation of the particular business," will be determined on the basis of all the pertinent facts surrounding each particular situation. It is anticipated that this concept of a bona fide occupational qualification will have limited scope and application. Further, as this is an exception to the Act it must be narrowly construed.

(b) An employer asserting a BFOQ defense has the burden of proving that (1) the age limit is reasonably necessary to the essence of the business, and either (2) that all or substantially all individuals excluded from the job involved are in fact disqualified, or (3) that some of the individuals so excluded possess a disqualifying trait that cannot be ascertained except by reference to age. If the employer's objective in asserting a BFOQ is the goal of public safety, the employer must prove that the challenged practice does indeed effectuate that goal and that there is no acceptable alternative which would better advance it or equally advance it with less discriminatory impact.

(c) Many State and local governments have enacted laws or administrative regulations which limit employment opportunities based on age. Unless these laws meet the standards for the establishment of a valid bona fide occupational qualification under section 4(f)(1) of the Act, they will be considered in conflict with and effectively superseded by the ADEA.

§ 1625.7 Differentiations based on reasonable factors other than age.

(a) Section 4(f)(1) of the Act provides that

* * * it shall not be unlawful for an employer, employment agency, or labor organization * * * to take any action otherwise prohibited under paragraphs (a), (b), (c), or (e) of this section * * * where the differentiation is based on reasonable factors other than age * * *.

(b) No precise and unequivocal determination can be made as to the scope of the phrase "differentiation based on reasonable factors other than age." Whether such differentiations exist must be decided on the basis of all the particular facts and circumstances surrounding each individual situation.

(c) When an employment practice uses age as a limiting criterion, the defense that the practice is justified by a reasonable factor other than age is unavailable.

(d) When an employment practice, including a test, is claimed as a basis for different treatment of employees or applicants for employment on the grounds that it is a "factor other than" age, and such a practice has an adverse impact on individuals within the protected age group, it can only be justified as a business necessity. Tests which are asserted as "reasonable factors other than age" will be scrutinized in accordance with the standards set forth at Part 1607 of this Title.

(e) When the exception of "a reasonable factor other than age" is raised against an individual claim of discriminatory treatment, the employer bears the burden of showing that the "reasonable factor other than age" exists factually.

(f) A differentiation based on the average cost of employing older employees as a group is unlawful except with respect to employee benefit plans which qualify for the section 4(f)(2) exception to the Act.

§ 1625.8 Bona fide seniority systems.

Section 4(f)(2) of the Act provides that

* * * It shall not be unlawful for an employer, employment agency, or labor organization * * * to observe the terms of a bona fide seniority system * * * which is not a subterfuge to evade the purposes of this Act except that no such seniority system * * * shall require or permit the involuntary retirement of any individual specified by section 12(a) of this Act because of the age of such individual. * * *

(In the case of employees covered by a collective bargaining agreement which was in effect on September 1, 1977, which was entered into by a labor organization (as defined by section 6(d)(4) of the Fair Labor Standards Act), the provisions of this section with respect to involuntary retirement of individuals between the ages of 65 and 70 were effective upon the termination of the collective bargaining agreement or January 1, 1980, whichever occurred first.) (See also § 1625.9 (d) (e), and (f).)

(a) Though a seniority system may be qualified by such factors as merit, capacity, or ability, any bona fide seniority system must be based on length of service as the primary criterion for the equitable allocation of available employment opportunities and prerogatives among younger and older workers.

(b) Adoption of a purported seniority system which gives those with longer service lesser rights, and results in discharge or less favored treatment to those within the protection of the Act, may, depending upon the circumstances, be a "subterfuge to evade the purposes" of the Act.

(c) Unless the essential terms and conditions of an alleged seniority system have been communicated to the affected employees and can be shown to be applied uniformly to all of those affected, regardless of age, it will not be considered a bona fide seniority system within the meaning of the Act.

(d) It should be noted that seniority systems which segregate, classify, or otherwise discriminate against individuals on the basis of race, color, religion, sex, or national origin, are prohibited under Title VII of the Civil Rights Act of 1964, where that Act otherwise applies. The "bona fides" of such a system will be closely scrutinized to ensure that such a system is, in fact, bona fide under the ADEA.

§ 1625.9 Prohibition of involuntary retirement.

(a)(1) As originally enacted in 1967, section 4(f)(2) of the Act provided: "It shall not be unlawful * * * to observe the terms of a bona fide seniority system or any bona fide employee benefit plan such as a retirement, pension, or insurance plan, which is not a subterfuge to evade the purposes of this Act, except that no such employee benefit plan shall excuse the failure to hire any individual * * *." The Department of Labor interpreted the provision as "Authoriz[ing] involuntary retirement irrespective of age: *Provided*, That such retirement is pursuant to the terms of a retirement or pension plan meeting the requirements of section 4(f)(2)." *See* 29 CFR 860.110(a), 34 FR 9709 (June 21, 1969). The Department took the position that in order to meet the requirements of section 4(f)(2), the involuntary retirement provision had to be (i) contained in a bona fide pension or retirement plan, (ii) required by the terms of the plan and not optional, and (iii) essential to the plan's economic survival or to some other legitimate business purpose—i.e., the provision was not in the plan as the result of arbitrary discrimination on the basis of age.

(2) As revised by the 1978 amendments, section 4(f)(2) was amended by adding the following clause at the end: "and no such seniority system or employee benefit plan shall require or permit the involuntary retirement of any individual specified by section 12(a) of this Act because of the age of such individual * * *." The Conference Committee Report expressly states that this amendment is intended "to make absolutely clear one of the original purposes of this provision, namely, that the exception does not authorize an employer to require or permit involuntary retirement of an employee within the protected age group on account of age" (H.R. Rept. No. 95-950, p. 8).

(b)(1) The amendment applies to all new and existing seniority systems and employee benefit plans. Accordingly, any system or plan provision requiring or permitting involuntary retirement is unlawful, regardless of whether the provision antedates the 1967 Act or the 1978 amendments.

(2) Where lawsuits pending on the date of enactment (April 6, 1978) or filed thereafter challenge involuntary retirements which occurred either before or after that date, the amendment applies.

(c) The amendment protects all individuals covered by section 12(a) of the Act. Accordingly, before January 1, 1979 (the effective date of the amendment to section 12(a) which raised the upper age limit to 70), the amendment applied to individuals who were at least 40 years of age but less than 65 years of age. On and after that date it applies also to individuals who are at least 65 years of age but less than 70 years of age, unless otherwise exempt.

(d)(1) To allow time for the adjustment of collective bargaining agreements, the 1978 amendments provide that

* * * in the case of employees covered by a collective bargaining agreement which is in effect on September 1, 1977, which was entered into by a labor organization (as defined by section 6(d)(4) of the Fair Labor Standards Act of 1938), and which would otherwise be prohibited by the amendment (to section 12 of the Act), the amendment (to section 4(f)(2) of the Act) shall take effect upon the termination of such agreement or on January 1, 1980, whichever occurs first * * *

(Pub. L. 95-256, section 2(b), 92 Stat. 189)

(2) This delay of up to one year in the effective date of the amendment to section 4(f)(2) applies only to the protection afforded against involuntary retirement and affects only individuals who have attained 65 years of age but not 70 years of age on and after January 1, 1979. Such individuals may not be involuntarily retired unless (i) the retirement age specified in the plan is 65 or above; (ii) the retirement is authorized by the express terms of a bona fide seniority system or a bona fide employee benefit plan which is not a subterfuge to evade the purposes of the Act; and (iii) those terms have been adopted no later than September 1, 1977 and are pursuant to a collective bargaining agreement in effect on September 1, 1977. "Bona fide" shall have the same meaning as in § 860.120(b), as amended, 44 FR 30658 (May 25, 1979).

(3) Where a collective bargaining agreement expired prior to September 1, 1977, and a new agreement was signed subsequent to that date effective retroactively to the expiration date of the previous agreement, the exemption does not apply. The expressed congressional intent was to exempt only those agreements which had been "negotiated" before September 1, 1977 (see S. Rept. No. 95-493, 95th Cong., 1st Sess. (1977), p. 11; H.R. Rept. No. 95-527, Part 1, 95th Cong., 1st Sess. (1977), pp. 8-9).

(e) The exemption of up to one year is inapplicable after the expiration of the collective bargaining agreement in effect on September 1, 1977, whether or not the agreement is extended or renewed. The exemption is in no event applicable after January 1, 1980.

(f) Neither section 4(f)(2) nor any other provision of the Act makes it unlawful for a plan to permit individuals to elect early retirement at a specified age at their own option. Nor is it unlawful for a plan to require early retirement for reasons other than age.

§ 1625.10 Reserved for costs and benefits under employee benefit plans.

For currently applicable interpretations, see 29 CFR 860.120.

* * * * *

§ 1625.13 Apprenticeship programs.

Age limitations for entry into bona fide apprenticeship programs were not intended to be affected by the Act. Entry into most apprenticeship programs has traditionally been limited to youths under specified ages. This is in recognition of the fact that apprenticeship is an extension of the educational process to prepare young men and women for skilled employment. Accordingly, the prohibitions contained in the Act will not be applied to bona fide apprenticeship programs which meet the standards specified in §§ 521.2 and 521.3 of this chapter.

[FR Doc. 81-28222 Filed 9-28-81; 8:45 am]

BILLING CODE 6570-06-M

Federal Register
Vol. 44, No. 226
Wednesday,
November 21, 1979

Rules and Regulations

§ 1625.11 Exemption for employees serving under a contract of unlimited tenure.

(a)(1) Section 12(d) of the Act, added by the 1978 amendments, provides: "Nothing in this act shall be construed to prohibit compulsory retirement of any employee who has attained 65 years of age but not 70 years of age, and who is serving under a contract of unlimited tenure (or similar arrangement providing for unlimited tenure) at an institution of higher education (as defined by section 1201(a) of the Higher Education Act of 1965)."

(2) This exemption from the Act's protection of covered individuals took effect on January 1, 1979, and is repealed on July 1, 1982 (see sections 3(b)(1) and 3(b)(3) of the Age Discrimination in Employment Act Amendments of 1978, Pub. L. 95–256, 92 Stat. 189). Individuals who attain age 65 prior to July 1, 1982 and all of whose job duties and responsibilities cease prior to that date will not be considered outside the exemption merely because their contract (or similar arrangement) providing for unlimited tenure expires on or after July 1, 1982.

(b) Since section 12(d) is an exemption from the nondiscrimination requirements of the Act, the burden is on the one seeking to invoke the exemption to show that every element has been clearly and unmistakably met. Moreover, as with other exemptions from the ADEA, this exemption must be narrowly construed.

(c) Section 1201(a) of the Higher Education Act of 1965, as amended by 20 U.S.C. 403(b), provides in pertinent part:

The term "institution of higher education" means an educational institution in any state which (1) admits as regular students only persons having a certificate of graduation from a school providing secondary education, or the recognized equivalent of such certificate, (2) is legally authorized within such State to provide a program of education beyond secondary education, (3) provides an educational program for which it awards a bachelor's degree or provides not less than a two-year program which is acceptable for full credit toward such a degree, (4) is a public or other nonprofit institution, and (5) is accredited by a nationally recognized accrediting agency or association approved by the Commissioner (of Education) for this purpose or, if not so accredited, (A) is an institution with respect to which the Commissioner has determined that there is satisfactory assurance, considering the resources available to the institution, the period of time if any, during which it has operated, the effort it is making to meet accreditation standards, and the purpose for which this determination is being made, that the institution will meet the accreditation standards of such an agency or association within a reasonable time, or (B) is an institution whose credits are accepted on transfer by not less than three institutions which are so accredited, for credit on the same basis as if transferred from an institution so accredited.* * *

The definition encompasses almost all public and private universities and two- and four-year colleges. The omitted portion of the text of section 1201(a) refers largely to one-year technical schools, which generally do not grant tenure to employees, but which, if they do, are also eligible to claim the exemption.

(d)(1) Use of the term "any employee" indicates that application of the exemption is not limited to teachers, who are traditional recipients of tenure. The exemption may also be available with respect to other groups, such as academic deans, scientific researchers, professional librarians and counseling staff, who frequently have tenured status.

(2) The Conference Committee Report on the 1978 amendments expressly states that the exemption does not apply to Federal employees covered by section 15 of the Act (H.R. Rept. No. 95–950, p. 10).

(e)(1) The phrase "unlimited tenure" is not defined in the Act. However, the almost universally accepted definition of academic "tenure" is an arrangement under which certain appointments in an institution of higher education are continued until retirement for age of physical disability, subject to dismissal for adequate cause or under extraordinary circumstances on account of financial exigency or change of institutional program. Adopting that definition, it is evident that the word "unlimited" refers to the duration of tenure. Therefore, a contract (or other similar arrangement) which is limited to a specific term (for example, one year or 10 years) will not meet the requirements of the exemption.

(2) The legislative history shows that Congress intented the exemption to apply only where the minimum rights and privileges traditionally associated with tenure are guaranteed to an employee by contract or similar arrangement. While tenure policies and practices vary greatly from one institution to another, the minimum standards set forth in the 1940 Statement of Principles on Academic Freedom and Tenure, jointly developed by the Association of American Colleges and the American Association of University Professors, have enjoyed widespread adoption or endorsement. The 1940 Statement of Principles on academic tenure provides as follows:

(a) After the expiration of a probationary period, teachers or investigators should have permanent or continuous tenure, and their service should be terminated only for adequate cause, except in the case of retirement for age, or under extraordinary circumstances because of financial exigencies.

In the interpretation of this principle it is understood that the following represents acceptable academic practice:

(1) The precise terms and conditions of every appointment should be stated in writing and be in the possession of both institution and teacher before the appointment is consumated.

(2) Beginning with appointment to the rank of full-time instructor or a higher rank, the probationary period should not exceed seven years, including within this period full-time service in all institutions of higher education; but subject to the proviso that when, after a term of probationary service of more than three years in one or more institutions, a teacher is called to another institution it may be agreed in writing that his new appointment is for a probationary period of not more than four years, even though thereby the person's total probationary period in the academic profession is extended beyond the normal maximum of seven years. Notice should be given at least

one year prior to the expiration of the probationary period if the teacher is not to be continued in service after the expiration of that period.

(3) During the probationary period a teacher should have the academic freedom that all other members of the faculty have.

(4) Termination for cause of a continuous appointment, or the dismissal for cause of a teacher previous to the expiration of a term appointment, should, if possible, be considered by both a faculty committee and the governing board of the institution. In all cases where the facts are in dispute, the accused teacher should be informed before the hearing in writing of the charges against him and should have the opportunity to be heard in his own defense by all bodies that pass judgment upon his case. He should be permitted to have with him an advisor of his own choosing who may act as counsel. There should be a full stenographic record of the hearing available to the parties concerned. In the hearing of charges of incompetence the testimony should include that of teachers and other scholars, either from his own or from other institutions. Teachers on continuous appointment who are dismissed for reasons not involving moral turpitude should receive their salaries for at least a year from the date of notification of dismissal whether or not they are continued in their duties at the institution.

(5) Termination of a continuous appointment because of financial exigency should be demonstrably bona fide.

(3) A contract or similar arrangement which meets the standards in the 1940 Statement of Principles will satisfy the tenure requirements of the exemption. However, a tenure arrangement will not be deemed inadequate solely because it fails to meet these standards in every respect. For example, a tenure plan will not be deemed inadequate solely because it includes a probationary period somewhat longer than seven years. Of course, the greater the deviation from the standards in the 1940 Statement of Principles, the less likely it is that the employee in question will be deemed subject to "unlimited tenure" within the meaning of the exemption. Whether or not a tenure arrangement is adequate to satisfy the requirements of the exemption must be determined on the basis of the facts of each case.

(f) Employees who are not assured of a continuing appointment either by contract of unlimited tenure or other similar arrangement (such as a state statute) would not, of course, be exempted from the prohibitions against compulsory retirement, even if they perform functions identical to those performed by employees with appropriate tenure.

(g) An employee within the exemption can lawfully be forced to retire on account of age at age 65 or above. In addition, the employer is free to retain such employees, either in the same position or status or in a different position or status: *Provided,* That the employee voluntarily accepts this new position or status. For example, an employee who falls within the exemption may be offered a nontenured position or part-time employment. An employee who accepts a nontenured position or part-time employment, however, may not be treated any less favorably, on account of age, than any similarly situated younger employee (unless such less favorable treatment is excused by an exception to the Act).

§ 1625.12 Exemption for bona fide executive or high policymaking employees.

(a) Section 12(c)(1) of the Act, added by the 1978 amendments, provides: "Nothing in this Act shall be construed to prohibit compulsory retirement of any employee who has attained 65 years of age but not 70 years of age, and who, for the 2-year period immediately before retirement, is employed in a bona fide executive or a high policymaking position, if such employee is entitled to an immediate nonforfeitable annual retirement benefit from a pension, profit-sharing, savings, or deferred compensation plan, or any combination of such plans, of the employer of such employee which equals, in the aggregate, at least $27,000."

(b) Since this provision is an exemption from the non-discrimination requirements of the Act, the burden is on the one seeking to invoke the exemption to show that every element has been clearly and unmistakably met. Moreover, as with other exemptions from the Act, this exemption must be narrowly construed.

(c) An employee within the exemption can lawfully be forced to retire on account of age at age 65 or above. In addition, the employer is free to retain such employees, either in the same position or status or in a different position or status. For example, an employee who falls within the exemption may be offered a position of lesser status or a part-time position. An employee who accepts such a new status or position, however, may not be treated any less favorably, on account of age, than any similarly situated younger employee.

(d)(1) In order for an employee to qualify as a "bona fide executive," the employer must initially show that the employee satisfies the definition of a bona fide executive set forth in § 541.1 of this chapter. Each of the requirements in paragraphs (a) through (e) of § 541.1 must be satisfied, regardless of the level of the employee's salary or compensation.

(2) Even if an employee qualifies as an executive under the definition in § 541.1 of this chapter, the exemption from the ADEA may not be claimed unless the employee also meets the further criteria specified in the Conference Committee Report in the form of examples (see H.R. Rept. No. 95-950, p. 9). The examples are intended to make clear that the exemption does not apply to middle-management employees, no matter how great their retirement income, but only to a very few top level employees who exercise substantial executive authority over a significant number of employees and a large volume of business. As stated in the Conference Report (H.R. Rept. No. 95-950, p. 9):

Typically the head of a significant and substantial local or regional operation of a corporation [or other business organization], such as a major production facility or retail establishment, but not the head of a minor branch, warehouse or retail store, would be covered by the term "bona fide executive." Individuals at higher levels in the corporate organizational structure who possess comparable or greater levels of responsibility and authority as measured by established and recognized criteria would also be covered.

The heads of major departments or divisions of corporations [or other business organizations] are usually located at corporate or regional headquarters. With respect to employees whose duties are associated with corporate headquarters operations, such as finance, marketing, legal, production and manufacturing (or in a corporation organized on a product line basis, the management of product lines), the definition would cover employees who head those divisions.

In a large organization the immediate subordinates of the heads of these divisions sometimes also exercise executive authority, within the meaning of this exemption. The conferees intend the definition to cover such employees if they possess responsibility which is comparable to or greater than that possessed by the head of a significant and substantial local operation who meets the definition.

(e) The phrase "high policymaking position," according to the Conference Report (H.R. Rept. No. 95-950, p. 10), is limited to "* * * certain top level employees who are not 'bona fide executives' * * *." Specifically, these are:

* * * individuals who have little or no line authority but whose position and responsibility are such that they play a significant role in the development of corporate policy and effectively recommend the implementation thereof.

For example, the chief economist or the chief research scientist of a corporation typically has little line authority. His duties would be primarily intellectual as opposed to executive or managerial. His responsibility would be to evaluate significant economic or scientific trends and issues, to develop and recommend policy direction to the top executive officers of the corporation, and he would have a significant impact on the ultimate decision on such policies by virtue of his expertise and direct access to the decisionmakers. Such an employee would meet the definition of a "high policymaking" employee.

On the other hand, as this description makes clear, the support personnel of a "high policymaking" employee would not be subject to the exemption even if they supervise the development, and draft the recommendation, of various policies submitted by their supervisors.

(f) In order for the exemption to apply to a particular employee, the employee must have been in a "bona fide executive or high policymaking position," as those terms are defined in this section, for the two-year period immediately before retirement. Thus, an employee who holds two or more different positions during the two-year period is subject to the exemption only if each such job is an executive or high policymaking position.

(g) The Conference Committee Report expressly states that the exemption is not applicable to Federal employees covered by section 15 of the Act (H.R. Rept. No. 95–950, p. 10).

(h) The "annual retirement benefit," to which covered employees must be entitled, is the sum of amounts payable during each one-year period from the date on which such benefits first become receivable by the retiree. Once established, the annual period upon which calculations are based may not be changed from year to year.

(i) The annual retirement benefit must be immediately available to the employee to be retired pursuant to the exemption. For purposes of determining compliance, "immediate" means that the payment of plan benefits (in a lump sum or the first of a series of periodic payments) must occur not later than 60 days after the effective date of the retirement in question. The fact that an employee will receive benefits only after expiration of the 60-day period will not preclude his retirement pursuant to the exemption, if the employee could have elected to receive benefits within that period.

(j)(1) The annual retirement benefit must equal, in the aggregate, at least $27,000. The manner of determining whether this requirement has been satisfied is set forth in § 1627.17(c).

(2) In determining whether the aggregate annual retirement benefit equals at least $27,000, the only benefits which may be counted are those authorized by and provided under the terms of a pension, profit-sharing, savings, or deferred compensation plan. (Regulations issued pursuant to section 12(c)(2) of the Act, regarding the manner of calculating the amount of qualified retirement benefits for purposes of the exemption, are set forth in § 1627.17 of this Chapter.)

(k)(1) The annual retirement benefit must be "nonforfeitable." Accordingly, the exemption may not be applied to any employee subject to plan provisions which could cause the cessation of payments to a retiree or result in the reduction of benefits to less than $27,000 in any one year. For example, where a plan contains a provision under which benefits would be suspended if a retiree engages in litigation against the former employer, or obtains employment with a competitor of the former employer, the retirement benefit will be deemed to be forfeitable. However, retirement benefits will not be deemed forfeitable solely because the benefits are discontinued or suspended for reasons permitted under section 411(a)(3) of the Internal Revenue Code.

(2) An annual retirement benefit will not be deemed forfeitable merely because the minimum statutory benefit level is not guaranteed against the possibility of plan bankruptcy or is subject to benefit restrictions in the event of early termination of the plan in accordance with Treasury Regulation 1.401–4(c). However, as of the effective date of the retirement in question, there must be at least a reasonable expectation that the plan will meet its obligations.

[FR Doc. 79–36003 Filed 11–20–79; 8:45 am]
BILLING CODE 6570-06-M

EQUAL EMPLOYMENT OPPORTUNITY COMMISSION

29 CFR Parts 850, 1627

Records To Be Made or Kept Relating to Age; Notices To Be Posted; Administrative Exemptions; Recodification of 29 CFR Part 850

AGENCY: Equal Employment Opportunity Commission.

ACTION: Final rule.

SUMMARY: Pursuant to Reorganization Plan No. 1 of 1978, 43 FR 19807 (May 9, 1978), responsibility and authority for enforcement of the Age Discrimination in Employment Act of 1967, as amended, 29 U.S.C. 621 et seq. was transferred from the Department of Labor to the Equal Employment Opportunity Commission. The transfer became effective and the Commission assumed enforcement of this Act on July 1, 1979.

In order to assist the Commission in the performance of its duties under the Act and in order to provide for continuity in enforcement of the Act, the Commission has adopted, with only minor changes to reflect the transfer of authority to the Commission, the recordkeeping requirements and administrative exemption provisions of the Department of Labor as set forth in 29 CFR Part 850.

EFFECTIVE DATE: July 2, 1979.

FOR FURTHER INFORMATION CONTACT:
Constance L. Dupre, Associate General Counsel, Legal Counsel Division, Office of the General Counsel, Room 2254, EEOC, 2401 E Street, N.W., Washington, D.C. 20506, (202) 634-6595.

Signed this 27th day of June, 1979.

For the Commission.

Eleanor Holmes Norton,
Chair, EEOC.

Accordingly, the adopted regulations of the Equal Employment Opportunity Commission, 29 CFR Part 1627, read as follows:

PART 1627—RECORDS TO BE MADE OR KEPT RELATING TO AGE: NOTICES TO BE POSTED: ADMINISTRATIVE EXEMPTIONS

Subpart A—General

Sec.
1627.1 Purpose and scope.

Subpart B—Records to be Made or Kept Relating to Age; Notices To Be Posted

1627.2 Forms of records.
1627.3 Records to be kept by employers.
1627.4 Records to be kept by employment agencies.
1627.5 Records to be kept by labor organizations.
1627.6 Availability of records for inspection.
1627.7 Transcription and reports.
1627.8–1627.9 [Reserved]
1627.10 Notices to be posted.
1627.11 Petitions for recordkeeping exceptions.

Subpart C—Administrative Exemptions

1627.15 Administrative exemptions; procedures.
1627.16 Specific exemptions.

Authority: Sec. 7, 81 Stat. 604; 29 U.S.C. 626; sec. 11, 52 Stat. 1066, as amended, 29 U.S.C.; sec. 2, Reorg. Plan No. 1 of 1978, 43 FR 19807.

§ 1627.1 Purpose and scope.

(a) Section 7 of the Age Discrimination in Employment Act of 1967 (hereinafter referred to in this part as the Act) empowers the Commission to require the keeping of records which are necessary or appropriate for the administration of the Act in accordance with the powers contained in section 11 of the Fair Labor Standards Act of 1938. Subpart B of this part sets forth the recordkeeping and posting requirements which are prescribed by the Commission for employers, employment agencies, and labor organizations which are subject to the Act. Reference should be made to section 11 of the Act for definitions of the terms "employer", "employment agency", and "labor organization". General interpretations of the Act and of this part are published in Part 1625 of this chapter. This part also reflects pertinent delegations of the Commission's duties.

(b) Subpart C of this part sets forth the Commission's rules under section 9 of the Act providing that the Commission may establish reasonable exemptions to and from any or all provisions of the Act as it may find necessary and proper in the public interest.

Subpart B—Records To Be Made or Kept Relating to Age; Notices To Be Posted

§ 1627.2 Forms of records.

No particular order or form of records is required by the regulations in this Part 1627. It is required only that the records contain in some form the information specified. If the information required is available in records kept for other purposes, or can be obtained readily by recomputing or extending data recorded in some other form, no further records are required to be made or kept on a routine basis by this Part 1627.

§ 1627.3 Records to be kept by employers.

(a) Every employer shall make and keep for 3 years payroll or other records for each of his employees which contain:
(1) Name;
(2) Address;
(3) Date of birth;
(4) Occupation;
(5) Rate of pay, and
(6) Compensation earned each week.

(b)(1) Every employer who, in the regular course of his business, makes, obtains, or uses, any personnel or employment records related to the following, shall, except as provided in subparagraphs (3) and (4) of this paragraph, keep them for a period of 1 year from the date of the personnel action to which any records relate:

(i) Job applications, resumes, or any other form of employment inquiry whenever submitted to the employer in response to his advertisement or other notice of existing or anticipated job openings, including records pertaining to the failure or refusal to hire any individual,

(ii) Promotion, demotion, transfer, selection for training, layoff, recall, or discharge of any employee,

(iii) Job orders submitted by the employer to an employment agency or labor organization for recruitment of personnel for job openings,

(iv) Test papers completed by applicants or candidates for any position which disclose the results of any employer-administered aptitude or other employment test considered by the employer in connection with any personnel action,

(v) The results of any physical examination where such examination is considered by the employer in connection with any personnel action,

(vi) Any advertisements or notices to the public or to employees relating to job openings, promotions, training programs, or opportunities for overtime work.

(2) Every employer shall keep on file any employee benefit plans such as pension and insurance plans, as well as copies of any seniority systems and merit systems which are in writing, for the full period the plan or system is in effect, and for at least 1 year after its termination. If the plan or system is not in writing, a memorandum fully outlining the terms of such plan or system and the manner in which it has been communicated to the affected employees, together with notations relating to any changes or revisions thereto, shall be kept on file for a like period.

(3) In the case of application forms and other preemployment records of applicants for positions which are, and are known by applicants to be, of a temporary nature, every record required to be kept under subparagraph (1) of this paragraph shall be kept for a period of 90 days from the date of the personnel action to which the record relates.

(4) When an enforcement action is commenced under section 7 of the Act regarding a particular applicant or employee, the Commission or its authorized representative may require the employer to retain any record required to be kept under subparagraph (1), (2), or (3) of this paragraph which is relative to such action until the final disposition thereof.

§ 1627.4 Records to be kept by employment agencies.

(a)(1) Every employment agency which, in the regular course of its business, makes, obtains, or uses, any records related to the following, shall, except as provided in subparagraphs (2) and (3) of this paragraph, keep them for a period of 1 year from the date of the action to which the records relate:

(i) Placements;

(ii) Referrals, where an individual is referred to an employer for a known or reasonably anticipated job opening;

(iii) Job orders from employers seeking individuals for job openings;

(iv) Job applications, resumes, or any other form of employment inquiry or record of any individual which identifies his qualifications for employment, whether for a known job opening at the time of submission or for future referral to an employer;

(v) Test papers completed by applicants or candidates for any position which disclose the results of any agency-administered aptitude or other employment test considered by the agency in connection with any referrals;

(vi) Advertisements or notices relative to job openings.

(2) In the case of application forms and other preemployment records of applicants for positions which are, and are known by applicants to be, of a temporary nature, every record required to be kept under subparagraph (1) of this paragraph shall be kept for a period of 90 days from the date of the making or obtaining of the record involved.

(3) When an enforcement action is commenced under section 7 of the Act regarding a particular applicant, the Commission or its authorized representative may require the employment agency to retain any record required to be kept under subparagraph (1) or (2) of this paragraph which is relative to such action until the final disposition thereof.

(b) Whenever an employment agency has an obligation as an "employer" or a "labor organization" under the Act, the employment agency must also comply with the recordkeeping requirements set forth in § 1627.3 or § 1627.5, as appropriate.

§ 1627.5 Records to be kept by labor organizations.

(a) Every labor organization shall keep current records identifying its members by name, address, and date of birth.

(b) Every labor organization shall, except as provided in paragraph (c) of this section, keep for a period of 1 year from the making thereof, a record of the name, address, and age of any individual seeking membership in the organization. An individual seeking membership is considered to be a person who files an application for membership or who, in some other manner, indicates a specific intention to be considered for membership, but does not include any individual who is serving for a stated limited probational period prior to permanent employment and formal union membership. A person who merely makes an inquiry about the labor organization or, for example, about its general program, is not considered to be an individual seeking membership in a labor organization.

(c) When an enforcement action is commenced under section 7 of the Act regarding a labor organization, the Commission or its authorized representative may require the labor organization to retain any record required to be kept under paragraph (b) of this section which is relative to such action until the final disposition thereof.

(d) Whenever a labor organization has an obligation as an "employer" or as an "employment agency" under the Act, the labor organization must also comply with the recordkeeping requirements set forth in § 1627.3 or § 1627.4, as appropriate.

§ 1627.6 Availability of records for inspection.

(a) *Place records are to be kept.* The records required to be kept by this part shall be kept safe and accessible at the place of employment or business at which the individual to whom they relate is employed or has applied for employment or membership, or at one or more established central recordkeeping offices.

(b) *Inspection of records.* All records required by this part to be kept shall be made available for inspection and transcription by authorized representatives of the Commission during business hours generally observed by the office at which they are kept or in the community generally. Where records are maintained at a central recordkeeping office pursuant to paragraph (a) of this section, such records shall be made available at the office at which they would otherwise be required to be kept within 72 hours following request from the Commission or its authorized representative.

§ 1627.7 Transcriptions and reports.

Every person required to maintain records under the Act shall make such extension, recomputation or transcriptions of his records and shall submit such reports concerning actions taken and limitations and classifications of individuals set forth in records as the Commission or its authorized representative may request in writing.

§ 1627.8–1627.9 [Reserved]

§ 1627.10 Notices to be posted.

Every employer, employment agency, and labor organization which has an obligation under the Age Discrimination in Employment Act of 1967 shall post and keep posted in conspicuous places upon its premises the notice pertaining to the applicability of the Act prescribed by the Commission or its authorized representative. Such a notice must be posted in prominent and accessible places where it can readily be observed by employees, applicants for employment and union members.

§ 1627.11 Petitions for recordkeeping exceptions.

(a) *Submission of petitions for relief.* Each employer, employment agency, or labor organization who for good cause wishes to maintain records in a manner other than required in this part, or to be relieved of preserving certain records for the period or periods prescribed in this part, may submit in writing a petition to the Commission requesting such relief setting forth the reasons therefor and proposing alternative recordkeeping or record-retention procedures.

(b) *Action on petitions.* If, no review of the petition and after completion of any necessary or appropriate investigation supplementary thereto, the Commission shall find that the alternative procedure proposed, if granted, will not hamper or interfere with the enforcement of the Act, and will be of equivalent usefulness in its enforcement, the Commission may grant the petition subject to such conditions as it may determine appropriate and subject to revocation. Whenever any relief granted to any person is sought to be revoked for failure to comply with the conditions of the Commission, that person shall be notified in writing of the facts constituting such failure and afforded an opportunity to achieve or demonstrate compliance.

(c) *Compliance after submission of petitions.* The submission of a petition or any delay of the Commission in acting upon such petition shall not relieve any employer, employment agency, or labor organization from any obligations to comply with this part. However, the Commission shall give notice of the denial of any petition with due promptness.

Subpart C—Administrative Exemptions

§ 1627.15 Administrative exemptions; procedures.

(a) Section 9 of the Act provides that, "In accordance with the provisions of subchapter II of chapter 5, of title 5, United States Code, the Secretary of Labor * * * may establish such reasonable exemptions to and from any or all provisions of this Act as he may find necessary and proper in the public interest."

(b) The authority conferred on the Commission by section 9 of the Act to establish reasonable exemptions will be exercised with caution and due regard for the remedial purpose of the statute to promote employment of older persons based on their ability rather than age and to prohibit arbitrary age discrimination in employment. Administrative action consistent with this statutory purpose may be taken under this section, with or without a request therefor, when found necessary and proper in the public interest in accordance with the statutory standards. No formal procedures have been prescribed for requesting such action. However, a reasonable exemption from the Act's provisions will be granted only if it is decided, after notice published in the **Federal Register** giving all interested persons an opportunity to present data, views, or arguments, that a strong and affirmative showing has been made that such exemption is in fact necessary and proper in the public interest. Request for such exemption shall be submitted in writing to the Commission.

§ 1627.16 Specific exemptions.

(a) Pursuant to the authority contained in section 9 of the Act and in accordance with the procedure provided therein and in § 1627.15(b) of this part, it has been found necessary and proper in the public interest to exempt from all prohibitions of the Act all activities and programs under Federal contracts or grants, or carried out by the public employment services of the several States, designed exclusively to provide employment for, or to encourage the employment of, persons with special employment problems, including employment activities and programs under the Manpower Development and Training Act of 1962, as amended, and the Economic Opportunity Act of 1964, as amended, for persons among the long-term unemployed, handicapped, members of minority groups, older workers, or youth. Questions concerning the application of this exemption shall be referred to the Commission for decision.

(b) Any employer, employment agency, or labor organization the activities of which are exempt from the prohibitions of the Act under paragraph (a) of this section shall maintain and preserve records containing the same information and data that is required of employers, employment agencies, and labor organizations under §§ 1627.3, 1627.4, and 1627.5, respectively.

[FR Doc. 79–20336 Filed 6–29–79; 8:45 am]

BILLING CODE 6570-06-M

Accordingly, new §§ 1625.11, 1625.12, 1627.17, and new paragraph (c) of § 1627.1 are added to Title 29, Code of Federal Regulations.

Subpart A—General

§ 1627.1 Purpose and scope.

* * * * *

(c) Subpart D of this part sets forth the Commission's regulations issued pursuant to section 12(c)(2) of the Act, providing that the Secretary of Labor, after consultation with the Secretary of the Treasury, shall prescribe the manner of calculating the amount of qualified retirement benefits for purposes of the exemption in section 12(c)(1) of the Act.

* * * * *

Subpart D—Statutory Exemption

§ 1627.17 Calculating the amount of qualified retirement benefits for purposes of the exemption for bona fide executives or high policymaking employees.

(a) Section 12(c)(1) of the Act, added by the 1978 amendments, provides: "Nothing in this Act shall be construed to prohibit compulsory retirement of any employee who has attained 65 years of age but not 70 years of age, and who, for the 2-year period immediately before retirement, is employed in a bona fide executive or a high policymaking position, if such employee is entitled to an immediate nonforfeitable annual retirement benefit from a pension, profit-sharing, savings, or deferred compensation plan, or any combination of such plans, of the employer of such employee, which equals, in the aggregate, at least $27,000." The Commission's interpretative statements regarding this exemption are set forth in § 1625 of this chapter.

(b) Section 12(c)(2) of the Act provides:

In applying the retirement benefit test of paragraph (a) of this subsection, if any such retirement benefit is in a form other than a straight life annuity (with no ancillary benefits), or if employees contribute to any such plan or make rollover contributions, such benefit shall be adjusted in accordance with regulations prescribed by the Commission, after consultation with the Secretary of the Treasury, so that the benefit is the equivalent of a straight life annuity (with no ancillary benefits) under a plan to which employees do not contribute and under which no rollover contributions are made.

(c)(1) The requirement that an employee be entitled to the equivalent of a $27,000 straight life annuity (with no ancillary benefits) is satisfied in any case where the employee has the option of receiving, during each year of his or her lifetime following retirement, an annual payment of at least $27,000, or periodic payments on a more frequent basis which, in the aggregate, equal at least $27,000 per year: *Provided, however,* That the portion of the retirement income figure attributable to Social Security, employee contributions, rollover contributions and contributions of prior employers is excluded in the manner described in paragraph (e) of this section. (A retirement benefit which excludes these amounts is sometimes referred to herein as a "qualified" retirement benefit.)

(2) The requirement is also met where the employee has the option of receiving, upon retirement, a lump sum payment with which it is possible to purchase a single life annuity (with no ancillary benefits) yielding at least $27,000 per year as adjusted.

(3) The requirement is also satisfied where the employee is entitled to receive, upon retirement, benefits whose aggregate value, as of the date of the employee's retirement, with respect to those payments which are scheduled to be made within the period of life expectancy of the employee, is $27,000 per year as adjusted.

(4) Where an employee has one or more of the options described in paragraphs (c) (1)–(3) of this section, but instead selects another option (or

options), the test is also met. On the other hand, where an employee has no choice but to have certain benefits provided after his or her death, the value of these benefits may not be included in this determination.

(5) The determination of the value of those benefits which may be counted towards the $27,000 requirement must be made on the basis of reasonable actuarial assumptions with respect to mortality and interest. For purposes of excluding from this determination any benefits which are available only after death, it is not necessary to determine the life expectancy of each person on an individual basis. A reasonable actuarial assumption with respect to mortality will suffice.

(6) The benefits computed under paragraphs (c)(1), (2) and (3) of this section shall be aggregated for purposes of determining whether the $27,000 requirement has been met.

(d) The only retirement benefits which may be counted towards the $27,000 annual benefit are those from a pension, profit-sharing, savings, or deferred compensation plan, or any combination of such plans. Such plans include, but are not limited to, stock bonus, thrift and simplified employee pensions. The value of benefits from any other employee benefit plans, such as health or life insurance, may not be counted.

(e) In calculating the value of a pension, profit-sharing, savings, or deferred compensation plan (or any combination of such plans), amounts attributable to Social Security, employee contributions, contributions of prior employers, and rollover contributions must be excluded. Specific rules are set forth below.

(1) *Social Security.* Amounts attributable to Social Security must be excluded. Since these amounts are readily determinable, no specific rules are deemed necessary.

(2) *Employee contributions.* Amounts attributable to employee contributions must be excluded. The regulations governing this requirement are based on section 411(c) of the Internal Revenue Code and Treasury Regulations thereunder (§ 1.411(c)–(1)), relating to the allocation of accrued benefits between employer and employee contributions. Different calculations are needed to determine the amount of employee contributions, depending upon whether the retirement income plan is a defined contribution plan or a defined benefit plan. Defined contribution plans (also referred to as individual account plans) generally provide that each participant has an individual account and the participant's benefits are based solely on the account balance. No set benefit is promised in defined contribution plans, and the final amount is a result not only of the actual contributions, but also of other factors, such as investment gains and losses. Any retirement income plan which is not an individual account plan is a defined benefit plan. Defined benefit plans generally provide a definitely determinable benefit, by specifying either a flat monthly payment or a schedule of payments based on a formula (frequently involving salary and years of service), and they are funded according to actuarial principles over the employee's period of participation.

(i) *Defined contribution plans.*—(A) *Separate accounts maintained.* If a separate account is maintained with respect to an employee's contributions and all income, expenses, gains and losses attributable thereto, the balance in such an account represents the amount attributable to employee contributions.

(B) *Separate accounts not maintained.* If a separate account is not maintained with respect to an employee's contributions and the income, expenses, gains and losses attributable thereto, the proportion of the total benefit attributable to employee contributions is determined by multiplying that benefit by a fraction—

(1) The numerator of which is the total amount of the employee's contributions under the plan (less withdrawals), and

(2) The denominator of which is the sum of the numerator and the total contributions made under the plan by the employer on behalf of the employee (less withdrawals).

Example: A defined contribution plan does not maintain separate accounts for employee contributions. An employee's annual retirement benefit under the plan is $40,000. The employee has contributed $96,000 and the employer has contributed $144,000 to the employee's individual account; no withdrawals have been made. The amount of the $40,000 annual benefit attributable to employee contributions is $40,000 × $96,000/$96,000 + $144,000 = $16,000. Hence the employer's share of the $40,000 annual retirement benefit is $40,000 minus $16,000 or $24,000—too low to fall within the exemption.

(ii) *Defined benefit plans*—(A) *Separate accounts maintained.* If a separate account is maintained with respect to an employee's contributions and all income, expenses, gains and losses attributable thereto, the balance in such an account represents the amount attributable to employee contributions.

(B) *Separate accounts not maintained.* If a separate account is not maintained with respect to an employee's contributions and the income, expenses, gains and losses attributable thereto, all of the contributions made by an employee must be converted actuarially to a single life annuity (without ancillary benefits) commencing at the age of forced retirement. An employee's accumulated contributions are the sum of all contributions (mandatory and, if not separately accounted for, voluntary) made by the employee, together with interest on the sum of all such contributions compounded annually at the rate of 5 percent per annum from the time each such contribution was made until the date of retirement. *Provided, however,* That prior to the date any plan became subject to section 411(c) of the Internal Revenue Code, interest will be credited at the rate (if any) specified in the plan. The amount of the employee's accumulated contribution described in the previous sentence must be multiplied by an "appropriate conversion factor" in order to convert it to a single life annuity (without ancillary benefits) commencing at the age of actual retirement. The appropriate conversion factor depends upon the age of retirement. In accordance with Rev. Rul. 76–47, 1976–2 C.B. 109, the following conversion factors shall be used with respect to the specified retirement ages:

Retirement age:	Conversion factor percent
65 through 66	10
67 through 68	11
69	12

Example: An employee is scheduled to receive a pension from a defined benefit plan of $50,000 per year. Over the years he has contributed $150,000 to the plan, and at age 65 this amount, when contributions have been compounded at appropriate annual interest rates, is equal to $240,000. In accordance with Rev. Rul. 76–47, 10 percent is an appropriate conversion factor. When the $240,000 is multiplied by this conversion factor, the product is $24,000, which represents that part of the $50,000 annual pension payment which is attributable to employee contributions. The difference—$26,000—represents the employer's contribution, which is too low to meet the test in the exemption.

(3) *Contributions of prior employers.* Amounts attributable to contributions of prior employers must be excluded.

(i) *Current employer distinguished from prior employers.* Under the section 12(c) exemption, for purposes of excluding contributions of prior employers, a prior employer is every previous employer of the employee except those previous employers which are members of a "controlled group of corporations" with, or "under common control" with, the employer which forces the employee to retire, as those terms are used in sections 414 (b) and 414(c) of the Internal Revenue Code, as modified by section 414(h) (26 U.S.C. 414(b), (c) and (h)).

(ii) *Benefits attributable to current employer and to prior employers.* Where the current employer maintains or contributes to a plan which is separate from plans maintained or contributed to by prior employers, the amount of the employee's benefit attributable to those prior employers can be readily determined. However, where the current employer maintains or contributes to the same plan as prior employers, the following rule shall apply. The benefit attributable to the current employer shall be the total benefit received by the employee, reduced by the benefit that the employee would have received from the plan if he or she had never worked for the current employer. For purposes of this calculation, it shall be assumed that all benefits have always been vested, even if benefits accrued as a result of service with a prior employer had not in fact been vested.

(4) *Rollover contributions.* Amounts attributable to rollover contributions must be excluded. For purposes of § 1627.17(e), a rollover contribution (as defined in sections 402(a)(5), 403(a)(4), 408(d)(3) and 409(b)(3)(C) of the Internal Revenue Code) shall be treated as an employee contribution. These amounts have already been excluded as a result of the computations set forth in § 1627.17(e)(2). Accordingly, no separate calculation is necessary to comply with this requirement.

EQUAL EMPLOYMENT OPPORTUNITY COMMISSION

29 CFR Part 1625

Interpretations; Age Discrimination in Employment Act; Correction

AGENCY: Equal Employment Opportunity Commission.

ACTION: Final rule correction.

SUMMARY: On November 21, 1979, the Equal Employment Opportunity Commission published in the **Federal Register** two final interpretations under the Age Discrimination in Employment Act of 1967, as amended, 29 U.S.C. 621 *et seq.* (FR DOC 79–36003, 44 FR 66791). Inadvertently, the amendatory language did not indicate that Part 1625 was being added to the Code of Federal Regulations. This document corrects the amendatory language and makes an additional correction of a typographical error appearing in the final document.

FOR FURTHER INFORMATION CONTACT:
John J. Pagano, Supervisory Attorney, Office of the General Counsel, Legal Counsel Division, EEOC, Room 2254, 2401 E Street, N.W., Washington, D.C. 20506 (202) 634–6595.

Correction: The paragraph following the signature of Eleanor Holmes Norton, Chair of the EEOC, which appears at 44 FR 66797, is hereby amended to read:

"Accordingly, new Part 1625 is added to Title 29 of the Code of Federal Regulations, consisting at this time of Section 1625.11 and 1625.12. Section 1627.17 and paragraph C of § 1627.1 are also added."

In addition, the EEOC hereby corrects a typographical error appearing in the last numbered section on 44 FR 66793. That section is hereby corrected to read:

(i) Current employer distinguished from prior employers. Under the section 12(c) exemption, for purposes of excluding contributions of prior employers, a prior employer is every previous employer of the employee except those previous employers which are members of a "controlled group of corporations" with, or "under common control" with, the employer which forces the employee to retire, as those terms are used in sections 414(b) and 414(c) of the Internal Revenue Code, as modified by Section 415(h) (26 U.S.C. 414(b), (c) and 415(h)).

For the Commission,
Eleanor Holmes Norton,
Chair, Equal Employment Opportunity Commission.

[FR Doc. 80–19586 Filed 6–27–80; 8:45 am]
BILLING CODE 6570-06-M

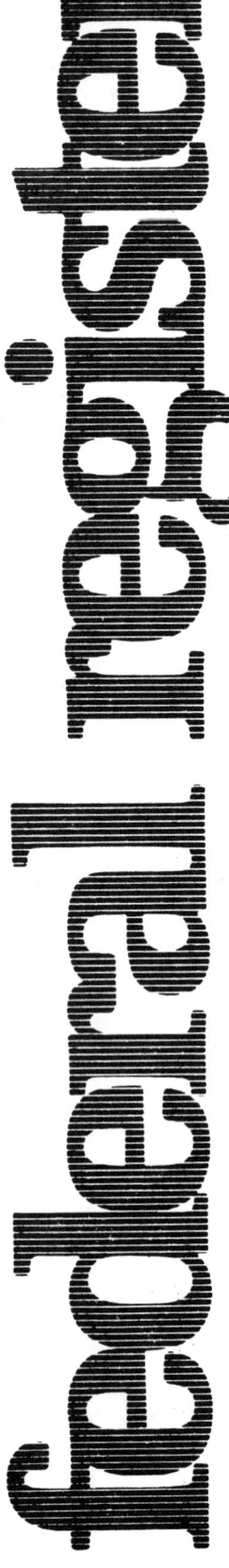

Friday
May 25, 1979

Part XI

Department of Labor

Wage and Hour Division

Employee Benefit Plans; Amendment to Interpretative Bulletin

DEPARTMENT OF LABOR

Wage and Hour Division

29 CFR Part 860

Employee Benefit Plans; Amendment to Interpretative Bulletin

AGENCY: Wage and Hour Division, Labor.

ACTION: Amendment to Interpretative Bulletin.

SUMMARY: The Interpretative Bulletin on the Age Discrimination in Employment Act of 1967, as amended ("ADEA" or "Act"), sets forth various interpretations which indicate the construction of the ADEA that the Department of Labor believes to be correct and which will guide it in the performance of its administrative and enforcement duties under the Act. After enactment of the Age Discrimination in Employment Act Amendments of 1978, Pub. L. 95-256, 92 Stat. 189 (approved April 6, 1978), the Department of Labor published in the **Federal Register** of September 22, 1978, a proposed amendment to the Interpretative Bulletin with respect to employee benefit plans. After considering carefully numerous written comments as well as testimony at a hearing on the proposed amendment, the Department has revised the original proposal, which it now publishes in final form.

DATES: Effective date: May 25, 1979. Since this is an interpretative rule or statement of policy, the 30-day delay in effective date as prescribed in section 553(d) of title 5, U.S. Code, does not apply. The enforcement policy that will be followed by the Department of Labor and by the Equal Employment Opportunity Commission under this interpretative bulletin is explained in more detail below in part 9 of the preamble. The Equal Employment Opportunity Commission, which will take on administrative and enforcement responsibility for the ADEA effective July 1, 1979, concurs with this enforcement policy.

FOR FURTHER INFORMATION CONTACT: Francis V. LaRuffa, Jr., Chief, Branch of Age Discrimination, Wage and Hour Division, U.S. Department of Labor, 200 Constitution Avenue, NW., Room S-3028, Washington, D.C. 20210, telephone 202-523-7640. (This is not a toll-free number.)

For additional copies of this interpretation, contact: Office of Information and Consumer Affairs, Employment Standards Administration, U.S. Department of Labor, 200 Constitution Avenue, NW., Room C-4331, Washington, D.C. 20210, telephone 202-523-8743. (This is not a toll-free number.)

SUPPLEMENTARY INFORMATION: The Department of Labor published its proposed amendment to § 860.120 of the Interpretative Bulletin on the ADEA on September 22, 1978 (see 43 FR 43264). This section of the Interpretative Bulletin deals with employee benefit plans under section 4(f)(2) of the Act, 29 U.S.C. 623(f)(2).

Prior to the 1978 amendments, when the Act protected individuals between the ages of 40 and 65, section 4(f)(2) provided:

(f) It shall not be unlawful for an employer, employment agency, or labor organization * * *

(2) to observe the terms of * * * any bona fide employee benefit plan such as a retirement, pension, or insurance plan, which is not a subterfuge to evade the purposes of this Act, except that no such employee benefit plan shall excuse the failure to hire any individual * * *

In fashioning the section 4(f)(2) exception with respect to employee benefit plans, Congress explicitly recognized that the cost of providing certain benefits to older workers is greater than providing those same benefits to younger workers. To require that the same benefits be provided to all workers without regard to age, Congress feared, would discourage the employment of older workers or would unduly burden the employer and thereby jeopardize the continued maintenance and operation of such plans. As explained by Senator Javits during passage of the original bill in 1967, section 4(f)(2) is "particularly significant," "since, in its absence, employers might actually have been discouraged from hiring older workers because of the increased costs involved in providing certain types of benefits to them" (S. Rept. 723, 90th Cong., 1st Sess. (1967), p. 14; 113 Cong. Rec. 31254-31255). Senator Javits also stated: "The meaning of this provision is as follows: An employer will not be compelled under this section to afford to older workers exactly the same pension, retirement, or insurance benefits as he affords to younger workers" (113 Cong. Rec. 31255). In a similar vein, Representative Daniels pointed out that section 4(f)(2) was "designed to maximize employment possibilities without working an undue hardship on employers in providing special and costly benefits" (113 Cong. Rec. 34727). See also Hearings before the Senate Labor Subcommittee on S. 830 and S. 788, 90th Cong., 1st Sess., 1967, pp. 27-30, 53, 106-107.

The Department's original interpretation of section 4(f)(2), as published in the **Federal Register** on June 21, 1969 (34 FR 9709), and as republished in successive editions of the Code of Federal Regulations (CFR), reflected the congressional purpose underlying section 4(f)(2) in setting forth the general rule governing employee benefit plans falling within the exception:

* * * A retirement, pension, or insurance plan will be considered in compliance with the statute where the actual amount of payment made, or cost incurred, in behalf of an older worker is equal to that made or incurred in behalf of a younger worker, even though the older worker may thereby receive a lesser amount of pension or retirement benefits, or insurance coverage.* * *

[29 CFR 860.120(a)(1977).]

The 1978 amendments, in addition to increasing the maximum age of those individuals protected by the Act from 65 to 70 (and making other changes not relevant here), added a final clause to section 4(f)(2) so that it now reads:

(f) It shall not be unlawful for an employer, employment agency, or labor organization— * * *

(2) to observe the terms of * * * any bona fide employee benefit plan such as a retirement, pension, or insurance plan, which is not a subterfuge to evade the purposes of this Act, except that no such employee benefit plan shall excuse the failure to hire any individual, and no such * * * employee benefit plan shall require or permit the involuntary retirement of any individual specified by section 12(a) of this Act because of the age of such individual * * *.

The principal purpose of this amendment was to make clear that "the exception does not authorize an employer to require or permit involuntary retirement of an employee within the protected age group on account of age" (H. Rept. No. 95-950, 95th Cong., 2d Sess. (1978), p. 8 (ADEA Conference Report)).

In amending section 4(f)(2) Congress also made clear that the Department should issue more comprehensive guidance with respect to section 4(f)(2), particularly because of the increase in the maximum age level of those covered by the Act. See 124 Cong. Rec. H 2271 (daily ed. Mar. 21, 1978) (remarks of Rep. Hawkins); 124 Cong. Rec. S. 4451 (daily ed. Mar. 23, 1978) (remarks of Sens. Williams and Javits). The increase in the maximum age level of those covered has raised questions about many common benefit practices affecting employees at age 65. In the absence of comprehensive guidance, these questions would have to be answered by the Department, and by the courts, on a potentially lengthy, costly and uncertain case-by-case basis.

The congressional requests for more comprehensive guidance from the Department were accompanied by a reiteration of the purposes of section 4(f)(2), reflecting the statements as described above which were made during the original enactment of the ADEA. Most significant was the following statement by Senator Javits, who was minority manager of the original ADEA and the 1978 amendments (124 Cong. Rec. S. 4450–S. 4451, daily ed., March 23, 1978):

> The purpose of section 4(f)(2) is to take account of the increased cost of providing certain benefits to older workers as compared to younger workers.
> Welfare benefit levels for older workers may be reduced only to the extent necessary to achieve approximate equivalency in contributions for older and younger workers. Thus a retirement, pension, or insurance plan will be considered in compliance with the statute where the actual amount of payment made, or cost incurred in behalf of an older worker is equal to that made or incurred in behalf of a younger worker, even though the older worker may thereby receive a lesser amount of pension or retirement benefits, or insurance coverage. This is consistent with the following statement I made during the November 6, 1967 floor consideration of the original act:
>> The amendment relating to * * * employee benefit plans is particularly significant: Because of it an employer will not be compelled to afford older workers exactly the same pension, retirement, or insurance benefits as younger workers and thus employers will not, because of the often extremely high cost of providing certain types of benefits to older workers, actually be discouraged from hiring older workers. At the same time, it should be clear that this amendment only relates to the observance of bona fide plans. No such plan will help an employer if it is adopted merely as a subterfuge for discriminating against older workers.
> The Department of Labor intends to promulgate comprehensive regulations in order to provide guidance in this regard for sponsors of employee benefit plans and the Secretary is urged to act as soon as possible.

Senator Williams, the majority manager, agreed that Senator Javits' statement "accurately reflects congressional intent in this regard." *Id.* at S. 4451.

Statements to the same effect were made during House floor debate by Congressman Hawkins (124 Cong. Rec. H. 2270–H. 2271, daily ed., March 21, 1978), Congressman Pepper (*id.* at H. 2275), Congressman Weiss (*id.* at H. 2276) and Congressman Waxman (*id.* at H. 2277). All of these statements indicate the congressional understanding of the language of section 4(f)(2), as originally enacted and as amended, which condemns any benefit practice which is "a subterfuge to evade the purposes of this Act." That understanding was succinctly stated by Congressman Waxman:

> I am hopeful, however, that employers do not terminate capable and healthy older workers from benefit plans solely on the basis of age. In the absence of actuarial data, which clearly demonstrates that the costs of this service are uniquely burdensome to the employer, such a policy constitutes discrimination and a conscious effort to evade the purposes of the act. (*Id.* at 2277.)

The legislative history of the 1978 amendments establishes one exception to the otherwise uniform rule under section 4(f)(2) that age-based reductions in employee benefit plans must be justified by actuarially significant cost considerations. That exception is with respect to certain retirement plans—both defined contribution plans and defined benefit plans. The legislative history makes clear that

> an employer will be permitted under the act, as amended, to maintain a defined contribution plan—other than a plan which is merely supplemental to a defined benefit or defined contribution plan maintained by the employer—which precludes employer and, if applicable, employee contributions to such a plan subsequent to an employee's attainment of the plan's normal retirement age. [124 Cong. Rec. S. 4450, daily ed., March 23, 1978, remarks of Sen. Javits.]

This statement by Senator Javits, with which Senator Williams concurred, is identical in all material respects to a statement by Congressman Dent with which Congressman Hawkins concurred (see 124 Cong. Rec. H. 2271, daily ed., March 21, 1978).

The legislative history also makes clear that under the ADEA, as amended, an employer maintaining a defined benefit retirement plan is not required (1) to credit, for purposes of benefit accrual, those years of service which occur after an employee has attained the normal retirement age under the plan; (2) to adjust actuarially the benefit accrued as of normal retirement age for an employee who continues to work beyond that age; (3) to commence benefits at normal retirement age when an employee's actual date of retirement is later; or (4) to provide for the accrual of benefits under such a plan during any years of service by an employee after normal retirement age. (See S. Rept. No. 95–493, 95th Cong., 1st Sess. 14–16 (1977); 123 Cong. Rec. H. 9977, daily ed., September 23, 1977.)

The Department of Labor's proposed interpretation, based on this legislative history, resulted in numerous comments from the public. These comments have been detailed and useful. They have convinced the Department that its proposed interpretation is in need of certain modifications and clarifications. Accordingly, as is explained in more detail below, several changes have been made in the interpretation.

In the preamble to the proposed interpretation, the Department discussed seven general questions that had arisen with respect to employee benefit plans under the ADEA, and it then explained how it had proposed to resolve them. The discussion below of the various comments received by the Department is grouped under the same headings. In addition, two other important issues raised by the comments are discussed below under headings 8 and 9 in the preamble. The first of these issues is whether the failure of the ADEA to preempt State age discrimination laws insulates such laws, to the extent that they relate to employee benefit plans, from the preemption provisions in section 514 of the Employee Retirement Income Security Act of 1974 (ERISA), 29 U.S.C. 1144.

The second issue not discussed originally, but which is discussed below, is the effective date of this amendment to the interpretative bulletin.

1. *What Kinds of Employee Benefit Plans Fall Within Section 4(f)(2)?*

The preamble and the proposed interpretation stated that section 4(f)(2) applies only to plans in which age is an actuarially significant factor in plan design, and used the example of group term life insurance to illustrate the kind of plan encompassed by this principle. The original proposal also stated that age is not an actuarially significant factor in the design of time off with pay plans, such as paid vacations and paid sick leave.

The comments on this aspect of the proposed interpretation were not numerous. Several commenters asserted that age is a significant actuarial cost factor in sick leave plans, particularly where such plans are separately insured. These same commenters questioned whether the Department, in formulating its position, had overlooked such plans or had intended to challenge the validity of the cost data with respect to such plans. The commenters requested clarification of the Department's position with respect to this issue.

The Department's original statement was intended to refer to those numerous paid sick leave plans which are not insured. Such plans do not fall within section 4(f)(2). An uninsured paid sick leave plan, like a paid vacation plan, is simply not an "employee benefit plan such as a retirement, pension, or insurance plan" as described in section 4(f)(2). However, there may be certain insured sick leave plans whose design is such that age is an actuarially significant cost factor. In terms of their cost, these plans are frequently similar to short-term disability plans. Where such plans exist and where the employer can show clearly that the cost of providing older workers with the same benefits as younger workers is higher because of age, then the benefits for older workers can be correspondingly reduced, in accordance with the principles contained in this § 860.120. The final interpretation reflects this approach by describing as "uninsured" those paid sick leave plans which are outside the scope of section 4(f)(2).

Other comments requested that the Department define the term "employee benefit plan" in order to make clear what plans fall within section 4(f)(2) and what plans do not. Some commenters suggested using the same definition as in section 3(3) of the Employee Retirement Income Security Act (ERISA), 29 U.S.C. 1002(3). In the Department's view, however, it would not be appropriate to use the ERISA definition, because it encompasses plans which are maintained to provide vacation benefits, prepaid legal services and certain other benefits whose cost does not increase with the age of the employee participant. The Department believes that it is sufficient to rest with its original statement, in view of the change in the reference to paid sick leave.

A major part of the comments received pointed out the absence of any discussion in the proposed interpretations of employee-pay-all plans which employers sometimes offer to their employees. It is clear that an employee-pay-all plan is subject to the provisions of section 4(a)(1) of the Act, since such a plan is one of the "terms, conditions, or privileges of employment" with respect to which discrimination on the basis of age is forbidden. Regardless of who pays for an employee benefit plan, it is available to employees of the employer and is therefore governed by the section 4(a)(1) prohibition against discrimination.

However, it does not follow that the level of benefits available to older workers under an employee-pay-all plan must be no less than those available to younger workers. Section 4(f)(2) of the ADEA permits a reduction in the level of benefits for older workers where the cost of supplying the same level of benefits to older workers as to younger workers would be higher. There is no reason why a reduction in the level of benefits for older workers which would be permissible under a plan paid for in whole or in part by an employer should not also be permissible under an employee-pay-all plan. Accordingly, the interpretation takes the position that section 4(f)(2) applies to employee-pay-all plans. In such a plan, benefits for older workers may be reduced to the same extent and according to the same principles as apply to employee-paid plans.

The application of the ADEA to employee-pay-all plans raises not only the question of the level of benefits; it raises also the question of the costs paid by employees for those benefits. Regardless of whether benefits for older workers under an employee-pay-all plan are at the same level as or lower than benefits for younger workers, older workers cannot be required to pay more for the particular level of benefits they receive than the actual cost of those benefits. Requiring older workers to pay more than the actual cost of the benefits is plainly discrimination based on age, and no provision of the ADEA excuses such a practice.

These positions with respect to employee-pay-all plans are reflected in the interpretation below.

2. *What Kinds of Cost Data May Be Relied on To Show That Age is an Actuarially Significant Factor in Plan Design?*

The proposed interpretation took the position in § 860.120(d)(1) that an employer may rely on data which show the actual cost to him of providing the particular benefit in question. The proposal also stated, however, that where such data do not exist or where the universe of employees is too small to be statistically significant, reasonable actuarial data on benefit costs for similarly situated employees can be relied on.

This proposed interpretation, in requiring that employers rely on their own cost data in most instances, was intended to prevent employers from relying on other cost data which do not accurately reflect their own experience, even though such other data might be accurate with respect to other employers or groups of employers. In other words, the approach was designed to prevent potential abuses in the use of cost data.

Those who commented on this aspect of the proposed interpretation had several points to make. Some commenters noted that the Department's approach would prevent an employer from relying on cost data for a larger group of similarly situated employees (except where an employer's own workforce is too small to be statistically significant). This approach was criticized as being unnecessarily restrictive, particularly since a larger group of similarly situated employees would be likely to be more representative of a particular employer's experience over the years. In this connection, some commenters observed that an employer forced to rely on its own cost experience might have to make adjustments in benefit levels each year, as a result of an unusually high or low number of deaths, illnesses or other events insured against in the previous year.

Another commenter requested that the Department state explicitly that where little or no reliable cost information is available—as may be the case with respect to some benefits after age 65—reasonable projections from cost data for younger ages be permitted.

After reviewing the comments and considering the orginal proposal afresh, the Department has decided to permit an employer to make adjustments in benefits on the basis of any reasonable data on benefit costs. In order to be considered reasonable, the data relied upon must reflect approximately the actual cost to the employer, over a representative period of years, of the benefits in question. Under this standard, an employer may rely on his own cost data for a representative period of years; this longer period will serve to reduce the cost impact of unusually high or low incidences of events insured against in a single year. An employer may also rely on cost data for a larger group of similarly situated employees. However, where an employer which is a self-insurer, or which is experience-rated by an insurance company, incurs costs which are significantly different from costs for similarly situated employees, the cost data for the similarly situated employees will not be considered reasonable as a basis for approximating the particular employer's benefit costs. This approach is adopted in § 860.120(d)(1) below.

The interpretation also makes clear that where reliable cost information is not yet available, reasonable projections may be made from existing cost data.

3. *May comparisons of benefit costs at different age levels be made with respect to the benefit package as a whole, or must the cost comparison be made on a benefit-by-benefit basis?*

The proposed interpretation required that all cost comparisons be made on a benefit-by-benefit basis, not on an overall "benefit package" basis. The rejection of the "benefit package" approach was based on two major concerns: (1) that its application could deprive individual employees of benefits of particular value to them in a way unjustified by the age-related costs of those benefits, and (2) that it would be a less workable standard for compliance.

Comments in this area have sharply questioned the appropriateness of the Department's proposed rejection of the benefit package approach. These comments have also urged that if the Department persists in the benefit-by-benefit approach, it should clarify what it means by a "benefit."

In advocating a benefit package approach, commenters made several general points. First, several commenters stated that the legislative history does not explicitly rule out a benefit package approach; its only explicit requirement is that payments made or costs incurred by employers for employee benefit plans for older workers must be no less than for younger workers.

Second, numerous commenters contended that the more restrictive benefit-by-benefit approach would deprive not only employers, but also employees (including older employees), of the flexibility to design a package of fringe benefits responsive to their particular needs. Specifically, an employer who makes equal contributions at all age levels for each fringe benefit whose cost goes up with age may find that his employees want a package of benefits forbidden by the proposed interpretation.

Thirdly, commenters emphasized that group insurance plans of any type cannot be tailored to fit the individual needs of each employee. Generalities based on the needs of average or typical employees must be used in the design of such plans.

Finally, various commenters asserted that the purported convenience of being able to determine compliance with section 4(f)(2) by examining each employee benefit plan in isolation was an insufficient basis on which to forbid the use of a benefit package approach.

After a careful review of the legislative history in the light of these various comments, the Department has concluded that an exclusive adherence to the benefit-by-benefit approach is not warranted.

Although the legislative history does not compel a benefit-by-benefit approach exclusively, there is clear support for such an approach. Thus, Senator Javits described benefit plans one by one in indicating the compliance standard applicable to "a retirement, pension or insurance plan * * *" (124 Cong. Rec. S 4450, daily ed., March 23, 1978, emphasis added). Also in 1978, Congressman Waxman, apparently referring to health insurance, condemned reductions for older workers "[i]n the absence of actuarial data which clearly demonstrates that the costs of *this* service are uniquely burdensome to the employer" (124 Cong. Rec. H 2277, daily ed., March 21, 1978, emphasis added). Moreover, the 1978 legislative history specifies a particular rule with respect to one type of benefit—retirement or pension benefits—without reference to other benefits or costs. All of these indications point to a benefit-by-benefit approach.

Nevertheless, this legislative history need not be read as rejecting a benefit package approach altogether, since it does not appear that Congress had the opportunity to consider the matter fully. Certainly there is no explicit rejection of a benefit package approach.

Moreover, the language and purposes of the act itself suggest that in some circumstances a benefit package approach should be permitted. The language of section 4(f)(2) condones a benefit arrangement which is "not a subterfuge to evade the purposes of [the] Act," and section 2(b) declares that one of those purposes is "to help employers and workers find ways of meeting problems arising from the impact of age on employment." One way of "meeting problems arising from the impact of age on employment" is to make sure that there is enough flexibility under section 4(f)(2) so that (1) older workers can continue to have the same level of certain fringe benefits which are particularly valuable to them as do younger workers, and (2) employers can avoid higher fringe benefit costs for older workers which would otherwise result by reducing the level of some other benefit or benefits more than the benefit-by-benefit approach would permit. This approach would meet the purposes of both section 2(b) and section 4(f)(2), provided that the costs of the benefits were no less for older workers than for younger workers, and provided that the benefits provided were not a subterfuge to evade the purposes of the ADEA.

Accordingly, the interpretation permits a benefit package approach, which is subject to certain restrictions which are described in detail under heading 7 of this preamble, as well as in § 860.120(f). These restrictions are designed to assure that the greater flexibility of the benefit package approach is used to provide older workers with a benefit package which meets their needs at least as well as the benefit-by-benefit approach, if not better.

Benefit-by-Benefit Approach

In accepting the benefit package approach, the Department does not thereby reject the benefit-by-benefit approach. The benefit package approach, even with its restrictions, is designed to afford greater flexibility in the design of employee benefits than the benefit-by-benefit approach would have provided, but many employers may find that the benefit-by-benefit approach is a simpler means by which to assure compliance with the ADEA. For this reason, the precise application of the benefit-by-benefit approach must be defined.

Many comments indicated uncertainty or confusion as to the precise meaning of a "benefit" under the benefit-by-benefit approach. Some commenters seemed to believe that the Department intended a "plan-by-plan" approach. Many others suggested that the approach be understood to look at benefits on an "event-by-event" basis (that is, to take together all benefits available to an employee for a particular event—death, disablement, etc.). The Department acknowledges the ambiguity of the proposed interpretation. The Department also acknowledges that it anticipated a somewhat flexible definition of a "benefit" which would have permitted the substitution for older employees of similar benefits meeting the same basic need.

The Department now believes, however, that the desired flexibility—that is, flexibility that will better meet the needs of employees—may be and should be justified on a benefit package approach. The Department therefore now takes a strict view of a "benefit" under the benefit-by-benefit approach. The Department specifically rejects the suggestion that the benefit-by-benefit approach should be understood as an "event-by-event" approach which would ignore differences in the forms of benefits available for a particular event. Adjustments in benefits under the benefit-by-benefit approach are to be made in the amount of the benefit, not in its form. Where benefits *are* different in form or otherwise, they must stand up to a benefit package analysis. This is all explained more fully under heading 7 below and in § 860.120(f).

(4) *May the Level of a Benefit be Reduced on the Basis of the Average Cost of the Benefit for all Employees Within an Age Range (Such as 65 to 70 years Old), or Must the Cost of the*

Benefit be Calculated on a Year-by-Year Basis?

The proposed interpretation took the position in § 860.120(d)(3) that cost comparisons and adjustments must be made on a year-by-year basis. The purpose behind this approach was to avoid a large and sudden reduction in benefits for employees reaching a certain age which could not be justified by cost considerations with respect to that age.

The great majority of comments received took issue with this interpretation. Many comments noted that it has long been the practice in the insurance industry to price insurance on the basis of average costs in five-year age brackets, rather than on the basis of yearly costs. The same practice, it was pointed out, is reflected in section 79 of the Internal Revenue Code and Treasury Regulations thereunder. To change from the normal five-year average price approach to the Department's proposed approach, these commenters stated, would add to the administrative burden of maintaining such plans and of communicating changes in benefit levels to participants.

Several commenters also noted that under a five-year average cost approach, older employees within each age bracket would receive a *higher* level of benefits than under a year-by-year approach; conversely, younger employees within each age bracket would receive less. Accordingly, it was pointed out, the five-year bracketing approach, viewed in a broader perspective of an employee's total years of service with an employer, would be no more harmful to older employees than a year-by-year cost approach.

The Department has rejected an average cost approach based on periods of longer than five years. Some commenters suggested that a 10-year period be permitted, and others suggested that reductions in benefits at age 65 be based on the average cost of those benefits for a 25-year period (from ages 40 to 65). Such approaches, however, would lead to the drastic reductions in benefit levels at older age groups which the Department has sought to avoid.

Another comment requested that the interpretation make clear that cost-based reductions in benefit levels could start at any age—not just at age 65. (This comment may have been prompted by the example given in § 860.120(d)(3), which was of reductions starting at age 65.)

After reviewing the various comments and reassessing the original proposal, the Department has decided to permit up to a five-year average cost approach, which is reflected in the interpretation below. Of course, a year-by-year approach or any other approach using age brackets of less than five years is also an acceptable form of compliance. The interpretation also states explicitly that reductions in benefit levels, if cost-justified, may begin at any age. Examples of this approach are given in the interpretative bulletin itself.

5. *Where the Government pays for certain benefits to employees on the basis of age—such as Medicare beginning at age 65—may an employer to that extent cease to provide those same benefits under his employee benefit plan, even though as a result the cost to the employer of providing medical benefits to older employees may be less than for younger employees?*

The interpretation permits such coordination of benefits, even though the availability of the Government-paid benefits may be based on age, provided that, when the Government-paid benefits are included, older employees still enjoy no less of a benefit than younger employees. It is in the nature of many employee benefit plans to respond to individual needs, and it would seem reasonable for such plans to take into account the extent to which individual needs are met by other benefits provided by the Government. This principle applies not only to Medicare, but also to Social Security disability and old-age and other such government-provided benefits.

Some comments in this area have validly pointed out that "Government-paid" benefits are ultimately paid for by employees and employers as a result of payroll deductions, taxes and similar devices. The Department did not intend to imply otherwise in using that shortened expression to describe such benefits.

The basic position expressed in the proposed interpretation has not been changed, except insofar as the interpretation seemed to disapprove any adjustment in health insurance coverage which did not simply offset (or "carve-out") Medicare benefits actually paid from regular health plan benefits. As indicated in the specific discussion of health insurance below, the Department is taking the position that plans which "supplement" rather than "carve-out" Medicare benefits are permissible where the total health benefit for employees over 65 is no less favorable than that for employees under 65.

6. (a) *May an employer require that an older employee make greater contributions into a benefit plan as a condition of employment?*

The interpretation below, like the proposed interpretation, answers this question in the negative. The Department remains convinced that to impose such a requirement as a condition of *employment* would violate the special restrictions in section 4(f)(2). Such a requirement would force older workers, if they wanted to continue working, to accept less take-home pay as a result of higher contributions and in addition would impose an impermissible impediment to employment. Such a practice is illegal under the ADEA.

(b) *May an employer require that an older employee make greater contributions into a benefit plan as a condition of participation in the plan, in order for the employee to be able to receive the same level of benefits as a younger employee?*

The proposed interpretation answered this question in the negative, on the ground that the language and legislative history of section 4(f)(2) indicated that the provision contemplated adjustments in benefits, not adjustments in pay or in employee contributions which are a condition of participation in an employee benefit plan.

Upon reconsideration of this proposed position, and after reviewing comments, the Department of Labor has concluded that its original position is essentially correct. However, some refinements in that position are necessary, because in the Department's view there are very limited circumstances under which an older employee, in order to receive the same level of benefits as a younger worker, can be required, as a condition of continued participation, to contribute a greater amount than the younger worker.

In most situations, the Department continues to believe that a violation of the ADEA would occur if an older employee were required to contribute more than a younger employee for the same level of benefits. As indicated under heading 6(a) above, where participation in the employee benefit plan is *mandatory*, such a practice would violate the ADEA, because older workers, on the basis of age, would have no option but to receive less take-home pay than younger workers.

Where participation in the employee benefit plan is *voluntary*, somewhat different considerations apply. In such a situation, older workers are free to avoid reductions in take-home pay by declining to participate in the employee benefit plan. However, even where older workers voluntarily agree to participate in such a plan, the plan would not be considered lawful where the cost of such participation to older workers is discriminatory on the basis of age. In order to avoid discriminatory costs, the proportion of the total premium borne by older workers cannot be more than that borne by younger workers.

The application of this principle can be illustrated with respect to the three different contribution arrangements for employee benefit plans in which participation is voluntary. The first such arrangement is one in which the employee-participant pays for the entire benefit in question. In such employee-pay-all plans, as noted under heading (1) above, it would not by unlawful to require older workers to contribute the full amount of the cost increase with age. In such a plan, older employees are treated no less favorably than younger employees, since all participants in the plan are required to pay the entire cost of the benefit, regardless of age. Employees are simply denied the advantage of continued membership in the plan if they are unwilling or unable to pay their own way like everyone else.

The second type of contribution arrangement in employee benefit plans in which participation is voluntary is the non-contributory (or "employer-pay-all") plan. In such plans, older employees cannot be required to contribute towards any of the age-related cost increase. If no employee-participants are required to make any contributions, there is obviously no age-based discrimination against older workers. However, if older workers are required to make contributions but younger workers are not, a violation of the ADEA would result. Such a requirement is discriminatory, even though the employer's contribution is no less for older than for younger workers, because in order to obtain any benefit from that contribution older workers must put in money of their own (that is, receive less take-home pay) whereas younger workers need not. (Of course, as explained elsewhere, an employer can reduce the level of benefits for older workers in order to avoid age-related increases in costs.)

The third type of contribution arrangement in employee benefit plans in which participation is voluntary is the contibutory plan, in which the employer and the employee share the premium cost. In such a plan, in order to avoid discrimination based on age, the proportion of the total premium borne by older workers cannot be more than that borne by younger workers. This principle can perhaps best by illustrated by a concrete example.

Assume a contributory group insurance plan to which the employer and the employee each contribute 50 percent of the total premium of $20 per month per employee, during a certain five-year age range. Further assume that in the next five-year age range the total premium increases to $30 per month per employee. The employee contribution could be required to increase to as much as $15 per month, since this amount is no more than 50 percent of the total premium cost, as is paid by the younger workers. The employer's contribution could not be less than $15 per month. It could not be lower—such as $10—since then the employee contribution would have to be greater than 50 percent of the total premium cost—in the example, $20. This would be discriminatory because in order to obtain any benefit from the employer's contribution older employees would have to match it with $2 of their own (out of their take-home pay) for every $1 of the employer's contribution, whereas younger employees would only have to match it dollar-for-dollar. The only way the employer contribution could be held at $10 would be by decreasing the level of benefits so that the total premium remained at $20 and the employee contribution at $10. (Alternatively, the employer could decrease coverage by a lesser amount—for example, so that the total premium increased to just $24. The employee contribution could be required to increase in relation to the resulting total increase—in the example, to up to $12.)

However, as the interpretation makes clear, older employees could be given the option, as individuals, to make the additional contribution necessary to prevent the reduction in benefits otherwise justified. Thus, the employee contribution could be permitted at employee option, but could not be required as a condition of participation in the plan, to increase to $20 in order to fund, along with the $10 employer contribution, the unreduced level of benefits whose total cost is $30.

7. How Would Section 4(f)(2), As Amended, Apply to Various Employee Benefit Plans?

The application of section 4(f)(2) to various employee benefit plans depends on whether reductions in benefit levels are justified by means of the benefit-by-benefit approach or by the benefit package approach. Under the benefit-by-benefit approach, as outlined above, reductions in the level of one benefit—such as group term life insurance—must be justified by an increase in the cost of that particular benefit, regardless of any adjustment in the levels of other benefits. The discussion in part A below describes the limits on reductions in benefit levels for four of the most common types of employee benefit plans—group term life insurance, group health insurance, long-term disability, and retirement plans—under the benefit-by-benefit approach. Employers who meet these standards (as set forth more precisely in § 860.120(f)) will be considered in compliance with section 4(f)(2). Although not specifically discussed herein, other plans within section 4(f)(2), such as short-term disability and accidental death and dismemberment, are subject to the same general principles.

Where reductions in any individual benefit are greater than those permitted under the benefit-by-benefit approach, such reductions must meet the standards of the benefit package approach. These standards are described in part B below.

A. Benefit-by-Benefit Approach.—(1) *Group term life insurance.* Where the level of group term life insurance benefits is reduced, on the basis of age, in direct correlation to the age-based increase in cost, no violation of the ADEA will result. The reduction may be made on the basis of average costs over a period of up to five years, but no longer. Where the level of group term life insurance benefits is based on the employee's wages or salary, such as two times base pay, increases in the cost of such coverage for older workers which are caused by increases in wages or salary cannot be taken into account. The reason for this is that such increases are not directly related to age. The interpretation sets forth examples of permissible adjustments in the level of group term life insurance benefits.

(2) *Health insurance.* It is still the Department's understanding that ordinarily health insurance coverage does not vary significantly with age up to age 65. Where employees are not now subject to mandatory retirement at that age, coverage after that age is almost invariably reduced to take account of Medicare. In view of the availability of Medicare starting at age 65, the interpretation takes the position that reductions in total health benefits (Medicare plus benefits from other sources) for employees age 65 to 70 will generally not be justified.

Comments and hearing testimony in this area have emphasized that there is more than one approach to the adjustment of health insurance coverage to take account of Medicare. The Department clearly intended to permit what is called a "carve-out" approach, under which regular health plan benefits are directly offset by benefits paid under

Medicare. Under this approach employees over 65 receive the same total health benefits as those under 65.

Other common approaches do not simply offset Medicare benefits actually paid but rather attempt to anticipate what will be paid under Medicare and supplement them with benefits which Medicare is not anticipated to pay. Under these approaches, which might be generally referred to as "supplement" approaches, employees over 65 might not receive the same total health benefits as those under 65: of some benefits (for example, professional service for which Medicare pays less than anticipated) they may receive less, and of some benefits (for example, prescription drugs not covered by either Medicare or the regular health plan but covered by the "supplement" plan) they may receive more.

Comments and hearing testimony have suggested that "supplement" approaches are used rather than the "carve-out" approach for administrative reasons, that they are not based on age stereotypes, and that they are not regarded as necessarily less favorable to employees. The Department takes the position that such Medicare "supplement" plans are a permissible alternative to a "carve-out" plan, provided that (1) their cost to the employer is no less than a "carve-out" plan would be, and (2) taken with Medicare benefits, they provide no less favorable benefits on an overall basis than a "carve-out" plan.

The specific question has been raised whether, in adjusting health insurance benefits to take account of Medicare, an employer may assume that eligible employees have taken advantage of available Medicare coverage. The Department takes the position that employers may not make such an assumption, unless they inform each eligible employee of the need to apply for Medicare coverage and provide any necessary assistance for making an application for benefits. Furthermore, where the employer's regular health plan requires no employee contribution or an employee contribution less than that required for Medicare "Part B" coverage, the employer must pay or contribute toward the "Part B" contribution so as to make the total benefits available to employees over 65 on the terms on which they are available to employees under 65. However, the employer's total contribution for Part B and the carve-out or supplemental plan would not have to be greater than the employer's highest contribution for health benefits for employees of any age under 65.

Some comments have suggested that some employers may be able to prove that despite the availability of Medicare their health insurance costs are higher for employees age 65 to 70 than for any younger employee group. Presumably any such employers would be ones with unusually comprehensive health insurance plans. In any case, the burden will be on any employer which reduces total health benefits for employees age 65 to 70 to produce sound and specific costs data to justify the reduction.

(3) *Long-term disability.* The proposed interpretation stated that age-based reductions in the level of benefits under long-term disability plans are permissible only where justifiable by age-related cost considerations. To supplement this position two alternatives were stated and comments were solicited with respect to the reasonableness of either or both. The first approach prohibited the cutting off of long-term disability benefits, on the basis of age, before age 70. The second alternative allowed benefit payments under long-term disability plans to cease at age 65 if the employee was disabled at age 60 or less, or to cease after five years (except that no payments need be made beyond age 70) with respect to disabilities occurring after age 60. A detailed explanation was offered for each of these alternatives in the supplementary information accompanying the proposed interpretation.

Almost every comment received by the Department offered views on the subject of long-term disability benefits. Most of these pointed out (as the Department was aware) that both alternative interpretations would have treated as unlawful the past practice under these plans of ceasing benefits at age 65 or at the age of eligibility for a full actuarially unreduced pension (if that age was other than age 65). Under this practice, workers who were disabled after age 65 or after normal retirement age would receive no long-term disability benefits at all. Thus, the employer would incur no long-term disability costs for such employees, whereas he would incur costs for younger employees. Section 4(f) (2) does not permit this treatment of older workers under the benefit-by-benefit approach, since workers can now continue working until age 70. The past practice would also adversely affect workers who are disabled just before age 65 or normal retirement age. Their benefits might cover only a few months, whereas workers who are disabled somewhat earlier would receive benefits for several years. Under a benefit-by-benefit analysis, this difference in treatment cannot be justifed under section 4(f) (2).

The Department has reassessed the two proposed alternatives thoroughly, and has concluded that although both are acceptable means of compliance, they are not the only options available.

The first alternative, in forbidding a cut-off in disability benefit payments until age 70, would have permitted an employer to avoid age-based benefit cost increase only by reducing the *level* of benefits. Another way of adhering to section 4(f) (2) cost justification principles is to reduce the *duration* of long-term disability payments. Under this approach, the minimum required duration of disability payments would depend upon the age at which an employee is disabled. For example, suppose an employee who is disabled at age 35 is entitled to long-term disability payments until age 65. In order to satisfy section 4(f) (2), the cost to the employer of insurance providing disability payments for an employee who is disabled at age 45, for example, must be no less than the cost to the employer of disability insurance for the 35-year-old. The same rule would apply to employees disabled at any other age.

The final interpretation set forth below, reflecting this approach, permits an employer to cut off disability payments at age 65 (or, for example, at normal retirement where that is not age 65) for workers who are disabled at relatively early ages. However, in order to assure equal costs in support of workers who are disabled at relatively later ages, the duration of their disability payments may have to extend beyond age 65. For any such older worker who is disabled before age 70, the employer must expend in support of his or her disability coverage an amount no less than the greatest amount expended in support of coverage for any younger worker. Where equal costs in support of disability coverage for older workers result in lesser benefits for such workers, the lesser benefits can be in the form of a shorter duration of benefits but at the same level as for younger workers.

A concrete example of this approach can be given. Suppose an employer, in line with a common practice in the past, cut off long-term disability coverage at age 65 for workers disabled at any age before age 65. It is likely that the greatest cost of such a plan, in terms of net annual claims costs, was for workers who were disabled at about age 61. (After age 61, the greater the age of the employee at the time of disablement, the less the cost of coverage until age 65, because the duration of the disability payment declines more rapidly as a function of age than the probability of disablement increases.) In order to assure that workers who are disabled after age 61 have equal costs expended in support of their long-term disability coverage, their coverage must extend beyond age 65. The extent of the coverage depends on the age at which they are disabled and the rate of disablement at that age.

Statistics on the rate of disablement for employees over age 65 are scanty, but data are available for employees disabled just before age 65. Some information on this subject came from a comment prepared by the insurance company which provides group long-term disability insurance to more employers than any other insurer in the United States. Although the Department of Labor has not independently verified the accuracy of the insurance company's data or the assumptions on which they were computed, the data indicate how the duration of benefits could be reduced to avoid increases in costs. For any employer who cuts off long-term disability coverage at age 65 for workers who are disabled at age 61 or younger, the greatest cost expended for this benefit, if applied to workers disabled at later ages, would yield the following durations of benefits:

Age at disablement	Duration of benefits (in years)
61 or younger	To age 65
62	3½ years
63	3
64	2½
65	2
66	1¾
67	1½
68	1¼
69	1

If these statistics are based on reasonable actuarial data and reasonable extrapolations therefrom, then a long-term disability plan which provides at least this duration of benefits would be in compliance with section 4 (f) (2) under a benefit-by-benefit analysis. Thus, the Department's proposed second alternative, although it was not originally suggested on the basis of cost data, would be in compliance with section 4(f) (2). There are clearly other possible forms of compliance which are likewise somewhat more generous than the data would minimally require. For example, a plan might provide for benefits to age 65 or for four years, whichever is later (except that no benefits would have to extend past age 70). Another plan might provide for benefits to age 67 or for three years, whichever is later (except that no benefits would have to extend past age 70).

(4) *Retirement plans.* Comments and hearing testimony in this area have focused largely on the treatment of defined contribution plans. (The term "defined contribution plan" as used herein is synonymous with individual account plan.)

The proposed interpretation took the position that a defined contribution plan which was not "supplemental" could provide for the cessation of employer contributions after normal retirement age. Commenters have taken a variety of positions, including the following:

(1) That the distinction between "supplemental" and other defined contribution plans ought to be abandoned and all such plans treated alike, and

(2) That all "money purchase" plans ought to be deemed not to be "supplemental" and all other defined contribution plans (for example, profit-sharing plans) deemed "supplemental."

After reviewing these and other comments, the Department has concluded that, although in need of some clarification, the proposed interpretation was essentially correct.

The Department believes it should not ignore the clear legislative history which distinguishes between "supplemental" and other plans. In the absence of any indication that a specific technical meaning was intended, the Department has attempted to give the word "supplemental" its ordinary meaning. In response to specific comments and questions, the Department wishes to clarify its interpretation on one point, consistent with the ordinary meaning of the word "supplemental." The point concerns the situation where an employer has more than one retirement plan, but no one employee participates at one time in more than one plan. While the proposed interpretation might have been read to say otherwise, the Department would not in that situation deem any plan to be "supplemental," since as to any employee no plan "supplements" another. However, when any one employee participates at one time in more than one plan, as to that employee every plan but one is supplemental.

Another point raised by the comments relating to "supplemental" plans concerns what are sometimes called "floor" plans. A floor plan has a defined contribution component, but if the benefits available from that component are below a certain "floor" level, then extra benefits up to the "floor" level are provided. Some comments have suggested that a "floor" plan is a single plan with no "supplemental" plan involved; other comments have suggested that it is two plans with the defined benefit plan being "supplemental." On the basis of information now available to the Department of Labor, it will not necessarily take the position that a floor plan constitutes more than one plan, nor is it in a position to state an appropriate rule on floor plans generally.

Several comments asserted that the proposed interpretation appeared to be inconsistent with ERISA because it would have permitted an employer maintaining a non-supplemental defined contribution plan to exclude from participation in such a plan, on the basis of age, any employee who was hired after reaching normal retirement age. In this connection, section 202(a)(2) of ERISA (29 U.S.C. 1052(a)(2)) provides, in pertinent part:

No pension plan may exclude from participation (on the basis of age) employees who have attained a specified age, unless—
(A) the plan is a—(i) defined benefit plan, or (ii) target benefit plan (as defined under regulations prescribed by the Secretary of the Treasury) * * *

(See also section 410(a)(2) of the Internal Revenue Code, 26 U.S.C. 410(a)(2).) To the extent that "participation" within the meaning of section 202(a)(2) of ERISA would entail employer contributions, adherence to the rule provided in the legislative history of the ADEA Amendments of 1978 could not justify non-compliance with this (or any other) provision of ERISA. The interpretation states merely that it is not a violation of the ADEA to follow the rules it sets forth. However, in order to avoid any confusion on this point, § 860.120(f)(4) has been revised to state simply that no contributions need be made to a non-supplemental defined contribution plan on behalf of an employee hired after normal retirement age. Any specific determination as to compliance with the provisions of ERISA dealing with "participation" in defined contribution plans or as to compliance with Section 410 of the Code must be made by the Internal Revenue Service.

Some comments have raised questions as to the treatment of investment gains and losses and employee termination forfeitures in defined contribution plans. Because the legislative history refers only to the cessation of contributions after normal retirement age, the Department takes the following positions with respect to defined contribution plans:

(1) Older employees, including those working past normal retirement age, should receive no less favorable treatment because of age with respect to investment gains and losses than younger employees.

(2) Where employee termination forfeitures are not used to reduce employer contributions, they should not be allocated less favorably because of age to older employees, including those working past normal retirement age, than to younger employees.

With respect to defined benefit plans, many comments have raised questions as to the treatment of salary increases and benefit improvements after normal retirement age. The 1978 legislative history indicates an understanding that no adjustment to an accrued benefit under a defined plan is required on account of employment after normal retirement age. Accordingly, the interpretation takes the position that employees working past normal retirement age need not receive the advantage from salary increases and benefit improvements that other active employees receive.

It would not follow, however, that employees working past normal retirement age could be denied the advantage of a benefit improvement for current retirees. While the ADEA does not require that an employee get a greater benefit by choosing to work rather than to retire after normal retirement age, it does not permit an employee to be given a lesser benefit because of that choice, although the benefit may be paid later (beginning at the later actual retirement age). (Similarly, the payment of benefits may be suspended during reemployment. See ERISA section 203(a)(3)(B). See also 43 FR 59098, December 19, 1978.) To provide a lesser (and not merely later) retirement benefit would obviously discourage employees from continuing their employment and would be deemed a subterfuge to evade the purposes of the Act.

Questions have also been raised about the integration of Social Security benefits with defined benefit plan benefits. The Department takes the position that such integration is permissible, consistent with the general principles on the coordination of benefits where Government-paid benefits are available, with one limitation. For employees who actually retire at normal retirement age, the general practice is not to decrease defined benefit plan benefits because of a subsequent increase in Social Security benefits. (See ERISA Section 206(b).) In light of the principle discussed in the previous paragraph, the Department also takes the position that where an employee working past normal retirement age is denied because of age any upward adjustment in defined benefit plan benefits which is given younger active employees, that employee may not suffer any reduction in plan benefits because of an increase in Social Security benefits which current retirees would not suffer. Thus, where years of service in a benefit formula are "frozen" because of age at normal retirement age, the offset from plan benefits of Social Security benefits must generally also be "frozen" at that age. On the other hand, a plan need not "freeze" the Social Security offset at any age prior to actual retirement for employees who are given the full advantage of benefit adjustments (due to greater years of service, salary increases and benefit improvements) up to actual retirement age.

Finally, questions have been raised as to whether retirement benefits need to be paid to employees receiving long-term disability benefits who reach normal retirement age. Some comments have stated that an employee receiving both disability and retirement benefits might receive more than his or her full working salary. The legislative history makes clear that retirement benefits need not commence until actual retirement. The interpretation takes the position that an employee receiving long-term disability benefits as a salary replacement may be deemed not to have "actually retired" and therefore need not receive both benefits simultaneously.

B. *Benefit Package Approach.* A benefit package approach to compliance under section 4(f)(2) offers greater flexibility than a benefit-by-benefit approach. In essence it permits deviations from a benefit-by-benefit approach so long as the overall result is (1) no lesser cost to the employer and (2) no less favorable benefits for employees. As previously noted, part of the legal basis for a benefit package approach is the statutory purpose "to help employers and workers find ways of meeting problems arising from the impact of age on employment." In order to assure that such an approach is used for the benefit of older workers and not to their detriment, and is otherwise consistent with the legislative intent, it must necessarily be subject to limitations. These limitations are set forth in the interpretation and explained below:

(1) *A benefit package approach may apply only to employee benefit plans which fall within section 4(f)(2).* In other words, a benefit package approach does not expand the intended scope of section 4(f)(2).

(2) *A benefit package approach may not apply to a retirement or pension plan.* Such plans are of course within the scope of section 4(f)(2). However, as previously noted, the 1978 legislative history sets forth specific and rather comprehensive rules governing such plans. Unlike the general principles with respect to other plans under section 4(f)(2), these rules are not tied to actuarially significant cost considerations but are intended to deal with the special funding arrangements of retirement or pension plans, which were of concern to Congress. See, e.g., S. Rept. 95–493, 95th Cong., 1st Sess. (1977), pp. 13–16. It would be a departure both from the general principles of section 4(f)(2) and from the specific legislative history to apply a benefit package approach, which is based on the general cost principles, to a retirement or pension plan, which is specifically governed by other rules.

The interpretation therefore takes the position that variations from the special rules are not justified by variations from the benefit-by-benefit approach in other benefit plans. Thus, for example, an employer who does not make an age-based reduction in group term life insurance which could be justified under a benefit-by-benefit approach may not justify on that (or any other) basis an age-based reduction in employees' annual accrual of pension benefits prior to normal retirement age. Similarly, the interpretation takes the position that variations from the special rules governing pension and retirement plans do not justify variations from the benefit-by-benefit approach in other benefit plans. For example, an employer who does not cease pension accrual at normal retirement age (as a benefit-by-benefit approach would permit) may not justify on that basis a reduction in group term life insurance benefits greater than would be justified under a benefit-by-benefit approach.

(3) *A benefit package approach may not be used to justify reductions in health benefits greater than would be justified under a benefit-by-benefit approach.* Such benefits would appear to be a particular importance to older workers in meeting "problems arising from the impact of age" and were clearly of particular concern to Congress. Congressman Waxman stated in the 1978 legislative history that "[w]hile the conference committee did not specifically address the status of health benefits to older workers protected under this act," reductions should not be made "[i]n the absence of

actuarial data which clearly demonstrates that the costs of this service are uniquely burdensome to the employer" (124 Cong. Rec. H 2277, daily ed., March 21, 1978, emphasis added).

On the basis of this legislative history and the comments received on the original proposal, the interpretation below takes the position that the "benefit package" approach may not be used to reduce health insurance benefits by more than is warranted by the increase in the cost to the employer of those benefits alone. This position is set forth in § 860.120(f)(2). Any greater reduction would be deemed "a subterfuge to evade the purposes of [the] Act."

(4) *A benefit reduction greater than would be justified under a benefit-by-benefit approach must be offset by another benefit available to the same employees.* Thus, for example, a benefit available to all employees may not be "traded off" for a benefit available to relatively few. Otherwise, some employees could suffer clear age discrimination in that they would be deprived because of age of one benefit without any offsetting benefit being made a avilable to them.

(5) *Employers who wish to justify benefit reductions under a benefit package approach must be prepared to produce data to show that those reductions are fully justified.* Thus employers must be able to show that deviations from a benefit-by-benefit approach do not result in lesser cost to them or less favorable benefits to their employees. Obviously, the greater the deviation from a benefit-by-benefit approach, the greater will be the burden on the employer to show that older employees are being helped rather than hurt.

8. *What is the relationship of the ADEA and ERISA to State age discrimination laws?*

The ADEA does not preempt State age discrimination laws. See Section 14(a), 29 U.S.C. § 633(a). See also S. Rept. No. 95–493, 95th Cong., 1st Sess. (1977), p. 5–7. The question has arisen in the comments whether such State laws—to the extent that they relate to employee benefit plans—are nonetheless superseded under section 514 (a) of ERISA, 29 U.S.C. § 1144(a). This question was discussed by Senators Javits and Williams during floor consideration of the 1978 ADEA Amendments:

Mr. JAVITS. Finally, Mr. President, it is understood that just as these age discrimination amendments do not interfere with ERISA, State age discrimination in employment laws also are not to interfere with ERISA. The ADEA itself, as pointed out in the Senate Report, does not preempt such State age dis [crimination laws. However, there should] be no question that the preemption rules of section 514(a) of ERISA shall be determinative regarding the preemption of State age discrimination laws which directly or indirectly establish requirements relating to employee benefit plans.

ERISA's preemption of State age discrimination laws shall be determined without regard to section 514(d) of ERISA or the fact that the ADEA does not itself preempt State law.

Mr. WILLIAMS. I concur in my friend's observations as they accurately state the controlling principles of law in this regard. Federal law will preempt State age discrimination statutes only to the extent that those laws relate to an employee benefit plan described in section 4(a) of ERISA and are not exempt under section 4(b) of ERISA. [124 Cong. Rec. S4451, daily ed., March 23, 1978. The portion in brackets was inadvertently omitted from the March 23, 1978, statement, but it was corrected on April 4, 1978 (see 124 Cong. Rec. S4767).]

9. *Effective Date and Enforcement.*

This interpretation indicates the construction of the law which the Department of Labor believes to be correct and which will guide it in the performance of its administrative and enforcement duties under the Act unless and until it is otherwise directed by authoritative decisions of the Courts or concludes, upon reexamination of the interpretation, that it is incorrect. See 29 CFR 860.1.

This interpretation is effective immediately. It replaces as of this date the less specific interpretation in old § 860.120.

With respect to benefit practices *prior* to this date, no employer will be subject to back wage liability for failure to comply with the new interpretation if the employer can prove that the noncompliance was "in good faith in conformity with and in reliance on" the old interpretation or on an opinion letter of the Wage and Hour Administrator. See section 10 of the Portal-to-Portal Act of 1947, as amended, 29 U.S.C. 259, which applies to actions under the ADEA. ADEA section 7(e)(1), 29 U.S.C. 626(e)(1).

As noted above, the old interpretation provided in relevant part:

A retirement, pension, or insurance plan will be considered in compliance with the statute where the actual amount of payment made, or cost incurred, in behalf of a older worker is equal to that made or incurred in behalf of a younger worker, even though the older worker may thereby receive a lesser amount of pension or retirement benefits, or insurance coverage.

While the old interpretation was less specific than the new, the Department believes that some benefit practices could *never* be proved to have been in good faith in conformity with and in reliance on the old interpretation. One such practice would be a total cut-off on the basis of age of various benefits for employees between ages 40 and 65 or, since January 1, 1979, for employees between age 40 and 70.

With respect to benefit practices *after* the effective date of the new interpretation, appropriate enforcement policy will be determined on a case-by-case basis. Section 7(b) of the ADEA provides that before instituting any action, the Secretary of Labor shall attempt to eliminate any alleged unlawful practice and to effect voluntary compliance, through informal methods of conciliation, conference, and persuasion. 29 U.S.C. 626(b). Some comments have stated that it may be difficult to achieve prompt voluntary compliance with the new interpretation through any quick amendment of an employee benefit plan, particularly where such a plan is insured. These comments have emphasized the time involved in amending or creating insured employee benefit plans, particularly where changes cannot be made without the approval of a regulatory agency, such as a State insurance commission. This and other problems in achieving prompt compliance may appropriately be considered in the conciliation of individual cases. It will also be appropriate to consider whether prompt compliance could feasibly be achieved in spite of these problems through, for example, existing insurance products or partial self-insurance.

Finally, it should be noted that all the benefit practices specifically permitted under the proposed interpretation published September 22, 1978, would be in compliance with the final interpretation published now.

The Equal Employment Opportunity Commission, which will take on administrative and enforcement responsibility for the ADEA effective July 1, 1979, concurs with the interpretation and with this statement regarding enforcement.

This document was prepared under the direction and control of C. Lamar Johnson, Deputy Administrator, Wage and Hour Division. The principal authors were James B. Leonard, Counsel for Legal Advice, and Thomas J. Allen, Attorney, Office of the Solicitor, and Sandra K. Bollhoefer, Wage-Hour Analyst, Wage and Hour Division. They were assisted by staff from the Office of the Solicitor and the Wage and Hour Division.

Accordingly, § 860.120 of Title 29, Code of Federal Regulations, is amended as follows:

§ 860.120 Costs and benefits under employee benefit plans.

(a) (1) *General.* Section 4(f)(2) of the Act provides that it is not unlawful for an employer, employment agency, or labor organization "to observe the terms of * * * any bona fide employee benefit plan such as a retirement, pension, or insurance plan, which is not a subterfuge to evade the purposes of this Act, except that no such employee benefit plan shall excuse the failure to hire any individual, and no such * * * employee benefit plan shall require or permit the involuntary retirement of any individual specified by section 12(a) of this Act because of the age of such individuals." The legislative history of this provision indicates that its purpose is to permit age-based reductions in employee benefit plans where such reductions are justified by significant cost considerations. Accordingly, section 4(f)(2) does not apply, for example, to paid vacations and uninsured paid sick leave, since reductions in these benefits would not be justified by significant cost considerations. Where employee benefit plans do meet the criteria in section 4(f)(2), benefit levels for older workers may be reduced to the extent necessary to achieve approximate equivalency in cost for older and younger workers. A benefit plan will be considered in compliance with the statute where the actual amount of payment made, or cost incurred, in behalf of an older worker is equal to that made or incurred in behalf of a younger worker, even though the older worker may thereby receive a lesser amount of benefits or insurance coverage. Since section 4(f)(2) is an exception from the general non-discrimination provisions of the Act, the burden is on the one seeking to invoke the exception to show that every element has been clearly and unmistakably met. The exception must be narrowly construed. The following sections explain three key elements of the exception: (i) What a "bona fide employee benefit plan" is; (ii) what it means to "observe the terms" of such a plan; and (iii) what kind of plan, or plan provision, would be considered "a subterfuge to evade the purposes of [the] Act." There is also a discussion of the application of the general rules governing all plans with respect to specific kinds of employee benefit plans. For a discussion of the provisions in section 4(f)(2) forbidding the failure to hire any individual or the involuntary retirement of any individual, see § 860.110 of this chapter.

(2) *Relation of section 4(f)(2) to sections 4(a), 4(b) and 4(c).* Sections 4(a), 4(b) and 4(c) prohibit specified acts of discrimination on the basis of age. Section 4(a) in particular makes it unlawful for an employer to "discriminate against any individual with respect to his compensation, terms, conditions, or privileges of employment, because of such individual's age * * *." Section 4(f)(2) is an exception to this general prohibition. Where an employer under an employee benefit plan provides the same level of benefits to older workers as to younger workers, there is no violation of section 4(a), and accordingly the practice does not have to be justified under section 4(f)(2).

(b) *"Bona fide employee benefit plan."* Section 4(f)(2) applies only to bona fide employee benefit plans. A plan is considered "bona fide" if its terms (including cessation of contributions or accruals in the case of retirement income plans) have been accurately described in writing to all employees and if it actually provides the benefits in accordance with the terms of the plan. Notifying employees promptly of the provisions and changes in an employee benefit plan is essential if they are to know how the plan affects them. For these purposes, it would be sufficient under the ADEA for employers to follow the disclosure requirements of ERISA and the regulations thereunder. The plan must actually provide the benefits its provisions describe, since otherwise the notification of the provisions to employees is misleading and inaccurate. An "employee benefit plan" is a plan, such as a retirement, pension, or insurance plan, which provides employees with what are frequently referred to as "fringe benefits." The term does not refer to wages or salary in cash; neither section 4(f)(2) nor any other section of the Act excuses the payment of lower wages or salary to older employees on account of age. Whether or not any particular employee benefit plan may lawfully provide lower benefits to older employees on account of age depends on whether all of the elements of the exception have been met. An "employee-pay-all" employee benefit plan is one of the "terms, conditions, or privileges of employment" with respect to which discrimination on the basis of age is forbidden under section 4(a)(1). In such a plan, benefits for older workers may be reduced only to the extent and according to the same principles as apply to other plans under section 4(f)(2).

(c) *"To observe the terms" of a plan.* In order for a bona fide employee benefit plan which provides lower benefits to older employees on account of age to be within the section 4(f)(2) exception, the lower benefits must be provided in "observ[ance of] the terms of" the plan. As this statutory text makes clear, the section 4(f)(2) exception is limited to otherwise discriminatory actions which are actually prescribed by the terms of a bona fide employee benefit plan. Where the employer, employment agency, or labor organization is not required by the express provisions of the plan to provide lesser benefits to older workers, section 4(f)(2) does not apply. Important purposes are served by this requirement. Where a discriminatory policy is an express term of a benefit plan, employees presumably have some opportunity to know of the policy and to plan (or protest) accordingly. Moreover, the requirement that the discrimination actually be prescribed by a plan assures that the particular plan provision will be equally applied to all employees of the same age. Where a discriminatory provision is an optional term of the plan, it permits individual, discretionary acts of discrimination, which do not fall within the section 4(f)(2) exception.

(d) *"Subterfuge."* In order for a bona fide employee benefit plan which prescribes lower benefits for older employees on account of age to be within the section 4(f)(2) exception, it must not be "a subterfuge to evade the purposes of [the] Act." In general, a plan or plan provision which prescribes lower benefits for older employees on account of age is not a "subterfuge" within the meaning of section 4(f)(2), provided that the lower level of benefits is justified by age-related cost considerations. (The only exception to this general rule is with respect to certain retirement plans. See paragraph (f)(4) of this section.) There are certain other requirements that must be met in order for a plan not to be a subterfuge. These requirements are set forth below.

(1) *Cost data—General.* Cost data used in justification of a benefit plan which provides lower benefits to older employees on account of age must be valid and reasonable. This standard is met where an employer has cost data which show the actual cost to it of providing the particular benefit (or benefits) in question over a representative period of years. An employer may rely in cost data for its own employees over such a period, or on cost data for a larger group of

similarly situated employees. Sometimes, as a result of experience rating or other causes, an employer incurs costs that differ significantly from costs for a group of similarly situated employees. Such an employer may not rely on cost data for the similarly situated employees where such reliance would result in significantly lower benefits for its own older employees. Where reliable cost information is not available, reasonable projections made from existing cost data meeting the standards set forth above will be considered acceptable.

(2) *Cost data—Individual benefit basis and "benefit package" basis.* Cost comparisons and adjustments under section 4(f)(2) must be made on a benefit-by-benefit basis or on a "benefit package" basis, as described below.

(i) *Benefit-by-benefit basis.* Adjustments made on a benefit-by-benefit basis must be made in the amount or level of a specific form of benefit for a specific event or contingency. For example, higher group term life insurance costs for older workers would justify a corresponding reduction in the amount of group term life insurance coverage for older workers, on the basis of age. However, a benefit-by-benefit approach would not justify the substitution of one form of benefit for another, even though both forms of benefit are designed for the same contingency, such as death. See § 860.120(f)(1) of this section.

(ii) *"Benefit package" basis.* As an alternative to the benefit-by-benefit basis, cost comparisons and adjustments under section 4(f)(2) may be made on a limited "benefit package" basis. Under this approach, subject to the limitations described below, cost comparisons and adjustments can be made with respect to section 4(f)(2) plans in the aggregate. This alternative basis provides greater flexibility than a benefit-by-benefit basis in order to carry out the declared statutory purpose "to help employers and workers find ways of meeting problems arising from the impact of age on employment." A "benefit package" approach is an alternative approach consistent with this purpose and with the general purpose of section 4(f)(2) only if it is not used to reduce the cost to the employer or the favorability to the employees of overall employee benefits for older employees. A "benefit package" approach used for either of these purposes would be a subterfuge to evade the purposes of the Act. In order to assure that such a "benefit package" approach is not abused and is consistent with the legislative intent, it is subject to the limitations described in § 860.120(f), which also includes a general example.

(3) *Cost data—Five year maximum basis.* Cost comparisons and adjustments under section 4(f)(2) may be made on the basis of age brackets of up to 5 years. Thus a particular benefit may be reduced for employees of any age within the protected age group by an amount no greater than that which could be justified by the additional cost to provide them with the same level of the benefit as younger employees within a specified five-year age group immediately preceding theirs. For example, where an employer chooses to provide unreduced group term life insurance benefits until age 60, benefits for employees who are between 60 and 65 years of age may be reduced only to the extent necessary to achieve approximate equivalency in costs with employees who are 55 to 60 years old. Similarly, any reductions in benefit levels for 65 to 70 year old employees cannot exceed an amount which is proportional to the additional costs for their coverage over 60 to 65 year old employees.

(4) *Employee contributions in support of employee benefit plans—*

(i) *As a condition of employment.* An older employee within the protected age group may not be required as a condition of employment to make greater contributions than a younger employee in support of an employee benefit plan. Such a requirement would be in effect a mandatory reduction in take-home pay, which is never authorized by section 4(f)(2), and would impose an impediment to employment in violation of the specific restrictions in section 4(f)(2).

(ii) *As a condition of participation in a voluntary employee benefit plan.* An older employee within the protected age group may be required as a condition of participation in a voluntary employee benefit plan to make a greater contribution than a younger employee only if the older employee is not thereby required to bear a greater proportion of the total premium cost (employer-paid and employee-paid) than the younger employee. Otherwise the requirement would discriminate against the older employee by making compensation in the form of an employer contribution available on less favorable terms than for the younger employee and denying that compensation altogether to an older employee unwilling or unable to meet the less favorable terms. Such discrimination is not authorized by section 4(f)(2). This principle applies to three different contribution arrangements as follows:

(A) *Employee-pay-all plans.* Older employees, like younger employees, may be required to contribute as a condition of participation up to the full premium cost for their age.

(B) *Non-contributory ("employer-pay-all") plans.* Where younger employees are not required to contribute any portion of the total premium cost, older employees may not be required to contribute any portion.

(C) *Contributory plans.* In these plans employers and participating employees share the premium cost. The required contributions of participants may increase with age so long as the *proportion* of the total premium required to be paid by the participants does not increase with age.

(iii) *As an option in order to receive an unreduced benefit.* An older employee may be given the option, as an individual, to make the additional contribution necessary to receive the same level of benefits as a younger employee (provided that the contemplated reduction in benefits is otherwise justified by section 4(f)(2)).

(5) *Forfeiture clauses.* Clauses in employee benefit plans which state that litigation or participation in any manner in a formal proceeding by an employee will result in the forfeiture of his rights are unlawful insofar as they may be applied to those who seek redress under the Act. This is by reason of section 4(d) which provides that it is unlawful for an employer, employment agency, or labor organization to discriminate against any individual because such individual "has made a charge, testified, assisted, or participated in any manner in an investigation, proceeding, or litigation under this Act."

(6) *Refusal to hire clauses.* Any provision of an employee benefit plan which requires or permits the refusal to hire an individual specified in section 12(a) of the Act on the basis of age is a subterfuge to evade the purposes of the Act and cannot be excused under section 4(f)(2).

(7) *Involuntary retirement clauses.* Any provision of an employee benefit plan which requires or permits the involuntary retirement of any individual specified in section 12(a) of the Act on the basis of age is a subterfuge to evade the purpose of the Act and cannot be excused under section 4(f)(2).

(e) *Benefits provided by the Government.* An employer does not violate the Act by permitting certain benefits to be provided by the Government, even though the availability of such benefits may be based on age. For example, it is not necessary for an employer to provide health benefits which are otherwise provided to certain employees by Medicare. However, the availability of benefits from the Government will not justify a reduction in employer-provided benefits if the result is that, taking the employer-provided and Government-provided benefits together, an older employee is entitled to a lesser benefit of any type (including coverage for family and/or dependents) than a similarly situated younger employee. For example, the availability of certain benefits to an older employee under Medicare will not justify denying an older employee a benefit which is provided to younger employees and is not provided to the older employee by Medicare.

(f) *Application of section 4(f)(2) to various employee benefit plans.*

(1) *Benefit-by-benefit approach.* This portion of the interpretation discusses how a benefit-by-benefit approach would apply to four of the most common types of employee benefit plans.

(i) *Life insurance.* It is not uncommon for life insurance coverage to remain constant until a specified age, frequently 65, and then be reduced. This practice will not violate the Act (even if reductions start before age 65), provided that the reduction for an employee of a particular age is no greater than is justified by the increased cost of coverage for that employee's specific age bracket encompassing no more than five years. It should be noted that a total denial of life insurance, on the basis of age, would not be justified under a benefit-by-benefit analysis. However, it is not unlawful for life insurance coverage to cease at age 70 or upon separation from service, whichever occurs first.

(ii) *Health insurance.* Ordinarily, health insurance coverage has not varied significantly with age up to age 65. The great variety of health insurance plans makes it difficult to offer a general guideline as to when, if ever, reductions in coverage might be justified by increased costs. Such reductions may not, however, be concentrated on certain items so as to make coverage less attractive to older workers.

(A) With respect to employees eligible for Medicare, it is not unlawful for an employer to "carve-out" from its own health insurance plan those benefits actually paid for by Medicare. Under such a "carve-out" approach, Medicare assumes primary responsibility for health care expenses under the employer's regular health insurance plan; the regular plan pays only for those expenses it insures against which are not actually paid for by Medicare. It is also not unlawful for an employer to place employees eligible for Medicare in a separate health insurance plan which supplements Medicare, *provided* (1) that the cost to the employer for such a supplemental plan is not less than the cost which would be expended to include such individuals in the regular health plan (with a Medicare "carve-out") and (2) that the supplemental plan provides benefits which are no less favorable than an employee eligible for Medicare benefits would receive under the employer's regular health insurance plan.

(B) An employer may not assume that eligible employees have taken advantage of available Medicare coverage, unless the employer informs each eligible employee of the need to apply for Medicare coverage and provides any necessary assistance for making an application for benefits. Furthermore, where the employer's regular health plan requires no employee contribution or an employee contribution less than that required for Medicare "Part B" coverage, the employer must pay or contribute toward the "Part B" contribution so as to make the total benefits available on terms which are no less favorable for employees over 65 than for employees under 65. However, the employer's total contribution for "Part B" and the "carve-out" or supplemental plan would not have to be greater than the employer's highest contribution for health benefits for employees of any age under 65.

(C) As a result of the savings to employers when benefits are available through Medicare, reductions in total health benefits for employees age 65 to 70 will generally not be justified. The total denial on the basis of age of employer-provided health benefits for older employees not eligible for Medicare would never be justified. It is not unlawful, however, for health insurance coverage to cease at age 70 or upon separation from service, whichever occurs first.

(iii) *Long-term disability.* It has been common in the past to cut off long-term disability benefits for all disabled employees and long-term disability coverage for all active employees at age 65. Since the Act protects employees and their expectations of employment from discrimination up to age 70, this practice can no longer be justified under a benefit-by-benefit approach. Under such an approach, where employees who are disabled at younger ages are entitled to long-term disability benefits, there is no cost-based justification for denying such benefits altogether, on the basis of age, to employees who are disabled at older ages. It is not unlawful to cut off long-term disability benefits and coverage on the basis of some non-age factor, such as recovery from disability. Nor is it unlawful to terminate benefits or coverage, on the basis of age, at age 70. Reductions on the basis of age before age 70 in the level or duration of benefits available for disability are justifiable only on the basis of age-related cost considerations as set forth elsewhere in this section. An employer which provides long-term disability coverage to all employees until the age of 70 may avoid any increases in the cost to it that such coverage for older employees would entail by reducing the level of benefits available to older employees. An employer may also avoid such cost increases by reducing the duration of benefits available to employees who become disabled at older ages, without reducing the level of benefits. In this connection, the Department would not assert a violation where the level of benefits is not reduced and the duration of benefits is reduced in the following manner:

(A) With respect to disabilities which occur at age 60 or less, benefits cease at age 65.

(B) With respect to disabilities which occur after age 60, benefits cease 5 years after disablement or at age 70, whichever occurs first. Cost data may be produced to support other patterns of reduction as well.

(iv) *Retirement plans.* (A) *Participation.* No employee hired prior to normal retirement age may be excluded from a defined contribution plan. With respect to defined benefit plans not subject to the Employee Retirement Income Security Act (ERISA), Pub. L. 93-406, 29 U.S.C. 1001, 1003 (a) and (b), an employee hired at an age more than 5 years prior to normal retirement age may not be excluded from such a plan unless the exclusion is justifiable on the basis of cost considerations as set forth elsewhere in this section. With respect to defined benefit plans subject to ERISA, such an exclusion would be unlawful in any case. An employee hired less than 5 years prior to normal retirement age may be excluded from a defined benefit plan, regardless of whether or not the plan is covered by ERISA. Similarly, any employee hired after normal retirement age may be excluded from a defined benefit plan.

(B) *Benefits.* In addition to the requirements as set forth elsewhere in this section, the following special rules apply to benefits provided under a retirement plan.

(*1*) A defined contribution plan may provide for the cessation of employer contributions after the normal retirement age of any participant in the plan. A defined contribution plan may also provide that no employer contributions shall be made on behalf of an employee who is hired after normal retirement age. However, these provisions apply only with respect to plans which are not "supplemental." Any defined contribution plan is deemed "supplemental" with respect to any employee who is a participant in it as well as in a defined benefit plan maintained by the employer. Where an employer has no defined benefit plan but two or more defined contribution plans, all but one of the defined contribution plans are "supplemental" with respect to those employees who are participants in them. The one defined contribution plan which is not "supplemental" could provide for the cessation of employer contributions after normal retirement age. The employer can designate which one of the defined contributions plans is not "supplemental".

(*2*) In a defined contribution plan, investment gains and losses and employee termination forfeitures are typically allocated to individual accounts instead of being used to reduce employer contributions. Where this is done, the allocations shall not be made less favorably on the basis of age to older employees (including those continuing to work past normal retirement age) than to younger employees. This rule shall apply regardless of whether or not the defined contribution plan is "supplemental."

(*3*) A defined benefit plan may fail to credit, for purposes of benefit accrual, service which occurs after an employee's normal retirement age.

(*4*) A defined benefit plan need not adjust actuarially the benefit accrued as of normal retirement age for an employee who continues to work beyond that age. (A defined contribution plan would have to pay the balance in the individual account.)

(*5*) A defined benefit plan need not provide for the accrual of benefits for an employee who continues to work after normal retirement age.

(*6*) A defined benefit plan may provide, and may be amended to provide, that retirement benefits will commence at the actual date of retirement rather than at normal retirement age for employees who choose to work beyond normal retirement age. Employees receiving long-term disability benefits as a salary replacement may be deemed not to have "actually retired" and therefore need not be simultaneously provided with retirement benefits.

(*7*) A defined benefit plan need not take into account salary increases and benefit improvements under the plan which take place after an employee reaches the normal retirement age specified in the plan with respect to those employees continuing their employment beyond that age. However, benefit improvements for retirees may not be denied to such employees who do not receive the advantage of benefit accruals and increases given younger employees.

(*8*) A defined benefit plan which includes offsets for Social Security and which ceases benefit accruals or any other increases at the normal retirement age specified in the plan may not offset the benefit receivable by such employees at actual retirement with the amount of Social Security benefit receivable at that time if that amount is greater than it was at the cessation of accruals. The total retirement benefit must be calculated on the basis of a Social Security benefit no greater than that receivable at the time when benefit accruals ceased under the employer's plan.

(2) *"Benefit Package" Approach*

A "benefit package" approach to compliance under section 4(f)(2) offers greater flexibility than a benefit-by-benefit approach by permitting deviations from a benefit-by-benefit approach so long as the overall result is no lesser cost to the employer *and* no less favorable benefits for employees. As previously noted, in order to assure that such an approach is used for the benefit of older workers and not to their detriment, and is otherwise consistent with the legislative intent, it is subject to limitations as set forth below:

(i) *A benefit package approach shall apply only to employee benefit plans which fall within section 4(f)(2).*

(ii) *A benefit package approach shall not apply to a retirement or pension plan.* The 1978 legislative history sets forth specific and comprehensive rules governing such plans, which have been adopted above. These rules are not tied to actuarially significant cost considerations but are intended to deal with the special funding arrangements of retirement or pension plans. Variations from these special rules are therefore not justified by variations from the cost-based benefit-by-benefit approach in other benefit plans, nor may variations from the special rules governing pension and retirement plans justify variations from the benefit-by-benefit approach in other benefit plans.

(iii) *A benefit package approach shall not be used to justify reductions in health benefits greater than would be justified under a benefit-by-benefit approach.* Such benefits appear to be of particular importance to older workers in meeting "problems arising from the impact of age" and were of particular concern to Congress. Therefore, the "benefit package" approach may not be used to reduce health insurance benefits by more than is warranted by the increase in the cost to the employer of those benefits alone. Any greater reduction would be a subterfuge to evade the purpose of the Act.

(iv) *A benefit reduction greater than would be justified under a benefit-by-benefit approach must be offset by another benefit available to the same employees.* No employees may be deprived because of age of one benefit without an offsetting benefit being made available to them.

(v) *Employers who wish to justify benefit reductions under a benefit package approach must be prepared to produce data to show that those reductions are fully justified.* Thus employers must be able to show that deviations from a benefit-by-benefit approach do not result in lesser cost to them or less favorable benefits to their employees. A general example consistent with these limitations may be given. Assume two employee benefit plans, providing Benefit "A" and Benefit "B." Both plans fall within section 4(f)(2), and neither is a retirement or pension plan subject to special rules. Both benefits are available to all employees. Age-based cost increases would justify a 10% decrease in both benefits on a benefit-by-benefit basis. The affected employees would, however, find it more favorable—that is, more consistent with meeting their needs—for no reduction to be made in Benefit "A" and a greater reduction to be made in Benefit "B." This "trade-off" would not result in a reduction in health benefits. The "trade-off" may therefore be made. The details of the "trade-off" depend on data on the relative cost to the employer of the two benefits. If the data show that Benefit "A" and Benefit "B" cost the same, Benefit "B" may be reduced up to 20% if Benefit "A" is unreduced. If the data show that Benefit "A" costs only half as much as Benefit "B", however, Benefit "B" may be reduced up to only 15% if Benefit "A" is unreduced, since a greater reduction in Benefit "B" would result in an impermissible reduction in total benefit costs.

(g) *Relation of ADEA to State laws.* The ADEA does not preempt State age discrimination in employment laws. However, the failure of the ADEA to preempt such laws does not affect the issue of whether section 514 of the Employee Retirement Income Security Act (ERISA) preempts State laws which related to employee benefit plans.

Signed at Washington, D.C. on this 22nd day of May 1979.

C. Lamar Johnson,
Deputy Administrator, Wage and Hour Division.

[FR Doc. 79-16550 Filed 5-23-79; 10:25 am]

BILLING CODE 4510-27-M

DATE DUE